AF779549

SUBSTANCE ABUSE ASSESSMENT, INTERVENTIONS AND TREATMENT SERIES

SOCIAL DRINKING: USES, ABUSES AND PSYCHOLOGICAL FACTORS

Substance Abuse Assessment, Interventions and Treatment Series

Men and Addictions: New Research
Lyman J. Katlin (Editor)
2009. ISBN: 978-1-60692-098-5

Preventing and Reducing Underage Drinking
Nathaniel P. Marquis (Editor)
2009. ISBN: 978-1-60692-588-1

Social Drinking: Uses, Abuses and Psychological Factors
Katherine T. Everly and Eva M. Cosell (Editor)
2009. ISBN: 978-1-60876-219-4

SUBSTANCE ABUSE ASSESSMENT, INTERVENTIONS AND TREATMENT SERIES

SOCIAL DRINKING: USES, ABUSES AND PSYCHOLOGICAL FACTORS

KATHERINE T. EVERLY
AND
EVA M. COSELL
EDITORS

Nova Science Publishers, Inc.
New York

Copyright © 2010 by Nova Science Publishers, Inc.

All rights reserved. No part of this book may be reproduced, stored in a retrieval system or transmitted in any form or by any means: electronic, electrostatic, magnetic, tape, mechanical photocopying, recording or otherwise without the written permission of the Publisher.

For permission to use material from this book please contact us:
Telephone 631-231-7269; Fax 631-231-8175
Web Site: http://www.novapublishers.com

NOTICE TO THE READER

The Publisher has taken reasonable care in the preparation of this book, but makes no expressed or implied warranty of any kind and assumes no responsibility for any errors or omissions. No liability is assumed for incidental or consequential damages in connection with or arising out of information contained in this book. The Publisher shall not be liable for any special, consequential, or exemplary damages resulting, in whole or in part, from the readers' use of, or reliance upon, this material.

Independent verification should be sought for any data, advice or recommendations contained in this book. In addition, no responsibility is assumed by the publisher for any injury and/or damage to persons or property arising from any methods, products, instructions, ideas or otherwise contained in this publication.

This publication is designed to provide accurate and authoritative information with regard to the subject matter covered herein. It is sold with the clear understanding that the Publisher is not engaged in rendering legal or any other professional services. If legal or any other expert assistance is required, the services of a competent person should be sought. FROM A DECLARATION OF PARTICIPANTS JOINTLY ADOPTED BY A COMMITTEE OF THE AMERICAN BAR ASSOCIATION AND A COMMITTEE OF PUBLISHERS.

LIBRARY OF CONGRESS CATALOGING-IN-PUBLICATION DATA

Social drinking : uses, abuses, and psychological factors / editors, Katherine T. Everly and Eva M. Cosell.
p. cm.
Includes index.
ISBN 978-1-60876-219-4 (hardcover)
1. Drinking of alcoholic beverages--Social aspects. 2. Alcoholism--Social aspects. 3. Violence. I. Everly, Katherine T. II. Cosell, Eva M.

HV5035.S62 2009
362.292'2--dc22

2009034043

Published by Nova Science Publishers, Inc. ✝ New York

Contents

PREFACE

Social drinking refers to casual drinking in a social setting without an intent to get drunk. Social drinking plays an important (but not traditional) role in such social functions as dating, and marriage. For example, a person buying another a drink at a singles bar is a gesture that one is interested in the other and often initiates conversation, or at least flirtation. Bad news is often expressed through a drink, whilst good news is often celebrated by having a few drinks. Buying someone a drink is a gesture of goodwill, and can be used as an expression of gratitude or mark the resolution of a dispute--to bury the hatchet, so to say. The physical act of going to a comfortable setting with friends is a large part of sharing a drink in the above situations. This new and important book gathers the latest research from around the globe in the study of social drinking and discusses several topics such as: social drinking during pregnancy can lead to fetal alcohol spectrum disorder, social influence on adolescent alcohol use, behavioral strategies for reducing high-risk drinking among college students, and others.

Chapter 1 - New Zealand has a very strong culture for the consumption of alcohol. In the midst of this cultural behaviour is the belief amongst young women especially, that their drinking patterns are termed 'social drinking', whereas in fact and as my research has shown, their consumption of alcohol actually equates to 'binge drinking' (intake of large volumes of alcohol on a single occasion) albeit during festive seasons celebrated in the family homestead with family and friends. As a result, alcohol when consumed during pregnancy, has the potential to produce a baby affected by fetal alcohol spectrum disorder (FASD), although women in society are generally unaware of this condition. Indeed, FASD is not viewed as a mainstream health issue by the New Zealand government, even though it was 'discovered' over three decades ago.

Eight New Zealand birth mothers who had given birth to offspring neurodevelopmentally disabled by FASD were interviewed both in the South and North Islands of New Zealand during 2006. Their stories are the main focus of this chapter. The women describe their struggles to nurture, educate, as well as obtain a medical diagnosis of FASD for their offspring in an oppressive, discriminating and stigmatising society.

Chapter 2 - An extensive literature has demonstrated that many adolescents and young adults engage in drinking behavior, resulting in acute and chronic negative consequences (e.g., unintentional injuries, arguments, unplanned and/or unprotected sexual activities, trouble with police/authorities, poor academic/work performance, suicide, and death), and alcohol dependence. Social influence is foremost among the causes attributed to the initiation and maintenance of alcohol use during this period. This chapter reviews a number of prominent theories of social influence that are directly relevant to drinking behavior among adolescents and young adults. For each theory, a brief description is provided, followed by relevant research related to adolescent and young adult drinking. Theoretical implications for preventative interventions are also discussed. Highlighted theories include: social learning theory, social cognitive theory, alcohol expectancy theory, problem behavior theory, social comparison theory, social identity theory, self-derogation theory, the theory of reasoned action, the theory of planned behavior, prototype willingness model, deviance regulation theory, peer cluster theory, and reactance theory.

Chapter 3 - Alcohol is among one of the most commonly used substances among young people in Western culture. Nationally representative survey data (n=44,346) on students from the United States (US) show that alcohol use is extremely common, with 75% of students surveyed reporting consumption of alcohol (more than just a few sips) by the end of high school [Johnston, O'Malley, & Bachman, 2002]. According to the 2005 US National Survey on Drug Use and Health (NSDUH) [SAMHSA: Substance Abuse and Mental Health Services Administration, 2007], 28.2% of 12-20 year olds reported drinking alcohol in the past month. Of these, 18.8% were binge drinkers (i.e., 5 or more drinks on the same occasion) and 6% were heavy drinkers (i.e., binge drinking on at least 5 days in the past month). Prevalence statistics from other industrialised countries show similarly frequent levels of alcohol use and misuse in young people [Babor et al., 2003].

The burden associated with drinking in young people is considerable, accounting globally for five percent of all deaths of people aged between 5 and 29 years of age [Editorial, 2008; Jernigan, 2001]. Additionally, research suggests underage and binge drinking among young people is associated with a number of acute and long-term negative outcomes including poor school performance, engaging in risky behaviours, physical injury, memory loss, learning deficits, and an increased risk of developing alcohol dependence [Miller, Naimi, Brewer, & Everett Jones, 2007]. Alcohol related harm is a major component of preventable health and social costs experienced by young people [Cagney & Palmer, 2007b].

Individual, school, community and family characteristics have been identified as risk factors for the development of adolescent alcohol use [Hawkins, Catalano, & Miller, 1992]. Whilst this chapter briefly reviews these areas, the predominant focus will be on the role of the family. It is widely acknowledged that the family plays a critical role in the development and socialisation of alcohol use in young people. A considerable body of empirical work has been dedicated to understanding the role of the family, particularly parenting influences on adolescent alcohol initiation and patterns of alcohol use. This chapter will review a range of theorised familial influences on adolescent drinking. In particular, the impacts of three key areas of social influence by parents will be examined: (1) parental supply of alcohol use; (2) parental attitudes to drinking; and, (3) parental modeling of alcohol use on adolescent drinking outcomes. Finally, the implications and recommendations for working with parents and families to delay alcohol initiation and prevent alcohol misuse are overviewed.

Chapter 4 - Polydrug use is common among patients in opioid maintenance programs. Heroin users often abuse alcohol, which may deteriorate the outcome of opioid maintenance treatment.

Excessive alcohol consumption among opioid maintenance patients has been associated with quality of life impairments and with serious social and health costs. Patients who are dependent both on illicit drugs and alcohol may have a poorer treatment outcome than patients without alcohol problems. The clinical and psychosocial treatment of these patients presents challenging work for the clinician. Therefore, treatment outcomes may be further improved if clinical subtypes of substance abusers could be identified and matched to an adequate treatment program.

In this study we aim to assess the prevalence of a drinking problem and analyse the cognitive and behavioural features of problematic alcohol use in opioid addicts according to Cloninger and Lesch's alcoholism typologies in a sample of 102 heroin-dependent patients in Opioid Maintenance Treatment. This sample was selected in the Addiction Unit of the Psychiatric Service of Santa Maria University Hospital, in Lisbon-Portugal.

Results show that alcohol use and alcohol-related problems are frequent among heroin-dependent patients. Study clinical descriptors discriminate Cloninger's type I and type II drinking problem and confirm this binary alcoholism classification in this population. Heroin-dependent patients classified as Cloninger′s type II problem drinkers showed a more severe cognitive-behaviour profile than those with a type I alcohol problem, concerning alcohol-taking situation prototypes, beliefs and expectancies about alcohol effects. Data only allows preliminary results about the Lesch's alcoholism classification

This cognitive and behavioural multidimensional assessment has relevant indicators to diagnose different drinking problems among the opioid maintenance programs population. It may improve intervention and treatment outcomes, reducing current health and psychosocial damage associated with an alcohol-abusing lifestyle.

Chapter 5 - As many as 1/3 of women in the general population and 50% of women seen in primary care experience abuse by an intimate partner during adulthood. The consequences of having experienced intimate partner violence (IPV) are quite alarming. Female IPV victims represent one of the largest traumatized populations in the U.S. More than 60% of women who present to domestic violence shelters meet criteria for posttraumatic stress disorder.

Alcohol use among female victims of IPV is common in the form of heavy, moderate or episodic drinking and appears to be both an outcome of and a risk factor for trauma. Researchers have found that female victims of IPV use drinking to cope with a variety of symptoms associated with trauma and PTSD. Motives for drinking among females with PTSD include coping with anxiety, managing conflict with others, and dealing with sleep problems. Overall, research suggests that drinking is used as a method to cope with psychological distress related to PTSD rather than to create positive experiences. While drinking may serve to decrease the intensity of uncomfortable posttraumatic symptoms, this relief is only temporary. In the long-term, using substances has been associated with increased psychological distress, functional impairments, adverse health outcomes, and greater vulnerability to revictimization. It is important to understand the relationship between drinking, IPV, and IPV-related posttraumatic distress to help prevent and treat alcohol and other trauma related problems in women who have been abused.

In this chapter, we review the problems commonly associated with IPV, psychosocial treatments designed to help IPV victims, and research regarding the relationship between drinking and IPV. First, we review the prevalence of drinking and alcohol problems associated with IPV for women who are in the abusive relationship, transitioning out of such a relationship, and women who have terminated the abusive relationship. We then discuss the role of drinking in IPV and in trauma more generally. We review the literature on empirically supported psychosocial interventions for these three stages of IPV (i.e., current relationship, transitioning out, and terminated relationship) and organize our discussion around these three stages as well. Finally, we make recommendations for future research, specifically addressing the need for alcohol-related interventions for IPV victims.

For the purposes of this article, we address female victims of male violence. The review is focused in this way for a number of reasons: 85% of IPV victims are women, women suffer more severe physical injuries after IPV than men, and mental health sequelae for battered men have not been well researched. Little is known about mental health consequences of same-sex partner violence.

Chapter 6 - The primary goal of this study was to identify characteristics of licensed drinking establishments that predict alcohol sales to obviously intoxicated barroom patrons. Of particular interest was the relationship between "secondary servers" of alcohol and irresponsible alcohol service. Relying on a structured observation guide listing a large number of variables believed to be related to irresponsible alcohol service, trained observers spent a total of 444 hours collecting data in 25 licensed drinking establishments in Hoboken, New Jersey. Observations took place at two separate time periods, 7:30pm – 10:30pm and 11:00pm – 2:00am, on Thursday, Friday, and Saturday nights. Ordinary least squares (OLS) regression analyses revealed "number of secondary servers" as the strongest predictor of alcohol service to obviously intoxicated patrons in Hoboken barrooms. Another significant predictor of alcohol service to intoxicated patrons in this study was the presence of "aversive environmental stimuli" within licensed premises, such as excessive heat, smoke, and crowding. Several prevention strategies aimed at reducing irresponsible alcohol service in bars and associated problems with alcohol-related harm are proposed.

Chapter 7 - Despite the fact that alcohol use is associated with high risk of adverse health and social effects great majority of teenagers drink alcoholic beverages. For this reason and because of data indicating good psychosocial functioning of adolescents who use but not abuse alcohol, alcohol drinking may be treated as an important factor in "the development to adulthood".

The aim of the study was to assess changes in the prevalence of social drinking (moderate drinking with peers) and other patterns of alcohol use ("risky", "solitary", "family" and "other" drinking) by adolescents in the past 20 years. Analysis were based on the data from the study aimed at monitoring trends in alcohol and other drug use by Warsaw 15-year-olds. The survey was repeated every four years, from 1988 to 2008, with comparable sampling approach and core questions. The sample size varied from above 3000 in 1988 to 1244 in 2008. In 2004 and 2008 some questions concerning adolescents lifestyle and mental health were added what allow to compare lifestyles of adolescent abstainers, social drinkers and other alcohol users.

Study results indicate that since the late 80's majority of Warsaw adolescents have been social drinkers (30%-40% of the population). Recently the prevalence of social drinking decreased (to 26%) while the increase of alcohol abstinence rates (from 11% in 2000 to 18% in 2008) and risky drinking among boys (from 14% in 1988 to 24% in 2008) was observed. Alcohol use alone is more prevalent among boys (4% to 7% across years) than girls (2% to 4%), while drinking with parents - among girls (16% - 22%) than boys (13% - 17%).

Regression analysis indicate that social drinkers lifestyle differs from other adolescents lifestyle in many aspects: they spend more time out of home, less time on their school homework, smoke more cigarettes and more often participate in parties were illicit drugs are used than abstainers and those, who drink alcohol with parents (family drinkers). Their cigarette use and partying is less intensive than in case of risky drinkers (those who abuse alcohol in peers company). Risky and solitary drinkers are at the higher risk of developing alcohol related problems. The finding that teenagers who drink alcohol in moderate quantities in company of parents (family drinkers) is associated with less risk of negative social and health consequences than drinking with peers, solitary or even being an abstainer, suggests the revision of zero-tolerance approach.

Chapter 8 - Protective behavioral strategies (PBS) are cognitive-behavioral strategies that can be used to reduce high-risk drinking and related negative consequences. Such strategies may be useful to include in intervention efforts targeted at college students, who have been identified as a population at-risk for dangerous alcohol consumption. The purposes of this chapter are therefore to (a) review the research on college student alcohol use, (b) address existing research findings on the relationship between PBS and college student drinking, (c) discuss ways in which PBS have been incorporated into clinical interventions, and (d) provide recommendations for future research and clinical efforts in the area.

Chapter 9 - The scientific community has long been aware of the relation between alcohol consumption and aggression through anecdotal and experimental evidence. Correlational studies have linked alcohol consumption to an increased likelihood of committing acts of aggression, including spousal abuse, sexual assault, and murder. Further, a meta-analysis of thirty experimental studies on alcohol and aggression supported a causal relationship between alcohol consumption and aggressive behavior. By examining rates of crime in which alcohol was involved, predicted that if alcohol consumption per capita decreased by 10%, there would be a 1% decrease in homicide, a 6% decrease in sexual assault, a 6% decrease in assault, and a 9% decrease in robberies nationwide. This potential for the reduction of violent crime offers a compelling argument for the continuation of research into the mechanisms through which alcohol increases the propensity to aggress.

Despite the growing body of evidence that alcohol consumption facilitates aggression, the effect appears to be more complicated than pure psychopharmacology. That alcohol influences aggressive behavior appears to be at least partially due to the anticipated effects of alcohol, as placebos can produce behavioral changes that reflect a person's expectations. In particular, people who believe that they have consumed alcohol have been shown to engage in greater retaliation against an aggressive confederate. Such findings support the notion that the mere belief that one has consumed alcohol contributes significantly to the behavioral effects of alcohol consumption.

Recent experimental efforts have looked beyond the placebo effect to examine the extent to which cues that prime alcohol expectancies, in the absence of alcohol consumption itself, can influence aggressive behavior. Of course, the propensity of alcohol consumption to increase aggressive behavior is not consistent across the population, as the majority of people who consume alcohol do not aggress. While some of this variance can be explained by physiological differences, there is also evidence that cognitive processes moderate the link between alcohol consumption and aggression. Alcohol outcome expectancies in particular, may partially account for individual differences in the alcohol consumption – aggression link.

Chapter 10 - Drinking alcohol is a socially accepted behaviour; however, it becomes a social problem when it exceeds the accepted social boundary as identified as alcohol misuse. Alcohol misuse includes three patterns of alcohol use: hazardous alcohol use, harmful alcohol use, and alcohol dependence. Implemented in 1995, adults were encouraged to drink within the recommended daily limit which was 3-4 units for men and 2-3 units for women to prevent incidence associated with alcohol misuse. There was a dose-response link between quantity of alcohol use and alcohol attributed diseases in men and between heavy alcohol use and traffic accidents. Drinking alcohol "sensibly" by adhering with this recommended quantity of alcohol by English government appears to be an effective way to protect adults from physical harm induced by alcohol misuse.

Reflecting this public health campaign of "sensible alcohol use", recent alcohol related statistics in England showed that the proportions of adult men's hazardous alcohol use and alcohol dependence were slightly reduced from the past figures. However, the prevalence of harmful alcohol use in men was not changed, and adult women's patterns of alcohol misuse were not changed at all. Moreover, the prevalence of mild alcohol dependence in women increased by nearly 1% compared with the past figure. According to the Health Survey for England 2007, around 30 to 40% of adults reported that they heard about the measurement for alcohol intake, "units", yet they did not know the recommended daily limit for alcohol intake for adults of either gender. These indicate that public message of "sensible drinking" has not yet been reached to all of the population and therefore English public has not been responding well to reduce incidence and consequence of alcohol misuse. This figure shows that an urgent need for public education about recommended quantity of alcohol use.

While it is necessary to educate public for quantity of sensible alcohol use, the public health message of "sensible drinking" tended to emphasise quantity of alcohol use over frequency of alcohol use. However, low quantity of alcohol use was found to have increased risk of developing cirrhosis, cancer, and cardiac arrhythmia. It also did not alcohol dependent drinkers from mortality. Long-term alcohol use, even it is only one drink a day, increased incidence of cancer among adult women. In addition, individuals who reported to have misused alcohol also reported to have drunk excessively in more than one occasion. It is possible that a longitudinal effect of alcohol use on alcohol dependence appears not to follow the dose-response pattern because frequency and quantity related adolescent drinking patterns were risk for adult alcohol dependence for men, whereas adult women's alcohol dependency was associated with frequent adolescent alcohol use. Although the trend is declining, in England about 13% of adult men and 7% of women reported to have consumed alcohol daily and 6% of the sampled adults showed symptoms of alcohol dependence. Based on these findings, alcohol studies are required to include both quantity and quantity in their models of alcohol use to better understand the complex mechanisms of alcohol use and misuse.

Moreover, researchers need to examine the effects exerted by social factors on alcohol use and misuse, given the documented link between social positions and alcohol misuse Adding the relevant social context into behaviour oriented alcohol use and misuse would assist researchers to better understand the dimensions of quantity and frequency of alcohol use. In turn, it will assist to develop empirically supported effective alcohol related interventions. Alcohol related social factors can be at the level of individual, family, and society which are woven into individual life time alcohol use and misuse. Adopting the lifecourse approach is likely to capture complex socially patterned alcohol use and misuse which develop and change over time. This approach is also effectively to assess the effect of long term alcohol use and the trajectory of drinking patterns on physical and psychological health.

Chapter 11 - "An alcoholic is always one drink away from a drunk" is one of many catch-phrases of the popular organization Alcoholics Anonymous. AA upholds a popular view of alcoholism – that it is a disease and abstinence is the only effective goal for preventing relapse. In other words, a sip of alcohol is assumed to lead to irresistible cravings for more.

However, many individuals with alcohol use disorders (AUDs) are not interested in abstinence or are unable to commit to it (Gastfriend, Garbutt, Pettinati, and Forman, 2007). In fact fewer than 20 percent of individuals with AUDs choose to follow an abstinence-based treatment program Controlled drinking (or "moderation"), by contrast, aims to reduce a person's alcohol consumption and minimize the potential harm associated with drinking.

This topic – abstinence vs. controlled drinking – remains among the most contentious in the field of substance abuse treatment. Current clinical standards for treatment of AUDs in the US typically recommend complete abstinence, especially for those with alcohol dependence. Controlled drinking, though, is employed widely in the UK and other European countries as a treatment goal.

Chapter 12 - A large segment of the population drinks moderately. It is called social or "safe" drinking. Social drinkers usually drink not more than 2-3 units of alcohol per day. The Royal College of Physicians, Psychiatrists, and General Practitioners advise a safe weekly limit of alcohol intake of 21 units (168 g) for men and 14 units (112 g) for women. Although binge drinkers can remain within safe weekly limits of alcohol consumption, bingeing-induced harm is reliably observed. Binge drinking is characterized by the consumption of alcohol leading to intoxication (drinking to get drunk), often measured as having more than 5/4 (men/women) number of drinks on one occasion or bringing blood alcohol concentration (BAC) above 0.08 gram percent in about 2 hrs. Other binge measures include drinking over half the "sensible" number of units per week (1–14 units per week for women and 1–21 for men), or double the recommended daily guidelines in one session. Binge drinking occurs in a third of the drinking occasions and increases the risk for numerous acute adverse health and social events including alcohol poisoning, acute myocardial infarction, injuries, accidents, suicide, interpersonal violence, etc. However, for most bingeing people, none of the abovementioned health and social harms result and drinkers think they remain within the recommended "safe" weekly limits of alcohol consumption or think their drinking is social or slightly risky at the worst. The Royal College of Physicians points out that "one third of the population is drinking at potentially hazardous levels". Nothing unusual in that since an increasing number of working young adults use alcohol as a recreational drug, tending to concentrate their drinking at weekends. The type of drinks preferred in single drinking episodes are beer and spirits. Moderate drinking has been proven to be beneficial and this pattern seems to be less than risky. In terms of total alcohol consumption most of binge drinkers can be classified as moderate drinkers or social drinkers. However, binge drinking is characterized by occasional high alcohol intake, being much more intensive during the single episode than social drinking. Thus binge drinking is referred to as hazardous or even a harmful pattern of drinking. Moreover, few studies compare "bingeing" to episodic heavy drinking or even to a heavy drinking. As there is a wide variation in individual susceptibility to alcohol-induced harm, the "safe" limits for alcohol intake seem to be controversial. Although, the term binge drinking is usually considered a subset of at-risk (hazardous) drinking, the term of hazardous drinking is often used loosely to cover also the forms of drinking that cause harm- even if minimal. Thus, other alternative terms of binge drinking/risky single occasion drinking appeared e.g. heavy episodic drinking, heavy sessional drinking or simply heavy drinking. Routine laboratory tests are not sensitive enough to detect harmful effects of single occasion drinking, since pronounced changes are only measurable after very high and prolonged ethanol consumption. However an acute high alcohol intake has been shown to increase moderately serum level of aspartate aminotransferase in healthy subjects or elevated other biomarkers as salivary, serum and urinary β-hexosaminidase, hemoglobin-associated acetaldehyde or salivary immunoglobulin A. Thus, it may be concluded that the binge drinking session can induce harmful effects, even if acute adverse health and social events are not apparent and drinkers remain within the recommended "safe social" weekly limits of alcohol consumption. Changes in laboratory tests, after bingeing, can help us in fully understanding the implications of the binge drinking session within a broader context, e.g. in context of more effective opportunities for intervention. Evidence exists for the effectiveness of "brief intervention" in reduction in binge drinking episodes per month. In general populations questionnaires and physical examination are superior for alcohol-related problems screening. The value of biomarkers in screening appears insufficient to justify their cost but little is known about biofeedback properties of such a markers. Providing the results of elevated laboratory test together with the specific information about binge drinking to the patient may enhance the impact on the patient's drinking behaviour with possible risk or harm reduction. Saliva-based testing in particular shows much promise, since material can be obtained in a simple non-invasive way.

In: Social Drinking: Uses, Abuses and Psychological Factors ISBN: 978-1-60876-219-4
Editors : K. T. Everly, E. M. Cosell, pp. 1-100 © 2010 Nova Science Publishers, Inc.

Chapter 1

'SOCIAL DRINKING' DURING PREGNANCY CAN EQUATE TO FETAL ALCOHOL SPECTRUM DISORDER (FASD)

Jenny Salmon*

Department of General Pratice and Primary Health Care,
University of Auckland, New Zeland

DESCRIPTIVE PARAGRAPH

New Zealand has a very strong culture for the consumption of alcohol. In the midst of this cultural behaviour is the belief amongst young women especially, that their drinking patterns are termed 'social drinking', whereas in fact and as my research has shown, their consumption of alcohol actually equates to 'binge drinking' (intake of large volumes of alcohol on a single occasion) albeit during festive seasons celebrated in the family homestead with family and friends. As a result, alcohol when consumed during pregnancy, has the potential to produce a baby affected by fetal alcohol spectrum disorder (FASD), although women in society are generally unaware of this condition. Indeed, FASD is not viewed as a mainstream health issue by the New Zealand government, even though it was 'discovered' over three decades ago.

Eight New Zealand birth mothers who had given birth to offspring neurodevelopmentally disabled by FASD were interviewed both in the South and North Islands of New Zealand during 2006. Their stories are the main focus of this chapter. The women describe their struggles to nurture, educate, as well as obtain a medical diagnosis of FASD for their offspring in an oppressive, discriminating and stigmatising society.

* *albeit the research having been carried out when the author was in the Department of Psychological Medicine at the University of Otago, Dunedin, New Zealand*

Introduction

This chapter presents the findings from a three-year study carried out from 2002-2005, which explored and described the 'lived' experiences and perceptions of eight New Zealand birth mothers, from pregnancy onwards, of a child/ren diagnosed with fetal alcohol spectrum disorder (FASD). By using a feminist lens, it also describes the impact of disability on the mothers' offspring and themselves in the midst of patriarchal professionals, stigmatisation, oppression and discrimination. This is important because, although much has been written about parents' and professionals' views of the effects of disability on children, no studies to date within New Zealand have sought the views of the birth mothers' of offspring diagnosed with FASD.

Importantly, I begin the chapter by addressing alcohol issues in relation to FASD, followed by risk and then I turn to the drinking patterns of New Zealand's women. Next, historical events in relation to the disability are presented followed by discussion relating to the features of the disorder, diagnostic confirmation and terms used. The cost of the disability together with incidence and prevalence rates are then addressed.

As the study draws on insights and ideas from two fields – disability studies and feminism – I then present these. The issues of narratives and motherhood and mothering are also discussed as these relative to feminism, as does the doctor-patient relationship.

Conducting the study, which follows, includes such issues as the methodological approaches used. Ethical considerations are then considered. Finally, I present and discuss the findings from my work.

Research Background

Alcohol and Fetal Alcohol Spectrum Disorder

Heavy maternal alcohol intake is a major perinatal risk, but unfortunately, it is difficult for obstetricians and gynaecologists to detect. Consequently, pregnant women, worldwide, continue to consume this teratogenic (poisonous) substance that freely crosses the placenta at the full concentration that is ingested by the woman, entering the circulatory system of the fetus. Thus, the mixing of alcohol with pregnancy can result in FASD, which is the umbrella term in usage today, whereby the fetus may suffer neurological, developmental and neuropsychiatric deficits (O'Malley et al, 2002).

Children at the severe end of the spectrum (with the complete phenotype) have been defined as having fetal alcohol syndrome (FAS). A large body of scientific literature (experimental studies with laboratory animals, case/control studies of children of alcoholic mothers and well-controlled epidemiological studies with large cohorts of children), has substantiated the existence of many specific fetal alcohol effects/disorders that can be traced to prenatal alcohol in both experimental animal studies and in studies on groups of children (Streissguth, 1997) with deficits being found in most systems, including the dopaminergic, noradrenergic, serotonergic, cholinergic, glutamatergic, GABAergic and histaminergic systems.

Streissguth (1997), being a leader in this field of research, reported that alcohol can have a direct toxic effect on the rapidly-developing cells of the embryo and fetus. Prenatal alcohol exposure can damage the developing embryo and fetus in many different ways, causing a whole spectrum of effects. Some of these effects are observable in the newborn baby (eg poor suckling ability, heart defects, low birth weight), which is substantiated by the participating birth mothers in my study. Others, however, are detectable only within the framework of an appropriate developmental stage or a specific environment. For example, hyperactivity is contingent on walking ability; attentional and learning problems become apparent in the classroom.

Most individual fetal alcohol effects are not unique to alcohol in the sense that only alcohol can cause them, but they are justifiably called and diagnosed as 'alcohol-related neurodevelopmental disorders' (ARND) because research has shown that prenatal alcohol exposure significantly increases the rate of their occurrence. ARND refers to various neurological abnormalities such as problems with communication skills, memory, learning ability, visual and spatial skills, intelligence and motor skills (Williams, 2006). So these individuals and those who lack 'the face of FAS' (ie morphology), often also experience developmental delays, attention deficits, learning disabilities, self-injurious behaviours, impulsivity and emotional and social adaptive disturbances (Sampson et al, 1997; Streissguth, 1997). They typically exhibit specific characteristics that may increase their risk for criminal behaviour. Examples include poor impulse control, information processing deficits, inability to relate behaviour to consequences, lack of a sense of connection to societal rules, poor short-term memory, poor sense of personal boundaries, confusion under pressure, difficulty grasping abstract concepts, inability to manage anger and poor judgment (McCreight, 1997).

In addition to the characteristics mentioned above, other potential domains that can be affected include sensory problems (eg tactile defensiveness and oral sensitivity), pragmatic language problems (eg difficulty reading facial expression, poor ability to understand the perspectives of others) and difficulty responding appropriately to common parenting practices (eg not understanding cause-and-effect discipline) (NCBDDD, CDCP, DHHS, 2004). These individuals may also exhibit naivete and a tendency to be easily led by others. Children with FASD are commonly not mentally retarded but present complex learning disabilities, especially a mixed receptive-expressive language disorder with deficits in social cognition and communication (reminiscent of sensory aphasia and apraxia), working memory problems and frequently, a mathematics disorder. Secondary disabilities are those believed to occur as a result of primary disabilities and are revealed as mental health problems, school dropout and trouble with the law (Koren et al, 2003). Comorbid psychiatric conditions include anxiety, mood, conduct or explosive disorders (O'Malley and Nanson, 2002). Incidences of inappropriate behaviours are poor judgment and difficulty perceiving social cues (LaDue et al, 1992).

Stratton et al (1996) stated that people with FASD are born with it. FASD is a birth defect that has its primary effect on the brain. Some people with FASD are slightly affected and manifest only mildly dysfunctional behaviour, whilst others are severely affected; devastatingly disabled in their ability to cope with even simple day-to-day interactions. FASD is a birth defect whether or not it is noticeable at birth. One does not outgrow FASD, although the manifestations may change with age. As Kerns et al (1997) stated "The degree of abnormality in any one measure can vary greatly between individuals and can change with time in the same individual. For example, people with FASD can have intelligence quotients

(IQs) from well within the normal range, to the severely mentally handicapped range (Kernes et al, 1997). The Mattson et al study (1997) demonstrated that the average IQ for a child with FAS was 74. However, Streissguth et al's 1996 study ascertained that the average IQ for individuals with FAS as 79 (range from 20 [indicating severe mental retardation]) to 120 (indicating above average intelligence) with an IQ score ranging from 49 to 142 (mean of 90) for those individuals with fetal alcohol effects (FAE), partial fetal alcohol effects (pFAE) or ARND (Streissguth, 1997).

The physical anomalies of the condition can be slight or quite striking. Some people with FASD live fairly normal lives if given adequate and structured support throughout their lives, whereas others are severely impaired. The defects may or may not be apparent or easily diagnosed at birth. Each individual with FASD has his or her own special needs, problems, behaviour, cognitive disorders and capabilities. Sometimes other disorders can co-exist with FASD such as autism, conduct disorder and oppositional defiant disorder (NCBDDD, CDCP, DHHS).

Because children with FASD are reportedly extremely active, the most common behaviour associated with this disability is attention-deficit hyperactivity disorder (ADHD) which was first identified in Heinrich Hoffman's 19th Century descriptions of 'Fidgety Phil' (Gardner, 2000; O'Malley and Nanson, 2002). ADHD has been diagnosed in about half of children with FASD, becoming apparent usually at or near school age. Frequently these children exhibit impaired social adaptive ability and impaired executive functions which reflect prefrontal cortex dysfunction (Koren et al, 2003). Individuals with FASD also tend to have difficulty with the encoding of information and flexibility (shifting) aspects of attention whereas children with ADHD typically display problems with focus and sustaining attention (NCBDD, CDCP, DHHS). This is not to say that individuals with FASD do not appear to display hyperactivity – because their impulsivity may lead to increased activity levels.

Some research, however, has shown that the attention problems for children with FASD do not seem to fit the classic pattern of ADHD and O'Malley and Nanson (2002) argue that there may be no link between FASD and ADHD. They further state that the clinical quality of ADHD in children with FASD often differs from that of children without FASD. For children with FASD, ADHD is more likely to be the earlier-onset, inattention subtype – as defined according to DSM-IV 314.00, 314.01 (American Psychiatric Association Diagnostic and Statistical Manual for Mental Disorder) – with comorbid developmental, psychiatric and medical conditions (O'Malley and Nanson, 2002).

The societal burden of FASD is immense, in terms of suffering, lost productivity and excess medical and educational expenses (Lupton et al, 2004). Identification of women at risk for consuming alcohol during pregnancy is critical to the design of interventions for reducing the adverse effects of alcohol on both women and their children.

The Risk

Although the teratogenic effects of alcohol are now believed to be well known, the alcohol consumption required to create those effects is still being studied and it has been shown by Streissguth in her longitudinal study begun in 1974 of a birth cohort of nearly 500 children with varying levels of exposure from birth to adulthood, that prolonged exposure to excessive amounts of alcohol is not necessary to create developmental disabilities, this being substantiated by one birth mother in my study. Streissguth's study also showed that nearly one per hundred babies grew up to have either FAS or ARND, that 60% of the adolescents and adults with these conditions have had major disruptions in their schooling and that 60% have been in trouble with the law – a fact that Dr Streissguth points out is "certainly not true of any other birth defect" and "…people just don't realize how many children and adults are affected by prenatal alcohol exposure" – a statement that is fully supported by my study participants.

Importantly, some sources state that the risk is highest in the early stages of pregnancy, the actual severity of the effects of prenatal alcohol exposure depends on interactions between maternal and fetal physiology and genetics, timing and duration of fetal exposure, pattern of maternal drinking and a number of maternal lifestyle factors, including higher maternal age, lower education level, cocaine use, smoking, custody changes, lower socio-economic status and paternal drinking and drug use at the time of pregnancy (Sood et al, 2001) as well as reduced access to pre- and post-natal care and services, inadequate nutrition and a poor developmental environment (eg stress, abuse, neglect). However, evidence shows that binge drinking (5 drinks or more on an occasion) creates the greatest risk of FASD (Maier and West, 2001). Of note, is that Pierce and West (1986) demonstrated that blood alcohol level rather than the amount of alcohol consumed, is critical for producing fetal damage. FASD studies consistently report that women who have had one child with FASD and who continue to drink, have progressively more severely affected children with subsequent pregnancies (May et al, 1983; Davis and Lipson, 1984; Abel, 1988).

There are currently, no reliable means to confirm maternal drinking using biochemical markers for pregnancy (Chudley et al, 2005). The great tragedy, of course, of this cognitive disability is that it is 100% preventable (Stratton et al, 1996, p.17). As one New Zealand paediatrician stated "As a society we feel strongly that children and young people should not consume alcohol, that we have laws designed to prevent this, why then do we have so much difficulty in preventing an unborn child from consuming alcohol?" (Marks, 1996). At present, there appears to be no answer to this question.

The Drinking Patterns of New Zealand's Women

Because of its strong culture of heavy alcohol use, this toxic substance plays a very important part in New Zealanders' lives, where *alcohol abuse* is considered to be normal *social drinking* (Salmon, 2006; 2007; 2008). So, amongst its pregnant women, there are high levels of alcohol consumption (>4 standard drinks per week) as well as 16-24 year-old females (Marks, 1996; Ministry of Health NZ, 2007a). Nearly a quarter of those young women aged between 18 and 19 years who drink, consume sufficient to feel drunk at least once a week (Ministry of Health NZ, 2001). Therefore, women are most likely to be drinking heavily at ages when fertility and sexual activity is high. As Mathew et al (2001) commented "By the early seventies, drinking beer and wine seemed to be an integral part of the teenage way of life in the Western World". This may be because medical and health advice on drinking during pregnancy continues to be inconsistent despite the official guideline of no intake of alcohol whilst pregnant, planning pregnancy and when breastfeeding (Ministry of Health NZ, 2006). Importantly, however, this has implications far beyond the acute risk of harm to the individual drinker and the immediate risk that it may also pose to the fetus should the drinker be pregnant at the time of consumption.

Of interest is the drinking behaviour of New Zealand women during pregnancy:

- A 1994 national study in New Zealand showed 41.6% of pregnant women consumed alcohol during pregnancy. Hazardous drinking was not confined to any one socioeconomic group (Counsell et al, 1994).
- A 1999 nutrition report on 500 pregnant women in New Zealand showed that 29% continued to drink alcohol after their pregnancy was confirmed. Of the 24% of women who regularly drank to intoxication before pregnancy recognition, 11% continued to do so throughout pregnancy (Watson and McDonald, 1999).
- A survey of midwives reported that 36% of pregnant adult clients and 82% of pregnant teenage clients drank during their pregnancy (Mathew et al, 2001).
- A 2002 study reported that a quarter of pregnant New Zealand women at 24 weeks report consuming alcohol in the previous 7 days (McLeod et al, 2002). The study found that women who were older, had previous pregnancies, a tertiary education and higher income levels, were more likely to drink.
- In 2004, 82.4% of women drinkers reported having stopped alcohol intake during pregnancy. No significant differences were found between Maori and non-Maori (NZ Ministry of Health, 2007a).
- A 2006 study on the awareness of the effect of alcohol use during pregnancy (Parackal et al, 2006) showed that more than 50% of women were of the opinion that if a pregnant woman wanted to drink, then some alcohol was safe in pregnancy. Nearly 20% of all women had binged at least on one occasion in pregnancy, most having done so before they realised they were pregnant.

In the absence of individual assessments, it is unclear whether drinking during pregnancy in New Zealand is actually decreasing or whether fewer women are reporting it owing to their awareness of the issue and possible associated stigma if admitting to drinking. Clearly if 50% of women believe that some alcohol during pregnancy is safe, then some will be more likely to drink themselves (Alcohol Healthwatch, 2007). Certainly, general directions for limiting the harm caused by alcohol were set by the National Alcohol Strategy 2000-2001 (Alcohol Advisory Council of NZ, 2001a) in which a number of initiatives were directed specifically towards reducing the consumption of alcohol by pregnant women. (Alcohol Advisory Council of NZ, 2001b) Four years later ALAC suggested that drinking pattern, rather than the average number of drinks per week, was likely to be the most significant factor affecting adverse pregnancy (Alcohol Advisory Council of NZ, 2005).

How Much Alcohol?

Importantly, there has been confusion over how much alcohol a pregnant woman could safely consume. Whereas mothers who are alcoholic or abusing alcohol during pregnancy are at highest risk of having children with FASD, even *social-drinking* women are at risk of having children with subtle, yet long-lasting neurodevelopmental problems. Because medical researchers have not been able to say for certain what the safe level of alcohol use is for pregnant women, many service providers argue that any alcohol use must be considered risky behaviour (Tait, 2000). In this respect, the New Zealand Government in 2007, erring on the side of caution, called for 'zero' consumption of alcohol by pregnant women. This, in contrast to the statement made by the United States Institute of Medicine (IoM, 1996) which said "While alcohol is the necessary teratogen, it alone may not be sufficient to produce FASD in humans or birth defects in animals. As with most teratogens, not every fetus exposed to significant amounts of alcohol is affected. The outcomes might be modulated by numerous biologic and environmental factors" (Tait, 2003).

Interestingly, whilst the Royal College of Obstetricians and Gynaecologists (UK) in 2001 recommended limiting alcohol consumption to no more than one standard drink per day, Sood et al in the same year, suggested that prenatal exposure to small amounts of alcohol – as low as one standard drink per day, where a standard drink contains about 0.5 oz of ethanol alcohol (eg 360 mL [12 oz] of beer, 150 mL [5 oz] of wine or 45 mL [1.5 oz] of spirits – has some neurobehavioural effects on the offspring. Since the precise lower threshold for ethanol embryopathy is unknown, pregnant women should be advised to abstain from all alcohol use if possible (Loock et al, 2005).

Previously and of note, is that based on two prospective longitudinal studies conducted in Seattle and Detroit, Jacobson and Jacobson (1994) attempted to arrive at a threshold for any manifestation of *in utero* alcohol exposure. On review of these studies, the authors supported the suggestion that *seven standard drinks per week* is a threshold for the manifestation of most neurobehavioural effects, which include attentional, memory, fine and gross motor skill problems, language problems and academic problems (especially in arithmetic) and problems with speed of information processing. Furthermore, these occur against a background of behavioural problems that include impulsivity, poor comprehension, poor frustration tolerance, a rigid problem-solving approach that makes new situations difficult and unpredictable behaviour (Streissguth, 2001). Using the margin of safety factor of 10, they concluded that 0.35oz of absolute alcohol or one drink in 10 days could be considered as safe. In 1996, Abel reported that there existed *no* danger to the child with *one* single drink – 13g absolute alcohol/per day, which is certainly argued against today.

Astoundingly, the Royal New Zealand College of Obstetricians and Gynaecologists Guideline for alcohol and pregnancy (1998) clearly stated that "There is no conclusive evidence of adverse effects in either growth or IQ at levels of consumption below *15 units* per week". Interestingly, a prospective study performed on 9,236 pregnant women in Paris, showed higher risks for still birth and intra-uterine growth retardation to be associated with heavy *beer* drinkers in comparison with *wine* or *wine/beer* drinkers (Kaminski et al, 1978).

Historical Events

Until 1968, the relationship between prenatal alcohol and developmental disabilities was essentially unknown. Although there were historical references linking drinking and birth defects, it was not common knowledge that drinking during pregnancy could be harmful to the child. However, historically, the human race has associated alcohol intake by women of childbearing age with harmful effects on the outcome of pregnancy. The Romans, being the traditional producers and retailers of alcohol, meted out severe punishment to women if they touched a drop of that stuff (Abel, 1998). The enlightened Europeans were more tolerant to their women drinking alcohol (Paton, 1997). Interestingly, the teratogenic effects of alcohol on pregnancy and therefore, the fetus, were realized thousands of years ago, to the time of Aristotle (Curtis, 1994; Abel, 1999) and even in the most well-read book in the world, "*The Bible*", it is written that when the wife of Manoah was informed that she would bear a son, she was told to "Beware and drink no wine or strong drink…" (Judges 13, verses 4,7, 1952).

A Report by the College of Physicians to the British Parliament in 1726 claimed that "Parental drinking is a cause of weak, feeble and distempered children" (Plant, 1985, p.9). This was followed by a report from the British House of Commons in 1834, which described infants born to alcoholic mothers as sometimes having a starved, shriveled and imperfect look as well as looking old (as though they had numbered many years) (Goodacre, 1965). Eighteenth Century London, during the gin epidemic (1720-1750), was also targeted by medical historians in their search for FAS evidence and especially William Hogarth's *'Gin Lane'* (Plant, 1985, p.10), which some authors alleged reflected an awareness of the facial characteristics of the syndrome. Abel (2001) refuted this by stating "While the gin epidemic undoubtedly resulted in the increased birth of weak and sickly children, claims about Hogarth's awareness of the stigmata of FAS are unfounded…" An historical review of the American and British literature by Warner and Rosett (1975), showed that observations made during this period of time, were followed by warnings of the 19th Century medical writers that *parental* drinking could damage the fetus.

However, Warren and Bast (1988) highlighted the work of Sullivan into alcohol-related birth defects (ARBD) with his research on 600 children born to 120 female alcohol Liverpool Prison (UK) inmates. He concluded that these women produced children characterized by a pattern of birth defects of increasing severity and higher rates of miscarriage; there was a tendency for healthier infants to be born when gestation occurred in prison (thus indicating abstinence as prevention); these children were not productive members of society as they aged and male alcoholism was not a factor in producing the abnormalities. [The male alcoholism idea would, of course, be totally argued against today]. Thus this 1899 paper would appear to be the earliest description for this constellation of features.

Clinically, the 'discovery' of FASD is said to be relatively recent (Hoyme et al, 2005) even though the disability has been in existence for over three decades. Indeed, in 1968, Lemoine et al in France reintroduced the apparently ignored, unrecognized or misunderstood concept of adverse outcomes resulting from fetal alcohol exposure when they published a report that described some of the common problems among well over 100 children of women who drank heavily. Although the authors documented many of the physical and behavioural patterns among those children, they drew few conclusions. That article did not present definitive diagnostic criteria and the observations did not lead to recognition of FASD in France or elsewhere in Europe (Hoyme et al, 2005). Interestingly, Lemoine in 1997 (cited J FAS, 2003) stated that during his medical studies, which started in 1935, "We were taught without any doubt that it *(parental* alcoholism*)*, had *no* teratogenic effects, although sometimes written with a caution against conception while intoxicated". Of note is that Lemoine et al used the word *parental* alcoholism rather than *maternal* alcoholism.

So, it was not until the late '60s and early '70s that clinicians began to see a definite connexion and not until 1973 that the first clinical study establishing a relationship was made by two Americans, Kenneth Jones and David Smith, who observed from a study of eight children born with serious developmental disabilities and a specific pattern of birth defects that could have been caused by gestational development. The children's mothers came from various ethnic groups and had nothing in common except their alcohol abuse, thus Jones and Smith's study not only noted the connexion between prenatal alcohol and developmental disabilities, but gave it a name – fetal alcohol syndrome, which remains as a clinical diagnosis today.

Features of the Disorder

The features of FASD are growth deficiency, a specific pattern of facial features and some central nervous system (CNS) damage. FASD involves a specific pattern of fetal alcohol effects occurring in unison, a pattern of features that has not, as a group, been associated with any other prenatal condition (Streissguth, 1997) and as such, is diagnosed when children meet the following criteria:

- Growth deficiency, pre- or postnatally, for height or weight or both
- A specific pattern of minor anomalies that includes a characteristic face, generally defined as short palpebral fissures (eye slits), a flat midface, a short upturned nose, a smooth or long philtrum (the ridges running between the nose and the lips) and a thin upper lip
- Some CNS damage, including microcephaly (small size of the brain), tremors, hyperactivity, fine or gross motor problems, attentional deficits, learning disabilities, intellectual or cognitive impairments or seizures. Streissguth (1997) posited that mental retardation and developmental delays also qualify as CNS criteria but…are not necessary for diagnosis

Facial signs of FASD are most evident between eight months and eight years of age; hence, their vague appearance in the newborn should not be mistinterpreted. Other physical malformations may also occur in FASD, although the frequency and occurrence of these malformations is poorly defined. These can range from cardiac, skeletal, renal, ocular and auditory (Koren et al, 2003). Additional characteristics may include clinodactyly (curved fifth finger), "hockey stick" palmar crease (upper crease in the palm curves upward ending between the index and third fingers) and "railroad track" appearance to upper margin of the ear (flattened upper ear margin that parallels the horizontal crease below it) (Wattendorf and Muenke, 2005).

Diagnostic Confirmation and Terms Used

Diagnosing FASD among children and adults historically has presented physicians with a challenge. Even cases of full-blown FAS often go undetected at birth and later in life (Little et al, 1990; Stratton et al, 1996). Children with less severe phenotypes in the FASD continuum present an even greater diagnostic challenge, because often the physical signs are more subtle (Astley and Clarren, 2000). These less severe types of FASD are much more common than

FAS however and may affect >1% of all children born in the United States (Sampson et al, 1997).

Aase et al (1995) argued that although the positive results of making this diagnosis are well known, the consequences of mis-diagnosis frequently have been over-looked. For example, inaccurate diagnosis of an alcohol-related disability may lead to stigmatization of mothers of labeled children, although it may be unclear whether prenatal alcohol exposure led to the children's problems. Mis-diagnosis also can lead to inaccurate and potentially damaging labeling and inappropriate treatment and referral by schools and social service agencies (see findings). Finally, once a diagnosis of an alcohol-related disability has been made, the search for other causes of an affected child's disabilities often is abandoned. Therefore, an inaccurate diagnosis can result in a lack of premature termination of diagnostic studies to determine the true cause and specific nature of the disabilities.

It is stated (Roberts and Nanson, 2000) that partial fetal alcohol syndrome (pFAS) requires a confirmed history of prenatal alcohol exposure, facial dysmorphology and either growth retardation or CNS abnormalities, that ARND requires a confirmed history of prenatal alcohol exposure and evidence of CNS abnormalities and that ARBD (which denotes the presence of congenital anomalies, as referred to above [Koren et al, 2003]), requires a confirmed history of prenatal alcohol exposure. However, the US IoM 1996 nomenclature (to reflect current knowledge in the field) had previously eliminated the term FAE (Canadian Paediatric Society, 2002) because it lacked specificity and sensitivity (Roberts and Nanson, 2000), proposing instead an establishment of a category for assigning the FAS diagnosis without maternal history (Leslie and Roberts, 2004). The term FAE was first used in 1978 in reference to the cognitive or behavioural problems, growth aberration or physical (dysmorphic) deviations that occurred at higher frequencies in alcohol-exposed populations than in unexposed populations (Clarren and Smith, 1978; Hanson et al, 1978).

It was also stated (Roberts and Nanson, 2000) that FAS *without* confirmed maternal exposure requires evidence of facial dysmorphology, growth retardation and CNS dysfunction. The CNS is often the most debilitating of the three areas of impairment and may include structural abnormalities of the brain, neurological problems such as impaired motor skills, poor coordination and visual problems and behavioural and/or cognitive problems such as mental handicaps, learning difficulties, poor impulse control, problems in social perception together with problems in memory, attention, reasoning and judgment.

Because of several problems with the IoM criteria for diagnosis, Astley and Clarren (2000) sought to develop a more objective set of diagnostic criteria for FASD which were published in 2000. These diagnostic criteria are commonly referred to as the Washington criteria because they were formulated through reviews of the medical records of 1014 children diagnosed with FAS through the Washington State Fetal Alcohol Syndrome Diagnostic and Prevention Network. Their criteria retain the 4 commonly accepted key diagnostic features of FASD, ie growth deficieny, characteristic FAS facial phenotype, CNS damage/dysfunction and alcohol exposure in utero. The degree to which each of these 4 factors is present for any given child is ranked on a 4-point Likert scale with 1 representing the complete absence of the feature and 4 representing a classic presentation of the feature. Each child is assigned a 4-digit diagnostic code, with each digit corresponding to the degree to which 1 of the 4 main features of FASD is present. Two hundred and fifty-six possible combinations (ranging from 1111 to 4444) result and are collapsed into 22 diagnostic categories (termed A through V). The authors of this system noted that, because a number of categories differ only with respect to the amount of prenatal alcohol exposure, there are only 9 unique diagnostic outcomes. These diagnostic outcomes range from no cognitive/behavioural or sentinel physical findings detected to FAS (Astley and Clarren, 2000).

Hoyme et al (2005) would argue however, that although the Washington system appears to be extremely accurate in placing each child into a specific diagnostic category within the spectrum of alcohol-associated abnormalities, the myriad of diagnostic categories is confusing and the system is impractical for routine use in clinical practice. They believe that an ideal classification system for FASD would allow accurate diagnoses of affected individuals by minimizing the false-positive and false-negative rates, precisely defining diagnostic categories, taking genetic and family histories into account, using a multidisciplinary approach (including careful behavioural and neuropsychological assessments) and creating straightforward, understandable, practical terms that could be applied easily in local settings.

Cost of the Disability

FASD is irreversible and is said to be the leading known cause of mental retardation in the Western World (Murphy-Brennan and Oei, 2001). It is also said to be the leading cause of developmental and cognitive disabilities among Canadian children and has surpassed Down syndrome, spina bifida and cerebral palsy in estimated prevalence in the United States (Canadian Paediatric Society, 2002). Even though FASD is stated to be fully preventable, the Public Health Agency of Canada (2005) believes this to be an over-simplification of the problem, suggesting that any woman can 'just say no' to consuming alcohol, ignoring the dynamics of addiction and the burden of other health and social problems that many women face (Poole, 2000). This idea had been previously mooted by Stratton et al (1996, p.17) who argued:

> "It sounds simple: women who drink excessively while pregnant are at high risk for giving birth to children with birth defects. Therefore, to prevent these defects, women should stop drinking during all phases of pregnancy. Alternatively, women who drink alcohol should not become pregnant unless and until they can control their drinking. More than [30] years ago, when fetal alcohol syndrome (FAS) was first described in the published medical literature, there were high hopes for its prevention.
>
> In fact, this has not been simple and the biomedical and public health communities are still struggling to eliminate a birth defect that should be absolutely preventable."

The cost of failing to prevent FASD is significant. New cases of FASD could conservatively be costing New Zealand $3.5 million annually in extra medical, educational and social services. This does not include the cost of secondary disabilities (Streissguth et al, 1997) that can develop if the individual is not receiving adequate and appropriate care according to need (Alcohol Healthwatch, 2007).

International estimates vary. The US estimates the life-time health-care costs for one individual with FAS at 1.4 million (Lupton et al, 2004). In Canada, using an estimated life-time care cost of $1 million per person, the calculation for FAS alone costs Canadian taxpayers an extra $4 billion every year across all systems (Clarren, 2007). This estimate is based on the annual Canadian birth rate and a FAS prevalence rate of 1 per 1000 live births (4,000 babies born with FAS). Of note and by way of comparison, May et al (2007) found a FAS rate of 3.7-7.4 per 1000 and a FASD rate of 20-40 per 1000 in 5-6 year old pupils in Italian schools.

Without appropriate knowledge and skill for services and families to manage the needs of persons with FASD appropriately, the unmet needs of individuals will inevitably result in increased cost and duplication of ineffective services across lifetimes and generations. The cost of diagnosis, early intervention and ongoing support by appropriately trained personnel within services would likely be much less than the cost of not identifying and treating appropriately individuals affected by FASD. If lifetime care costs for FAS and FASD were calculated together with a higher estimated prevalence rate (which is quite likely given the current drinking culture in New Zealand), then it can be assumed that FASD is costing New Zealand an enormous amount of avoidable revenue expenditure, not unlike that now recognised in Canada and the US (Alcohol Healthwatch, 2007).

Incidence and Prevalence

Incidence and prevalence rates of FASD vary widely (Glasgow, 1996; Roberts and Nanson, 2000) and are difficult to estimate in many countries. This is equally true of New Zealand, where a national registry of such cases is not held, the New Zealand Ministry of Health stating that 'there is no such thing as a notifiable disability' (The Paediatric Society of NZ, 2004; MoH, 2007b). Interestingly, a lack of evidence of the prevalence and incidence of FASD in New Zealand has been cited as the reason why health policy and programmes have not been developed to prevent and/or treat FASD in this country (Alcohol Healthwatch, 2007), yet FASD is not routinely screened for in infancy and early childhood. In contrast, all newborns (2,500 per year) are screened for FASD in France, with selected infants examined by a neonatologist (Sampson et al, 1997).

The Alcohol and Public Health Research Unit (1999) stated that they believed FASD was under-recognised and under-reported in New Zealand with low public awareness of risks (see findings). Only about half general practitioners (GPs) and obstetricians routinely advise women about alcohol consumption at the first antenatal contact (Leversha and Marks, 1995; Fetal alcohol NZ, 2004). Of note, is that the majority of affected children in New Zealand are in foster home/adopted care and adopted Russian orphans comprise a significant proportion of the affected children (Leversha and Marks, 1995). However, a report drawn up in 2006 (Parackal et al, 2006) argue that the incidence of FASD in New Zealand has not yet been established or estimated.

The first study to report the possible prevalence of FASD in New Zealand was the one performed in 1993 by Leversha and Marks (1995). They reported 63 children (under the age of 10) in paediatric care diagnosed with FASD based on maternal alcohol abuse and dysmorphic features in the child. An additional 78 children were diagnosed, but were not under paediatric care. 130 children with recognised ARBD were under paediatric care. Compared to the incidence rate of FAS in overseas studies, Leversha and Marks (1995) estimated the actual number per year of FAS cases to be 20-114 (0.3-1.9:1,000), ARND 354 (5.9:1,000), cerebral palsy 120 (2:1,000), Down syndrome 60 (1:1,000) and cystic fibrosis 20

(1:3000). The FASD figures are in keeping with those reported by the New Zealand Paediatric Surveillance Unit (NZPSU) in 2004 who predicted between 20 and 112 children are born each year in New Zealand with the disability. This figure is considerably less than the expected rate from overseas figures and it is not clear whether New Zealand does actually have a lower prevalence than overseas or whether the estimate is just low and thus falsely reassuring.

A 21/2 year study performed by the New Zealand Paediatric Surveillance Unit ending December 2001 (2002), concluded that there were 62 valid reports of new cases or suspected FAS (97% were from the North Island and New Zealand born) - 39% of cases were New Zealand European, 45% Maori, 8% Pacific, 8% Unknown and 8% Other (predominantly Russian). Information received on 24 (83%) stated: 9 definite cases of FAS were reported; the remainder were suspected FAS but awaiting further investigation or assessments over time; the diagnosis was usually suspected by the notifying paediatrician: however, other agencies also suspected the diagnosis facilitated referral (2 by Special Education Services, 2 by Child, Youth and Family services [CYF], 2 by mental health professionals and one by the child's parents; 20 children were born in New Zealand and the remaining 4 in Russia; 7 of the 24 were living with their biological parents, 7 living with family and the remainder adopted or in foster care; of the 20 children born in New Zealand, 11 were of Maori and 9 of European ethnicity.

The prevalence of FAS in the US has been estimated to be 0.5 to 2 cases per 1,000 live births and FASD as 9.1 cases per 1000 live births (Public Health Agency of Canada, 2005). It is also recognized that there are higher rates in Indigenous populations (O'Leary, 2004) and in North America, Aboriginal heritage is a risk factor for FAS and ARBD, creating methodological problems (Tait, 2003). Importantly, Hoffman and Shanske (2003) stated that many factors must be considered when discussing incidence, ie maternal age, socio-economic and health status, race, drug use, the rate of abortion, educational background, as well as factors affecting data reporting. Also, of course, FASD epidemiology data (Stratton et al, 1996) can be confounded by inconsistencies of diagnostic criteria, reluctance to diagnose, lack of diagnostic expertise, surveyed population, migration, whilst other individuals go undiagnosed.

However, although there is no clear national data available to indicate the likely FASD incidence and cost burden to New Zealand services and families, anecdotal evidence suggests that individuals with the disability are continuing to come to the attention of health, educational and social service professionals and are being referred to other services for ongoing assistance, most of which are not equipped to respond adequately or appropriately (Symes, 2004; Salmon, 2007). So, what does 'disability' mean? This is now discussed.

The Meaning of Disability

Ballard (1994) argued that disability is sometimes thought of as a personal problem, as something that someone 'has', but this is not how many of those directly involved view it. For them, disability is a social issue and they say that they experience disability as discrimination that keeps them out of schools (an important gateway to employment [Cahill, 1991]), out of the workforce and out of the mainstream of community life".

In New Zealand around 12,000 people are said to be 'intellectually handicapped' or 'intellectually disabled' (Ballard, 1994), so that by these very descriptions, people are oppressed and discriminated against. These are the people who are denied access to normal classroom activities, normal school curricula, limited in employment opportunities and described by professionals (gatekeepers to the required disability services) as trouble-makers, uneducable, dumb or deviant. These people so labeled then engaged in the self-fulfilling prophecy whereby they act out their stigmatizing and oppressive roles. Therefore, it can be seen that disability from this perspective, is socially created. This meant (Ballard, 1994) that the experience of disability is in large part a product of the institutional practices of society expressed in education, health, employment and other aspects of community life (see findings).

It also followed that the person who is societally labeled as 'disabled' is also seen by the medical professionals as being in a state of 'illness' (as is the pregnant woman), rather than viewed in terms of 'wellness' and is therefore, categorized as such (Woollett and Marshall, 1997). The reality is, of course, that every disabled person is a human being, a unique individual with his or her own individual problems and needs and the only way professionals and the wider community can learn to understand is to listen to them and their parents as they share their feelings.

Unfortunately, offering disabled people the opportunity to speak as experts on their own lives had not up until the early 1970's, gained favour (Thomas, 1999), so that children and their families were a largely invisible group as far as politicians, policy makers and the general public were concerned. It was only in the 1970s, as a result of growing public concern about thalidomide, that disabled children and their families found themselves anywhere near the public policy agenda (Thomas, 1999). Concern in the UK media and among politicians and the general public over thalidomide was further reinforced by awareness of the consequences of vaccine damage, which resulted in greater recognition of the problem of all disabled children and their families and generated some political will to take action (Baldwin and Carlisle, 1994). As a result, various acts were drawn up to meet the needs of the disabled child, but a discussion on these is outside the realm of this chapter, so I now address the two models of disability which my work drew on – the medical model of disability and the social model of disability. I then discuss a new medical model: the morphological model of disability.

Models of Disability

The Medical Model of Disability

Disability has been defined in various different ways over the years; not surprisingly, these definitions have been influenced by varying historical, social and ideological practices. So, historically, there has been a strong link between disability and medical care and as Duchan (2001) stated "the medical model has served us well...but before we become complacent in thinking that we now have it exactly right, we need to consider the challenges of other models to the well-worn medical approach". Like Murphy (1990), I personally believed that in the field of FASD, the paradigm did not allow for the child and its family to be seen and cared for at an holistic level, this being substantiated by Suchman et al (1988) when they stated:

> Only when the medical model itself embodies the wholeness of a human being's experience, can it guide clinicians and patients towards complete healing.

Rioux, writing in 1994, emphasized that "For the first 80 years of this century, the policy and research agenda in disability was driven first by biomedical concerns" (p.1). Similarly, Duchan (2001) stated that the medical model is made up of causal chains, of primary, secondary and tertiary causes with the primary cause often being seen as the original cause. It is frequently depicted as a problem at the biological level. The symptoms of diseases are often cast in psychological terms. A final link to the causal chain is usually seen as a social one – a language problem causes a person to withdraw from social situations or be excluded from them by others.

Medical practices, organized around the medical model, presumed that the physician's task is to diagnose diseases, to discover their causes and symptoms and design treatments. The treatments are aimed at eliminating or minimizing the symptoms of the disease or the cause of the disease or the disease itself, hence the paradigm also being referred to as the 'disease model' (Reger, 1972). Of language used within the medical model, Reger (1972) argued that "the term 'disease' itself is seldom used: other terms such as dysfunction, disorder, disturbance or maladaption are used instead" (p.9). Somewhat later, however, Hearle (1980, p.25) did in fact, refer to FASD as a 'disease'. This shows how language used within the literature on this condition has reflected people's thinking within a medical model of disability: a thinking that in today's society can be seen as potentially outmoded and damaging. Outmoded because societal values and feelings are not visible and damaging because the child is labelled and damaging because of its tendency to blame the 'victim' (the disabled person). The person becomes deconceptualized in the sense of being seen in biological and physiological terms. Outmoded too because it does not view the individual holistically: it forgets to take into account the 'wellness' part or what that person is feeling.

The medical model involves diagnosing and assessing as a result of which, people with disabilities are usually given a clinical label, which have tended to view disabled people as 'sick' and 'impaired', so that this paradigm is still particularly suited to society's paternalistic doctors. However, as the birth mothers in my study have demonstrated, the medical construction of disability is not simply a stigmatizing label that rationalizes social disadvantage. It is something that mothers can use to ground the very claim of disability – a claim that might prove better than alternative constructions of the child with FASD, such as lazy, mediocre student, dumb, or a troublemaker.

The medical model has moreover, been shown to encompass its own words and language as applied to FASD, eg imbecile, but as Reger (1972) explained, the language of the medical model has shaped the way in which society views people with disabilities. Rapp (1994) commented that 'medical language employs a great authority and cannot always be used to respond to the resources and questions particular women bring to this encounter' (p.28). She pointed out that medical language is not neutral and that 'medical discourse protects medical staff from the sad and disorientating experience of their patients, allowing the routinization of services' (p.210). Further, Anspach (1993, pp.104-105) posits that the 'process of communicating prognostic information across class lines may introduce subtle transformations in connotative meanings...Thus, between the discourse of medicine and the vernacular (of mothers), lies the realm of connotative meaning'.

Rioux (1994, p.1) argued that the medical model is an individualized account of disability because it focuses on relieving society of its responsibility for disability since disability is defined in biological, physical or psychological terms – and is therefore, a personal construct. The 'problem' of disability is not a societal problem, but a personal problem – 'an individual problem rather than...a social relationship'. Feminists and other advocates for disabled people would, however, argue that disability is socially constructed, hence the emergence of the social model of disability, now discussed.

The Social Model of Disability

Briefly, this paradigm proposes that disability is created by society's barriers and by discrimination (Shakespeare, 1998) prejudice, oppression and the denial of agency and autonomy. To put it simply, the problem is not the person with disabilities; the problem is the way that normalcy is constructed to create the 'problem' of the disabled person. The social model locates the impediments to a high quality of life not within the body of the disabled person (such that the person should be cured, put out of his/her misery or prevented from being born in the first place), but rather within the society that discriminates against persons with disabilities (Landsman, 2005).

According to Oliver (1990) this model gives no consideration to the issue of the ideology of 'normality' nor to the idea that the environment could be changed rather than the individual. Certainly in the case of the FASD-affected child, the birth mothers in my study, changed the environment within the household in order to meet the needs of their offspring because they realized that they could not change their cognitively-impaired child. Interestingly, Landsman (2005) stated that for strong advocates of the social model, parents are often seen as misplacing their efforts on correcting the impairment rather than on addressing the disabling conditions of society.

The birth mothers' understandings in this present study, steeped in the everyday experience of interdependency, may converge with efforts within disability studies to reexamine the identity of disability and create a more inclusive world. This inclusive world may be attained by virtue of a new paradigm – the morphological model – which, by definition, fits neatly within the domain of FASD.

The Morphological Model of Disability

As I have demonstrated, both the medical model and the social model of disability have substantial drawbacks in creating better lives for people with disabilities: the first denies the value of difference and the effects of discrimination and the second denies any place for prevention and cure. From the birth mothers' narratives, it would seem that a third model – a morphological model of disability – could best help with effective intervention in the field of FASD. This model being termed such since FASD, as stated previously, is a collection of physical, neurological and *morphological* disabilities caused in part (Vedder, 2005) by heavy maternal drinking during pregnancy.

Vedder's (2005) new paradigm is based on Elizabeth Wilson's feminist practice that replaces 'the body' with morphology, which "is best understood not as originary fixed anatomy or as secondary or gendered production, but as a particular biocultural instantiation of the body...[M]orphology has the idea of 'this biological body' already written within it" (Wilson, 1998, p.64). The concept of morphology, in other words, allows society to think about 'the body' as the confluence of biological and social/cultural forces interacting over time. Although Wilson's project specifically addresses the brain, her argument may also equally apply to the fetus, so that under the definition of the morphological body, the fetus is neither a socially-produced phantasm nor an obviously biological and determined entity (Vedder, 2005). Therefore, the body is thus not simply biological or simply social, but biological, social and *temporal*: the body is *produced* (Shilling, 1993, p.111). Because the fetus is produced rather than being stable and given, this offers new possibilities for FASD-intervention and new ways of conceptualizing a model of disability which allows for intervention at both individual and social levels. Vedder (2005) argued that because FASD is caused through a combination of individual action (maternal drinking) and social context..., it is a particularly appropriate example for exploring the ethics and efficacy of different interventions.

So, the morphological model of disability which seeks to combine the social and the biological, highlights the multiple ways society might intervene in disability without devaluing dis(en)abled people and while acknowledging the important social dimension to disability (Vedder, 2005). This means that with FASD, intervening at the level of maternal behaviour is one possibility, but intervening here does not ensure the health or welfare of the fetus. Alternatively, as a lack of prenatal education and care impinges on fetal health, making obstetrical visits accessible economically, geographically and psychologically would go a long way towards improving the health of all fetuses as well as the health of all pregnant women.

Importantly, as analyses of the women participants' memoirs of living with and nurturing their offspring disabled by FASD would appear to highlight the importance and value of Wilson's morphological theory, it follows that a morphological model based on her concept would allow for thinking in terms of prevention and cure whilst still valuing difference and disability. Respecting difference and disability is about attending to the broader conditions that affect not only disability but also the health and welfare of *all* people.

Women's Research

I now discuss feminism and how this perspective fits naturally into the qualitative paradigm in relation to women's research – in this case, research by a female researcher using women, who are also birth mothers, as the participants – those who continue to remain an oppressed group within society by virtue of their gender and who, generally unwittingly, cope daily with 'invisibility' and 'voicelessness' in their quest to nurture their disabled offspring to the best of their ability. Smith (1987) argued that women have difficulty claiming authority for themselves and their own voices, because we live in a world intellectually dominated by men and we take for granted that our thinking needs to be validated by others. Consequently, our opinions tend to meet the approved standards, which are, of course, set by men.

Feminist Research

Reinharz (1992) stated quite clearly that “feminism is a perspective; not a research method”. Therefore, I used feminism as such and employed the most widely used research tool – the one-to-one, face-to-face interview (Madriz, 2003) which gives ‘voice’ to women so that that they can communicate their lived experiences through ‘narratives’ or ‘story-telling’ – stories that reveal their private, interiorized emotional and intimate worlds – stories that reveal inequalities within society and the health and educational systems together with inequalities of knowledge being perpetuated within the doctor-patient relationship (Leversha and Marks,1995).

As Clandinin and Connelly (1994, p.416) commented “Thus we say that people by nature lead storied lives and tell stories of those lives, whereas narrative researchers (myself included), describe such lives, collect and tell stories of them and write narratives of experience” after having initially analysed the data. However, in order to acquire the data and as Eisner (1991) pointed out “It is necessary to get in touch with the reality and context of a situation before one can hope to understand it and effect any useful interventions or changes.” Belenky et al (1986) believed that by inviting women to tell their own stories, without interruption, they can control and develop their responses within terms that have meaning to them.

The feminist perspective was also used as a theory to generate ideas from the research partiipants in order to build and shape my motivational study. Thus and as Clandinin and Connelly (1994, p.415) documented:

> When persons note something of their experience, either to themselves or to others, they do so not by the mere recording of experience over time, but in storied form. Story is, therefore, neither raw sensation nor cultural form; it is both and neither. In effect, stories are the closest we can come to experience as we and others tell of our experience. A story has a sense of being full, a sense of coming out of a personal and social history.

Feminist perspectives on women’s health research challenge the axioms of the scientific method that is the predominant research paradigm used in the medical field (Clifford-Walton, 1998). The scientific method refers to “quantitative” research which believes in rationality and universalism; a belief that there is order in the world. Feminists believe that in the scientific method - where the researcher decides the research question, the data to be collected, the mode of analysis and the dissemination of the results – the researched are disempowered. Feminists see this as unethical as they feel that research should be done for women, by women and with women (Oakley,1981; Stanley and Wise, 1983) in keeping with my own work. Much of the research in the past had been carried out by men on all-male samples (Oakley, 1981) and generalisations had been made from those findings about women (Rosser, 1992). This of course, was unacceptable because, as has been shown, women's social construction is entirely different from that of men, as is their biological makeup.

One of the major difficulties feminists have with the scientific method is the dichotomy drawn between subject and object (Cook and Fonow, 1986). The scientific method separates the researcher from the object of the study, denying that the researcher occupies a definite place within society and seeing the object as excluding personal-subjectivity based knowledge. This leaves the position of the researcher and the relationship of the researched, unexamined – another reason for my chosen methodology as it allowed me to gain an essential rapport with the women – a rapport of honesty and trust, which ultimately allowed for the breakdown of barriers to communication between the women and myself.

Feminists do not show the concern over the *generalisability* of research results exhibited by those pursuing the scientific method, as they see each research project as illustrating a partial view of the world, the whole picture being made up of many differing perspectives (Clifford-Walton, 1998). Clifford-Walton (1998) further believed that feminists see the collection of any data as a basis on which to start asking questions and to draw attention to issues that need to be further researched.

It is stated that the researcher should, ideally, pass all their writing to the participants to check that it accords with their world view and the researched's own words should be used wherever possible so that the reader can come to their own conclusions about what was meant (Lather, 1986a; 1986b; Opie, 1989). I, being totally committed to such statement, carried through these measures.

Acker et al (1983, p.434) stated that the active voice of the subject should be heard in the final account and the theoretical reconstructions must be able to account for the investigator as well as those being researched, although it is acknowledged that it is 'impossible to create a research process that completely erases the contradictions in the relationship between the researcher and the researched'. Acker et al (1983) also stressed that we must not impose our definitions of reality on those we research, this being supported by myself.

Finch (1986) argued that "only studies of natural situations ("naturalistic" setting) can show what it is 'actually like' and reflect the subjective reality of people or the social meanings of their actions" and this certainly proved so for me when interviewing in a participant's house, I observed one child with FASD. The 'naturalistic' setting for six out of the eight birth mothers was their own home where they felt secure. In contrast, positivistic (traditional/scientific) researchers are unable to study meanings, as they are not directly observable. The interpretation of meanings are heavily context dependent.

Cotterill (1992) in her work explored some of the negative aspects of feminist interviewing by contrasting her experiences with those of Oakley (1981) and Finch et al (1983), her main points being: a) disagreement about how shared experience as women overcomes other barriers; b) using friendship as a measure of success; c) the moral dilemma of exploiting friendship. She also outlined how the woman researcher can herself be as vulnerable as the women she is studying and initially, I admit that I felt thus during my first interview, but this soon subsided as I became more and more aware that the birth mothers just longed to tell their stories. Cotterill (1992) further believed that while all women, as a consequence of their gender, share important experiences, these are not sufficient to overcome other structural barriers such as age, class, status, race and disability.

Before a participant is willing to share personal information, they will place the interviewer in a particular position and in this connexion, I established my rapport with the birth mothers by being an openly articulate, caring and humanistic registered nurse with a friendly smile and a sense of humour; an 'older' birth mother of fraternal twins, who occupied the same socially-oppressed status as themselves whilst 'mothering'. I also demonstrated a working knowledge of the phenomenon under study. This presentation was a most necessary access into the research 'field'.

As Cotterill (1992, p.596) speculated "The 'friendly stranger', unlike a friend, does not exercise social control over respondents because the relationship exists for the purpose of the research and is terminated when the interviews are complete". Cotterill (1992, p.600) disagreeing with Finch (1993) on the social indicators of friendship argues "Rapport cannot be said to exist on the basis of hospitality; often this is less to do with empathy between women than an indication of conventional ideas about good manners". Consequently, as I was always offered a cup of tea before commencing each interview, my integrity and intuition did not lead me to believe that I was being offered friendship, since I would have reciprocated the same hospitality and on the other hand, a 'friend' would not normally arrive carrying a tape-recorder, ask questions which caused the women to recall highly distressing life events and then leave.

Feminists challenge medical research because of their different beliefs about knowledge, their awareness of the influence of the researcher on the whole research process and the concern of many feminists with agendas of social change (Clifford-Walton, 2003). Acker et al (1983, pp.424-425) argued that feminists view 'people as active agents in their own lives and as such constructors of their social worlds'. They (together with myself) recognise the objects of research as subjects in their own rights and the research relationship as one being differentiated by power.

For women (and other groups) it is believed that research participants should gain knowledge from the research and become empowered to make changes in their lives. Research that does not have an agenda of change would be seen by feminists as purely exploitative and reinforcing the *status quo* (Acker et al, 1983). However, feminists... and other qualitative researchers, have different epistemological beliefs. They see knowledge as being historically, culturally and politically situated and being socially constructed as each person filters what they see and experience through their own previous experiences (Bleier, 1986; Lather, 1986a; 1986b; Hawkesworth, 1989). Where feminists do stray from traditional science is in their privileging of women's experience, knowledge, feelings and opinions (Stanley and Wise, 1983; Lather, 1986a, 1986b; Oakley, 1990; Hall and Stevens, 1991) and as Lather (1986b, p.68) stated "They make 'gender' a fundamental category for our understanding social order".

I shared some of my own personal information with the birth mothers, this being known as reciprocity (Oakley, 1981), but as Cotterill (1992, p.595) argued, this will not totally guarantee avoidance of what she described as 'best face phenomenon' and discusses people's responses to the research experience – characterized as a social interaction in an unfamiliar situation in which behaviour is not formally prescribed, whereby part of the participants' coping strategies accommodate the researcher by giving socially acceptable answers to questions instead of revealing views which are kept private in a belief that they will be unacceptable to others. When participants referred to me by my name, I believed that I had broken down the barrier, this being endorsed when the first answers uttered by a few of the women were changed later on, thus revealing some of the women's most inner privatizations. Because the women used narratives to inform me, I now comment on this.

Narratives

Smith (1993) stated that narratives have long been of interest in accessing individuals' experience and reflections of the past. Narratives have been particularly attractive to feminist researchers wishing to explore the experiences of women 'hidden from history' as well as means to access women's voices. However, as Hollway and Jefferson (2000, p.35) argued:

> Eliciting stories from people is not always a simple matter, especially from those who feel their lives lack sufficient interest or worth to justify 'a story'.

Polkinghorne (1991, p.135) described 'narratives' as the ways 'individuals construct private and personal stories linking diverse events of their lives into unified and understandable wholes. These are stories about the self. They are the basis of personal identity and self-understanding and they provide answers to the question "Who am I?"' Byrne (2000), suppporting Polkinghorne (1991), believed that approaching processes of subject construction through narrative allows for the acknowledgement of the constructed, flexible and fictionalised nature of the process of accounting for the self. Narrative approaches also enable the exploration of processes of subjection - the ways in which certain subject positions are discursively available for individuals to occupy, eg the birth mothers of this present study. To be asked about one's life is, to some extent, to be asked to give an account of one's self. It is also to produce an account which is explicitly or implicitly a story, an act of creation. In telling the story of her self, the narrator claims the position of the subject for her fictionalised self and accounts for her subjectivity. However, she does it through accessing the available resources or techniques of the self.

Riessman (1993) stated that story telling, to put the argument simply, is what we do with our research materials and what informants do with us. The story metaphor emphasizes that we create order, construct texts in particular contexts. Narrative analysis takes as its object of investigation the story itself. The purpose is to see how respondents in interviews impose order on the flow of experience to make sense of events and actions in their lives. The methodological approach, as used by me, examined the informant's story and analyzed how it was put together, the linguistic and cultural resources it drew on and how it persuaded a listener of authenticity. Studying narratives is additionally useful for what they revealed about social life - culture "speaks itself" through an individual's story. It is possible too, to examine gender inequalities, racial oppression and other practices of power that may be taken for granted by individual speakers, as my work did.

Narrators speak in terms that seem natural, but we can analyze how culturally and historically contingent these terms are (Rosenwald and Ochberg, 1992). Nature and the world do not tell stories – ndividuals do. Telling a narrative about one's life involves making oneself the subject of the story, claiming both intelligibility and agency for oneself. It often involves taking a particular approach to the self - as experiencing transformation and change, as the feminist perspective dictates. However, I acknowledged that some lived experiences are extremely difficult to speak about and Roth (1993) confirmed this. On the other hand and as Isak Dinesen believed "All sorrows can be borne if we can put them into a story" (quoted in Arendt, 1958, p.175). Could this be one reason amongst many others, why the birth mothers were so eager to tell me their stories?

Importantly, women's personal narratives embody and reflect the reality of difference and complexity and stress the centrality of gender to human life and thought. They are, therefore, critical to the elaboration of a more finely nuanced understanding of humanity and to a reconstruction of knowledge that admits the fact and value of difference into its definition (Personal Narratives Group, 1989, p.163).

To consolidate, narrative plays a crucial, but ancillary role – by leading physicians to recognize the moral dimension in every medical encounter, it helps to ground difficult medical decisions in the concreteness and specificity of each patient's life (Frank, 1995, pp155-156), but how does this link with motherhood and mothering? What do male physicians really know about motherhood and mothering (Marshall, 1991), since they have not lived the experience (an exclusively female pursuit) and what are society's attitudes towards such a state of affairs in a patriarchal society?

Motherhood and Mothering

Shorter (1991) contended that until this century, women were victimized by their own bodies and that the demands of constant childbirth, abortions and other gynaecological conditions, were instrumental in maintaining women in an inferior social position. We will now explore these issues employing a feminist perspective and as Belenky et al (1986) argued:

> feminists are beginning to articulate the values of the female world and to reshape the disciplines to include woman's voice, while continuing to press for the right of women to participate as equals in the male world.

Gilligan (1982) however, in her conventional feminine voice, would state that in actuality, women do not speak in a different voice: they have no voice at all. Conventional feminine goodness means being voiceless as well as selfless within society. In most societies, women are expected to become mothers and motherhood is construed as 'normal' and 'natural' by virtue of their female identity. The societal emphasis on motherhood as being normal and natural implies that women who are childless are to be considered 'abnormal' and 'unnatural' and their voices are often silenced (Ireland, 1993; Morell, 1994; Sandelowski, 1991; 1993; 1995; Woollett, 1991). Secondly, women are expected by society, to ensure by their nurturing practices, as 'good' mothers, that their children are well adjusted and become competent members of society, but why should it be the dominant 'male' group who defines them as such?

Although society acknowledges the diversity of motherhood and mothering, some settings are theorized as 'good' and more appropriate than others. Gilligan (1982) is supported in the literature by O'Barr et al (1990, p.2) who argued 'motherhood as an institution has been named by the authorative voice not of women, but of patriarchal culture.' These authors contended that failing to recognise the cultural construction of female oppression causes women to label themselves negatively and proscribes recognition of the conditions necessary for successful, confident parenting. Women not only make sense of their 'problem' mothering in ways that recognize how they are considered by others, but also by resisting and challenging ideas about the inadequacy of their mothering. So how does society view the mothering skills of birth mothers' of a child/ren disabled with FASD?

A variety of aspects of mothering have been identified as influencing children's development and linked to children's cognitive, social or emotional development, but those aspects that researchers explore vary according to their theoretical position. In general, society argues that 'good' mothering, ie mothering associated with children's competence, adjustment, and development – is responsive and child-centred (Burman, 1994; Woollett and Phoenix, 1991), but do these adjectives equally apply to birth mothers' of a child/ren with FASD? Ribbens (1994) similarly argued that 'good' mothering also involves being directive, socializing, listening to and guiding children along with monitoring and controlling their activities to ensure that they behave well, perform effectively and fit into society. Unfortunately, even when the former activities were practised by the birth mothers, there was no guarantee that their offspring would behave well, perform effectively and fit into society – in fact, the opposite was generally the case.

Ideas about motherhood and mothering provide a framework within which women make sense of mothering and their practices as mothers. Women [usually] consider motherhood a source of satisfaction, enjoyment and pleasure, but they also experience it as costly in terms of time and energy and because they are expected to subordinate their needs and identities to those of their children (Obermann and Josselson, 1996) – even more so when the child has FASD, necessitating frequent GP and hospital visitations as a result of their medicalized beginning. However, women's own accounts (Woollett and Phoenix, 1996), suggest powerfully that their experiences are moderated by the circumstances of their lives, the settings in which they mother and their social relations.

These settings, according to Furstenberg et al (1987) and Phoenix (1991a, 1991b) include the age at which women become mothers, their relationships and support for mothering (Silva, 1996; Silverstein and Phares, 1996), how many children they have (Munn, 1991), their health and able-bodiedness (Thomas, 1999) and their other roles, including employment (Birns and Hay, 1988; Brannen and Moss, 1991; Gilbert, 1994; Glenn, et al, 1994). From my findings, I support these ideas.

Woollett and Marshall (2001, p.174) argued that most women become mothers in their twenties and thirties, with relatively few 'young' mothers. This statement is not supported by the findings of my work, as the majority of the participants were in their 'teens when they first became mothers. These researchers further stated that young mothers, especially those under the age of 16 years, are considered problematic because motherhood disrupts their education. This obviously is true, but what of those 16 year old FASD-affected mothers-to-be who do not want to continue at school because they are oppressed and discriminated against by teachers and the educational systems? (see findings).

Since the birth mothers were frequently in and out of GP surgeries and hospitals with their disabled offspring, I now discuss the doctor-patient relationship using a feministic lens.

Doctor-Patient Relationship

It is assumed that the doctor is the knowledgeable, powerful, responsible person and the patient incompetent and in need of care (Gray, 2002). The word 'patient' has two definitions in the Shorter English Dictionary: 'one who is under medical treatment' and 'one who suffers patiently' or 'a person...to whom something is done', but there is no need for a person who is suffering to be powerless. Interestingly, doctors were not always powerful and in the 19th Century, their social status was low – lower than that of the clergy or the legal profession, but as science provided more knowledge for clinicians, their authority increased (Gray, 2002). This is not to say that patients gave up their beliefs, but they certainly deferred overtly to the power of authority of the doctor, even though his science was often flawed... (Gray, 2002) and still is today, as evidenced by the birth mothers' utterances.

Gray (2002) believed that an intelligent patient (herein mothers advocating for their offspring) focusing on one disease, can soon become familiar with its concepts, terminology and evidence. Also that many patients are better educated than clinicians and even though the doctor may have better esoteric knowledge at the start of the patient's journey, the patient can soon overtake the clinician. Gray's (2002) beliefs are upheld by the birth mothers' stories and as Sherwin (1998) maintained:

> The very large gap in life experience between physicians who are, byvirtue of their professional status, relatively privileged members of society and some of their seriously disadvantaged patients, makes the likelihood of the former anticipating the specific information needs of the latter, questionable (p.27).

The shift of power from patient to physician occurred relatively recently, during the second half of the 20th Century. Alongside this power difference – men have more than women (Goodwin and Fiske, 2001) – there remains the power difference in communication within agencies by male doctors towards their female patients and hitherto, the birth mothers' of offspring with FASD, who are not listened to when advocating for their disabled child/ren. Professor Kleinman at Harvard, emphasized that the most difficult skill of all for doctors and even nurses, was the skill of listening. That may be so, but under patriarchy, female authentic voices are ignored.

Gilligan (1982) further contended that while women and men may ostensibly speak the same language and indeed, assume they hold the same meanings, in fact, the dissimilarities of self and social relationships between them cause an incongruity in the language which impedes communication and limits the potential for care and cooperation in relationships. She agreed with Spender (1985) when she said that the failure to see the different reality of women's lives and to hear the differences in their voices, stems in part from the assumption that there is a single mode of social experience and interpretation (Gilligan, 1982, p.173). This idea is enhanced by Hoagland (1988, p.14) when she declared that "language is a tool of oppression, for we remain trapped in oppression when we perceive only what the oppressors perceive, when we are restricted to their values and categories". If there are differences in everyday discourse, those differences are exaggerated and exacerbated within the circumstances of medical encounters, where two differently socialised cultural groups (ie women and male doctors), interact.

Comparing normal conversations with medical discourse, Fisher (1986, p.59) believed that balanced participation is not expected within the framework of the medical exchange. She found the asymmetry of the doctor-patient discourse (as reflective of the doctor-patient relationship), highlights the importance of context and power relationships when she stated "obscured is a language pattern: during medical encounters, language use is structured by the authority of the medical role". That is to say, that language in the form of discourse can serve differing purposes – it can illuminate a situation as well as obfuscate or increase uncertainty. It is a locus of power in the medical encounter as substantiated by the birth mothers'accounts.

Helle (1991) suggested that one of the ways in which power and domination are reinforced is by excluding forms of expression relevant to women's experience from 'legitimate' forms of representation and as I believed, by keeping relevant information concerning their child, from them. Todd (1989), being an author who perceived that the hierarchical nature of the doctor-woman-patient relationship was but a mirror of generally held societal attitudes, advocated that a society's values develop historically and are deeply embedded in institutional arrangements and individual consciousness. Further, Spender (1985), writing on the use of language to construct reality and meaning, argued that by assuming the male as a norm, female experience remains not only unacknowledged, but unrecognised and therefore, invisible and discounted. Todd (1989) also argued that doctors and patients bring to their interactions complex internalizations of larger societal expectations. Physicians carry with them assumptions about women which have been nurtured for many generations and are difficult to change even in these times of increased awareness (p.43). This arguable rings true today with two birth mothers being viewed as 'neurotic' by their GPs.

Sherwin (1992) claimed that even in cases where a woman, who is not ill, brings in a family member for medical care, she may still be dismissed as incapable of coming to an appropriate decision when speaking on behalf of the patient (in this instance, her disabled child):

> In a sexist society where women are regularly denied the status of competent reasoners, where patients are typically women and where physicians are mostly men, that physicians experience patients as lacking in reason does not constitute reliable evidence that patients really are incapable of the reasoning that is required to arrive at reliable decisions about their own [*or their children's*] care (p.142). (my emphasis).

The doctor's influence appears to be mediated by the relationship that develops with the patient and the need for a new style of practice has been clearly described by one of the people who has studied the work of the physician in most detail, Howard Brody (1994), who wrote:

> In medicine, especially a male-dominated world of medicine, close relationships seem scary and potentially overwhelming, whereas isolation seems safe. Our own sense of safety in emotional distance has probably led us to be overeager to hear the message of detached concern, with the emphasis on the detached rather than the concern. It might be time to explode the myth of getting too close to the patient as a serious danger of attending carefully to the patient's story and affect.

Both research-based evidence and the patient's narrative are important, but for feminists, the latter may be more important than the former. So from this statement do we ascertain that women and feminists are the healers (Ehrenreich and English, 1973) on the basis that they are society's minority who call for stories to be unfolded on the lived experiences of women, through research? These questions now lead onto addressing the qualitative research and the methodological approaches used in my study.

Conducting the Research

Introduction

As Oliver (1992) argued, the medical model of disability is strongly linked with a positivist research methodology, which until recently, has largely dominated research within the social sciences and the disability field. Quantitative research efforts are based on positivism, but are ill-suited for addressing the social or health relevance of same (Stainbach and Stainbach, 1984). Since feminist emancipatory research seeks to explore the lived experiences of women through their memoirs, using a qualitative methodology, this project has adopted this stance in order to explore the lived experiences of birth mothers' of a child/ren disabled with FASD (Denzin and Lincoln, 2003, p.12).

I now address the defining features of qualitative research which are well-documented in the literature and discuss these defining features in terms of my study, along with specific procedures involved.

Methodological Approach

A qualitative paradigm, a feminist theory and a phenomenological perspective were adopted to explore the retrospective experiences of eight New Zealand-resident multipara biological mothers aged 18 and over who had nurtured or were still living with an affected child or children. The protocols in this project were approved by the University of Otago (Dunedin, New Zealand) Human Ethics Committee and involved consultation work with a sub-group of birth mothers.

The mothers had nine affected offspring amongst them aged from 8 ½ to 30 years – two males had FAS, three males had FAE, two females had FAS, one female had FAE and one female had pFAE plus ADHD. All individuals had been diagnosed by a medical professional. All interviews were analysed using the constant comparative method (Strauss and Corbin, 1994) which is inherent within grounded theory methodology. Validity was informed through triangulation, participant-checking and closeness of 'fit' (see p.66).

The study produced several emergent hypotheses. The birth mothers described concerns for their offspring relating to health, social, educational, judicial and professionals' lack of knowledge. Some mothers believed that *social drinking* was different from binge-drinking and was not as hazardous. Society felt that the mothers were the cause of the individual's behaviour which included lying, stealing, hyperactivity, aggressiveness, destructiveness, sexual promiscuity: cognitive issues being attention-deficit, absence of fear, diminished memory and comprehension together with inability to acknowledge and understand consequences (Table 1). Of the fifteen sub-themes that emerged, four were categorized as key themes (Table 3). Forty-eight recurring themes/words were identified and are inter-related with each other to some degree (Table 4). The mothers' characteristics are to be found in Table 2: their profiles appear on page 74, with all names being fictitious. The themes identified are written in the first person to ensure easy reading, accuracy of narrative together with checking by the participants.

Present Study

Since the purpose of my study was to establish the experiences of New Zealand birth mothers' of offspring with FASD, a qualitative methodology was utilized, which allowed me to explore and capture the depth and richness that comes from individuals' experiences, namely, the small, sub-group of women themselves, by virtue of field focusing using an open-ended interview technique, which was in keeping with the interpretive nature (Miller and Dingwall, 1997) of the chosen method.

Table 1. CNS structural and functional effects by age that can be alcohol related

Age	Effects
Newborn:	Microcephaly, jitteriness, opisthotonos (hyper-extension of body with arched back), seizures, tremors, weak suck, umpredictable and dis-rupted sleep/wake cycles, hypotonia, hypertonia, poor state regulation, decreased vigorous bodily activity, hyperacusis (lower hearing threshold), failure to thrive (given adequate opportunity), poor habituation (difficulty tuning out redundant stimuli), EEG abnormalities
Infancy:	Delayed development in one or more areas, head-banging and/or body rocking, poor fine motor or gross motor control, neurological dysfunction (including cerebral palsy)
Preschool:	Hyperactivity, poor eye-hand coordination, poor balance, poor tandem gait, central auditory dysfunction, delayed or perseverative language, mental retardation
Early school age	Attentional impairments, learning disabilities, arithmetic disabilities, specific cognitive disabilities, deficits in higher order receptive and expressive language, poor impulse control
Later school age and adolescence	Memory impairments, difficulties with judgment, difficulties with abstract reasoning, poor adaptive functioning

Source: Streissguth, Bookstein, Sampson and Barr, 1993.
Note: Items are listed at the age at which they might be observed for the first time.

Table 2. Mothers' Characteristics

	Age	*Alcoholic Partner*	*Professional Occupation*	*Birth Mother's Father Alcoholic*	*Birth M other Alcoholic*
Oldest group 1970's births					
1975 Mary	64	Yes	No	No	No
1975 Miriam	52	No	Yes	No	No
Middle group 1980's births					
1980 Martha	42	Yes	No	Yes (+ brother)	Yes
1988 Rebecca	41	Yes	Yes	No	No
1987 Esther	38	Yes	No	Yes	No
Youngest group 1990's births					
1993 Ruth	32	Yes	No	Yes	No
1995 Sarah	31	Yes	No	No	No
1996 Naomi	29	Yes + drugs	No: unemployed medical problem	No	No

Table 3. The Study's Core Categories, Categories and Recurring Themes/Words

Core Category	Category	Recurring Themes/Words No.
1. It's the mother's fault		
	*lack of knowledge	34, 35, 36, 38, 40, 42, 44, 46
	*the mothers drank in pregnancy	34, 35, 37, 38, 40, 42, 46
	*pregnancy/labour/birth different	34, 35, 38, 41, 42, 44
2. Medical and health professionals abandon the mothers		
	*mothers left 'to it'	33, 34, 35, 36, 37, 39, 42, 43, 44
	*mothers viewed subjectively/violation of rights	34, 35, 36, 37, 42, 43, 44
	*mothers not listened to	34, 35, 36, 37, 39, 42, 43, 44, 47
	*mothers want a diagnosis for their child	34, 35, 36, 37, 38, 39, 42, 43, 44, 46
	*mothers learn to cope with child's neurodevelopmental problems	1, 2, 3, 4, 5, 6, 7, 8, 9, 10, 11, 12, 13, 14, 15, 16, 17, 19, 20, 21, 24, 26, 28, 34, 35, 37, 44, 46, 47
3. Birth Mothers and their children are unsupported in the educational system		
	*mothers not listened to by teachers	4, 5, 6, 7, 9, 13, 14, 18, 23, 27, 28, 31, 33, 34, 36, 37, 39, 42, 43, 48
	*child's behaviour not understood by teachers	1, 2, 4, 5, 6, 9, 13, 14, 15, 16, 17, 19, 20, 22, 23, 24, 25, 26, 28, 29, 31, 34, 36, 37, 39, 48
	*children should be taught according to their educational needs	22, 23, 24, 25, 27, 28, 29, 30, 31, 33, 34, 39, 42, 43, 48
	*child is frustrated and not included in classroom	1, 2, 4, 5, 6, 9, 10, 11, 12, 13, 14, 15, 16, 17, 18, 20, 21, 22, 23, 24, 25, 26, 27, 28, 29, 30, 31, 32, 33, 34, 35, 36, 37, 39, 48
	*child has few friends	1, 2, 22, 32, 34
4. Birth Mothers are the cause of criminal behaviour		
	*police blame the mothers for the child's behaviour	1, 4, 6, 9, 14, 17, 23, 24, 25, 26, 32, 33, 36, 37, 39, 45
	*police have little or no knowledge of the syndrome	1, 2, 4, 6, 9, 14, 15, 16, 17, 19, 20, 23, 24, 25, 26, 32, 33, 36, 37, 45, 46, 48

Table 4. Recurring Themes/Words

1. Odd/different/not normal/retarded/dumb
2. Sexually promiscuous
3. Perfect/good baby

4. Spoilt/lazy/naughty child
5. Lack of concentration
6. Difficult behaviour
7. Sensitive
8. Floppy/rigid
9. Missing link
10. Cries++
11. Sleep pattern disturbance
12. Lazy suck/feeding problems
13. Delayed milestones
14. Learning problems
15. No sense of time
16. Fearless/risk taker/no fear of heights
17. Lack of foresight/poor judgement
18. Special
19. Truant
20. Restlessness
21. Tactile defensiveness
22. Child's feelings ignored
23. Gets in with wrong individuals/attracted to other FAS individuals
24. Alcohol/drug use by child
25. Child's lack of trust in the professionals
26. The child steals/crook/liar
27. Child held back in school system
28. Child doesn't fit in at playgroups/kindergarten
29. Child viewed as 'clown' in mainstream schooling
30. Homework/overload/'special'/not set at correct academic level of child
31. Separation/integration within the educational system
32. Animals/cars/young children
33. Violence against child
34. Social workers/health professionals/teachers
35. Language/power of the medical professionals
36. Burden on society
37. Labelling
38. General Practitioner surgeries/ante-natal clinics hold no literature on the syndrome
39. Violation of the child's rights
40. Women didn't know they were pregnant
41. Fast/shock birth
42. Frustration of the mothers in relation to the professionals/systems
43. Women didn't know about FAS/FAE
44. Women's intuition
45. Male doctors
46. Police/policing system/legal system
47. Alcohol/drug use by other family members
48. Violence against mothers
49. Employment/job stability

Through the use of a feminist lens, a voice was given to eight women, whose truths of their personal narratives are the truths revealed from their lived experience in the context of their real positions and social relationships. It is because they are women and mothers that they have a particular interpretation; "when women construct the adult domain, the world of relationships emerges and becomes the focus of attention and concern" (Gilligan, 1982, p.167).

In concordance with the inductive nature of qualitative research and grounded theory analysis, as a research design, which allowed me to generate hypotheses, no particular outcomes or products were sought as the issues had not been defined beforehand. Therefore, the purpose was to establish the issues according to the participants themselves. Moreover, a strength of a qualitative paradigm is that it enables a picture of the person within their sociocultural context to be developed, in contrast to traditional (quantitative) research which often focuses on a small number of discrete variables (Krefting and Krefting, 1991).

I also chose qualitative methodology to work from within as it allowed for the incorporation of a feminist standpoint which embodies an acknowledgement of the significance of gender and gender asymmetry as a basic feature of all social life, is conducted with the aim of creating social change, challenges the myth of scientific objectivity, accepts that the intersubjectivity of the researcher will and can, enchance the research process and the outcome and has concern for the ethical implications of research (Mies, 1983; Cook and Fonow, 1986; Smith and Nobel-Spruell, 1986).

Because FASD is not recognised in New Zealand as a main stream disability, it was anticipated that the number of birth mothers would be relatively small. Also, coupled with this notion, was the fact that many children with FASD are either adopted, cared for by foster parents or "significant others" (NZ Paediatric Surveillance Unit, 2004), making it extemely difficult to locate the birth mothers who are still caring for their disabled offspring. For these reasons, it would have been unrealistic to aim for reliability or generalizability of the data in the statistical or technical sense. Instead, the present study's focus was on originality coupled with establishing the validity of the data and meaningful findings or results, which would improve society's knowledge and understanding of FASD and what the birth mothers' experiences had been in nurturing offspring with this condition.

Use of a Qualitative Research Method and Design

Qualitative methodology is not the property of any one theoretical paradigm or discipline. As Bogdan and Biklen (1982) stated "All qualitative research, in some way, reflects a phenomenological perspective where 'researchers in the phenomenological mode attempt to understand the meaning of events and interactions to ordinary people in particular situations'" (p.31). Patton (1987) believed that qualitative methods are particularly oriented towards "exploration" and "discovery" (p.15) and are "derived most directly from the ethnographic and field study traditions of anthropology and sociology" (p.19). So, it was deemed a suitable paradigm to work within for the purposes of my study. Miller and Crabtree (1992) endorsed the beliefs of Patton (1987) by stating that within the qualitative paradigm there are different disciplinary perspectives which have evolved out of the main social science framework. These give rise to distinct methodologies which tend to reflect their epistemological foundations, eg. the anthropological field has developed the strategies of ethnography and ethnoscience; psychology has given us hermeneutics and sociology created grounded theory and symbolic interactionism.

Because I am a registered nurse and therefore, a health professional, I chose qualitative methodology as the paradigm in which to identify the experiences of birth mothers' of offspring with FASD in New Zealand, since qualitative research also combines the science and artistic natures of nursing to enhance understanding of the human health experience (Burns and Grove, 1993). Qualitative research focuses on process rather than on outcomes/products according to Bogdan and Biklen (1982), who further believed that it is descriptive, employing the "use of expressive language and the presence of voice in the text" (Eisner,1991, p.36). Neither does it seek to measure by numbers or bring a statistical analysis to the data (Smythe, 2000).

Similarly, Boyd (1990, p.183) stated that qualitative research involves broadly stated questions about human experiences and realities, studied through sustained contact with people in their natural environments, generating rich, descriptive data (expressive language and voice in the text) that helps us to understand their experiences. The data, therefore, is collected in words or pictures which cannot be separated from the research process. Data results include direct quotations to illustrate and substantiate findings and I myself, in accordance with this remark, documented my findings thus from the raw data, ie unadulterated text.

As qualitative methods focus on meaning, they permit the interviewer to study "selected issues, cases or events in depth and detail" (Patton, 1987, p.9). For this reason, a wealth of detailed information is usually produced about a much smaller number of people or situations (Eisner, 1991; Patton, 1990), my study being reliant on eight women, as stated.

In contrast to the quest for quantitative data, it has been argued that "the flavour of the particular situation, individual, event or object is lost" (Eisner, 1991, p.38); that from data, is a need to be statistically treated, emerges "a description of relationships, almost disconnected from the particulars from which the data were originally secured" (Eisner, 1991, p.38). Eisner (1991) also believed that where quantitative studies lose the flavor of research attempts, qualitative studies tend to provide the flavor. In this way, qualitative research methods focus on 'validity' in establishing results or findings. In other words, the researcher searches for other participants who experienced (or observed or heard about) the same event and listens to their accounts and interpretations thereby improving evidence for descriptive validity (Johnson and Christensen, 2004).

Methodologically, the qualitative research approach utilises case studies, participant observation and the use of interview techniques while drawing on a tradition of inquiry concerned primarily with exploring, describing and explaining human experiences (Lincoln and Guba, 1985; Patton, 1990). The qualitative approach is characterized by the study of the real world situation in a non-manipulative and non-controlling manner.

The qualitative paradigm is broad and can be a number of things, including inductive and holistic ideologies: it is used to describe a phenomenon in detail, but is not normally employed to answer such questions that will prove causality or to supply answers to questions such as 'how much?" or 'how many?" as these require statistical answering, which is the domain of quantitative methodology. So, qualitative research questions are more appropriate to trying to gain an understanding of people or events. As a strategy, qualitative research is founded on the belief that human beings react not only to events that happen to them, but also act upon and create meaning in their experiences (Avis, 1995). It assumes that a full and adequate knowledge of human experiences cannot be grasped until the researcher has understood the symbolic world within which the research participants live (Patton, 1990). Additionally, it assumes that those who have particular experiences are the best placed to be the most knowledgeable about what events are significant in their lives and what they mean to them (DePoy and Gitlin, 1998).

In relation to the field of FASD, the "people who have the experiences" will be the birth mothers, foster parents, carers and significant others of offspring suffering from the disability, effects or any of the other spectrum of anomalies, in knowing what is most significant about an experience and its impact on the individual. Thus, qualitative research allows the adoption of a humanistic approach, where individual circumstances or unique episodes can be incorporated into the findings.

This methodology also has particular relevance to my study since it provided a flexibility by which the participants could reveal their experiences around a particularly disabling disability. As such, it provided an appropriate method by which a better understanding of the human experiences around the impact of the disability on an individual's life could be developed through direct and repeated contacts over time (DePoy and Gitlin, 1998).

Another important theoretical assumption underlying the approach of qualitative research was the concept that multiple realities exist. An individual's view of reality is largely determined by his/her psychological processes and/or the existence of social structures which transcend an individual's experience (Avis, 1995; DePoy and Gitlin, 1998). For example, from a professional health worker's point-of-view and as has previously been written, the social structure for women is very different from that of men by the sheer virtue of their gender. Women and especially mothers, are rendered "voiceless" in a male dominated society even when they are advocating for their disabled child for whom their intuition tells them there is something "wrong", "not quite right" or "different" about their offspring.

Within the practice of qualitative research, it is acknowledged that human experience is complex and cannot be understood solely by quantitative methods upon which the scientific paradigm for research has been built. Surveys, random sampling techniques and the use of control groups are not necessarily seen as applicable to the quest of understanding complex human experiences and their meaning for individuals, such as the experiences of birth mothers of a child/ren with FASD. Neither can this method be used to describe or to gain insight into people's attitudes, values and opinions, nor explore the interpretations and meanings that they place upon their lives (Ryan and Denz-Penhey, 1996).

In this study, as with other qualitative research, I employed an empathetic and non-judgmental stance toward the emerging data which was critical to the furthering of the understanding of the complex situation under study, one of its elements being "How do the birth mothers cope with their child affected by FASD?" The primary task was to depict the social world as it exists for those being investigated through the use of direct quotations (determined by what I, as the author, deemed worthy) or excerpts which captured participants' reality and acted as the equivalent to the numerical data reported in quantitative studies, which according to Stainbach and Stainbach (1984, p.400) are 'ill-suited for addressing the social or educational relevance of research efforts."

Qualitative researchers are able to observe, interview, record, describe, interpret and appraise settings as they are (Eisner, 1991, p.33). This is referred to as the "natural

setting" by Bogdan and Biklen (1982), who believed that to "divorce the act, word or gesture from its context is...to lose sight of significance" (p.27). Therefore, the emphasis is on design procedures to gain "real", "rich" and "deep" data (Stainbach and Stainbach, 1984) as there is no statistical test of significance to determine if results 'count': in the end, what 'counts' is a matter of judgement (Eisner, 1991, p.39). Research design is defined by Easterby-Smith et al (1990, p.21) as "...overall configuration of a piece of research: what kind of evidence is gathered from where and how such evidence is interpreted in order to provide good answers to the basic research question(s)".

The final element of qualitative research relates to the criteria for judgement of the study and as Eisner (1991) posited "Qualitative research becomes believable because of its coherence, insight and instrumental utility" (1991, p.39).

Use of Phenomenology

Phenomenology, being my choice of design, for reasons as described, was also classified by Omery (1983) as an approach and a philosophy, its purpose being to describe the world as experienced by the participants of the study ('life-world') and to understand the personal meaning of the phenomena as constructed from their 'lived experiences'. In other words, it is an attempt to enter another's world as defined by themselves; not as one would presume it to be. It is not limited by the experiences and perceptions of researchers, allowing them to identify everything they already know in relation to their research question and put it to one side (bracketing) (Giorgi 1970, p.162), so that it does not 'contaminate' the study (Smythe, 2000). Thus, as mentioned briefly previously, a tenet of this approach to research is the necessity of accounting for the presence of the researcher in the process, the reason being:

> It is neither practical nor ethical to eliminate from scrutiny our own membership in society with its accompanying realm of sense-making. While considering a distant interpretation from ours, we cannot suspend, remove or contain our interpretive practices as matter of conscious effort, irrespective of our research pursuits. Even if we could, such distancing would deny authenticity to the very realm of experiences that we permit the other (Silvers, 1982, p.244).

Explaining the phenomenon under study is always interpreted through the filter of our own 'biographies' – we can only understand others in the context of our own social knowledge (Darroch and Silvers, 1982). Referring to a researcher's biography is however, not necessarily to make reference to a personal 'autobiography', but "rather it is through the researcher's biography as a cultural memory (cultural memory as the selection and signification of the structures of experience) that understanding as the meaning of another's experience...is made possible" (pp.16-17).

Phenomenology's usefulness is in that it reveals the taken-for-granted nature of everyday experience (Smythe, 2000) whereas, a different approach, such as a structured interview or questionnaire, could lead to narrowing of the elements of the experience. Thus, phenomenology enabled the participants to give a detailed picture of their experiences without researcher-imposed constraints, enabling me to obtain a broader view as the participant's own reality was described.

Phenomenological researchers do not, however, generally assume that individuals are completely unique. More technically speaking, phenomenological researchers do not just study the variant structures of an experience (the unique part of an individual's experience that varies from person to person). Phenomenologists generally assume that there is some commonality in human experience and they seek to understand this commonality, as with my own experience of childbirth and motherhood vis-a-vis the lived experience for the mothers interviewed for this work. This commonality of experience is called an essence or invariant structure of the experience and is universally present in particular instances of a phenomenon (van Manen, 1990). Phenomenology does not accept that duplication of data is necessary to prove the validity of the results and to reiterate, this study did not seek to generalize results, which is the domain of quantitative research methods.

Emerson (1981), referring to validation techniques, believed them not to be tests, but opportunities for reflexive elaboration. By being in the phenomenological mode, I was able to instigate and utilize the interviewing technique in order to investigate the lived experiences of a very particular subset of women - the birth mothers' of offspring with FASD – as there was to date, no research from within New Zealand on the specific phenomena from the birth mothers' point-of-view. So, in other words, I was trying to make the world of problematic lived experience of the interviewed birth mothers, directly available to the reader and thus produce a plausible story. Denzin (1989) confirmed thus:

> "to make the world of problematic lived experience of ordinary people directly available to the reader, the inter-actionist interprets these worlds. The research methods of this approach include open-ended, creative interviewing; document analysis; semiotics; life-history; life-story; personal experience and self-story construction; participant observation and thick description".

As Becker (1958) also pointed out in his classic piece on 'inference and proof', the challenge is to convert these sense data into an explanation of the situation and as Strong (1979, p.250) posited 'the best we can hope for in this world, even if we study practical reasoning, is a plausible story'.

Phenomenology can trace its intellectual roots back to a philosophical tradition conceived by the German philosopher, Edmund Husserl, at the beginning of the 20th Century (Baron, 1985; Baker Wuest and Stern, 1992; Morse and Field, 1996), when he and his associates were dissatisfied with the contemporary acceptance of the dominant concept of Cartesian dualism. They argued that by accepting the tenet of 'rational' science as being capable of understanding the world in its entirety, science was precluded from helping people understand themselves and their world as they lived in it. While not intending to denigrate the achievements of modern science, Husserl believed that those achievements needed to be placed into a more fully human context as did Baron (1985) who proclaimed that:

> By taking seriously questions about the world as experienced (rather than taking scientific description to be the world of all that is), phenomenologists seek to reunite science with life and to explore the relationship between the abstract world of the sciences and the concrete world of human experience (p.608).

Use of Grounded Theory

Grounded theory is a reaction against the positivist trends of the 'great men' theories of Weber, Durkheim, Cooley, Mead and others whose work focused on testing them in the 1950s and 1960s (Kinach,1995). Therefore, the 'fathers' of this reaction/approach, Glaser and Strauss (1967), argued that the prevailing emphasis on theory testing neglected the process of theory generation, as well as stressing the idea that theory emerged from and was grounded in, data. However, Glaser and Strauss have fallen out about what it (grounded theory) really is and the nature of the research strategy they promoted in the 1960's (Denzin and Lincoln, 2003). This concept they described as 'a strategy for handling data in research, providing modes of conceptualization for describing and explaining' plus the fact that constant comparison allows for drawing on literature and theorizing in the area under study as well as the more obvious comparison of data with data and data with emerging conceptual categories (Melia, 1997) that would describe and explain the phenomenon under study. I therefore, believed that the original justification lay in grounded theory, which, according to Melia (1997), is an accepted practice in the analysis of qualitative data.

Several explanatory or conceptual categories (or sub-categories/themes) would be integrated around a core category and so the theory would emerge. The core category/theme (ie the central idea, event or happening) is defined as the phenomenon (Pandit, 1996). The idea was to follow-up conceptually fruitful avenues and allow emergent concepts to dictate the direction and nature of the data collection, which was described by Glaser (1978) as a process of 'theoretical sensitivity', whereby data collection and analysis went on side by side until a core category emerged and was 'saturated' (Glaser and Strauss, 1967).

If there is room for dispute between the founders, it is not surprising that qualitative methods become so complicated, as I experienced. Glaser and Strauss now clearly have different views about the essential nature of the analytical strategy which they co-originated: indeed, if we were to accept Glaser's version, they may have had different understandings from the outset! (Melia, 1997). Glaser (1992: p.43) argued:

> "Strauss's method of labelling and then grouping is totally unnecessary, laborious and is a waste of time. Using constant comparison method gets the analyst to the desired conceptual power, quickly, with ease and joy. Categories emerge upon comparison and properties emerge upon more comparison. And that is all there is to it."

Because in the main (ibid, p.31) and for the reason that 'theoretical saturation' did not figure in Corbin and Strauss's (1990) method, I adopted the works of the latter two researchers as the study's approach which is, albeit, based on the originators' works and which still utilized the associated analytical procedures of the constant comparative method (as opposed to content analysis, which *presupposes* what will come out of the raw data) and theoretical sensitivity, which go beyond the interview data themselves to a more conceptual level (Melia, 1997), but still allowed for the plausible collection of data to explain the lived experience of the birth mothers of offspring with FASD within their worlds.

A further reason for the implementation of Strauss and Corbin's (1990) grounded theory ideas from the beginning of the project, as opposed to Glaser and Strauss's, was because there would only be eight participants under study and therefore, there was no guarantee from the outset that "theoretical" saturation would be achieved. Also, the use of Strauss and Corbin's

(1990) concept allowed me to "freely develop the method". The accounts were grounded in the data supplied by the birth mothers, as the participants of the study, yet moved to an analytical level beyond the raw data themselves and as such, the data 'jumped' (ie stood out with themes/words like "class clown" and "dumb", as opposed to being 'pushed', ie forcing (Glaser, 1992 p.43).

The grounded theory method was chosen also to guide the data collection and analyses for this study for three reasons:

a) Grounded theory would provide an effective and systematic framework around which the analysis and interpretation of the vast amount of descriptive data expected to be generated, could be manipulated, through the use of coding techniques and the constant comparative method (Bailey, 1997; Dubouloz, Egan, Vallerand and von Zweck, 1999; de Laine, 1997; Young and Ensing, 1999);
b) as a new area of qualitative research, the use of a qualitative approach would help ensure that any emerging theories were based on the participant-generated data and not based on any preconceived ideas or biases that I myself, as the researcher, may hold (Glaser and Strauss, 1967; Glaser, 1992; Honey, 2000);
c) as a major objective of the study was to develop a theoretical framework by which the birth mothers' experiences of offspring with FASD would be forthcoming and demonstrated, grounded theory was well-suited, given its emphasis on theory development (Creswell, 1998; DePoy and Gitlin, 1998) and as Glaser and Strauss (1967, p.45) argued, it is "the process of data collection for generating theory whereby the analyst jointly collects, codes and analyses his data and decides what data to collect next and where to find them, in order to develop his theory as it emerges.

In adopting a qualitative research method, I acknowledged the major criticisms of the grounded theory approach, as cited above.

Recruitment Strategies

Participants for the study were recruited on the basis of their ability and willingness to provide detailed descriptions and reflections of their lived experiences in conceiving, giving birth to and nurturing a child/ren with FASD (Denzin and Lincoln, 2003). No mother under the age of 18 could be considered and all women had to be resident within New Zealand. The sample was of necessity, purposeful (Patton, 1990), as entry criteria into the study was clearly defined. My recruiting agency was Fetal Alcohol Support Trust in Hamilton. The other participants into the study were recruited via the technique of 'snowballing' and as such, three birth mothers of a child with FASD were then located in the South Island following interviewing participants in the North Island. One woman enrolled herself into the study on the basis that she believed her child suffered from FAE and since she was an outspoken advocate and support person for the condition, she was enrolled into the study.

I initially contacted seven potential participants via letter together with an information sheet, outlining the study and also inviting them to participate. A stamped-addressed envelope was also enclosed for the return-slip to be sent to my department. Upon receipt of the returned slip, the participants were contacted via telephone and email to enable further explanation about the study and to organize appropriate appointment times when to meet and interview the women.

Moreover, as previously stated and in accordance with the practice of Strauss and Corbin's grounded theory principles (1994), recruitment of participants, data collection and data analysis *did not* occur simultaneously (this latter being the premise of the founding-fathers, Glaser and Strauss). However, open coding (which refers to the process of discovering and categorizing phenomena under study and then developing properties that will describe each category), was applied because I was unclear about which concepts or experiences would be relevant to the emerging theory. This procedure allowed for openness rather than specificity, to guide the initial sampling process (Strauss and Corbin, 1990).

Once the initial category outlines had been formed and their dimensions developed, the coding procedures of axial coding and selective coding were applied. Axial coding aims to uncover and validate any relationships that exist between the categories or concepts developed thus far. In the final steps of selective coding, persons or sites under study are specifically chosen in order to maximise research opportunities for verifying emerging relationships between categories and/or for filling in poorly-developed categories (Creswell, 1998; Strauss and Corbin, 1997).

Interview Schedule

The interviews, which were carried out over a six week period and in keeping with qualitative research and grounded theory, used broad, open-ended questions, covering the areas of pregnancy, birth, post-partum and onwards. As King (1994, p.14) argued "the goal...is to see the research topic from the perspective of the interviewee and to understand how and why he or she comes to have this particular perspective". Pseudonyms have been used for the birth mothers and their offspring, so as to maintain anonymity. Because the demographics of several of the women could have made them identifiable, specific details about the families are not disclosed. Some of the interviews took place with the FASD child present. However, where a child was present during the interview, much patience had to be exercised by me during transcription. At no point was I requested to turn-off the recorder for privacy reasons.

Being a somewhat 'theoretically-sensitive' (Johnston and Christensen, 2004, p.383) researcher and knowing that I was dealing with a sensitive area (which could upset the birth mother when retrospectively visiting the phenomena under study), a counsellor was made available at the end of a telephone during each interview. However, this facility proved not to be required. All interviews were carried out and transcribed by myself, from additional shorthand notes and from tape-recordings and although this was an extremely arduous task at times, it proved to be a valuable exercise in itself as I was able to 'hear' the voices of the women which immediately allowed me to reflect on the interview and capture the 'reliving' of the accompanying non-verbal language utilized by them and the ease at which they were able to report the issues at hand.

Since five of the eight interviews were conducted in the participant's own home, an informal atmosphere was easily created which effected an easy, confident, trustworthy and intimate relationship between two oppressed women and as Finch (1993, p.170) contended, "both parties share a subordinate structural position by virtue of their gender". Added to this, the space between conducting the interviews and transcription of same (which ranged from between two weeks and two months), afforded an opportunity to gain critical distance between the women's words (as spoken) and my reactions to them, thus enabling 'dialogue reflection' to produce the emergence of new perceptions.

Because the women appeared to be so eager to talk to me, they were also invited to share their perceptions of and experiences around FASD from the moment of conception of their disabled offspring until the present day, describing details of particular events, situations and people involved. It is noted here that women are almost always enthusiastic about talking (referred to by Oakley, 1981, as 'therapeutic') to a woman researcher (Finch, 1984; Finch, 1993, p.167) as they have few opportunities to talk about themselves in depth and often welcome the chance to share their lives with an interested listener. Oakley (1981, pp.50-51) further posited that her research showed husbands, mothers, friends, etc did not provide a sufficiently sympathetic or interested audience for a detailed recounting of the experiences and difficulties of motherhood.

Additional probes were used where necessary to expand the discussion to ensure all relevant issues were addressed and that the mothers had the opportunity to express their views. The flexible and progressive nature of grounded theory enabled participants to be asked extra questions to further verify findings. Such questioning aimed to explore the various data possibilities inherent in a given situation and thus enabled the researcher to develop the appropriate richness and variations of the different concepts necessary to develop a grounded theory (Strauss and Corbin, 1998).

All transcripts were sent back to the individual women, so that they could review, validate and edit the manuscripts as appropriate to themselves, but none of the women chose to make any alterations. This process is referred to as *participant review* or *member checking* (Johnson and Christensen, 2004) and formed part of the *triangulation* process. All transcripts, being verbatim, were therefore, unadulterated by me and so included usage of the "ums', 'ahs' (LaFrance, 2001, p.250) and 'you know' to allow for the clarity and meaning of dialogue and narrative as recorded by each woman which in turn, allowed for the conveyance of the richness of their speech. Also the transcripts, using an ellipse to indicate a gap, were punctuated in a manner designed to acknowledge the speech style as spoken by each woman and are not therefore, grammatically corrected.

In keeping with what I, as the researcher employed and as Reinharz (1992) so rightfully stated, one should '...respect the intention behind women's words and learn to listen to phrases such as 'you know' as a request for understanding. If we do not understand, we must say so; if we do understand, we must say *what* we understand' (p.40, original emphasis).

Data Collection

I met with the participants at a time and place convenient to themselves – generally in their own home. However, one interview took place in a motel room, one in the private rooms of a counsellor and the other in the private office of child health professionals. The mothers were informed that they could stop the interview at any time and could decline to answer any question. Questions such as "Please tell me about your experiences of your pregnancy with your child with FASD" were used with other topic areas relating to labour, birth, post-partum period and onwards. Most interviews, which were audiotaped (so as to glean the narratives' richness as closely as possible to the form in which it was recorded/transcribed [Bogdan and Biklen, 1982, p.28], but in opposition to Glaser's recommendations) with the approval of the interviewee, were between one and one-and-a-half hours in duration, having obtained written, informed consent beforehand.

As data collection progressed, additional themes were added, as new areas of interest emerged. After each bout of data collection, the key issues were noted down and remembered. A review of the documented medical histories, as given by two birth mothers, was later carried out by me to add further clarification to the collected data.

Data Analysis

Using the grounded theory approach as devised and amended by Corbin and Strauss (1990) together with the adoption, in part, of Bob Dick's (2002) framework, each transcribed interview, was read in its entirety to ensure that the context of the interview material had been maintained and to enable reflection by me on the interview process in order that the overall sense of the account from each woman was gained (Rose, 1998). Then, employing the constant comparative method (or 'open' coding, ie, the asking of questions and the making of comparisons [similarities with and differences from other units of categorised data], thereby fracturing the data into concepts and categories), I compared interview with interview and watched for theory to emerge. Theory emerged following the identification of key units of data which described each woman in terms of her lived experience of being a birth mother of a child with FASD (inductive analysis), at which point, data was then compared to theory. Inductive analysis ensures that the themes or categories of analysis being generated come directly from the data. That is to say, the themes or categories emerged from the data rather than being imposed on the data *a priori* to collection or analysis (Patton, 1990; Pandit, 1996).

The results of the comparisons were written in the margin of the note-taking as 'coding' and as such, represented the operations by which data were broken down, conceptualised and put back together in new ways, by making connexions between a category and its sub-categories. This latter operation is appropriately termed by Corbin and Strauss (1990) as 'axial' coding and refers to the process of developing core categories and their sub-categories (Pandit, 1996) and as Corbin and Strauss (1990, p.57) stated "It is the central process by which theories are built from data", 'selective' coding involving the integration of the developed categories.

The second interview was then coded with the first interview and the subsequent interviews (plus data from field notes, medical documentation) were coded with the emerging theory in mind (constant comparison - initially comparing data set to data set: later comparing data set to theory). Categories were then identified (themes or variables) and their properties (sub-categories) and were highlighted with different coloured pens, ie a different colour for each different theme and the same colour for the same theme or variable. Ultimately and using a pair of scissors, these highlighted areas were cut out of each interview transcript and pinned onto a large memorandum board, each piece of paper representative of a flow chart with its appropriately-coloured units of data at the bottom and all other coloured sub-categories and categories emanating upwards, until finally, a core category emerged.

On coding, which I did by taking a sentence of each interview at a time and examining it, certain theoretical propositions occurred, ie links between categories (the "cornerstones" of developing theory) and in some cases, core categories, the latter being central to the study, as they have the greatest explanatory power. In most cases, the core category proved to be that which had high frequency of mention by the birth mothers and which was connected to many of the other categories which emerged: eg, many of the women stated that their child suffered "*lack of foresight*" (theme or category) and that the child's behaviour was such, that *"discipline meant nothing"* (variable of the transcribed raw data). These significant units of information then, when taken to a higher sub-category, became *"mothers' learn to cope with child's neurodevelopmental problems"*. The higher order or 'core' category in this case became *'Medical and health professionals abandon the mothers"*.

Following identification of a core category, any such coding of sentences which did not relate to it ceased and accordingly, only one core category was focused on at any one time, thus enabling coding for the core category, plus other connected categories as well as properties of both (Dick, 2002) and as Strauss and Corbin (1990, p.124) posited "The core category must be the sun, standing in orderly systematic relationships to its planets." Therefore, as the categories and the properties emerged, they and their links to the core category, provided the theory and thus, notes of these were written down on 125mm x 75mm sized and lined, filing cards (one for each participant), this procedure being known as 'memoing' (Dick, 2002).

As the data collection and coding proceeded, the codes and the memos accumulated and the sample was added to via theoretical sampling where this was attained, thereby strengthening the emerging theory by defining the properties of the categories and how those mediate the relationship of category to category. Theoretical sampling also increased the diversity of the sample by searching for different properties, so that when a core category and its linked categories 'saturated', I no longer added to them, although as stated previously, I did not set out with this intention, based on the fact that purposive sampling would be low in numbers.

Following this procedure and in the knowledge that the sample is emergent, as is the theory and the method generally, sorting was then carried out by grouping all memos, like with like, and sequenced into an order to enable theory to become clearest, at which point, the literature, as it became relevant, was accessed. The order of the sorted memos provided a skeleton from which to work, together with many words for my study. Thus, over time (and thankfully, there did come a time after much patience and persistence, when things became clearer), this emergent, grounded theory study worked through the following, mostly-overlapping phases: data collection, note taking, coding, memoing, sorting and writing.

Together, these phases of data analysis resulted in a critical review of the data, leading to the formation of a grounded theory of birth mothers' experiences of a child/ren with FASD. This newly-developed theory was then compared with existing theories to determine if it had anything significant to add to the work. As a theory, grounded in raw data, the findings should have two basic qualities: firstly, there should be a closeness of 'fit' between the theoretical construct and the field being studied in the real world and secondly, the 'end product' or theory developed, should be understandable to the research participants.

In order to test the validity of the emerging theoretical construct, *triangulation* of data interpretation was peformed (see below). Consequently, I did not begin with a theory and then prove it – rather I began with an area of study and that which was relevant to the area, was allowed to emerge (Stauss and Corbin, 1990, p.23) and as Eisenhardt (1989, p.545) posited "overall, tying the emergent theory to existing literature enhances the *internal validity*...and theoretical level of the theory building from the research...because the findings often rest on a very limited number of cases", in keeping with this study.

Validation of the Data

Within the qualitative paradigm, I am, as the researcher, expected to determine the trustworthiness or credibility of any given account (Lincoln and Guba, 1985) and in this regard, I again used *triangulation* (which makes use of multiple and different sources of data to check the accuracy of the subjects' interpretation of the collected data/provide extra data for further analysis) was employed by means of matching and contrasting the primary information source (ie the interviews) with participant checking and observation (when it proved available within the naturalistic setting), the relevant medical notes, as given to me by the birth mothers and by the regular writing of field notes, thoughts, ideas and any telephone conversations with the participants during the course of the study.

A categorized list of the participants' characteristics (profiles) was also considered by myself to add to the triangulation process. The medical records can be considered an historical account of the children's (and by extension, the birth mothers') lived experience, participant observation is a contemporary account of life (ie a 'snapshot') as it is currently being lived and the interviews served as a bridge with retrospective memories merging into the present lived experience.

Since the participants had their typed interview notes sent back to them so that they could judge the accuracy of the account and make any alterations and rectifications as necessary, this process is usually considered the most critical technique for establishing the *credibility* of obtained qualitative data (Creswell, 1998).

Participant observation was considered to be an additional primary data gathering device. The members of any group or sub-group, are influenced by assumptions that they take for granted which reflect the unique culture of a given group so rather than relying on the group members' perception, participant observation affords the researcher direct access to these assumptions, eg research has shown that many men with employed partners assume that they are doing half the household chores, but observing what men and women actually do in the home proves that the situation is really quite different.

As stated by Waddington (1994), participant observation is best suited to research projects which emphasize the importance of human meanings, interpretations and interactions where the phenomenon under investigation is generally obscured from public view (p.108) as with FASD and its derivatives and especially more so now that consultant paediatricians and other diagnostic health professionals are diagnosing the disability as ADHD. This apparently, in order not to label (or stigmatise) the child and thereby not burden the birth mother with 'guilt' (Elvin-Nowak, 1999), but as one quite vocal participant stated:

> "I do not feel guilty about having given birth to a child with FAS because I knew nothing about this syndrome when I was pregnant and I don't want my child diagnosed ADHD when he is actually FAS because I want the correct treatment for him".

The ability to access some of the children's medical notes served a dual purpose - on a technical note it was for triangulation, but it also filled-in information in relation to a birth mother's memories, either corroborating them or giving a different picture. Also as part of the triangulation process, I was in regular verbal communication with FAST in Hamilton because of its workers' extensive experience of working with children, adolescents and adults disabled by FASD. These workers were respectfully requested to comment on the validity of the present findings as well as the summary of results of findings which were sent to the birth mothers.

During the data collection and analysis stage, attention was directed to avoid and test out personal biases by myself (Patton, 1990). My two main supervisors were given access to the raw data (sets of transcripts and concurrent coding) to check my interpretations against the data themselves in order to further check for data validity. The criteria of internal validity, external validity and reliability do not equate to qualitative studies – these are the domain of quantitative research – and as such, alternative measures of verification, accompanied by more appropriate terms of reference (Patton, 1990; Morse and Field, 1996; Miller and Crabtree, 1992) are proferred by Beck (1993) who equated the former with what she described as credibility of the results. By this she meant not only the participants, but others who had also experienced the phenomenon under study, would recognise vividly the described experiences as their own. Beck (1993, p.264) also substituted fittingness for internal validity, which she defined as measuring how well the working hypothesis or propositions 'fit' into a context other than the one from which they were generated. Beck (1993) also substituted reliability for auditability, this being the ability of another researcher to follow successfully, the audit trail to understand the research process and therefore, the conclusions reached.

Validation of the Findings Revisited

A major threat to the use of retrospective qualitative research methodology in this study, was that the women participants were having to recall a major turning point in their lives, a major, sensitive, dramatic event – an event, whereby correct recall for events could be somewhat clouded or distorted if the biological mothers had been heavy drinkers, but on the other hand and in light of the continuum of events being problematic for both the mother and her offspring, memories for such events do not normally fade with time, as all participants demonstrated, except one, who had at the time of conception, pregnancy, labour and early child-rearing, been alcoholic. However, this woman still demonstrated good retrospective recall for many major events associated with her children, as her narratives bear witness to.

Participants Checking and Closeness of 'Fit'

All women were sent a copy of the qualitative research study findings, as agreed and also for comment. On the whole, participants said that the findings represented the experiences of birth mothers' with offspring with FASD. The general sense of agreement is reflected in the comment below made by Mary, the oldest study participant (Berryman, 1991; Berryman et al, 1995): *Absolutely wonderful...worthy of a book.*

The results obtained from participants' checking suggested a good closeness of 'fit' between my interpretations of the data and the participants' own perception of their experiences. Furthermore, the summary of the findings appeared understandable to the research participants. No amendments were made to the original data interpretations.

Validity Checking with Experienced FASD Health Workers

As a further test of validity of the data gathered, a copy of the transcribed data was sent to Fetal Alcohol Support Trust in Hamilton for review. These workers described the work as '*excellent*'.

Ethical Considerations

As Fontana and Frey (1994, p.372) stated "Because the objects of inquiry in interviewing are human beings, extreme care must be taken to avoid any harm to them". These authors outlined three factors which must be taken into ethical consideration when researching with human participants, viz: informed consent, right to privacy, protection from harm. These factors were carefully considered in my study, as follows:

Informed Consent

All participants signed an informed consent form to indicate that they had understood the purposes of the study. The informed consent form outlined that their participation was entirely voluntary, that they could withdraw from the study at any time without any harm to themselves or the study, that they would have access to the interview transcript to review, delete or change wording or statements, that the audiotaped data would be destroyed after a period of five years in accordance with university policy, that there was no anticipated risk or harm involved, but if discomfort or stress was involved in recall, that a professional counsellor would be on hand (via the telephone), that the results may well be published and that their anonymity would be preserved to the extent that this was possible. The informed consent form further stated that participants agreed to take part in the study and was signed and dated before interviews took place.

Right to Privacy

As this study was low in subject numbers, anonymity was assured by way of pseudonym usage for all women and their offspring, plus the non-detailing of family demographics. Any identifying features were accounted for and thus, removed. These points were communicated to the women prior to written consent being obtained. The themes identified are written in the first person to ensure easy reading, accuracy of narrative together with checking by the participants.

Protection from Harm

It was not anticipated that there would be any harm or risk experienced by the participants in my study. Participants were asked to relate their lived experiences as a birth mother of a child/ren with FASD. They were asked to discuss only particular issues or personal information specific to themselves and their offspring and to refrain from using the names of other women or children known to them who also had FASD. All participants were informed of their right to withdraw from the study at any time, their right not to address any question that they chose not to answer, their right to revise or withdraw what they had stated, if necessary and lastly, their right to anonymity and confidentiality. The women were also notified of the addresses and telephone numbers of myself, as the researcher and her two supervisors, should any stress, harm or concerns arise in relation to their participation in the study.

In conclusion, it should be stated that there was no direct benefit or greatly ensuing improvement in the women's situation as a result of their study participation. They were simply asked to share their experiences in anticipation of educating and rendering their knowledge to prospective and future would-be mothers. It is also noted that Finch (1993, p.176) believed ways should be devised to ensure that information given so readily in interviews will not be used ultimately against the collective interests of women. This statement is fully endorsed by myself.

Finally, Cotterill (1992, p.603) sums the initial part of the research process up well by stating "family women are extremely difficult to recruit, do not constitute a 'captive' group and have nothing to lose by saying 'No'". In this vein therefore, I did indeed, consider myself extremely fortunate in not only locating the birth mothers, but more importantly, in their agreeing without hesitation, to participate in my study.

The Findings

Introduction

Women and their families are usually joyous when a baby is born which is healthy, but for the mothers who give birth to a child suffering from FASD, this is not generally the case and even if the child is not diagnosed immediately after birth, the woman's intuition is quite remarkable in informing her that there is something "wrong" or "different" about the new offspring she is nurturing even when the medical profession appeared to be unaware of it or were unable to acknowledge it. These are the birth mothers who experienced a different transition to motherhood than other women, through the auspices of their offspring being viewed as different from other babies as well as being different from their own healthy and non-compromised siblings; these differences becoming more pronounced as the child grows and milestones (Batshaw, 2002) are not met. As Reibel (2004) stated:

> Childbirth is a pivotal moment in a woman's life in terms of both her identity as a woman and as a mother. How she feels about her role in bringing forth a new life will shape her reactions to these aspects of herself. Her birth experience has the potential to create either a positive or negative start to her journey and her carers can strongly influence how she feels

> after 'leaving' this unique occurrence and embarking on mothering. For some the joy of childbirth will remain with them, instilling a sense of empowerment and determination in their lives. For others, particularly those who have been patronised and frightened into working against their instincts, their memories of childbirth will not only be tainted but may provoke problems with bonding, breastfeeding, the capacity to cope with the demands of a baby in the short or long term, or their sense of self.

Because of the FASD child's medicalised beginning in the world, the individual was seen to be frequently in and out of hospitals and general practitioner surgeries which, because of their very essence of business amongst peoples – staff and patients – there was a great cacophony in amongst the midst of which, the medical model of disability was practised by physicians (usually male): the paradigm which provided the dominant voice of the latter – the "real" story by simple virtue of their indoctrination into saving lives rather than "listening" to the patient or the patient's 'significant other', which in this context, was the child's biological mother – a biological mother whose voice struggled to be heard above the noise and din of the hospital's physical environment, a voice which struggled to compete with the physician's medical story – this is the woman's story – the true story – the story that formed the basis of my work and the one that indeed, should be listened to and taken notice of with empathetic ears and then acted upon by the welfare state and medical and health professisonals.

Participants' Profiles

The ages of the eight participants at interview ranged from 29 to 64 years. Seven of the women were divorced with six of them being in second marriages. All the women were born in New Zealand. A range of occupations was evident amongst the women, with only two holding positions requiring professional qualifications. Although I cannot address in depth the group's profiles, because of confidentiality issues, I felt that the following short biographical sketches would give some insight in the hope that the reader may get to 'know' the women participants.

Older Age Participants

Mary (64) is now divorced, single and living in her own home. She was born to elderly parents who were in their 40's at the time. Mary's parents were 'wine with dinner' drinkers only. She has one brother. Because Mary worked hard, doing long shifts at a stretch, she ultimately became the manageress of a canteen. Mary married an Englishman whose culture was to drink 'socially' at the weekend in the local pub. He would take Mary along with him. He became an alcoholic. At the age of 35, Mary gave birth to her fourth and last child, a boy, who was, at the age of 22, diagnosed as having fetal alcohol syndrome. Mary said that she thought her family was complete with two daughters, the first-born having died early in life. She was very surprised when she discovered that she was pregnant for a fourth time.

Miriam (52) has always been involved in the care and education of young children, ultimately becoming the owner-operator of an early childcare centre. She has now changed direction in life and lectures on fetal alcohol spectrum disorder. Miriam comes from a non-drinking, supportive family. Her husband is an engineer and is non-alcoholic. She has one caring and supportive brother. She herself seems to be a very supportive and caring mother who maintains good family dynamics. She gave birth to three children, the middle child being a boy, whom she delivered at the age of 22. At the age of 20, this child was diagnosed firstly with ARND, then FAS and finally, FAE by different medical professionals.

Middle Age Participants

Martha (42), who is one of three siblings, described herself as 'alcoholic', but added that she "hadn't drunk for about 15 years and won't drink now". She described her father as an alcoholic, as well as one of her two brothers. Her mother does not drink. Martha said she started drinking at the age of 14 and was introduced to ethanol by her brother. She drank throughout pregnancy and experienced toxaemia. She is the birth mother of two daughters who are aged 26 and 24 years. The youngest is said to have FAE. She gave birth to her first child when she was 16 years old. The children's father was an alcoholic. Martha has remarried and works alongside her non-drinking husband in a social work capacity. At the age of 15 and after only nine months in her first job, which was that of a shorthand-typist, Martha was sacked. She said that drinking was to blame. This happened to her again when she was 16 and in her second office job. She then got a job in the forestry industry, pruning trees. Martha had strict organization and routine within her household while rearing her girls. She said that sometimes though, she was unable to accompany them to school because of her drinking. She would wait outside the front gate for another person to come along with her children and then send her two children off to follow on behind this group.

Rebecca (41) has been married to her second husband for 15 years and from whom she has a step-daughter, aged 20. She is the biological mother of two children: one male, aged 17 years by her first husband and one female aged 11 years by her second husband. Rebecca said that her eldest child, a breech, but natural delivery, was diagnosed with FAE at the age of 14. Rebecca's first husband was an alcoholic. She said that this caused the marriage to break-up when her son was two years old. While she worked, she put her son into care, but he later came to live with her at weekends. Rebecca was educated to sixth-form level before going into an office where she eventually became the office manager. She then gained a position as a bank manager, following which, she changed direction and trained as a herbal therapist since her son was affected by high allergies.

Esther (38) was born and bred in Dunedin. She has one sister and five brothers. Esther stated that she "dropped out" of school at the age of 15 because she was "not academic" and had no interest in the system. She described herself as coming from a long line of alcoholics. Her father is an alcoholic. Her husband is a recovering alcoholic and he too, comes from a long line of alcoholics and drug-users. Esther is a hotel room attendant and cleaner. She is the biological mother of three sons whose ages ranged from 8 and-a-half-years to 15 years. Esther stated that she used to drink heavily on five nights out of seven. The 15 year-old child is said to be 'fetal alcohol'.

Younger Age Participants

Ruth (32), who is the youngest of six siblings, lives on a farm with her second husband who is the farm manager. She is the assistant farm manager. Presently, she is also undertaking a social work course at her local polytechnic. At the age of 20 she gave birth to her first child, a girl, born of her first husband, who was an alcoholic. This man was also violent towards

Ruth. Her daughter was later diagnosed with FAS. Ruth now has two other children by her second husband, both of whom are girls and who are in foster care. The first daughter is cared for by Ruth's mother who lives locally. Ruth's parents split up when she was eight years old. She described her father as an alcoholic.

Sarah (31), who is an adopted child with three older brothers, described her educational status as "nil". She left school in order to get a job and gave birth to her first child at the age of 21. he child, a boy, was conceived of an alcoholic father following a "binging" session. Sarah lives on a small farm with her husband, who is not the father of her first-born child. He is the father of their other two children. Following the birth of her first child, Sarah suffered from post-natal depression, but did not require any medication. She said that she did not suffer from this condition afer the birth of her other two children. Initially, when caring for her first child, Sarah lived next door to her parents and her mother helped her out tremendously with the baby.

Naomi (29) is one of four siblings, all of whom are female. She finished school at the eginning of the fifth form when she was aged 15 and went to work. Although her arents worked in the drinking industry, they were and remain, non-alcoholic. Naomi lives with her husband. She is unable to work now because of a medical condition. She is the birth mother of five children whose ages range from eight-and-a-half years to 13 years of age. She had her eldest child, a boy, when she was 16 years old. Her youngest child, a girl, is believed to have FAE. The father of this child was 17 when she was born. Naomi said he "did drugs" and drank only occasionally. He was tragically killed in a road traffic accident at the age of 19 and-a-half years. Naomi described herself as "not being a big drinker" and said that when she was pregnant with her first child, she "went off alcohol". However, on moving to the other end of town with her first partner, Naomi says she "got in with the wrong crowd" and consequently "hooked up with alcoholics". She said that she will shortly be moving again, with her family, in order that she can receive appropriate hospital care and treatment for her medical condition.

The Birth Mothers' Stories

Because grounded theory allowed for the data to be told in story-form, this is how the birth mothers' narratives are now presented.

Core Category One - It's the mother's fault

The research participants in this study all talked about having responsibility for their child's disability, although some did not experience guilt. Some mothers also felt that others blamed them without cause. Seven mothers stated that they did not know that alcohol could have a disastrous neurodevelopmental effect on the unborn child. All eight women acknowledged that they had never heard of FAS or FAE when they were pregnant with their disabled children.

Lack of Knowledge

Mary, the eldest participant, said that she eventually found out about FAS when her son was an adult. She purchased a computer and delved into the research on the web:

> Nobody had ever heard of FAS. You get away with it...it's Russian Roulette - you seem to get away with it when you're very young and your body's healthy.

Miriam, another older participant, found out about the syndrome when she was watching TV. The programme was the televised version of a book entitled "The Broken Cord" by Michael Dorris, a solo foster parent of a boy with FAS. The boy's behaviours were very similar to those of her son, so she believed that Tom had the same disability. Miriam then told her husband about it:

> ...And so, we talked quite thoroughly that night about the whole thing and of course, we knew nothing about fetal alcohol.

Esther, although categorized into the middle age range, which meant that her affected child was born in the 1980's, also supported the comments made by the other two older women:

> I didn't know anything about fetal alcohol effects or syndrome until I came to the coast...I actually cannot recall where the information came from that it wasn't good to drink, but I knew that it wasn't ok. But you're not told that.
>
> You're told "Do you smoke?" "How many cigarettes would you have a day?" I wasn't asked, even though I was pregnant,"How many alcoholic drinks have you had?"

Martha, who also had her child in the 1980's, similarly said that she knew nothing about the syndrome and its effects on the developing fetus. She did wonder though whether her memory might have failed her because of the fact that she had previously been an alcoholic:

> I wouldn't have had a clue. Well, I was pretty young...Well, I can't remember anything being said to me about it...Whether they said it and I didn't want to hear it, I don't know.

Rebecca, who is of a similar age to Martha, said that she found out about FAS/FAE by watching a programme on TV. After watching this programme, she got in touch with Fetal Alcohol Support Trust, who sent her some literature. She wished she had known about FAS earlier:

> Just wish that back when I was pregnant the emphasis was made don't drink any alcohol as I was into heavy drinks. I wish that there had been emphasis on it. There was definitely not any mention of FAE/FAS back then.

It is of interest that Naomi, the youngest participant, who delivered her affected child in the 1990's – in fact, 21 years after the birth of Mary's child - reinforced the remarks made by all the other mothers. However, she felt that she may be to blame for her child's disablement even although initially she did not know about FAS/FAE:

> No, no, I didn't know about it until now, yeah...exactly, but I know at the end of the day, I put it down to two things. I was not aware that I was doing damage to the child's brain and secondly, I had my own choice, but I just didn't know. I wouldn't have done it otherwise, I wouldn't have put her at risk...and I got 'hooked up' with some undesirables and yeah, got

pregnant and drunk and I honestly...I didn't consider the fact that it could harm the child. I just thought everyone was doing it - it can't be that bad...actually if someone said "If you drink, Naomi, you're going to hurt your baby" that would be it, I wouldn't drink.

But there was nothing like that in the conversation of people talking.

Ruth, another younger participant, whose two eldest daughters were affected by alcohol wondered whether she was just 'naive' in not knowing about FAS/FAE:

...and I didn't even realize at the time...that alcohol could really damage a fetus. I wasn't aware at that time...I never thought at the time when I was carrying the girls, that I could have done any permanent damage to them.

Many of the women believed that there should have been health information regarding FAS/FAE freely available to them, so that they would have been left in no doubt about the devastating effects of alcohol on the unborn child. Naomi felt very strongly about this:

At antenatal, it needs to be said...and scare the living shit out of these women. ...either they want a normal baby or they're going to have a child...that's going to need special needs for the rest of their life. To what extent, is totally up to you with how much you drink. They need to be told this...It needs to be right in your face, like it gives you a (bang - noise made)! Oh, my gosh!! They've got to bring this right up to the surface...It is in everyone's best interest, because when you have a FAS child, it just does not affect the parent, it affects the grandparents, the aunties...their friends, it affects everyone and that's just at this beginning part of their life - let's not talk about the rest of their life!

The Mothers Drank In Pregnancy

Because the participating women were unaware of FAS/FAE (albeit some knew that it was not good to drink during pregnancy, but didn't know why), they consumed alcohol during their pregnancies, with some not aware that they had conceived until near the end of the first trimester. One of the younger participants, Ruth, said:

...and when I got pregnant with the girls, I was drinking quite heavily, as you do when you've just turned 18, you know, it's a normal thing for teenagers to do...and I didn't know I was pregnant until I was 3-4 months pregnant, so...

Naomi also became pregnant as a teenager having got in with the 'wrong crowd'. She said of her pregnancy:

I drunk every night of the week, almost, yeah...I just lost...absolutely lost the plot!

Whilst Sarah commented that she continued to drink throughout her pregnancy because she had been told no different:

I was only five-six weeks pregnant when I found out...me and a friend of mine, had a really, really big night at the pub and I drank nine jugs of beer and had a smoke - marijuana - and whatever follows on after that...Yeah, but it was almost as if I wasn't pregnant at all.

Interestingly, both Esther and Rebecca, who are in the middle age range, suffered contraceptive failure as a result of binge-drinking:

> Yeah, but I had a binge when I was about three-and-a-half to four weeks pregnant with him. My husband and I were both drinking heavily. I didn't know I was pregnant until I was eight weeks. I was on contraceptives...(sigh).

Once Rebecca knew she was pregnant, her attitude towards drinking changed:

> I obviously conceived him over...festivities time. In fact, I remember the night I fell pregnant with him, in which I had actually been drinking tequila...my birth control pill did not obviously work because I was violently ill, but I didn't actually know I was pregnant until another six weeks later, when I thought "Ghee,I haven't cycled"...so I didn't drink right from the time I knew, but there would have been a portion I would have drank probably five-six weeks after conception before I realized I had been drinking pre-pregnancy, quite heavily obviously, married to an alcoholic - did the same thing!

Martha, the third mother in this same age range, drank through both her pregnancies, with only her youngest girl being affected by alcohol, although both girls were fathered by the same man.

Only three of the participants came from families who drank. Seven participants had husbands or partners who drank heavily or were drug-users. Consequently, some of the families were disrupted and Mary, who drank socially at weekends, sought shelter in a Salvation Army refuge with her son:

> I married a man who later turned out to be an alcoholic and a rather bad-tempered one at that...He liked to go to the pub regular - a sort of a Saturday night thing...and I worked 'till about five months and we still went Saturday nights down to the pub - that was our big social centre - apart from one church, that was it and one shop.
>
> My husband would go early and I'd give the girls their tea. Nobody worried about if they were left home alone then. That was culture and socialization. My husband was brought up in England...Yeah and his parents drunk and I think he was FAS too...I don't think my mother ever went into a pub in her life.

Five of the other participants, like Mary, also suffered marriage or partner break-ups, but Miriam has remained in a stable relationship with her husband. Like Mary, Miriam too drank 'socially', as it was part of her culture. Miriam believed that it was her 'cultural' drinking pattern at Christmas and the New Year which had created her alcohol-affected son.

Martha's family drank heavily and she said that she believed one of her brothers had influenced her into drinking:

> Probably my brother introduced me to alcohol and then I gravitated to older people because they always had alcohol and I always set out to make sure that whoever I was with drunk alcohol...My father would have been alcoholic. He wouldn't say so, but he was very dependent on alcohol. Mum doesn't drink - she might have a sherry occasionally.

Esther, like Martha, associated with 'heavy drinkers' and used drugs, but stopped 'partying' when she became pregnant:

> I drank a lot when I was younger. From Thursday through Sunday, I would be drinking heavily. I associated with people who drank heavily and used drugs and I sort of stopped

> partying when I got pregnant with my oldest child. I was 22 when I had him, yeah and his father...is an alcoholic as well and he drinks today still. He drinks a lot. My father is an alcoholic. My background is basically from alcoholics: we have a long line of alcoholics on my side.
>
> My husband is a recovering alcoholic and he too, comes from a long line of alcoholics and drug-users, yeah.

Ruth, one of the younger participants, grew up in a 'split family' and also had an alcoholic father:

> ...so I grew up in a split family, seeing my dad whenever I could and he was an alcoholic - so I grew up around alcohol. It was a norm to have a drink...

Naomi was raised by parents who worked in the drinking industry, but interestingly, neither parent drank:

> They worked in the drinking industry - like my mother was a bar-tender and my father was a bouncer and a bar-tender, but they never drunk themselves, yeah. So that's interesting...If they did, it might have been a drink at Christmas.

The two other younger participants were either informed by their partner or a family member that it was alright to drink and that just one drink or drinking 'in moderation' would not harm the fetus. As Sarah explained:

> I didn't know I was pregnant when I was having that big session...After that, my partner at the time, said to me that it was OK to drink beer but not spirits -just one or two glasses a week...So I used to go to the pub and have a couple of beers, then just drink orange juice after that...He said it was OK to drink...because he's been in a previous marriage and he's got two children and his wife drank through the pregnancy and it didn't cause any problems, so there's no reason why I can't do it. Well, that was his theory and I was only 20, so I was not old enough to know the difference...so I just carried on, you know...

A member of Naomi's extended family encouraged her to drink even when she herself believed it to be unwise, although she did not know why:

> ...so I wasn't drinking at that stage...I remember saying "Oh, no, I shouldn't be drinking". "Oh, we all drunk with our children. There's nothing wrong with them". ...That's what everybody was saying to me.

Naomi's partner took drugs and it appeared that his drug-taking also influenced her to drink alcohol whenever they were out of an evening:

> He done more drugs than anything. Marijuana! He did drink, but he wasn't a heavy drinker, no...He might have had one drink a week...but he smoked drugs every day. Yeah, yeah, done marijuana every day...So it was just when I was pregnant with Pippa. If we went out, he would do the drugs and I would just drink...Yeah, so that's pretty much what it was about.

Ruth wanted to terminate her pregnancy, so drank heavily in the hope of aborting the fetus:

> Knowing the old wives tales that if you drink enough, you'll lose...you'll have a miscarriage. I drank like a fish for the first four months trying to get rid of it.
>
> On quite a few times I went on quite big binges to try and end the pregnancy...

Pregnancy/Labour/Birth Different

All the women participants were multiparous (ie, had given birth to other live children). Therefore, they were able to compare the pregnancy, labour and birth of their disabled child with that of their other offspring. Two pregnancies were unintended because contraceptive use by the women failed. All the women, except Martha, mentioned that the pregnancy, birth and labour of the disabled child was in some way different from their experiences with their other children and that the child had a lower birth weight and a low Apgar score*. Two children were delivered with the umbilical cord around their neck and one child was a breech delivery.

Miriam recalled that she was somewhat astounded at being pregnant and was surprised at her child's fast birth:

> The pregnancy came very fast. There's only 22 months between my first two children, so it was quite unexpected ...the pregnancy seemed to go quite well. Tom came round about on time. He was a pound lighter than the eldest girl and a bit smaller. His birth was very fast.

Similarly, Esther, who experienced threatened miscarriages, underwent a fast birth with her disabled son:

> ...And his was a traumatic pregnancy. I threatened to miscarry I don't know how many times. I had severe Braxton-Hicks from 18 weeks.
>
> He was a very fast delivery...the cord, the whole deal...I had what they call a 'shock' birth with him because he was born so quickly...within an hour of my first contraction too...he was here!

Of the younger participants, it was Naomi who experienced a fast birth with her daughter, being born prematurely and with a low Apgar score:

> I do remember that there were things that were slightly out of character, but I didn't know if it was the state that I was in...as in if I was "Piss-crook". ... I look back at my pregnancy now and I don't know how she bloody survived! I drunk night after night after night! Um, it was a very quick birth, yeah...She was a bit prem...about two-three weeks...just 6lb 7oz...No she didn't get 10 [Apgar score]...
>
> I think she got 6...7...Actually, I vaguely remember her literally screaming!

*A numerical expression of an infant's condition, usually determined at 60 seconds after birth, based on heart rate, respiratory effort, muscle tone, reflex irritability and colour.

Sarah, another younger participant, who had an over-due birth, was the only mother to have suffered from post-natal depression, but it was not clear as to whether this was as a result of her not wanting the baby. She experienced a long labour:

> ...no problems throughout the whole pregnancy until right at the very end when he stopped moving, so the doctors decided to induce...me when I was four days over...and nearly a 15 hour labour! The birth went quite well as far as births go, I suppose. He cried quite quickly after he was born...
>
> I went through a period of reasonably deep depression after I had him because I was young and he'd ruined my life...I was stuck at home every night, you know...yeah...It just sort of all caught up in the end and I went "Bang, crack, pop" and said 'I don't want this baby: take it away!" It [Apgar score] was reasonably low when he first came out...was only about 5 or 6 ...he didn't cry for about 30 seconds...

Esther believed that she too had experienced a long and painful labour, requiring her to do more work in the delivery of her son:

> It was the worst birth of the three! It was the longest, yeah and it had more pain attached to it...Oh, yes, yes, it was a natural birth...[went on for]...six hours, which people say isn't a long time, but it is to me, because I was only three with my first and an hour with my second, so it was a long time...and it was really quite an intense delivery...The pain was more intense...I had to do a lot more work to deliver him than what I had to do with the other two...

Like Sarah, Martha said that she did not really want her baby because her circumstances were not right. Martha also said that the only difference between her two pregnancies was that she experienced toxaemia with her second child, but not with her first-born:

> I guess circumstances were kind of different during the pregnancy because my husband left me half-way through and I lost a stone in weight, yeah, so, err...and then she was 7lb 2oz [full-term]...Yeah, same amount of time, same birth - had to be started, hmm, I didn't get toxaemia with her though...Yeah, definitely [cried]...It was more about me then - I didn't really want her...

Rebecca's experience was similar to that of Sarah in that her child became over-due and was a delivered as a breech with a low Apgar score:

> He was actually 43 weeks, not 40 week term. He had a fairly low birth weight of 2,735g which equates to 6lb 1oz...he had fully dislocated hips at birth and he had a fairly turbulent time because he was a fully breech baby,which I delivered naturally and his Apgar score was actually 6, which I believe is quite low.

Ruth's first and second pregnancies with her two affected children were similar to each other:

> With the two oldest ones...it was totally different to Tania's because with Tania's, got no morning sickness, but with Abby and Faith, I was croaking along, right up until about two months before I had them and I don't know whether it's to do with...the fact that they've got problems, or what it was, whether that had anything to do with it, but I often wonder...and my labour!

Mary was in labour for six hours which she believed was not lengthy. She recounted with humour what her doctor and husband were doing whilst she laboured:

> The birth was quite difficult. I can remember going in about 11 – so Jamie was born, I think, about 5 o'clock in the morning, so it wasn't a long labour, but it was different than, you know, the girls...It was much more painful and very uncomfortable, much different. It was in the middle of the Soccer World Cup...the doctor and my husband are yelling out from the TV room "Hang on, wait!, wait!"...yeah, yeah, mm,but there was a panic - they put a blood pressure on my arm at one stage but nobody ever told me what that was about...The delivery, in the end, I remember getting fed up and got off the bed because there wasn't anyone around - they were all watching the soccer! So I went into the toilet and because I was standing up, he decided he'd be born, so that was a good thing and his head came out while I was in the toilet, so then, of course, panic, panic, so then they delivered me and he was 6lb 7oz, I think, but he didn't seem to need any extra care ...Yeah, well, you know, it was just different, but then I put that down to him being a boy, after the girls, you see...

Core Category Two - Medical and Health Professionals Abandon the Mothers

During pregnancy, labour, delivery and the post-natal period, the participants found themselves in the midst of many different medical and health professionals. The women expected that these professionals would show empathy and be supportive of them as well as knowledgeable. However, the women did not experience this and were left to cope the best way they could with their 'different' child.

Mothers Left 'to it'

All the women in this study felt unsupported. Health professionals were unable to meet their needs and the special needs of their children. The women were also left unsupported because the medical professionals did not give any information or explanation for why certain things are happening to their children. This caused much anxiety and stress, which was experienced by all the women in the study to some degree especially when witnessing for the first time their child's unpredictable behaviour.

Mary recalled that after she split-up from her alcoholic husband, she was at her 'wit's end' trying to cope with her son. So, acknowledging that she required help and support, went to the Department of Child, Youth and Family with all the custody orders for her child. She found them to be unsupportive and ineffective.

Ruth also inferred that she felt unsupported in her parenting and consequently, tried a sleep programme which actually caused more difficulty for herself:

> ...Abby would scream up to 10 hours because I did that sleep book programme by Dr Green and each night you had to leave the baby screaming a little bit longer and one night, we got up to 10 hours. She'd scream and we'd just go in and tuck her back in and back out, like you're supposed to and I thought "10 hours solid - poor baby" and she's still got that determination today if she doesn't want anything.

Ruth and Naomi, both in the youngest age range, had fairly out-going and out-spoken daughters, but because Ruth was unable to cope with Abby's untoward behaviours, she was placed in care by social services, where she was abused. She told her mother that she had said the following to her social worker:

> ..."you social workers are supposed to protect me and you stuck me in a place where I get attacked. Mum wouldn't let this happen to me".

Martha stated that she too, felt totally lost and unsupported whilst trying to rear her daughter, who also displayed behavioural determination.

Five of the women believed that their children were seen as 'different' from other children. Miriam, acknowledged that Tom was 'different' and could be 'rigid' as well as 'floppy'. She was frustrated in her and her husband's efforts to rear their son:

> But by this time, of course, we'd stopped going to ask people about what to do with this kid, because the system didn't help anyway...And you start to get really cranky with them [child] and then you start to lose it and say "You'd better listen to me!". It's terribly frustrating,..In the end you start to give up on it and think, you know, well maybe there is nothing wrong with this child, but he was very different..and very rigid and floppy, depending on where he was at.

Ruth commented that her daughter had been different right through babyhood:

> ...right through babyhood, she's been different, because they could never put it down to what it was until last year, when she got her diagnosis.

Naomi, Martha and Rebecca each stated that their offspring (being misunderstood) was viewed as a 'very good baby', that he/she 'slept a lot', 'wouldn't cry' and was the 'perfect baby'. As Naomi commented:

> ...and absolutely everyone can tell that she's different, she's special - she's different from all the others.

Like Mary and Miriam, Naomi also wondered whether her baby was deaf:

> I remember looking at her...her eyes were huge! I remember these big, black eyes, just really looking at me...But for the first seven to eight months of her life, she was a 'perfect' baby...she would just lie in the...basinette and not even cry. She was totally not like any other children. As she started getting older, I used to put her in the play-pen and she'd sit there and play all by herself even if there was only one toy in there. She would not groan...I did actually wonder whether she was deaf...I remember everyone used to say to me "My gosh! What a perfect child". She'd just lie in bed - she wouldn't scream and she wouldn't cry.
>
> She just did her own thing and I could put her on the floor for an hour - I'd be in the same room - and she wouldn't flinch. ....She was a very low maintenace child until she was about eight years and eight months old.

In regard to untoward and different behaviours, many of the women said that they had witnessed oppositional defiance and aggression from their child, with three participants experienced violence from their sons. On the other hand and in stark total contrast, was the fact that the same individual had an innate softness to its nature, which Esther explained she experienced of her son, Reuben.

Mothers Viewed Negatively/Violation of Rights

Because the biological mother of the disabled child drank in pregnancy, the medical and health professionals with whom they came into contact, tended to view them judgmentally and with a somewhat negative attitude. Also during birth, some participants believed their carers were unsympathetic to their pain, thereby showing no empathy. Esther said of her carers:

> She got my legs and she just put her hands on them and let them...and they shot back and I remember I said to her "If you flipping well touch me again, I'll get up and break your bloody neck" and my partner at the time, just looked and he sort of took a few steps back: it was like "Well, this must really hurt, so I'm getting out of the way" and then when he was delivered...'cause he had the cord round his neck...and he was blue and I ripped and I was hightly upset. I was gutted...But I had a nurse prior to that and I quite...I'm not a violent person, but I quite literally could have got off the bed and punched her. She was just...really awful to me.

Sarah recounted how she became frustrated with the health professionals who were trying to teach her how to breast feed her baby, they being totally unaware of the fact that the child, being disabled by the syndrome, had a sucking problem:

> They got her in [La Leche League] and I had these things dangling from my nipples and I thought "Oohh" . I just turned and said to them "Look, I can't be bothered with this. If this is what breast feeding is cracked up to be, I'm not doing it", so that was it...Yeah, yeah, got one of them too [lactation nurse] and you know, I'd just had enough by then.

Because Ruth was young and naive, she always did what the doctor said, never questioning anything, even if she did not understand. She was also not informed about what was happening to her baby:

> ...the most frightening experience for me...when she was only two days old and it wasn't until years later, I found out that they flew her from Whangarei to Auckland to have a head scan done because they had tested her for Down's Syndrome because she was born with very slanted eyes - your typical Down's Syndrome face, but not the extra chromosome. Yeah, so they couldn't find out what was wrong with her...they just said to my family and I "Oh, she's going for some tests: you can't go with her". And at 18-19, you're very naive and you don't question anything, you know. If a doctor says to me "You can't go", you just accept that. Uhm and I'll tell you now, it was the longest morning I've had in my life because we knew something was wrong with her, but we didn't quite know what it was or what it would be or entail for us as parents of her.

Another hospital birthing encounter to complement that of Ruth, followed by a clinic encounter was experienced by Esther, who recounted male doctors' attitudes towards her:

> I remember when I had the eldest child, I yelled because I didn't know what I was in for and I yelled and he said to me "Sweetheart, put your energy into pushing. It can't hurt that much" and I remember looking at him and I said "What would you know, you're a male". When I was pregnant with the youngest one, I had a male GP and he thought he knew it all and I told him that until he gave birth, to shut up.

Miriam's GP was very negative towards her when she sought his help and advice in regard to her disabled child. Miriam said she was basically labelled as 'neurotic' and told to take a pill and go home.

Naomi experienced a similarly negative remark from her GP when she sought assistance and advice regarding her disabled daughter:

> Isn't this [health] system screwed up? Well, I'm anti my G.P. to be perfectly honest, because for four-and-a-half years he's told me that "I'm a hyperchondriac.There is nothing wrong with me. Blow into a paper bag and take these antidepressants". I would not take the antidepressants, did not blow into a paper bag, had fluid on my lungs and 12 hours to live!

The experiences within the hospital system for both Rebecca and her son, were made more intense when she discovered that a male hospital doctor had given Isaac, who was an allergy-sufferer, a tetanus injection without her prior knowledge or agreement. Rebecca felt this to be a violation of her rights as Isaac's mother on the basis that she believed her disabled son did not have the cognitive ability to make a correct and independent decision:

> Isaac said that they gave him an injection and I'd got a really bad feeling that it wasn't just an injection for the pain and it wasn't: it was tetanus and diptheria...and I went off 'my lolly' ...I actually had to take him to a homeopath and get him detoxed because he was a high allergy sufferer.
>
> Their argument [health professionals] was that he was of sound mind and body, that he was 14 and he could make his own decision...They had decided there was no breach and that I was just an 'overly concerned mother'.
>
> ...I felt that my rights as a parent had been violated and I felt that my son was incompetent: the fact that I suspected that he had FAE... I was his caregiver, therefore, I should be consulted, but they didn't take that into consideration...you know, this is a 14 year old boy, who's ...not that good with conversation. So this is what they did and...really, really...to me, that actually blew my faith of, you know...

Mothers not listened to

Because of the mothers' general lack of knowledge together with patriarchy and subjectivity within the medical and health arenas, the mothers were in general, not listened to by health professionals. This appeared to be especially so when the mother encountered a health conversation with a male doctor. Miriam described one of her experiences with a GP:

> With the feet, when I went for my six week check-up, he just took one look at the baby and said "he's fine". The feet were very abnormal at this stage, but he was quite happy to let me go out of the door until I stopped and said "I really think that you ought to do something with his feet" and then he looked at them and goes "Oh, yeah, they are quite bad, aren't they? ... So with that, he sent me to Auckland Hospital and Tom was put into fibre plaster casts from

the knee through to the toes and I had to go to Auckland Hospital every week until he was six months old to have these changed.

Esther was totally dissatisfied with the negative encounters and conversations she had with her male GP in relation to her son, Reuben's disabilities, saying to him:

> I'll find a real doctor who knows that he's talking about...so it's really frustrating, really frustrating.

Sarah recalled her doctor asking her what was wrong with her son, John, when he had lost some considerable weight:

> We rang the doctor up and he took one look at John and said "Why's he doing this?" and I said "I don't know, he's feeding ok", so doctor says "Oh, I'll send him to Invercargill" and he ended up screaming the whole time he was there.

Ruth recalled her call to the social worker regarding her daughter being sexually abused at school by a boy pupil. The social worker's attitude was extremely negative:

> I rang the social worker the next day. She didn't believe it - she thinks Abby was making it all up. From November, when it happened, right through December, she made Abby go to school with him. He did it to her another four times and in late December, early January, she tried to take an overdose of pills here. I rang the social worker and asked her to come out and talk to Abby two days before she did it. She came out and said to me "There's nothing wrong with the child - she's just attention-seeking!"

Mothers Want a Correct Diagnosis

Because there is a close link between ADHD, the birth mothers' were frequently given this diagnosis for their FASD-affected child by the medical professisonals. It was also a common occurrence by the professionals to confuse FASD with Down Syndrome because of the similar facial characteristics. Esther recalled this happening to her son back in the 1980's when she consulted a paediatrician for a diagnosis in keeping with her alcohol consumption:

> I said to him that I had a binge with him and that I drank with the youngest one and told him about their behaviours. I took photos because it's quite evident, particularly in the youngest one - his eyes wide apart, no philtrum, thin top lip - and he said to me "Oh, I don't like to put that on mothers. I don't like to put that guilt on them". My exact words to him were "I don't feel guilty because I didn't know I was pregnant, so I have nothing to feel quilty about. But I do need my children to have a proper diagnosis. I don't want my kids, you know, diagnosed ADHD" because I don't believe Reuben is ADHD...I know of other children who have ADHD and his behaviours are similar, but there's also a lot of differences with them, you know, and um, I came out of there so peeved off - I was really frustrated ...Yeah and this one said "Oh, yes, definitely ADHD and I said
>
> "Well, what about the youngest one?" "Well maybe he's just" and I said to him "He's doing this and this and this". "Spoilt, youngest children don't do that", that's what he said to me.

Esther also recollected that in another encounter with her GP, he advised her incorrectly in relation to the fetus's development and prognosis:

I remember saying to the doctor "Oh, my God, I was drinking two weekends ago, yeah"...He said "The baby will be fine because it was only one weekend". I said "Oh, no, I had a real night on it."

Mary, like Esther, on seeking advice from the medical and health professisonals in relation to her son, Jamie, was informed that he was 'spoilt'. They had disregarded the fact that he couldn't talk:

> Everytime I asked anybody - nurses, the doctor - "Oh, he's spoilt", you know. "He's getting all his own way" - tantrums and stamping feet. They thought he was deaf. Well, he went to the audiology clinic and did all the tests and they said "There was probably certain high frequency ranges he couldn't hear". It suited him to be. I don't know whether it's part of the FAS thing or not...'cause he wouldn't talk, too.

Miriam, in her unerring and unquestioning attempt to get to the source of Tom's problems, was given three different diagnoses (including Down Syndrome), sending her into 'a swim'. She stated that it was the worst time in her life. The differing diagnoses had been made by different medical practitioners all of whom were in the FASD field:

> He had a look at him and said that he really didn't have a problem with the alcohol syndrome and that he would put him down to developmental behaviour and alcohol exposure, which is ARND. Being re-diagnosed again was a problem for us, as you can well imagine...He actually said he's Down's Syndrome, but he's not...and he said "Have you ever had any evidence...personally to prove that women can drink minimal alcohol and have a child with the syndrome? You should have heavy alcohol for the syndrome"...You see in those days, I didn't ask them what they knew: they just so bombarded me with all the stuff and I wouldn't say anything because I wouldn't ask questions.

A further encounter with a psychiatrist by Miriam and her son, Tom, produced the following somewhat negative, statement:

> "There's something about him [Tom] that's not quite right" and I said "I've been telling people that for years, but nobody told me what it was". He said "He's got no knowledge about his world". Well, this just brought it home. I'd never ever known anybody who didn't know anything about his world. He said "If you can get him to 35 and just teach him the basics of living, you'll be doing very well".

However, society would appear not to have moved very far forwards because what medical practitioners there are available at present, are still diagnosing incorrectly or will not diagnose at all, this being confirmed by FASD group-support person, Esther:

> I have one mum who's not long had baby number five. She's a chronic alcoholic...the eldest one would be very close to FAS, one's FAE, the other two are FAS, but the youngest one is difficult to tell, but he too, is going to be a borderline FAS-child. He's very floppy and... he's certainly not on a par with the other babies. She cannot get a diagnosis and yet she's said "I'm an alcoholic. I drank heavily with my children", you know...I mean it's really hard here. We need someone to come down...specifically to do diagnosing of FAE...and

> someone who knows what they're talking about...If the child lives on the coast and you want to get a diagnosis and you say "Hey, I drank, can we look at this?" "Oh, no, your child won't have that. Your child's got oppositional defiance. Your child's got ADHD. Your child has bipolar"...you know... "Your child has everything else..." but they will not say FAE and I actually had one supposed psychologist say to me one day"Why would you want to label your child with that?" and I said "Why do you want to label my child ADHD?"

Mothers Learn to Cope with Child's Neurodevelopmental Problems

Since alcohol freely crosses the placenta, the neural tube of the developing fetus is devastatingly affected, so that the baby can be born with both physical and cognitively disabling abnormalities.

Rebecca stated that her son, Isaac, was born with 'clicking' hips, but the medical and health professisonals appeared to be unconcerned:

> He had fully dislocated hips at birth...Uunfortunately, no-one actually told me that I should have gone and seen someone about having a little bit of...not physiotherapy, but something similar, to see how his hips were working because now I actually have a son who cannot squat...because his... Achilles' tendons were never developed and he was always an ungainly child who could not skip.

Medical conditions frequently become manifest in the FAS/FAE child as a result of their neurodevelopmental abnormalities. Esther's son Reuben, turned yellow:

> ...and they thought he had something wrong with his liver 'cause he was very yellow and he was just getting worse... They ran tests on him, did bloods and they put it down to breast milk jaundice. Well, I didn't believe that - that's just doctors who can't find out why, so they just...

Other medical medical conditions mentioned by the women were constant ear infections for which grommets were generally placed, adenoiditis, chest and eye infections, apnoea attacks, sight,dental and feeding problems, asthma, breathing difficulties and hayfever. Isaac's sight was a problem for him and a source of distress for his mother, Rebecca:

> When he was little, he had this lazy eye...but not lazy as in vision, as his eye wasn't as open as the other one, but we didn't know that he couldn't see properly... He did get diagnosed as having an eye problem...Oh, you couldn't get him to read...but when he got his first glasses, we came out and he said "Ooohh, is that what that sign says up there?" Then when we got him home he said..."Kitchen stove: it's smooth, it's not wrinkly down the side". So obviously...everything had a sharp edge and I wondered why things that he made never had square edges.

Esther stated that her son was taking inhalers for his asthma at the age of nine months. He also experienced extensive dental problems:

> He's got incredibly chalky teeth... They've all got wee chips out of them...the back ones, because he was crunching a lolly. But then my other kids, they could crunch a lolly and their teeth would be fine. He's actually snapped one...Mmh [sigh].

Another child who suffered dental problems was Pippa, who, according to her mother, seemed to have a high pain threshold:

> She doesn't know what pain is. She had a tooth capped – no anaesthetic and all she did was like this with her hands [Naomi demonstrating].

Delayed walking and other delayed milestones appeared to be an issue for seven of the children. Martha's child, however, walked at what she described as 'early', ie one year. She felt though that this was probably because she did a lot of walking with her two daughters.

Although Isaac was still not walking properly at 14 months, Rebecca believed it to be because he had been put into a 'frog splint' to reduce his 'clicking hips'. Ruth's daughter, Abby, did not start walking properly "'till she was two-and-a-half". Reuben, was also a late walker according to his mother, Esther:

> ...he was about 14 months when he walked, you know, like started taking steps by himself...He didn't crawl as such....he pulled himself around on his elbows and yeah and he was quite slow to walk and always falling over.

Mary, Esther, Naomi, Miriam, Ruth and Sarah said they had experienced sleeping problems with their children, in so much as the child did not sleep well, but that once the offspring was asleep, he/she would sleep for abnormally long periods. The children also appeared to require long periods of time in which to 'wind down'. John was one such child:

> Right from eight days old, he'd sleep for 12 hours! It was getting him to sleep that was the problem. I just couldn't do it...My mother used to come over and rock him to sleep every night...but he wouldn't wake up so that I could feed him...Then when the Plunket Nurse said to me "You'll have to wake him up", I started waking him up and then I'd be up all night feeding him...he had a lazy suck. Whereas the baby's got to work at the breast, on the teat, it just runs out and you don't have to do much.

Delayed speech and language were also commented upon by Mary, Rebecca, Esther and Sarah. Both Mary and Miriam felt that their child's delayed speech/language was related to a hearing problem. Miriam took Tom to a doctor in Australia where she and her family were living at the time:

> He said "I think there's something in his hearing that's not right", so we took him for a test and sure as eggs, there was something with his hearing, so within a week, he'd got him into hospital and did an operation... it wasn't just grommets -and when Tom came out of surgery, the air-conditioner clicked in and he was still under the effects of the anaesthetic and he just put his hands up over his ears and "squinched" his face up and said 'Oh, no!" So he had his hearing at that stage...age six or seven and then after that, his language...definitely developed a lot...I'd go to the doctor (NZ) and I would query the hearing because he was doing things like turning my face to him all the time. He would lie on my chest so that he could hear the vibrations. He'd lie on the floor so he could hear the vibrations and that was what he was doing in the surgery when the doctor picked it up: that was the **one** doctor that could pick it up! So, with all the others, I'd take him along and they would sort of say, "We'll send him along for a hearing thing, but it wasn't a specialist hearing place... and he'd be tested and he'd be fine.

Sarah's son, John, had difficulty verbally communicating with others owing to a cognitive problem which had produced a stutter:

> He's got quite a bad stutter... It's only when he's excited - it's all buzzing through the brain too fast and he can't get the words out and he's thinking of the next word before the word before is out... So I tell him to stop and think what he wants to say and then say it.

Unrelenting crying and inability to feed by the child presented major issues to women in all age ranges. Mary commented that although her accident-prone son, Jamie, was difficult to feed, he eventually out-grew his unrelenting crying:

> He cried, he cried and he cried, you know and everyone was saying "Oh, it's because he's a boy." He would only sleep for a couple of hours, you know and he was restless, he was hyper...it sort of went on and on and on...he just gradually grew out of it - there wasn't anything you could pin down, but he just wasn't a normal baby. Yeah, yeah, you could just feel it, yeah and then everybody says "Oh, the girls have spoilt him", yeah... but even feeding him was difficult because you'd have half a bottle and then an hour later, he'd want the rest of it, you know, that sort of thing, mmh...He crawled about 14 months and he got into everything. Nothing was a danger - fire! And he kept having accidents - broken arms, broken legs and that, you know.

Sarah, like Mary, also experienced unrelenting crying and feeding problems with her son:

> ...but they had to tap him on the bottom of his feet to make him cry...and then he never stopped crying after that [laughter].He had a lazy suck as well. I'd just feed continuously.
>
> I gave up feeding when he was 18 days old...he'd lost over a pound in weight and he was bottle-fed from there on. He cried and cried and just cried all the time: never seemed to be happy and I assume that's just the alcohol getting out of his system...

Instead of crying, Tom screamed, as Miriam laughingly recalled:

> He was a very irritable baby and had an extremely high-pitched scream. He used to sound like a little piglet. Very hard to feed and sicked-up a lot.

Getting Reuben to eat was a constant battle for Esther because he didn't like the feel of certain foods in his mouth (tacticle defensiveness):

> He was quite an incredibly fussy eater. He'll eat anything with pasta...he won't eat any red meat, he won't eat chicken - he'll eat a little bit of fish, he won't eat vegies.
>
> He used to love broccoli... and then he mentioned that it made the roof of his mouth feel funny, so then he wouldn't eat it.

Pippa was the same too, according to Naomi, because she experienced tacticle defensiveness:

> She doesn't eat meat... She tells everyone she's a vegetarian...She tells me its because of the taste. "I don't like it in my mouth" is what she tells me, yeah.
>
> She eats a bit of chicken...yeah. She won't eat sausages. She just absolutely hates meat.

According to Rebecca, her son Isaac, experienced hypersenstitive reactions to certain foods, one of these being peanuts:

> Isaac actually can't have peanuts...because they make him feel really, really strange...I mean he eats anything, but he doesn't like peanuts for that reason...and he says "Mum, they're getting stuck in my throat and I can't breathe properly"...He said "I don't like that feeling".

Because of cognitive impairment, John did not dress according to the prevailing climate or weather conditions. As Sarah recalled:

> He's got no dress sense whatsoever...Like the other day, it was freezing and with a really cold, bitterly wind and it was raining and he came out of the bedroom with his shorts, T-shirt and sandals on. So I said "John, look outside. What's the weather doing mate?" "Well, it's not too bad in here, Mum. If I go outside, I might have to get changed". I said "Well, why don't you get changed now?", because it was only like 12 degrees inside...

Martha, Sarah, Esther and Naomi all stated that their affected children were very sensitive and as such, required careful handling. Naomi also commented that Pippa was very secretive and not scared of things or people. Her mother added that she had no fear and didn't fear consequences, which was similar to the behaviour of Jamie, Mary's child, who always told his mother everything that was going on in his life. Mary therefore, believed that Jamie would never make a criminal. Tom, however, according to his mother, could be quite withdrawn at times, even though he hurt other children for no apparent reason. Tom too, would take diabolical risks and not see danger, even though he was told it could be dangerous, Miriam said. Sarah, likewise, had experienced risk taking behaviours by her son, John:

> He took a knife off to school...Yeah, so that's the thing I'm up against all the time. Lighting a bag of cement in the garage to see how well it burns and I wonder how dad's going to react if I cut the tunnel house up?
>
> He's done some pretty shocking things: he's done some pretty funny things too.

It was not just the sons of the women who demonstrated 'risk taking' behaviours, as Ruth experienced with one of her daughters. Ruth said that Abby's 'risk taking' generally took place in shops or supermarkets:

> She used to pull all the racks over as I pushed her in the pushchair. The worst experience I've ever had of that was at the supermarket when she pulled a whole lot of clothes over and I growled at her and the shop assistant shouted "Eh you, you should control that kid better." And I walked out ...there were tears rolling down...and coming 20, 21...Well, being a solo parent, you know, my heart...they didn't know what it's like, you know.

All the women mentioned that their offspring suffered from memory problems, so that they were constantly reminding them to do things, otherwise they did not get done. Esther and Martha said they went to the extent of making wall-hanging charts/lists of what t heir children needed to do every day, in an attempt to keep daily structure within the household. The two mothers hung the charts/lists in appropriate places within the home where they could be constantly seen by the affected children.

Esther made a list for Reuben and his non-affected siblings which she hung on a wall in the house:

> They have their routine because I work and I walk out of the door to go to work when they go to school. So they know that they have to get out of bed.I did have it on the wall, but I notice that they've taken it down... A list - get out of bed, go to the toilet, go into your room, get your uniform on, make your bed, open both big windows, open little window - everything. I have everything written down and the middle one saying to me "Do you think I'm bloody dumb?"
>
> I said 'No, I don't, but if I don't write it down, you can't remember". He cannot remember to do everything.

Pippa couldn't remember to do everything either, as Naomi recounted:

> We can go to town - "Pippa, for goodness sake, where're your shoes?" "I don't want my shoes". Really it's because she can't find them. She doesn't know where she has left them. We'll be sitting in the car ready to go to school "Pippa" - I always ask her if she's got her bag and her books. "No".
>
> "Well go and get them. Hurry up", you know.

According to Sarah, John never remembered to hand-in his homework or clear out his school-bag:

> He does all of his homework, but he never gives it in. I don't like to go into his bag because that's his property... but about every two-three weeks, I will go through his bag and find how many pairs of socks and how many sweat shirts he's got in it and why his bag is looking so full and bulk. He's got about six sweat-shirts and half-a-dozen pairs of socks in and a mouldy apple at the bottom and sandwiches that he never ate from three days ago.

Miriam recounted the experiences she and her son had because of his memory problems:

> Tom became a very, very good swimmer, but he could never remember to catch the bus to school or he'd lose his clothes and miss buses, so at the age of seven, he didn't have the ability to remember.

Core Category Three - Birth Mothers and their Children are Unsupported in The Educational System

All women in this study believed that their childen had suffered as a result of poor or incorrect educational facilities, programmes and teachers being unable to meet the child's special and individual needs as well as their own. This created much frustration and stress amongst the children and their families. Consequently, the children suffered a disrupted school experience.

Mothers Not Listened to by Teachers

Because the women and their affected children were seen as a burden on the educational system they were generally viewed negatively and without empathy by school-teachers. Therefore, the teachers took no interest in the child and could not be bothered to listen to the birth mother. As a result, the child had no interest in the classroom situation and became unmotivated, disruptive and ultimately, a truant. According to Mary, Jamie was one such child:

> He didn't fit in at playgroups or kindergartens. I'd send him, but they'd usually send him home because he'd want to fight or take one of the kid's lunches, you know...hmm. They reckoned he was a 'spoilt little brat', mm [laughter] mm. But he went to school and he had difficulty...he couldn't spell 'cat' or 'dog', but he could spell 'hippopotamus' and 'rhinoceros'...It was just the way his brain worked, you see, mmh...The other ones [teachers] couldn't be bothered, you know, so he didn't do good at school...He was a truant, he was known by the police...Well, he was just one of those kids, you know, he wouldn't be told - discipline didn't mean anything. I'd take him into Boys' High in the one gate and see him in there and he'd be out of the other gate - roaming the on the verge of it [expulsion] all the time.

Martha said that her daugher, Jessica, had experienced a similarly frustrated and disrupted school experience, with the teachers keen to see her leave the institution:

> Just behavioural attitude [teachers' thought] - takes up too much time...
>
> Trying to work out how they get her to go and...so they did...that was high school. When she got to Form 1...her concentration was noticeably going...and yeah, she just wasn't on the ball at all. She started not wanting to go to school...No concentration span, difficult behaviour...yeah. Just kind of be in a world of her own you couldn't get into...she was frustrated and once she'd got behind, I think her understanding of herself is she is useless and she can't do it anyway, so she's not going to try. She actually left school at 14. The school couldn't wait to get rid of her in the end. She got an exemption to leave. Didn't like it there and she wasn't going anyway.

Faith, Ruth's eldest daughter, suffered similarly at school, the result, amongst other things, being that she suffered depression and was ultimately removed from the classroom by her mother:

> She's had problems ever since she started school. She has severe behavioural learning problems. She started intermediate and wasn't at a level where she should be starting intermediate. They [school] don't want to know and then you're left with this kid that's got to be schooled...Faith kept getting suspended.
>
> Faith got very depressed, so I took her to my doctor who told me to take her out of school, which is what I did and...stress! I was told it was a good school.
>
> Marjorie and I went and told them Faith's problems and they said "Oh, OK, we'll get the help she needs; not a problem. We'll put everything in" and they hadn't!

Another child who suffered a disrupted school experience was Pippa, the daughter of Naomi, the youngest woman of all the participants. This showed that there had been no radical change in the educational system meeting the needs of FAS/FAE children during the past 20 years. Pippa's schooling experience also demonstrated that her teachers had very little knowledge of the syndrome from which she suffered, as Naomi recalled:

> I have spoken to the teacher. She said "Oh, well, she doesn't...she doesn't look like a FAS child" and I said "Well, I know she doesn't, but she's been in reading recovery ever since she started school here and now she's on her...second year of teacher's aide" and I said "It's doing nothing at all. She's still not even reading". She doesn't know the alphabet and she's eight. She can only count probably to 30 and that's it...she has her special homework from the teacher's aide...but she never does it. She gets her sister to do it. Yeah and they thought "Oh, Pippa!" and I said "I can't believe that you women are teachers". I said "This girl has, for the last month, got her sister doing it. Do you honestly think that she's capable of doing this amount of work?" "Oh, oh, oh..." and I said "Yeah, I thought not".

Martha stated that although Jessica's teachers had a negative attitude towards her, the school's principal, who had a special way with children, did not. She, like Tom, was good in the pool:

> Yeah, the only thing she liked going to school for was the water-polo team and the principal of that particular school at the time, was really good with the kids - gave them some sort of special attention. He just seemed to have the knack and it was also special teams, so she was on that special team.

Rebecca was the only mother who spoke in support of the teachers, but then, she had been listened to by the school, who acted upon what she had said about her son, Isaac needed:

> He has a wonderful teacher. She just needs a huge medal. She's done such wonders with him and thank goodness the school *listened* to what I said and they've kept him with her this year... 'Cause he's due to go to high school next year, which worries me. He cannot handle going from one thing to another very quickly.

Child's Behaviour not Understood by Teachers

Since the teachers had little or no knowledge of FASD, the disabled child, by virtue of its untoward behaviour was labelled as lazy, naughty, spoilt or dumb. They appeared not to be able to comprehend that the child's behaviour was not of his/her own making - that it is a neurodevelopmental and cognitive disorder.

Tom's teacher was one such individual, as Miriam recounted:

> That particular very old male teacher decided to teach Tom some lessons and apparently made him pick up his desk and chair on top of each other, carry them to the foyer and then the kids could file past and laugh at him...I think those experiences of him being at school were 'horrific'.

Naomi stated that the teachers of Pippa, not acknowledging that FAS/FAE children have a very short attention-span together with memory deficits, believed her to be lazy and naughty:

> "Pippa is darn-right just lazy" and I said "She's not lazy, she's alcohol fetal effects" and I said "You, as a teacher, should be up with the play of this kind of stuff, because how many other children are you labelling, when this is actually what the problem is?"

Because Isaac asked to sit up the front of the classroom in order to see the blackboard clearly, he was, like Pippa, classified as naughty by his teachers. However, according to Rebecca, the fact was that he couldn't see properly:

> Yes, he actually asked to be up the front so that he could see the blackboard. They [teachers] said he was "Naughty", he was "A naughty boy", but when he got his new glasses.......

On the basis that the teachers did not give John the structured attention he required, he attempted to gain it by 'acting out', the consequence of which, was classroom disruption. As Sarah described:

> He'll snap his pencil or roll it to get attention. He'll throw bits of paper at the kids to distract them if they're working...He'll crawl underneath his desk and make silly noises and more noises and tell the teacher he needs to go to the toilet and take half-an-hour to come back because he's in the toilet throwing paper on the roof.

Although Pippa had a urinary problem, she was not allowed by her teachers, to go to the toilet when she needed to, making Naomi very frustrated:

> She wasn't allowed to go to the toilet. She had to wait 'till interval and I said "Pippa, you tell your teacher that your mother said that if you need to go to the toilet, you go to the toilet right now! You just get up, Pippa and you go to the toilet. You do not have to be told by your teacher that you're not allowed to go when you need to go to the toilet". I said "This is unacceptable"...especially when my kidneys are screwed up and Pippa has already got kidney problems as it is.

Three of the boys (excluding Jamie) became 'class clowns' because the teachers did not give them the special attention they required. Sarah believed that John had become one such boy:

> Yes, he's the 'class clown'...he thinks the kids think he's really funny, so he just keeps doing it. Yes, he likes to be the centre of attention: he does something to make him become the centre. They all laugh and think it's great - it's a great joke, but of course, he gets into trouble for it. He's been known to climb on the roof of the school before and "Look at me everyone, I can fly!, standing on the edge of the roof.

Miriam, however, had specific views in relation to Tom being the 'class clown':

> This, of course, is what happens to a lot of children who are not making it on the social scene and the educational scene in the classroom. They then become the 'class clown' and he gets them to laugh and laugh and that's what the teachers appear to be upset about.

Children Should be Taught According to their Educational Needs

As a result of the teachers failing to recognise that the child's cognitive ability does not equate to the child's chronological age, the individual was given schoolwork which was not in keeping with his/her educational age. The child was also given too much homework and became overloaded, as with Abby, one of Ruth's disabled daughters:

> She came home and you know, went to school and she was overloaded there. Then she started intermediate and she wasn't at a level where she should be starting intermediate because...they hadn't done anything. They were sending her home with homework she couldn't do and I wasn't doing it with her.

Pippa too, was overloaded with schoolwork by her teachers, causing her to become frustrated. Naomi said that her daughter wanted to be back in her safe zone ie kindergarten where she had been given special attention by one of the teachers there:

> Just completely...overwhelmed...she just can't do it. But to get her to sit down for that long anyway...is very hard. She just doesn't...understand that you need to be able to read and write in this world. She doesn't believe it.
>
> She just wants to go back to Kindy, because obviously, it's a safe zone for her...She doesn't care about school. "It's too hard, Mum. I just can't read, I can't learn. It's too hard".

Child Is Frustrated and not Included in the Classroom

Since the disabled child appears not to fit into the classroom scene, it tends to become frustrated a result of which, is that the child is excluded by the teachers and the other children. Miriam, Ruth, Sarah, Naomi and Martha believed that their children were frustrated in mainstream schooling. Tom was also tormented by the other children and excluded from the classroom, as Miriam recalled:

> He was in intermediate school and he was terribly, terribly tormented by these children and so frustrated at one stage - he was locked out of the class-room by other children.

Naomi felt that Pippa was not only 'picked on' by the teachers, but was, like Tom, tormented, requiring more help from them in the classroom so that she did not become frustrated in her efforts to get things right:

> "You're not doing that right!". Pippa said "I don't know how to do it" and she said "You're just being lazy and I don't like lazy children". So Pippa went and told the Principal that she will not stay in that class because the teacher hates her. Yeah and then she just sat down and cried, because she was so frustrated because no-one's doing anything. So now, this year, they've got to apply for more help for her because she needs one-to-one...It makes me angry, because this teacher sounds as if she's just bloody 'picking' on her...These teachers are tormenting our children - like Pippa. Does she have problems? Does she have problems? It's because she's high maintenance...I don't think they understand the full potential of what's going on.

Similarly, Abby ended up crying and believing that she was dumb as a result of being frustrated by the teachers. Ruth recalled:

> I said to Marjorie "I'm not going to do this. I'm not going to put Abby through that". Anyway, the teacher...unbeknown to me, was giving Abby hell and she broke down in tears one night...and said "Mum, am I dumb?"

However, Sarah believed that John had got more help from the teachers in his new school than he had previously:

> Yeah and they know not to give him more than one instruction at a time, because if they give him two or three instructions, he'll only hear the last one they said...He wasn't doing very well at school...he's about 20 months behind...There's only about 14 or 15 kids in the class and they've got a full-time teacher's aide in the room, so he's got a lot more here than what he's ever had in town. In town it was most difficult...and they know that they've got to give him short tasks, otherwise, he's never going to get finished.

Child Has Few Friends

Owing to the behavioural problems of the disabled child, other children tended not to include them amongst their friends. The FAS/FAE child was seen to have a tendency towards friendships with other FAS/FAE children. As Mary believed "FAS-kids mix with other FAS kids". They also sought comfort from animals, collecting items or have bondings with much younger children. Pippa called her so-called friends, her 'best friends', as Naomi explained:

> Friends, aren't friends, they're her 'best' friends! Or, she'll go through the stage of ..."I have no friends. Nobody likes me. Nobody likes me because Carla plays with Fiona now. She's not playing with me and so I have to go and play with Tina". But you're dead-right, she goes through friends all the time or maybe not go through friends...she classes them differently all the time. "Caroline's my best friend", then she gets very upset that Caroline goes and plays with another friend. I don't know if that's anything to do with this condition, but...you know, she loves animals...Pippa loves horses and ponies...she carries her horse 'photos around: she sleeps with them.

Tom would appear to have experienced similar relationship problems to those of Pippa. Miriam recounted that he too liked animals as well as being totally focused on cars:

> Throughout his school-life, he's never been able to settle with friends and I remember as a pre-schooler, I had him back at school one day, for the rest of the morning. But he didn't stay, came out and he said "Mummy, those are my friends" and "I collect snails now". They meant so much to him that they're his friends. Yeah, so he just has a thing for these animals, so yeah...Now a lot of these children have a thing that they're totally focused on and he was totally focused on cars. We had so many of them, I wouldn't have known if there were any in there that weren't his or not, you know...

Sarah stated that John loved the company of smaller children, even though he couldn't keep his friendships for very long:

> Oh, he loves kids, loves them. He'll make friends, but he can't keep them...
>
> Well he might keep that friend for two or three days, then he'd do something to upset them and they'll not want anything to do with him and he'll move onto the next one...But the school's working with him on that as we've been quite frustrated because there's only about 30 kids at the school these days.
>
> As he goes from one kid to the next, by the end of the year, he's not going to have any friends and no-one's going to want to know him or have anything to do with him...so I've made the school aware of that.

Jamie, similarly, liked the friendship of smaller children, but collected different items from those of Tom, as Mary explained:

> ...he collects furniture. Now, I don't know whether that's a FAS thing or a Taurus thing, but he does collect fridges, TVs, dressing tables and of course, he's in debt. Then he got, you know, dragged before the courts and the job they gave him to do after school was working in a children's home for three months. He liked it and they liked him and they wanted him to stay permanent. He just loved it and it was supposed to be a punishment!
>
> He's always been great with young kids. He loved kids 'cause you see, he was the 'big brother' then, you know, the power thing - important. He still loves that.

Core Category Four - Birth Mothers are the Cause of Criminal Behaviour

Children affected by fetal alcohol spectrum disorder can easily get into trouble with the police and the legal system, based on the premise that they do not have the cognitive ability to connect cause with effect, are unable to learn from previous experiences, have a high need for social interaction, but lack the social and cognitive skills for such long-term relationships, know little about the world in which they live and as such, are unaware that there are laws and systems put in place by the government to protect citizens.

Police Blame the Mothers for the Child's Behaviour

Although the birth mothers are seen to make numerous attempts at controlling, influencing and educating their children in the differences between right and wrong and their consequences, their efforts generally fail to have the desired effect. In some cases, unfortunately, the primary option for structure offered by society becomes that provided by penal institutions. It is not uncommon for the child to participate in petty crime, for which the mother is blamed.

Mary, who worked full-time, recalled her encounter with the police when they inferred by their communication that she was to blame for Jamie's behaviour:

> I'm trying to work and he was pinching my car and pinching my little scooter and things like that. Taking off at nine and of course, they said, you know "Why aren't you watching him?" and I said "You have to sleep sometimes."

Police Have Little or No Knowledge of the Syndrome

Because the police believed that all children at some stage in their lives may steal, the FASD child was put into this group, the police, in general, being unaware that the offending individual was suffering from the effects of the syndrome, of which they had little or no knowledge. Consequently, the courts are not likely to recognise the person's cognitive disability and behaviour problems so that the individual is misunderstood and misinterpreted, being labelled as stubborn, obnoxious, lazy, having antisocial personality disorder or given other judgmental and inaccurate labels. The individual may become involved with gangs, but more often as a 'fringe' member or 'gopher', which is what happened to Jamie following a few altercations with the police. As Mary said of her son:

...and he joined the local gang,...and you know, he was very excited - "But they've given me adventure, Mum and a Triumph motorcycle!" [laughter].

Real criminal gang and the reason they gave him the bike was so he'd do their drug running ...you see, mm and...he was in a terrible state. "I don't like this, Mum". "Well, you were told, weren't you?" "They won't let me sleep."

He was a Prospect - that's the ones that want to be a gang person, you see. So he ran away, but being Jamie, he forgot he had the King Pad's keys with him and he had his patch on and that patch is their sacred mark... Mmh, he came in that window one night - he'd run away. One of his jobs that made him run away was they were making cannabis oil and they sent him up to the airport to pinch four huge drums of isopropylene...

Jamie experienced further involvement with the Australian police when he was shot by a member of the Commacero gang. This negative event however, proved to have a somewhat positive outcome for him:

...evidently the group of young Muslims circled him. He'd taken to carrying a knife and there was a bit of a brawl. He ended up in prison and that's where he got diagnosed as FAS...and that's in Sydney and you know, Aussie's terribly behind.

Sarah, in an attempt to stop John from stealing, sought the advice and help of the local police by taking him to the police-station:

He'd nicked my husband's watch...taken it to school...I think it was just his way of being closer to us - I'm not sure. We told him that he can't do it and he just wouldn't take 'No' for an answer. So we told him that if he was going to do it again, he would go and see the police with us. Anyway, we took him to see the local community cop. He told John that if his Mum had to bring him back, he wasn't going to be very nice the next time he saw him. So that sort of knocked him off his perch a little bit.

Likewise, Reuben was taken to the local police station by his mother because he stole from and had lied to her. Esther said:

He's an awesome liar! He took a $50 note and a $20 note from my purse...

I thought "God, I'm losing the plot. A note's gone missing" and I thought "Oh, I must have used it"...A couple of days later he took a $20 and I thought "Oh, the little bugger." This time the drawer was left open and I said to him "Where's that money?" "I've only got a 50 and a 20". Well, I thought he had a $20 note and a 50c piece. He had the $50 note as well! He has no conception on...the value of money...so I took him down the police station. We had a marvellous police officer and he showed him the pink cell and gave him a stern talking to. He walked out and the tears were rolling down his cheeks and he said to me "I'm really sorry, mummy. I'll never do it again" and I said "OK. Well it had better not happen again" knowing it would. We walked out the door and he said to me "When you bring me down next time, they're going to lock me in that pink cell, you know. I quite like that pink cell. It's a nice wee room, eh?" And I thought that didn't work.

Miriam stated that her son did not learn from past experience, so that the crime was committed again and again:

Money was disappearing and my husband and I set traps...it was him that was doing the stealing! Well, this just blew us away. We got him to give some money back he'd taken...He

> was really angry with us, so he went off and two days later it happened again...Nothing we could do would stop him. It was terrible!

Naomi said that Pippa lied to her and other people, following her daughter's offending, even though she had told her that she must not steal and that she must always tell the truth:

> ...she goes "Look what I've got" and I said "Where'd you get that from?" She goes "I found it" I said "Pippa, you've got that from the car. That's stealing.
>
> You really shouldn't steal...You can't take other people's money"...
>
> "I never stole any money, Mum, I found it". "Well show me where you found it". "No, I can't remember".

On a final note, but without being classified as a core category – rather a category – the majority of the birth mothers mentioned that they worried about their child's future. As this is an important category/theme, it is now addressed.

Since the offspring may have dabbled in drugs, alcohol and petty crime whilst still at school and whilst living within the family household, it became a major worry to the birth mothers of what might happen to their disabled child when he/she left the security of the educational institution for the outside world: a world which the disabled individual knew little about. The women feared that their son or daughter, on finding their independece, would violate the law: a law which failed to understand the neurodevelopmental behaviours of the affected individual. Another worry for the women was that their disabled offspring lacked the social and communication skills necessary to become a valued member of society and in order to become an independent individual, the child must secure gainful employment. The mothers worried that their children would not secure paid positions because of the individual's instability and unreliability.

Jamie was also given another job by the police, which really suited him, even though it was supposed to be a form of punishment. As his mother, Mary recounted:

> Jamie was in prison last year for drink-driving from the accident in his 4WD and he was full of boose and drugs. Sure he liked it - he fell on his feet! After four days - "Oh, you're a trained arborist" We'll give him his own chain-saw - he can take them down [trees] and he was spending all day at the beach!

Some universal factors are protective against problems with employment, namely, a diagnosis before the age of six, longer time in a stable and nurturing home, longer duration in each household and not being a victim of violence. Tom, coming from a caring and stable family environment had moved on from collecting small cars to driving the 'proper' thing. As Miriam stated "He drives trucks. We're back to the driving thing - cars!" Isaac, who was once told by his school principal that he wouldn't even get a job as a street cleaner if he applied for it, secured paid employment on leaving school early. Rebecca said:

> Isaac is a free agent now that I have little control over as he has been working since he left school before the end of his 5th form level, which is coming up totwo-and-a-half years. He is still working at a meat works.

Jessica loved the job she obtained on leaving school early because she found she could do it and having gained self-confidence, self-esteem and identity, believed she could achieve even higher positions. According to Martha:

> She worked in a milk factory, yeah, something really simple. She actually loved it, because she could do it! Yeah and she was really surprised. She'd done those courses that when the kids drop out of school, they've got nowhere to go and met lots of kids in the same situation. I think she decided that she can do it, so...She's working in an office, yeah, doing the accounts on the computer...She left all her jobs - cleaning, housemaiding and in a cafe bar and went back to school, last year, yeah.

None of the children in this study was given an early diagnosis, yet the four who left school secured paid positions of employment and lived independent of their families. Tom married and lived with his wife, who was a teacher of eight-year-old children. They are soon to become parents. Jamie fathered a child who was born with six fingers on each hand and six toes on each foot, an abnormality apparently, in keeping with the Tudors' era.

DISCUSSION

Introduction

The disability story of parents needs to be heard; it will inform our knowlege of "How people come to adopt stories" (Corker and French, 1999 cited Fisher 1972, p.235) as well as shedding light on the epistemology of 'difference'. Most importantly, the act of telling one's story is a crucial first step toward what bell hooks (1984; 1990) has called a 'coming to voice' (Corker and French, 1999 p.118). Therefore and to reiterate, the aim of this original work was to explore, using a standpoint feminist perspective on disability (Fawcett, 2000), eight birth mothers' experiences of being pregnant with, giving birth to and nurturing a child with FASD by giving 'voice' to this oppressed sub-group of women.

Through the documentation of their narratives, which are veracious stories – veracious stories because they come from the 'voices' of the birth mothers themselves – the struggling women who have had to fight long and hard against state systems that society and public policy have imposed, without knowledge for and irrespective of, those individuals afflicted by this devastatingly disabling condition and the hierarchical non-listening professisonals operating within them – for the sakes of nurturing and educating their disabled child/ren and more often than not, without any help whatsoever from those systems which purportedly operate to support the child and family unit. These mothers therefore, found themselves at the intersection of competing discourses. That is to say, they nurtured their children in a society that devalued and medicalized the lives of individuals with disabilities as well as giving them a stigmatized label.

The publicly available discourses of disability and identity are inherent in the medical model of disability and the social model of disability. Within the medical model of disability, children are developmentally delayed (Landsman, 2005) – in keeping with all nine disabled children born to the women participants. However, Oliver (1990) would deem it to be society itself which creates the disability within an individual by virtue of held attitudes, beliefs, values, discrimination and oppression. In short, disability, for these mothers, was viewed as a 'personal tragedy' (Sullivan, 1991) and a social problem or 'burden' for the rest of society (Barnes and Mercer, 2003), which kept the affected individual [frequently] out of schools...and out of the mainsteam of community life (Ballard, 1994 cited Cahill, 1991).

My work has argued in favour of incorporating a social aspect into medical professionals' ways of thinking so that all disabled individuals may be viewed in terms of a relatively healthy person as opposed to one who is ill. Therefore, it seemed legitimate that a morphological model of disability (Vedder, 2005) based on Elizabeth Wilson's feminist theory of morphology, which seeks to combine the social and the biological and which highlights the multiple ways in which professionals might intervene in disability without devaluing dis(en)abled individuals, whilst at the same time acknowledging the importance of the social dimension to disability, be appropriated. This is deemed to be an ideal model since it also takes into consideration the ways in which FASD is socially constructed through prejudicial assumptions about facial morphology.

This qualitative research study has produced several emergent hypotheses by the valid employment of grounded theory. Of the fifteen sub-themes which emerged, four were categorized as key themes with all women responding to lack of knowledge for the syndrome, maternal guilt/blame laying and diagnosis, support networks, education, health, the policing and judicial systems, employment and independence (Table 3). Forty-eight recurring themes/words were identified (Table 4). As a result, various relative issues and problems associated with the disabled child and its family have been raised, thereby confirming, as well as adding to, the existing body of knowledge in this field. Some of these issues find wide support in the literature such as the lack of teaching strategies available, the primary and secondary disabilities, the importance of an integrated teaching approach and the complexities involved in making a diagnosis of FASD. Because there is no FASD diagnosis in the current American Psychiatric Association: Diagnostic and Statistical Manual of Mental Disorders (DSMIV), this means that mental health professionals have to rely on personal experience for screening. Other issues raised relate to the incorrect behavioural conception of the cognitively-disabled individual by the policing and judicial systems, violation of mothers' and childrens' rights, the importance of appropriate and adequate support networks for the family of a child with the syndrome and issues concerning labelling, child abuse, promiscuity, stealing, lying, risk-taking, daily structuring, unpredictability, lapses in memory, adoption and fostering together with lack of printed information on the syndrome within society. All fifteen sub-categories/themes, although identified separately, are in fact, inter-related with each other to some degree, this becoming evident upon reading of the text.

The women were aged between 19 and 35 years when they delivered their disabled child, which is in keeping with Marks' (1996) statement that women are most likely to be drinking heavily at ages when fertility is high. As previously noted, two boys were diagnosed with FAS, three boys with FAE, two girls with FAS (one being classified as ADHD by a medical professional), one girl with FAE and one girl with pFAE and ADHD. The spread across the sexes therefore, is equal. Seven of the eight babies had low Apgar scores at birth with an average of 6 (out of 10) being achieved. Interestingly, seven of the eight babies were of low birth weight – their average weight being 6lb 2oz. All eight multipara women described their pregnancies as differing in various ways from their other pregnancies with doctors (usually male) intervening in their labours. Since the majority of the doctors (operating within the context of the medical model of disability) used medical language which the mothers did not understand, it was felt that patriarchy and oppression of women remained in vogue on the maternity wards as knowledge by the doctors was power.

I now discuss issues relative to the mothers' narratives, taking each section in turn:

It's the Mother's Fault

A most disturbing issue which emerged from the findings was that 87.5% of the women had never heard of and knew nothing about, fetal alcohol spectrum disorder prior to or during their pregnancies. Only one woman was aware that alcohol should not really be consumed when pregnant, although she was totally unaware that it could have a disastrous neurodevelopmental effect on the unborn child. All eight women stated that had they known about the syndrome prior to or during pregnancy, they would never have drunk alcohol or continued to consume it. It is of concern that one birth mother was informed by her general practitioner that her baby would be fine because she had only had one binge-drinking session. None of the mothers was aware that their partner or husband's heavy drinking pattern could affect his sperm (lowered testosterone levels) and it's count (DNA [deozyribonucleic acid] permanently altered), which is classified as a marker for neurodevelopmental abnormality of the fetus, ie learning. According to Evensen (1996-2002), the male cannot cause FASD, but other birth defects can be present owing to the defective sperm, ie, small baby. Abel (1998) posited that other drugs associated with alcohol abuse are potential risk factors and contribute to alcohol's impact on the fetus, eg marijuana, cocaine, caffeine (p.180). Out of the nine affected babies born to the participants, only one was not of low birth weight. Interestingly, this was Martha's baby. Whilst in this vein, it is noted that all the women stated that their child was different and was viewed as 'different' by other people, the difference generally being seen in the child's behaviour, since physical disparities are 'invisible' to the lay-person.

Society believed the mother to be responsible for the child's difference and so 'mother-blaming' becomes encompassed within the social model of disability. It is because of the mothers' responsibilities and proximity to their children which have tended to make them the prime suspects when things are seen to go wrong in their children's lives (Read, 2003). However, Ong-Dean (2005) stated that advice books warn that parent-blaming is a common approach to disability, but that this is an illegitimate attempt to blame families, driven by moralism, not scientific understanding. Lewis, Strauss and Lehtinen (1960) wrote of [h]ow often...the parents of a brain-injured child [are] told by grandparents or other relatives "There's not a thing wrong with that child; you're just spoiling him". This statement echoed one of the participant's memoirs (Mary), who was told likewise about her son's behaviour by medical, health and educational professionals and as Brutten, Richardson and Mangel (1973) argued "Teachers, psychologists and physicians also appear as learning-disability skeptics who blame parents". This comment is supported by Nevin et al (2002) whose Canadian survey on physicians' knowledge of FASD concluded that they needed more education about the syndrome as they are not confident about being able to make a diagnosis. So, after 36 years, Brutten et al's claim still rings true today.

Although it is said that women have a natural tendency to decrease the amount of alcohol they consume during pregnancy, three of the mothers in this study did not do so, with one woman dramatically increasing her amount of alcohol consumption in an attempt to abort the fetus. A New Zealand study carried out by Clissold et al (1991) in Dunedin and using lifestyle behaviours questionnaires during pregnancy within one week of giving birth, concluded from the 183 returned questionnaires that before pregnancy 58% of the women drank alcohol, consuming 4.0 (6.6) glasses per week. At full-term, 19% of the sample was still drinking alcohol, but these women were now only consuming 1.7 glasses per week: only 1% of the total sample was drinking more than five glasses a week at full-term (p.111). Clissold et al (1991) concluded that the women had little difficulty in reducing alcohol consumption during pregnancy and in any case, consumption of alcohol pre-pregnancy was generally low (p.112).

The findings from my work, albeit a small sample of women, challenges the work of Clissold et al – in as much as consumption of alcohol pre-pregnancy amongst the study's participants, was high – as do the statistics from the 2002/03 New Zealand Survey (MOH, 2004) which indicate that the proportion of female drinkers aged 16 to 17 years who consumed larger amounts of alcohol (defined as four drinks or more) on a typical occasion *doubled* from 10% in 1995 to 21% in 2000. Surveys of drinking conducted in 1995 and 2000 by the Alcohol and Public Health Research Unit (APHRU) showed increases in both the frequency of drinking and the amount drunk by female drinkers with the amount drunk on a typical occasion also increasing across all age groups, especially in females aged 16 to 24 years. A further New Zealand study performed by Counsell et al (1994) found that 41.6% of New Zealand women consumed alcohol during their pregnancy. Of this 41%, when compared with the 58.4% of abstainers, it was found that they tended to be older, have higher educational qualifications, lower parity, higher socioeconomic status and be European or Maori (p.278). Alarmingly, 18.7% of these women were consuming alcohol on a regular basis of more than once a week - supporting this project's findings. Marks (1996) study also showed that over 40% of New Zealand women continue to consume alcohol during pregnancy. Marks (1996) further argued that whilst this is less than half the total of New Zealand's pregnant women, it cannot be ignored.

A finding of much importance by my work was that seven of the women were either married or partners of heavy drinkers/alcoholics with six of the women coming from drinking families. Seven of the mothers said that the pregnancy, labour and birth with their disabled child was different from that experienced with their other offspring, but the author is unclear as to whether this is related to the fact that the unborn child had consumed alcohol because there is no literature that could be found to support this finding. My study has also shown that even when using contraceptive methods, women who are heavy drinkers, can still unintentionally, become pregnant. This finding is supported in the literature by Jackson (2002) who stated that about half of pregnancies are unintended and up to one in ten women may not recognise their pregnancy until the second trimester, thus inadvertently exposing the fetus to alcohol during its early development. This latter recognition also supported the birth mothers' memoirs.

Counsel et al (1994) concluded that programmes needed to be developed in New Zealand to reduce the amount of alcohol consumption amongst women during pregnancy. As my study suggests, whatever methods were drawn up to prevent women from drinking have not succeeded. Therefore, Counsel et al statement of 1994 is endorsed, but amended by all women research participants who state that *no* alcohol should be consumed by a pregnant woman. The birth mothers also felt that all women of childbearing age, should be banned from purchasing alcohol purchase and banned by law from its consumption. The women believed that public awareness, information and education needs to be readily available about the disability at all ante-natal classes, GP surgeries, the media, so that no woman is left in any doubt about the consequences of alcohol upon the unborn child.

My study participants believed that certain sub-groups of society's women require to be targeted – those who come from heavy alcohol-consuming families, women who are already heavy, binge or dependent drinkers, social/cultural drinkers, teenage girls, women who have mental health issues and/or drug-users. These recommendations therefore, encompass a much broader target area than that suggested by Counsell et al (1994). Overseas research has also emphasized targeting 'high risk' women such as alcoholics, certain ethnic minority groups and those of low socioeconomic status.

Interestingly, in 1982 Clarren stated "If women can be appropriately warned of alcohol's dangers and can abstain from alcohol, this unfortunate disorder can be eliminated" (p.45). Unfortunately, it fell on 'deaf ears' until fairly recently, when the United States Government, followed closely by France, put warning labels on alcohol. I myself called for the NZ Government to address the issue by adopting the same trend (Salmon, 2004) in the hope that women will abstain from consuming alcohol during their fertile years, especially since those methods or means which were adopted in the past, have obviously failed. The New Zealand Government was also called upon last year by a consensus of opinion and signatures in both the North and South Islands, to classify FASD as a 'notifiable' condition in order that a database can be established and all FASD births recorded. In echoing the remarks made by Belenky et al (1986), this too, fell on 'deaf ears'.

Medical and Health Professionals Abandon the Mothers

The women were dismayed and frustrated by the medical and health care professisonals who were unwilling or unable to respond to their needs, the offspring's needs and their compassion for their children. The medical and health support networks were viewed as a failure with many gaps being identified by the women: the major one appearing to be a lack of diagnostic professionals and services – in particular medical diagnosis and neurodevelopmental/behavioural/psychological assessment. Even where a service might exist, coverage and access is uneven and often does not extend to rural or remote communities.

The women stated that it was the experience of other parents which represented almost the major source of help and understanding regarding what is needed, what is not needed, what works and what does not work and who understands FASD in each community and who does not. In other words and as Landsman (2005) stated "The women get to know who the experts are". This idea was supported by Wright back in 1981, who said "The affected child's family will need ongoing supportive services to help them disentangle the host of emotions they will feel and effectively confront the difficulties of living with a FASD child" (p.7). This statement confirms that of Short and Hess (1995) who believed that the demand placed upon caregivers and families with a FASD member is relentless.

Because the women realized that they could not change the cognitive impairment and behavioural issues of their child, they intuitively changed their attitudes toward the individual, so that he/she too became a valued member of the family unit – the 'special one'. In order to bring some sort of order to the household, the women 'knowingly', put structure in place, eg, charts or lists as aides-memoire. It was through the mothers' intimate relationship with their offspring, that they became aware the child's behaviour was not of its own conscious making and thus came to understand and learn from their son or daughter, ultimately becoming an earnest advocate and mediator in amongst the many medical and health encounters they experienced. The birth mothers also described how they interceded in a host of other ways between their disabled child and people and circumstances that fostered misunderstanding of them and their needs (Read, 2003) eg, right of consent. The women's experiences are supported in the literature by Wekselman et al (1995) who believed that caregivers need to have a clear understanding of FASD in order to reframe their perspective of their stubborn and uncooperative child, to that of a child with a CNS impairment. It needs to be noted that the child's unpredictable behaviour arises because his/her brain is not able to function properly in the area of orientation in time and space, the dysfunctional consequence of which is appointments are missed and social cues are misperceived. The resultant behavioural attitude as perceived by society is one of 'cannot be bothered' by the affected individual with 'time appearing to be of no essence.' In fact, stimulus overload is more likely the cause unless drugs are being used.

Another issue of much concern to the women was of the consequences for the child of incorrectly identifying the syndrome. For the appropriate recognition and intervention strategies to occur, the FASD child requires to be diagnosed correctly, which also bodes well for the future. However, there would still, three decades after identification of the disorder, appear to be many difficulties and uncertainties for the medical professionals involved in making the FASD diagnosis. Possibly because FASD is a complex of morphological and behavioural characteristics as opposed to a single, unifying observable feature (Umbreit and Ostrow, 1980 cited Shelton and Cook, 1993, p.45), being further complicated by a lack of a single biological marker (Morse et al, 1992 cited Wekselman et al, 1995, p.296). Alternatively and as my work has shown, a medical professional may not make the correct FASD diagnosis because he/she does not wish to 'label' the child, since 'labelling' brings about a possible issue of guilt and blame laying on the mother. All women participants stated that they had experienced great difficulty in obtaining a diagnosis for their child from a diagnostic medical professional, creating much frustration for them because they were constantly fighting the system. This major issue is commented upon in the literature by Leslie and Roberts (2001) who stated that "Even when childen are suspected of being affected by FASD, getting a diagnosis is a major challenge". However, when the participants did receive a proper diagnosis for their child, they expressed much relief because as well as knowing what was actually wrong with the child, it also, as Landsman (2005) stated, "Made sense of confusing behaviours they had observed and had thought were the consequence of their own poor mothering skills".

Identification in infancy is possible through attention to growth measures and to common manifestations (ie, feeding problems, irritability and unpredictable patterns of sleeping and eating) that may be due to withdrawal from alcohol and make the baby hard to care for (Aase, 1994; Stratton et al, 1996). More often than not, the doctor gave, according to many of the participants, an incorrect diagnosis – usually ADHD, so as not to lay blame or guilt on the mother, although there are traits with FASD which are comparable with ADHD (Coles et al, 1997). Niccols (1994) observed "The behavioural disorder most frequently noted in clinical papers and research reports describing children with FASD is ADHD...[and] during the preschool period, hyperactivity is present in 85% of children with FASD" (p.99). Short and Hess (1995) believed that FASD individuals are often viewed as similar to ADHD children 'possibly due to a similarity in CNS irregularities' (p.24). Other researchers have acknowledged that individuals with FASD are socially engaging, outgoing, friendly and chatty, especially in the younger age groups (Abkarian, 1992; Burgess and Streissguth, 1992; Streissguth and Giunta, 1988 cited Niccols, 1994), which tends to mask their disability.

In Shilts's (1999) book, she wrote of one of her two sons "...I didn't want to hear he was attention deficit. That meant he was impulsive and prisons are full of people with impulsive control problems". When she finds out that her son has FAS she claims "The adolescent years for fetal alcohol syndrome children are pretty bad: lying, stealing, criminal activity, lack of empathy, low motivation, depression, fourth grade level reading and third grade level math is about all they can do" – all in keeping with the lived experiences of the birth mothers of my study.

Landsman's (2005) research also confirmed the views of my birth mothers', in that upon hearing their child diagnosed with a developmental delay or disability, many mothers argued that the child is mislabelled in as much as the child demonstrated behavioural and cognitive abnormalities. They tell 'the doctor is wrong' stories, in which they describe being given misdiagnoses and dismal predictions that are later proven wrong by a child, as my work has demonstrated. In resisting the placement of their child in the marked category, many mothers point to contradictory prognoses given by different physicians and therapists (Landsman, 2005). In this respect, Miriam was given three differing diagnoses for her son, Tom, whom she believed to be FAE because he did not display the facial characteristics of the syndrome. At one stage, even Down Syndrome was suggested, as was the case for another woman participant prior to the correct diagnosis being made.

Ong-Dean (2005) states that in order to arrive at the proper diagnosis, parents may, in fact, need to take the lead. Landsman (2005) confirmed that many doctors are reluctant to give diagnoses they perceive to be painful to parents. However, Niccols (1994, p.103) argues that even when a physician considers the diagnosis, it may be dismissed because there is a general belief that the FASD label is not needed for the child's treatment and may place an unfair and overwhelming burden of guilt upon the mother. The women's narratives in general, do not support Niccols's finding since most neither felt guilty nor responsible – neither did they feel they were entirely to blame for their child's disability on the basis that there was lack of public information available on the condition. The birth mothers would argue that Niccols (1994) statement is incorrect in that a FASD child within New Zealand *does* require a correct diagnosis in order to receive the necessary treatment and welfare benefits.

Intertwined with battling to obtain the correct diagnosis of FASD from a medical practitioner, is the issue that the women felt oppressed and belittled by the male doctors they encountered in the health systems. This state of affairs is in keeping with most mothers of children who are disabled: not just children disabled by FASD (Read, 2003). Christensen (1996) stated that "For much of this century the lives of people with disabilities have been dominated by the medical profession. As a group their identity was defined for them in terms of sickness, involving pathology or disorder. They were labelled as deaf, dumb, blind, mentally deficient, spastic". However, medical terminology inevitably intersected with social values and cultural norms at the time...with the medical language of disability soon becoming the social language of insult and disparagement ie, moron, idiot, imbecile. The women participants' experiences are in keeping with these remarks in that they too met with negativity, judgmental and uncaring attitudes because their child was seen to be disabled. Also the medical language that the doctors used (generally male: supported by Barnes and Mercer [2003]), was hierarchical and the mothers did not understand it – neither did they question it because and as Vedder (2005) argues, "They felt devalued...being undermined as complex beings".

Read (2003 cited Strong (1979, p.128) explored key features of the interactions between staff and parents (mostly mothers) in his study of paediatric consultations:

> Here parents were both excluded and controlled. They might be partners but they were not equals and the balance of power within the bureaucratic format was one of the most striking features. Although some parents had some rights to question and to criticize they could only use these within an overall context of medical dominance. The technical authority given to the doctors was matched by an equivalent authority to control almost every aspect of the consultant's shape, sequence and timing.

Read (2003 cited Strong, 1979) also observed that while the women might be assumed by staff to be loving and competent in their role as mothers, it was also almost universally taken for granted that they were ignorant of those things deemed to be in the area of competence of the professional. Correspondingly, whatever the reality of the competence of the staff, they both assumed and were granted the mantle of 'expert' as the birth mothers soon realized. Because of this mantle, the professionals are seen as the gatekeepers (Moore et al, 1998) to the welfare, health and educational services that disabled individuals require.

Vedder (2005) further believed in relation to FASD, that the medical model offers intervention which undermines the humanity of dis(en)abled patients. Consequently, the doctors, purportedly having the knowledge, retained the power (Fawcett, 2000), so that patriarchy remained in vogue in each medical encounter the participants experienced – a byproduct of the medical model of disability and its usage by male doctors, for whom it is well-suited (Fawcett, 2000). As a consequence, the mothers became 'voiceless'. However, feminism dictated that women be given a 'voice', listened to and recognized as full moral agents, capable of understanding and acting on information by virtue of their value systems. Graham (1980) suggested that by listening to mothers talk about their lives, helps to fill a theoretical vacuum by bridging the gap between the abstract analysis of feminism and those everyday experiences in women's lives that feminism tries to address.

As Duff (1981) stated "Being emotionally troubled does not make parents unintelligent, nor does it prevent them from using the intelligence they have" (p.316). It therefore, becomes a self-fulfilling prophecy, that women are incapable of making intelligent, informed decisions when they have insufficient information on which to base these because no-one will take the time to explain what they have a right and a need to know – they become stymied by patriarchy.

As statistics have shown, the health field remains dominated by males and that society retains gender inequalities – inequalities which feminism maintains women and especially mothers, are still viewed as an oppressed group of people, an 'invisible' group of women who are not listened to by health and medical professionals.

Birth Mothers and Their Children are Unsupported in the Educational System

Disagreements and conflicts of interest over appropriate education within the disability arena are commonly reported by mothers of disabled children (Read, 2003 cited Rogers, 1986a, 1986b; Audit Commission 1992; Haylock et al. 1993; Beresford 1994b). In keeping with this statement, all women participants, even through their 'battling' experiences, believed that the educational system had, overall, failed to meet the needs of their offspring, so that each individual, after entering mainsteam schooling, experienced a disrupted education. The mothers' narratives clearly stated that a major concern was lack of progress by their son or daughter. The mothers' beliefs and concerns are supported in the literature by Streissguth (1997, p.109) who stated that students with disrupted school experiences had twice as many learning and behaviour problems as those without disrupted school experiences and that more than 60% of the adolescents...had had a disrupted school experience.

Niccols (1994) stated that some researchers have claimed it 'essential' to identify the specific and specialised needs of children with FASD and develop a set of educational and developmental strategies tailored to meet these needs. This has not transpired and the teachers still tend to remain reliant upon educational practices drawn up for children with other developmental disabilities, which are generally unsuccessful (Carmichael Olson and Burgess, 1997). The mothers also recognized these issues when they stated that the disabled child should be taught according to its educational needs and not its chronological age: this because the teachers are still not au fait with the spectrum of cognitive and neurobehavioural challenges which FASD encompasses. The mothers are supported in the literature by Ballard (1999) who firmly stated that "Those children who have a disability (including intellectually), their needs are often not met, or at least not met without there having to be seemingly endless advocacy by parents, disability groups...and other professionals".

Because the teachers lack knowledge about the condition, they do not comprehend that the child's behaviour is not of its own making. The child therefore, is viewed as a troublemaker, a time-waster and ineducable. These findings support those made by Oliver (1990 cited Barns and Mercer, 2003, p.44), which shows that within New Zealand, the educational system appears not to have changed much from the United Kingdom in fifteen years. Consequently, instead of appropriate teaching strategies being drawn up to meet the slow-learning child's needs, the individual is ridiculed by some of their contemporaries and teachers, as was Tom. Tom's experience is supported in the literature by Turnbull and Turnbull (1978), further indicating that the New Zealand educational system's attitudes towards disability have not changed over the past 26 years. As Streissguth (1998) posited "Students who inappropriately express their needs are often misunderstood and ridiculed or goaded by fellow students and viewed as troublemakers by administrators and teachers". These comments strengthen as well as support the experiences of the birth mothers and their children. Streissguth (1998) further posited "In the absence of a meaningful 'causal event', it is unlikely that the 'brain damage' hypothesis will be brought into play by most observers (eg, teachers). The diagnosis or knowledge of significant prenatal alcohol exposure might be enough for the observer to generate the correct hypothesis, but only if the observer actually understands the meaning of FASD or the significance of prenatal alcohol exposure". It is believed by the women that the teachers see FASD as a 'hidden' disability when compared with other disabilities, because only with FAS are there observable facial anomalies.

The mothers also stated that more help and resources were required within the classroom so that the affected child could receive one-to-one support, care and attention in the mainsteam schooling system as opposed to 'special education' systems which arose out of the response to the 'special needs' of those unable to cope in the mainstream sector (Barnes and Mercer, 2003 cited Warnock, 1978). The critics of special education believe that the system is deeply implicated in the oppression of people with impairments and should be abolished (Barnes and Mercer, 2003).

Ballard (1994) argued that what is frequently ignored in education circles, are the wishes of the parents and of people with disabilities. For example, their request for integration over segregation, for regular education over special education, has often gone unheeded or been rejected. Yet they know that segregated education is not particularly 'special' in the education it provides, nor is it equitable or effective. Ballard (1994) further stated that the Government's Special Education Service called for an end to separate, special education and a commitment to an inclusive education system in which every student was a valued and full participant in ordinary mainstream classrooms throughout the education system. Inclusion is not a policy of assimilation, but of valuing diversity. Also, the right to inclusion does not mean that a person or group *has* to take part. Many people who are deaf, for example, see separate education for deaf children as essential for retaining deaf language and culture. Therefore, the difference between forced segregation and choosing to be part of a separate organization, lies in the right of the person to choose to be included or not.

The mothers perceived that the child's challenging behaviour was a burden on the teacher and that the individual took up too much classroom time. As Read (2003) summed up in her study of 12 West Midlands (UK) women who cared for their disabled child "Their work as mediators trying to obtain services for their children was ongoing and often time-consuming and stressful. Some of the mothers had difficulty in finding out basic information about their child's entitlements and others discovered quite significant services by chance. Even when they succeeded, things rarely happened easily and there was usually something to be challenged, sorted out or chased up". This statement is a typical example of the experiences of the birth mothers in my study.

Another issue of concern for the birth mothers was that the structure put in place within the household is not counter-balanced by that of the classroom. A structured environment is vital to a child with FASD, as is only being given small tasks at a time by teachers. Unless the child is totally structured in the classroom and receives the attention and help that is required with school-work and especially mathematics, it becomes frustrated, followed by a tendency to 'act out' which culminates in much classroom disruption, as the mothers' stories bear witness to. As a result, the child, yet again, is often excluded from general activities within the classroom, suffers loneliness, has few friends and frequently feels dumb and useless (as confirmed by the birth mothers). Segregation of disabled children is reported by Read (2003), who stated "The process has been documented whereby historically disabled children and adults have consistently been segregated into separate educational, health and social care institutions, a practice which to some degree persists today". Christensen and Rizu (1996) argued that "Many students are identified as disabled, stigmatized or excluded not because their personal characteristics necessitate this, but because schooling is structured in such a way that student diversity beyond very narrow prescribed limits cannot be accommodated". Because every child needed to be socialized in order to fit into the environment and society, the disabled child required to be included in all classroom, curricula or wider school activities.

Birth Mothers are the Cause of Criminal Behaviour

Some of the women participants felt that because their disabled child had been involved in the policing or legal systems, they were unjustifiably viewed as 'bad mothers' and as such, they were the culprits for the criminal behaviours the offending individual displayed. However, according to those birth mothers who experienced the legal or policing systems with their offspring, they (the people within the systems) were, in general, not au fait with FASD and thus, the courts are not likely to recognise the person's cognitive disability and behaviour problems. The consequence is that the individual is misunderstood, misinterpreted and labelled as stubborn, obnoxious, having anti-social personality disorder or given other judgmental and inaccurate labels. The birth mothers also believed that the individual's unpredictable memory lapses and gains happened just often enough to convince those who were not au fait with FASD, that they were deliberate 'behaviours' made manifest under the control of the affected offspring. The reality, of course, is very different as no one is more frustrated by the situation than the disabled individual, who has to continually deal with other people's reactions. Telling the truth, making sense of situations and responding to requests, therefore, become difficult and even when information has been successfully stored and accessed, the individual must be able to interpret what it needs to do with that information.

As the birth mothers' narratives have shown, although FASD children know right from wrong, they cannot relate cause to an effect. Neither do they have regard for the consequences of their actions. According to Streissguth (1998), it is the lack of appropriate interventions and structures not put in place early in life and maintained across the life span which is the cause for FASD children to become involved in the legal system since many of these individuals are at high risk from birth through to their adult years.

It should be noted that the UK Law Commission (1995) maintained that individuals whose mental capacity is severely impaired are not able to understand, retain or accept information, nor to reasonably foresee the results of their actions. Accordingly, the actions of all individuals with learning disabilities are seen to be qualitatively and quantitatively different from those who are not seen to have learning difficulties and who deliberately take risks with hazards attached (Fawcett, 2000). Streissguth (1998) also believed that trouble with the law is usually strongly related to disrupted school experiences. Those individuals who do not experience disrupted school experiences were less likely to be in trouble with the law. As my work has confirmed, all the disabled children of the women participants had experienced a disrupted school experience.

A study performed in British Columbia by Conry and Fast in 1999 revealed FASD individuals to be highly suggestible, often having a negative self-imagine and almost always getting caught by the legal system because they can't plan ahead. Because Mary's son could not plan ahead, he was caught by the legal system. Conry and Fast (2000) purported that these individuals have poor adaptive behaviour, poor language ability, they acquiesce when they don't understand, confabulate because their memory is faulty and fail to reason through issues. They further report that approximately 25% of youth prison populations in British Columbia are FASD-affected and 50% have other disabilities, resulting in a high representation of disabled youth who are now labelled criminal. Somewhat earlier, Zakreski (1998) stated that Nanson and four colleagues authored a 1996 study on FASD in Saskatchewan in which they examined 207 cases over a two-year period. In concluding that the incidence of FASD had not dropped in the province during the past 20 years, despite efforts to inform the public of the danger of drinking while pregnant, they also stated that "One of the ironies is that children with FASD often make model prisoners". In terms of the justice system handling individuals with this, one of the things they fail to understand is that FASD people do very well in structured environments.

Often people are fooled in the early stages of treatment into thinking somebody is doing really well, not realising that they're doing really well because all the opportunities for them not to do well are taken care of in a structured program. There is a point where the individual with FASD falls apart again. Nanson et al (1996) findings supported the lived experience of

Mary and her son, who "fell on his feet" whilst in prison in Australia and also whilst undertaking community work in a children's home for his offending.

CONCLUSION

In keeping with Bogdan and Biklen's theory (1982, p.29) on qualitative research whereby "You are not putting together a puzzle, whose picture you already know. [Rather] you are constructing a picture which takes shape as you collect and examine the parts", so my study has produced a colourful and powerful picture, which has been achieved by the identification and usage of common themes across the eight birth mothers' narratives as building blocks. It showed how the birth mothers became fierce advocates for their disabled children as they struggled and battled against societal prejudice, oppression and discrimination so as to acquire from welfare, educational and policing systems, what they believed their children needed in order to survive in the outside world. The mothers, by virtue of their responsibility towards, interconnectedness (Gilligan, 1982; Noddings, 1990) with and very experience of their child, are the ones who became the *experts* in knowing and meeting their offsprings' needs rather than and as posited by Turnbull and Turnbull (1989) the 'so-called experts'.

As Murray and Penman (1996) categorically stated "Our children are the ones who teach us about the issues. They give us the opportunities to learn and understand. They give us determination and confidence. They give us hope and courage. They show us how it can be done...Our children are teaching us how to be their allies". The mothers took responsibility for caring work because it was the...'only thing they could do' and because of their gender they operated within 'the extended caring role' when mothers of children with disabilities extend their caring to a broader societal concern (Traustadottir, 1993).

The birth mothers have shown how the very word 'disability' (which presents the child as 'defective' [Read, 2003]), becomes located within the discourses of the medical profession and society under the paradigms of the medical and social models of disability. My study believed that the morpthological model would be a better workable paradigm within the FASD arena, especially since the medical model fails to take into account the positive qualities mothers attribute to their children and it commits women to participate in exhausting and sometimes demoralizing efforts to change their own children. The social model is effective in exposing societal barriers to full participation, yet it provided parents little guidance about how to ensure that adequate social change will take place in time to positively affect their own child's life. The social model also allowed for value difference and disability, but failed to allow for thinking in the realm of prevention and cure which the morphological model provided, whilst still valuing difference and disability. In this context therefore, public policy and agencies are required to attend to the broader conditions which affected not only disability, but also the health and welfare of all people.

Through my valid use of a feminist perspective, some of the mothers demonstrated how they finally found their voices in amongst the knowledge-power relationships of the doctors, medical practitioners, health workers and even, the teachers. The mothers found that they were able to make sense of their lived experiences with their disabled child and therefore, their actions by virtue of their interactions and connexions with the medicalization and socialization processes and those professionals working within them. It is interesting to note that these same issues are in keeping with the experiences of birth mothers' of children with other disabilities, eg Lesch Nyhan Syndrome (Pritchard, 2005, p.87), Down Syndrome, Rett Syndrome, autism, Fragile-X, as found in the plethora of literature on disability. However, it must be stated that FASD is not genetically constructed, as is the case with many other intellectual disabilities. The only issue which was not of joint acknowledgement, as described by the birth mothers, was that there was insufficient literature within society relating to alcohol consumption by pregnant women and FASD.

There may be a general awareness in the public at large of adverse effects of alcohol consumption by pregnant women, but as has been shown, people generally do not know about FASD. This proved to be of major concern for the women participants who believed that greater public awareness of the syndrome was imperative. They believed that certain public sectors and agencies required targeting for alcohol education, which included all medical, health, social and education professionals and that all ante-natal clinics, GP surgeries, women's health and mental health clinics, alcohol and drug clinics should carry literature on the syndrome. It was felt that all alcoholic beverages should carry a warning label, as with cigarettes. The mothers also felt that a government registry should be set-up to act as a notifiable-case dossier and to aid in statistical information analysis of the syndrome within New Zealand, as this as yet, does not exist. Interestingly, one mother, who felt so strongly about curtailing pregnant women from drinking, called for a law to be established whereby *all* women of child-bearing age, should not consume alcohol and that if they did so, they should pay a penalty for their offending. Only by total abstinence from the consumption of alcohol by all women worldwide, will FASD be prevented. There are few disabilities with as much potential for prevention as FASD since it is 100% preventable and occasioned only by women's alcohol consumption.

With regards to the issue of meeting the children's educational needs, since programmes drawn up in the past have generally failed, the mothers, now being the experts, called for appropriate *individual* intervention programmes to be drawn-up for each FASD-affected child, using one-to-one teacher aide, but still located within mainstream schooling as opposed to segregation, which alienates the child from the socialization process – a process which is so necessary for the child's future development and employment prospects. The women participants also called for increased numbers of professionals who are able to undertake correct diagnostic testing for FASD.

An important, positive fact which emerged is that of the four children of the birth mothers' who left school, seeking paid employment, all found positions within the workforce relatively easily, albeit of low job status, with one offspring still in his first job after two-and-a-half years, thus demonstrating reliability and stability in his independent life. This is in contrast to Reid and Bray's (1997) statement that traditionally people with intellectual disabilities have been excluded from paid work, but in keeping with Barnes and Mercer (2003, p.47) who said that "Disabled people are particularly under-represented in the professions and management, where there are higher earnings and greater job security and opportunities for promotion. Conversely, disabled people are over-represented in low-skilled, poorly paid, less secure jobs".

An interesting issue of societal importance which was raised is that all the birth mothers, except for one, experienced family breakdown, felt to be by the participants, as a result of the consumption of alcohol by the father of the FASD-affected child. This finding is in contrast to the findings of the study by Bray et al (1979, p.174) which explored 15 fathers' experiences of children with disabilities, when they concluded that family breakdown was not prevalent in the group and the evidence that a child with a disability significantly increases the chances of marriage breakdown (cited Beresford, 1994a), is equivocal. It should also be noted that the role of fathers in reproduction is understudied and should be of great significance to disability studies. I believe that future research should address this omission.

In conclusion, the findings I have presented represent an important step in furthering the understanding the lives of children with FASD in the midst of societal prejudice, oppression, stigmatisation and discrimination. The women's personal experiences, as reported by me, provided order and a measure of cohesion in terms of the experiences that mothers with a child with FASD undergo to nurture and educate their offspring so that it has the best possible opportunity of fitting into and being a valued member of society. It is hoped that my emancipatory work, which has given *voice* to the birth mothers' of offspring disabled by FASD, may advance the knowledge of professionals working with individuals and their families within the FASD arena and provide an impetus for future research in the field.

REFERENCES

Aase, J.M. (1994). Clinical recognition of FAS: Difficulties of detection and diagnosis.*Alcohol Health and Research World.* 18(1), 5-9.

Aase, J.M., Jones, K.L. and Clarren, S.K. (1995). Do we need the term 'FAE'? *Pediatrics,* 95, 428-430.

Abel, E.L. (1980). Fetal alcohol syndrome: Behavioural teratology. *Psychological Bulletin* 87(1), 29-50.

Abel, E.L. (1988). Fetal alcohol syndrome in families (commentary). *Neurotoxicology and Teratology,* 10, 12.

Abel, E.L. (1996). Moderate drinking during pregnancy: cause for concern? *Clinica Chimica. Acta,* 246: 149-154.

Abel, E.L. (1998). *Fetal alcohol abuse syndrome.* New York: Plenum Press.

Abel, E.L.(1999). Was the fetal alcohol syndrome recognized by the Greeks and Romans? *Alcohol Alcohol,* 34, 868-872.

Abel, E. L. (2001). Gin Lane: Did Hogarth know about Fetal Alcohol Syndrome? *Alcohol and Alcoholism,* 36(2): 131-134.

Abkarian, G. G. (1992). Communication effects of prenatal alcohol exposure. *Journal of Communication Disorders.* 25(4), 221-240.

Acker, J., Barry, K., Esseveld, J. (1983). Objectivity and truth: problems in doing feminist research. *Women's Studies International Forum.* 6(4): 424-425.

Alcohol Advisory Council of New Zealand, MoH (2001a). *National Alcohol Strategy 2000-2003.* Wellington: Alcohol Advisory Council of NZ and Ministry of Health.

Alcohol Advisory Council of New Zealand, MoH (2001b). *Baby or the bottle? Alcohol.org.nz.* The newsletter of the Alcohol Advisory Council of New Zealand. Te Panei a te Kaunihera Whakatupato Waipiro o Aotearoa, 2-4.

Alcohol Advisory Council of New Zealand (2005). *The burden of death, disease and disability due to alcohol in New Zealand.* Occasional publication No. 23, Wellington: *www.alac.org.nz* and *www.waipiro.org.nz*

Alcohol Healthwatch (2007). *Fetal Alcohol Spectrum Disorder in New Zealand: Activating the awareness and intervention continuum.* Newmarket, Auckland.

Alcohol and Public Health Research Unit, Auckland (1999). *Advice for purchasing strategy on public health issues: alcohol harm reduction.* Runanga, Wananga, Hauora me te Paekaka, PB 92019, Auckland.

Anspach, R. R. (1993). *Deciding who lives: Fateful choices in the intensive-care nursery.* Berkeley: University of California Press.

Arendt, H. (1958). *The Human Condition.* Chicago: University of Chicago Press.

Astley, S.J. and Clarren, S.K. (2000). Diagnosing the full spectrum of fetal alcohol-exposed individuals: introducing the 4-digit diagnostic code. *Alcohol Alcohol,* 35, 400-410.

Avis, M. (1995). Valid arguments? A consideration of the concept of validity in establishing the credibility of research findings. *Journal of Advanced Nursing.* 22, 1203-1209.

Bailey, D. M. (1997). *Research for the health professional: A practical guide.* Philadelphia: F. A. Davis.

Baker, C., Wuest, J. and Stern, P. N. (1992). Method slurring: The rounded theory/phenomenological example. *Journal of Advanced Nursing,* 17(11): 1355-1360.

Baldwin, S. and Carlisle, J. (1994). *Societal support for disabled children and their families: a review of the literature.* Edinburgh, UK: HMSO.

Ballard, K. (1994) (Ed.). *Disability, family, whanau and society.* Palmerston North, NZ: Dunmore Press Ltd.

Ballard, K. (1999). Concluding thoughts. In K. Ballard (Ed.) *Inclusive Education:International voices on disability and justice.* (pp.167-180). London: Falmer Press.

Barnes, C. and Mercer, G. (2003). *Disability.* Cambridge, UK: Polity Press.

Baron, R. J. (1985). An introduction to medical phenomenology: I can't hear you while I'm listening. *Annals of Internal Medicine,* 103, 606-611.

Batshaw, M.L. (2002) (5th Ed). *Children with Disabilities.* Baltimore, Maryland: Paul H. Brookes Pub. Co. Inc.

Beck, C. T. (1993). Qualitative research: The evaluation of its credibility, fittingness and auditability. *Western Journal of Nursing Research.* 15(2): 263-266.

Becker, H. S. (1958). Problems of inference and proof in participant observation. *American Sociological Review.* 23: 652-660.

Belenky, M. F., Clinch, B. M., Goldberger, N. R. and Tarule, J. M. (1986). *Women's waysof Knowing: The development of self, voice and mind.* USA: Bergin and Harvey Pubs, Inc.

Beresford, B. (1994a). Resources and Strategies: How parents cope with the care of a disabled child. *Journal of Child Psychology and Psychiatry,* 35, 171-209.

Beresford, B. (1994b). *Positively Parents: Caring for a severely disabled child.* London: HMSO.

Berryman, J. (1991). Perspectives on later motherhood. In Phoenix, A., Woollett, A. and Lloyd, E. (Eds.), *Motherhood: Meanings, practices and ideologies* (pp.103-122). London: Sage.

Berryman, J., Thorpe, K. and Windridge, K. (1995). *Older mothers: Conception, pregnancy and birth after 35.* London: Pandora Press.

Birns, B. and Hay, D. F. (Eds.). (1988). *The different faces of motherhood.* New York: Plenum Press.

Bleier, R. (1986). Lab coat: robe of innocence or klansman's sheet? In T. de lauretis (Ed.) *Feminist Studies/Critical Studies.* London: Macmillan Press.

Bogdan, R. C. and Biklen, S. K. (1982). *Qualitative Research for Education: An Introduction to Theory and Methods.* Boston: Allyn and Bacon, Inc.

Boyd, C. O. (1990). Qualitative Approaches to Research. In G. LoBiondo-Wood and J. Haber (Eds). *Nursing Research: Methods, Critical Appraisal and Utilization*, 181-210. St. Louis: Mosby Year Book.

Brannen, J. and Moss, P. (1991). *Managing mothers: Dual earner household after maternity leave.* London: Unwin.

Brody, H. (1994b). The Four Principles and Narrative Ethics. In *Principles of health care ethics.* R. Gillon (Ed.). Chichester: John Wiley and Sons.

Brutten, M. Richardson, S.O. and Mangel, C. (1973). *Something's Wrong with My Child:A Parents' Book about Children with Learning Disabilities.* New York: Harcourt Brace Jovanich Inc., 76.

Burgess, D. M. and Streissguth, A. P. (1992). Fetal alcohol syndrome and fetal alcohol effects: Principles for educators. *Phi-Delta-Kappan.* 74(1), 24-30.

Burman, E. (1994). *Deconstructing developmental psychology.* London: Routledge.

Burns, N. and Grove, S. (1993). *The Practice of Nursing Research (2nd Ed.).* London: W. B.Saunders.

Byrne, B. (2000). White lives: gender, class and 'race' in contemporary London. *School of Social and Political Science.* Brighton: University of Sussex, UK.

Cahill, M. (1991). *Exploring the experience of disability.* Wellington: Health Services Equal Employment Opportunities Development Unit.

Canadian Paediatric Society (2002). Fetal alcohol syndrome: position statement II. (2002-01). *Paediatric Child Health,* 7(3), 161-174.

Carmichael Olson, H. and Burgess, D.M. (1997). Early intervention for children prenatally exposed to alcohol and other drugs. In M.J. Guralnick (Ed.), *The Effectiveness of Early Intervention* (pp.109-145). Baltimore: Paul Brookes Pub. Co.

Christensen, C. (1996). Disabled, handicapped or disordered: what's in a name? In C. Christensen and F. Rizvi (Eds.), *Disability and the dilemmas of education and justice* (pp.63-78). Buckingham, UK: Open University Press.

Christensen, C. and Rizu, Fazal (1996). *Disability and the Dilemmas of Education and Justice.* Buckingham, UK: Open University Press.

Chudley, A.E., Conry, J., Cook, J.L., Loock, C., Rosales, R. and LeBlanc, N. (2005). Fetal Alcohol Spectrum Disorder: Canadian Guidelines for Diagnosis. *CMAJ,* 172 (Suppl 5).

Clandinin, D.J. and Connelly, F.M. (1994). Personal experience methods. In N.K. Denzin and Y. S. Lincoln (Eds). *Handbook of Qualitative Research.*Thousand Oaks, C.A: Sage Publications.

Clarren, S.K. and Smith, D. (1978). The fetal alcohol syndrome. *N.Eng.J.Med,* 298, 1063-1067.

Clarren, S. K. (1982). The diagnosis and treatment of fetal alcohol syndrome. *Comprehensive Therapy.* 8(10), 41-46.

Clarren, S.K. (2007). *The Western and Northern Canadian approach to diagnostic, intervention and prevention research.* Plenary session at the 2nd international conference on fetal alcohol spectrum disorder: Research policy and practice around the world. Inter-professional Continuing Education, University of British Columbia.

Clifford-Walton, V. A. (1998). Feminist Perspectives on Women's Health Research. In Romans, S. E. (Ed.) *Folding Back the Shadows.* Dunedin, NZ: University of Otago Press.

Clissold, T.L., Hopkins, W.G. and Seddon, R.J. (1991). Lifestyle behaviours during pregnancy. *New Zealand Medical Journal.* 104, 111-112.

Coles, C. D. et al (1997). A comparison of children affected by prenatal alcohol exposure and attention deficit, hyperactivity disorder. *Alcoholism: Clinical and Experimental Research.* 21(1), 150-161.

Conry, J. and Fast, D. K. (2000). *Fetal alcohol syndrome and the criminal justice system.*British Columbia Fetal Alcohol Syndrome Resource Society: Vancouver, BC.

Cook, J. A. and Fonow, M. M. (1986). Knowledge and women's interests: Issues of epistemology and methodology in feminist sociological research. *Sociological Inquiry.* 56(1): 2-29.

Corbin, J. and Strauss, A. (1990). Grounded theory research: Procedures, canons and evaluative criteria. *Qualitative Sociology.* 13, 3-21.

Corker, M. and French, S. (Eds.) (1999). *Disability Discourse.* Buckingham, UK: Open University Press.

Cotterill, P. (1992). Interviewing women: Issues of friendship, vulnerability and power. *Women's Studies International Forum.* 15(5/6): 593-606.

Counsell, A., Smale, P. and Geddes, D. (1994). Alcohol consumption by New Zealand women during pegnancy. *The New Zealand Medical Journal,* 107(982), 278-281.

Creswell, J. W. (1998). *Qualitative inquiry and research dessign: Choosing among five traditions.* Thousand Oaks: Sage Publications.

Curtis, J. (1994). *Alcohol and pregnancy: information for health professionals.* Alcohol Advisory Council of New Zealand.

Darroch, V. and Silvers, R. J. (1982). Biography and discourse. *Interpretive human studies: An introduction to phenomenological research.* Darroch, V. and Silvers, R. J. (Eds.), Washington DC: University Press of America.

Davis, A. and Lipson, A.A. (1984). Challenge in managing a family with fetal alcohol syndrome. *Clinical Pediatrics,* 23, 304.

de Laine, M. (1997). *Ethnography: Theory and applications in health research.* Sydney: MacLellan and Petty.

Denzin, N. K. (1989) (3rd Edn.). *The research act: A theoretical introduction to sociological methods.* Englewood Cliffs, NJ: Prentice Hall.

Denzin, N. K. and Lincoln, Y. S. (Eds) (2003) (2nd Edn.). *Collecting and Interpreting Qualitative Materials.* Thousand Oaks, California: Sage Pubs Inc.

DePoy, E. and Gitlin, L. (1998). *Introduction to research: Multiple strategies for health and human services.* St Louis: Mosby Year Book.

Dick, Bob (2002). Grounded theory: a thumbnail sketch. [On line] Available at http://www/scu.edu.au/schools/gcm/ar/arp/grounded.html

Dorris, M. (1998). *The Broken Cord* in *Biography* 21(4), 421-444. Also Harper and Row, 1989, New York.

Dubouloz, C-J., Egan, M., Vallerand, J. and von Zweck, C. V. (1999). Occupational therapists' perceptions of evidence-based practice. *American Journal of Occupational Therapy.* 53, 445-453.

Duchan, J. F. (2001). *Learning Leveling and Leveling Learning.* Graduation Speech, May 12. Department of Communicative Disorders and Sciences. *http://www.acsu.buffalo.edu/duchan/leveling.html*

Duff, R. S. (1981). Counselling families and deciding care of severely defective children: A way of coping with 'medical Vietnam'. *Pediatrics* 67(3): 315-320.

Easterby-Smith, M., Thorpe, R. and Lowe, A. (1990). *Management research: An introduction.* London: Sage Publications.

Ehrenreich, B. and English, D. (1973). *Witches, midwives and nurses: A history of women healers.* New York: The Feminist Press.

Eisner, E. W. (1991). *The Enlightened Eye: Qualitative Inquiry and the Enhancement of Educational Practice.* New York: MacMillan Publishing Co.

Elvin-Nowak, Y. (1999). *Accompanied by guilt: Modern motherhood the Swedish way.*Stockholm: Stockholm University.

Emerson, R. M. (1981). Observational field work. *Annual Review of Sociology*,7: 351-378.

Evensen, D. (1996-2002). Beginning at the Beginning: Understand the biological basis for FAS. *Project facts: fetal alcohol consultation and training services.* http://www.fasalaska.com

Fawcett, B. (2000). *Feminist Perspectives on Disability.* Essex, UK: Prentice Hall.

Fetal Alcohol NZ (FANZ) (2004). www.everybody.co.nz

Finch, J. and Groves, D. (1983) (Eds.). *A Labour of Love: Women, work and caring.* UK: Routledge and Kegan Paul.

Finch, J. (1984). It's great to have someone to talk to: The ethics and politics of interviewing women. In Bell, C. and Roberts, H. (Eds.), *Social researching: Politics, problems, practice* (pp.70-87). London: Routledge and Kegan Paul.

Finch, J. (1986). *Research and Policy: The uses of qualitative methods in social and educational research.* London: Falmer Press.

Finch, J. (1993). It's great to have someone to talk to: ethics and politics of interviewing women. *Social research: Philosophy, politics and practice.* In Hammersley, M. (Ed.). London: Sage Pubs Ltd.

Fisher, S. (1986). *In the patient's best interest: Women and the politics of medicaldecisions.* New Brunswick: Rutgers University Press.

Fontana, A. and Frey, J. H. (1994). Interviewing: The art of science. In Denzin, N. K. and Lincoln, Y. S. (Eds.). *Handbook of qualitative research* (pp.361-376). Thousand Oaks, A: Sage.

Frank, A. W. (1995). *The wounded storyteller: Body, illness and ethics.* Chicago:University of Chicago Press.

Furstenberg, F. F., Brooks-Gunn, J. and Morgan, S. P. (1987). *Adolescent mothers in later life.* Cambridge, UK: Cambridge University Press.

Gardner, J. (2000). Living with a child with fetal alcohol syndrome. *MCN,* 25(5), Sept/Oct.

Gilbert, L. A. (1994). Reclaiming and returning gender to context: Examples from studies of heterosexual dual-career families. *Psychology of Women Quarterly*, 18, 539-558.

Gilligan, C. (1982). *In a different voice: Psychological theory and women's development.* USA: Harvard University Press.

Giorgi, A. (1970). *Psychology as a human science: A phenomemologically-based approach.* New York: Harper and Row.

Glaser, B. G. (1978). *Theoretical sensitivity: advances in the methodology of grounded theory*. Mill Valley, CA: Sociology Press.

Glaser, B. G. (1992). *Basic of grounded theory analysis. emergence vs forcing*. Mill Valley, CA: Sociology Press.

Glaser, B. G. and Strauss, A. L. (1967). *The discovery of grounded theory: Strategies for qualitative research.* New York: Aldine De Gruyter.

Glasgow, G. (1996). The incidence of fetal alcohol syndrome in New Zealand. *New Zealand Medical Journal.* 109(1014), 18.

Glenn, E. N., Chang, G. and Forcey, L. R. (Eds). (1994). *Motherhood: Ideology, experience and agency.* New York: Routledge.

Goodacre, K. (1965). *Guide to the Middlesex Sessions Records 1549-1889: prepared for the Standin.* London (UK): Greater London Records Office, 1965, 785.

Goodwin, S. A. and Fiske, S. T. (2001). Power and Gender: The Double-Edged Sword of Ambivalence. In Unger, R. K. (Ed.) *Handbook of the Psychology of Women and Gender,* New York: John Wiley and Sons, Inc.

Gray, J. A. Muir. (2002). *The resourceful patient.* Oxford, UK: eRosetta Press.

Hall, J. M. and Stevens, P. E. (1991). Rigor in feminist research. *Advances in NursingScience* 13(3): 16-29.

Hanson, J.W., Streissguth, A.P. and Smith, D.W. (1978). The effects of moderate alcohol consumption during pregnancy on fetal growth and morphogenesis. *J.Pediatr,* 92,457-460.

Hawkesworth, M. E. (1989). Knowers, knowing, known: Feminist theory and claims of 'truth'. *Signs: Journal of Women in Culture and Society*, 14(3): 533-557.

Hearle, J. M. (1980). Conference on fetal alcohol syndrome. *Quality Review Bulletin.* 6(8), 24-29.

Helle, A. P. (1991). Reading women's autobiographies: A map of reconstructed knowing. *Stories lives tell: Narrative and dialogue in education.* Witherell, C. and Noddings, N. (Eds.). New York: Teacher's College Press.

Hoagland, J. A. (1988). *Lesbian ethics: Towards new value.* USA: Institute of Lesbian Studies.

Hoffman, J.D. and Shanske, A. (2003). Trends in fetal alcohol syndrome. *International Pediatrics,* 18(2), 114-118.

Hollway, W. and Jefferson, T. (2000). *Doing Qualitative Research Differently. Freeassociation narrative and the interview method.* London: Sage Publications.

Honey, A. (2000). Psychiatric vocational rehabilitation: Where are the customers' views? *Psychiatric Rehabilitation Journal.* 23, 270-279.

hooks, b. (1984). *Feminist theory from margin to center.* Boston: South End Press.

hooks, b. (1990). *Yearning: Race, gender and cultural politics.* Boston: South End Press.

Hoyme, H.E., May, P.A., Kalberg, W.O., Kodituwakku, P., Gossage, P., Trujillo, P.M., Buckley, D.G., Miller, J.H., Aragon, A.S., Khaole, N., Viljoen, D.L., Jones, K.L. and Robinson, L.K. (2005). A practical clinical approach to diagnosis of fetal alcohol spectrum disorders: clarification of the 1996 Institute of Medicine criteria. *Pediatrics,* 115(1), 39-47.

Institute of Medicine (1996). *Fetal alcohol syndrome: diagnosing, epidemiology, prevention and treatment.* Washington, DC: National Academy Press.

Ireland, M.S. (1993). *Reconceiving motherhood: Separating motherhood from female identity*. New York: Guildford Press.

Jackson, R.J. (2002). *The Challenge of Fetal Alcohol Syndrome: overcoming secondary disabilities.* Eds. Streissguth, A. and Kanter, J. Seattle: University of Washington Press.

Jacobson, J.L. and Jacobson, S.W. (1994). Prenatal alcohol exposure and neurobehavioural development: where is the threshold? *Alcohol Health and Research World,* 18(1), 30-36.

Johnson, B. and Christensen, L. (2004). *Educational Research. Quantitative, Qualitative and Mixed Approaches (2nd Edn).* Boston: Pearson Education, Inc.

Jones, K.L. and Smith, D.W. (1973). Recognition of the fetal alcohol syndrome in early infancy. *Lancet,* 2, 999-1001.

Jones, K. L. (1986). Fetal alcohol syndrome. *Pediatrics in Review.* 8(4), 122-126.

Judges (1952). *The Holy Bible.* London: Collins.

Kaminski, M., Rumeau, C., Schwartz, D. (1978). Alcohol consumption in pregnant women and the outcome of pregnancy*Alcoholism: Clinical and Experimental Research,* 2(2), 155-163.

Kernes, K.A., Don, A., Mateer, C.A. and Streissguth, A.P. (1997). Cognitive deficits in nonretarded adults with fetal alcohol syndrome. *Journal of Learning Disabilities,* 30(6), 685-693.

Kinach, B. M. (1995). Grounded Theory as scientific method: Haig-inspired reflections on educational methodology. *Philosophy of Education Society 1996-2001.* Vanderbilt University.

King, N. (1994). The qualitative research interview. *Qualitative method in organizational research.* Cassell, C. and Symon, G. (Eds.). USA: Sage Publications, Inc.

Koren, G., Nulman, I., Chudley, A.E. et al (2003). Fetal alcohol spectrum disorder. *CMAJ,* 169(11), 1181-1185.

Krefting, L. and Krefting, D. (1991). Leisure activities after a stroke: An ethnographic approach. *American Journal of Occupational Therapy.* 45, 214-222.

LaDue, R.A., Streissguth, A.P., Randels, S.P. (1992). *Clinical considerations pertaining to adolescents and adults with fetal alcohol syndrome.* In T.B. Sonderegger (Ed.).Perinatal substance abuse: research findings and clinical implications. Baltimore: The Johns Hopkins University Press, 104-131.

LaFrance, M. (2001). Gender and Social Interaction. In Unger, R. K. (Ed.) *Handbook of the Psychology of Women and Gender.* New York: John Wiley and Sons, Inc.

Landsman, G. (2005). Mothers and Models of Disability. *Journal of Medical Humanities*, 26, Nos. 2/3, 121-139.

Lather, P. (1986a). Research as praxis. Harvard Educational Review. 56(3): 257-277.

Lather, P. (1986b). Issues of validity in openly ideological research: Between a rock anda soft place. *Interchange.* 17(4): 63-84.

Lemoine, P., Harrousseau, H., Borteyru, J.P. and Menuet, J.C. (1968). Les enfants de arents alcholiques. Anomalies observeas. A propos de 127 cas. *Quest Medical*, 21, 476-482.

Lemoine, P. (1997). The history of alcoholic fetopathies. *J FAS Int* 2003; 1:e2.

Leslie, M. and Roberts, G. (2001). *Enhancing Fetal Alcohol Syndrome (FAS)-relatedIntervention at the Prenatal and Early Childhood Stages in Canada.* Canadian Centre on Substance Abuse: Ottawa.

Leslie, M. and Roberts, G. (2004). *Nurturing change. Working effectively with high-risk women and affected children to prevent and reduce harms associated with FASD.*

Canadian Centre on Substance Abuse, Ottawa, ON. www.ccsa.ca/fas and www.mothercraft.org

Leversha, A. M. and Marks, R. E. (1995a). Alcohol and pregnancy: Doctors attitudes, knowledge and clinical practice. *The New Zealand Medical Journal*, 108: 428-30.

Leversha, A. M. and Marks, R. E. (1995b). The prevalence of fetal alcohol syndrome in New Zealand. *New Zealand Medical Journal*. 108(1013), 502-505.

Lewis, R.C., Strauss, A.A. and Lehtinen, L.E. (1960). *The Other Child: The BrainInjured Child, a Book for Parents and Laymen.* New York: Grune and Stratton, 81.

Lincoln, Y. S. and Guba, E. G. (1985). *Naturalistic inquiry*. California: Sage Publications Inc.

Little, B.B., Snell, L.M., Rosenfeld, C.R., Gilstrap, L.C.III, Gant, N.F. (1990). Failure to recognize fetal alcohol syndrome in newborn infants. *Am J Dis Child.* 144, 1142-1146.

Loock, C., Conry, J., Cook, J.L. et al (2005). Identifying fetal alcohol spectrum disorder in primary care. *CMAJ*, 172(5).

Lupton, C., Burd, L., Harwood, R. (2004). Cost of fetal alcohol spectrum disorders.*American Journal of Medical Genetics Part C: Seminars in Medical Genetics,* 127C(1), 42-50.

Madriz, E. (2003). Focus Groups in Feminist Research. In N. K. Denzin and Y. S. Lincoln (Eds.) (2nd Edn.), *Collecting and Interpreting Qualitative Materials* (p.364). London: Sage Publications.

Maier, S.E. and West, J.R. (2001). Drinking patterns and alcohol-related birth defects. A*Alcohol Research and Health,* 25.

Marks, R. (1996). Fetal alcohol syndrome: A New Zealand perspective. *New Ethicals,* 9-13.

Marshall, H. (1991). The social construction of motherhood: An analysis of childcare and parenting manuals. In Phoenix, A., Woollett, A. and Lloyd, E. (Eds.), *Motherhood: Meanings, practices and ideologies* (pp.66-85).

Mathew, S., Kitson, K. and Watson, P. (2001). Assessment of risk of foetal alcohol syndrome and other alcohol related effects in New Zealand: A survey of midwives in New Zealand. Institute of Food Nutrition and Human Health, Massey University, Palmerston North, NZ.

Mattson, S., Riley, E., Gramling, L. et al. (1997). Heavy prenatal alcohol exposure with or without physical features of fetal alcohol syndrome leads to IQ deficits. *Journal of Pediatrics,* 131, 718-721.

May, P.A., Hymbaugh, K.J., Aase, J.M., and Samet, J.M. (1983). Epidemiology of fetal alcohol syndrome among American Indians of the Southwest. *Sociol Biology,* 30,374-387.

McCreight, B. (1997). *Recognizing and managing children with fetal alcohol syndrome/fetal alcohol effects: A guidebook.* Washington DC: CWLA Press.

McLeod, D., Pullon, S., Cookson, T. and Cornford, E. (2002). Factors influencing alcohol consumption during pregnancy and after giving birth. *The New Zealand Medical Journal,* 115(1157).

Melia, K. M. (1997). *Producing 'Plausible Stories': Interviewing Student Nurses.*In Context and Method in Qualitative Research, Miller, G. and Dingwall, R. (Eds.).London: Sage Publications.

Mies, M. (1993). Towards a methodology for feminist research. *Social research: Philosophy, politics and practice*. Hammerseley, M. (Ed.). London: Sage Publications Inc.

Miller, W. L. and Crabtree, B. F. (1992). Primary care research: A miltimethod typology and qualitative road map. *Doing qualitative research.* Miller, W. L. and Crabtree, B. F. (Eds.). USA: Sage Publications, Inc.

Miller, G. and Dingwall, R. (Eds.) (1997). *Context and Method in Qualitative Research.* London: Sage Publications.

Ministry of Health (2001). Minimising alcohol and other drug related harm. *NZ Government.*

Ministry of Health (2006). Food and nutrition guidelines for healthy, pregnant and breastfeeding women: A background paper. *NZ Government.*

Ministry of Health (2007a). Alcohol use in New Zealand: Analysis of the 2004 New Zealand Health Behaviour Survey – Alcohol Use 2007. *NZ Government.*

Ministry of Health (2007b). National drug policy 2007-2012. *NZ Government.*

Moore, M., Beazley, S. and Maelzer, J. (1998). *Researching Disability Issues.* Buckingham, UK: Open University Press.

Morell, C. M. (1994). *Unwomanly conduct: The challenges of intentional childlessness.* New York: Routledge.

Morse, B. A., Idelson, R. K., Sachs, W. H., Weiner, L. and Kaplan, L. C. (1992).Pediatricians' perspectives on fetal alcohol syndrome. *Journal of Substance Abuse.* 4, 187-195.

Morse, J. M. and Field, P. A. (1996). *Nursing research: The application of qualittiveapproaches.* 2nd Edn. London: Chapman and Hall.

Munn, P. (1991). Mothering more than one child. In Phoenix, A., Woollett, A. and Lloyd, E. (Eds), *Motherhood: Meanings, practices and ideologies.* London: Sage.

Murphy, S. A. (1990). Human responses to transitions: A holistic nursing perspective. *Holistic Nursing Practice,* 4, 1-7.

Murphy-Brennan, M.G. and Oei, T.P.S. (2001). Is there evidence to show that fetal alcohol syndrome can be prevented? *Journal of Drug Education,* 29(1), 5-24.

Murray, P. and Penman, J. (1996). *Let our children be.* Sheffield, UK: Parents with Attitude.

National Center on Birth Defects and Developmental Disablities, Centers for Disease Control and Prevention, Department of Health and Human Services (2004). *Fetal alcohol syndrome: guidelines for referral and diagnosis.* Department of Health and Human Services.

Nevin, A. C., Parshuram, C., Nulman, I., Koren, G. and Einarson, A. (2002). A survey of physicians knowledge regarding awareness of maternal alcohol use and the diagnosis of FAS. *BioMed Central Family Practice,* 3: 2.

New Zealand Paediatric Surveillance Unit (2002). Establishment and first year of operation. *NZ Public Health Report,* 6(6).

New Zealand Paediatric Surveillance Unit (2004). http://webnz.co.nz:8001/paediatrics/nzpsu /FAS%20protocol.htm

Niccols, G.A. (1994). Fetal alcohol syndrome: Implications for psychologists. *Clinical Psychology Review.* 14(2), 91-111.

Noddings, N. (1990). Stories in dialogue: Caring and interpersonal reasoning. *Stories lives tell: Narrative and dialogue in education.* Witherell, C. and Noddings, N. (Eds). New York: Teachers College Press.

Oakley, A. (1981). Interviewing women, a contradiction in terms? In Roberts, H. (Ed.), *Doing Feminist Research* (pp.30-61). London: Routledge and Kegan Paul.

Oakley, A. (1990). *A case of maternity: Paradigms of women as maternity cases. Ties that bind: Essays on mothering and patriarchy.* O'Barr, J. F., Pope, D. and Wymer, M. (Eds.). Chicago: University of Chicago Press.

O'Barr, J. F., Pope, D. and Wymer, M. (1990). *Introduction. Ties that bind: Essays on mothering and patriarchy.* O'Barr, J. F., Pope, D. and Wymer, M. (Eds). Chicago:University of Chicago Press.

Obermann, Y. and Josselson, R. (1996). Matrix of tensions: A model of mothering. *Psychology of Women Quarterly*, 20, 341-359.

O'Leary, C.M. (2004). Fetal alcohol syndrome: diagnosis, epidemiology and developmental outcomes. *J Paediatr Child Health,* 40(1-2), 2-7.

Oliver, M. (1990). *The Politics of Disablement.* Basingstoke, UK: Macmillan.

Oliver, M. (1992). Changing the social relations of research production? *Disability,Handicap and Society*, 7(2), 101-114.

O'Malley, K.D. and Nanson, J. (2002). Clinical implications of a link between fetal alcohol spectrum disorder and attention-deficit hyperactivity disorder. *CanJPsychiatry,* 47(4), 349-353.

Omery, A. (1983). "Phenomenology: A method for nursing research." *Advances in Nursing Science*, 5(2): 49-63.

Ong-Dean, C. (2005). Reconsidering the Social Location of the Medical Model: An Examination of Disability in Parenting Literature. *Journal of Medical Humanities,* 26, Nos. 2/3, 141-158.

Opie, A. (1989). Qualitative methodology, deconstructive readings, appropriation of the 'other' and empowerment. Paper presented at Sociology Association of Aotearoa (New Zealand) Conference, Wellington.

Overholser, J. C. (1990). Fetal alcohol syndrome: A review of the disorder. *Journal of Contemporary Psychotherapy*. 20(3), 163-176.

Pandit, N. R. (1996). The creation of theory: A recent application of the grounded theory method. *The Qualitative Report,* 2(4). *http://www.nova.edu/ssss/QR/QR2/pandit.html*

Parackal, S., Parackal, M., Fergusson, E. and Harraway, J. (2006). *Report on awareness of the effects of alcohol use during pregnancy among New Zealand women of childbearing age.* University of Otago, Dunedin, NZ.

Paton, A. (1997). Women and Alcohol: Contemporary and Historical perspectives.*British Medical Journal.* 314(7101): 197.

Patton, M. Q. (1987). *How to Use Qualitative Methods in Evaluation.* California: Sage Pubs.

Patton, M. Q. (1990). *Qualitative Evaluation and Research Methods (Second Edition)*.California: Sage Pubs.

Personal Narratives Group (1989) (Eds). *Interpreting women's lives: Feminist theory and personal narratives.* USA: Indiana University Press.

Phoenix, A. (1991a). Mothers under twenty: Outsider and insider views. In Phoenix, A., Wollett, A. and Lloyd, E. (Eds.), *Motherhood: Meanings, practices and ideologies* (pp.86-102). London: Sage.

Phoenix, A. (1991b). *Young mothers?* Cambridge, England: Polity.

Pierce, D.R., West, J.R. (1986). Blood alcohol concentration: a critical factor for producing fetal alcohol effects. *Alcohol.* 3: 269-272.

Plant, M. (1985). *Women, Drinking and Pregnancy.* Tavistock Publications Ltd., London.

Polkinghorne, D. E. (1991). Narrative and Self-Concept'. *Journal of Narrative and Life History.* 1(2and3): 135-153.

Poole, N. (2000). *Evaluation report to the Sheway project for high-risk pregnant and parenting women.* Vancouver, BC: British Columbia Centre of Excellence for Women's Health.

Pritchard, M. (2005). Can there be such a thing as a 'wrongful birth'? *Disability and Society,* 20(1), 81-93.

Public Health Agency of Canada (2005). *Summary report national thematic workshop on FASD.*

Rapp, R. (1994). The power of 'positive' diagnosis: Medical and maternal discourses on amniocentesis. *Representations of motherhood.* Bassin, D., Honey, M. and Kaplan, M. M. (Eds). New Haven: Yale University Press.

Read, J. (2003). *Disability, the Family and Society: Listening to mothers.* Berkshire: UK: Open University Press.

Reid, P.M. and Bray, A. (1997). Paid work and intellectual disability. *Journal of Intellectual and Developmental Disability,* 22(2), 87-96.

Reger, R. (1972). The medical model in special education. *Psychology in the Schools.* 9, 8-12.

Reibel, T. (2004). The language of birth: How words colour women's experiences. *Birth Issues* 13(1)

Reinharz, S. (1992). *Feminist Methods in Social Research.* New York: Oxford University Press.

Ribbens, J. (1994). *Mothers and their children: A feminist sociology of child rearing.* London: Sage.

Riessman, C. K. (1993). *Narrative Analysis: Qualitative Research Methods, Vol. 30, Parts I* and *II.* London: Sage Publications.

Rioux, M. H. (1994). New research directions and paradigms: Disability is not measles. In M. H. Rioux and M. Bach (Eds.), *Disability is not Measles: New Research Paradigms in Disability* (pp.1-7). L'Institut Roeher Institute.

Roberts, G. and Nanson, J. (2000). *Best practices. Fetal alcohol syndrome/fetal alcohol effects and the effects of other substance use during pregnancy.* Health Canada.

Rose, L. E. (1998). Gaining control: Family members relate to persons with severe mental illness. *Research in Nursing and Health,* 21, 363-373.

Rosenwald, G. C. and Ochberg, R. L. (1992). Introduction: Life stories, cultural politics and self-understanding. In G.C. Rosenwald and R. L. Ochberg (Eds.), *Storied lives: The cultural politics of self-understanding.* New Haven, CT: Yale University Press.

Rosser, S. (1992). Are there feminist methodologies appropriate for the natural sciences and do they make a difference? *Women's Studies International Forum,* 15(5/6): 535-550.

Roth, S. (1993). Speaking the unspoken: A work-group consultation to reopen dialogue. In E. Imber-Black (Ed.), *Secrets in families and family therapy.* New York: Norton.

Royal College of Obstetricians and Gynaecologists (2001). Alcohol consumption in pregnancy. http://www.rcog.org.uk

Ryan, K. and Denz-Penhey, H. (1996). Qualitative research in medical practice. *New Zealand Medical Journal,* 109(1018), 87-88.

Salmon, J. V. (2004). Mothers to be: do not let one drop pass your lips. *Otago Daily Times.* September 20: Allied Press Co., Dunedin, New Zealand.

Salmon, J.V. (2006). Fetal Alcohol Syndrome: New Zealand Birth Mothers' Experiences. *NZ Addiction Treatment Research Monograph.* Research Proceedings from the Cutting Edge Conference, Sept., Wellington, NZ.

Salmon, J.V. (2007). *New Zealand Birth Mothers' Experiences.* Wellington, NZ: Dunmore Pubs.

Salmon, J.V. (2008). Fetal Alcohol Syndrome: New Zealand Birth Mothers' Experiences. *Can J Clin Pharm,* 15(2): e191-213.

Sampson, P., Streissguth, A., Bookstein, F. et al (1997). Incidence of fetal alcohol syndrome and prevalence of alcohol-related neurodevelopmental disorder. *Teratology,* 56, 317-326.

Sandelowski, M. (1991). Telling stories: Narrative approaches in qualitative research. *Image: Journal of Nursing Scholarship.* 23(3), pp.161-166.

Sandelowski, M. (1993). *With child in mind: Studies of the personal encounter with infertility.* Philadelphia: University of Pennsylvania Press.

Sandelowski, M. (1995). Focus on Qualitative Methods: Sample size in qualitative research. *Research in Nursing and Health,* 18: 179-183.

Shakespeare, T. (1998). Choice and Rights: Eugenics, Genetics and Disability Equality. *Disability and Society,* 13(5): 670.

Shelton, M. and Cook, M. (1993). Fetal alcohol syndrome: Facts and prevention. *Preventing School Failure.* 37(3), 44-46.

Sherwin, S. (1992). *No longer patient: Feminist ethics and health care.* Philadelphia: Temple University Press.

Sherwin, S. (1998). A relational approach to autonomy in health care. *The politics of women's health: Exploring agency and autonomy.* Sherwin, S. (Ed). Philadelphia: Temple University Press.

Shilling, C. (1993). *The Body and Social Theory.* London: Sage Publications.

Shilts, D. (1999). *Love is a Start: The Real Challenges of Raising Children with Emotional Disorders.* Portland: LookAgain Publishing.

Short, R. H. and Hess, G. C. (1995). Fetal alcohol syndrome: Characteristics and remedial implications. *Developmental Disabilities Bulletin.* 23(1), 12-29.

Shorter, E. (1991). *Women's bodies: A social history of women's encounter with health, ill-health and medicine.* New Brunswick: Transaction Publishers.

Silva, E. B. (1996). *Good enough mothering? Feminist perspectives on lone motherhood.* London: Routledge.

Silvers, R. J. (1982). A silence within phenomenology. *Interpretive human studies: An introduction to phenomenological research.* Darroch, V. and Silvers, R. J. (Eds.), Washington DC: University Press of America.

Silverstein, L. B. and Phares, V. (1996). Expanding the mother-child paradigm: An examination of dissertation research 1986-1994. *Psychology of Women Quarterly,* 20, 39-54.

Smith, B. and Noble-Spruell, C. (1986). An overview of feminist research perspectives. *Gender reclaimed! Women in social work.* Marchant, H. and Wearing, B. (Eds.). NSW: Hale and Iremonger.

Smith, D. (1987). *The everyday world as problematic: A feminist sociology.*Toronto: University of Toronto Press.

Smith, S. (1993). Who's talking/who's talking back? The subject of personal narrative. *Signs: Journal of Women in Culture and Society.* 18(21): 392-407.

Smythe, L. (2000). Making sense of qualitative research. *Kai Tiaki NZ*, 8(5): 16-18.

Sood, B., Delany-Black, V., Covington C., Nordstrom-Klee, B., Ager, J., Templin, T. et al (2001). Prenatal alcohol exposure and childhood behaviour at age 6 to 7 years: 1 dose-response effect. *Pediatrics,* 108(2):e34.

Spender, D. (1985) (2nd Edn.). *Man Made language.* London: Pandora Press.

Stainbach, S. and Stainbach, W. (1984). Broadening the research perspective in special education. *Exceptional Children*, 50(5), 400-409.

Stanley, L. and Wise, S. (1983). *Breaking Out: Feminist Consciousness and FeministResearch.* London: Routledge and Kegan Paul.

Stratton, K., Howe, C. and Battaglia, F. (Eds.) (1996). *Fetal alcohol syndrome. Diagnosis, epidemiology, prevention and treatment.* Institute of Medicine. Washington: National Academy Press.

Strauss, A. and Corbin, J. (1990). *Basics of Qualitative Research: Grounded Theory Procedures and Techniques.* Newbury Park, California: Sage Publications Inc.

Strauss, A. and Corbin, J. (1994). Grounded theory methodology: An overview. In Denzin, N. K. and Lincoln, Y. S. (Eds.), *Handbook of qualitative research* (pp.273-285). Newbury Park, CA: Sage Publications Ltd.

Strauss, A. and Corbin, J. (1997). *Grounded theory in practice*. Thousand Oaks, CA: Sage Publications Ltd.

Strauss, A. and Corbin, J. (1998) (2nd Edn.). *Basics of Qualitative Research: Techniques and Procedures for Developing Grounded Theory.* London: Sage Publications.

Streissguth, A.P., Bookstein, F.L., Sampson, P.C. and Barr, H.M. (1993). *The enduring effects of prenatal alcohol exposure on child development: Birth through seven years, a partial least squares solution.* Ann Arbor, MI: University of Michigan Press.

Streissguth, A.P. (1997). *Fetal alcohol syndrome: a guide for families and communities.* Baltimore: Paul H. Brookes Publishing Co.

Streissguth, A.P., Barr, H., Kogan, J. et al (1997). Primary and secondary disabilities in fetal alcohol syndrome. In Streissguth, A.P., Kanter, J. (Eds.). The challenge of fetal alcohol syndrome: overcoming secondary disabilities. Seattle: University of Washington Press, 14-39.

Streissguth, A. P. (1998). A Fetal Alcohol Behavior Scale. *Alcoholism: Clinical andExperimental Research,* 22(2): 325-333.

Streissguth, A.P. (2001). Recent advances in fetal alcohol syndrome and alcohol use in pregnancy. In Agarwal, D.P. and Seitz, H.K. (Eds.), *Alcohol in health and disease.* NY: Marcel Dekker, Inc.

Strong, P. M. (1979). *The Ceremonial Order of the Clinic*. London: Routledge.

Suchman, A. L. and Matthews, D. A. (1988) What makes the patient-doctor relationship therapeutic? Exploring the connexional dimension of medical care. *Annals of Int. Medicine*. 108: 125-130.

Sullivan, M. (1991). From personal tragedy to social oppression: The medical model and social theories of disability. *New Zealand Journal of Industrial Relations*. 16, 845-850.

Symes, M. (2004). The legacy of prenatal exposure to alcohol: fetal alcohol spectrum disorder: The New Zealand situation. Doctoral thesis, medical anthropology, *Massey University, Albany, NZ.*

Tait, C.L. (2000). A study of the service needs of pregnant addicted women in Manitoba. Winnipeg: Manitoba Health.

Tait, C.L. (2003). Fetal alcohol syndrome among Aboriginal people in Canada: review and analysis of the Intergenerational links to residential schools. Ottawa, Ontario: Aboriginal Healing Foundation.

The New Zealand Paediatric Surveillance Unit (2002). *New Zealand Public Health Report,* 6(6).

Thomas, C. (1999). *Female forms: experiencing and understanding disability.* Buckingham, UK: Open University Press.

Thomas, C. (1999). *Female Forms: Experiencing and understanding disability.* Buckingham, UK: Open University Press.

Todd, A. D. (1989). *Intimate adversaries: cultural conflict between doctors and womenpatients.* Philadelphia: University of Pennsylvania Press.

Traustadottir, R. (1993). Mothers who care: Gender, disability and family life in *Perspectives on Disability* (2nd Edn) (1993) by Nagler, M.: Palo Alta, CA: Health Markets Research.

Turnbull, A.P. and Turnbull, H.R. (1978). *Parents speak out: Views from the other side of the 2-way mirror.* Columbus, Ohio: Merrill Pub. Co.

van Manen, M. (1990). *Researching lived experience: Human science for an action pegagogy.* London, Ontario: State University of New York Press.

Vedder, J. (2005). Constructing Prevention: Fetal Alcohol Syndrome and the Problem of Disability Models. *Journal of Medical Humanities,* 26, Nos. 2/3, 107-120.

Waddington, D. (1994). Participant observation. *Qualitative method in organizational research.* Cassell, C and Symons, G. (Eds). USA: Sage Publications, Inc.

Warner, R.H. and Rosett, H.L. (1975). The effects of drinking on offspring. *Journal of Studies on Alcohol,* 36(11), 1395-1425.

Warren, K.R. and Bast, R.J. (1988). Alcohol-related birth defects: an update. *Public Health Reports,* 103(6), 638-642.

Watson, P. and McDonald, B. (1999). *Nutrition during pregnancy. Report to the Ministry of Health.* Massey University, Auckland, NZ.

Wattendorf, D.J. and Muenke, M. (2005). Fetal alcohol spectrum disorders. *American Family Physician,* 72, 279-285.

Wekselman, K., Spiering, K., Hetteberg, C., Kenner, C. and Flandermeyer, A. (1995). Fetal alcohol syndrome from infancy through childhood: A review of the literature. *Journal of Pediatric Nursing.* 10(5), 296-303.

Williams, S.J. (2006). Is there justice in the juvenile justice system? Examining the role of fetal alcohol spectrum disorders.*Justice Policy Journal,* 3(1).

Wilson, E. (1998). *Neural Geographies: Feminism and the Microstructure of Cognition.*New York: Routledge, 15.

Woollett, A. (1991). Having children: Accounts of childless women and women with reproductive problems. In Phoenix, A, Woollett, A and Lloyd, E. (Eds.), *Motherhood: Meanings, practices and ideologies* (pp.47-65). London: Sage.

Woollett, A. and Marshall, H. (1997). Accounts of pregnancy and childbirth. In Yardley, L. (Ed.), *Material discourses of health and illness* (pp.176-198). London: Routledge.

Woollett, A. and Marshall, H. (2001). Motherhood and mothering. In Unger, R.K. (Ed.), *Handbook of the psychology of women and gender* (pp.170-182). New York: John Wiley and Sons, Inc.

Woollett, A. and Phoenix, A. (1991). Psychological views of motherhood. In Phoenix, A., Woollett, A. and Lloyd, E. (Eds.), *Motherhood: Meanings, practices and ideologies* (pp.28-46). London: Sage.

Woollett, A. and Phoenix, A. (1996). Motherhood as pedagogy: Developmental psychology and the accounts of mothers of young children. In Luke, C. (Ed.), *Feminisms and pedagogies of everyday life* (pp.80-102). New York: State University of New York Press.

Wright, J. M. (1981). Fetal alcohol syndrome: The social work connection. *Health and Social Work*. 6(1), 5-10.

Young, S. L. and Ensing, D. S. (1999). Exploring recovery from tge perspective of people with psychiatric disabilities. *Psychiatric Rehabilitation Journal*. 22, 219-213.

Zakreski, D. (1998). Almost half of young offenders suffer from birth defect. *The Saskatoon Star Phoenix,* March 10.

In: Social Drinking: Uses, Abuses and Psychological Factors ISBN: 978-1-60876-219-4
Editors : K. T. Everly, E. M. Cosell, pp. 101-139 © 2010 Nova Science Publishers, Inc.

Chapter 2

THEORIES OF SOCIAL INFLUENCE ON ADOLESCENT AND YOUNG ADULT ALCOHOL USE

Melissa A. Lewis[1][1]***, Clayton Neighbors***[1]***, Kristen P. Lindgren***[2]***,***
Kaitlin G. Buckingham[1] ***and Melissa Hoang***[1]

1. Department of Psychiatry and Behavioral Sciences ,
University of Washington, WA, USA
2. Department of Psychology University of Richmond, VA, USA

ABSTRACT

An extensive literature has demonstrated that many adolescents and young adults engage in drinking behavior, resulting in acute and chronic negative consequences (e.g., unintentional injuries, arguments, unplanned and/or unprotected sexual activities, trouble with police/authorities, poor academic/work performance, suicide, and death), and alcohol dependence. Social influence is foremost among the causes attributed to the initiation and maintenance of alcohol use during this period. This chapter reviews a number of prominent theories of social influence that are directly relevant to drinking behavior among adolescents and young adults. For each theory, a brief description is provided, followed by relevant research related to adolescent and young adult drinking. Theoretical implications for preventative interventions are also discussed. Highlighted theories include: social learning theory, social cognitive theory, alcohol expectancy theory, problem behavior theory, social comparison theory, social identity theory, self-derogation theory, the theory of reasoned action, the theory of planned behavior, prototype willingness model, deviance regulation theory, peer cluster theory, and reactance theory.

INTRODUCTION

[1] Please send correspondence concerning this chapter to Melissa A. Lewis, Department of Psychiatry and Behavioral Sciences, Box 354944, University of Washington, Seattle, WA 98195. Phone: 206-221-6932 Fax: 206-616-1705 E-mail: lewisma@u.washington.edu.

Alcohol continues to be the most widely used substance by American youth. Results from the 2008 Monitoring the Future survey found that the proportions of 8th, 10th, and 12th graders who reported drinking an alcoholic beverage in the 30-day period prior to the survey were 16%, 29%, and 43%, respectively (Johnston, O'Malley, Bachman, and Schulenberg, 2009). Moreover, research has shown that adolescence is the most common time for the initiation of alcohol use, with 39% of 8th graders having initiated alcohol use and 58% of 10th graders having initiated alcohol use. By the time high school students graduate, over 70% will have initiated alcohol use (Johnston et al., 2009). Alcohol use among adolescents is a concern, because it is a contributor to the top causes of death for youth: unintentional injuries, homicides, and suicides (Heron, 2007). Moreover, preventing or delaying the initiation of alcohol use of adolescents is of importance as research has shown that earlier initiation is related to problems in brain development and neurocognitive disadvantages, such as reduced hippocampal volumes and poorer performance on memory and spatial tasks (Brown and Tapert, 2004; Squeglia, Jacobus, Tapert, 2009). Alcohol use in adolescence is also associated with an increased risk of developing alcohol dependence (Buchmann et al., in press; Grant et al., 2006; Grant and Dawson, 1997; Hingson, Heeren, Winter, 2006). For example, Buchmann and colleagues (in press) found that the age of first drink significantly predicted high-risk drinking in young adults (number of standard drinks, frequency of drinking occasions, frequency of heavy drinking occasions, and AUDIT scores). In addition, Grant and Dawson (1997) found that youth who initiated alcohol use prior to age 14, had a 41% chance of developing alcohol dependence during their lifetime compared to individuals who waited until the age of 21 to initiate alcohol use, whose chances were reduced to 10%.

Alcohol use and associated risks are also prevalent among young adults (Bingham, Shope, and Tang, 2005; Courtney and Polich, 2009; Hingson, Heeren, Winter, and Wechsler, 2005; Hingson, Heeren, Zakocs, Kopstein, and Wechsler, 2002; O'Malley and Johnston, 2002; Schulenberg and Maggs, 2002; Slutske, 2005; Substance Abuse and Mental Health Services Administration [SAMHSA], 2008; White et al., 2006). Furthermore, college students between the ages of 18 to 22 are more likely than their non-college peers to have used alcohol in the past month and to have engaged in heavy-episodic drinking. Although individuals who drink heavily in high school are less likely to attend college, alcohol use among college students increases more rapidly and eventually surpasses that of non-college peers (Bachman, Wadsworth, O'Malley, Johnston, and Schulenberg, 1997). For example, past month alcohol use was reported by 63.7% of college students in comparison to 53.5% of non-college individuals (SAMHSA, 2008). Moreover, 43.6% of college students report heavy-episodic drinking (defined as five or more drinks in a row during the previous two weeks) compared to 38.4% of their non-college peers (SAMHSA, 2008). Research continues to demonstrate that not only are young adults engaging in heavy drinking but also that they are experiencing considerable alcohol-related negative consequences including as poor class/work attendance, property damage, hangovers, trouble with authorities, injuries, unprotected sex, sexual assault, and death (Abbey, Zawacki, Buck, Clinton, and McAuslan, 2004; Hingson, Heeren, Winter, and Weschsler, 2005; Wechsler, Davenport, Dowdall Moeykens, and Castillo, 1994).

Because of the high prevalence rates of alcohol use and the number of negative consequences associated with alcohol use, drinking among adolescents and young adults presents an enormous public health concern. In 2007, the Acting Surgeon General of the United States issued a *Call to Action To Prevent and Reduce Underage Drinking* (U.S. Department of Health and Human Services, 2007). In addition, the National Institute on

Alcohol Abuse and Alcoholism has an underage drinking research initiative that aims to intensify research, evaluation, and outreach efforts regarding underage drinking. A key to preventing alcohol use and related negative consequences in adolescents and young adults is gaining a better understanding of why individuals initiate and continue to engage in those behaviors.

Overview of Chapter

Prior research has demonstrated that social influence is foremost among the causes attributed to the initiation and maintenance of alcohol use during adolescence and young adulthood (Baer, 2002; Baer, MacClean, and Marlatt, 1998; Borsari and Carey, 2001; Hawkins, Catalano, and Miller, 1992). Social influence factors include parents, family, peers, society and culture. This chapter reviews a number of prominent theories of social influence that are relevant to drinking behavior among adolescents and young adults. For each theory, a brief description is provided, followed by selected research related to adolescent and young adult drinking. Theoretical implications for preventative interventions are also discussed. Highlighted theories include: social learning theory, social cognitive theory, alcohol expectancy theory, problem behavior theory, social comparison theory, social identity theory, self-derogation theory, the theory of reasoned action, the theory of planned behavior, prototype/willingness model, deviance regulation theory, peer cluster theory, and reactance theory.

Social Learning Theory and Social Cognitive Theory

Social learning theory applies to several theories of human behavior proposed by various prominent psychologists. These principles of learning are integrated with cognitive psychology in order to explain how social and personal factors relate to the environment. One of the most influential contributors of social learning theory is Albert Bandura (Bandura, 1969, 1977, 1986). According to social learning theory (Bandura, 1969, 1977) and later extended to social cognitive theory (Bandura, 1986), people's acquisition and maintenance of behaviors, including but not limited to health and risk behaviors, are dependent upon the interrelationships among behavior, environmental factors, and personal factors (cognitive, affective, and biological events). Social learning/cognitive theory is comprised of four major constructs: differential reinforcement, vicarious learning, cognitive processes and reciprocal determinism. Each of these principles or constructs may be applied to enhance our understanding of alcohol use among adolescents and young adults.

Differential reinforcement occurs when consequences are applied for a behavior dependent on stimulus conditions or environmental setting. Differential reinforcement is used to help explain why people's behavior often changes in different environmental settings. Positive and negative reinforcement as well as punishment are often received from the environment or from the self depending on environmental setting. For example, if an adolescent drinks alcohol at a party with friends, he may experience feelings of relaxation, participate in and enjoy social exchanges with peers, and receive social approval. However, if an adolescent drinks alcohol at home with parents, he may still experience relaxation but will likely receive disapproval and possible consequences from his parents. Whether or not an adolescent or young adult will abstain or initiate alcohol use, or continue or stop alcohol use, is dependent on past, present and future anticipated rewards and punishments attached to abstinence and alcohol use. The more an adolescent or young adult perceives alcohol use as positive and the *less* he/she experiences negative consequences for alcohol use and holds attitudes that are disapproving of alcohol use, the more likely he/she is to engage in alcohol use.

Vicarious learning (modeling). Bandura also proposed that the acquisition of behavior can occur through observation of others or by communication with others. In other words, not only will direct reinforcement increase the likelihood of engaging in that behavior, but vicarious learning (e.g., seeing someone else reinforced), or modeling, of a behavior will also increase the likelihood of behavior. When applied to adolescent and young adult drinking behavior, one's drinking behavior can be affected by observing others' drinking behavior or attitudes, as well as by observing the outcomes of others' drinking behavior. Social learning/cognitive theory posits that adolescents and young adults acquire their behaviors and beliefs about alcohol from their role models, especially close friends and parents. Thus, drinking behaviors, alcohol-related expectancies and evaluations, drinking self-efficacy, and drinking refusal self-efficacy can all be acquired from the observation and modeling of role models who use and who do not use alcohol.

Experimental research has demonstrated that modeling can be predictive of alcohol consumption among adolescents and young adults. In a meta-analytic review of the literature, Quigley and Collins (1999) found that modeling had a significant effect on alcohol consumption, blood alcohol concentration, and volume per sip, such that participants increased their alcohol consumption when exposed to a heavy-drinking model in comparison to a no-model control condition and a light-drinking model. More recently, Larsen and colleagues (2009) examined the role of modeling in relation to alcohol consumption among college students in the Netherlands. Students were exposed to either a control, light-drinking, or heavy-drinking same-sex model. Unlike previous research in which participants were obligated to consume alcohol (Quigley and Collins, 1999), a design was used such that students were allowed to drink alcohol but were also allowed to choose non-alcohol beverages. Findings indicated that participants consumed significantly greater amounts of alcohol when exposed to heavy-drinking models in comparison to non-drinking and light-drinking models. Additionally, Engels and colleagues (2009) examined whether portrayal of alcohol images in movies and commercials on television promotes alcohol consumption. Male students in the Netherlands were assigned to watch a movie clip with two commercial breaks and were allowed to drink non-alcohol or alcoholic beverages. Participants were randomly assigned to one of four conditions that varied by movie (few vs. many alcohol portrayals) and commercials (alcohol not present vs. alcohol present). Participants in the many alcohol portrayals and alcohol present commercials consumed an average of 1.5 more glasses of alcohol than those in the control condition with no alcohol portrayals. Together, these experimental studies provide evidence of a causal relationship between modeling and alcohol consumption.

When examining the influence of role models, non-experimental research supports that adolescents and young adults may learn to use substances by modeling drinking behavior of parents, siblings, and peers (Andrews, Hops, and Duncan, 1997; Borsari and Carey, 2001;

Casswell, Pledger, and Pratap, 2002; Duncan, Duncan, and Strycker, 2006; Latendresse et al., 2008). For example, a longitudinal study conducted by Casswell and colleagues (2002) found that parental drinking at the age of nine was found to predict offspring drinking trajectories. Additionally, a longitudinal study of young adults demonstrated that peer use of alcohol predicted binge drinking and problem use by young adults, providing evidence for a causal role of peer influence on drinking behaviors (Andrews, Tildesley, Hops, and Li, 2002).

According to social learning/cognitive theory, cognitive processes are posited to mediate environmental events and behavior. These processes include encoding, organizing, and retrieving information, all of which are postulated ultimately to regulate behavior. Thus from this viewpoint, the environment provides an individual with information that is then cognitively processed, and that, in turn, determines an individual's behavioral response. Once an individual has acquired a behavior, self-regulation and self-efficacy plays a role in future engagement of that behavior. Self-regulation is the capability of arranging environment incentives and producing consequences for one's behavior. Self-efficacy is an individual's beliefs regarding the likelihood that he or she can engage in a behavior in order to produce a desired outcome.

In relation to drinking behavior, self-efficacy is often defined as confidence in one's abilities to drink or to not drink in a given situation, or across situations. According to social learning/cognitive theory, role models can shape both drinking self-efficacy and drinking refusal self-efficacy. For example, observing a peer refusing to use alcohol can enhance one's drinking refusal self-efficacy: the peer models the skills necessary to avoid using alcohol. Drinking refusal self-efficacy has been found to relate to alcohol consumption when examined in adolescent and young adult samples. For example, Epstein, Zhou, Bang, and Botvin (2007) found that adolescents who had greater decision-making skills, drinking refusal skill techniques, and skills related to resisting media influences were less likely to engage in future drinking. Young and colleagues (2006, 2007) found that drinking refusal self-efficacy specific to social pressure (e.g., when someone offers you a drink), emotional relief (e.g., when you are feeling upset), and opportunistic drinking (e.g., when you are by yourself) were negatively associated with alcohol consumption in adolescents and college students.

Reciprocal determinism. Bandura (1969) used the term "reciprocal determinism" to describe the interactive relationships among behavior, environmental factors, and personal factors. Briefly, reciprocal determinism suggests that change in one factor is shaped by the other two factors and vice versa. For example, change in drinking behavior is shaped by environmental and personal factora and vice versa. One's drinking behavior can also affect one's environment and peer groups, such that those who drink may select social environments in which drinking occurs or have close friends who also drink. These social environments and peers will then affect subsequent drinking behavior.

Many studies have supported the concept of reciprocal determinism among samples of adolescents and young adults. Curran, Stice, and Chassin (1997) examined reciprocal determinism in peer influences and alcohol use in an adolescent sample. Findings supported both peer socialization and peer selection: early levels of peer alcohol use were associated with later adolescent alcohol use and earlier adolescent alcohol use was associated with later levels of peer alcohol use. Research has also evaluated reciprocal determinism in personal factors, such as alcohol expectancies (see Alcohol Expectancy Theory), and alcohol use among adolescents (Mitchell, Beals, and Kaufman, 2006; Sher, Wood, Wood, and Raskin, 1996; Smith, Goldman, Greenbaum, and Christiansen, 1995). For example, Mitchell and colleagues (2006) found that in a sample of Native American adolescents and young adults, alcohol use and outcome expectancies were interrelated, providing support for reciprocal determinism between this two constructs.

Read, Wood, and Capone (2005) examined reciprocal determinism in social influence, alcohol use and related negative consequences among young adults transitioning to college. Findings indicated a reciprocal relationship between active and passive social influence and alcohol use. Specifically, pre-matriculation alcohol use offers and social modeling predicted sophomore year alcohol use, and pre-matriculation alcohol use predicted sophomore year alcohol use offers and social modeling. However, when examining alcohol-related negative consequences, environmental selection was supported rather than reciprocal determinism. Specifically, alcohol-related negative consequences at pre-matriculation predicted alcohol use offers and social modeling during sophomore year, but only social modeling at pre-matriculation was marginally associated with alcohol-related negative consequences during sophomore year. Thus, this study provided support for reciprocal determinism for alcohol use, but not alcohol-related negative consequences. Additional research is needed to further evaluate reciprocal determinism in consequences associated with drinking among adolescents and young adults.

Summary and implications. Social learning/cognitive theory suggests that the acquisition and maintenance of health and risk behaviors results from the interrelationships among behavior, environmental factors, and personal factors. Primary constructs of this theory have received support from alcohol literature pertaining to adolescents and young adults, which suggests that interventions that address the impact of social influence on drinking by including drinking refusal skills training and drinking moderation strategies may be beneficial (Larimer et al., 2007; Schinke, Cole, and Fang, 2009). For example, recent research found that drinking moderation strategies mediated the efficacy of a mailed alcohol feedback intervention (Larimer et al., 2007) in a sample of college students. Participants who received the intervention were more likely to use protective behavior strategies (such as limiting the number of alcoholic drinks consumed or using a designated driver) more frequently and the use of protective behavior strategies was associated with subsequent reductions in alcohol use. In addition, social learning/cognitive theory suggests that prevention efforts should try to make role models who approve of or use alcohol less salient and role models who disapprove of or do not use alcohol more salient.

Alcohol Expectancy Theory

Alcohol expectancy theory originates from basic psychological theories and was extended to the domain of alcohol. More technically known as alcohol expectancy *outcome* theory (see Goldman, Del Boca, and Darkes, 1999; Jones, Corbin, and Fromme, 2001), the theory is derived from general expectancy outcome theory, which incorporates both basic principles of learning as well as cognitive constructs (e.g., Bandura, 1977; MacCorquodale and Meehl, 1953; Rotter, 1954; Tolman, 1932). Briefly, expectancy outcome theories propose that behavior is governed not only by reinforcement and punishment (basic learning theory) but also by one's expectations of the future (positive or negative) reinforcement outcomes associated with engaging in that behavior. It is argued that the reinforcement outcomes associated with a behavior can be learned and are stored in memory and that one's expectations of those outcomes influence future behavior. Consistent with social learning models (e.g., Bandura, 1969, 1977, 1986), these expectancies can be learned through direct and indirect experience. There is ongoing debate regarding the extent to which these expectancies are consciously versus non-consciously held and/or whether their influence on behavior is "automatic" or "spontaneous," but theory proponents appear to agree that expectancies have, at a minimum, a significant automatic or non-conscious component (see Goldman et al., 1999; Thush and Wiers, 2007).

Regarding applications of expectancy outcome theories to alcohol, specifically; the behavior (alcohol consumption) is predicted to occur as a function of one's expectations of reinforcement outcomes. Alcohol outcome expectancies (AOE) are predicted to *vary across* persons as a function of their learning histories – i.e., to the extent that individuals have similar/different drinking experiences, they will have similar/different AOEs. They are also predicted to vary *within persons* as a function of their learning histories --i.e., to the extent that a person has different experiences with or makes changes to their drinking over time, that person's AOEs will change. Finally, although at first glance, AOE theory may seem an unlikely representative of social influence theories *per se*, it is important to note that some of the effects of alcohol are psychological (versus pharmacological) and that AOEs appear to be learned from peers, parents, mass media as well as from direct experience with alcohol (see Abrams and Niaura, 1987; MacAndrew and Edgerton, 1969; Maisto, Carey, and Bradizza, 1999). Accordingly, it can be stated that AOEs are, at least partially, a product of and/or subject to social influence.

Consistent with theories of AOE, people can develop AOEs well before they begin to drink. For example, AOEs have been measured in children as young as eight years of age, and research suggests that there are critical periods – in particular, late childhood and early adolescence – for the development of AOEs (Dunn and Goldman, 1998; Miller, Smith, and Goldman, 1990). It also appears that as children's AOEs shift as they age and mature into drinking– e.g., ., they seem to change from having largely negative AOEs to more positive AOEs (Miller et al., 1990; Schell, Martino, Ellickson, Collins, and McCaffrey, 2005). As suggested by AOE theories, children's and adolescents' AOEs (a) are correlated with alcohol use, exposure to alcohol advertisements, and peer and parental use and approval of use (see Martino, Collins, Ellickson, Schell, and McCaffrey, 2006); and (b) predict incremental variance in drinking behavior, particularly with respect to the quantity (vs. frequency) of drinking (see Jones et al., 2001). Moreover, adolescents' pre-drinking AOEs have been found to predict changes in drinking in prospective studies (Goldman et al., 1999; Jones et al., 2001). Finally, advanced statistical methods enable the testing of models that specify reciprocal prospective relations between adolescents' AOEs and their drinking behaviors. Consistent with AOE theory, there is evidence of a reciprocal relationship between alcohol use and AOE, providing support for the claim that changes in expectancies predict changes in drinking and vice-versa (e.g., Mitchell et al., 2006; Sher et al., 1996; Smith et al., 1995).

Research on young adults, which largely focuses on college students, also indicates that AOEs are associated with alcohol consumption, including problematic drinking (see Baer, 2002; Ham and Hope, 2003; Jones et al., 2001). It appears that positive AOEs are most commonly and consistently linked to alcohol consumption (Baer, 2002; Ham and Hope, 2003; but see also Jones et al., 2001), and that AOEs predict future drinking behavior over time (Blume, Schmaling, and Marlatt, 2003; Carey, 1995; Kidorf et al., 1995, cf. Ham and Hope, 2003). Other studies have found that negative AOEs also are positively correlated with college students' alcohol consumption and that they predict incremental variance in drinking above and beyond positive AOEs (e.g., Jones et al., 2001, Valdiva and Stewart, 2005). Related to these findings is a debate within the alcohol field about (a) which AOEs are "truly" negative from the point of view of those being studied and (b) whether measurement of AOEs should also include assessments of a person's evaluation of the AOE (i.e., is the AOE positive or negative?) (e.g., Fromme, Stroot, and Kaplan, 1993). Consistent with these issues, Neighbors and colleagues (2007) found that negative AOEs, in comparison to positive AOEs, are uniquely and positively predictive of alcohol-related problems. Neighbors et al. also found that viewing negative AOE more positively was associated with more alcohol-related problems. Beyond AOE valence and measurement concerns, recent research has also turned to identifying moderators of AOE, including gender (Jones et al., 2001), anxiety sensitivity (O'Connor, Farrow, and Colder, 2008), self-efficacy (Gilles, Turk, and Fresco, 2006), and sexual orientation (Hatzenbuehler, Corbin, and Fromme, 2008) and examining AOE as a mediator (e.g., Goldman et al., 1999; Hatzenbuehler, et al., 2008; McCarthy, Aarons, and Brown, 2002).

Summary and implications. AOEs seem to be consistent predictors of adolescent and young adult drinking. However, many important questions remain. First and foremost, there is a debate in the field about the importance of AOEs – i.e., what proportion of variance in drinking do AOEs account for. Although some argue that AOEs can account for as much as 50% of the variance (see Del Boca and Darkes, 2001; Goldman et al., 1999), others (e.g., Jones et al., 2001) argue that proportion is actually much smaller, with an upper bound of 25% and a lower bound of 1-2%. This issue is particularly complex (and resolution is beyond the scope of this chapter) as there are multiple measures of AOEs and drinking behaviors and multiple strategies for data analysis. In addition, there are important questions about the measurement of AOEs. The majority of studies assess AOEs using self-report measures that draw upon more controlled, introspective, cognitive processes (see Thush and Wiers, 2007, for an exception); however, AOEs very likely have a strong automatic cognitive component which may better be assessed using alternative measures (e.g., implicit measures). Also related to the issue of measurement are findings that AOEs are context-specific. At least two studies have found differences in AOEs as a function of setting (a laboratory versus a college bar) (see Wall et al., 2000; Wall et al., 2001). These findings not only have implications for measurement but also for intervention efforts. Previous reviews have reached contradictory findings with respect to the efficacy of targeting AOEs for interventions (see Goldman et al., 1999; Jones et al., 2001) and increased construct and methodological clarity would likely be extremely useful.

Problem Behavior Theory

Problem behavior theory (PBT) was initially proposed by Richard Jessor in the late 1960s (e.g., Jessor, Graves, Hanson, and Jessor, 1968) and revised to its most widely known form in the 1970s (e.g., Jessor and Jessor, 1977). PBT is a psychosocial and developmental approach for understanding problem behavior in adolescents and it has evolved over time. Because our treatment of PBT is necessarily brief, we refer interested readers elsewhere for more detailed descriptions (e.g., Jessor, 1987; 1998; Jessor, Donovan, and Costa, 1991; Jessor and Jessor, 1977). PBT is psychosocial and developmental in nature, and at its core, it suggests that the extent to which one engages in problem behaviors is predicted by one's "proneness to deviance," also called "unconventionality" (Donovan and Jessor, 1985; Jessor and Jessor, 1977). Deviance proneness is conceptualized as stemming from personality, perceived environmental, and behavioral systems. The former two are postulated to exert their influences both proximally and distally. PBT also proposes that each of the three systems is composed of variables that instigate or promote engaging in problem behaviors as well as variables that control *against* or inhibit engaging in problem behaviors. Ultimately, PBT holds that it is the *balance* of instigations and controls across these three systems that constitutes deviance proneness and predicts engagement in problem behaviors (Jessor, 1987).

What constitutes "problem behavior" in the eyes of PBT is contextual – i.e., problem behaviors are conceptualized to vary as a function of one's age and of current societal norms (Jessor, 1987; Jessor and Jessor, 1977). For example, consuming a single alcoholic beverage at age eight is a social norms transgression and thus, would be conceptualized as a problem behavior, whereas consuming a single alcoholic beverage at age 28 is not a social norms transgression, and thus would not be conceptualized as a problem behavior. Thus it is not simply engaging in a behavior, per se, that renders it problematic, but rather it is engaging in that behavior earlier than expected that renders the behavior problematic. Notably, PBT holds that deviance proneness leads to engagement in a broad constellation of problem behaviors (e.g., delinquency, alcohol use, problem drinking, tobacco use, illicit drug use, and early sexual behavior) rather than a single behavior or circumscribed set of behaviors. Thus, PBT holds that a single syndrome of problem behavior is predicted by the psychosocial construct of deviance proneness (Jessor and Jessor, 1977). This single syndrome has been proffered to explain the positive correlations in adolescents between a variety of behaviors such as alcohol use, tobacco use, illicit drug use, and sexual activity (e.g., Jessor, 1987). Finally, PBT also predicts that proneness to engage in problem behaviors is negatively associated with engagement in conventional behaviors (e.g., religious service attendance, school attendance, and other prosocial behaviors).

As stated above, PBT has evolved over time. The most recent formulation of PBT (e.g., Jessor, 1991) extended to health related behaviors. Parts of the 1991 reformulation were, in essence, semantic – i.e., the constructs of control agents have been reconceptualized as protective factors, and instigations have been reconceptualized as risk factors – in order to better match the terminology of health psychology and behavioral medicine. Thus, consistent with the earlier formulations, protective factors decrease the likelihood of engaging in a problem behavior and risk factors increase the likelihood of engaging in problem behavior. Some of the reformulation did go beyond semantics. Most importantly, protective factors (formerly control agents) were hypothesized to play an additional role. Not only were they predicted to decrease the likelihood of engaging in a problem behavior, but they were also predicted to moderate or attenuate the effect of exposure to risk factors (Jessor, 1991). In addition, the behavioral domain of the model has been expanded to include not only the prediction of problem behaviors but also the prediction of health behaviors and prosocial behaviors. Finally, in its modern form, PBT includes biology and genetics among its risk and protective factors (see Jessor, 1998), indicating that it may, ultimately, be better characterized as a bio-psycho-social-developmental model of risk behavior.

Because the focus of our chapter is on alcohol use, our review of the research findings will focus primarily on predictions and findings from PBT related to alcohol, with a brief discussion of the debate over whether problem behaviors do or do not represent a single syndrome. When used to predict adolescent alcohol use and problem drinking – the latter typically defined as a function of drinking to intoxication as well as having experienced at least one negative consequence from alcohol – PBT typically accounts for upwards of 30% of the variance (e.g., Costa, Jessor, Turbin, 1999; Jessor, 1987; Hays, Stacy, and DiMatteo, 1987), with much of the variance explained by having friends who used alcohol and/or other substances. Similarly, when used to predict heavy episodic drinking in college students, risk and protective factors (as specified by the 1991 reformulation of PBT) accounted for approximately 25% of the variance after controlling for sociodemographic variables (Jessor, Costa, Krueger, and Turbin, 2006). Support has also been found for the role of protective factors as moderators of the effects of risk factors in both college (e.g., Jessor et al, 2006) and adolescent samples (Costa et al., 1999; Jessor et al., 1995). In addition, consistent with PBT, studies have also shown that deviant behaviors in adolescence predict drinking problems in adulthood (e.g., Clapper et al., 1995; DeCourville, 1995). Finally, PBT also hypothesizes that problem behaviors will be positively related to one another and negatively related to conventional behavior. In their study of six different samples of adolescents collected over a 20-year period, Donovan and colleagues (1999) reported results consistent with those predictions. Moreover, their findings indicated relatively consistent patterns of correlations among problem behaviors within and across each sample.

Research on PBT is characterized by several strengths. First, the studies tend to include large samples, typically ranging upwards of 800 (e.g., DeCourville, 1995; Jessor et al., 2006). Second, they tend to be longitudinal in nature, allowing for analysis related to transitioning into a problem behavior and maturing out of it. Some studies have also striven to recruit ethnically diverse samples (e.g., Costa et al., 1999), which allows for investigation of the generalizability of the model. Finally, as statistical methods and computer software packages have become more sophisticated and wide-spread, data analytic strategies have matured. Early tests of PBT tended to rely primarily on multiple correlation techniques (e.g., Jessor, 1987) whereas more recent studies have relied on more advanced statistics, including structural equation models, latent class models, and multidimensional scaling (e.g., Basen-Engquist et al., 1996; DeCourville, 1995; Willoughby et al., 2004).

Despite its strengths, PBT faces certain challenges both with respect to drinking, in particular, and to the model, more generally. Regarding the former, in PBT, problem behaviors are conceptualized as transgressions of norms. Although drinking under the age of 21 is illegal and a transgression in that sense, adolescent and young adult alcohol consumption is *statistically* normative (e.g., Baer et al., 1998; Johnston, O'Malley, Bachman, and Schulenberg, 2008, 2009). For example, more than half of 10th graders report having used alcohol in their lifetimes and more than half of 12th graders report having been drunk (Johnston et al., 2009); 72% of college students report having been drunk and 80% of young adults report having been drunk (Johnson et al., 2008). In addition, despite PBT's premise that problem behavior is a single syndrome, there have been contrary findings which suggest that multiple factors (vs. a single factor) may better fit the data (e.g., Basen-Engquist et al., 1996; Gillmore et al., 1991; Willoughby et al., 2004). In addition, others have found support for a single syndrome but, contray to PBT, also found that problem behaviors were not negatively correlated with conventional behaviors (e.g., Farrell et al., 1992). Concerns have also been raised about the extent to which individual problem behaviors actually co-occur because of data analytic strategies that rely on correlations and therefore may not provide accurate predictions of the co-occurrence of problem behavior (Willoughby et al., 2004).

Moreover, some studies that have tested the full PBT model have found that it did not fit the data as well as an abridged model (e.g., DeCourville, 1995). Finally, there is also mixed evidence with respect to PBT's generalizeabilty, with some studies finding it a better fit for White male adolescents from the U.S. than for Blacks or White females (e.g., Basen-Engquist et al., 1996) and others reporting a good fit for U.S. (Donovan et al., 1999; Jessor et al., 2003) and Chinese adolescents (Jessor et al., 2003).

Summary and implications. PBT is a comprehensive psycho-social developmental theory for predicting adolescent problem behavior. Research findings indicate that its three systems (e.g., personality, perceived environment, and behavioral) explain a substantial amount of variance in alcohol use and problem drinking. Consistent with other social influence theories, findings testing PBT indicate the influence of friends and other models on drinking. Although not unique to PBT, such influences can be and often are targets for intervention. Unanswered questions with respect to PBT include the extent to which problem behaviors should or should not be conceptualized as a single syndrome. As discussed above, problem behaviors may better be conceptualized as several factors versus a single syndrome, and covariance among problem behaviors does not necessarily indicate co-occurrence. These issues have important treatment implications in terms of whether alcohol use should be targeted individually versus as a part of a larger constellation of maladaptive behaviors. Finally, generalizeabilty issues remain important concerns and future studies should continue to test PBT's applicability to populations beyond White American adolescents and young adults.

Social Comparison Theory

Social comparison theory was proposed by Leon Festinger in 1954. The original theory was formal and structured with nine hypotheses, eight corollaries, and eight deviations. The theory's basic premise is that people have a natural drive to evaluate themselves and, in the absence of objective criteria, compare themselves with other people. Much of the original theory considered with whom and on what dimensions people engage in social comparison. More than six decades of subsequent research (social comparison theory is cited in more than 3500 articles) has extended the theory considerably and most social influence theories acknowledge social comparison theory as an underlying foundation. Dimensions of social comparison that have been studied in detail include motivations for comparison, choice of comparison target, and effects of social comparison.

Although Festinger emphasized the desire to have an accurate self-evaluation as a motive, much subsequent research suggests that people also engage in social comparison as a means of self-improvement or ego-enhancement (Collins, 1996; Wills, 1981). Helgeson and Mickelson (1995) found direct support for the existence of these three motives, as well as three others (common bond, altruism, and self-destruction) by having participants list possible reasons why they themselves or anyone else might want to make social comparisons in response to a threatening event.

Choice of comparison target has also received extensive attention and overlaps with the literature evaluating motivations for engaging in social comparisons. Wills' (1981) downward comparison theory suggests that individuals may compare themselves with others who are of lower standing as a means of enhancing the self. Classic views suggested that lateral comparisons were motivated by accuracy whereas upward comparisons were motivated by self-improvement (Festinger, 1954; Wheeler, 1966). Subsequent research has shown that the specific choice of a comparison target, with respect to relative standing, is moderated by a number of situational and contextual variables, and there is no simple, general formula for the relationship between whom one compares with and why (e.g., Collins, 1996).

Similarly, the direction of comparison is associated with affect and esteem-related consequences. The traditional view (Suls and Wheeler, 2000) suggests that upward comparisons are most often associated with reduced positive affect, increased negative affect, and experienced as esteem-threatening. In contrast, downward comparisons are presumed most often associated with favorable affect and esteem-related outcomes. Here again, additional evidence has indicated that the impact of upward and downward comparisons are not so simple, and either direction can be associated with positive or negative consequences to the self, depending on context (Buunk, Collins, Taylor, VanYperen and Dakof, 1990; Collins 1996).

Relatively little research has *formally* evaluated social comparison theory in the context of alcohol use. There have been at least four edited books dedicated to social comparison theory (Buunk and Gibbons, 1997; Stapel and Blanton, 2007; Suls and Wheeler, 2000; Suls and Wills, 1991), and only one of the included papers has a distinct alcohol focus. Stapel and Blanton (2007) include a reprint of a study in which Schroeder and Prentice (1998) evaluate dpluralistic ignorance as a means of reducing drinking. Pluralistic ignorance and other constructs such as social norms (see Social Identity Theory) are implied and implicitly connected to social comparison theory but are not central to social comparison theory Related, a compelling argument can be made that social comparison theory is the field in which many, if not most, perspectives related to social influence on alcohol are imbedded. For example, a considerable body of research has evaluated peer influences on adolescents, which are among the strongest predictors of adolescent substance use (e.g., Hawkins, Catalano, and Miller, 1992). Similarly, social norms are among the strongest influences of drinking among college students (Neighbors, Lee, Lewis, Fossos, and Larimer, 2007). Among young adults there is an extensive literature indicating strong peer influences on drinking generally and in specific situations (Borsari and Carey, 2001). Moreover, most conceptualizations of peer influence require social comparisons as an integral part of the influence process. In order for others to have indirect influence on us (as opposed to direct requests to engage in a particular behavior), we must consider their expectations. Thus, on the one hand it might be suggested that there are few studies focusing on social comparison and drinking among adolescents and young adults. However,, on the other hand, it also might be suggested that there are few studies related to social influence on drinking in this population that are not related to social comparison theory.

Summary and implications. There are a number of promising directions for evaluating alcohol consumption in the context of social comparison theory. It would be worthwhile to reformulate existing findings related to peer social networks among adolescents, which are associated with drinking and other risk behaviors, in the context of social comparison theory (see review of Peer Cluster Theory). Examining social comparison processes as a function of maturation would provide ideas about how to tailor social influence approaches to prevention developmentally. In general, social comparison theory provides a rich theoretical foundation that is seldom formally evaluated in the context of drinking despite the potential practical implications for intervention development. We recommend more lab-based social comparison studies where alcohol use is used as the comparison dimension.

Social Identity Theory

Social identity theory (SIT; Tajfel and Turner, 1986) describes the role of self-conception in relation to group membership, group processes, and intergroup relations. SIT was developed by Henri Tajfel in collaboration with John Turner. According to SIT and related theories, such as self-categorization theory (Turner, Hogg, Oakes, Reicher, and Wetherell, 1987), people view themselves and others as group members with a common or shared social identity, which is primarily comprised from group memberships. Individuals strive to maintain a positive social identity that is largely derived from positive comparisons between the in-group and relevant out-groups. SIT is composed of four primary elements: categorization, identification, comparison, and psychological distinctiveness. Categorization occurs when we place ourselves and others into categories, such as student, Asian, female, or fraternity member. The social category to which one belongs provides a definition of who one is based on the defining characteristics of the category (identification). People have a number of category memberships that vary in importance to the self, which serves to bolster self-esteem. Self-enhancement guides social categorization such that self-enhancement can be achieved by making comparisons between the in-group and relevant out-groups in ways that favor the in-group. Finally, psychological distinctiveness suggests that people desire to have a social identity that is distinct from yet positively compares with other groups.

Individuals have cognitive representations of social categories (i.e., prototypes) that consist of attributes that define one group and distinguish it from other groups. As such, category representations accentuate intragroup similarities and intergroup differences. Because prototypes tend to be shared by people within one group, they have group prototypes or group norms related to the in-group and relevant out-groups. In order for social categorization to influence normative behavior, categorization must be salient, such that individuals must psychologically identify with their in-group in the specific context. Thus, SIT proposes that norms and behaviors are tied to groups that are most salient (Christensen, Rothgerber, Wood, and Matz, 2004).

Although SIT as a whole has not been formally evaluated when applied to alcohol use, prior research examining alcohol use among adolescent and young adults has supported the notion that norms and behaviors are tied to salient referent groups. Several research studies have shown that normative perceptions of more proximal groups (e.g., same-sex peers, close friends), in comparison to more distal groups (e.g., typical student), are associated with alcohol use (Larimer et al., in press; Lewis and Neighbors, 2004; Lewis, Neighbors, Oster-Aaland, Kirkeby, and Larimer, 2007; Yanovitsky, Stewart, and Lederman, 2006). For example, Larimer and colleagues (2009) evaluated whether descriptive drinking normative perceptions (i.e., the perceived prevalence of drinking behavior) varied based on specificity of the normative referent group at three levels (gender, race, and residence), and whether normative perceptions for more specific reference group norms were associated with alcohol consumption. Results indicated that participants distinguished between different referent groups when estimating descriptive drinking norms. Moreover, results demonstrated that perceived norms for more specific groups were uniquely related to participants' own alcohol consumption. Perceived norms at all three levels of specificity significantly added to the prediction of participants' own drinking, even when controlling for relevant covariates such as demographics and perceived norms for typical students.

Research conducted by Neighbors and colleagues (2009) found that the relationship between perceived descriptive drinking norms and alcohol consumption was moderated by level of identification with the normative referent (e.g., typical same-sex student, typical same-race student, and typical same-Greek status student). Findings indicated that when examining these relationships for all three normative referent groups, descriptive drinking normative perceptions for the normative referent were more strongly associated with alcohol consumption when participants reported feeling closer to (i.e., stronger identification with) to the normative referent.

Similarly, Reed and colleagues (2007) evaluated the relationships among identity and perceived injunctive drinking norms (i.e., perceptions of how much others approve or accept of drinking behavior) for friends, other university peers, and Greek members. Results suggested that when these relationships were examined among friends, perceived injunctive drinking norms were positively associated with consuming more drinks per occasion, and that was especially true as identification with friends increased. For other university peers, identification was associated with drinking only for those who perceived other university students as more approving of drinking behavior (medium and high levels of approval). For Greek normative referents, identification was associated with drinking only for those who perceived Greek members as strongly approving of drinking behavior. Together, findings from Larimer and colleagues (in press), Neighbors and colleagues (2009), and Reed and colleagues (2007) support SIT such that the relationship between both perceived descriptive and injunctive normative drinking behavior with alcohol consumption may depend on how strongly students identify with the normative referent.

SIT's concept that categorization must be salient in order to influence normative behavior has also been applied to social norms interventions for adolescent and young adult alcohol use. Universal social norms marketing interventions (e.g., DeJong et al., 2006; Perkins and Craig, 2006; Perkins, Haines, and Rice, 2005) attempt to correct overestimated normative perceptions for relevant peer groups by presenting accurate norms messages on a large scale (e.g., 85% of students on this campus drink 0-1-2-3 or at most 4 drinks when they party), often through campus newspaper ads, emails, posters, and/or flyers. Research on social norms marketing has produced equivocal support. Some findings demonstrate support for social norms marketing as an effective intervention for reducing alcohol consumption (e.g., DeJong et al., 2006; Mattern and Neighbors, 2004; Perkins and Craig, 2006; Perkins et al., 2005) and other research concludes partial or no support (e.g., Clapp, Lange, Russell, Shillington, and Voas, 2003; Thombs and Hamilton, 2002; Wechsler, Lee, Nelson, and Lee, 2003; Werch et al., 2000).

Personalized normative feedback is also a social norms approach to reducing alcohol use, which attempts to correct overestimated normative misperceptions by presenting individual feedback regarding the student's own drinking, the student's perception of others' drinking, and others' actual drinking (Lewis and Neighbors, 2007; Lewis, Neighbors, Oster-Aaland, Kirkeby, and Larimer, 2007; Neighbors, Larimer, and Lewis, 2004; Neighbors, Lewis, Bergstrom, and Larimer, 2006). Personalized intervention strategies using normative comparisons have generally yielded promising results showing reductions in normative perceptions of peer drinking and reductions in drinking behavior (Carey, Scott-Sheldon, Carey, DeMartini, 2007; Larimer and Cronce, 2002, 2007; Walters and Neighbors, 2005).

Many personalized feedback interventions have incorporated other components, such as review of risk factors, expectancy challenge, and blood alcohol concentration information

(Carey et al., 2007; Larimer and Cronce, 2002, 2007); thus evaluation of single component personalized feedback interventions are necessary. A handful of studies have evaluated the effects of personalized normative feedback as a single component intervention (Lewis and Neighbors, 2007; Lewis, Neighbors et al., 2007; Neighbors et al., 2004; Neighbors et al., 2006). These studies have all demonstrated that personalized normative feedback is effective at reducing normative perceptions and drinking behavior. When examining personalized normative feedback in relation to SIT, Lewis and Neighbors (2007) evaluated gender-nonspecific and gender-specific versions of a brief personalized normative feedback intervention aimed at reducing alcohol consumption among college students. Consistent with SIT, findings indicated that gender-specific personalized normative feedback was especially effective at reducing drinking for women who more strongly identified with their gender at a two-month follow-up.

Summary and implications. According to SIT, adolescents and young adults form social identities based on group membership, or categorization. Identification with in-groups, and comparison with in-groups and relevant out-groups aid in making these social identities distinct for individuals. Aspects of SIT have been applied to etiology and prevention research. Specifically, salience of the in-group is often a moderator of the relationship between social norms and alcohol use. For example, prior research has demonstrated that more closely identifying with relevant normative referents is associated with increased normative perceptions for drinking behavior as well as increased personal alcohol use. In addition, research evaluating preventative interventions has found that personalized normative feedback is more effective in certain instances when identification with the normative referent is stronger. Additional research is needed to extend these findings to adolescent and non-college young adult populations.

Self-Derogation Theory

Self-derogation theory is a broad theory that describes the interplay between socialization factors, self-esteem, deviant behavior, and associations with deviant peers (Kaplan, 1982; 1987; 2001). The theory suggests, among adolescents, a number of factors may contribute to the development of low self-esteem, self-rejection, and rejection of the norms and values endorsed by the broader society. These factors, in turn, may motivate adolescents to engage in deviant behaviors, including alcohol and drug use, and seek out similarly deviant peers. Under these circumstances, involvement with and acceptance by deviant peers provides a means of restoring or enhancing an adolescent's sense of self-worth.

A number of social, familial, cultural, and intrapersonal factors have been proposed to increase the likelihood of self-rejection (i.e., self-derogation; Kaplan, 2001). These include peer rejection, parental neglect and poor family cohesion, academic failure, stigmatization, and inadequate coping skills, among others. Adolescents who feel disenfranchised from conventional society and who do not fit in with main stream peers lose motivation to conform to societal norms. They may respond with reactance and rejection of conventional values (see Reactance Theory) whereby they engage in deviant behaviors. In other words, having failed to fit in with the main stream, these adolescents engage in deviant behaviors as an alternative response pattern. They may concurrently seek out others who have similarly rejected conventional norms (see Peer Cluster Theory), which is predicted increase deviant behaviors and self-worth.

The model is difficult to test in its entirety because it is a process model and requires longitudinal data spanning the period of adolescence. The breadth of the theory provides considerable overlap with other theoretical perspectives and bodies of research regarding risk and protective factors (Hawkins, Catalano, and Miller, 1992; also see Problem Behavior Theory) as well peer influences on alcohol and other substance use (Oetting and Beauvais, 1987). For example, a considerable body of evidence supports associations between family factors (e.g., attachment, parental support, parental monitoring, and family conflict) and alcohol and other substance use (Bray, Adams, Getz, and Baer, 2001; Petraitis, Flay and Miller, 1995).

The relationship between self-esteem and alcohol has been somewhat mixed although higher self-esteem has been prospectively associated with less alcohol and other substance use in adolescence (Stein, Newcomb, and Bentler, 1987). In college students, morally-based self-esteem, and esteem based on God's love, has been associated with less drinking (Lewis, Phillipi, and Neighbors, 2007 Luhtanen and Crocker, 2005) whereas self-esteem based on appearance has been associated with increased drinking (Luhtanen and Crocker, 2005). More central to the theory are how self-esteem, peer associations, and deviant behaviors are associated over time.

Mason (2001) found direct support for this aspect of self-derogation theory, finding delinquency to be associated with growth in self-esteem among adolescent boys who were initially low in self-esteem. The measure of delinquency did not however include alcohol and other substance use. More recently, in a longitudinal sample of American Indian adolescents, Radin and colleagues (2006) found that low self-worth was associated with alcohol-related problems and that this relationship was mediated by associations with deviant peers in earlier, but not later adolescence. In later adolescence self-esteem and peer deviance had direct associations with alcohol-related problems. Using latent growth analysis, Radin and colleagues also found some support for a comprehensive model of self-derogation theory. Specifically, family cohesion, family conflict, and academic competence were associated with initial self-worth and changes in self-worth in expected directions. Self-worth and increases in self-worth were associated with lower peer deviance. Peer deviance and changes in peer deviance were, in turn, associated with drinking and changes in drinking. Thus, risk factors were associated with lower self-worth, which was in turn, associated with peer deviance and subsequent alcohol use. Radin and colleagues (2006) did not, however, find any support for affiliation with deviant peers having positive effects on changes in self-worth.

Summary and implications. Self-derogation theory shares a number of commonalities with other theories of social influence (e.g., Problem Behavior Theory, Reactance Theory and Peer Cluster Theory) but also makes some unique predictions regarding the potential incentives of substance use and affiliation with other substance users among adolescents who feel rejected from conventional society. The theory's primary implications for intervention are in the identification of risk factors and potential issues to be addressed among deviant adolescents. The theory has been primarily examined in adolescents and is presumed to be most relevant to this time period. However, future research examining the potential long term affects of self-derogation into young adulthood would be worthwhile.

Theory of Reasoned Action and Theory of Planned Behavior

The theory of reasoned action, developed by Ajzen and Fishbein (TRA; Ajzen and Fishbein, 1980; Fishbein and Ajzen, 1975), was designed to predict and explain human behavior in specific contexts. This theory suggests that behavior is determined by intentions to perform the behavior, and that intentions are a function of attitude toward the behavior and subjective norms toward the behavior. Ajzen extended the TRA to the theory of planned behavior (TPB; Ajzen, 1988, 1991) such that perceived behavioral control, together with behavioral intentions, can be used directly to predict behavior.

According to the TRA and the TPB, the best predictor of a behavior is intention to engage in that behavior. Thus, intentions are considered to be the immediate antecedent of reasoned and planned behavior. Intentions are determined by attitudes toward the specific behavior (i.e., beliefs about consequences or attributes of the behavior), subjective norms toward the specific behavior (i.e., beliefs about how important others will view the specific behavior), and perceived behavioral control (i.e., one's perceptions of their ability to perform a given behavior). An assumption of these theories is that the more favorable the attitude and the subjective norm, and the greater the perceived behavioral control, the stronger the intentions to perform the behavior. Furthermore, the stronger the intention to engage in a behavior, the more likely one will do so. According the TPB, behavioral intentions are only predictive of behavior when the behavior is perceived as being under one's volitional control (i.e., if the person can decide to engage or not engage in the behavior).

Armitage and Connor (2001) reviewed the research on the TPB and found that across studies the TPB accounted for 27% to 39% of the variance in behavior and intentions, respectively. In addition, they found that the subjective norm construct was generally a weaker predictor of intentions in comparison to attitudes and perceived behavioral control, which was in part due to poor measurement and the need to expand the subjective norm component of the model. When applied specifically to adolescent and young adult alcohol use, both the TRA and the TPB are empirically supported (Connor, Warren, Close, and Sparks,1999; Collins and Carey, 2007; Huchting, Lac, LaBrie, 2008; Johnston and White, 2003; Kam, Matsunaga, Hecht, and Ndiaye, 2009; Kuther and Higgens-D'Alessandro, 2003; Marcoux and Shope, 1997; McMillan and Connor, 2003; Norman, Armitage, and Quigley, 2007; Norman and Conner, 2006; O'Callaghan, Chant, Callan, and Baglioni, 1996; Schlegal, D'Avernas, Zanna, DeCourville, and Manske, 1992).

However, despite the empirical support of the TRA and the TPB when applied to alcohol use among adolescents and young adults, as well as across a wide range of other behaviors, a major shortcoming of these models is their inability to account fully for the influence of past behavior on alcohol use intentions and future alcohol use. Prior research has shown that past behavior is one of the strongest predictors of intentions and future behavior, explaining variance over and above that accounted for by the TPB variables (Ajzen, 1991; Conner and Armitage, 1998; Ouellette and Wood, 1998). For example, Conner and Armitage (1998) reported that the addition of past behavior to the TPB variables explains, on average, an additional 7% of the variance in intention and 13% of the variance in behavior.

Recent research has examined the role of past behavior in the TPB. For example, Collins and Carey (2007) examined the TPB in an undergraduate student sample, and found that self-efficacy and attitudes significantly predicted intentions, and that intentions to engage in heavy-episodic drinking predicted future heavy-episodic drinking. However, subjective norms were not found to be predictive of intentions. Findings further indicated that a model including past heavy-episodic drinking did not provide a better fit than the model excluding past behavior. The authors concluded that a TPB model excluding past behavior, which is more parsimonious and theory driven, may provide better prediction of heavy-episodic drinking among college drinkers than a model including past behavior.

Norman and Conner (2006) examined the TPB in relation to heavy-episodic drinking among college students. Findings indicated that attitude, self-efficacy, and perceived control were predictive of heavy-episodic drinking intentions. Findings indicated the TPB to be predictive of intentions to engage in heavy-episodic drinking over the next week, explaining an additional 66% of the variance in intentions when controlling for age and gender. Attitude, self-efficacy, and perceived control were significant predictors. Furthermore, results indicated that additional variance was explained by past behavior, and that past behavior moderated the associations between attitude and intention and intentions and behavior. Weaker relationships were found as frequency of past behavior increased. The authors explained that this finding is consistent with the idea that repeatedly performing a behavior leads to a reduction in the amount of deliberative processing, and thus, attitudes are less important when determining intentions as the frequency of past behavior increases. Similarly, intentions become less important in determining behavior as the frequency of past behavior increases. Thus, while research is examining the role of past behavior in relation to the TRA and the TPB, findings are mixed as to whether including past behavior enhances the predictability of these two models.

Summary and implications. According to the TRA and the TPB, alcohol use among adolescents and young adults is predicted by intentions to use alcohol, which are predicted by attitudes toward alcohol, subjective norms related to alcohol, and perceived behavioral control. The results of the above studies confirm the predictive validity of the TPB in relation to alcohol-related intentions and behavior among adolescents and young adults. Furthermore, research literature on the TRA and the TPB suggest that preventative interventions should target favorable attitudes toward alcohol use, such as alcohol-expectancy challenge interventions (for a review see Carey et al., 2007; Larimer and Cronce, 2002; 2007). In addition, perceived subjective norms for alcohol use should be targeted. Prior research has shown that subjective norms are often misperceived such that adolescents and young adults perceive important others' as more approving of alcohol use than they actually are (Borsari and Carey, 2001; Carey, Borsari, Carey, and Maisto, 2006; Suls and Green, 2003). Providing accurate subjective normative information for alcohol use may reduce perceived approval of alcohol use, and in turn lower intentions and behavior. Finally, preventative interventions could provide skills aimed at increasing drinking-refusal self-efficacy (for a review see Carey et al., 2007; Larimer and Cronce, 2002; 2007).

Prototype/Willingness Model

The prototype/willingness model is used to explain complex health behaviors in adolescents and young adults. (Gerrard, Gibbons, Houlihan, Stock, and Pomery, 2008; Gibbons, Gerrard, Blanton, and Russell, 1998), and is based on theories of social cognition and primarily draws from the TRA. The prototype-willingness model is a dual-processing model that posits that there are two related yet independent paths, a reasoned path and a social reaction path, to risky health behaviors for adolescents and young adults. The reasoned path represents a deliberative style of processing, similar to that proposed in the theory of reasoned action. Within this path, actions are premeditated and planned (analytic processing) and are a function of behavioral intentions. Attitudes and subjective norms toward the behavior predict intentions. In contrast, the social reaction path represents a different style of processing, one that is more heuristic-based or experiential (heuristic processing). This pathway of the model suggests that there are times (more so for adolescents) when behavior is unintended, and is rather less deliberative and often occurs from being in situations that facilitate risky behaviors. Once in these risky situations, it is not reasoned decision making (behavioral intentions), but behavioral willingness that determines behavior. Risk prototypes (e.g., the typical drinker) and behavioral willingness (i.e., an openness to engaging in risky behavior) are two key components of the social reaction path. Behavioral willingness predicts behavior, and is a function of risk images or prototypes. Unlike the TRA, previous behavior is included in the model as a predictor of attitudes, subjective norms, and risk images.

There are several basic assumptions of the prototype/willingness model. One basic assumption is that adolescent and young adult health risk is usually volitional (their choice), but is often not planned or even intentional. Prior research has shown that adolescents and young adults who engaged in a risky behavior, will have previously reported no intention to engage in that risky behavior in the future (Gibbons et al., 1998). Gerrard and colleagues (2008) suggest that this discrepancy between intentions and behavior is not due to misrepresentation of intentions but rather is a reflection of images of who engages in drinking behavior.

A second major assumption of the prototype/willingness model is that adolescents and young adults have distinct social images or cognitive representations (prototypes) of the type of person their age who engages in specific risk behaviors (typology of a person rather than a description). These social images or prototypes are associated with behavioral willingness, such that the more favorable the image of a drinker than the more likely they are to engage in alcohol use and to accept the social consequences as being seen as a drinker. Prior research has supported the social reaction path of the prototype/willingness model when applied to adolescent and young adult alcohol use (Andrews, Hampson, Barchley, Gerrard, and Gibbons, 2008; Blanton, Gibbons, Gerrard, Conger, and Smith, 1997; Gerrard et al., 2002; Rivis, Sheeran, and Armitage, 2006; Spijkerman, van den Eijnden, Vitale, and Engels, 2004). For example, Andrews and colleagues (2008) found that adolescents' prototypes of drinkers were either indirectly related to alcohol use through willingness or were directly related to alcohol use.

An additional assumption of the prototype/willingness model is that the relationship between intentions and behavior becomes stronger than the relationship between willingness and behavior over time. Thus, as adolescents and young adults age and become more experienced, decision making tends to shift from a more reactive process (social reaction path) to a more reasoned one (reasoned path). Although this assumption has not yet been tested when applied to adolescent and young adult alcohol use, it has been supported in various other high-risk behaviors including condom use, smoking, and skipping class (Gerrard et al., 2008).

Finally, according to the prototype/willingness model, prototypes are easier to change when younger, and specifically in those who do not engage in the risk behavior. Thus, change is more likely before the development of prototypes and a stable behavior pattern.

Interventions designed to change prototype images at an early age are likely to be effective in decreasing willingness to engage in alcohol use, and subsequently alcohol use (Gerrard et al., 2006). When evaluated among adolescents, Gerrard and colleagues (2006) found support for a prototype-willingness model based intervention. This study examined a dual-focus prevention intervention aimed to delay the onset of alcohol use and to reduce alcohol consumption among African American adolescents. Findings indicated that two-years following the intervention, changes in alcohol consumption were mediated by two paths, the reasoned path and the social reaction path. The reasoned path demonstrated that the intervention influenced intentions to drink by increasing parenting behaviors related to alcohol. The social reaction path provided evidence that the intervention decreased willingness to drink by decreasing the favorability of drinker images. Furthermore, changes in intentions and willingness were independently associated with alcohol consumption at the two-year follow-up. The authors suggest that taking a dual-process approach to preventative interventions that targets both intentions and willingness is likely to be more effective than targeting either alone.

Although change in alcohol use becomes more difficult as prototypes develop and as individuals have more experiences or stable patterns of alcohol use, it may still be possible to alter drinker images and change drinking behavior into adulthood. For example, Gibbons and colleagues (2005) found that among college students and young adults that interventions can reduce the favorability of the image of a sun bather or typical person who uses a tanning booth, and thus reduce willingness to be exposed to UV rays. Interventions applying the prototype/willingness model still need to be evaluated for reducing alcohol use among young adults.

Summary and implications. The prototype/willingness model is a dual-process model that incorporates a reasoned, intentional approach to predicting behavior as well as a more reactive approach to predicting behavior. Research has provided support for these two pathways in predicting alcohol use in adolescents and young adults. Moreover, research has shown that prevention interventions aimed at reducing intentions and willingness to drink are effective in reducing drinking in adolescents. Additional research is needed to replicate these findings in preventing and/or reducing drinking in young adults.

Deviance Regulation Theory

Developed by Blanton and colleagues, Deviance regulation theory (DRT; Blanton, Stuart, VandenEijnden, 2001; Blanton and Christie, 2003) presents a novel perspective on social influence. While most theories of social influence assume that conformity lies at the root of social influence, DRT suggests that deviance, rather than conformity, is a more central motivator. This theory offers compelling rationale that it is what makes us different that defines us, to ourselves, and to others. More specifically, DRT suggests that individuals attempt to maintain positive images by seeking to deviate from social norms in a positive way and by avoiding deviation from social norms that are viewed negatively. Consistent with classic attribution perspectives (Jones and Davis, 1965; Kelley, 1967) the theory suggests that distinctive actions (i.e., counter-normative alternatives) receive greater weight in impression formation and are therefore most strongly considered in the regulation of social behaviors. In essetence, behaving the same way everyone else does has little impact on one's social identity. Rather, it is when behavior is distinctive that others alter their impressions of themselves which, in turn, has implications for their personal identify and sense of self-worth (Leary, Tambor, Terdal, and Downs, 1995). Distinctiveness can be either positive or negative depending on the prevailing attitudes and values of the self and the reference group. For example, being the only person not drinking alcohol at a keg party may result in negative social distinction. Similarly, excessive drinking at a formal social gathering where few people are drinking is also likely to constitute negative social distinction.

Blanton, Stuart, and VandenEijnden (2001) conducted several experiments testing hypotheses derived from DRT. In one of these studies they randomly assigned participants to receive information suggesting that getting a flu shot was normative (i.e., most students get flu shots) or non-normative (i.e., few students get flu shots). Some students received positively framed persuasive messages (i.e., getting a flu shot is good) whereas others received negatively framed persuasive messages (i.e., not getting a flu shot is bad). Consistent with their theoretical framework, the two conditions that were most strongly associated with intentions to get a flu shot were the normative negatively framed condition (i.e., most students get flu shots and not getting a flu shot is bad) and the non-normative positively framed condition (i.e., few students get flu shots and getting a flu shot is good). In another one of these studies they found the identical pattern regarding willingness to have unprotected sex. In this study Blanton and colleagues (2001) measured participants' perceived norms regarding condom use and then, two weeks later, exposed them to either positively framed messages (using condoms is good) or negatively framed messages (not using condoms is bad). Students who believed condom use was relatively rare were most unwilling to have unprotected sex when they were exposed to positively framed messages. Students who believed condom use was relatively common were most unwilling to engage in unprotected sex when they received negatively framed messages.

DRT also suggests that inferences about prevalence are made on the basis of how messages are framed. For example, Stuart and Blanton (2003) found that prevalence estimates for condom use were higher among participants who were exposed to a negatively framed message (i.e., having sex without a condom is stupid) compared with participants who were exposed to a positively framed message (i.e., using condoms is smart). Thus, according to DRT, just as prevalence estimates influence the impact of positively versus negatively framed messages (Blanton et al., 2001), positively versus negatively framed messages influence prevalence estimates.

Although no published empirical research to date has directly evaluated DRT in the context of alcohol use, there have been speculations regarding its applicability to norms based alcohol interventions for adolescents (Blanton and Burkley, 2008) and college students (Blanton, Koblitz, and McCaul, 2008). In the context of discussing DRT's application to adolescents, Blanton and Burkley (2008) describe an unpublished study examining the effects of exposure to positively versus negatively framed messages about healthy drinking on college students drinking intentions. They reported that negatively framed messages reduced drinking intentions among students with little drinking history, as would be expected assuming these students are more likely to believe healthy drinking is the norm and that unhealthy drinking is a negative behavior. They further reported that, among students with extensive drinking backgrounds, exposure to negatively framed messages was not only ineffective, but was iatrogenic, increasing drinking intentions. Assuming these students were more likely to believe that drinking is good and common, this finding would not support

DRT, but would be more consistent with suggestions that heavy drinking students may be more defensive and reactive to pejorative alcohol statements (Neighbors, Palmer, and Larimer, 2004). Thus, while preliminary evidence suggests this theory may be applicable to drinking, it may be more applicable to universal prevention and messages to adolescents and/or young adults who have a limited drinking history.

Summary and implications. The primary limitation of DRT is the relatively small number of studies evaluating hypotheses derived from the theory. Perhaps more importantly, none of the published studies to date have evaluated the impact of messages on actual behavior change but have been limited to studying intentions or willingness to engage in health-related behaviors. Thus, to date, there is no efficacy data for prevention/interventions strategies derived from this theory. Moreover, it has yet to be explored in detail in the context of alcohol use. In contrast, DRT has a number of appealing characteristics which make it well worthy of inclusion. It is one of the most novel and innovative perspectives on social influence to be offered in recent years. Whether correct or incorrect the theory offers clear straight forward and theoretically rich hypotheses about how to frame alcohol interventions, for adolescents and young adults. Current approaches to alcohol interventions, understandably, tend to emphasize what works in changing behavior often at the expense of theoretical innovation. However, the ability to continue to develop new and better approaches for interventions rests on theoretical innovation, and DRT is a promising candidate.

Peer Cluster Theory

Peer cluster theory, first introduced by Oetting and Beauvais (1986), is a psychosocial model that proposes that socialization factors associated with adolescent development interact to create peer clusters that either support or discourage alcohol and other substance use. The peer cluster, different from the broader and more loosely associated peer group, is a small and cohesive unit of friends that serves as the dominant sphere of influence, that shapes adolescent behavior (Oetting and Beauvais, 1987). While peer cluster theory recognizes other factors in the adolescent social network that either increase or decrease the probability of alcohol and drug involvement, these elements only indirectly affect substance use to the extent that they influence the selection of a peer cluster (Oetting and Lynch, 2006). More specifically, this theory identifies several psychosocial characteristics that motivate drug use, including social structure, socialization links, and psychological characteristics. Again, these factors only lay the groundwork for the formation of either a substance-using or a substance-abstaining peer cluster (Oetting and Beauvais, 1986). Moreover, it is primarily peer clusters that "shape and determine attitudes, values, and beliefs about drugs…and, to a great extent, determine the actual drug-taking behaviors (Oetting and Beauvais, 1987)."

According to peer cluster theory, in order to successfully treat a substance-abusing adolescent, the counselor must first separate the individual from his or her substance-using peer cluster. The counselor must also address the original psychosocial elements that established the vulnerability to substance involvement. If these elements remain strong in the adolescent's life, then the adolescent remains susceptible. Peer cluster theory posits that alcohol and drug treatment approaches that do not stress changes in peer associations first and foremost, will ultimately, be ineffective (Oetting and Beauvais 1986).

In their study of 415 eleventh and twelfth grade students, Oetting and Beauvais (1987) confirmed two of their primary hypotheses about socialization characteristics and substance use. The first of these hypotheses was that socialization characteristics are significantly correlated with substance use, indicating that theories of substance use should not neglect the influence of psychosocial characteristics. The second hypothesis, supported by the results of this study, was that peer substance associations were preeminent among psychosocial factors predicting adolescent substance use. The results of Swaim, Oetting, Edwards and Beauvais' (1989) study of 563 high school students similarly indicated that peer substance associations were highly predictive of adolescent substance use. Moreover, emotional distress was found to be associated with substance use only indirectly through peer substance use. Finally, Bray, Adams, Getz, and McQueen (2003) investigated patterns of adolescent alcohol use in their longitudinal study of 6,048 students in the Southwestern United States. Among the goals of the study was to examine the relationship between peer alcohol use and adolescent alcohol use. Results of this study mirrored those in the previously mentioned two studies: peer alcohol use influenced youth drinking. Additionally, findings of this research emphasized the importance of studying the longitudinal relationships between peer alcohol use and youth alcohol consumption, while also taking into consideration the capacity for change and growth.

Related to peer cluster theory, in the prevention domain, social resistance skills training has been an effective component of many empirically supported primary prevention strategies (Botvin, 2000). Similarly, building efficacy for social resistance has been incorporated in empirically supported treatments for alcohol (e.g., Marlatt and Donovan, 2005). Both domains acknowledge the powerful influence of close peers on alcohol and other substance use and provide practical strategies for resisting this influence.

Summary and implications. In sum, peer cluster theory stresses the strong influence of close peers on the use of alcohol and other substances, especially among adolescents and further suggests the value of incorporating some aspect of the peer cluster into alcohol interventions. Peer cluster theory has important implications for interventions targeting adolescent and young adult alcohol use. Peer cluster theory suggests interventions centering solely on the individual, and neglecting the social network, will be ineffective. Small group interventions targeting either the peer cluster directly or incorporating supportive peers in interventions are a natural extension of peer cluster theory. Some concerns have been raised regarding the potential for high-risk peers to influence one another negatively in adolescent group interventions (Dishion, McCord, and Poulin, 1999), however a meta-analysis examining the validity of this concern revealed little support (Weiss et al., 2005). More recently, Tevyaw, Borsari, Colby, and Monti (2007) evaluated a peer enhanced brief motivational intervention and found support for the inclusion of peers in targeting alcohol use among college students. Specifically, relative to an individual brief motivational intervention, a brief motivational intervention with a supportive friend present resulted in greater reductions in drinking and alcohol related problem and higher satisfaction ratings. Future studies might also explore individual-centered interventions that seek to incorporate friends, who are part of the alcohol-using peer cluster.

Reactance Theory

Reactance theory (RT) was formulated in the 1960s (Brehm, 1966), and suggests that reducing or threatening to reduce a person's freedom will result in arousal – so-called "motivational arousal." RT further argues that people are motivated to reestablish or regain their freedoms through non-compliance. Psychological reactance is, therefore, a motivational *state* that leads people to remove threats to their freedom, regain their freedom, and prevent such threats from occurring again. The original formulation of RT specifies that reactance is best understood as a state versus a trait (Brehm, 1966). Others have argued that reactance could also be understood as an individual difference variable, suggesting that some people may be more reactant than others, and much of that research has sought methods to identify and intervene with "reactant" clients or patients (Beutler et al., 1991; Dillard and Shen, 2005; Shoham-Salomon and Hannah, 1991). This view of RT as trait is controversial and inconsistent with the original formulation of RT, and findings are mixed, at best (see Shoham, Trost, and Rohrbaugh, 2004). Accordingly, the present review will limit its scope to (a) consideration of RT as a state and (b) RT's application to adolescent and young adult alcohol use.

It would seem that RT would have substantial application to alcohol research, in general – (e.g., intervention and prevention efforts can be considered to be attempts to reduce a person's freedom to drink) and to alcohol research on adolescents and young adults in particular (e.g., in the U.S. a myriad of legal and public health efforts have been launched at restricting or limiting adolescents and young adults' access to, consumption of, and consequences from alcohol). In addition, adolescents and young adults are thought be, from a developmental perspective, at a period in their lives in which rebellion and questioning authority are normative (see Arnett, 2000). Surprisingly, little research formally tests RT with respect to alcohol use. Instead, most research seems either to capitalize on opportunities for naturalistic experiments (e.g., changes in drinking laws) or to offer RT as a possible post hoc explanation for study findings or survey trends. There appears to be a recent resurgence of interest in RT within the field of health communication, which may presage additional research within alcohol studies.

With respect to naturalistic experiments, two changes in laws – one raising the minimum age for purchase and public possession to 21 and the second requiring warning labels on alcoholic beverages – provided opportunities to investigate whether restrictions on young adults' and adolescents' freedom to drink would result in more drinking as a means of restoring that freedom. In both instances, findings have been mixed. Related to the former, two studies of students at post-secondary school institutions (e.g., colleges, community colleges, technical schools, etc.) been conducted. One found that students who were not of legal age consumed more than students who were of age and that a higher percentage of students underage were drinkers as compared to students who were of age (Engs and Hanson, 1989),. A second found, more drinking among students who were not of age as compared to those who were but no difference in the use of illicit drugs among students who were and were not of legal drinking age (arguably because there were no recent or new changes in laws regulating them) (Allen, Sprenkel, and Vitale, 1994). In contrast, however, at least two studies found that drinking did not change substantially either one month (e.g., Gordon and Minor, 1992) or one year (e.g., Perkins and Berkowitz, 1989) after changes to the minimum purchase age went into effect. Gordon and Minor (1992), however, argued that those underage "needed time" to regain their lost freedom to drink and examined another group 13 months after the law change. Although they found an increase in drinking, it is unclear if that finding is due to method effects – e.g., the study asked specifically and directly about alcohol consumption before and after the law change, possibly creating strong demand characteristics. Similar to findings related to changing the purchase age, warning label findings have been equivocal, suggesting, at best, that the labels neither increase nor decrease consumption (see Andrews, 1995; MacKinnon, Nohre, Cheong, and Stacy, 2001).

Beyond changes in law, RT has also been considered in light of the recent emphasis on social norms marketing approaches to alcohol education and prevention (e.g., DeJong et al., 2006 see also Social Identity Theory). In particular, it has been suggested that social norms marketing campaigns may "misfire" or "boomerang" and create reactance among (heavier) drinking adolescents and young adults (e.g., Cameron and Campo, 2006; Campo and Cameron, 2006). A study by Campo and Cameron (2006) found some support for college-wide social norms marketing campaigns resulting in more negative health attitudes about one's own drinking (e.g., being less likely to endorse that "drinking to get drunk is a bad idea") and that more such attitudes were more likely to occur in the heaviest drinkers. Similarly, a study of an Australian government-backed alcohol campaign, which essentially targeted injunctive norms about drinking and drinking-related consequences, found that although many college students liked the campaign and thought it was effective, other students were very negative about it (e.g., Ricciardelli and McCabe, 2008). The authors suggested that many of the negative remarks were consistent with RT – e.g., students do not want to be told what to do or do not care or will drink regardless. A significant limitation of the aforementioned studies, however, is that none assessed pre-, post, or follow-up drinking *behaviors*.

Within the field of health communications more broadly, there has been some experimental work as to what makes health-oriented messages (some of which were alcohol-related) more persuasive and less likely to elicit reactance (e.g., Dillard and Shen, 2005; Miller, Lane, Deatrick, Young, and Potts, 2007; Rains and Turner, 2007). Consistent with RT, findings suggest that (a) more controlling messages are perceived negatively by college students and (b) "restorative" postscripts, which remind readers that it is their choice whether or not to follow the message's advice, are perceived positively (Miller et al., 2007). In addition, another study suggests that a smaller sized request is also associated with less reactance (Rains and Turner, 2007). However, none of the aforementioned studies included post-tests or follow up assessments of actual drinking or other health behaviors.

Summary and implications. Ultimately, findings are mixed with respect to RT, and even studies with findings supportive of RT typically cannot rule out alternative interpretations or make claims about changes in actual behavior due to methodological limitations. Moreover, recent studies seem to focus exclusively on college students; thus, the implications for adolescents and young adults not attending college are unclear. However, the recent resurgence in the health communication literature is promising; it is hoped that future studies will continue to assess messages about alcohol consumption, to go beyond college populations and to measure and link RT directly to drinking behavior and consequences. Moreover, findings from those studies suggest that some current alcohol intervention strategies (e.g., motivational interviewing: Miller and Rollnick, 1991, 2002) may be particularly useful because (a) therapists specifically tell clients that they can choose not to change (i.e., retain their freedom to drink) and (b) therapists are instructed to avoid eliciting resistance and defensiveness and to change tactics immediately if either occurs. In addition, given the likelihood that the most extreme college drinkers are less likely to attend drinking interventions (see Neighbors, Palmer, and Larimer, 2004), it seems vitally important for continued and more methodologically rigorous research on reactance theory and alcohol use.

CONCLUSION

As reviewed within this chapter, there are a number of theoretical models that place importance on social influence in relation to decision making and behavior. Specifically, this chapter reviewed theories of social influence in relation to etiology and prevention of adolescent and young adult alcohol use. One criterion of success of a psychological theory is its explanatory, predictive, and generative power. A key to preventing alcohol use and associated negative consequences in adolescents and young adults is gaining understanding as to why individuals initiate and continue to engage in those behaviors. Thus, when applied to alcohol use, a successful theory can explain alcohol use, predict alcohol use, and provide a basis for innovation to produce additional empirical research. Some of the theories reviewed in this chapter had more explanatory, predictive, and generative power when applied to the etiology of adolescent and young adult alcohol use, such as social learning theory, social cognitive theory, alcohol expectancy theory, problem behavior theory, social identity theory, the theory of reasoned action, the theory of planned behavior, and prototype willingness model as compared to social comparison theory, self-derogation theory, deviance regulation theory, peer cluster theory, and reactance theory. While having weaker explanatory, predictive, or generative power may be associated with when the theory was developed or how broad the theory is, future experimental and longitudinal research is needed for these latter theories to solidify their application to alcohol use among adolescents and young adults.

An additional criterion for a good psychological theory is its value at addressing the conditions that necessitated the creation of the theory – i.e., prevention of alcohol use in adolescents and young adults. As indicated above, it appears as if many of these theories have empirical support related to the etiology of alcohol use in adolescents and young adults. However, reviewing this literature highlights that many of these theories have not been evaluated in the context of prevention of alcohol use in adolescents and young adults, such as social comparison theory, self-derogation theory, deviance regulation theory, and reactance theory. As such, future research is needed to apply these theories of social influence by testing the efficacy of theoretically-based preventative interventions aimed to reduce alcohol use among adolescents and young adults.

Although each of these theories of social influence is distinct, many of these theories have similarities or overlapping components, such as the theory of reasoned action and the prototype/willingness model. Thus, additional research is needed to test competing theories of social influence when applied to etiology and prevention of adolescent and young adult alcohol use. Related, we can have greater confidence in conclusions that are derived from different sources. Common factors arising from multiple theories of social influence as related to alcohol include the importance of peers, family environment and socialization (i.e., risk and protective factors), social norms, and behavior as a means of distinguishing one's self or one's group. It seems clear that each of these factors plays an important influencing the drinking of adolescents and young adults. However, more research is needed to consider their mutual and interactive influences across perspectives and to consider how these factors might be used in combination in the development of alcohol interventions.

Alcohol use among adolescents and young adults continues to be problematic, thus creating a need for etiology and presentation research. Many of the theories presented in this chapter are useful in terms of understanding why adolescents and young adults initiate and engage in alcohol use as well as considering how to best reduce the incidence of alcohol use among these populations.

Author Note

Manuscript preparation was supported by National Institute on Alcohol Abuse and Alcoholism Grants K01AA016966 (awarded to M. A. Lewis), R01AA014576 (awarded to C. Neighbors), and K99AA017669 (awarded to K. P. Lindgren).

References

Abbey, A., Zawacki, T., Buck, P. O., Clinton, A. M., and McAuslan, P. (2004). Sexual assault and alcohol consumption: What do we know about their relationship and what types of research are still needed? *Aggression and Violent Behavior, 9,* 271-303.

Abrams, D. B., and Niaura, R. S. (1987). Social learning theory. In Blane, H. T. and Leonard, K. E. (Eds.), *Psychological Theories of Drinking and Alcoholism* (pp. 131-178). New York: Guildford.

Ajzen, I. (1988). *Attitudes, personality, and behavior.* Chicago: Dorsey Press.

Ajzen, I. (1991). The theory of planned behavior. *Organizational Behavior and Human Decision Processes, 50,* 179-211.

Ajzen, I., *and* Fishbein, M. (1980). *Understanding attitudes and predicting social behavior.*Englewood Cliffs, NJ: Prentice Hall.

Allen, D., Sprenkel, D., and Vitale, P. (1994). Reactance theory and alcohol consumption laws: Further confirmation among collegiate alcohol consumers. *Journal of Studies on Alcohol, 55,* 34-40.

Andrews, J. (1995). The effectiveness of alcohol warning labels: A review and extension. *American Behavioral Scientist, 38,* 622-632.

Andrews, J. A., Hampson, S. E., Barckley, M., Gerrard, M., and Gibbons, F. X. (2008). The effect of early cognitions on cigarette and alcohol use during adolescence. *Psychology of Addictive Behaviors, 22,* 96-106.

Andrews, J. A., Hops, H., and Duncan, S. C. (1997). Adolescent modeling of parent substance use: The moderating effect of the relationship with the parent. *Journal of Family Psychology, 11,* 259-270.

Andrews, J. A., Tildesley, E., Hops, H., and Li, F. (2002). The influence of peers on young adult substance use. *Health Psychology, 21,* 349-357.

Armitage, C. J., and Conner, M. (2001). Efficacy of the theory of planned behaviour: A meta-analytic review. *British Journal of Social Psychology, 40,* 471-499.

Arnett, J. J. (2000). Emerging adulthood: A theory of development from the late teens through the twenties. *American Psychologist, 55,* 469-480.

Bachman, J. G., Wadsworth, K. N., O'Malley, P. M., Johnston, L. D., and Schulenberg, J. (1997). *Smoking, drinking, and during use in young adulthood: The impacts of new freedoms and new responsibilities.* Mahwah, NJ: Lawrence Erlbaum Associates.

Baer, J. S. (2002). Student factors: Understanding individual variation in college drinking. *Journal of Studies on Alcohol, 14* (Suppl. 14), 40-53.

Baer, J. S., MacClean, M. G., and Marlatt, G. A. (1998). Linking etiology and treatment for adolescent substance use: Toward a better match. In R. Jessor (Ed.), *New perspectives on adolescent risk behavior* (pp.182-220). New York, NY US: Cambridge University Press.

Bandura, A. (1969). *Principles of behavior modification.* New York: Holt, Rinehart, and Winston.

Bandura, A. (1977). *Social learning theory.* Englewood Cliffs, NJ: Prentice Hall.

Bandura A. (1986). *Social foundations of thought and action: A social cognitive theory.* Englewood Cliffs, NJ: Prentice Hall.

Basen-Engquist, K., Edmundson, E., and Parcel, G. (1996). Structure of health risk behavior among high school students. *Journal of Consulting and Clinical Psychology, 64,* 764-775.

Beutler, L. E., Mohr, D. C., Grawe, K., Engle, D., and MacDonald, R. (1991). Looking for differential treatment effects: Cross-cultural predictors of differential psychotherapy efficacy. *Journal of Psychotherapy Integration, 1,* 121-141.

Bingham, C. R., Shope, J. T., and Tang, X. (2005). Drinking behavior from high school to young adulthood: Differences by college education. *Alcoholism: Clinical and Experimental Research, 29,* 2170-2180.

Blanton, H., and Burkley, M. (2008). Deviance regulation theory: Applications to adolescent social influence. In M. J. Prinstein and K. A. Dodge (Eds.), *Understanding peer influence in children and adolescents* (pp. 94-121). New York, NY US: Guilford Press.

Blanton, H. and Christie, C. (2003). Deviance regulation: A theory of action and identity. *Review of General Psychology, 7,* 115-149.

Blanton, H., Gibbons, F. X., Gerrard, M., Conger, K. J., and Smith, G. E. (1997). Role of family and peers in the development of prototypes associated with substance use. *Journal of Family Psychology, 11,* 271-288.

Blanton, H., Koblitz, A., and McCaul, K. D. (2008). Misperceptions about norm misperceptions: Descriptive, injunctive, and affective 'social norming' efforts to change health behaviors. *Social and Personality Psychology Compass, 2/3,* 1379-1399.

Blanton, H., Stuart, A. E., and VandenEijnden, R. J. J. M. (2001). An introduction to deviance-regulation theory: The effect of behavioral norms on message framing. *Personality and Social Psychology Bulletin, 27,* 848-858.

Blume, A., Schmaling, K., and Marlatt, A. (2003). Predictors of change in binge drinking over a 3-month period. *Addictive Behaviors, 28,* 1007-1012.

Borsari, B., and Carey, K. B. (2001). Peer influences on college drinking: A review of the research. *Journal of Substance Abuse, 13,* 391-424.

Botvin, G. J. (2000). Preventing drug abuse in schools: Social and competence enhancement approaches targeting individual-level etiologic factors. *Addictive Behaviors, 25,* 887-897.

Bray, J. H., Adams, G. J., Getz, J. G., and Baer, P.E. (2001). Developmental, family, and ethnic influences on adolescent alcohol usage: A growth curve approach. *Journal of Family Psychology, 15,* 301-314.

Bray, J. H., Adams, G. J., Getz, J. G., and McQueen, A. (2003). Individuation, peers, and adolescent alcohol use: A latent growth analysis. *Journal of Consulting and Clinical Psychology, 71,* 553-564.

Brehm, J. W. (1966). *A theory of psychological reactance.* San Diego, CA: Academic Press.

Brown, S. A., and Tapert, S. F. (2004). Adolescence and the trajectory of alcohol use: Basic to clinical studies. *Annals New York Academy of Sciences, 1021,* 234-244.

Buchmann, A. F., Schmid, B., Blomeyer, D., Becker, K., Treutlein, J., Zimmermann, U. S., et al. (in press). Impact of age of first drink on vulnerability to alcohol-related problems: Testing the marker hypothesis in a prospective study of young adults. *Journal of Psychiatric Research.*

Buunk, B. P., Collins, R. L., Taylor, S. E., Van Yperen, N. W., and Dakof, G. A. (1990). The affective consequences of social-comparison - either direction has its ups and downs. *Journal of Personality and Social Psychology, 59,* 1238-1249.

Buunk, B. P., and Gibbons, F. X. (1997). *Health, coping, and well-being: Perspectives from social comparison theory.* Mahwah, NJ US: Lawrence Erlbaum Associates Publishers.

Cameron, K. A., and Campo, S. (2006). Stepping back from social norms campaigns: Comparing normative influences to other predictors of health behaviors. *Health Communication, 20,* 277-288.

Campo, S., and Cameron, K. A. (2006). Differential effects of exposure to social norms campaigns: A cause for concern. *Health Communication, 19,* 209-219.

Carey, K. B. (1995). Alcohol-related expectancies predict quantity and frequency of heavy drinking among college students. *Psychology of Addictive Behaviors, 9,* 236–241.

Carey, K. B., Borsari, B., Carey, M. P., and Maisto, S. A. (2006). Patterns and importance of self-other differences in college drinking norms. *Psychology of Addictive Behaviors, 20,* 385-393.

Carey, K. B., Scott-Sheldon, L. A. J., Carey, M. P., and DeMartini, K. S. (2007). Individual-level interventions to reduce college student drinking: A meta-analytic review. *Addictive Behaviors, 32,* 2469-2494.

Casswell, S., Pledger, M., and Pratap, S. (2002). Trajectories of drinking from 18 to 26 years: Identification and prediction. *Addiction, 97,* 1427-1437.

Christensen, P. N., Rothgerber, H., Wood, W., and Matz, D. C. (2004). Social norms and identity relevance: A motivational approach to normative behavior. *Personality and Social Psychology Bulletin, 30,* 1295-1309.

Clapp, J. D., Lange, J. E., Russell, C., Shillington, A., and Voas, R. B. (2003). A failed norms social marketing campaign. *Journal of Studies on Alcohol, 64,* 409-414.

Clapper, R., Buka, S., Goldfield, E., and Lipsitt, L. (1995). Adolescent problem behaviors as predictors of adult alcohol diagnoses. *International Journal of the Addictions, 30,* 507-523.

Collins, R. L. (1996). For better or worse: The impact of upward social comparison on self-evaluations. *Psychological Bulletin, 119,* 51-69.

Collins, S. E., and Carey, K. B. (2007). The theory of planned behavior as a model of heavy episodic drinking among college students. *Psychology of Addictive Behaviors, 21,* 498-507.

Conner, M., and Armitage, C. J. (1998). Extending the theory of planned behavior: A review and avenues for further research. *Journal of Applied Social Psychology, 28*, 1429–1464.

Conner, M., Warren, R., Close, S., and Sparks, P. (1999). Alcohol consumption and the theory of planned behavior: An examination of the cognitive mediation of past behavior. *Journal of Applied Social Psychology, 29*, 1676-1704.

Costa, F. M., Jessor, R., and Turbin, M.S. (1999). Transition into adolescent problem drinking: The role of psychosocial risk and protective factors. *Journal of Studies on Alcohol, 60*, 480-490.

Courtney, K. E., and Polich, J. (2009). Binge drinking in young adults: Data, definitions, and determinants. *Psychological Bulletin, 135*, 142-156.

Curran, P. J., Stice, E., and Chassin, L. (1997). The relation between adolescent alcohol use and peer alcohol use: A longitudinal random coefficients model. *Journal of Consulting and Clinical Psychology, 65*, 130-140.

DeCourville, N. H. (1995). Testing the applicability of problem behavior theory to substance use in a longitudinal study. *Psychology of Addictive Behaviors, 9*, 53-66.

DeJong, W., Schneider, S. K., Towvim, L. G., Murphy, M. J., Doerr, E. E., Simonsen, N. R., et al. (2006). A multisite randomized trial of social norms marketing campaigns to reduce college student drinking. *Journal of Studies on Alcohol, 67*, 868-879.

Del Boca, F. K., and Darkes, J. (2001) Is the glass half full or half empty? An evaluation of the status of expectancies as causal agents. *Addiction, 96*, 1681-1683

Dillard, J., and Shen, L. (2005). On the nature of reactance and its role in persuasive health communication. *Communication Monographs, 72*, 144-168.

Dishion, T. J., McCord, J., and Poulin, F. (1999). When interventions harm: Peer groups and problem behavior. *American Psychologist, 54*, 755–764.

Donovan, J. E., and Jessor, R. (1985). Structure of problem behavior in adolescence and young adulthood. *Journal of Consulting and Clinical Psychology, 53*, 890-904.

Donovan, J., Jessor, R., and Costa, F. (1999). Adolescent problem drinking: Stability of psychosocial and behavioral correlates across a generation. *Journal of Studies on Alcohol, 60*, 352-361.

Duncan, S. C., Duncan, T. E., and Strycker, L. A. (2006). Alcohol use from ages 9 to 16: A cohort-sequential latent growth model. *Drug and Alcohol Dependence, 81*, 71-81.

Dunn, M. E., and Goldman, M. S. (1998). Age and drinking-related differences in the memory organization of alcohol expectances in 3rd-, 6th-, 9th-, and 12th-grade children. *Journal of Consulting and Clinical Psychology, 66*, 579–585.

Engels, R. C. M. E., Hermans, R., Baaren, R. B., Hollenstein, T., and Bot, S. M. (2009). Alcohol portrayal on television affects actual drinking behaviour. *Alcohol and Alcoholism, 44*, 244-249.

Engs, R., and Hanson, D. (1989). Reactance theory: A test with collegiate drinking. *Psychological Reports*, *64*, 1083-1086.

Epstein, J. A., Zhou, X. K., Bang, H., and Botvin, G. (2007). Do competence skills moderate the impact of social influences to drink and perceived social benefits of drinking on alcohol use among inner-city adolescents? *Prevention Science, 8*, 65-73.

Farrell, A., Danish, S., and Howard, C. (1992). Relationship between drug use and other problem behaviors in urban adolescents. *Journal of Consulting and Clinical Psychology, 60*, 705-712.

Festinger, L. (1954). A theory of social comparison processes. *Human Relations, 7*, 117-140.

Fishbein, M., and Ajzen, I. *(1975). Belief, attitude, intention, and behavior: An introduction totheory and research.* Reading, MA: Addison-Wesley.

Fromme, K., Stroot, E., and Kaplan, D. (1993). Comprehensive effects of alcohol: Development and psychometric assessment of a new expectancy questionnaire. *Psychological Assessment, 5,* 19-26.

Gerrard, M., Gibbons, F. X., Brody, G. H., McBride Murry, V., Cleveland, M. J., and Wills, T. A. (2006). A theory-based dual-focus alcohol intervention for preadolescents: The strong African American families program. *Psychology of Addictive Behaviors, 20,* 185-195.

Gerrard, M., Gibbons, F. X., Houlihan, A. E., Stock, M. L., and Pomery, E. A. (2008). A dual-process approach to health risk decision making: The prototype willingness model. *Developmental Review, 28,* 29-61.

Gerrard, M., Gibbons, F. X., Reis-Bergan, M., Trudeau, L., Vande Lune, L. S., and Buunk, B. (2002). Inhibitory effects of drinker and nondrinker prototypes on adolescent alcohol consumption. *Health Psychology, 21,* 601-609.

Gibbons, F. X., Gerrard, M., Blanton, H., and Russell, D. W. (1998). Reasoned action and social reaction: Willingness and intention as independent predictors of health risk. *Journal of Personality and Social Psychology, 74,* 1164-1180.

Gibbons, F. X., Gerrard, M., Lane, D. J., Mahler, H. I. M., and Kulik, J. A. (2005). Using UV photography to reduce use of tanning booths: A test of cognitive mediation. *Health Psychology, 24,* 358–363.

Gilles, D. M., Turk, C. L., and Fresco, D. M. (2006). Social anxiety, alcohol expectancies, and self-efficacy as predictors of heavy drinking in college students. *Addictive Behaviors, 31,* 388-398.

Gillmore, M. R., Hawkins, J. D., Catalano, R. F., Day, L. E., Moore, M., and Abbott, R. (1991). Structure of problem behaviors in preadolescence. *Journal of Consulting and Clinical Psychology, 59,* 499–506.

Goldman, M. S., Del Boca, F., and Darkes, J. (1999). Alcohol expectancy theory. In K. E. Leonard and H. T. Blane (Eds.), *Psychological Theories of Drinking and Alcoholism (2nd ed.)* (pp. 203-246). New York: Guilford.

Gordon, R., and Minor, S. (1992). Attitudes toward a change in the legal drinking age: Reactance versus compliance. *Journal of College Student Development, 33,* 171-176.

Grant, B. F., and Dawson, D. A. (1997). Age at onset of alcohol use and its association with DSM-IV alcohol abuse and dependence: Results from the National Longitudinal Alcohol Epidemiologic Survey. *Journal of Substance Abuse, 9,* 103-110.

Grant, J. D., Scherrer, J. F., Lynskey, M. T., Lyons, M. J., Eisen, S. A., Tsuang, M. T., et al. (2006). Adolescent alcohol use is a risk factor for adult alcohol and drug dependence: Evidence from a twin design. *Psychological Medicine, 36,* 109-118.

Ham, L., and Hope, D. (2003). College students and problematic drinking: A review of the literature. *Clinical Psychology Review, 23,* 719-759.

Hatzenbuehler, M., Corbin, W., and Fromme, K. (2008). Trajectories and determinants of alcohol use among LGB young adults and their heterosexual peers: Results from a prospective study. *Developmental Psychology, 44,* 81-90.

Hawkins, J. D., Catalano, R. F., and Miller, J. Y. (1992). Risk and protective factors for alcohol and other drug problems in adolescence and early adulthood: Implications for substance-abuse prevention. *Psychological Bulletin, 112,* 64-105.

Hays, R. D., Stacy, A. W., and DiMatteo, M. R. (1987). Problem behavior theory and adolescent alcohol use. *Addictive Behaviors*, *12*, 189-193.

Helgeson, V. S., and Mickelson, K. D. (1995). Motives for social comparison. *Personality and Social Psychology Bulletin, 21,* 1200-1209.

Heron, M. P. (2007). *Death: Leading causes for 2004.* National Vital Statistics Reports, 56, 1-96. Hyattsville, MD: National Center for Health Statistics.

Hingson, R. W., Heeren, T., and Winter, M. R. (2006). Age at drinking onset and alcohol dependence. *Archives of Pediatrics and Adolescent Medicine, 160,* 739-746.

Hingson, R., Heeren, T., Winter, M., and Wechsler, H. (2005). Magnitude of alcohol-related mortality and morbidity among U.S. college students ages 18-24: Changes from 1998 to 2001. *Annual Review of Public Health, 26,* 259-279.

Hingson, R. W., Heeren, T., Zakocs, R. C., Kopstein, A., and Wechsler, H. (2002). Magnitude of alcohol-related mortality and morbidity among U.S. college students ages 18-24. *Journal of Studies on Alcohol, 63,* 136-144.

Huchting, K., Lac, A., and LaBrie, J. W. (2008). An application of the theory of planned behavior to sorority alcohol consumption. *Addictive Behaviors, 33*, 538-551.

Jessor. R. (1987). Problem-behavior theory, psychosocial development, and adolescent problem drinking. *British Journal of Addiction, 82,* 331-342.

Jessor, R. (1991). Risk behavior in adolescence: A psychosocial framework for understanding and action. *Journal of Adolescent Health, 12,* 597-605.

Jessor, R. (1998). *New perspectives on adolescent risk behavior.* New York, NY US: Cambridge University Press.

Jessor, R., Costa, F., Krueger, P., and Turbin, M. (2006). A developmental study of heavy episodic drinking among college students: The role of psychosocial and behavioral protective and risk factors. *Journal of Studies on Alcohol, 67,* 86-94.

Jessor, R., Donovan, J. E., and Costa, F. M. (1991). *Beyond adolescence: Problem behavior and young adult development.* New York: Cambridge University Press.

Jessor, R., Graves, T. D., Hanson, R. C., and Jessor, S. L. (1968). *Society, personality, and deviant behavior: A study of a tri-ethnic community*. New York: Holt, Rinehart and Winston.

Jessor, R., and Jessor, S. L. (1977). *Problem behavior and psychosocial development: A longitudinal study of youth.* New York: Academic Press.

Jessor, R., Turbin, M. S., Costa, F. M., Dong, Q., Zhang, H., and Wang, C. (2003). Adolescent problem behavior in China and the United States: A cross-national study of psychosocial protective factors. *Journal of Research on Adolescence, 13,* 329–360.

Jessor, R., Van Den Bos, J., Vanderryn, J., Costa, F. M., and Turbin, M. S. (1995). Protective factors in adolescent problem behavior: Moderator effects and developmental change. *Developmental Psychology*, *31*, 923-933.

Johnston, L. D., O'Malley, P. M., Bachman, J. G., and Schulenberg, J. E. (2008). *Monitoring the Future national survey results on drug use, 1975–2007: Volume II, College students and adults ages 19–45* (NIH Publication No. 08-6418B). Bethesda, MD: National Institute on Drug Abuse.

Johnston, L. D., O'Malley, P. M., Bachman, J. G., and Schulenberg, J. E. (2009). *Monitoring the Future national results on adolescent drug use: Overview of key findings, 2008* (NIH Publication No. 09-7401). Bethesda, MD: National Institute on Drug Abuse.

Johnston, K. L., and White, K. M. (2003). Binge-drinking: A test of the role of group norms in the theory of planned behaviour. *Psychology and Health, 18*, 63-77.

Jones, B., Corbin, W., and Fromme, K. (2001). Half full or half empty, the glass still does not satisfactorily quench the thirst for knowledge on alcohol expectancies as a mechanism of change. *Addiction, 96*, 1672-1674.

Jones, E. E., and Davis, K. E. (1965). From acts to dispositions: The attribution process in person perception. In L. Berkowitz (Ed.), *Advance in experimental social psychology* (pp. 220-266). New York: Academic Press.

Kam, J. A., Matsunaga, M., Hecht, M. L., and Ndiaye, K. (2009). Extending the theory of planned behavior to predict alcohol, tobacco, and marijuana use among youth of Mexican heritage. *Prevention Science, 10*, 41-53.

Kaplan, H. B. and Johnson, R. J. (2001). *Social deviance: Testing a general theory*. New York: Kluwer/Plenum.

Kaplan, H. B., Johnson, R. J., and Bailey, C. A. (1987). Deviant peers and deviant behavior: Further elaboration of a model. *Social Psychology Quarterly*, 50, 277-284.

Kaplan, H. B., Martin, S. S., and Robbins, C. (1982). Application of a general theory of deviant behavior: Self-derogation and adolescent drug use. *Journal of Health and Social Behavior, 23*, 274-294.

Kelley, H. H. (1967). Attribution theory in social psychology. *Nebraska Symposium on Motivation, 15,* 192-238.

Kidorf, M., Sherman, M. F., Johnson, J. G., and Bigelow, G. E. (1995). Alcohol expectancies and changes in beer consumption of first-year college students. *Addictive Behaviors, 20,* 225–231.

Kuther, T. L., and Higgins-D'Alessandro, A. (2003). Attitudinal and normative predictors of alcohol use by older adolescents and young adults. *Journal of Drug Education, 33,* 71-90.

Larimer, M. E., and Cronce, J. M. (2002). Identification, prevention, and treatment: A review of individual-focused strategies to reduce problematic alcohol consumption by college students. *Journal of Studies on Alcohol, 14,* 148-163.

Larimer, M. E., and Cronce, J. M. (2007). Identification, prevention, and treatment revisited: Individual-focused college drinking prevention strategies 1999-2006. *Addictive Behaviors, 32,* 2439-2468.

Larimer, M. E., Kaysen, D. L., Lee, C. M., Kilmer, J. R., Lewis, M. A., Dillworth, T., Montoya, H., and Neighbors, C. (2009). Evaluating levels of specificity in normative referents in relation to personal drinking behavior. *Journal of Studies on Alcohol and Drugs,s16,* 115-121.

Larimer, M. E., Lee, C. M., Kilmer, J. R., Fabiano, P. M., Stark, C. B., Geisner, I. M., et al. (2007). Personalized mailed feedback for college drinking prevention: A randomized clinical trial. *Journal of Consulting and Clinical Psychology, 75,* 285-293.

Larsen, H., Engels, R., Granic, I., and Overbeek, G. (2009). An experimental study on imitation of alcohol consumption in same-sex dyads. *Alcohol and Alcoholism, 44,* 250-255.

Latendresse, S. J., Rose, R. J., Viken, R. J., Pulkkinen, L., Kaprio, J., and Dick, D. M. (2008). Parenting mechanisms in links between parents' and adolescents' alcohol use behaviors. *Alcoholism: Clinical and Experimental Research, 32*, 322-330.

Leary, M. R., Tambor, E. S., Terdal, S. K., and Downs, D. L. (1995). Self-esteem as an interpersonal monitor - the Sociometer Hypothesis. *Journal of Personality and Social Psychology, 68,* 518-530.

Lewis, M. A. and Neighbors, C. (2004). Gender-specific misperceptions of college student drinking norms. *Psychology of Addictive Behaviors, 18,* 334-339.

Lewis, M. A. and Neighbors, C. (2007). Optimizing personalized normative feedback: The use of gender-specific referents. *Journal of Studies on Alcohol and Drugs, 68,* 228-237.

Lewis, M. A., Neighbors, C., Oster-Aaland, L., Kirkeby, B. S., and Larimer, M. E. (2007). Indicated prevention for incoming freshmen: Personalized feedback and high-risk drinking. *Addictive Behaviors, 32,* 2495-2508.

Lewis, M. A., Phillippi, J., and Neighbors, C. (2007). Morally based self-esteem, drinking motives, and alcohol use among college students. *Psychology of Addictive Behaviors, 21,* 398-403.

Luhtanen, R. K., and Crocker, J. (2005). Alcohol use in college students: Effects of level of self-esteem, narcissism, and contingencies of self-worth. *Psychology of Addictive Behaviors, 19,* 99-103.

MacAndrew, C., and Edgerton, R. B. (1969). *Drunken comportment: A social explanation.* Oxford, England: Aldine.

MacCorquodale, K., and Meehl, P. E. (1953). Preliminary suggestions as to a formalization of expectancy theory. *Psychological Review, 60,* 55-63.

MacKinnon, D. P., Nohre, L., Cheong, J., and Stacy, A. W. (2001). Longitudinal relationship between the alcohol warning label and alcohol consumption. *Journal Studies on Alcohol, 62,* 221-227.

Maisto, S., Carey, K., and Bradizza, C. (1999). Social learning theory. *Psychological theories of drinking and alcoholism (2nd ed.)* (pp. 106-163). New York: Guilford Press.

Marcoux, B. C. and Shope, J. T. (1997). Application of the theory of planned behavior to adolescent use and misuse of alcohol. *Health Education Research, 12,* 323-331.

Marlatt, G. A. and Donovan, D. M. (2005). *Relapse prevention: Maintenance strategies in the treatment of addictive behaviors (2nd ed.).* New York: Guilford Press.

Martino, S., Collins, R., Ellickson, P., Schell, T., and McCaffrey, D. (2006). Socio-environmental influences on adolescents' alcohol outcome expectancies: A prospective analysis. *Addiction, 101,* 971-983.

Mason, W. A. (2001). Self-esteem and delinquency revisited (again): A test of Kaplan's self-derogation theory of delinquency using latent growth curve modeling. *Journal of Youth and Adolescence, 30,* 83-102.

Mattern, J. L.,and Neighbors, C. (2004). Social norms campaigns: examining the relationship between changes in perceived norms and changes in drinking levels. *Journal of Studies on Alcohol, 65,* 489-493.

McCarthy, D., Aarons, G., and Brown, S. (2002). Educational and occupational attainment and drinking behavior: An expectancy model in young adulthood. *Addiction, 97,* 717-726.

McMillan, B., and Conner, M. (2003). Using the theory of planned behaviour to understand alcohol and tobacco use in students. *Psychology, Health and Medicine, 8,* 317-328.

Miller, C. H., Lane, L. T., Deatrick, L. M., Young, A. M., and Potts, K. A. (2007). Psychological reactance and promotional health messages: The effects of controlling language, lexical concreteness, and the restoration of freedom. *Health Communication Research, 33,* 219-240.

Miller, P. M., Smith, G. T., and Goldman, M. S. (1990). Emergence of alcohol expectancies in childhood: A possible critical period. *Journal of Studies on Alcohol, 51*, 343–349.

Miller, W. R., and Rollnick, S. (1991). *Motivational interviewing: Preparing people to change addictive behavior.* New York: Guilford.

Miller, W. R., and Rollnick, S. (2002). *Motivational interviewing: Preparing people for* change (2nd ed.). New York: Guilford.

Mitchell, C. M., Beals, J., and Kaufman, C. E. (2006). Alcohol use, outcome expectancies, and HIV risk status among American Indian youth: A latent growth curve model with parallel processes. *Journal of Youth and Adolescence, 35*, 729-740.

Neighbors, C., LaBrie, J. W., Hummer, J. F., Lewis, M. A., Lee, C. M., Desai, S., et al. (2009). Group identification as a moderator of the relationship between social norms and alcohol consumption. Manuscript submitted for publication.

Neighbors, C., Larimer, M. E., and Lewis, M. A. (2004). Targeting misperceptions of descriptive drinking norms: Efficacy of a computer delivered personalized normative feedback intervention. *Journal of Consulting and Clinical Psychology, 72*, 434-447.

Neighbors, C., Lee, C. M., Lewis, M. A., Fossos, N., and Larimer, M. E. (2007). Are social norms the best predictor of outcomes among heavy-drinking college students? *Journal of Studies on Alcohol and Drugs, 68,* 556-565.

Neighbors, C., Lewis, M. A., Bergstrom, R. L., and Larimer, M. E. (2006). Being controlled by normative influences: Self-determination as a moderator of a normative feedback alcohol intervention. *Health Psychology, 25,* 571-579.

Neighbors, C., Palmer, R. S., and Larimer, M. E. (2004). Interest and participation in a college student alcohol intervention study as a function of typical drinking. *Journal of Studies on Alcohol, 65,* 736-740.

Norman, P., Armitage, C. J., and Quigley, C. (2007). The theory of planned behavior and binge drinking: Assessing the impact of binge drinker prototypes. *Addictive Behaviors, 32*, 1753-1768.

Norman, P., and Conner, M. (2006). The theory of planned behaviour and binge drinking: Assessing the moderating role of past behaviour within the theory of planned behaviour. *British Journal of Health Psychology, 11*, 55-70.

O'Callaghan, F. V., Chant, D. C., Callan, V. J., and Baglioni, A. (1996). Models of alcohol use by young adults: An examination of various attitude–behavior theories. *Journal of Studies on Alcohol, 58*, 502–507.

O'Connor, R. M., Farrow, S., and Colder, C. R. (2008). Clarifying the anxiety sensitivity and alcohol use relation: Considering alcohol expectancies as moderators. *Journal of Studies on Alcohol and Drugs*, *69*, 765-772.

O'Malley, P. M., and Johnston, L. D. (2002). Epidemiology of alcohol and other drug use among

American college students. *Journal of Studies on Alcohol, 14,* 23-39.

Oetting, E. R., and Beauvais, F. (1986). Peer cluster theory: Drugs and the adolescent. *Journal of Counseling and Development*, *65*, 17-22.

Oetting, E. R., and Beauvais, F. (1987). Peer cluster theory, socialization characteristics, and adolescent drug use: A path analysis. *Journal of Counseling Psychology, 34,* 205-213.

Oetting, E. R., and Lynch, R. S. (2006). Peers and the prevention of adolescent drug use. In Z. Sloboda and W. J. Bukoski (Eds.), *Handbook of drug abuse prevention: Theory, science, and practice* (pp.101-127). New York, NY: Springer.

Ouellette, J. A., and Wood, W. (1998). Habit and intention in everyday life: The multiple processes by which past behavior predicts future behavior. *Psychological Bulletin, 124,* 54-74.

Perkins, H., and Berkowitz, A. (1989). Stability and contradiction in college students' drinking following a drinking-age law change. *Journal of Alcohol and Drug Education, 35,* 60-77.

Perkins, H. W., and Craig, D. W. (2006). A successful social norms campaign to reduce alcohol misuse among college student-athletes. *Journal of Studies on Alcohol, 67,* 880-889.

Petraitis, J., Flay, B. R., and Miller, T. Q. (1995). Reviewing theories of adolescent substance use: Organizing pieces in the puzzle. *Psychological Bulletin, 117,* 67-86.

Perkins, H. W., Haines, M. P., and Rice, R. (2005). Misperceiving the college drinking norm and related problems: A nationwide study of exposure to prevention information, perceived norms and student alcohol misuse. *Journal of Studies on Alcohol, 66,* 470-478.

Quigley, B. M., and Collins, R. L. (1999). The modeling of alcohol consumption: A meta-analytic review. *Journal of Studies of Alcohol, 60,* 90-98.

Radin, S. M., Neighbors, C., Walker, P. S., Walker, R. D., Marlatt, G. A., and Larimer, M. E. (2006). The changing influences of self-worth and peer deviance on drinking problems in urban American Indian adolescents. *Psychology of Addictive Behaviors, 20,* 161-170.

Rains, S. A., and Turner, M. M. (2007). Psychological reactance and persuasive health communication: A test and extension of the intertwined model. *Health Communication Research, 33,* 241-269.

Read, J. P., Wood, M. D., and Capone, C. (2005). A prospective investigation of relations between social influences and alcohol involvement during the transition into college. *Journal of Studies on Alcohol, 66,* 23-34.

Reed, M. B., Lange, J. E., Ketchie, J. M., and Clapp, J. D. (2007). The relationship between social identity, normative information, and college student drinking. *Social Influence, 2,* 269-294.

Ricciardelli, L., and McCabe, M. (2008). University students' perceptions of the alcohol campaign: "Is getting pissed getting pathetic? (Just ask your friends)". *Addictive Behaviors, 33,* 366-372.

Rivis, A., Sheeran, P., and Armitage, C. J. (2006). Augmenting the theory of planned behaviour with the prototype/willingness model: Predictive validity of actor versus abstainer prototypes for adolescents' health-protective and health-risk intentions. *British Journal of Health Psychology, 11,* 483-500.

Rotter, J. (1954). *Social learning and clinical psychology.* Englewood Cliffs, NJ: Prentice-Hall, Inc.

Substance Abuse and Mental Health Services Administration. (2008). *Results from the 2007 National Survey on Drug Use and Health: National findings.* Office of Applied Studies. Rockville, MD.

Schell, T., Martino, S., Ellickson, P., Collins, R., and McCaffrey, D. (2005). Measuring developmental changes in alcohol expectancies. *Psychology of Addictive Behaviors, 19,* 217-220.

Schinke, S. P., Cole, K. C. A., and Fang, L. (2009). Gender-specific intervention to reduce underage drinking among early adolescent girls: A test of a computer-mediated, mother-daughter program. *Journal of Studies on Alcohol and Drugs, 70,* 70-77.

Schlegel, R. P., D'Avernas, J. R., Zanna, M. P., DeCourville, N. H., and Manske, S. R. (1992). Problem drinking: A problem for the theory of reasoned action? *Journal of Applied Social Psychology, 22,* 358–385.

Schroeder, C. M., and Prentice, D. A. (1998). Exposing pluralistic ignorance to reduce alcohol use among college students. *Journal of Applied Social Psychology, 28,* 2150-2180.

Schulenberg, J. E., and Maggs, J. L. (2002). A developmental perspective on alcohol use and heavy drinking during adolescence and the transition to young adulthood. *Journal of Studies on Alcohol, 14,* 54-70.

Sher, K. J., Wood, M. D., Wood, P. K., and Raskin, G. (1996). Alcohol outcome expectancies and alcohol use: A latent variable cross-lagged panel study. *Journal of Abnormal Psychology, 105,* 561-574.

Shoham, V., Trost, S., and Rohrbaugh, M. (2004). From state to trait and back again: Reactance theory goes clinical. *Motivational analyses of social behavior: Building on Jack Brehm's contributions to psychology* (pp. 167-185). Mahwah, NJ US: Lawrence Erlbaum Associates Publishers.

Shoham-Salomon, V., and Hannah, M. T. (1991). Client-treatment interaction in the study of differential change processes. *Journal of Consulting and Clinical Psychology, 57,* 590-598.

Slutske, W. (2005). Alcohol use disorders among U.S. college students and their non-college-attending peers. *Archives of General Psychiatry, 62,* 321-327.

Smith, G. T., Goldman, M. S., Greenbaum, P. E., and Christiansen, B. A. (1995). Expectancy of social facilitation from drinking: The divergent paths of high-expectancy and low-expectancy adolescents. *Journal of Abnormal Psychology, 104,* 32-40.

Spijkerman, R., van den Eijnden, R. J. J. M., Vitale, S., and Engels, R. C. M. E. (2004). Explaining adolescents' smoking and drinking behavior: The concept of smoker and drinker prototypes in relation to variables of the theory of planned behavior. *Addictive Behaviors, 29,* 1615-1622.

Squeglia, L. M., Jacobus, J., and Tapert, S. F. (2009). The influence of substance use on adolescent brain development. *Clinical EEG and Neuroscience Journal, 40,* 31-38.

Stapel, D. A., and Blanton, H. (2007). *Social comparison theories: Key readings*. New York: Psychology Press.

Stein, J. A., Newcomb, M. D., and Bentler, P. M. (1987). Personality and drug use: Reciprocal effects across four years. *Personality and Individual Differences, 8,* 419-430.

Stuart, A. E., and Blanton, H. (2003). The effects of message framing on behavioral prevalence assumptions. *European Journal of Social Psychology, 33,* 93-102.

Suls, J., and Green, P. (2003). Pluralistic ignorance and college student perceptions of gender-specific alcohol norms. *Health Psychology, 22,* 479-486.

Suls, J., and Wheeler, L. (2000). *Handbook of social comparison: Theory and research.* (vols.2000) Dordrecht, Netherlands: Kluwer Academic Publishers.

Suls, J., and Wills, T. A. (1991). *Social comparison: Contemporary theory and research.* Hillsdale, NJ England: Lawrence Erlbaum Associates, Inc.

Swaim, R. C., Oetting, E. R., Edwards, R. W., and Beauvais, F. (1989). Links from emotional distress to adolescent drug use: A path model. *Journal of Consulting and Clinical Psychology, 57*, 227-231.

Tajfel, H., and Turner, J. C. (1986). The social identity theory of intergroup behavior. In S. Worchel and W. G. Austin (Eds.), *Psychology of intergroup relations* (pp. 7-24). Chicago: Nelson-Hall.

Tevyaw, T. O., Borsari, B., Colby, S. M., and Monti, P. M. (2007). Peer enhancement of a brief motivational intervention with mandated college students. *Psychology of Addictive Behaviors, 21,* 114-119.

Thombs, D. L., and Hamilton, M. J. (2002). Effects of a social norm feedback campaign on the drinking norms and behavior of Division I student-athletes. *Journal of Drug Education, 32*, 227-244.

Thush, C., and Wiers, R.W. (2007). Explicit and implicit alcohol-related cognitions and the prediction of future drinking in adolescents. *Addictive Behaviors, 32,* 1367-1383.

Tolman, E. (1932). *Purposive behavior in animals and men.* London England: Century/Random House.

Turner, J. C., Hogg, M. A., Oakes, P. J., Reicher, S. D., and Wetherell, M. S. (1987).*Rediscovering the social group: A self-categorization theory.* Oxford, UK: Blackwell.

U.S. Department of Health and Human Services. (2007). *The Surgeon General's Call to Action To Prevent and Reduce Underage Drinking.* Department of Health and Human Services, Office of the Surgeon General. Washington, DC.

Valdivia, I., and Stewart, S.H. (2005). Further examination of the psychometric properties of the comprehensive effects of alcohol questionnaire. *Cognitive Behaviour Therapy, 34*, 22-33.

Wall, A., Hinson, R., McKee, S., and Goldstein, A. (2001). Examining alcohol outcome expectancies in laboratory and naturalistic bar settings: A within-subject experimental analysis. *Psychology of Addictive Behaviors, 15*, 219-226.

Wall, A., McKee, S., and Hinson, R. (2000). Assessing variation in alcohol outcome expectancies across environmental context: An examination of the situational-specificity hypothesis. *Psychology of Addictive Behaviors, 14*, 367-375.

Walter, S. T., and Neighbors, C. (2005). Feedback interventions for college alcohol misuse: What, why and for whom? *Addictive Behaviors, 30,* 1168-1182.

Wechsler, H., Davenport, A., Dowdall, G., Moeykens, B., and Castillo, S. (1994). Health and behavioral consequences of binge drinking in college: A national survey of students at 140 campuses. *Journal of the American Medical Association, 272,* 1672-1677.

Wechsler, H., Lee, J. E., Nelson, T. F., and Lee, H. (2003). Drinking and driving among college students: The influence of alcohol-control policies. *American Journal of Preventive Medicine, 25*, 212-218.

Weiss, B., Caron, A., Ball, S., Tapp, J., Johnson, M., and Weisz, J. R. (2005). Iatrogenic effects of group treatment for antisocial youths. *Journal of Consulting and Clinical Psychology, 73,* 1036–1044.

Werch, C. E., Pappas, D. M., Carlson, J. M., DiClemente, C. C., Chally, P. S. and Sinder, J. A. (2000). Results of a social norm intervention to prevent binge drinking among first-year residential college students. *Journal of American College Health, 49,* 85-92.

Wheeler, L. (1966). Motivation as a determinant of upward comparison. *Journal of Experimental Social Psychology, 2,* 27-31.

White, H. R., McMorris, B. J., Catalano, R. F., Fleming, C. B., Haggerty, K. P., and Abbott, R. D. (2006). Increases in alcohol and marijuana use during the transition out of high school into emerging adulthood: The effects of leaving home, going to college, and high school protective factors. *Journal of Studies on Alcohol, 67,* 810-822.

Willoughby, T., Chalmers, H., and Busseri, M. (2004). Where is the syndrome? Examining co-occurrence among multiple problem behaviors in adolescence. *Journal of Consulting and Clinical Psychology, 72*, 1022-1037.

Wills, T. A. (1981). Downward comparison principles in social psychology. *Psychological Bulletin, 90,* 245-271.

Yanovitzky, I., Stewart, L. P., and Lederman, L. C. (2006). Social distance, perceived drinking by peers, and alcohol use by college students. *Health Communication, 19*, 1-10.

Young, R. M., Connor, J. P., Ricciardelli, L. A. and Saunders, J. B. (2006). The role of alcohol expectancy and drinking refusal self-efficacy beliefs in university student drinking. *Alcohol and Alcoholism, 41*, 70-75.

Young, R. M., Hasking, P. A. Oei, T. P. S. and Loveday, W. (2007). Validation of the drinking refusal self-efficacy questionnaire: Revised in an adolescent sample (DRSEQ-RA). *Addictive Behaviors, 32*, 862-868.

In: Social Drinking: Uses, Abuses and Psychological Factors ISBN: 978-1-60876-219-4
Editors : K. T. Everly, E. M. Cosell, pp. 141-175 © 2010 Nova Science Publishers, Inc.

Chapter 3

ADOLESCENT DRINKING: THE SOCIAL INFLUENCE OF THE FAMILY

Elizabeth Maloney, Delyse Hutchinson, Laura Vogl, Cecilia Essau, and Richard Mattick
University of New South Wales, Sydney, NSW, Australia

ABSTRACT

Alcohol is among one of the most commonly used substances among young people in Western culture. Nationally representative survey data (n=44,346) on students from the United States (US) show that alcohol use is extremely common, with 75% of students surveyed reporting consumption of alcohol (more than just a few sips) by the end of high school [Johnston, O'Malley, & Bachman, 2002]. According to the 2005 US National Survey on Drug Use and Health (NSDUH) [SAMHSA: Substance Abuse and Mental Health Services Administration, 2007], 28.2% of 12-20 year olds reported drinking alcohol in the past month. Of these, 18.8% were binge drinkers (i.e., 5 or more drinks on the same occasion) and 6% were heavy drinkers (i.e., binge drinking on at least 5 days in the past month). Prevalence statistics from other industrialised countries show similarly frequent levels of alcohol use and misuse in young people [Babor et al., 2003].

The burden associated with drinking in young people is considerable, accounting globally for five percent of all deaths of people aged between 5 and 29 years of age [Editorial, 2008; Jernigan, 2001]. Additionally, research suggests underage and binge drinking among young people is associated with a number of acute and long-term negative outcomes including poor school performance, engaging in risky behaviours, physical injury, memory loss, learning deficits, and an increased risk of developing alcohol dependence [Miller, Naimi, Brewer, & Everett Jones, 2007]. Alcohol related harm is a major component of preventable health and social costs experienced by young people [Cagney & Palmer, 2007b].

Individual, school, community and family characteristics have been identified as risk factors for the development of adolescent alcohol use [Hawkins, Catalano, & Miller, 1992]. Whilst this chapter briefly reviews these areas, the predominant focus will be on the role of the family. It is widely acknowledged that the family plays a critical role in the development and socialisation of alcohol use in young people. A considerable body of empirical work has been dedicated to understanding the role of the family, particularly parenting influences on adolescent alcohol initiation and patterns of alcohol use. This chapter will review a range of theorised familial influences on adolescent drinking. In particular, the impacts of three key areas of social influence by parents will be examined: (1) parental supply of alcohol use; (2) parental attitudes to drinking; and, (3) parental modeling of alcohol use on adolescent drinking outcomes. Finally, the implications and recommendations for working with parents and families to delay alcohol initiation and prevent alcohol misuse are overviewed.

INTRODUCTION

Prevalence and Patterns of Adolescent Drinking

Alcoholic beverages have been among the most widely used substances by adolescents in most Western societies. The use of alcohol is both a popular and a generally accepted activity among adolescents. Drinking is regarded as integral to a night out and heavy drinking is used by some young people to establish and maintain friendships. In fact, it is the 'group' aspect of the drinking session that makes getting drunk fun for many adolescents.

The number of epidemiological studies on the prevalence of alcohol use in adolescents has been accumulative in recent years. Methodological differences, however, in the assessment instruments, age groups, countries, and settings make it difficult to make a direct comparison of findings across studies [Essau, Barrett, & Pasquali, 2002]. Furthermore, the introduction of "alcopops" (i.e., soft drinks with a small amount of alcohol) and bottled mixed drinks in the mid-1990s has changed the patterns of adolescent alcohol use, making it difficult to compare the trends in drinking. Alcopops and mixed drinks are among the most popular alcoholic drinks, accounting for a significant increase in alcohol consumption among 13- to 16-year olds [Roberts, Blakey, & Tudor Smith, 1999; Ter Bogt, van Dorsselaer, & Vollebergh, 2002]. Among females drinking at high risk levels, for example, there was a four-fold increase (21% to 78%) in consumption rates of premixed spirits over a four year period (2000-2004), with similar but less pronounced trends for males [King, Taylor, & Carroll, 2005].

It is well recognised that cross-national comparisons are also likely to be less precise if they are not collected as part of a co-ordinated study (Babor et al 2003). To address such a limitation the World Health Organisation commenced the World Mental Health survey initiative [Degenhardt et al., 2008]. The aim of this initiative was to utilise the same methodology to collect data on the prevalence and correlates of a wide variety of mental and substance disorders across the world. Although considerable effort was expended to ensure that countries from every region in the world were represented in the consortium, some areas are yet to be represented (e.g., French speaking West Africa). Cross-national survey data has however, been collected from 17 countries, with a combined sample size of 85,052 participants from the Americas (Colombia, Mexico, United States), Europe (Belgium, France, Germany, Italy, Netherlands, Spain, Ukraine), Middle East and Africa (Israel, Lebanon, Nigeria, South Africa), Asia (Japan, People's Republic of China) and Oceania (New Zealand). Although this survey does not specifically address alcohol use in adolescence, it does show that lifetime prevalence of alcohol use was reported by the majority of respondents in the Americas, Europe, Japan and New Zealand, while considerably smaller proportion had ever used alcohol in the Middle East, Africa and China. The median age of onset was between 16-19 years of age for alcohol in all countries except South Africa, where the median was 20 years of age. Alcohol use by 15 years of age was also far more common in European countries than in the Middle East and Africa. Results revealed that by age 21, the vast majority of young adults in European countries (76-99%), Japan (92%), New Zealand (94%) and the Americas had begun using alcohol. Given the concentration of alcohol use in these regions of the world, this review will focus specifically on the consumptions of alcohol by adolescents in some of the countries within these regions.

Alcohol use in the US

In the US, alcohol use in adolescence has been assessed by two extensive national epidemiologic studies of drug use: the Monitoring the Future study (MTF) [Johnston et al., 2002] and the National Survey on Drug Use and Health (NSDUH) [SAMHSA: Substance Abuse and Mental Health Services Administration, 2003], which was previously called the National Household Survey on Drug Abuse.

For the MTF study, more than 46,000 US students in grades 8 (~13 years of age), 10 (~15 years of age), and 12 (~17 years of age) in almost 400 secondary schools were surveyed in 2008 [Johnston, O'Malley, Bachman, & Schulenberg, 2009]. Alcohol use remained very common. By the end of high school about three-quarters (72%) of the students reported consuming alcohol. The annual prevalence of alcohol drinking among 8th, 10th, and 12th graders were 32.1%, 52.5%, and 65.5%, respectively. Of these adolescents, 0.7%, 1%, and 2.8% of the 8th, 10th, and 12th graders, respectively, used alcohol on a daily basis. Almost half (45.6%) of the 12th graders and 12.7% of the 8th graders reported having been drunk at least once in their life. The rate for binge drinking (i.e., having 5 or more drinks in a row at least once in the past 2 weeks; the definition of a standard drink in the US is 14 grams of ethanol) was 8.1% for 8th, 16% for 10th, and 24.6% for 12th graders.

Despite alcohol use being common among adolescents, in the MTF study a general decline in the use of alcohol was noted since peaks in use during the mid-1990s. The proportional declines were smaller for the older than the younger students. The greater long-term decline in use among 8th graders could have been related to the greater decline in the reported availability of alcohol. The percentage of the 8th graders who reported being drunk also continued to decline.

The National Survey on Drug Use and Health (NSDUH), directed by the Substance Abuse and Mental Health Services Administration (SAMHSA), provides annual estimates of prevalence, incidence, demographic distribution of use of illicit drugs, alcohol, and tobacco among those living in the United States aged 12 or older. In its 2007 survey, 67,870 interviews were carried out across the 50 states. According to the 2007 survey [SAMHSA, 2008], the prevalence of current alcohol use among youths aged 12 to 17 was 15.9%. The rates for binge and heavy drinking were 9.7 and 2.3 percent for 12 to 17 year olds respectively. More than half (56.3%) of current drinkers aged 12 to 20 reported that their last use of alcohol (past month use) was in someone else's home; while 29.4% reported that it was in their own home. The past month prevalence for alcohol use differs across ethnic groups. Specifically, among 12 to 20 year olds, past month alcohol use rates were highest among whites (32%), followed by American Indians or Alaska Natives (28.3%); the lowest rates were found among Asians (16.8%).

Alcohol use in Japan

Many adolescents in Japan consume alcohol despite it being illegal to consume alcohol under the age of 20 years. This is evident from a nation-wide survey which has been conducted on adolescent alcohol use in Japan in 1996, 2000 and 2004 [Osaki et al., 2009]. In each of the survey years, between 1-2% of Japanese junior (12-15 years of age) and senior high schools (15 -18 years of age) were randomly selected to participate. In 2004 this meant that 102,451 students completed the survey (response rate: 60.7% junior high school, 67.7% senior high school). In 2004, 53.3% of male and 57% of female junior high school students reported having used alcohol in their lifetime. In senior high, 25% of males and 77% of females reported lifetime alcohol use. Weekly alcohol use was reported by 3.9% of male and 2.9% of female junior high students and 10% of male and 6.5% of female senior school students. For all senior and junior students the prevalence of daily alcohol use was less than 1%. In terms of drinking to intoxication (defined by 6 drinks and over; the definition of a standard drink in Japan is 19.75 grams of ethanol) 7.2% of junior males and 5.6% of females reported such behaviour. In the senior school sample, 21.3% of males and 12.1% of females reported drinking to intoxication. Of the alcohol related harms assessed (vomiting, fighting, black out, trouble with police, scalding by parent), the most frequent harms reported were vomiting, black out and scolding by parents. In examining the patterns of alcohol user over time by Japanese adolescents, the prevalence of lifetime, current and weekly alcohol use has decreased in the 2004 survey in comparison with the 1996 and 2000 survey results.

Alcohol use in Europe

Most information on the prevalence of alcohol use among adolescents across Europe has come from the European Schools Project on Alcohol and other Drugs (ESPAD) [Morgan et al., 1999]. This survey collects data on adolescent alcohol and drug use (from 1995) in 26 European countries. Since 1995, ESPAD has been conducted every four years. In its latest version (i.e., 2007) the survey was conducted in 35 European countries with over 100, 000 students. The 2007 survey found that: (i) The majority (90%) of students reported having drank alcohol at least once in their lifetime; (ii) Approximately one quarter reported regular alcohol use (i.e., at least 40 times in their lifetime), and (iii) Countries with the highest percentages of students indicating that they have been drunk 10 times or more include Denmark, the Isle of Man and the United Kingdom. The lowest rates of frequent intoxication were reported in countries such as Armenia, Cyprus, Portugal, Romania, Greece, Italy and Belgium (<5%). The results suggest that cultural factors play an important role and account for some of the difference in the frequency of alcohol consumption across European countries. For example, in some countries, alcohol is associated with socializing and cultural celebrations. Additionally, some countries (e.g., Greece) do not have any age limit on the sale of alcohol [Kokkevi et al., 2007].

There are numerous smaller scale studies and government surveys conducted in different European countries such as in England [e.g. Bellis et al., 2006], the Netherlands [De Zwart, Monshouwer, & Smit, 2000; Poelen, Scholte, Engels, Boomsma, & Willemsen, 2005], in Germany [Essau, Karpinski, Petermann, & Conradt, 1998; Wittchen, Nelson, & Lachner, 1998], and in Poland [Sprawozdanie, 2006]. Overall, the results showed similar findings to those reported in the ESPAD, with few exceptions. Notable was an increase in the prevalence of binge drinking (daily intake of more than 6-8 and 4-6 units for men and women respectively) in England [Essau, Mohiyeddini, & Bray, 2009], which has been regarded as related to the introduction of the new Licensing Act 2003 which came into effect in November 2005 [Parlimentary Office of Science and Technology (POST), 2005]. The new law allows the extension of opening times to 24 hours seven days a week for licensed venues, with the argument that extending opening times may reduce the practice of 'stocking up' with alcohol shortly before closing time, and that by staggering the closing times, the number of people disgorging on the streets could be reduced.

Another interesting finding was the significant increase in the rate of alcohol use among adolescents in Poland after the transformation of the political system in 1989 from a socialist to a capitalist system, and following Poland's accession to the European Union in 2004 [Bokszczanin, Essau, & O'Callaghan, 2009]. In comparison with the period before these political changes, the consumption of beer and vodka increased considerably among Polish adolescents.

Alcohol use in Australia and New Zealand

The Australian Secondary Students' Alcohol and Drug Survey (ASSAD) is a secondary school based survey conducted throughout Australia, which began in 1984 [White & Hayman, 2006b]. The 2005 survey showed a high percentage of alcohol use among adolescents, with 86% of the 14-year olds and 96% of the 17-year olds ever having tried alcohol in their life. Among current drinkers, a small proportion of 13-year olds (2%) and just under a quarter of 17-year olds (21%) reported consuming alcohol at a risky level (defined by the Australian Alcohol Guidelines, i.e., 7 or more drinks in one day for males and 5 or more drinks in one day for females; the definition of a standard drink in Australia is 10 grams of ethanol) on at least one occasion in the week prior to the survey. The survey found that females were most likely to consume premixed spirits, whereas males were more likely to consume beer. Parents were a common source of obtaining alcohol for both younger (39%) and older students (35%). The ASSAD surveys show a decline in the prevalence of current drinking among adolescents during the 1980s and then an increase in the 1990s, with no significant changes in 2005.

The ALAC Alcohol Monitor is a New Zealand survey which examines adult and youth drinking behaviour on a quarterly basis [Palmer, Fryer, & Kalafatelis, 2007c]. In the overall report for 2006-2007 surveys, a total of 1204 young people had been surveyed. Eighty-one percent of the 12-17 year olds reported having tried alcohol in their lifetime, with 52% reporting that they were current drinkers. According to this survey the average age at which young people reported "really" starting to drink alcohol was 13.8 years of age. One percent of 12-17 year olds reported drinking on a daily basis and 8% reported drinking 2-3 times per week. For those young people who consume alcohol, on the last drinking occasion they report drinking 6.1 standard drinks per occasion (the definition of a standard drink in New Zealand is 10 grams of ethanol). Forty-one percent reported drinking more than 5 standard drinks on the last drinking occasion, and 54% reported having ever consumed more than 5 standard drinks.

Burden Association with Adolescent Drinking

Research suggests underage and binge drinking among young people is associated with a number of acute negative outcomes including poor school performance, trouble with the police, engaging in risky behaviours (e.g. unprotected sexual intercourse, drink driving), physical injury, violence, use of illicit drugs, and suicidal behaviours [Kypri et al., 2009; Lavikainen, Ahlstrom, Metso, Nevalainen, & Lintonen, 2008; Miller et al., 2007; Swahn, Bossarte, & Sullivent, 2008; Wagner & Anthony, 2002]. Research has also identified a number of long-term harms associated with heavy alcohol use during adolescence including memory loss, learning deficits, and an increased risk of developing alcohol dependence [Miller et al., 2007]. Additionally, alcohol abuse/dependence in adolescents are often associated with impairment in various life areas such as negative interpersonal relationships, increase in family conflict, decline in academic functioning, antisocial behaviours and legal problems, failing to fulfil major role obligations, experiencing more psychological distress and recurrent social or interpersonal problems [Myers, Stewart, & Brown, 1998].

The consequences of risky drinking become more tangible when we consider that in the US in 2001, 3,170 deaths (from motor vehicle accidents, interpersonal violence, drowning, suicide, burns, alcohol poisoning) and over 2.5 million injuries could be attributed to underage drinking [Miller, Levy, Spicer, & Taylor, 2006]. Often alcohol consumption during adolescence is disregarded as a phase of experimentation that adolescents pass through in their transition to adulthood [Bonomo, Bowes, Coffey, Carlin, & Patton, 2004; Shanahan, Wilkins, & Hurt, 2002]. These figures suggest, however, that identifying and preventing alcohol misuse in young people is essential considering the high burden of harm identified and immense costs to society borne by such behaviour.

In addition to its proximal consequences, alcohol use early in life is associated with an increased risk of AUD and associated psychopathology in adulthood [Anthony & Petronis, 1995b; Dawson, Goldstein, Chou, Ruan, & Grant, 2008; Lewinsohn, Rohde, & Seeley, 1996]. Research suggests that if you delay the age of onset of alcohol use before the age of 14, each year delay in initiation decreases the risk of alcohol abuse (by 8%) and dependence (by 14%) [Grant, Stinson, & Harford, 2001]. Additionally, those who start drinking at an early age are also more likely to experience longer episodes of an alcohol use disorder, with greater symptom severity (including blackouts and tolerance), and go on to require treatment for alcohol abuse as an adult [Gruber, DiClemente, Anderson, & Lodico, 1996; Hingson, Heeren, & Winter, 2006]. Furthermore, adolescent alcohol abuse and dependence tend to be quite stable over time [Wagner & Tarolla, 2002], which suggests any negative developmental effects will extend into adulthood.

Despite substantial evidence suggesting that early-onset alcohol use leads to a quicker progression into alcohol dependence, the diverse nature of adolescent alcohol use makes it difficult to ascertain the direction of causality. Recent evidence suggests that early-onset alcohol use is an indicator of risk but not a direct cause of later alcohol dependence, with early-onset illicit drug use and other factors (e.g., behavioural problems, parental psychopathology, and family environment) contributing to the relationship [Behrendt, Wittchen, Hofler, Lieb, & Beesdo, 2009b; King & Chassin, 2007].

RISK FACTORS FOR THE DEVELOPMENT OF ADOLESCENT ALCOHOL USE

A large body of research has examined risks for alcohol problems in young people, however given space constraints, this section is not all-inclusive. The factors for which there was considerable empirical support were selected for review. It should be noted that one of the complexities in this field of research is that risk and protective factors frequently co-occur and interact in complex ways across time, serving to increase or decrease the relative risk for alcohol problems. Adolescents who develop alcohol problems typically report multiple risk factors at different developmental stages, and the relative importance of such risk factors shifts at different developmental stages [e.g., Jacob & Leonard, 1994].

Individual Factors

Research supports a number of individual risk factors for the development of adolescent alcohol use including early childhood emotional and behavioural problems, personality traits and temperament.

Behavioural and emotional problems during childhood and early adolescence have consistently been linked to the development of alcohol misuse in young people [Sher, 1994; Smart et al., 2005]. It is possible to split these problems roughly into two main categories: outwardly directed externalising problems, including symptoms of oppositional defiant disorder, attention deficit hyperactivity disorder, conduct disorder and antisocial personality disorder; or, inwardly directed internalising problems, including symptoms of anxiety and depression. A number of longitudinal studies both within Australia and internationally support the suggestion that childhood behavioural and emotional problems are risk factors for later alcohol abuse/dependence. For example, findings from the Seattle Social Development Project suggest that both externalising and internalising behaviours at age 10 are important predictors of alcohol abuse and dependence at age 21 [Guo, Hawkins, & Hill, 2001]. Additionally, data from the Mater University birth cohort study in Australia indicated that externalising but not internalising symptoms at age 14 years are significantly associated with alcohol use disorders at age 21 years, after controlling for other factors across three sensitive periods: birth, childhood and early adolescence [Alati et al., 2005].

There is also evidence to suggest that personality traits and temperament are important predictors of heavy drinking in young adults [Hawkins et al., 1992]. A birth cohort study, for example, found that youths characterised by high negative emotionality and low constraint at 18 years were predisposed to engage in alcohol abuse as well as a range of other health-risk behaviours at 21 years (violent crime, unsafe sex practices and dangerous driving habits) [Caspi, Begg, & Dickson, 1997].

School Environment or Peer Factors

Considering the amount of time children spend at school, it is not surprising that the school environment has been identified as contributing to the development of adolescent alcohol use. The major school risk factors which have been suggested as contributing to the development of substance use in adolescence include school failure, not completing secondary school and a low commitment to school [Hawkins et al., 1992; Loxley et al., 2004].

A Finnish longitudinal study found that problem drinking at age 26 was directly accounted for by poor school success at age 14 [Pulkkinen & Pitkanen, 1994]. Not completing secondary school has been identified as a risk factor for the initiation of substance use in adolescence; however, the evidence is unclear as to whether this relationship can be explained by earlier developmental influences [Loxley et al., 2004]. Retention in school, for example, is predicted by earlier behavioural problems and school adjustment, making it difficult to assess if a direct relationship to alcohol use exists [Loxley et al., 2004]. Additionally, a 10-year population-based longitudinal study found that the teacher's estimate of a child's problem behaviour at age 8 predicted frequent drunken behaviour during late adolescence [Niemela et al., 2006]. This finding highlights the potential role of the school system in identifying those at risk of adolescent problem behaviours, including alcohol misuse.

Theoretical models suggest that while parents are a primary source of influence on childhood, the influence of peers becomes increasingly important during adolescence [Jacob & Leonard, 1994]. Numerous studies have shown that peer alcohol use is a strong predictor of adolescent alcohol misuse [Sher, Grekin, & Williams, 2005]. It has been proposed that peer influence occurs through two main processes, socialisation and peer selection. Socialisation is the process by which an individual's behaviour is shaped and influenced through peer group association. This influence is thought to occur via modeling and imitation of specific behaviours, increased availability of and access to alcohol, and through value transmission and social reinforcement. Longitudinal studies have provided evidence for a direct effect of peers on the development of problematic drinking patterns. In a study by Fergusson and colleagues [1995], affiliation with substance using peers at age 15 was shown to directly predict alcohol abuse at age 16, after controlling for a range of confounders. A longitudinal study by Curran et al. [1997] found that not only were adolescent and peer alcohol use closely related but earlier levels of adolescent alcohol use predicted later changes in peer use, and vice versa.

Peer or friendship selection is the process by which adolescents choose friends with whom they share similar attitudes and behaviours. A three-wave longitudinal study by Reifman, Watson and McCourt [2006] found that greater presence of individuals considered 'drinking buddies' in a network predicted individual's own later drinking, providing support for the peer selection theory. In support for the socialisation theory discussed above, Reifman et al [2006] found that changes in average network drinking appeared to result from members with different drinking levels being added to and dropped from the network. The findings suggest that young people who share certain prior attributes tend to associate with one another and subsequently influence each other's drinking patterns as a result of continued association.

The relative contribution of parental and peer influences to adolescent alcohol use has been examined in numerous studies. When Reifman et al. [1998] compared the role of peers and parents in the prediction of drinking among adolescents they found peer drinking was the most significant predictor of progression to heavy drinking, followed by low parental monitoring. Similar findings were identified by Rai et al. [2003] in which peer and parental influence was compared using data from six cross-sectional studies conducted over ten years. The authors identified an increased risk for alcohol use in adolescents whose peers were involved in risky behaviours, and low parental monitoring was also associated with greater risk for alcohol use [Rai et al., 2003]. The evidence suggests that the effect of peers mediates the influence of parenting factors on adolescent alcohol use. In line with these conclusions, a recent review by Hayes and colleagues [2004b] suggested that peer effects become particularly important when parent-adolescent relationships are of poorer quality.

Research also suggests that while peer alcohol use is a risk factor for alcohol misuse during adolescence, young people at high risk for the development of alcohol use disorders are often part of more deviant peer networks [Sher et al., 2005]. These networks typically comprise of adolescents from dysfunctional or disadvantaged backgrounds and are characterised by involvement in both licit and illicit drug use, antisocial behaviour and aggression, school truancy, risky sexual behaviour and criminal involvement [Smart et al., 2005; Spooner, Hall, & Lynskey, 2001]. Longitudinal studies suggest that delinquent and substance using peer group affiliation is one of the strongest predictors of both antisocial behavioural patterns and substance use disorders in young people [Fergusson & Horwood, 1996; Fergusson et al., 1995; Hawkins et al., 1992]. Research also suggests that there is a complex range of childhood risks associated with the development of deviant peer affiliations including family social stratification (i.e., low socio-economic status, growing up in a problem neighbourhood), poor family functioning, parental substance use disorder, and individual behavioural predispositions including early anxiety and withdrawal, aggression, conduct problems and drug experimentation [Fergusson & Horwood, 1999; Jacob & Leonard, 1994; Smart et al., 2005].

In summary, the literature has highlighted a number of school environment factors which appear to contribute to the development of alcohol use among adolescents, including poor school performance and retention in school. While causal relationships cannot be determined it is possible that early developmental influences and behavioural problems play a role. There is also strong evidence to suggest that peers play an important role in the development of adolescent alcohol use and misuse. It has been suggested that this can occur through a number of processes, including peer selection, peer socialisation, and the formation of deviant peer networks. The relationships involved are complex, however, and it is likely that a range of childhood risk factors contribute to the formation of peer groups, including family functioning and socio-economic status, parental substance use, and individual behavioural and personality characteristics.

Community or Cultural Factors

Longitudinal research studies have typically ignored the influence of the community on the development of adolescent alcohol misuse in favour of risk factors at an individual or familial level. Community factors, however, can play a role. Evidence from cross-sectional studies suggests that increased levels of perceived neighbourhood disorder are related to increased levels of adolescent alcohol use [Wilson, Syme, Boyce, Battistich, & Selvin, 2005]. Other cross-sectional studies demonstrate the complex array of factors involved when assessing neighbourhood context including alcohol availability, poverty and social cohesion. A study by Duncan and colleagues [2002], for example, found that alcohol availability was higher in areas with elevated levels of poverty which was related to lower levels of social cohesion. Lower social cohesion was associated with an increased perception of neighbourhood problems with adolescent alcohol use, and in turn this perceived view was related to a higher arrest rate in the neighbourhood for adolescent alcohol use [Duncan et al., 2002].

A number of broader cultural factors have also been explored for the development of adolescent alcohol use including cultural norms, laws regarding adolescent alcohol use, differences among ethnic and minority groups, and youth living in rural or remote areas.

It has been suggested that cultural norms regarding adolescent alcohol use act as a powerful influence on adolescent drinking behaviour. Bjarnason and colleagues [2002] examined adolescent alcohol use in 11 European countries and found heavier patterns of use in countries where there are permissive attitudes, compared to countries where the cultural climate is less favourable toward youth alcohol use. A cross-national comparison (of Victoria, Australia; and Oregon and Maine, United States) by Beyers and colleagues [2004] also identified differences in cultural norms concerning patterns of adolescent alcohol use. The factors which were more strongly associated with risk for substance use in Australian adolescents reflected more tolerant norms and attitudes, whereas the risk factors identified for adolescents in the United States cohorts were reflective of social alienation, measured by individual factors such as academic failure, rebelliousness and poor social skills [Beyers et al., 2004]. Policy differences were suggested by the authors as a possible reason for the differences identified, i.e., American abstinence policies associated with punishment for use and Australian harm minimisation policies associated with greater tolerance toward experimentation with drug use [Beyers et al., 2004]. It is likely, however, that other factors, not accounted for in the research also contributed to differences identified (including laws relating to youth alcohol use and socialisation practices surrounding alcohol).

Laws regarding adolescent alcohol use have been shown to influence patterns of youth drinking by directly controlling the availability of alcohol, and indirectly through their effect on cultural attitudes [Hawkins et al., 1992]. There is now strong evidence from studies conducted in the United States, Canada, New Zealand and some other countries to show that decreasing the minimum legal age for both the purchase and use of alcohol can increase youth alcohol use and alcohol related harm [Fell, Fisher, Voas, Blackman, & Tippetts, 2008; Kypri et al., 2006; Shults et al., 2001; Wagenaar & Toomey, 2002]. These studies have monitored the prevalence and patterns of youth alcohol use and alcohol-related mortality and morbidity before and after policy changes to minimum drinking and purchase age laws. A study conducted in New Zealand by Kypri and colleagues [2006], for example, found that lowering the minimum legal purchase age for alcohol from 20 to 18 in 1999 was associated with significant increases in both alcohol-involved crashes and hospitalised injuries among adolescents. Similarly, a review by Shults and colleagues [2001] found that lowering the minimum legal drinking age produced a median increase of 10% in car accidents involving adolescents. Other American laws prohibiting the supply or sale of alcohol to minors (those younger than 21) and the law making it illegal to use a false identification card to purchase alcohol have been shown to reduce the ratio of drinking to nondrinking adolescent drivers involved in fatal crashes [Fell et al., 2008]. These studies support the view that laws regarding adolescent alcohol use are important and can influence risky adolescent drinking patterns and related harms. The evidence suggests that while laws can increase risk, they can also have a protective effect on adolescent drinking.

Research has also observed differences in levels of alcohol use among youth from particular cultural, ethnic or minority groups. Mortality rates attributable to alcohol abuse among indigenous youth in the United States are substantially elevated, particularly among American Indian adolescents (estimated at 15 times higher), compared to other ethnic groups [Mitchell, Beals, Whitesell, & et al, 2008]. While data from the United States shows Anglo Americans report greater prevalence of alcohol use, there are important differences in the patterns and consequences of alcohol use by ethnic minorities [Beauvais, 1998; Johnston et al., 2002]. With significant variation across tribes, Native Americans show the highest rate of harms related to alcohol abuse among any ethnic/indigenous group in the United States, including driving and other accidents and Fetal Alcohol Syndrome [e.g. Beauvais, 1998]. Alcohol has been identified as the most abused substance among African American adolescents, and its use appears to remain stable with increasing age instead of decreasing as it does among Anglo Americans [Henderson, Ma, & Shive, 2002]. Since young people are at higher risk for alcohol abuse and dependence than older individuals, these ethnic and indigenous minority groups are at elevated risk for the development of alcohol misuse and alcohol use disorders. While it has been suggested that differences in youth alcohol use among ethnic minorities in the United States may be a result of differences in family acculturation (i.e. parents who are less acculturated than their adolescents may experience a loss of parental control) [Spooner et al., 2001], there is little research examining ethnic differences in the risk factors for adolescent alcohol misuse in Australia. The research which has been conducted has produced inconsistent findings which are not surprising considering the complex array of risk factors to be considered and the wide range of the ethnic minority groups which could be studied internationally [Bersamin, Paschell, & Flewelling, 2005; Wallace Jr. & Muroff, 2002].

There is a considerable body of research indicating that young indigenous peoples in Australia are also at elevated risk for the development of alcohol problems. The proportion of young indigenous people who drink alcohol is lower than for non-indigenous Australian youth, however more young indigenous Australians consume alcohol at risky or harmful levels (34% versus 29%), with high risk drinking more common among young indigenous males [ABS: Australian Bureau of Statistics, 2006; Saggers & Gray, 1998]. Research has identified a number of risk factors which youth from indigenous communities are exposed to that are likely to contribute to higher rates of alcohol misuse including impoverishment, poor health, overcrowded housing, unemployment, lack of educational qualifications, high crime rates, racism, cultural bereavement and elevated rates of family violence and abuse [Spooner et al., 2001; Stanley, Tomison, & Pocock, 2003].

Australian and international data suggest that youth living in rural or remote areas are more likely to drink alcohol at high risk levels and are at a greater risk for alcohol related problems [ABS, 2006; Bond, Thomas, Toumbourou, Patton, & Catalano, 2000; Johnston et al., 2002]. While research has identified common risk factors for alcohol misuse among adolescents living in urban and rural areas (including peer and family influences), a number of additional factors associated with living in a rural area are thought to compound the risk [D'Onofrio, 1997]. These additional risks include greater economic disadvantage, more limited access to social supports and services, and vulnerability to external factors such as sudden loss of employment (i.e., extreme weather conditions prevent farming or closure of large industries) [D'Onofrio, 1997; Spooner et al., 2001].

In summary, while the literature is limited, a number of cross sectional surveys have highlighted the contribution of community factors in the development of adolescent alcohol misuse, including perceived neighbourhood disorder, poverty, social cohesion and availability of alcohol. Furthermore, the literature has explored the impact of broader cultural factors on adolescent alcohol use and misuse. Research suggests that it is likely that cultural norms in terms of attitudes towards youth drinking, government policies and laws all influence adolescent drinking behaviours. Additionally, research has identified differences in the prevalence of youth alcohol use and the risk factors associated with such use in minority groups, including indigenous or ethnic communities, and those living in rural or remote areas. These differences have important implications for the prevention of adolescent alcohol misuse among these communities.

Family Factors

A considerable amount of research has been conducted to better understand the role of the family and parenting factors in the development of adolescent alcohol misuse. This is not surprising when we consider that the family plays a fundamental role in many aspects of a child's development. The following section will summarise the literature on a range of proposed familial risk factors for alcohol use and misuse including poor family functioning, family structure (i.e family composition; dual, single or blended families) and low socioeconomic background, disruptions in parenting, and poor parent-adolescent relationship quality.

The evidence suggests that adolescents who develop alcohol related problems typically report problems in family functioning. These families are commonly characterised by high levels of family disorganisation (i.e., low levels of family organisation), more family conflict (and/or parent-child conflict specifically), low family support, low family control and greater levels of family stress [Bray, Adams, Getz, & Baer, 2001; Colder & Chassin, 1999; Duncan, Duncan, Biglan, & Ary, 1998; Foxcroft & Lowe, 1991]. It has been suggested that poor family functioning increases the risk for adolescent alcohol misuse by impacting negatively on parenting and disrupting child development and socialisation processes [Jacob & Leonard, 1994; Lowe, Foxcroft, & Sibley, 1993]. This hypothesis has received support from longitudinal research. Ary and colleagues [1999a; Ary, Duncan, Duncan, & Hops, 1999b] found that families with high levels of conflict had lower levels of parent-child involvement and poor parental monitoring, which made associations with deviant peers more likely. In turn these factors were strongly related to adolescent problem behaviours including engagement in substance use.

The research is limited on the impact of family structure or composition (i.e., families with either dual biological parents, single parent, or blended parents) on adolescent alcohol misuse. The evidence suggests that non-intact family status is associated with an increased risk for adolescent drinking [Bjarnason et al., 2002; Fergusson et al., 1995; Kuntsche & Silbereisen, 2004]. This has been shown, however, to be mediated by lower family socioeconomic status [Spooner et al., 2001]. Additionally, the experience of adverse and/or traumatic events (including childhood physical and sexual abuse, verbal arguments with parents, death of a close friend, or parent arrested/jailed) has been shown to be associated with the initiation and continuation of alcohol use, and the development of problematic adolescent alcohol use [Clark, Lesnick, & Hegedus, 1997; Deas & Thomas, 2002]. While the literature proposes that family disruption (i.e., changes to family structure or experience of an adverse family event) is likely to impact on adolescent alcohol use and misuse through a decline in family attachment, and the development of poor parent-child relationships, there is limited evidence to either support or refute this hypothesis [Miller, 1997; Needle, Su, & Doherty, 1990].

The research is unclear as to whether a direct relationship exists between socioeconomic status and youth alcohol use as inconsistent findings have been reported in the literature [Hayes et al., 2004b; Loxley et al., 2004; Williams, Sanson, Toumbourou, & Smart, 2000]. Inconsistent findings may be the result of the different indicators used to measure socioeconomic status including employment, education, personal income, occupational class etc. Lower family socioeconomic status has been associated with the development of youth drug use [Spooner et al., 2001]. Findings from the Christchurch Health and Development study suggest that adolescents who drank larger amounts of alcohol and displayed alcohol related problems at age 15 were more likely to come from a family characterised by lower social position (assessed from birth) [Fergusson, Lynskey, & Horwood, 1994]. Additionally, Lowry and colleagues found that as family income increased adolescents were less likely to engage in harmful patterns of alcohol consumption [Lowry, Kann, Collins, & Kolbe, 1996]. In contrast, a number of studies conducted in the United States and Europe have suggested that alcohol use is greater among adolescents from higher socioeconomic backgrounds [Hawkins et al., 1992; Loxley et al., 2004; Richter, Leppin, & Nic Gabbainn, 2006]. Other studies have found no or weak associations for adolescent alcohol misuse in lower socioeconomic groups [Poulton et al., 2002; Richter et al., 2006; Vereecken, Maes, & De Bacquer, 2004]. It has been suggested that alcohol use increases only when poverty is severe. When this is the case, however, it is likely that most other adolescent problem behaviours (e.g. delinquency, poor school performance) are also likely to increase [Hawkins et al., 1992].

Disruptions in Parenting

A number of parenting deficits have been empirically linked to adolescent alcohol misuse including low levels of parental support, parental monitoring, and parental control. Assessing the impact of these factors is complex given that theoretical models suggest they are often directly or indirectly linked to other individual (including biological and psychological factors) and broader environmental influences (including cultural and sociodemographic factors) [Hayes et al., 2004b; Jacob & Leonard, 1994]. Parenting deficits are also likely to impact on adolescent alcohol misuse through their impact on quality of the parent-adolescent relationship. The impact of these parenting deficits will be discussed in more detail in the following section.

SOCIAL INFLUENCE BY PARENTS ON ADOLESCENT ALCOHOL USE

The previous section suggested that parenting deficits are linked to adolescent alcohol misuse through their impact on the quality of the parent-adolescent relationship. The literature focuses on deficits in three key areas of parenting: parental support, parental monitoring and parental control.

Parental support includes constructs such as nurturing, attachment, acceptance, cohesion and love, and as such is a key dimension of effective parenting [Jacob & Leonard, 1994]. Research has consistently found that greater parental support and involvement predicts better adolescent functioning and fewer problem behaviours, including a lower risk of alcohol use [Ary et al., 1999a; Ary et al., 1999b; Barnes, Farrell, & Windle, 1987; Barnes, Reifman, Farrell, & Dintcheff, 2000; Barnes, Reifman, Farrell, Uhteg, & Dintcheff, 1994; Barrera Jr. & Li, 1996].

Parental monitoring refers to awareness and supervision of the child's activities in multiple domains (including friends, school and behaviour at home), and communication to the child that the parent is concerned about, and aware of such activities [Dishion & McMahon, 1998]. Both cross-sectional and longitudinal studies have found that poor parental monitoring is associated with adolescents initiating drinking at an earlier age, greater consumption of alcohol and increased risk for the development of problematic drinking patterns [Hayes et al., 2004b]. Longitudinal studies have also found that parental monitoring can mediate other family effects. For example, Barnes et al [2000] found that low levels of parental support were indirectly related to increasing adolescent alcohol misuse through poor parental monitoring. This finding suggests that children who are raised in a supportive environment may be more amenable to parental monitoring, and in turn less likely to engage in risky alcohol use in adolescence.

Parental control refers to active efforts by a parent to shape the behaviour of their child [Hayes et al., 2004b]. The evidence suggests that optimal functioning is related to a moderate degree of parental control, with both too little and too much control leading to behaviour problems during adolescence including risky drinking patterns. Additionally, research has shown the type of control is important. For example, a study by Barnes and Farrell [1992] found that more coercive control (including hitting and yelling) was associated with alcohol misuse in adolescence. Consistent with this, other studies have linked adolescent alcohol use to harsh parenting and discipline [Hayes et al., 2004b], although the links appear to be indirect and distal through their impact on other parenting behaviours, such as poor monitoring and poor parent-child relationship quality [e.g. Ary et al., 1999a; Ary et al., 1999b; Duncan et al., 1998].

It has been suggested that parent-adolescent relationship quality supports all aspects of parenting [Hayes et al., 2004b]. A healthy parent-adolescent relationship is believed to be important as it promotes and encourages open communication between parents and child, which provides a foundation for better parental monitoring and the setting of appropriate boundaries relating to alcohol use and other adolescent behaviour [Dishion & McMahon, 1998; Jacob & Leonard, 1994]. The evidence from longitudinal studies indicates that parent-adolescent relationship quality has both direct [Bray et al., 2001] and indirect (e.g., through its impact on parental monitoring and deviant peer associations) effects on the development of adolescent alcohol use and misuse [Ary et al., 1999a; Ary et al., 1999b; Barnes et al.,

2000]. For example, a study by Bray and colleagues [Bray et al., 2001] found that more positive parent-adolescent relationships were associated with a decrease in adolescent drinking across time, greater emotional autonomy and lower family stress and conflict. Conversely, adolescents who reported their alcohol use increased across time were more likely to report experiencing difficulties in the relationship with their parents, including emotional problems, separation and detachment, and greater conflict and family stress.

Parental Attitudes and Behaviours

Parent-adolescent relationship quality is an ongoing interplay between parents and adolescents, and can be heavily influenced by parental attitudes and behaviours. The impact of parental attitudes and behaviours on problematic patterns of alcohol use during adolescence will be discussed in more detail below. Specifically, the evidence relating to parental supply, attitudes and modelling of alcohol use will be discussed.

The vast majority of parents (95%) believe that it is their responsibility to teach their children, when, where, and how to drink alcohol [Taylor & Carroll, 2001]. This can be done implicitly or explicitly in a number of ways, including parents directly supplying alcohol to their adolescent children, parents expressing their attitudes about drinking and appropriate drinking behaviours to their children, or parental modeling through their own use of alcohol. This section of the review will explore the evidence on the impact of these three behaviours by parents on adolescent drinking outcomes.

Parental Supply of Alcohol use

In many western countries, parents are a major source of alcohol supply for young people [Australian Institute of Health and Welfare, 2005; Cagney & Palmer, 2007a; Hayes, Smart, Toumbourou, & Sanson, 2004a; King et al., 2005; Premier's Drug Prevention Council, 2005; Sanchez-Sosa & Poldrugo, 2001; Substance Abuse and Mental Health Services Administration, 2008; White & Hayman, 2006a]. Whether parents should supply alcohol to their children is contentious. One argument for supplying alcohol is for the purpose of teaching young people how to drink responsibly [Graham et al., 2006; Oreckin, 2005]. The Mediterranean countries are often held up as an example of how including alcohol into the everyday lives of young people has led to lower levels of harmful alcohol consumption. The contrary view is that supplying alcohol may lead to a reduction in the legal and monetary barriers to alcohol use, and inadvertently increase the risk for harmful patterns of consumption [Kypri, Dean, & Stojanovski, 2007; Lundborg, 2002; Toumbourou, Rowland, & Jeffreys, 2005]. There is also concern that alcohol may negatively impact on the developing adolescent brain and for this reason initiation to alcohol use by parents should be delayed. The evidence, however, in support of these different points of view is unclear and will be considered in terms of research on (1) the impact of parental supply on alcohol consumption and related harms, (2) implication from the Mediterranean model and, (3) the impact of alcohol on the developing adolescent brain.

The Impact on Alcohol Consumption and Related Harms

In the short-term, the evidence of the impact of parental supply on the frequency of adolescent alcohol consumption and average quantity consumed is equivocal, with a relatively equal amount of research suggesting it leads to increases as there is which suggests it leads to decreases [Dent, Grube, & Biglan, 2005; Fisher et al., 2006; Foley, Altman, Durant, & Wolfson, 2004; Jackson, Henriksen, & Dickinson, 1999; Lundborg, 2002, 2007; Resnick et al., 1997; van der Vorst, Engels, Meeus, & Dekovi, 2006; Van Zundert, Van Der Vorst, Vermulst, & Engels, 2006a; White & Hayman, 2006a; Yu, 2003]. The balance of evidence does, however, suggest that parental supply is associated with a reduction in drinking to excess on single occasions [Dent et al., 2005; Foley et al., 2004; King et al., 2005; Komro, Maldonado-Molina, Tobler, Bonds, & Muller, 2007; Lundborg, 2007; Palmer, Fryer, & Kalafatelis, 2007a, 2007b; Wagenaar et al., 1996]. The majority of this evidence, however, comes from cross-sectional research, making the direction of causality unclear. That is, parents may only supply alcohol to children they perceive to be more responsible and less likely to drink to excess, rather than vice-versa.

In the long-term, there is considerable evidence suggesting that early initiation to alcohol use is associated with a higher incidence and greater severity of alcohol related problems in later life [Anthony & Petronis, 1995a; Behrendt, Wittchen, Hofler, Lieb, & Beesdo, 2009a; DeWit, Adlaf, Offord, & Ogborne, 2000; Grant & Dawson, 1997; Hawkins et al., 1997; Hingson et al., 2006]. This is often used as a caution for parents not to supply. Other research, however, has demonstrated that adolescent alcohol consumption is only associated with problems confined to adolescence and does not extend to problems in adulthood once other important confounding factors (e.g., family history, intoxication at first use, delinquency) are taken into account [Warner & White, 2003]. A recent study also found that the higher the age of onset to alcohol use, the faster the transition to substance use problems [Behrendt et al., 2009a].

In summary, while there is evidence to suggest both short- and long-term impacts of parental supply on adolescent alcohol consumption, the evidence is conflicting and limited to cross-sectional designs. Further longitudinal research is clearly needed. The conflicting evidence makes the decision on whether to supply adolescents with alcohol a difficult one for many parents. The implications of the findings are discussed and a number of recommendations for parents and families have been noted below.

Implication from the Mediterranean Model

Research does not exist to directly compare the effects of parental supply of alcohol to minors across different countries with varying cultures and drug related policies. However, there are clearly different cultural positions and policies on drinking which may have implications for this important area of public health [Kuntsche, Rehm, & Gmel, 2004].

At a cultural level, in Europe, in the past it has been well accepted that there is a North-South gradient in patterns of drinking and binge drinking, which reflects the different positions of alcohol in society [Room & Makela, 2000]. Specifically, in the countries of Northern Europe, which are described as 'dry countries', alcohol consumption is characterized by infrequent but heavy episodes. This is contrasted with the Mediterranean countries which are described as 'wet countries', where alcohol consumption is integrated into everyday life (e.g., drinking with meals) [Kuendig et al., 2008]. It is often assumed that the lower rates of harmful adolescent alcohol consumption in Mediterranean countries are a direct result of this different cultural position where young people are introduced to alcohol in the family home as a part of everyday life.

In support of this assumption, results from the Health Behaviour in School-aged Children (HBSC) demonstrate that adolescents in Mediterranean countries do appear to have lower risk patterns of consumption than those in the Northern European counties. Specifically, HBSC study is large scale survey which has been conducted every four years since 1983/1984. In the survey conducted in 2001/2002, data was collected from 33 European countries, Canada and the United States of America [Schmid & Nic Gabhainn, 2004]. Among 15 year olds in this study, it was found that the highest prevalence of students reporting drunkenness at least twice in their lives was found in Denmark, Wales, Greenland, England and Finland, whereas the lowest prevalence was found in countries in the Mediterranean region such as Greece, Italy, France, Israel and the Former Yugoslav republic of Macedonia. In this survey it was found that for countries on the Mediterranean Sea, adolescents reported a relatively late onset and low proportion of drunkenness, but regular drinking was common. Likewise, in the survey conducted in 2005/2006 [Currie et al., 2008], among 15 year olds it was relatively more common to have reported a first drunken episode at the age 13 or younger in the Northern European countries as opposed to the Mediterranean countries. The proportion of 15 year olds reporting that they had been drunk twice or more was also higher in Northern European countries, whereas the rates in Southern Europe were relatively low.

Not all survey data collected from adolescents in Europe, however, completely and consistently support the pattern of consumption typified by this assumed North-South gradient in adolescent binge drinking. The European School Survey Project on Alcohol and other Drugs (ESPAD) is a survey conducted every 4 years in 35 European countries. This survey examines the drinking and other drug use patterns of over 100,000, 15-16 year olds. When this survey was conducted in 2003, the countries with the highest percentage of young people indicating they had had been drunk 20 times or more in their lifetime included the more traditionally 'dry countries' such as Denmark, Ireland, Isle of man, the United Kingdom, Estonia and Finland (26-36%). Those with the lowest rates included the Mediterranean countries such as Turkey, Cyprus, France, Greece and Portugal (i.e., 0-3%). This pattern of lower rates of consumption in the Mediterranean countries compared with the Northern countries was also mirrored in the prevalence of past 30 day drunkenness (i.e., subjective feeling of intoxication) and binge drinking (i.e., drinking more than 5 drinks on one occasion). In the 2007 survey [Hibell & Balakireva, 2009], however, this pattern was no longer as clear cut. Although the students in the majority of Mediterranean countries (with the exception of Spain) were less likely to report being drunk in their lifetime and past 30 days (i.e., subjective experience of intoxication), the clear difference between the Mediterranean and Northern regions could no longer be seen in rates of heavy episodic drinking (i.e., defined as consuming more than 5 drinks on a single occasion). Specifically, for the traditionally 'dry countries' the prevalence of young people in each country having consumed more than 5 drinks on one occasion during the last 30 days ranged between 34-61%. The range for Mediterranean countries was between 29-57%, with the prevalence in France being 43%. Given this more objective measure of consumption, these recent results make it harder to draw an association between the Mediterranean drinking culture and more restrained patterns of adolescent alcohol consumption. This one conflicting result, however, may also reflect the possibility that 'the concept of a drink' varied in different countries and will need to be more clearly clarified in future surveys.

In summary, the balance of evidence suggests that adolescents in Mediterranean countries demonstrate more restrained patterns of harmful alcohol consumption than those in Northern European countries. This, however, does not provide direct support for the notion that alcohol provided by parents with the family meal is protective against harmful patterns of alcohol consumption. The above surveys are cross-sectional and do not specifically measure cross-country differences in parental supply which means that such differences may reflect other factors. Nor do these observed patterns of consumption provide a consistent picture over time.

The Impact of Alcohol on the Developing Adolescent Brain

When considering the issue of parental supply of alcohol, it is also highly pertinent to address the impact of alcohol consumption on brain development as 'the brain undergoes considerable important sculpting and remodelling during the adolescent years' [Spear, 2004, p. 26]. Animal research suggests that adolescent brains may be more deleteriously affected by alcohol than a fully matured brain [Brown & Tapert, 2004]. In general, animal studies show that adolescents are more sensitive to memory and learning impairments produced by exposure to alcohol, but less sensitive to the sedation and temperature regulation effects of alcohol [Brown & Tapert, 2004; White, Ghia, Levin, & Swartzwelder, 2000]. The adolescent brain is also more vulnerable to frontal lobe damage [Crews, Mdzinarishvili, Kim, He, & Nixon, 2006]. The functioning of the frontal lobe during adolescence is vital as it plays a part in social and sexual behaviour, impulse control, motor functions, problem solving, working memory, language, judgement, planning abilities and motivation.

The information from human studies is less clear as it is not possible to determine the direction of causality. That is, evidence of an association between heavy alcohol use and damage to a certain brain region does not necessarily imply that the heavy alcohol use caused the brain damage. It is equally plausible that pre-existing brain damage resulted in greater drinking or that a third variable (e.g., depression) resulted in both heavy drinking and brain damage. The scant research which has been conducted on the adolescent brain has also been conducted on adolescents with alcohol-use disorders [National Health and Medical Research Council, 2009]. For this reason, it is not necessarily possible to extrapolate the results to non-clinical populations with low to moderate alcohol consumption as is most likely the case when we consider parental supply.

The research does, however, show that adolescents who have alcohol use disorders have reduced hippocampal volumes and a smaller prefrontal cortex [De Bellis et al., 2000; De Bellis et al., 2005]. The lower age of onset of alcohol consumption and greater duration of exposure to alcohol is also associated with greater reduction in hippocampal volume [De Bellis et al., 2000]. Heavy alcohol consumption during adolescence is associated with a number of functional impairments including deficits in learning new information and memory skills that worsen with continued drinking during early adulthood [Brown & Tapert, 2004]. Other functional changes that have been associated with adolescents with alcohol-use disorders include diminished attention, lower IQ and academic performance as well as minor deficits in verbal skills and impaired problem solving ability [For review see Brown & Tapert, 2004].

In summary, heavy drinking in adolescence is associated with numerous brain structural abnormalities and cognitive deficits. Although causality cannot be inferred from the existing human literature, animal studies strongly point to the causal influence of heavy alcohol use on impaired brain function. Furthermore, the adolescent brain may be more susceptible to the deleterious effects of heavy alcohol exposure than the fully matured adult brain. Unfortunately, there is a dearth of research on the effects of small or moderate alcohol use on the adolescent brain, which may be more typical of parental supply.

Clearly the jury is still out on determining the relationship between parental supply of alchol and the impact on adolescent alcohol use. Animal research on the impact of alcohol on the developing adolescent brain possibly provides the clearest unambiguous evidence. This evidence would suggest that parents should delay initiation to alcohol for as long as is feasible. Given the easy accessibility to alcohol in most western countries, this recommendation needs to be tempered against the evidence that early alcohol consumption initiated inside, rather than outside the family home is associated with a lesser risk of developing later problems [Warner & White, 2003].

Parental Attitudes to Drinking

Parental attitudes toward drinking can be viewed as an indirect means of social modeling. Parental attitudes may be communicated either overtly or tacitly through the setting of limits on behaviour or through the communication of values regarding alcohol use [Williams & Hine, 2002]. The evidence suggests that parents who drink alcohol are more likely to be more permissive toward alcohol use in their adolescent children [Hayes et al., 2004b]. More tolerant or lenient attitudes by parents in regard to alcohol use appear to be influential in determining adolescent alcohol initiation and the later transition to heavier drinking [Williams & Hine, 2002; Wood, Read, Mitchell, & Brand, 2004]. For example, Wood and colleagues [2004] found that the more permissive parents were in regard to adolescent alcohol use, the more likely their adolescents were to engage in heavy binge drinking.

Research also suggests that the provision of clear alcohol-specific rules by parents can impact on adolescent drinking behaviours [van der Vorst, Engels, Meeus, Dekovic, & Leeuwe, 2005; Van Zundert, van der Vorst, Vermulst, & Engels, 2006b; Wood et al., 2004]. For example, van der Vorst and colleagues [2007] found that the likelihood of drinking initiation was reduced if clear alcohol-specific rules were provided, regardless of the age of the adolescent. Once the adolescent has an established drinking pattern, the impact of alcohol-specific rules appears to decline. This suggests early involvement by parents is needed to influence later patterns of adolescent drinking. A study by Ennett and colleagues [2001] found that while alcohol initiation among adolescents was not influenced by providing alcohol-specific rules (and other parenting behaviours) escalation of use was. Other studies have noted the importance of parental communication styles. For example, Beck and colleagues [2003] found that willingness to talk to their mother, and reporting that their father's opinion of alcohol was important to them, were both associated with a reduced likelihood of adolescent drinking.

Parental Modeling of Alcohol use

Research has identified that alcohol use problems among family members, especially parents, is a key risk factor for adolescent alcohol misuse. Studies have consistently found that parents' own use of alcohol increases both the likelihood that their adolescent children will engage in alcohol use and the risk for more significant alcohol-related problems [Chassin, Rogosch, & Barrera, 1991; Ellis, Zucker, & Fitzgerald, 1997]. In fact, research indicates that the risk of alcohol misuse among children of alcohol dependent parents is four-fold in comparison to that of children with non-alcohol dependent parents [Chassin, Pitts, DeLucia, & Todd, 1999; Jacob, Windle, Seilhamer, & Bost, 1999; Weinberg, 1997]. It is likely that many inappropriate and harmful patterns of drinking are learned in the family. The evidence also suggests that children exposed to alcohol at home also tend to initiate alcohol use earlier and engage in problem drinking at a younger age than non-exposed children [Bonomo et al., 2001].

Longitudinal research has also demonstrated that less problematic, but frequent parental drinking is associated with negative adolescent outcomes. For example, data from the Australian Mater University birth cohort study show that maternal drinking (more than one glass of alcohol a day), assessed when the adolescent offspring were 14 years of age, was a strong predictor of alcohol use disorder in children at age 21, even after controlling for a range of biological, familial and interpersonal factors [Alati et al., 2005]. This suggests that social learning is likely to be an important determining factor.

There is now considerable evidence that genetic effects play a role in the development of alcohol problems, with genetic effects having been identified among children of alcohol dependent parents [Hawkins et al., 1992]. Russell [1990] found that males were 4 to 9 times more likely, and females were 2 to 3 times more likely to develop an alcohol use disorder if they had a family history of alcohol dependence. Both twin and adoption studies have supported these findings [Hawkins et al., 1992; Windle, 2008]. Biological linkages do not, however, account for all cases and other environmental factors should be taken into account [Hawkins et al., 1992]. Research suggests that family environmental effects do contribute to adolescent outcomes. For example, Jacob and colleagues [Jacob et al., 2003] found that low-risk environments (i.e., environments absent of parental alcohol dependence) can moderate the impact of high genetic risk in offspring for the development of alcohol use disorders. Other studies have reported similar conclusions in that it is likely that alcohol misuse in adolescents is the result of multiple genetic risk factors (rather than a single gene) which interact with environmental factors [Loxley et al., 2004; Weinberg, Rahdert, Colliver, & Glantz, 1998]. Research also suggests that among adolescents genetic risk may not be specific to substance use. It is likely that substance use is one of many possible negative behavioural outcomes among high risk adolescents with some genetic predisposition [Weinberg et al., 1998]. It has also been suggested that the more severe the substance use problem the larger the genetic contribution is likely to be [Glantz & Leshner, 2000; Loxley et al., 2004]. Attempting to separate the role of social and behavioural learning links in the transmission of alcohol problems is complex and it is likely that multiple pathways of influence exist.

Parenting practices, parenting deficits and peer influences appear to have a more direct impact on adolescent alcohol use than parental alcohol use disorders per se. For example, Dishion and colleagues [Dishion, Capaldi, & Yoerger, 1999] found that parental substance use did not have a unique influence on adolescent substance use after controlling for parenting practices (parenting skills and behaviour management) or peer influences. Similarly, a study by Barnes et al. [2000] found that parental alcohol abuse indirectly predicted adolescent alcohol use across time through lack of parental support and poor parental monitoring. This suggests that frequent or abusive drinking patterns impact negatively on parenting ability, which may then contribute to alcohol misuse among adolescents. Other longitudinal research suggests that parental alcohol use may influence adolescent drinking via the association with alcohol-using peers. Fergusson and colleagues [1995] found that parental alcohol use at child age 11 years did not directly predict problem drinking at 16 years. The effect of parental alcohol use on the risk of later problem drinking was actually mediated by adolescent peer relationships at age 15 years. This finding suggests that children exposed to alcohol use at home are more likely to associate with peers who also use alcohol. In turn, the risk of alcohol abuse at age 16 years was elevated by deviant peer associations.

Implications and Recommendations for Parents and Families

The research described above shows that alcohol use in adolescence is influenced by a range factors suggesting a multi-component approach is required to alter drinking behaviour [Galanter, 2006; Mitchell, Spooner, & Copeland, 2001]. This means that interventions would need to target changes in families, schools, peers, communities, social norms and laws, as well as the continuum of drinking behaviours linked to later drinking problems (i.e., delay adolescent initiation or experimentation and limit the progression to regular use, misuse and disordered patterns of drinking). Any effective prevention or intervention program would also need to systematically target identified risk and protective factors at critical developmental points. For example, in early childhood, preventative interventions would need to address childhood risk factors prior to drinking onset (including externalising behaviours, parenting skills, and the development of a healthy parent-adolescent relationship); whereas, in adolescence, interventions would need to address drinking onset and related drinking attitudes and behaviour co-occurring with other risk factors (including involvement in deviant peer friendships, and parent-adolescent relationship problems). Significant progress has been made over the last ten years in the development and evaluation of prevention and intervention strategies that aim to reduce alcohol use and misuse among adolescents [Galanter, 2006; Loxley et al., 2004; Mitchell et al., 2001; Tobler et al., 2000].

The Cochrane consortium conducted a review in 2003 of primary prevention programs for alcohol misuse among adolescents [Foxcroft, Ireland, Lister-Sharp, Lowe, & Breen, 2003]. This review identified only 3 out of 56 studies with demonstrated effective long-term benefits in alcohol reduction. One of the programs that showed the strongest effects was the *Strengthening Families Program (SFP)*, which was developed in the United States. The SFP is a family program that aims to prevent the initiation of alcohol use in adolescents, with widespread application among parents and children in the general community. The program comprises once-a-week sessions for families of 10- to 14-year-olds, which aim to enhance parental skills in nurturing, communication, and limit-setting, in addition to youth pro-social and peer resistance skills (7 sessions in total). The effectiveness of the SFP was tested by Spoth and colleagues [Spoth, Redmond, & Lepper, 1999] in a randomised control trial of 446 families (with sixth grade children). At the 1-year follow-up, significantly fewer children in the intervention group had initiated alcohol compared with children in the control group, with the treatment effect remaining evident at the 2-year follow-up [Spoth et al., 1999].

Given the limited evidence and controversial nature of parental supply it is not surprising that parents often express anxiety and confusion about how to address and manage drug and alcohol issues with adolescents. Although the research is somewhat limited and mixed, a number of important recommendations can be made to help guide parents. Children are often first introduced to alcohol in the family home so it is important that parents are aware of the opportunity this presents for prevention and management. Educating parents on the harms associated with early initiation to alcohol use is important considering there is no minimal legal age of consumption in many countries throughout the world (e.g., Australia, Denmark, Estonia, Iceland, Israel) which prohibits the supply of alcohol to minors by parents in their own home. If parents are concerned about how to introduce their children to alcohol, research suggests that delaying initiation is advisable. There will always be children that are likely to consume alcohol irrespective of parental rules and attitudes, and some parents may make the decision to provide alcohol. If this is the case, the research suggests that lesser quantities are preferable, and that adolescents are far more likely to drink at low-risk levels if under parental supervision than elsewhere. It is important to note that alcohol which is provided for parties is typically consumed at high risk levels, and such provision is best avoided.

The research literature also provides a number of other recommendations for what parents can do to decrease the risk of alcohol misuse and related harms. It is important that parents ensure they have a healthy relationship with alcohol. The research cited earlier suggested both genetics and parental modelling of alcohol use (particularly inappropriate and harmful patterns) play a role in the initiation of alcohol use and the onset of problem drinking in adolescents [Hawkins et al., 1992; Hayes et al., 2004b]. The evidence also suggests that maternal drinking plays an important role [Alati et al., 2005]. Additionally, parents who both drink alcohol and have more permissive attitudes towards drinking alcohol are more likely to have adolescents who consume alcohol at risky and high risk levels [Hayes et al., 2004b].

It is also important that parents try to develop a good quality parent-child relationship (which is characterised by trust, involvement, attachment and support, for example) as this has been shown to be an important protective factor against alcohol misuse in children [Hawkins et al., 1992; Hayes et al., 2004b; Windle, 2008]. Careful monitoring of a child/adolescent's behaviour and good open communication is recommended. It is important to note that parental monitoring does not refer to 'interrogating' a child/adolescent to ensure that a parent knows exactly what is happening. The capacity to effectively monitor a child's behaviour is based on a good quality parent-child relationship. It involves active supervision through open communication and displaying an interest about adolescent activities. It is also involves setting clear expectations, limits and establishing rules for appropriate behaviour [Hawkins et al., 1992; Hayes et al., 2004b; Loxley et al., 2004; Windle, 2008].

It is also recommended that parents discuss alcohol use specifically with adolescents which will not only help to make parental expectations clear, but will also assist in discrediting popular and unhelpful myths regarding alcohol use (for example, alcohol use will increase popularity among peers; every parent provides their child with alcohol; every teenager drinks alcohol to get drunk). Research has clearly shown that young people with positive expectations regarding the benefits that alcohol may afford are more likely to consume alcohol both now and in the future [Anderson et al., 2005; Brown, Christiansen, & Goldman, 1987; Christiansen & Goldman, 1983; Christiansen, Smith, Roehling, & Goldman,

1989; Kline, 1996]. The research suggests it is important for parents to honestly and accurately challenge such beliefs and expectations. If parents are unsure about adolescent queries regarding the harms associated with alcohol use, for example, learning together may help protect against harms. Additionally, a good behaviour management policy by parents is likely to delay alcohol initiation, and decrease the frequency of alcohol consumption by adolescents [Hawkins et al., 1992; Hayes et al., 2004b; Loxley et al., 2004; Windle, 2008]. A good behaviour management policy involves having clear explicit rules and boundary conditions for acceptable adolescent behaviour, with reasonable and consistently enforced consequences for when rules are broken. It is important to note that it does not involve punitive discipline, and to the other extreme, it should not be lax and overly permissive with unclear boundaries and inconsistent consequences.

CONCLUSION

Experimenting with alcohol use is extremely common among adolescents, with a small proportion consuming alcohol at harmful and/or excessive levels. This issue is of significant concern when the range of both short- and long-term harms associated with excessive alcohol use during adolescence is considered. This review has documented the individual, school environment, community/cultural and family characteristics identified as contributing to adolescent alcohol use and misuse. The main focus of the review was on the role of the family, particularly parenting issues, in the development and socialisation of alcohol use among adolescents. Specifically, the literature on the social influence of parents via the supply of alcohol to adolescents, their attitudes to drinking, and the modelling of alcohol use, was examined.

Using the available evidence a number of recommendations can be suggested to assist parents in decreasing the risk of adolescent alcohol misuse. These include:

1. Parents are not the only source of alcohol supply and the reality is that alcohol is available to adolescents if they choose to drink. It is suggested that if parents do supply adolescents with alcohol, preferably they should supply lesser quantities and should ensure parental supervision when the alcohol is consumed;
2. Parents should also monitor their own alcohol use and make sure that they only model low risk (or no) alcohol use to their children;
3. Parents should try to develop and maintain a good parent-child relationship. A healthy parent-child relationship should be developed from an early age and is typically characterised by clear and open communication;
4. Parents should set clear boundaries and expectations in terms of alcohol use by adolescents. Expectations and boundaries should be consistent with parental beliefs, and will probably differ for each family.
5. Parents should ensure there are clear, reasonable and consistent consequences for adolescents who break the rules set.
6. It is important for parents to monitor their children's activities through being involved in their life and knowing where they are at given times.

7. It is useful for parents to have open and honest conversations about alcohol with their children. These types of discussions are useful to question popular alcohol related myths.

References

ABS: Australian Bureau of Statistics. (2006). *Alcohol consumption in Australia: A snapshot 2004-05* (No. 4832.0.55.001). Canberra.

Alati, R., Najman, J. M., Kinner, S. A., Mamun, A. A., Williams, G. M., O'Callaghan, M. J., et al. (2005). Early predictors of adult drinking: A birth cohort study. *American Journal of Epidemiology, 162*, 1098-1107.

Anderson, K. G., Smith, G. T., McCarthy, D. M., Fischer, S. F., Fister, S., Grodin, D., et al. (2005). Elementary school drinking: The role of temperament and learning. *Psychology of Addictive Behaviors, 19*(1), 21-27.

Anthony, J. C., & Petronis, K. R. (1995a). Early-onset drug use and risk of later drug problems. *Drug & Alcohol Dependence, 40*(1), 9-15.

Anthony, J. C., & Petronis, K. R. (1995b). Early-onset drug use and risk of later drug problems. *Drug and Alcohol Dependence, 40*, 9-15.

Ary, D. V., Duncan, T. E., Biglan, A., Metzler, C. W., Noell, J. W., & Smolkowski, K. (1999a). Development of adolescent problem behavior. *Journal of Abnormal Child Psychology, 27*(2), 141-150.

Ary, D. V., Duncan, T. E., Duncan, S. C., & Hops, H. (1999b). Adolescent problem behavior: the influence of parents and peers. *Behaviour Research and Therapy, 37*(3), 217-230.

Australian Institute of Health and Welfare. (2005). *2004 National Drug Strategy Household Survey: First Results*.

Babor, T., Caetano, F., Casswell, S., Edwards, G., Giesbrecht, N., Graham, K., et al. (2003). *Alcohol: No Ordinary Commodity—A Consumer's Guide to Public Policy*. Oxford, U.K. : Oxford University Press.

Barnes, G. M., & Farrell, M. P. (1992). Parental support and control as predictors of adolescent drinking, delinquency, and related problem behaviors. *Journal of Marriage and the Family, 54*, 763-776.

Barnes, G. M., Farrell, M. P., & Windle, M. (1987). Parent-adolescent interactions in the development of alcohol abuse and other deviant behaviors. *Family Perspective, 21*, 321-335.

Barnes, G. M., Reifman, A. S., Farrell, M. P., & Dintcheff, B. A. (2000). The effects of parenting on the development of adolescent alcohol misuse: a six-wave latent growth model. *Journal of Marriage and the Family, 62*, 175-186.

Barnes, G. M., Reifman, A. S., Farrell, M. P., Uhteg, L., & Dintcheff, B. A. (1994). Longitudinal effects of parenting on alcohol misuse among adolescents. *Alcoholism: Clinical and Experimental Research, 18*, 507.

Barrera Jr., M., & Li, S. A. (1996). The relation of family support to adolescents' psychological distress and behavior problems. In G. R. Pierce, B. R. Sarason & I. G. Sarason (Eds.), *Handbook of social support and the family* (pp. 313-343). New York: Plenum Press.

Beauvais, F. (1998). American Indians and alcohol. *Alcohol Research and Health, 22*, 253-259.

Beck, K. H., Boyle, J. R., & Boekeloo, B. O. (2003). Parental monitoring and adolescent alcohol risk in a clinic population. *American Journal of Health Behavior, 27*(2), 108-115.

Behrendt, S., Wittchen, H., Hofler, M., Lieb, R., & Beesdo, K. (2009a). Transitions from first substance use to substance use disorders in adolescence: Is early onset associated with a rapid escalation? *Drug and Alcohol Dependence, 99*, 68-78.

Behrendt, S., Wittchen, H. U., Hofler, M., Lieb, R., & Beesdo, K. (2009b). Transitions from first substance use to substance use disorders in adolescence: Is early onset associated with rapid escalation? *Drug and Alcohol Dependence, 99*, 68-78.

Bellis, M. A., Hughes, K., Morleo, M., Tocque, K., Hughes, S., Allen, T., et al. (2006). *Patterns of risky alcohol consumption in North West teenagers and their implications for preventing alcohol-related harm* Liverpool, Merseyside: Centre for Public Health, Liverpool John Moores University.

Bersamin, M., Paschell, M. J., & Flewelling, R. L. (2005). Ethnic differences in relationships between risk factors and adolescent binge drinking: A national study. *Prevention Science, 6*(2), 127-137.

Beyers, J. M., Toumbourou, J. W., Catalano, R. F., Arthur, W. M., & Hawkins, J. D. (2004). A cross-national comparison of risk and protective factors for adolescent substance use: The United States and Australia. *Journal of Adolescent Health, 35*(1), 3-16.

Bjarnason, T., Andersson, B., Choquet, M., Elekes, Z., Morgan, M., & Rapinett, G. (2002). Alcohol culture, family structure and adolescent alcohol use: Multilevel modeling of frequency of heavy drinking among 15-16 year old students in 11 European countries. *Journal of Studies on Alcohol, 64*, 200-208.

Bokszczanin, A., Essau, C. A., & O'Callaghan, J. (2009). Alcohol use and abuse in Poland. In A. Browne Miller (Ed.), *The Praeger International Collection on Addictions*. New York: Greenwood Publishing Group.

Bond, L., Thomas, L., Toumbourou, J., Patton, G., & Catalano, R. (2000). *Improving the lives of young Victorians in our community: A survey of risk and protective factors*. Melbourne: Centre for Adolescent Health.

Bonomo, Y., Coffey, C., Wolfe, R., Lynskey, M., Bowes, G., & Patton, G. (2001). Adverse outcomes of alcohol use in adolescents. *Addiction, 96*(10), 1485-1496.

Bonomo, Y. A., Bowes, G., Coffey, C., Carlin, J. B., & Patton, G. (2004). Teenage drinking and the onset of alcohol dependence: a cohort study over seven years. *Addiction, 99*(12), 1520-1528.

Bray, J. H., Adams, G. J., Getz, J. G., & Baer, P. E. (2001). Developmental, family, and ethnic Influences on adolescent alcohol usage: A growth curve approach. *Journal of Family Psychology, 15*(2), 301-314.

Brown, S., Christiansen, B. A., & Goldman, M. S. (1987). The Alcohol Expectancy Questionnaire: an instrument for the assessment of adolescent and adult alcohol expectancies. *Journal of Studies on Alcohol, 48*(5), 483-491.

Brown, S. A., & Tapert, S. F. (2004). Adolescence and the trajectory of alcohol use: Basic clinical skills. *Annals of the New York Academy of Science, 1021*(234-244).

Cagney, P., & Palmer, S. (2007a). *The sale and supply of alcohol to under 18 year olds in New Zealand: A systematic overview of international and New Zealand literature*.

Cagney, P., & Palmer, S. (2007b). *The sale and supply of alcohol to under 18 year olds in New Zealand: A systematic overview of international and New Zealand literature* Alcohol Advisory Council of New Zealand.

Caspi, A., Begg, D., & Dickson, N. (1997). Personality differences predict health-risk behaviours in young adulthood: Evidence from a longitudinal study. *Journal of Personality and Social Psychology, 73*, 1052-1063.

Chassin, L., Pitts, S. C., DeLucia, C., & Todd, M. (1999). A longitudinal study of children of alcoholics: Predicting young adolescent substance use disorders, anxiety and depression. *Journal of Abnormal Psychology, 108*(1), 106-199.

Chassin, L., Rogosch, F., & Barrera, M. (1991). Substance use and symptomatology among adolescent children of alcoholics. *Journal of Abnormal Psychology, 100*(4), 449-463.

Christiansen, B. A., & Goldman, M. S. (1983). Alcohol-related expectancies versus demographic/background variables in prediction of adolescent drinking. *Journal of Consulting and Clinical Psychology, 51*(2), 249-257.

Christiansen, B. A., Smith, G. T., Roehling, P. V., & Goldman, M. S. (1989). Using alcohol expectancies to predict adolescent drinking behavior after 1 year. *Journal of Consulting and Clinical Psychology, 57*(1), 93-99.

Clark, D. B., Lesnick, L., & Hegedus, A. M. (1997). Traumas and other adverse life events in adolescents with alcohol abuse and dependence. *Journal of the American Academy of Child and Adolescent Psychiatry, 36*(12), 1744-1751.

Colder, C. R., & Chassin, L. (1999). The psychosocial characteristics of alcohol users versus problem users: Data from a study of adolescents at risk. *Development and Psychopathology, 11*, 321-348.

Crews, F. T., Mdzinarishvili, A., Kim, D., He, J., & Nixon, K. (2006). Neurogenesis in adolescent brain is potently inhibited by ethanol. *Neuroscience, 137*, 437-445.

Curran, P. J., Stice, E., & Chassin, L. (1997). The relation between adolescent and peer alcohol use: A longitudinal random coefficients model. *Journal of Consulting and Clinical Psychology, 65*, 130-140.

Currie, C., Gabhainn, S., Godeau, E., Roberts, C., Smith, R., Currie, D., et al. (2008). *Inequalities in young people's health: HBSC International Report from the 2005/2006 Survey*. Copenhagen: World Health Organisation.

D'Onofrio, C. N. (1997). The prevention of alcohol use by rural youth. In *Rural substance abuse: State of knowledge and issues*. Rockville, MD: NIDA Research Monograph no. 168.

Dawson, D. A., Goldstein, R. B., Chou, P. S., Ruan, J. W., & Grant, B. F. (2008). Age at first drink and the first incidence of adult-onset DSM-IV alcohol use disorders. *Alcoholism: Clinical and Experimental Research, 32*(12), 2149-2160.

De Bellis, M. D., Clark, D. B., Beers, S. R., Soloff, P. H., Boring, A. M., Hall, J., et al. (2000). Hippocampal volume in adolescent-onset alcohol use disorders. *American Journal of Psychiatry, 157*, 737-744.

De Bellis, M. D., Narasimhan, A., Thatcher, D. L., Keshavan, M., Soloff, P., & Clark, D. B. (2005). Prefrontal cortex, thalamus, and cerebellar volumes in adolescents and young adults with adolescent-onset alcohol use disorders and comorbid mental disorders. *Alcoholism: Clinical and Experimental Research, 29*, 1590-1600.

De Zwart, W. M., Monshouwer, K., & Smit, F. (2000). *Jeugd en Riskant Gedrag. Kerngegevens 1999. Roken, Drinken, Drugsgebruik en Gokken onder Scholieren vanaf*

Tien Jaar (Youth and Risky Behavior. Key data 1999. Smoking, drinking, drug use and gambling among scholars aged ten years and older). Utrecht: Trimbos-institutt.

Deas, D., & Thomas, S. (2002). Comorbid psychiatric factors contributing to adolescent alcohol and other drug use. *Alcohol Research and Health, 26*(2), 116-121.

Degenhardt, L., Chiu, W., Sampson, N., Kessler, R. C., Anthony, J. C., Angermeyer, M., et al. (2008). Toward a global view of alcohol, tobacco, cannabis, and cocaine use: Findings from the WHO World Mental Surveys. *PLoS Medicine, 5*(7), 1053-1065.

Dent, C. W., Grube, J. W., & Biglan, A. (2005). Community level alcohol availability and enforcement of possession laws as predictors of youth drinking. *Preventive Medicine, 40*(3), 355-362.

DeWit, D., Adlaf, E., Offord, D., & Ogborne, A. (2000). Age at first alcohol use: a risk factor for the development of alcohol disorders. *American Journal of Psychiatry, 157*(5), 745-750.

Dishion, T. J., Capaldi, D. M., & Yoerger, K. (1999). Middle childhood antecedents to progressions in male adolescent substance use: an ecological analysis of risk and protection. *Journal of Adolescent Research, 14*, 175-205.

Dishion, T. J., & McMahon, R. J. (1998). Parental monitoring and the prevention of child and adolescent problem behavior: a conceptual and empirical formulation. *Clinical Child and Family Psychology Review, 1*, 61-75.

Duncan, S. C., Duncan, T. E., Biglan, A., & Ary, D. (1998). Contributions of the social context to the development of adolescent substance use: a multivariate latent growth modeling approach. *Drug and Alcohol Dependence, 50*, 57-71.

Duncan, S. C., Duncan, T. E., & Strycker, L. A. (2002). A multilevel analysis of neighbourhood context and youth alcohol and drug problems. *Prevention Science, 3*(2), 125-133.

Editorial. (2008). Calling time on young people's alcohol consumption. *Lancet, 371*, 871.

Ellis, D. A., Zucker, R. A., & Fitzgerald, H. E. (1997). The role of family influences in development and risk. *Alcohol Health and Research World, 21*(3), 218-226.

Ennett, S. T., Bauman, K. E., Foshee, V. A., Pemberton, M., & Hicks, K. A. (2001). Parent-child communication about adolescent tobacco and alcohol use: What do parents say and does it affect youth behavior? *Journal of Marriage and the Family, 63*, 48-62.

Essau, C. A., Barrett, P., & Pasquali, K. (2002). Concluding remarks. In C. A. Essau (Ed.), *Substance abuse and dependence in adolescence*. London: Brunner-Routledge.

Essau, C. A., Karpinski, N. A., Petermann, F., & Conradt, J. (1998). Haufigkeit und Komorbiditat von Storungen durch Substanzkonsum. *Zeitschrift Kindheit und Entwicklung, 7*, 199-207.

Essau, C. A., Mohiyeddini, C., & Bray, D. (2009). Alcohol consumption and binge drinking in the United Kingdom. In A. Browne Miller (Ed.), *The Praeger International Collection on Addictions*. New York: Greenwood Publishing Group.

Fell, J. C., Fisher, D. A., Voas, R. B., Blackman, K., & Tippetts, S. A. (2008). The relationship of underage drinking laws to reductions in drinking drivers in fatal crashes in the United States. *Accident Analysis and Prevention, 40*, 1430-1440.

Fergusson, D. M., & Horwood, L. J. (1996). The role of adolescent peer affiliations in the continuity between childhood behavioural adjustment and juvenile offending. *Journal of Abnormal Child Psychology, 24*, 205-221.

Fergusson, D. M., & Horwood, L. J. (1999). Prospective childhood predictors of deviant peer affiliations in adolescence. *Journal of Child Psychology and Psychiatry, 40*, 581-592.

Fergusson, D. M., Horwood, L. J., & Lynskey, M. T. (1995). The prevalence and risk factors associated with abusive or hazardous alcohol consumption in 16-year-olds. *Addiction, 90*, 935-946.

Fergusson, D. M., Lynskey, M. T., & Horwood, L. J. (1994). Childhood exposure to alcohol and adolescent drinking patterns. *Addiction, 89*, 1007-1016.

Fisher, S. L., Bucholz, K. K., Reich, W., Fox, L., Kuperman, S., Kramer, J., et al. (2006). Teenagers are right--parents do not know much: an analysis of adolescent-parent agreement on reports of adolescent substance use, abuse, and dependence. *Alcoholism: Clinical & Experimental Research, 30*(10), 1699-1710.

Foley, K. L., Altman, D., Durant, R. H., & Wolfson, M. (2004). Adults' approval and adolescents' alcohol use. *Journal of Adolescent Health, 35*(4), 345.e317-326.

Foxcroft, D. R., Ireland, D., Lister-Sharp, D. J., Lowe, G., & Breen, R. (2003). Longer-term primary prevention for alcohol misuse in young people: a systematic review. *Addiction, 98*, 397-411.

Foxcroft, D. R., & Lowe, G. (1991). Adolescent drinking behaviour and family socialization factors: a meta-analysis. *Journal of Adolescence, 14*(3), 255-273.

Galanter, M. (Ed.). (2006). *Alcohol problems in adolescence and young adults: Epidemiology, neurobiology, prevention and treatment*. New York: Springer Science and Business Media.

Glantz, M. D., & Leshner, A. I. (2000). Drug abuse and developmental psychopathology. *Development and Psychopathology, 12*, 795-814.

Graham, M. L., Ward, B., Munro, G., Snow, P., Ellis, J., Graham, M. L., et al. (2006). Rural parents, teenagers and alcohol: what are parents thinking? *Rural & Remote Health, 6*(1), 383.

Grant, B., & Dawson, D. (1997). Age of onset of alcohol use and its association with DSM-IV alcohol abuse and dependence: Results from the National Longitudinal Alcohol Epidemiologic Survey. *Journal of Substance Abuse, 9*, 103-110.

Grant, B. F., Stinson, F. S., & Harford, T. C. (2001). Age at onset of alcohol use and DSM-IV alcohol abuse and dependence: a 12-year follow-up. *Journal of Substance Abuse, 13*, 493-504.

Gruber, E., DiClemente, R. J., Anderson, M. M., & Lodico, M. (1996). Early drinking onset and its association with alcohol use and problem behaviour in late adolescence. *Preventive Medicine, 25*, 293-300.

Guo, J., Hawkins, J. D., & Hill, K. G. (2001). Childhood and adolescent predictors of alcohol abuse and dependence in young adulthood. *Journal of Studies on Alcohol, 62*, 754-762.

Hawkins, J., Graham, J., Maguin, E., Abbott, R., Hill, K., & Catalano, R. (1997). Exploring the effects of age of alcohol use initiation and psychosocial risk factors on subsequent alcohol misuse. *Journal of Studies on Alcohol, 58*, 280-290.

Hawkins, J. D., Catalano, P., & Miller, J. Y. (1992). Risk and protective factors for alcohol and other drug problems in adolescence and early adulthood: implications for substance abuse prevention. *Psychological Bulletin, 112*, 64-105.

Hayes, L., Smart, D., Toumbourou, J., & Sanson, A. (2004a). *Parenting influences on adolescent alcohol use*: Department of Health and Ageing, Institute of Family Studies.

Hayes, L., Smart, D., Toumbourou, J. W., & Sanson, A. (2004b). *Parenting influences on adolescent alcohol use*. Research Report No. 10. Melbourne: Australian Institute of Family Studies, Commonwealth of Australia.

Henderson, G., Ma, G. X., & Shive, S. E. (2002). African American substance users and abusers. In G. X. Ma & G. Henderson (Eds.), *Ethnicity and substance abuse: Prevention and intervention*. Springfield, Illinois: Charles C. Thomas.

Hibell, B., & Balakireva, O. (2009). *ESAPD: The European School Survey Project on Alcohol and Other Drugs*. Stockholm.

Hingson, R. W., Heeren, T., & Winter, M. R. (2006). Age at drinking onset and alcohol dependence: Age at onset, duration and severity. *Archives of Pediatric Adolescent Medicine, 160*, 739-746.

Jackson, C., Henriksen, L., & Dickinson, D. (1999). Alcohol-specific socialization, parenting behaviours and alcohol use by children. *Journal of Studies on Alcohol, 60*, 362-367.

Jacob, T., & Leonard, K. E. (1994). Family and peer influences in the development of adolescent alcohol abuse. In R. Zucker, G. Boyd & J. Howard (Eds.), *Development of alcohol problems: Exploring the biopsychosocial matrix of risk.* [NIAAA Monograph No. 26, pp. 123-156]. Rockville, MD: National Institute on Alcohol Abuse and Alcoholism.

Jacob, T., Waterman, B., Heath, A., True, W., Bucholz, K. K., Haber, R., et al. (2003). Genetic and environmental effects on offspring alcoholism: new insights using an offspring-of-twins design. *Archives of General Psychiatry, 60*, 1265-1272.

Jacob, T., Windle, M., Seilhamer, R. A., & Bost, J. (1999). Adult children of alcoholics: Drinking, psychiatric, and psychosocial status. *Psychology of Addictive Behaviors, 13*(1), 3-21.

Jernigan, D. H. (2001). *Global status report: Alcohol and young people*. Geneva: World Health Organisation.

Johnston, L. D., O'Malley, P. M., & Bachman, J. G. (2002). *National Survey Results on Drug Use from the Monitoring the Future Study, 1975-2001, Vols. 1 and 2* (No. 02-5106 and 02-5107). Rockville, MD: National Institute on Drug Abuse.

Johnston, L. D., O'Malley, P. M., Bachman, J. G., & Schulenberg, J. E. (2009). *Monitoring the Future national results on adolescent drug use: Overview of key findings, 2008* (No. 09-7401). Bethesda, MD: National Institute on Drug Abuse.

King, E., Taylor, J., & Carroll, T. (2005). *Alcohol consumption patterns among Australian 15-17 year olds from 2000 to 2004*: Research Marketing Group.

King, K. M., & Chassin, L. (2007). A prospective study of the effects of age of initiation of alcohol and drug use on young adult substance dependence. *Journal of Studies on Alcohol and Drugs, 68*, 256-265.

Kline, R. B. (1996). Eight-month predictive validity and covariance structure of the Alcohol Expectancy Questionnaire for Adolescents (AEQ-A) for junior high school students. *Journal of Studies on Alcohol, 57*, 396-405.

Kokkevi, A. E., Arapaki, A. A., Richardson, C., Florescu, S., Kuzman, M., & Stergar, E. (2007). Further investigation of psychological and environmental correlates of substance use in adolescence in six European countries. *Drug and Alcohol Dependence, 88*, 308-312.

Komro, K. A., Maldonado-Molina, M. M., Tobler, A. L., Bonds, J. R., & Muller, K. E. (2007). Effects of home access and availability of alcohol on young adolescents' alcohol use. *Addiction, 102*(10), 1597-1608.

Kuendig, H., Plant, M. A., Plant, M. L., Miller, P., Kuntsche, S., & Gmel, G. (2008). Alcohol-related adverse consequences: cross-cultural variations in attribution process among young adults. *The European Journal of Public Health*, 1-6.

Kuntsche, E., Rehm, J., & Gmel, G. (2004). Characteristics of binge drinkers in Europe. *Social Science and Medicine, 59*, 113-127.

Kuntsche, E. N., & Silbereisen, R. K. (2004). Parental closeness and adolescent substance use in single and two parent families in Switzerland. *Swiss Journal of Psychology, 63*(2), 85-92.

Kypri, K., Dean, J. I., & Stojanovski, E. (2007). Parent attitudes on the supply of alcohol to minors. *Drug and Alcohol Review, 26*, 41-47.

Kypri, K., Paschall, M. J., Langley, J., Baxter, J., Cashell-Smith, M., & Bourdeau, B. (2009). Drinking and alcohol-related harm among New Zealand University Students: Findings from a national web-based survey. *Alcoholism: Clinical and Experimental Research, 33*(2), 307-314.

Kypri, K., Voas, R. B., Langley, J. D., Stephenson, S. C., Begg, D. J., Tippetts, A., et al. (2006). Minimum purchasing age for alcohol and traffic crash injuries among 15- to 19-year-olds in New Zealand. *American Journal of Public Health, 96*, 126-131.

Lavikainen, H., Ahlstrom, S., Metso, L., Nevalainen, J., & Lintonen, T. (2008). Relationship between negative experiences and drinking experience among 15- to 16-year-old adolescents in Finland. *European Addiction Research, 14*, 169-178.

Lewinsohn, P. M., Rohde, P., & Seeley, J. R. (1996). Alcohol consumption in high school adolescents: Frequency of use and dimensional structure of associated problems. *Addiction, 91*, 375-390.

Lowe, G., Foxcroft, D. R., & Sibley, D. (1993). *Adolescent drinking and family life (Vol. XI)*. PA, England: Harwood Academic Publishers/Gordon.

Lowry, R., Kann, L., Collins, J. L., & Kolbe, L. (1996). The effects of socio-economic status on chronic disease risk behaviors among US adolescents *Journal of the American Medical Association, 276*, 792-797.

Loxley, W., Toumbourou, J., Stockwell, T., Haines, B., Scott, K., Godfrey, C., et al. (2004). *The prevention of substance use, risk and harm in Australia: a review of the evidence*: The National Drug Research Institute and the Centre for Adolescent Health.

Lundborg, P. (2002). Young people and alcohol: an econometric analysis. *Addiction, 97*(12), 1573-1582.

Lundborg, P. (2007). Parents' willingness to provide alcohol and adolescents' alcohol use - Evidence from Swedish data. *Vulnerable Children and Youth Studies, 2*(1), 60 - 70.

Miller, J. W., Naimi, T. S., Brewer, R. D., & Everett Jones, S. (2007). Binge drinking and associated health risk behaviours among high school students'. *Pediatrics, 119*, 76.

Miller, P. (1997). Family structure, personality, drinking, smoking and illicit drug use: a study of UK teenagers. *Drug and Alcohol Dependence, 45*, 121-129.

Miller, T. R., Levy, D. T., Spicer, R. S., & Taylor, D. M. (2006). Societal costs of underage drinking. *Journal of Studies on Alcohol, 67*, 519-528.

Mitchell, C. M., Beals, J., Whitesell, N. R., & et al. (2008). Alcohol use among American Indian high school youths from adolescence and young adulthood: A latent markov model *Journal of Studies on Alcohol and Drugs, 69*, 666-675.

Mitchell, P., Spooner, C., & Copeland, J. (2001). *The role of families in the development, identification, prevention and treatment of illicit drug problems*. Canberra: NM&MRC.

Morgan, M., Hibell, B., Andersson, B., Bjarnason, T., Kokkevi, A., & Narusk, A. (1999). The ESPAD Study: implications for prevention. *Drugs: Education, Prevention and Policy, 6*, 243-256.

Myers, M. G., Stewart, D. G., & Brown, S. A. (1998). Progression from conduct disorder to antisocial personality disorder following treatment for adolescent substance abuse. *American Journal of Psychiatry, 155*, 479-485.

National Health and Medical Research Council. (2009). *Australian alcohol guidelines to reduce health risks from drinking alcohol*: Commonwealth of Australia.

Needle, R. H., Su, S., & Doherty, W. J. (1990). Divorce, remarriage, and adolescent substance use: A prospective longitudinal study. *Journal of Marriage and the Family, 52*(1), 157-169.

Niemela, S., Sourander, A., Poikolainen, K., Helenius, H., Sillanmaki, L., Parkkola, K., et al. (2006). Childhood predictors of drunkenness in late adolescence among males: a 10-year population-based follow-up study. *Addiction, 101*, 512-521.

Oreckin, M. (2005). You must be over 21 to drink in this living room. *Time, 165*(6), 142-143.

Osaki, Y., Tanihata, T., Ohida, T., Kanda, H., Suzuki, K., Higuchi, S., et al. (2009). Decrease in the prevalence of adolescent alcohol use and its possible causes in Japan: Periodical nationwide cross-sectional surveys. *Alcoholism: Clinical and Experimental Research, 33*(2), 247-254.

Palmer, S., Fryer, K., & Kalafatelis, E. (2007a). *ALAC Alcohol Monitor - Adults & Youth 2005-2006 Annual Report*. Wellington: Alcohol Advisory Council of New Zealand.

Palmer, S., Fryer, K., & Kalafatelis, E. (2007b). *ALAC Alcohol Monitor - Adults & Youth 2006-2007 Drinking Behaviours Report*. Wellington: Alcohol Advisory Council of New Zealand.

Palmer, S., Fryer, K., & Kalafatelis, E. (2007c). *ALAC Alcohol Monitor - Adults and Youth 2006-2007 Drinking Behaviours Report* (No. 3650): Research New Zealand.

Parlimentary Office of Science and Technology (POST). (2005). *Binge drinking and Public Health*. London.

Poelen, E. A. P., Scholte, R. H. J., Engels, R. C. M. E., Boomsma, D. I., & Willemsen, G. (2005). Prevalence and trends of alcohol use and misuse among adolescents and young adults in the Netherlands from 1993 to 2000. *Drug and Alcohol Dependence, 79*, 413-421.

Poulton, R., Caspi, A., Milne, B. J., Thomson, W., Taylor, A., Sears, M., et al. (2002). Association between children's experience of socioeconomic disadvantage and adult health: a life-course study. *Lancet, 360*(9346), 1640-1645.

Premier's Drug Prevention Council. (2005). *Victorian Youth Alcohol and Drug Survey 2004 Alcohol Findings*: Premier's Drug Prevention Council.

Pulkkinen, L., & Pitkanen, T. (1994). A prospective study of the precursors to problem drinking in young adulthood. *Journal of Studies on Alcohol, 55*, 578-587.

Rai, A. A., Stanton, B., Wu, Y., Li, X., Gallbraith, J., Cottrell, L., et al. (2003). Relative influences of perceived parental monitoring and perceived peer involvement on adolescent risk behaviours: An analysis of six cross-sectional data sets. *Journal of Adolescent Health, 33*(2), 108-118.

Reifman, A., Barnes, G. M., Dintcheff, B. A., Farrell, M. P., & Uhteg, L. (1998). Parental and peer influences on the onset of heavier drinking among adolescents. *Journal of Studies on Alcohol, 59*(3), 311-317.

Reifman, A., Watson, W. K., & McCourt, A. (2006). Social networks and college drinking: Probing processes of social influence and selection. *Personality and Social Psychology Bulletin, 32*, 820-832.

Resnick, M. D., Bearman, P. S., Blum, R. W., Bauman, K. E., Harris, K. M., Jones, J., et al. (1997). Protecting adolescents from harm. Findings from the National Longitudinal Study on Adolescent Health. *JAMA, 278*(10), 823-832.

Richter, M., Leppin, A., & Nic Gabbainn, S. (2006). The relationship between parental socio-economic status and episodes of drunkenness among adolescents: findings from a cross-national survey. *BMC Public Health, 6*(289).

Roberts, C., Blakey, V., & Tudor Smith, C. (1999). The impact of "alcopops" on regular drinking by young people in Wales. *Drug Education Prevention Policy, 6*, 7-15.

Room, R., & Makela, K. (2000). Typologies of the cultural position of drinking. *Journal of Studies on Alcohol, 61*(3), 475-483.

Russell, M. (1990). Prevalence of alcoholism among children of alcoholics. In M. Windle & J. S. Searles (Eds.), *Children of alcoholics: Critical perspectives* (pp. 9-38). New York: Guilford Press.

Saggers, S., & Gray, D. (1998). *Dealing with alcohol: Indigenous usage in Australia, New Zealand and Canada*. New York, US: Cambridge University Press.

SAMHSA (Substance Abuse and Mental Health Services Administration). (2008). *Results from the 2007 National Survey on Drug Use and Health: National Findings (NSDUH Series H-34, DHHS Publication No. SMA 08-4343)*. Rockville, MD: Office of Applied Studies, Department of Health and Human Services.

SAMHSA: Substance Abuse and Mental Health Services Administration. (2003). *Overview of Findings from the 2002 National Survey on Drug Use and Health.* Rockville, MD: Office of Applied Studies, Department of Health and Human Services.

SAMHSA: Substance Abuse and Mental Health Services Administration. (2007). *Results from The 2006 National Survey on Drug Use and Health: National Findings.* (No. SMA 07-4293). Rockville, MD: Office of Applied Studies, Department of Health and Human Services.

Sanchez-Sosa, J. J., & Poldrugo, F. (2001). Family and Cultural Influences on Alcohol and Young People. In E. Houghton & A. M. Roche (Eds.), *Learning About Drinking* (pp. 57-83). Lillington, Nc.: Edward Brothers.

Schmid, H., & Nic Gabhainn, S. (2004). 'Alcohol use'. In: Currie, C., Roberts, C., Morgan, A., Smith, R., Settertobulte, W., Samdal, O., And Barnekow Rasmussen, V. (Eds.) *Young People's Health in Context: Health Behaviour in School-Aged Children (HBSC) Study: International Report from the 2001/2002 Survey, Health Policy for Children and Adolescents*, No. 4, Copenhagen, Denmark: Regional Office for Europe, World Health Organization, 2004, pp. 73-83.

Shanahan, P., Wilkins, M., & Hurt, N. (2002). *A study of attitudes and behaviours of drinkers at risk*. Canberra.

Sher, K. (1994). Individual-level risk factors. In R. Zucker, G. Boyd & J. Howard (Eds.), *Development of alcohol problems: Exploring the biopsychosocial matrix of risk.* [NIAAA Monograph No. 26, pp. 123-156]. Rockville, MD.

Sher, K., Grekin, E. R., & Williams, N. A. (2005). The development of alcohol use disorders. *Annual Reviews of Clinical Psychology, 1*, 493-523.

Shults, R. A., Elder, R. W., Sleet, D. A., Nichols, J. L., Alao, M. O., Carande-Kulis, V., et al. (2001). Review of evidence regarding interventions to reduce alcohol-impaired driving. *American Journal of Preventive Medicine, 21*(Supplement 4), 66-88.

Smart, D., Richardson, N., Sanson, A., Dussuyer, I., Marshall, B., Toumbourou, J., et al. (2005). *Patterns and precursors of adolescent antisocial behaviour: Outcomes and connections*. Melbourne: Australian Institute of Family Studies.

Spear, L. P. (2004). Adolescent brain development and animal models. *Annals of the New York Academy of Science, 1021*, 23-26.

Spooner, C., Hall, W., & Lynskey, M. (2001). *Structural determinants of youth drug use. (ANCD Research Paper No. 2).* Canberra: Australian National Council on Drugs.

Spoth, R., Redmond, C., & Lepper, H. (1999). Alcohol initiation outcomes of universal family-focused preventative interventions: one- and two-year follow-ups of a controlled study. *Journal of Studies on Alcohol, 13* (Special Issue: Alcohol and the Family: Opportunities for Prevention), 103-111.

Sprawozdanie. (2006). *Report on realization of the Act on Upbringing in Sobriety and Counteracting Alcoholism from 1st January to 31st December 2005.* Warszawa: National Agency for Solving Alcohol Problems.

Stanley, J., Tomison, A. M., & Pocock, J. (2003). *Child abuse and neglect in Indigenous Australian communities*. Melbourne: Australian Institute of Family Studies.

Substance Abuse and Mental Health Services Administration. (2008). *Results from the 2007 National Survey on Drug Use and Health: National Findings*. Rockville, MD.

Swahn, M. H., Bossarte, R. M., & Sullivent, E. E. (2008). Age of alcohol use initiation, suicidal behaviour, peer and dating violence victimisation and perpetration among high-risk, seventh-grade adolescents. *Pediatrics, 121*(2), 297-305.

Taylor, J., & Carroll, T. (2001). Youth alcohol consumption: experiences and expectations. In Australian Institute of Criminology (Ed.), *Alcohol, Young Persons and Violence.* Canberra: Australian Institute of Criminology Research and Public Policy Series No 35.

Ter Bogt, T., van Dorsselaer, S., & Vollebergh, W. (2002). *Roken, Drinken en Blowen door Nederlandse Scholieren (11 t/m 17 jaar) 2001: Kerngegevens Middelengebruik uit het Nederlands HBSC-onderzoek. Smoking, drinking and smoking dope among Dutch scholars (11-17 year) 2001: Key data substance use from the Dutch HBSC study.* Utrecht: Trimbos-instituut.

Tobler, N. S., Roona, M. R., Ochshorn, P., Marshall, D. G., Streke, A. V., & Stackpole, K. M. (2000). School-based adolescent drug prevention programs: 1998 meta-analysis. *Journal of Primary Prevention, 20*, 275-335.

Toumbourou, J. W., Rowland, B., & Jeffreys, A. (2005). *Could an alcohol-abstinence focus through childhood and adolescence reduce alcohol-related harm?* Drug Info Clearinghouse, Number 13, 1-21.

van der Vorst, H., Engels, R., Meeus, W., & Dekovi, M. (2006). The impact of alcohol-specific rules, parental norms about early drinking and parental alcohol use on adolescents' drinking behavior. *Journal of Child Psychology & Psychiatry & Allied Disciplines, 47*(12), 1299-1306.

van der Vorst, H., Engels, R. C. M. E., Dekovic, M., Meeus, W., & Vermulst, A. A. (2007). Alcohol-specific rules, personality and adolescents' alcohol use: a longitudinal person-environment study. *Addiction, 102*, 1064-1075.

van der Vorst, H., Engels, R. C. M. E., Meeus, W., Dekovic, M., & Leeuwe, J. V. (2005). The role of alcohol-specific socialization in adolescents' drinking behaviour. *Addiction, 100*, 1464-1476.

Van Zundert, R., Van Der Vorst, H., Vermulst, A., & Engels, R. (2006a). Pathways to alcohol use among Dutch students in regular education and education for adolescents with behavioral problems: the role of parental alcohol use, general parenting practices, and alcohol-specific parenting practices. *Journal of Family Psychology, 20*(3), 456-467.

Van Zundert, R., van der Vorst, H., Vermulst, A. A., & Engels, R. C. M. E. (2006b). Pathways to alcohol use among dutch students in regular education and education for adolescents with behavioral problems : The role of parental alcohol use, general parenting practices, and alcohol-specific parenting practices. *Journal of Family Psychology, 20*(3), 456-467.

Vereecken, C. A., Maes, L., & De Bacquer, D. (2004). The influence of parental occupation and the pupils' educational level on lifestyle behaviors among adolescents in Belgium. *Journal of Adolescent Health, 34*, 330-338.

Wagenaar, A. C., & Toomey, T. L. (2002). Effects of minimum drinking age laws: Review and analyses of the literature from 1960 to 2000. *Journal of Studies on Alcohol, 14*(Supplement), 206-225.

Wagenaar, A. C., Toomey, T. L., Murray, D. M., Short, B. J., Wolfson, M., Jones-Webb, R., et al. (1996). Sources of alcohol for underage drinkers. *Journal of Studies on Alcohol, 57*(3), 325-333.

Wagner, E. F., & Tarolla, S. M. (2002). Course and Outcome. In C. A. Essau (Ed.), *Substance abuse and dependence in adolescence*. London: Brunner-Routledge.

Wagner, F. A., & Anthony, J. C. (2002). From first drug use to drug dependence: developmental periods of risk for dependence upon marijuana, cocaine, and alcohol. *Neuropsychopharmacology, 26*, 479-488.

Wallace Jr., J. M., & Muroff, J. R. (2002). Preventing substance abuse among African American children and youth: Race differences in risk factor exposure and vulnerability. *The Journal of Primary Prevention, 22*(3), 235-261.

Warner, L., & White, H. (2003). Longitudinal Effects of Age at Onset and First Dinking Situations on Problem Drinking. *Substance Use & Misuse, 38*(14), 1983-2016.

Weinberg, N. Z. (1997). Cognitive and behavioral deficits associated with parental alcohol use. *Journal of the American Academy of Child and Adolescent Psychiatry, 36*(9), 1177-1186.

Weinberg, N. Z., Rahdert, E., Colliver, J. D., & Glantz, M. D. (1998). Adolescent substance abuse: A review of the past 10 years. *Journal of the American Academy of Child and Adolescent Psychiatry, 37*(3), 252-261.

White, A. M., Ghia, A. J., Levin, E. D., & Swartzwelder, H. (2000). Binge pattern ethanol exposure in adolescent and adult rats: Differential impact on subsequent responsiveness to ethanol. *Alcoholism: Clinical and Experimental Research, 24*, 1251-1256.

White, V., & Hayman, J. (2006a). *Australian secondary school students' use of alcohol in 2005*: National Drug Strategy Monograph Series.

White, V., & Hayman, J. (2006b). *Australian secondary school students' use of alcohol in 2005*: National Drug Strategy Monograph Series No. 58. Canberra: Australian Government Department of Health and Ageing.

Williams, B., Sanson, A., Toumbourou, J. W., & Smart, D. (2000). *Patterns and predictors of teenagers' use of licit and illicit substances in the Australian Temperament Project cohort*. Melbourne: Reported commissioned by the Ross Trust.

Williams, P. S., & Hine, D. W. (2002). Parental behaviour and alcohol misuse among adolescents: A path analysis of mediating influences. *Australian Journal of Psychology, 54*, 17-24.

Wilson, N., Syme, L., Boyce, T., Battistich, V. A., & Selvin, S. (2005). Adolescent alcohol, tobacco, and marijuana use: The influence of neighborhood disorder and hope. *American Journal of Health Promotion, 20*(1), 11-19.

Windle, M. (2008). Transitions into underage and problem drinking: developmental processes and mechanisms between 10 and 15 years of age. *Pediatrics, 121*(4), S273-S289.

Wittchen, H. U., Nelson, C. B., & Lachner, G. (1998). Prevalence of mental disorders and psychosocial impairments in adolescents and young adults. *Psychological Medicine, 28*, 109-126.

Wood, M. D., Read, J. P., Mitchell, R. E., & Brand, N. H. (2004). Do parents still matter? Parent and peer Influences on alcohol involvement among recent high school graduates. *Psychology of Addictive Behaviors, 18*(1), 19-30.

Yu, J. (2003). The association between parental alcohol-related behaviors and children's drinking. *Drug & Alcohol Dependence, 69*(3), 253-262.

In: Social Drinking: Uses, Abuses and Psychological Factors ISBN: 978-1-60876-219-4
Editors : K. T. Everly, E. M. Cosell, pp. 177-206 © 2010 Nova Science Publishers, Inc.

Chapter 4

COGNITIVE-BEHAVIOURAL INDICATORS OF ALCOHOLISM PHENOTYPES IN PATIENTS IN OPIOID MAINTENANCE TREATMENT

Samuel Pombo[1] [1,2], Filipe Barbosa [2], Rosário Lourenço [2], Inês Benkovskaia [2], Joana Almeida [2] and Nuno Félix da Costa [1,2]

[1] Psychology Laboratory of Medical School University of Lisbon, Portugal
[2] Psychiatric Service of Santa Maria General Hospital of Lisbon, Portugal

ABSTRACT

Polydrug use is common among patients in opioid maintenance programs. Heroin users often abuse alcohol, which may deteriorate the outcome of opioid maintenance treatment.

Excessive alcohol consumption among opioid maintenance patients has been associated with quality of life impairments and with serious social and health costs. Patients who are dependent both on illicit drugs and alcohol may have a poorer treatment outcome than patients without alcohol problems. The clinical and psychosocial treatment of these patients presents challenging work for the clinician. Therefore, treatment outcomes may be further improved if clinical subtypes of substance abusers could be identified and matched to an adequate treatment program.

In this study we aim to assess the prevalence of a drinking problem and analyse the cognitive and behavioural features of problematic alcohol use in opioid addicts according to Cloninger and Lesch's alcoholism typologies in a sample of 102 heroin-dependent patients in Opioid Maintenance Treatment. This sample was selected in the Addiction Unit of the Psychiatric Service of Santa Maria University Hospital, in Lisbon-Portugal.

Results show that alcohol use and alcohol-related problems are frequent among heroin-dependent patients. Study clinical descriptors discriminate Cloninger's type I and type II drinking problem and confirm this binary alcoholism classification in this population. Heroin-dependent patients classified as Cloninger´s type II problem drinkers

1 Correspondence address to: Dr. Samuel Pombo, Serviço de Psiquiatria e Saúde Mental do Hospital de Santa Maria (Piso 3) - Av. Prof. Egas Moniz, 1649-028 Lisboa, Portugal. Tel: 21 780 5143; e-mail: samuelpombo@gmail.com.

showed a more severe cognitive-behaviour profile than those with a type I alcohol problem, concerning alcohol-taking situation prototypes, beliefs and expectancies about alcohol effects. Data only allows preliminary results about the Lesch's alcoholism classification

This cognitive and behavioural multidimensional assessment has relevant indicators to diagnose different drinking problems among the opioid maintenance programs population. It may improve intervention and treatment outcomes, reducing current health and psychosocial damage associated with an alcohol-abusing lifestyle.

INTRODUCTION

Opioid Maintenance Treatment (OMT) with methadone or buprenorphine is a broadly used form of substitute therapy, with effective results in heroin dependence trials (West et al., 2000; Stein et al., 2005; Soyka et al. 2008; Costa et al., 2008). Studies demonstrate that it retains patients in treatment, decreases heroin use and related crime and health problems (Bertschy, 1995; Mattick et al., 2003). Even so, in some cases treatment discharge is a common reality. Treatment discontinuation or dropouts seems to be associated with loss of contact with treatment services, non-compliance with program rules, death or other medical problems, transfer to another program and achievement of goals (Magura et al., 1998). In order to improve retention and to identify risk or dropout, treatment enhancement efforts should focus on patient motivation, therapeutic involvement and frequency of session attendance, and also on the therapist perceptions (Simpson et al., 1997). According to our experience, the attendance at a weekly psychotherapeutic group could help to sustain different emotional problems habitually associated with motivation to change, dropout or relapse.

Treating OMT patients with combined heroin, cocaine and alcohol problems is more challenging than working with clients with less opioid polydrug use (Rowan-Szal et al., 2000).

Polydrug use has been reported among substance abusers from treatment and community samples (Martin et al., 1996; Hubbard et al., 1997; Gossop et al., 2002a; Leri et al., 2003; Flannery et al., 2004; Booth et al., 2006; Malcolm et al., 2006; Byqvist, 2006; Darke et al., 2007). Certainly, the use of multiple substances might cause difficulties in the assessment and understanding of addiction (Gossop, 2001). For example, focusing on a single primary substance use possibly will obscure the overall picture of substance use behaviour if a concomitant substantial polydrug use exists. In the same way, studies also suggest that multiple dependencies may present a barrier to successful treatment interventions (Downey et al., 2000; Bovasso and Cacciola, 2003; Williamson et al., 2006). Results from a 33-year follow-up study of 581 heroin addicts, indicates that heavy alcohol use was associated with negative outcomes such as more frequent illicit drug use (Hser et al., 2001).

Empirical literature supports the clinical and treatment complications of polydrug use, in terms of greater psychopathology (Beswick et al., 2001; Sumnall et al., 2004; Booth et al., 2006; Malcolm et al., 2006; Medina and Shear, 2007); higher levels of health risk behaviors (Patterson et al., 2005); and difficulties in engaging in treatment (John et al., 2001).

Heroin users often drink alcohol excessively (Almog et al., 1993; Backmund et al., 2003). Curiously, while this behaviour often causes serious health costs (Gossop et al., 2002b), limited epidemiological data is available. In many cases, it seems that an alcohol problem represents a "minor charge" in a maintenance treatment of a major heroin problem. This "cognitive blindness" related to alcohol abuse in opioid addicts appears to be generalized also to these families, and certainly it could be more concerning if this process also took place in substance abuse therapists.

Approximately 20–50% of methadone maintained therapy (MMT) patients have alcohol-related problems (Rittmannsberger et al., 2000; Hillebrand et al., 2001; Backmund et al., 2003; Dobler-Mikola et al., 2005; Senbanjo et al., 2006; Stenbacka et al., 2007). Variations in prevalence are likely since different definitions of problematic alcohol use are employed and populations studied are heterogeneous (Ottomanelli, 1999; Srivastava et al., 2008). In addition, Ottomanelli (1999), states that "in order to evaluate the extent of alcohol abuse by methadone patients, it is essential to review the prevalence of alcohol abuse in the general population in order to have a comparison base". According to the author, the range for alcohol-abusing methadone patients does not appear to be substantially different from the range rates of "heavier drinkers" in the general population.

Studies demonstrate that preadmission levels of substance use (which includes alcohol) in treatments were predictive of post-admission levels of use (Hunt et al., 1986; Kaufman, 1982), with particular attention to alcohol. A larger history of heroin abuse and its pre-MMT daily consumption predicted additional chronic alcohol use during MMT (Dobler-Mikola et al., 2005). Fairbank et al., (1993) compared the consumption of six substances (cocaine, amphetamines, illegal methadone, marijuana, and chronic alcohol use) in methadone patients' in the 1 year prior to admission with the use of these substances at 1-year follow-up. The results showed decreased substance use in the follow-up year, except for alcohol use, which remained stable during the preadmission and follow-up years.

While contradictory literature exists saying that MMT reduces alcohol use by offering a means of stabilization (Maremmani et al., 2007) or leads to an increase in alcohol use during treatment (Srivastava et al., 2008) and upon discontinuation of treatment (Maremmani et al., 2007), a positive association has been found between alcohol use and relapse into illicit drugs (Stenbacka et al., 2007).

Alcohol dependence can deteriorate the outcome of methadone treatment (Ottomanelli, 1999; Gossop et al., 2006) and is associated with increased psychiatric symptoms (Westreich, 2005). Moreover, alcohol use appears to be associated with more illicit drug use, higher rates of drop-out and higher mortality rates (Joseph and Appel, 1985; Zador and Sunjic, 2000; Hillebrand et al., 2001; Teplin et al., 2007).

Patients who are dependent both on illicit drugs and alcohol may have a poorer treatment outcome than patients without alcohol problems, that is, cause involuntary discharge from treatment (Kreek, 1978; Caputo et al., 2000).

MMT patients often experience mood changes, anxiety and personality disorders, and multiple substance use disorders which are frequently exacerbated by alcohol use (Westreich, 2005). Excessive alcohol consumption among MMT patients has been associated with quality of life impairments (Senbanjo et al., 2006), with MMT program non-completion, and are more likely to engage in unprotected sex (Arasteh et al., 2008).

Several studies have shown that a greater percentage of MMT males than females abuse alcohol (Backmund et al., 2003; Stenbacka et al., 2007). It has been shown that methadone-using patients who drink excessively are at a significantly greater risk of getting cirrhosis, esophageal varices, other medical complications and death (Stimmel et al., 1972; Anglin et al., 1989). Higher death rates and medical illness have also been reported among alcohol-using patients on methadone (Rowan-Szal et al., 2000), with alcohol playing a significant role (Gossop et al., 2003). In hepatitis C infection, which is prevalent in patients on MMT, alcohol use causes more severe and rapidly progressive liver cirrhosis and hepatocellular carcinoma (Schiff, 1997).

It has been suggested that many MMT patients replace heroin with an increase of drinking (Anglin et al., 1989). Moreover, MMT patients who were also excessive alcohol users may need higher methadone doses (Ottomanelli, 1999), and also additional heroin and alcohol use can be reduced by higher methadone doses (Hartel et al., 1995; Maxwell and Shinderman, 1999). Some reports described the practice of "boosting," that is, combining the use of alcohol and methadone in order to obtain a qualitatively different euphoria experience that could not be obtained from either drug alone (Hunt et al. 1986). The interaction between alcohol and methadone metabolism has been evaluated and documented in several studies (see Kreek, 1990).

It has been suggested that MMT drinkers tend to engage in problematic community behaviours. Hunt et al. (1986) study results show that patients who were methadone-abusive drinkers were more likely to sell their methadone (16%) than the other methadone patients (10%). This behaviour may elicit other interpretations, such as selling methadone to obtain money for drug purchases or additional alcohol consumption to alleviate the discomfort that resulted from selling a daily methadone dose (Ottomanelli, 1999).

In a study it was found that the methadone and buprenorphine treatment was able to suppress alcohol use in heroin addicts (Nava et al., 2008). This effect was more evident at the 6th and 12th month of treatment in the patients that received the highest doses of buprenorphine (32 mg/day). The mechanism underlying the effects of the OMT on the reduction of alcohol intake is still unclear although there are some promising theories. In the light of the above evidence, we hypothesize that use of the highest doses of buprenorphine could represent a potential effective treatment for heroin addicts with alcohol dependence and a possible therapeutic option in methadone-maintenance patients with an uncontrolled increase in alcohol intake. Another hypothesis is, the awareness of the potential influence of MMT on alcohol consumption is important, as early recognition and treatment of alcohol dependence in patients could have a major impact on treatment outcomes.

A previous research documented the considerable lack of treatment for alcohol related problems that occur among patients in methadone maintenance (El-Bassel et al., 1993). These patients may be further more vulnerable and should be identified and helped to achieve permanent abstinence (Dobler-Mikola et al., 2005). If MMT units do not have a clear policy for screening alcohol problems, it is truly possible that some heavy drinking patients may remain undetected in the treatment setting. Hence, clinicians should screen all methadone-using patients for alcohol abuse and dependence, and offer appropriate combined pharmacological and psychosocial treatment. For instance, Srivastava et al., (2008) study results noticeably suggested that methadone maintenance programs should prioritize addressing the issue of alcohol use and abuse in methadone maintenance programs.

However, despite the beneficial effects of methadone, it has been suggested in other studies, that methadone treatment may lead to an increase in alcohol use and dependence (Green and Jaffe, 1977; Gelb et al., 1978; Kreek, 1984; D'Aunno and Vaughn, 1992; Backmund et al., 2003), which causes significant disability and places a large burden on health care resources. Thus, establishing the nature of the relationship between alcohol and opioids is important from a clinical perspective, as improved awareness would be useful in planning treatment for opioid dependent patients with concurrent alcohol use.

Schut et al.'s (1973) study of methadone outpatients asked participants about relative changes in alcohol consumption at different phases of drug use and treatment (first use of drugs, first use of narcotics, daily narcotic use, and on MMT treatment. Sixty-eight percent of patients reported that they did not use alcohol at all during daily narcotic use; however, after an average of 18 months on methadone treatment, only 38% reported not using any alcohol at all and 20% reported drinking more or much more than prior to treatment. Anglin et al. (1989), in their retrospective study of male heroin-addicted patients, found that alcohol consumption increased during methadone treatment. However, the authors concluded that the increased alcohol consumption observed in patients on MMT was not causally related to MMT because the increase was also observed in a non-MMT treatment group. They found an inverse relationship between alcohol use and narcotic use, i.e., alcohol use increased during any phase when opiate use decreased. The study included only patients who were no longer in treatment, suggesting that there would have been a time lapse between treatment and the time of the interview.

Fairbank et al. (1993) followed 513 heroin users admitted to MMT and found that there was a decline in the use of all substances (cocaine, amphetamines, tranquilizers, marijuana, and illegal methadone) at 1 year. Alcohol was a notable exception: Heavy alcohol use (defined as 5 drinks/day for the last 90 days) remained constant from pre-admission (28%) to follow-up 1 year later (26%), regardless of whether patients were still on methadone. Strain et al. (1996) randomized intravenous opioid-dependent patients to either buprenorphine or MMT and followed them for 16 weeks. The patients who were enrolled in the methadone arm did not have a statistically significant change at either 6 or 16 weeks in the alcohol component (including the number of days drinking to intoxication in the last 30 days) of their ASI (Addiction Severity Index) scores. Schottenfeld et al. (1998) also randomized patients to either methadone or buprenorphine and found that, after 22 weeks of maintenance, there was no significant effect of MMT on the number of reported days using alcohol and the number of standard drinks consumed. Gossop et al. (2000) followed a cohort of patients for a mean of 414 days and, using the UK Royal College of Psychiatrists' recommendations for sensible drinking, found that there was no change from intake to follow-up in the overall percentage of patients who were drinking above safe guidelines, although there was reduction in the use of illicit stimulant, benzodiazepine, or opiate. Strang et al. (2000) found that in their randomized controlled trial of patients randomized to oral or injectable methadone for 6 months, there was no change in the frequency of alcohol used in the last 30 days in either group, although benzodiazepine and crack/cocaine use decreased.

Substance abuse literature has pointed to the need for taxonomies for classifying different types of addictive behaviours. Over the past decades, many efforts have been made to differentiate substance abusers in more homogeneous subgroups, in order to better predict the future course of the disorder, the accuracy of psychological and neurobiological mechanisms and to promote treatments response effectiveness (Babor and Caetano, 2006; Dvorak et al., 2006; Pombo and Lesch, 2009). These methodologies used multivariate statistical models that take into account the synergetic effects of neurobiological conditions, personality traits, co-morbidity prevalence's, alcohol consumption patterns, psychopathology and other drug consumptions. The vast majority of this type of research focused on alcoholic individuals, with the purpose to elucidate the heterogeneity of alcoholic behaviours and resolve a probable treatment matching strategy. Until today, numerous typology models have been introduced, yet few achieved clinical and empirical relevance in alcohol addiction field as Cloninger et al. (1981), Babor et al., (1992) or Lesch et al. (1988). In literature, there are generally two basic phenotypes of alcohol dependent drinkers, defined as low-severity/vulnerability subgroup and high-severity/vulnerability subgroup (Babor and Caetano, 2006). The first one is characterized by a later onset of problem drinking, less severe alcohol dependence and alcohol related problems. The latter is characterized by an early onset of problem drinking, family history of alcoholism problems, antecedents of psychopathology and severe alcohol dependence and alcohol related problems. In this binary classification, low-severity/vulnerability alcoholics are in some way similar to Cloninger et al. (1981) type I and Babor et al. (1992) type A, and high-severity/vulnerability alcoholics are similar to Cloninger et al. (1981) type II and Babor et al. (1992) type B. This dicothomic approach has been validated by biologic and psychosocial measures. For example, Pombo et al., (2008a), in a Portuguese alcoholic outpatient sample, verified that Cloninger's type II patients showed lower levels of alcoholism psychological denial, when compared with type I. Reports also reveal different levels of a potential trait biomarker for alcoholism as Platelet MAO-B activity, with type II alcoholism showing low levels of platelet MAO-B activity when comparing with to type I (von Knorring et al., 1985, 1998; Pandey et al., 1988; Sullivan et al., 1990). Recently, MAO-B was related to hostility and cognitive nonverbal reasoning in type I alcohol dependent patients (Pombo et al., 2008b).

Based on a long-term prospective follow-up study of 18 years, the Lesch Alcoholic Typology (LAT) emerged as an over-two type solution, describing predictors for chronic alcoholism development. This model distinguished four evolutionary types depending on family history of alcoholism, previous personal psychopathology and neurobiological substratum. Thus, type I evidences the appearance of early withdrawal symptoms and craving, which can be associated with an endorphinical vulnerability. Type II shows suicidal intentions, anxiety and premorbid conflicts, with changes within the serotoninergic system. Type III typifies an aggressive and impulsive behaviour with the existence of psychiatric comorbidity. In this type a chronobiological change can be previewed. And finally, type IV shows premorbid organic cerebral lesions associated with a deterioration of individual's psychic, organic, and social sphere. Lesch et al., (1988) 4 subtype distinction were validated by neurobiologic, psychological and psychophysiologic measures and psychopharmacologic trials (Dvorak et al. 2006; Lesch et al. 2001; Walter et al. 2006; Pombo et al. 2007; Hillemacher and Bleich, 2008).

As Cardoso et al. (2006) pointed out, alcoholics with concomitant polydrug use reflect a hybrid subgroup not devoted most of the time to a particular psychoactive substance. The authors called this particular type of patients, Adictopathics. Indeed, the lifetime diagnosis of joint alcohol and drug abuse is high, with most common alcohol/drug combinations related to alcohol with cocaine, alcohol with marijuana, and alcohol with sedatives (Martin et al. 1996; Staines et al., 2001). Normally, this alcoholic polydrug life-style, which may involve the active involvement in drug networks, drug dealing, sex trading, promiscuity and other behavioural problems; may engage the patients in health risks associated with Sexually Transmitted Diseases (STD) and HIV infections (Windle and Scheidt, 2004; Cardoso et al., 2006).

At the moment, a broad range of empirical research has supported the employment of alcoholism typologies in clinical and research settings, with appealing results so far.

Therefore, considering the potential usefulness of alcoholism subtyping systems and the current generalization of polydrug consumption pattern among substance use populations, it will be an indispensable concern how these constructs perform in other substance abuse disorders. For example, recently, Pombo and Lesch (2009), studied the patient's classification overlap across the main multivariate alcoholic typologies, and found that addictopathic patients from NETER classification scheme, an alcoholic polydrug subtype, significantly positively correlate with Cloninger's subtype II.

With the intent to assess the replicability and generalizability of multidimensional alcoholism typological systems in other substance use disorders, Ball et al., (1995) support the Babor's distinction of type A and type B in a sample of cocaine abusers. According to the results of the study, 33% of the cocaine abusers were classified as type B, presenting higher rates of pre-morbid risk factors, more severe drug problems, concomitant alcohol abuse and psychiatric comorbidity, when compared with 67% of participants categorized as type A.

Social learning theory made an influential contribution to the understanding of substance use, abuse and dependence (Bandura, 1977).

General cognitive-behavioural models posit that there are relevant situational cues associated with drinking that influence alcohol-related beliefs and coping strategies effectiveness. In substance abusers, these operate as situationally relapse precipitants for alcohol use or other drugs, such as nicotine, cannabis, heroin or cocaine.

Identifying patient's high-risk cues for alcohol or drug abuse plays an essential role in cognitive-behavioral models of treatment. For example, collecting information about risk situations for alcohol use could be crucial to understand a patient's reasons to drink, difficulties to maintain sobriety after treatment and to generate an individually-tailored treatment program. Usually, high-risk situations that enhance the likelihood of substance use include intrapersonal events such as cognitions and emotional states, and interpersonal dimensions such as peer pressure. The pioneer and systematic work produced by Alan Marlatt and his colleagues (Marlatt and Gordon, 1985), give considerably support for an empirically-based typology of situations that present a high risk for relapse. Indeed, based on alcoholic's interviews following discharge from treatment programs, the authors demonstrated that client descriptions of their primary relapse episodes could be classified in 8 categories: Unpleasant Emotions (UE), Physical Discomfort (PD), Pleasant Emotions (PE), Testing Personal Control (TC), Urges and Temptations to Use (UT), Conflict with Others (CO), Social Pressure to Use (SP), and Pleasant Times with Others (PO).

The behavior effects of alcohol involve a complex interaction between biologic, pharmacologic and situational features, but also cognitive factors. Alcoholism research has been giving a particular attention to the influence of the cognitive variables on drinking decisions that maintain the excessive ingestion of alcohol and consent relapse in the alcoholic's treatment process.

The beliefs that drinkers hold about the effects of the alcohol use are referred to as alcohol expectancies. Through decades, cognitive models of addictions have been generally accepted that cognitions predict social drinking behaviour. Early in the nineties, Marlatt and Rohsenow (1980) draw the attention for the important role that the expectancies about the alcohol effects played in the mediation of ingestion and behavior during acute alcohol intoxication.

Social cognitive theories recognized that alcohol use behaviour is, in part, ruled by outcome expectancies connected to the perceived consequences of alcohol consumption.

These expectancies are cognitive representations of alcohol correlated reinforcement. Numerous studies have been established that both negative and positive outcomes of drinking behaviour are associated with alcohol consumption (Connors et al., 1988; Stacy et al., 1990; Jones and McMahon, 1992; Oei and Baldwin 1994; Brown et al. 1998; Oei et al., 1998; Finn et al. 2000).

Drinking expectancies generally included increased social assertiveness, sexual enhancement, cognitive enhancement, tension reduction, negative affective change and dependence, and a loss of control over alcohol consumption (Young and Knight, 1989).

To our days, little research has been conducted on the reasons, motivations and other individual and social factors that influence drinking behaviour among the MMT client population. As a matter of fact, normally individuals perceived their alcohol use as serving specific functions in the economy of their psychological function. For example, Hillebrand et al., (2001), study the association between alcohol effect and their specific functions among clients in methadone maintenance. The results (n = 50) confirm that drinking fulfil specific functions, with the highest prevalence's related to helping to relax (84%); stop feeling bored (68%); make yourself feel better when low or depressed (66%); forget problems (64%); help to get to sleep (54%); increase the effects of methadone or any other drug (30%); help to "get going" in the morning (28%); stop feeling sick in the morning (24%) and calm after using other drugs (24%).

Psychological models has been pointing out the importance of not approaching addictive behaviours as a mere symptomatic expression of intrapsychic faults or personality disorders, since this may lead to unfocused and sometimes incessant treatment processes. Consequently, attention has been draw to the psychosocial context of substance consumption, in which addicted behaviour occurs in relation to situational and environmental circumstances, beliefs and expectations or craving.

According to Gossop (1996), treatments should be focused on different and compatible goals, such as the reduction of psychosocial problems, directly and not-directly related to the drug problem, and the reduction of risk behaviours associated with the use of drugs. Nevertheless, psychosocial interventions in addictive patients should be given carefully, mainly if patients present a multifaceted polysubstance abuse pattern and therapists did not delineate a more personalized therapeutic program.

As Moos (2005) posits, psychological health-care providers intend to ease the pain of individuals in distress and help them overcome their substance use and mental problems. However, if we believe that treatment has curative power and contributes to patients' improvement, we must consider the thought that, at times, treatment also may have iatrogenic effects and contribute to patients' deterioration. Common deterioration rates appear to be seen in substance abuse programs with different theoretical orientations, such as cognitive-behavioural interventions. In this regard, we believe that it is important to analyse cognitive and behavioural features of alcohol consumption, such as craving, positive alcohol related-expectations or non identified high-risk situations to drink, that could determine potentials iatrogenic effects in the heroin dependent with concomitant alcoholism, if they were not taken into account in the psychosocial intervention. With a more comprehensively scan of alcohol related behaviours and cognitions, we may offer detailed keys to guidance in the design of individualized psychosocial interventions.

The aim of the study is to (1) screen problematic alcohol use in opiate addicts in maintenance treatment; (2) assess cognitive-behavioural key constructs of drinking such as craving, alcohol related beliefs and expectancies and high-risk situations; (3) measure how alcoholism typologies behave in opiate addicts with an alcohol problem and (4) assess these previous cognitive-behavioural key constructs of drinking across alcoholism subtypes.

Methods and Measures

The sample comprised 102 heroin-dependent patients, admitted in the Addiction Unit of the Psychiatric Service of Santa Maria University Hospital in Lisbon, Portugal.

During the outpatient therapeutical programme clinical and socio-demographic information was collected with a brief standardized interview. After that, the patients fulfil the Michigan Alcoholism Screening Test (MAST).The MAST is one of the most widely used screening instruments for the assessment of alcohol-related problems. Was developed by Selzer (1971) and validated to the Portuguese population by Serra and Lima (1979). This scale composed by 25 weighted yes/no items have been used as an epidemiological tool in prevalence surveys of general populations. In the second moment, only patients who score positive in the screening procedure (MAST positive) were eligible for the study. As a result, patients complete the Inventory of Drug Taking Situations adapted for alcohol (IDTS), the Alcohol Related Beliefs and Expectations Questionnaire (ABEQ), the Penn Alcohol Craving Scale (PACS) and the substance abuse and dependence disorders section of the Mini International Neuropsychiatric Interview (MINI). The MINI is a short, structured diagnostic interview for DSM-IV and ICD-10 psychiatric disorders, which takes approximately 15 minutes to administer. Patients were administered with the MINI to assess the presence of lifetime DSM-IV diagnoses of ***alcohol*** and ***drug*** use disorders.

Developed by Annis and Martin (1985), the Inventory of Drug-Taking Situations (IDTS), is a 50-item self-report questionnaire that provides a profile of the situations in which an individual has used a substance of abuse. The drug-taking situations assessed on the IDTS are based on Marlatt's 8-category classification system of common antecedents to drug use. The IDTS offer for each client a split profile of the situations in which a client has used a particular drug above the past year. The individual is assessed in relation to eight categories of high-risk situations: Unpleasant Emotions (UE), Physical Discomfort (PD), Pleasant Emotions (PE), Testing Personal Control (TC), Urges and Temptations to Use (UT), Conflict with Others (CO), Social Pressure to Use (SO), and Pleasant Times with Others (PT). IDTS also present a second order factor constitute by three global categories: 1. (N) Negative situations (combining UE, PD and CO); 2. (P) Positive situations (combining PE and PT) and 3. (T) Temptation situations (combining UT, SO and TC). Clients are asked to specify their frequency of drug use or heavy drinking in the past year. The IDTS is designed to assess the situational antecedents to the use of a wide variety of drugs (e.g. alcohol, cocaine, heroin, other narcotics, cannabis, hallucinogens, tranquilizers, sedative/hypnotics, solvents, stimulants), and could be used as both research and clinical tool (Turner et al., 1997).

The Alcohol Personal Beliefs and Expectancies Inventory (APBEI) is self-administered instrument constitute by 61 items, design to evaluate beliefs and expectancies related to alcohol effect. To each belief there are five categories of a possible answer (Likert type), from “I don’t agree” to “I completely agree”. The APBEI has demonstrated good characteristics of reliability and validity in alcohol user populations. The inventory reaches good psychometric properties with highly intern consistency: correlation coefficient was 0.973 to (Split-half), the Spearman-Brown coefficient was equal to 0.986 and the alpha Cronbach was equal to 0.984. Temporal stability was adequate with a Spearman coefficient of correlation equal to 0.764. Factorial analysis isolate 6 factors, that explain 62.62% of the total variance: (F1) Factor 1: Global Positive Effects and Facilitation of Social Interactions; (F2) Factor 2: Expectancies on Activation and Sexual Pleasure effects; (F3) Factor 3: Composed by items that translate expectancies on Positive Effects in Activity and Humour; (F4) Factor 4: Dimension of the expectancies of alcohol might work as Escape to Negative Emotional States; (F5) Factor 5: Translate expectancies of Sexual Disinhibition; and (F6) Factor 6: Express expectancies on alcohol related to Diminution of Negative Feelings about himself and of Evaluated Anxiety. A global result that corresponds to the total of all answers is also obtained This tool may be useful in several contexts, like in clinical practice with alcoholics or individuals with drinking problems, since it allows the operationalization of cognitive variables that are considered to influence behaviour decisions as drinking (Gouveia et al., 1993).

Alcohol craving is considered one of the core components of the cognitive-behavioural model of alcoholism and a strong predictor of relapse. Craving was assessed with the PACS (Flannery et al., 1999). This instrument is a 5-item self-administered scale designed to assess the alcohol craving severity (frequency, intensity, duration, resistance, and overall craving) during the previous week. In an alcoholic Portuguese outpatient population, the PACS have revealed good psychometric qualities (Pombo et al., *in press*).

Quantity-Frequency (QF) method was used in order to estimate the average number of drinking days over a certain period (typical week) and then to estimate the average number of drinks consumed per drinking day. The QF drinking variable was then calculated as the product result of those measures (in standard drinks) - average number of drinks per week. A standard drink was defined as one beer, one glass of wine, one glass or shot of liquor.

All subjects were evaluated in a face-to-face interview and asked directly about the items that comprise the operationalized criteria described by each alcoholism typology. Here we provide an overview of the clinical criteria and decision process for subtyping the Cloninger approach and the Lesch alcoholic typology. Patients subtype allocation for Cloninger et al. (1981) model follows the von Knorring et al. (1985) criteria. For type I were the presences of subjective drinking problems start after age 25, first treatment contact after age 30 and few social complications (legal, work problems). Type II included subjective drinking problems start before age 25, first treatment contact before age 30 and frequent social complications (legal, work problems). Decision procedure in the set was: when the specified criteria of each subtype (I or II) was present, subjects received a positive score in each item endorsed (+1), and, when the specified criteria was not in attendance, subjects received a negative score (-1). Afterwards, for patient's allocation purposes, algebraic sum of the items are performed and the quantitative scores were transformed into categorical data on the basis of higher total positive scores (or less negative) in each subtype. Sums equal to 0 were considered to be undiagnosed classification.

The classification procedure of the 4 alcoholism sub-types of Lesch et al. (1988) was based in a computerized Decision Tree. This PC-guided version of patient's allocation (Decision Tree) is nowadays available in computer software in most European languages, including Portuguese, and it has already been used in various international trials (Lesch et al., 2001; Hillmacher et al., 2006; Walter et al., 2006; Pombo et al., 2007; 2009). The descriptors for each type are as follow: Type I: social drinking develops to habitual drinking, medium abstinence syndrome occurs early, craving, positive family history for alcoholism and minimal social effects; Type II: alcohol consumption as a coping strategy against anxiety, suicidal intentions (mainly under the influence of alcohol) and no severe somatic alcohol related disorders or withdrawal; Type III: alcohol consumption as a form of self treatment (depression, sleep disorders), suicidal tendencies, psychiatric co-morbidity, aggressive behaviour even without alcohol and mild somatic withdrawal; and Type IV: cerebral disturbances or prenatal damage before the termination of brain development, grand mal seizures (not only during withdrawal), enuresis nocturnal, deterioration of individual's psychic, organic and social sphere.

All researchers that performed the subtyping procedure enclose clinical skills to assess addiction patients and scientific knowledge to manage the principles of each classification system.

In order to accurately identify drugs consumption in our sample; all patients were urine tested for the presence of heroin, cocaine and cannabis metabolites. The urine analysis procedure was performed by staff nurses of our Addiction Unit.

All subjects were informed about the study and given the consent for participation.

The exclusion criteria were: presence of serious physical disease, severe psychiatric disorder (schizophrenia and other psychotic disorders, dementia, delirium), state of alcoholic intoxication during assessment and marked cognitive deficit.

Statistical Analysis

Considering normally distributed data (Kolmogorov-Smirnov test) parametric methods were used to calculate numerical relations between data. Chi-square (2-vs-2), student's t test and ANOVA comparisons were used to study the relation between groups. Pearson correlational analysis technique was used to measure the strength of a supposed linear association between the variables. Statistical analysis was performed with Statistical Package for Social Sciences (SPSS-Version 12.0). Statistical significance was defined at $p < 0.05$.

Results

The sample comprised 102 opiate dependent patients, being 79.4% males (N=81) and 20.6% females (N=21). Age varied between 27 and 53 years, with a mean value of 41.5 years (SD = 6.7). Females (mean age =36.8 years) were significantly ($p<0.01$) younger than males (mean age = 42.7 years). The sample was entirely Caucasian (100%). Regarding marital status, 16.6 % were married, 61.8 % were single, and 20.6% were separated. Education ranged between 2 and 15 years, with a mean value of 7.2 years of school attendance (SD=2.8). Concerning occupational status, 33.3 % were active workers, 8.8 % were already retired and 57.8% were unemployed. No other significant differences ($p >0.05$) were found between genders and the socio-demographic features.

In what is considered maintenance for the treatment of heroin-dependent outpatients, 58.4% are allocated in the methadone subgroup, with daily mean dosages of 65.1 mg

(SD=22.7); and 41.6% are allocated in the buprenorphine group, with daily mean dosages of 7.4 mg (SD=2.4). The patients report a mean of 20.4 (SD=32.0) months of heroin abstinence.

Urine analysis showed that 14.6% of the patients score positive for opiate metabolites, 19.5% score positive for cocaine metabolites, and 52.4% score positive for cannabis metabolites (THC).

Of 102 patients enrolled, 45.1% (N=46) have ***positive MAST scores*** (greater than 7), indicating putative ***alcohol related problems.*** Socio-demographic characterization of this sample indicates that, 83.7% were males and 16.3% were females; 12.3 % were married, 65.3 % were single, and 22.4% were separated; education level has a mean value of 6.5 years of school attendance; 28.6 % were active workers, 16.3 % were already retired and 55.1% were unemployed. No significant differences (p >0.05) were found between populations with MAST positive and negative cut-point scores.

Concerning clinical characterization of the problematic alcohol use sample, data shows that the average age of drinking onset was 13.7 (SD=7.5), age of alcohol abuse onset was 13.8 (SD=3.6) and the age of alcohol dependence onset was 28.7 years (SD=6.1). Subjects reported an average number of drinks per week (QF) of 72.1 units (SD=62.0).

History of family alcoholism was positive in 47.9% of the cases, being 39.6% with a father or a mother (2.1%) with an alcohol problem and 2.1% with a grandmother or grandfather (12.5%).

Of the total sample, 39.2% had a lifetime diagnosis of alcohol dependence according to the criteria of DSM-IV (MINI diagnostic interview).

After the alcoholism screening, patients were subtyped according to the following classifications sets. The decision tree system of Lesch typology classified the alcohol dependents in the following way: 33.3 % as type II; 40.0 % as type III and 26.7 % as type IV. Dicothomic typology of Cloninger with the operacionalized criteria derived from von Knorring et al. showed that 67.4% of individuals were classified as type I and 32.6% as type II. The IDTS eight subscales profile and second order global categories showed the following mean scores: (UE) Unpleasant Emotions (9.8; SD=8.0); (PD) Physical Discomfort (3.2; SD=3.3), (PE) Pleasant Emotions (6.4; SD=4.3); (TC) Testing Personal Control (3.2; SD=3.1), (UT) Urges and Temptations to Use (3.4; SD=3.7); (CO) Conflict with Others (7.8; SD=7.3); (SO) Social Pressure to Use (3.8; SD=3.9); (PT) Pleasant Times with Others (4.6; SD= 4.4); 1. Negative situations (20.9; SD=18.4); 2. Positive situations (10.9; SD=8.8) and 3. Temptation situations (10.5; SD=10.8). Concerning APBEI, the mean scores for the factors are as follow: F1; mean equal to 60.4; SD=26.8; F2; mean equal to 22.3; SD=10.9; F3; mean equal to 32.5; SD=15.8; F4; mean equal to 27.8; SD=17.6; F5; mean equal to 7.1; SD=3.5; and F6; mean equal to 23.7; SD=16.8. The mean total score for the PACS was 5.6 (SD=6.6).

No significant relationships were found between alcohol related variables (MAST, QF, age onset) and maintenance treatment variables such as buprenorphine or methadone daily mean dosages and drug screening in urine analyses.

PACS total score significantly correlate positive with the following subscales of the IDTS: UE (r = 0.30*); PE. (r = 0.44**), CO. (r = 0.40**); SP. (r = 0.45**) and PT. (r = 0.51**). No significant correlations were found between APBEI and the PACS. Significant positive correlations were observed between the MAST total score and the IDTS subscales UE. (r = 0.40 **); UT. (r = 0.37*) and CO. (r = 0.45**). MAST total score also correlate with the factors F2. (r = 0.33*); F4. (r = 0.45**); F6. (r = 0.46**) and total score (r = 0.33*) of the APBEI. No significant correlations were established between the APBEI, PACS and IDTS and socio-demographic features such as age or education level. Several significant positive correlations were found between the APBEI and the IDTS in the heroin-dependent population with concomitant problem drinking. Table I shows the matrix correlations between IDTS and the APBEI scores.

Table I. matrix correlations between IDTS and the APBEI scores

PABEQ IDTS	F1	F2	F3	F4	F5	F6	T
UE	.52**	.55**	.61**	.25	.53**	.25	.55**
PD	.38*	.48**	.47**	.18	.46**	.21	.43**
PE	.36**	.52**	.50**	.13	.60**	.40	.40**
TC	.42**	.48**	.44**	.16	.46**	.23	.43**
UT	.55**	.68**	.57**	.52**	.60**	.51**	.67**
CO	.67**	.70**	.74**	.38**	.60**	.31**	.70**
SO	.42**	.64**	.47**	.23	.57**	.23	.48**
PT	.54**	.76**	.60**	.24	.68**	.19	.58**

** $p<0.01$; * $p<0.05$.

Taking into account the Cloninger et al., (1981) classification, the statistical comparative procedure disclosed the following results: Heroin-dependent patients classified as type II problem drinkers showed significative ($t=-2.6$; $p<.05$) higher scores in MAST (MAST total score equal to 18.1), when comparing to Heroin-dependent patients classified as type I problem drinkers (MAST total score equal to 12.1); Heroin-dependent patients classified as type II problem drinkers, started to abuse and depend on alcohol ($t=4.1$, $t=4.5$, respectively; $p<.01$) earlier (mean ages of 18.3 and 24.0 years, respectively), than Heroin-dependent patients classified as type I problem drinkers (mean ages of 24.6 and 32.6 years, respectively); Heroin-dependent patients classified as type II problem drinkers, reported significative ($t=-2.6$; $p<.05$) higher average number of drinks per week (QF equal to 106.7 units), when comparing to Heroin-dependent patients classified as type I problem drinkers (QF equal to 57.1 units).

For IDTS comparisons in type I and type II patients, total scores were used. Hence, heroin-dependent patients classified as type II problem drinkers showed significative higher scores in UE, PD, TC, UT, CO, N and T, when comparing to heroin-dependent patients classified as type I problem drinkers. Table II shows the IDTS scores according to Cloninger typology of alcoholism in heroin-dependent patients.

Regarding APBEI comparisons in type I and type II patients, results showed that heroin-dependent patients classified as type II problem drinkers showed significative ($p<0.05$) higher scores in positive F1; F3 and total score, when comparing to heroin-dependent patients classified as type I problem drinkers. Table III shows the APBEI scores according to Cloninger typology of alcoholism in heroin-dependent patients.

Table II. IDTS scores according to Cloninger typology of alcoholism in heroin-dependent patients

Cloninger Set vs. IDTS	Type I X	(SD)	Type II X	(SD)	t test	p
UE. unpleasant emotions	7.0	(6.5)	15.6	(7.5)	-3.8	0.01
PD. physical discomfort	2.3	(2.8)	4.9	(4.4)	-2.1	0.05
PE. pleasant emotions	6.4	(3.2)	6.7	(4.0)		ns
TC. testing personal control	2.4	(2.3)	4.8	(4.6)	-2.0	0.05
UT. urges and temptations	2.6	(2.7)	5.2	(4.6)	-2.2	0.05
CO. conflict with others	4.4	(5.0)	14.4	(8.4)	-4.8	0.01
SO. social pressure to use	3.3	(3.9)	5.0	(5.5)		ns
PT. pleasant times with others	4.0	(3.9)	5.8	(5.2)		ns
N. Negative situations	13.8	(12.3)	34.9	(18.8)	-.4.3	0.01
P. Positive situations	10.4	(7.4)	12.6	(8.6)		ns
T. Temptation situations	8.4	(7.8)	15.0	(14.1)	-1.9	0.05

Table III. APBEI scores according to Cloninger typology of alcoholism in heroin-dependent patients

Cloninger Set vs. APBEI	Type I X	(SD)	Type II X	(SD)	t test	p
F1.	52.9	(21.8)	75.8	(27.2)	-2.9	0.05
F2.	20.3	(8.3)	26.5	(13.9)		ns
F3.	27.1	(11.1)	42.9	(17.8)	-3.5	0.01
F4.	25.6	(20.2)	32.8	(11.8)		ns
F5.	6.7	(3.4)	8.0	(3.7)		ns
F6.	21.5	(19.5)	28.6	(10.1)		ns
Total score	122.7	(47.4)	172.3	(61.8)	-2.8	0.05

No significant differences ($p > 0.05$) were found between Cloninger subtypes and socio-demographic variables or others such as PACS, methadone or buprenorphine dosages, alcoholism family history or drug screening in urine analyses.

Lesch alcoholism classification in heroin dependent patients did not showed significant differences regarding APBEI, IDST and PACS; whereas we found a marginal statistical difference ($p<0.06$) related to the subscale CO of IDTS, in what type IV patients showed higher scores (mean equal to 12.5; SD=7.0), when comparing to type II patients (mean equal to 5.3; SD=7.7). We also observe a tendency to report higher scores in APBEI and IDST in type IV and type III patients, when comparing to type II patients, however, none of these differences were significant ($p>0.05$).

Discussion

Polysubstance use is an unequivocal realism in modern addictions, been the simultaneous use of alcohol in heroin-dependent populations one of the most frequently and problematic behaviour, since the alcohol problem often may remain hidden behind a more prominent illegal drug problem. This concern evidently augments when studies reported the considerable lack of treatment for alcohol related problems that occur among patients in opiate maintenance (El-Bassel et al., 1993).

Like in quite a few studies, the frequency of alcohol related problems in opioid addiction populations was high (Backmund et al., 2003; Rittmannsberger et al., 2000; Dobler-Mikola et al., 2005; Hillebrand et al., 2001; Senbanjo et al., 2006; Stenbacka et al., 2007). The alcohol abuse measurement procedure in our heroin-dependent population undergoing OMT, reached a high prevalence of problem drinking, whether this was achieved by a screening method as MAST cut-point score, or according to the diagnostic criteria of DSM-IV (substance abuse section of MINI). Definitely, alcohol use and alcohol-related problems was confirmed to be common among heroin-dependent patients, in what about half of the patients showed indications of problem drinking and approximately one third meet the lifetime diagnosis of alcohol dependence (Maddux and Elliot, 1975; Joseph and Appel, 1985; Ottomanelli, 1999; El-Bassel et al., 1993; Hillebrand et al., 2001; Stenbacka et al., 2007). Several studies highlight the importance of screening alcohol problems in order to prevent the major impact of his recurrent related-problems, especially if heavy drinking continued to remain undetected in the treatment setting. For example, opioid addicted individuals who abused alcohol had a longer arrest history, higher rate of mortality, greater involvement in secondary abuse of other drugs, more severe psychopathology in childhood, a larger prevalence's of antisocial or borderline personality disorders diagnoses, greater global impairment and are at greater risk of drug overdose (Rounsaville et al. 1982; Joseph and Appel, 1985; Roszell et al., 1986; El-Bassel et al., 1993; Chatham et al., 1995; Best et al., 1999). In addition, an alcohol abusing lifestyle could be particularly dangerous to exposure to HIV duo to the influence of alcohol effect. Certainly, patients who consume alcohol and illicit drugs have a higher probability of risk behaviours and subsequent HIV infection (Ottomanelli, 1992). Patients who drink heavily and participate in an OMT may also be at risk of combined Central Nervous System (CNS) depressant pharmacological effects of both substances. For instance, patients could drink to increase the effects of methadone. However, in this study there was no significant correlation between alcohol-related variables and methadone or buprenorphine dosages, which is not consistent with studies stating that MMT patients with associated excessive alcohol use may need higher methadone dosages (Ottomanelli, 1999) and that additional heroin and alcohol use can be reduced by higher methadone dosages (Hartel et al., 1995; Maxwell and Shinderman, 1999).

We also did not find any relationship between the alcohol-related variables and the drug screening in urine analyses, suggesting that alcohol-related problems was not associated with more illicit drug use, a result contrary to others reviews, that reported a positive association between alcohol use and relapse into illicit drugs (Stenbacka et al., 2007). They underlined as well that alcohol dependence can deteriorate the outcome of methadone treatment (Gossop et al., 2006; Ottomanelli, 1999).

It may be put forward that many opiate dependent individuals report the frequent use of alcohol to cope with psychological discomfort related to heroin addiction rehabilitation. Ottomanelli, (1999) points out that alcohol abuse appeared to be more directly related to biological variables (i.e., potentiator of other drugs, relaxant) and to psychological variables (i.e., stimulus to socialization, and psychopathology), which enhanced the conclusion that alcohol abuse by methadone patients is as much a function of the lifestyle of the addicted individual as a biological need to alleviate withdrawal distress.

As in previous studies focused in alcohol dependent populations, the subtype distribution prevalence's have distinguished the predominance of Cloninger's type I patients (2/3 patients), and Lesch's type II and III (Bleich et al. 2004; Carpenter and Hasin, 2001; Hillmacher et al., 2006; Lykouras et al. 1994; Pombo et al., 2007; Pombo and Lesch, 2009). Recently, a closer examination of patients' classification relationship between Lesch et al. subtypes and Cloninger et al. model found a moderate overlap between Lesch et al. type IV and von Knorring et al criteria of Cloninger Type II. The authors mention that these results may be explained by the overlap of some of the operacionalized criteria used to define each alcoholic subtype (Pombo and Lesch, 2009).

Approaching the alcoholic subtypes classification on a basis of a spectrum of severity, Cloninger type I and Lesch type II and III should be considered as a moderate severity subgroup and Cloninger type II and Lesch type VI as a high severity subgroup (Pombo and Lesch, 2009).

Craving can be defined as a strong desire/urge towards alcohol consumption. In the study analysis, PACS positively correlated with some subscales of the IDTS, which means that the heroin-dependent population with a drinking problem who reports more alcohol-related craving in the most recent week, tend to generally identify triggers to use alcohol associated with pleasant times with others, social pressure to use, conflict with others, pleasant and unpleasant emotions. These results suggested that alcohol craving is a regular associate of alcohol use emotional triggers. In some extent, these findings go in accordance with previous studies who found that alcohol dependent "cravers" showed significantly higher scores in negative emotions (Rubonis et al., 1994; Cooney et al., 1997; Litt et al., 2000; Andersohn and Kiefer; 2004) as depression, anxiety or aggressivity, supporting the concept of negative and positive craving - cognitive component of craving induced by negative and positive emotions (Pombo et al., *in press*). Contrary to expected, the PACS did not correlate with the Urges and Temptations to Use subscale of IDTS.

Concerning the Cloninger et al., (1981) classification, heroin-dependent patients classified as type II problem drinkers showed more alcohol-related problems, started to abuse and depend on alcohol earlier and reported higher average number of drinks per week, when comparing to heroin-dependent patients classified as type I problem drinkers. These results from the clinical profile of the sample clearly discriminate the type I and type II Cloninger's *et al.* (1981) approach and visibly validate this binary alcoholism classification in an opioid addiction population with concomitant alcohol abuse problem. According to this classification, type I patients, recognised as low-severity/vulnerability subgroup, are characterised by showing a later onset of the drinking problem and less alcohol related problems, and type II patients, acknowledged as high-severity/vulnerability subgroup, by an early onset of the drinking problem, family history of alcoholism problems, antecedents of psychopathology and severe alcohol related problems (Babor and Caetano, 2006).

Back in 1985, Marlatt and Gordon developed an empirical eight-category of excessive drinking situations based on the circumstances that surround the after-treatment relapse episode of the alcoholics. Comprehensive evaluations of relapse situations have been demonstrating negative situation triggers with a fundamental role in the alcohol consume (type II re)engagement. For example, the study of Marlatt and Gordon (1985) concluded that in 35% of the cases the relapses occur by triggers related to negative emotions, 16% interpersonal conflicts with others and 20% by social pressure. Another study concluded that 62–73% of relapse episodes are related to negative emotions and social pressure (Lowman et al., 1996). On the grounds of this work, cognitive and behavioral relapse prevention programs for the psychological treatment of addictions focus on training clients in identifying and coping with their own high-risk situations for heavy drinking. This intervention might be assist with the fulfillment of a psychometric tool as the IDTS that offers a broad profile of the situations in which a client has used alcohol in the past year. Certainly, according to Turner et al., (1997), the implementation of IDTS as a treatment planning tool in clinical practice offers the therapist an effortlessly administered aid to the detection of a patient's high-risk situations for use of a particular drug.

One of the main aims of this research was to assess how the cognitive-behavioural taxonomy of excessive drinking situations could respond to the dichotomic classification of alcohol abuse of Cloninger. So, when considering alcohol use triggers assessed by the scores of IDTS taxonomy, results showed that heroin-dependent patients classified as type II problem drinkers were significantly more likely to abuse on alcohol in situations related to UE, PD, TC, UT, CO, N and T, than those classified as heroin-dependent patients classified as type I problem drinkers. In general, heroin-dependent patients classified as type II problem drinkers reported a more severe alcohol-taking profile than those with type I alcohol problem. This fact goes in conformity with previous studies that found that high negative profile patients have elevated alcohol dependence scores (Annis and Graham, 1995; Turner et al., 1997). Nevertheless, with further examination we could observe that heroin-dependent patients classified as type II problem drinkers were much more vulnerable to negative situation triggers like intrapsiquic unpleasant emotions (e.g. anger, anxiety, depression) or interpersonal conflituality (e.g.., discussions with others), than heroin-dependent patients classified as type I problem drinkers. These results are consistent with Waldrop et al., (2007), who compared high-risk triggers and situations among persons with alcohol dependence or cocaine dependence, with or without posttraumatic stress disorder (PTSD). The authors observe that individuals with PTSD+ reported significantly greater substance use in response to negative situations, as compared to PTSD− individuals, supporting this finding with the self-medication theory, in which subjects who experience high rates of negative situations use substances in an attempt to minimize such symptoms. In line with this construction, that enhances the negative reward properties of alcohol, our current findings regarding alcohol use situational triggers and the Cloninger typology might be explain by the high severity profile of disease that typically characterized type II patients, notable by an early onset and frequent psychiatric comorbidity (Babor and Caetano, 2006; Pombo and Lesch, 2009).

These two different IDTS profiles identified from type I/II patients may prove to be suitable for research analysis, but also of greater relevance for clinical intervention within a cognitive-behavioural perspective. Indeed, from a cognitive and behavioural psychological standpoint, we may suggest the development of intervention strategies designed to increase patient's coping self-efficacy, in order to improve perceived internal control over alcohol use. This proposal should have particular focus in type II individuals, since they present a higher severity profile, particular vulnerable to negative situation triggers (e.g. anxiety, social pressure) and research indicates that the greater the level of alcohol dependence, the lower the confidence in the ability to resist the urge to drink heavily in high-risk situations, especially in situations involving unpleasant emotions and conflict with others (Sklar et al., 1997). For these patients, programmes that encourage stress management and social skills training may be essential. In the future we should afford empirical support for the hypothesis that type II patients present a lack of perceived control over alcohol use and a lower confidence in the ability to resist drinking heavily in high-risk situations.

Expectancies usually result form the drinker previous direct and indirect learning experiences with alcohol, and are presumed to be central in decisions to drink (Connors et al., 1988). Generally, drinkers were able to identify quite a few areas of alcohol effects. For example, reduction of negative emotional states, global positive effect, sexual activation, tension reduction, social anxiety reduction, or decreased loneliness and boredom. Almost certainly, drinkers may be more susceptible to use alcohol if they enclose the belief that the alcohol ingestion is an efficient way of dealing with the own negative emotions and facilitate a more affirmative social behaviour. All these expectancies are thought to operate in decision making processes and are hypothesized to have a prevailing independently effect on drinking behaviours. A broad evaluation of personal expectancies about the alcohol effect provides to the clinician a better understanding of the cognitive dimension of patient's decisions to drink and also allows a more accurate elaboration of therapeutic programs, mostly in populations with polysubstance use. In methadone maintenance patients, alcohol is predominantly used to fulfil specific functions as helping to relax; stop feeling bored; make yourself feel better when low or depressed; forget problems; help to get to sleep; increase the effects of methadone or any other drug; help to ''get going'' in the morning; stop feeling sick in the morning and calm after using other drugs.

As expected, APBEI discriminate individuals with different levels of problem drinking. Study revealed that heroin-dependent patients classified as type II problem drinkers endorse generally higher levels of alcohol related-expectancies, especially about positive global effects and social interaction facilitation and positive effects on activation and humour, when comparing to heroin-dependent patients classified as type I problem drinkers. This finding goes in accordance with numerous studies, who concluded that individuals who drink more and present a higher problem drinking severity have significantly more positive expectancies about the alcohol effects, which will result in desirable outcomes who promote the increase of alcohol use (Brown et al., 1985; Connors *et al.,* 1988; Stacy et al., 1990; Oei and Baldwin 1994; Brown et al. 1998; Oei et al., 1998; Finn et al. 2000).

Even though, it's important to question why type II patients, acknowledged to exhibit and recognized more alcohol related consequences, report higher levels of expectancies related to the putative alcohol effect when they face up higher levels of negative outcome effects. It seems that the behavioural and social consequences related to alcohol abuse did not influence as much alcohol related cognitions in type II problem drinkers. Self-medication hypothesis might attempt to explain this conception, given the fact that patients who experience more psychological distress, like type II patients (high-severity/vulnerability subgroup), may achieve more reward properties derived from the ability of alcohol play down such negative feelings and symptoms. Other alternative explanation implicates a particular cluster of personality traits that generally characterized type II patients – high novelty seeking and low harm avoidance. These traits reflecting impulsivity and desinhibition may account to a greater exploration of the environment and also make type II patients more vulnerable to pharmacological benefits of alcohol, which could enhance alcohol related cognitions.

These assertions recognized that cognitions could also account to sustain the higher prevalence's of alcohol related problems in type II patients. Indeed, the combination of positive cognitions related to alcohol effect with impulsivity, a poor inhibitory control quality that noticeably characterized Cloninger type II problem drinker's profile, could explain why these patients have difficulties in restrain problematic drinking and present a poorer prognosis.

Cognitions might predict alcohol use in several drinking situations. In fact, expectancies reported by alcohol users more often deal with intrapersonal and interpersonal conflicts in social situations (Connors et al., 1988). As predicted, APBEI positive correlates with IDTS subscales, with the significant coefficients ranging from a low 0.31 (APBEI total score vs. CO subscale of IDTS) to a high 0.74 (APBEI F4 vs. CO subscale of IDTS). These findings clearly suggest that patients who endorse more general positive beliefs and expectancies related to alcohol effect tend to drank heavily across more intra-inter personal situations. We may consider that in high risk-situations for alcohol use, beliefs and expectancies related to alcohol effect become more prominent, rising the vulnerability for drinking behaviour. As Connors et al. (1988) mention, "if an adequate coping response is not available or not emitted, there results a decreased sense of self-efficacy and concomitant positive outcome expectancies regarding alcohol, which taken together lead to an increased probability that the alcoholic will drink in that situation". In a study related to drinking outcome expectancies during relapse situations among male alcoholics, the authors reported that almost half of the expectancies reported dealt with drinking as an aid in coping with a social situation, another one-quarter of the expectancies dealt with drinking to gain control of a situation. Interestingly, in a recent report by Blume et al., (2006), it was concluded that cognitions about drinking may not only predict consumption patterns, but also may predict the experience of negative drinking consequences. According to the authors, a significant portion of recent consequences experienced by individuals were not necessarily related to drinking per se, but rather were related to cognitions; for instance, the expected effects of alcohol and the self-efficacy for successfully negotiating high-risk situations without drinking heavily.

Data reduction only allows preliminary results regarding the Lesch alcoholism classification in heroin dependent patients, in what observes a tendency in type IV patients to present a high severity profile regarding the cognitive and behavioural dimensions assessed. This tendency is congruent with a high severity subgroup as Lesch type IV patients (Pombo and Lesch, 2009).

In the study we should consider some limitations: Like in other studies, our data demonstrate a high prevalence of drinking problems among patients undergoing opiate maintenance treatment. However, comparisons across studies should be done cautiously, since diverse study methods have used different instruments to assess alcohol use and abuse, producing some heterogeneity in the results prevalence's. In the study we did not measure other psychological dimensions that could account for the differences in the IDTS profiles. In some extent, other possible explanation accounting for the differences in IDTS profiles between type I and type II patients could be the notion of motivation to change (Prochaska and DiClemente, 1986). Indeed, studies have argued that readiness to change account for the differentiation of IDTS drinking profiles, with more motivated people reporting higher overall IDTS scores or greater differentiation of IDTS subscales and least motivated showing low totals scores and undifferentiated profiles (Annis and Graham; 1995; Turner et al., 1997). As Turner et al. (1997) states, patients with lack of awareness of their drinking (pre-contemplation stage) would have little interest, and maybe little awareness of how their affective states and external circumstances influenced their alcohol use; on the other hand, patients that have made a decision to change (determination stage), would have paid more attention on their alcohol use patterns. Moreover, addiction denial could also provide another plausible interpretation for the differences in IDTS in the subtypes. Alcohol abuse denial defines the notion of the drinker refusal to acknowledge his pathological alcohol use or minimizing the relation between alcohol consumption and his psychological, organic and social problems. In psychodynamic terms, denial is usually considered as an unconscious ego defence mechanism. Other authors propose that alcoholic denial is more related to cognitive failure than an ego defence mechanism, consisting in a diminished capacity for insight, for example, due to executive function failure (Rinn et al., 2002). A recent study performed in alcoholic patients have demonstrated that Cloninger's type II patients reported lower levels of alcoholism denial, when compared with type I patients (Pombo et al., 2008a). Indeed, since type I patients tend to become more defensive regarding alcohol use it will be expected that they tend to refuse or turn hesitant in identifying their real high-risk situations, and as result, a lower and more undifferentiated IDTS profile could emerge. In the psychometric study of IDTS performed by Turner et al., (1997), other dimensions were found to influence IDTS scores. For example, the authors concluded that individuals who reported that they spend little time using unaccompanied and experience pressure from family or friends to use substances, had higher scores on the IDTS interpersonal subscales of PT and SP, while individuals who assumed spending more time using substances alone had elevations on the IDTS intrapersonal subscales of UE and PD.

We also may found some inconsistencies regarding the alcohol related expectancies in this population, since this association may vary by population heterogeneity, polysubstance use and levels and time-course of substance use.

The screening for drug metabolites in urine analyses, a procedure that incorporates the clinical routine of our addiction unit, was properly controlled by the nurse staff. Nevertheless, alcohol use was only assessed by patients self-reports providing a possible reliability limitation in the interview, given the fact that participants with an excessive alcohol use may tend to underestimate or deny alcohol consumption and related problems. Therefore, a more accurate determination of patient alcohol consumption levels, for example, urine analyses or liver function, should be performed. For example, Stenbacka et al., (2007), posits that most studies on MMT patients consider the alcohol use information based on records from interviews and questionnaires, and only occasionally using laboratory tests. Indeed, a recent study of the authors found a significant association between the number of alcohol-related diagnoses prior to treatment and a positive 5HTOL/5HIAA (sensitive biomarker of acute alcohol consumption) test during MMT.

It's also important to bring up some technical issues applying the Lesch classification procedure to opiate dependent patients who meet also the criteria for alcohol dependence, since items related to alcohol withdrawal or seizures could also be attached to a frequent behaviour in this population like higher levels of benzodiazepine use.

Finally, we should also consider limitations due to the relatively small sample size of the study, the heterogeneity of the population and the fact that gender differences were not examined due to small cell sizes. So, it's not clear without further evaluation that these data could be generalized to other populations of drinkers.

CONCLUSION

A range of different factors that differ from person to person influences aetiology and outcomes of addiction. In research and clinical practice, the evaluation of different functions such as screening, assessment, diagnosis, treatment planning and follow-up, are an essential step to identify behaviours and associated problems and to improve prevention and treatment in a population that often seeks help related to the misuse of substances (Hester and Miller, 2003).

Studies have been assembling empirical evidence for the treatment of alcohol dependence in general (Johnson and Ait-Daoud, 2000; Hester and Miller, 2003; Saitz, 2007), particularly relapse prevention pharmaceutical agents such as naltrexone and acamprosate. In the meantime, when we extend the clinical management of an alcohol problem to methadone-using patients, we may face several boundaries in the treatment outcome, mostly related to the complexity inherent to polysubstance use, abuse or dependence and also because we must consider the exception of a pharmacologically effective tool in the treatment of alcoholism such as naltrexone since it is contraindicated in methadone-using patients.

A more accurate clinical establishment of the nature of the relationship between alcohol and opioids, would be useful in planning treatment for opioid dependent patients with concurrent alcohol use, with particular focus on relapse prevention not only for heroin use but for other drugs and alcohol as well (Stenbacka et al., 2007; Srivastava et al., 2008).

The study concluded that in general, heroin-dependent patients classified as type II problem drinkers demonstrate a more severe alcohol-taking profile than those with a type I alcohol problem. Nevertheless, upon closer examination we were be able to identify different situation-specific prototypes of alcohol use, in which heroin-dependent patients classified as type II problem drinkers were much more vulnerable to negative situation triggers like intrapsiquic unpleasant emotions or interpersonal confliction, than heroin-dependent patients classified as type I problem drinkers. These high-risk situations in type II patients, along with more positive beliefs and expectancies about alcohol effect may increase the chance for ineffective coping responses with an unremitting alcohol abuse pattern. Therefore, these cognitive-behavioural indicators should help the clinician to better tailor the intervention in this particular population. Indeed, treatment outcomes may be further improved if clinical subtypes of substance abusers could be identified and matched to an adequate treatment. Given this potential impact, evidence comes from the observation that type A alcoholics have better outcomes in interactional treatment and do more poorly with coping skills training and in opposition, type B alcoholics had better outcomes with the coping skills treatment and worse outcomes with interactional therapy (Litt et al., 1992). To some extent, these findings from Litt et al. (1992) may have clinical implications in our study, since type A patients from Babor et al. (1992) and type I from Cloninger et al. (1981) are in some way similar (low-severity/vulnerability subgroup), as Babor et al. (1992) type B and Cloninger et al. (1981) type II (high-severity/vulnerability subgroup).

With a cognitive-behavioural multidimensional assessment of relevant indicators such as alcohol craving, type and degree of beliefs and expectations related to alcohol effects and the identification of taxonomic high-risk situations for alcohol use would enable the substance abuse psychological health-care to focus on the management of specific areas to prevent problem drinking and reduce current harm associated with their lifestyle. Indeed, the cognitive-behavioural measurement and conceptualization underlying the pathological drinking in heroin dependence is essential in the development of successful psychoeducational messages and relapse prevention strategies related to alcohol use. Cognitive-behavioural therapists should teach patients a broad range of coping skills to avoid or deal with the return of previous excessive alcohol use, such as problem solving, challenging distorted thoughts, relaxation, assertiveness, modelling and functional analysis. In cases following an assessment of specific alcohol-use functions reported by patients with polysubstance use pattern, the mental health clinicians, in interaction with patients, should encourage them to indentify high-risk situations in as much detail as possible and develop alternative ways of fulfilling these functions. Nevertheless, it is imperative to posit that these psychological strategies only succeed with patients if therapists always keep up efforts to build a good therapeutic relationship with them. For example, Dundon et al., (2008), focused on a factor that is common to all types of psychosocial treatments for substance abuse—the therapeutic alliance between the patient and the clinician. According to the authors, the therapeutic alliance reflects the nature and strength of the affective bond between patient and primary clinician in their collaboration in identifying and working toward the patient's treatment goals.

Future investigations need to be considered in order to continuously update the cognitive-behavioural background with new empirical findings about clinical subgroups and polysubstance abuse life courses.

References

Almog YJ, Anglin MD, Fisher DG. (1993) Alcohol and heroin use patterns of narcotics addicts: gender and ethnic differences. *Am J Drug Alcohol Abuse*;19:219–38.

Andersohn, F. and Kiefer, F. (2004). Depressive mood and craving during alcohol withdrawal: association and interaction. *German Journal Psychiatry*, 7, 6-11.

Anglin, M. D., Almog, I. J., Fisher, D. G., and Peters, K. R. (1989). Alcohol use by heroin addicts: Evidence for an inverse relationship. A study of methadone maintenance and drug-free treatment samples. *American Journal of Drug and Alcohol Abuse* 15, 191– 207.

Annis, H.M. and Martin, G. (1985). *Inventory of Drug-Taking Situations*. Toronto, Canada: Addiction Research Foundation.

Annis, H. M., and Graham, J. M. (1995). Profile types on the Inventory of Drinking Situations: Implications for relapse prevention counselling. *Psychology of Addictive Behaviours* 9, 176-182.

Arasteh, K., Des Jarlais, D.C., Perlis, T. (2008). Alcohol and HIV sexual risk behaviors among injection drug users. *Drug Alcohol Depend.* 95, 54–61.

Babor, T. F., De Hofmann, M. I., Boca, F. K., Hesselbrock, V., Meyer, R. E., Dolinsky, Z. S. and Rounsaville, B. (1992) Types of alcoholics, I: evidence for an empirically derived typology based on indicator of vulnerability and severity. *Archives of General Psychiatry* 49, 599-608.

Babor and Caetano (2006) Subtypes of substance dependence and abuse: implications for diagnostic classification and empirical research. *Addiction* 101(sup):104-110.

Backmund M, Schutz CG, Meyer K, Eichenlaub D, Soyka M. (2003) Alcohol consumption in heroin users, methadone-substituted and codeine-substituted patients-frequency and correlates of use. *Eur Addict Res*; 9:45–50.

Bandura, A. (1977) Self-efficacy: toward a unifying theory of behavioural change. *Psychological Review* 84, 191–215.

Ball S. A. Carroll K. M. ; Babor T. F ; Rounsaville B. (1995) Subtypes of cocaine abusers: support for a Type A-Type B distinction. *Journal of Consulting and Clinical Psychology* 63, 115-124.

Bertschy, G. (1995). Methadone maintenance treatment: An update. *European Archives of Psychiatry and Clinical Neuroscience* 245, 114–125.

Best, D., Gossop, M., Lehmann, P., Harris, J., and Strang, J. (1999). The relationship between overdose and alcohol consumption among methadone maintenance patients. *Journal of Substance Use* 4, 41– 44.

Beswick, T., Best, D., Rees, S., Coomber, R., Gossop, M., Strang, J., (2001). Multiple drug use: patterns and practices of heroin and crack use in a population of opiate addicts in treatment. *Drug Alcohol Rev.* 20, 201–204.

Bleich S, Bayerlein K, Reulbach U, Hillemacher T, Bönsch D, Mugele B, Kornhuber J, Sperling W. (2004) Homocysteine levels in patients classified according to Lesch's typology. *Alcohol and Alcoholism* 39(6), 493-498.

Blume AW, Lostutter T, Schmaling K, Marlatt A. (2003) Beliefs about drinking behavior predict drinking consequences, *Journal of Psychoactive Drugs* 35(3), 395–399.

Booth B, Leukefeld C, Falck R, Wang J, Carlson R, (2006). Correlates of rural methamphetamine and cocaine users: results from a multistate community study. *J. Stud. Alcohol* 67, 493–501.

Bovasso, G., Cacciola, J. (2003). The long-term outcomes of drug use by methadone maintenance patients. *J. Behav. Health Serv. Res.* 30, 290–303.

Brown SA, Goldman MS, Christiansen BA. (1985) Do alcohol expectancies mediate drinking patterns of adults? *Journal of Consulting and Clinical Psychology* 53, 512-19.

Brown SA, Carrello PD, Vik PW, Porter RJ. (1998) Change in alcohol effect and self-efficacy expectancies during addiction treatment. *Substance Abuse*; 19:155–67.

Byqvist, S., (2006). Patterns of drug use among drug misusers in Sweden gender differences. *Subst. Use Misuse* 41, 1817–1835.

Caputo F, Addolorato G, Domenicali M, Mosti A, Viaggi M, Trevisani F, Gasbarrini G, Bernardi M and Stefanini G , and The Services For Addiction Treatment (2002) Short-term methadone administration reduces alcohol consumption in non-alcoholic heroin addicts. *Alcohol Alcohol* 37, 164 –16 8.

Cardoso, J.M., Barbosa, A., Ismail, F. and Pombo, S. (2006) Neter Alcoholic Typology (NAT). *Alcohol and Alcoholism* 41, 133-139.

Carpenter KM, Hasin DS (2001) Reliability and discriminant validity of the type I/II and type A/B alcoholic subtype classifications in untreated problem drinkers: a test of the Apollonian-Dionysian hypothesis. *Drug and Alcohol Dependence* 63, 51-67.

Chatham, L. R., Rowan-Szal, G. A., Joe, G. W., Brown, B. S., and Simpson, D. D. (1995). Heavy drinking in a population of methadone-maintained clients. *Journal of Studies on Alcohol* 7, 417– 422.

Cooney, N.L., Litt, M.D., Morse, P.A., Bauer, L.O. and Gaupp, L. (1997). Alcohol cue reactivity, negative mood reactivity, and relapse in treated alcoholics men. *Journal Abnormal Psychology* 106, 243-250.

Connors G J; O'Farrell T J; Pelcovits M A. (1988). Drinking outcome expectancies among male alcoholics during relapse situations. *British journal of addiction* 83(5), 561-6.

Costa NF, Pombo S, Barbosa F. (2008) A propósito da avaliação clínica numa consulta de toxicodependências. *Toxicodependências* 14, 25-34.

Cloninger, C. R., Bohman, M. and Sigvardsson, S (1981). Inheritance alcohol abuse: cross fostering analysis of adopted men. *Archives of General Psychiatry* 38, 861868.

D'Aunno, T., and Vaughn, T. E. (1992). Variations in methadone treatment practices. Results from a national study. *Journal of the American Medical Association* 267, 253– 258.

Downey, K., Helmus, T., Schuster, C. (2000). Treatment of heroin-dependent poly-drug abusers with contingency management and buprenorphine maintenance. *Exp. Clin. Psychopharmacol.* 8, 176–184.

Darke, S., Ross, J., Teesson, M. (2007). The Australian Treatment Outcome Study ATOS: what have we learnt about treatment for heroin dependence? *Drug Alcohol Rev.* 26, 49–54.

Dobler-Mikola, A., Hattenschwiler, J., Meili, D., Beck, T., Boni, E., Modestin, J. (2005). Patterns of heroin, cocaine, and alcohol abuse during long-term methadone maintenance treatment. *J. Subst. Abuse Treat.* 29, 259–265.

Dundon W, Pettinati H, Lynch K, Xie H, Varillo K, Makadon C, Oslin D. (2008) The therapeutic alliance in medical-based interventions impatcs outcome in treating alcohol dependence. *Drug and Alcohol Dependence* 95, 230–236.

Dvorak A, Pombo S, Ismail F, Barbosa A, Cardoso JM, Figueira ML, Walter H, Lesch OM (2006). Tipologias da dependência do álcool e o seu significado para a terapêutica médica. *Acta Psiquiátrica Portuguesa* 52, 1693-1705.

El-Bassel, N., Schilling, R. F., Turnbull, J. E., and Su, K.-H. (1993). Correlates of alcohol use among methadone patients. *Alcoholism: Clinical and Experimental Research* 17, 681–686.

Fairbank, J.A., Dunteman, G.H., and Condelli, W.S. (1993). Do methadone patients substitute other drugs for heroin? Predicting substance use at 1-year follow-up. *American Journal of Drug and Alcohol*

Abuse 19, 465–474.

Flannery, B.A., Volpicelli, J.R. and Pettinati. (1999). Psychometric properties of the Penn Alcohol Craving Scale. *Alcoholism: Clinical Experimental Research* 8, 1289-1295.

Flannery, B., Morgenstern, J., McKay, J., Wechsberg, W., Litten, R. (2004). Cooccurring alcohol and cocaine dependence: recent findings from clinical and field studies. *Alcohol Clin. Exp. Res.* 28, 976–981.

Finn PR, Sharkansky EJ, Brandt KM, Turcotte N. (2000). The effects of familial risk, personality, and expectancies on alcohol use and abuse. *Journal of Abnormal Psychology* 109:122–133.

Gelb, A. M., Richman, B. L., and Anand, O. P. (1978). Quantitative and temporal relationships of alcohol use in narcotic addicts and methadone maintenance patients undergoing alcohol detoxification. *American Journal of Drug and Alcohol Abuse* 5, 191–198.

Gossop, M. (1996). Cognitive and behavioural treatments for substance misuse. In: Edwards G. and Dare C. (Ed.), *Psychotherapy, Psychological Treatments and the Addictions* (158-172). Great Britain. Cambridge University Press.

Gossop, M., Marsden, J., Stewart, D., and Rolfe, A. (2000). Patterns of improvement after methadone treatment: 1 year follow-up results from the National Treatment Outcome Research Study. *Drug and Alcohol Dependence* 60, 275–286.

Gossop, M. (2001). A web of dependence. *Addiction* 96, 677–678.

Gossop M, Marsden J, Stewart D. (2002a) Dual dependence: assessment of dependence upon alcohol and illicit drugs, and the relationship of alcohol dependence among drug misusers to patterns of drinking, illicit drug use and health problems. *Addiction* 97:169–78.

Gossop, M., Marsden, J., Stewart, D., Kidd, T. (2002b). Changes in use of crack cocaine after drug misuse treatment: 4–5 year follow-up results from the National Treatment Outcome Research Study NTORS. *Drug Alcohol Depend.* 66, 21–28.

Gossop, M., Stewart, D., Browne, N., and Marsden, J. (2003). Methadone treatment for opiate dependent patients in general practice and specialist clinic settings: Outcomes at 2-year follow-up. *Journal of Substance Abuse Treatment* 24, 313– 321.

Gossop M, Stewart D, Marsden J. (2006) Effectiveness of drug and alcohol counselling during methadone treatment: content, frequency, and duration of counselling and association with substance use outcomes. *Addiction* 101, 404–12.

Green, J., and Jaffe, J. H. (1977). Alcohol and opiate dependence; a review. *Journal of Studies on Alcohol* 38, 1274– 1293.

Hartel, D. M., Schoenbaum, E. E., Selwyn, P. A., Kline, J., Davenny, K., Klein, R. S., et al. (1995). Heroin use during methadone maintenance treatment: The importance of methadone dose and cocaine use. *American Journal of Public Health* 85, 83– 88.

Hester R. K. and Miller W.R. (2003). *Handbook of Alcoholism Treatment Approaches*. USA. Pearson Education Inc..

Hillebrand, J., Marsden, J., Finch, E., and Strang, J. (2001). Excessive alcohol consumption and drinking expectations among clients in methadone maintenance. *Journal of Substance Abuse Treatment* 21, 155–160.

Hillemacher T, Bayerlein K, Wilhelm J, Bönsch D, Poleo D, Sperling W, Kornhuber J, Bleich S. (2006) Recurrent detoxifications are associated with craving in patients classified as type I according to Lesch's typology. *Alcohol and Alcoholism* 41(1), 66-69.

Hillemacher, T. and Bleich, S. (2008) Neurobiology and treatment in alcoholism--recent findings regarding Lesch's typology of alcohol dependence. *Alcohol and Alcoholism* 43, 341-6.

Hser, Y. I., Anglin, M. D., and Powers, K. (1990). Longitudinal patterns of alcohol use by narcotics addicts. *Recent Developments in Alcoholism* 8,145– 171.

Hser YI, Hoffman V, Grella CE, Anglin MD. (2001) A 33-year follow-up of narcotics addicts. *Arch Gen Psychiatry* 58, 503 – 8.

Hubbard, R., Craddock, S., Flynn, P., Anderson, J., Etheridge, R., (1997). Overview of 1 year follow-up outcomes in the Drug Abuse Treatment Outcome Study DATOS. *Psychol. Addict. Behav.* 11, 261–278.

Hunt, D.E., Strug, D.L., Goldsmith, D.S., Lipton, D.S., Robertson, K., and Truitt, L. (1986). Alcohol use and abuse: Heavy drinking among methadone clients. *American Journal of Drug and Alcohol Abuse* 12, 147–164.

John, D., Kwiatkowski, C., Booth, R. (2001). Differences among out-of-treatment drug injectors who use stimulants only, opiates only or both: implications for treatment entry. *Drug Alcohol Depend.* 64, 165–172.

Johnson BA, Ait-Daoud N. (2000) Neuropharmacological treatments for alcoholism: scientific basis and clinical findings. *Psychopharmacology* 149, 327–44.

Jones, B. T. and McMahon, J. (1992) Negative and positive expectancies in lone and group problem drinkers. *British Journal of Addiction* 87, 929–930.

Joseph H, Appel P. (1985) Alcoholism and methadone treatment: consequences for the patient and program. *Am J Drug Alcohol Abuse* 11:37–53.

Kaufman, E. (1982). The relationship of alcoholism and alcohol abuse to the abuse of other drugs. *American Journal of Drug and Alcohol Abuse* 9, 1–17.

Kreek MJ. (1978) Medical complications between opiates and alcohol. Ann NY Acad Sci 362, 36 – 49.

Kreek, M. J. (1984). Opioid interactions with alcohol. *Advances in Alcohol and Substance Abuse* 3, 35–46.

Kreek, M.J. (1990). Drug interactions in humans related to drug abuse and its treatment. *Modern Methods in Pharmacology* 6, 265–282.

Leri, F., Bruneau, J., Stewart, J. (2003). Understanding polydrug use: review of heroin and cocaine co-use. *Addiction* 98, 7–22.

Lesch, O. M., Dietzel, M., Musalek, M., Walter, H. and Zeiler, K (1988). The course of alcoholism. Long-term prognosis in different Types. *Forensic Science International* 36, 121–138.

Lesch O, Riegler A, Gutierrez K, Hertling I, Ramskogler K, Semler B, Zoghlami A, Benda N, Walter H (2001). The European Acamprosate Trials: conclusions for research and therapy. *J Biomed Sci* 8, 89-95.

Litt MD, Babor TF, DelBoca FK, Kadden RM and Cooney NL (1992) Types of alcoholics: II. Application of an empirically derived typology of treatment matching, *Archives of General Psychiatry* 49, 609–614.

Litt, M.D., Cooney, N.L. and Morse, P. (2000). Reactivity to alcohol-related stimuli in the laboratory and in the field: predictors of craving in treated alcoholics. *Addiction* 95, 889-900.

Lowman, R., Allen, J., Stout, R. L., and Relapse Research Group (1996). Marlatt's taxonomy of relapse precipitants: Overview of procedures and results. *Addiction* 91, 51–72.

Lykouras L, Moussas G, Botsis (2004) Examination of type I/II alcoholism typology in a Greek hospital treatment population. *European Psychiatry* 19, 214-218.

Maddux, J. F., and Elliot, B. (1975). Problem drinkers among patients on methadone. American Journal of Alcohol Abuse 2, 245– 254.

Magura, S., Nwakeze, P.C.and Demsky S.Y. (1998). Preditors of Treatment Retention in Methadone Treatment. *Addiction* 93, 51-60.

Malcolm, B., Hesselbrock, M., Segal, B. (2006). Multiple substance dependence and course of alcoholism among Alaska native men and women. *Subst. Use Misuse* 51, 729–741.

Maremmani, I., Pani, P.P., Mellini, A., Pacini, M., Marini, G., Lovrecic, M., Perugi, G., Shinderman, M., (2007). Alcohol and cocaine use and abuse among opioid addicts engaged in a methadone maintenance treatment program. *J. Addict. Dis.* 26 (1), 61–70.

Marlatt, G. A. and Gordon, J. R. (Eds.) (1985). *Relapse prevention: Maintenance strategies in the treatment of addiction behaviour.* New York: Guilford Press

Marlatt, G. A. and Roseenow, D. J. (1980) Cognitive processses in alcohol use: expectancy and the alanced placebo design, In: N. K. Mello (Ed.) *Advances in Substance Abuse: behavioral and biological research.* 1, 159-199 (Greenwich, CT, JAI Press)

Martin, C. S., Clifford, P. R., Maisto, S. A. Earleywine M, Kirlsci L, Longabaugh R. (1996) Polydrug use in an inpatient treatment sample of problem drinkers. *Alcoholism: Clinical and Experimental Research* 20, 413–417.

Mattick, R. P., Breen, C., Kimber, J., and Davoli, M. (2003). Methadone maintenance therapy versus no opioid replacement therapy for opioid dependence. Cochrane Database of Systematic, 2.

Maxwell, S., and Shinderman, M. (1999). Optimizing response to methadone maintenance treatment: Use of higher-dose methadone. *Journal of Psychoactive Drugs* 31, 95– 102.

Medina, K., Shear, P. (2007). Anxiety, depression, and behavioural symptoms of executive dysfunction in ecstasy users: contributions of polydrug use. Drug Alcohol Depend. 87, 303–311.

Moos, R (2005). Iatrogenic effects of psychosocial interventions for substance use disorders: prevalence, predictors, prevention. *Addiction 100,* 595 – 604.

Nava F, Manzato E, Leonardi C, Lucchini A. (2008) Opioid maintenance therapy suppresses alcohol intake in heroin addicts with alcohol dependence: Preliminary results of an open randomized study. *Progress in Neuro-Psychopharmacology and Biological Psychiatry* 32, 1867–1872.

Oei TPS, Baldwin AR (1994) Expectancy theory: A two-process model of alcohol use and abuse. *Journal of Studies on Alcohol.* 55, 525-534.

Oei TPS, Fergusson S, Lee NK. (1998) The differential role of alcohol expectancies and drinking refusal self efficacy in problem and nonproblem drinkers. *Journal of Studies on Alcohol* 59, 704–11.

Ottomanelli, G. (1992). *HIV infection and intravenous drug use.* Westport, CT: Praeger

Ottomanelli G. (1999) Methadone patients and alcohol abuse. *J Subst Abuse Treat.* 16, 113–21.

Pandey, G.N., Fawcett, J., Gibbons, R., Clark, D.C., David, J.M. (1988) Platelet monoamine oxidase in alcoholism. *Biological Psychiatry* 24, 15-24.

Patterson, T., Semple, S., Zians, J., Strathdee, S. (2005). Methamphetamineusing HIV-positive men who have sex with men: correlates of polydrug use. *J. Urban Health* 82 (Suppl. 1), 120–126.

Pinto Gouveia, J., Ramalheira, C., Robalo, M., Borges, J. Almeida; J. (1993). Inventário de expectativas e crenças pessoais acerca do álcool. Psiquiatria Clínica *14*, 147-163.

Pombo, S., Reizinho, R., Ismail, F., Barbosa, A., Luísa Figueira, M., Neves Cardoso, J.M., Lesch, O.M. (2007). NETER Alcoholic 5 Subtypes: Validity with Lesch 4 Evolutionary Subtypes. *International Journal of Psychiatry in Clinical Practice*, 1-10.

Pombo, S., Reizinho, R., Ismail, F. and Neves Cardoso. J,M, (2008a). Denegação do alcoolismo nos subtipos I e II de Cloninger. *Análise Psicológica*, XXVI, 59-69.

Pombo, S., Levy, P., Bicho, M., Ismail, F., Cardoso, J.M.(2008b) Neuropsychological function and platelet monoamine oxidase activity levels in type I alcoholic patients. *Alcohol Alcohol* 43, 423–30.

Pombo S, Lesch OM. (2009) The alcoholic phenotypes among different multidimensional typologies: similarities and their classification procedures. *Alcohol Alcohol.* 44, 46-54

Pombo, S., Ismail, F. and Neves Cardoso. J,M. "Cravers" pelo álcool. Revista Psicologia, Saúde and Doenças (in press)

Prochaska, J.O. and DiClemente, C.C. (1986). Toward a comprehensive model of change. In: W. Miller and N. Heather (Eds.), *Addictive behaviours: Processes of Change*. New York: Plenum Press, 3-28.

Roszell, D. K., Calsyn, D. A., and Chaney, E. F. (1986). Alcohol use and psychopathology in opioid addicts on methadone maintenance. *American Journal of Drug and Alcohol Abuse* 12, 269– 278.

Rounsaville, B.J., Weissman, M.M., and Kleber, H.D. (1982). The significance of alcoholism in treated opiate addicts. *Journal of Nervous and Mental Disease* 170, 479–488.

Rowan-Szal, G. A., Chatham, L. R., and Simpson, D. D. (2000). Importance of identifying cocaine and alcohol dependent methadone clients. *American Journal on Addictions* 9, 38–50.

Rinn W, Desai N, Rosenblatt H, Gastfriend DR (2002). Addiction denial and cognitive dysfunction: a preliminary investigation. *J. Neuropsychiatry Clin Neuroscience.* 14, 52-57.

Rittmannsberger H, Silberbauer C, Lehner R, Ruschak M. (2000) Alcohol consumption during methadone maintenance treatment. *Eur Addict Res* 6:2–7.

Rubonis, A.V., Colby, S.M., Monti, P.M., Rosenow, D.J., Gulliver, S.B. and Sirota, A.D. (1994). Alcohol cue reactivity and mood induction in male and female alcoholics. *Journal Studies Alcohol* 55, 487-494.

Saitz, Richard (2007). Treatment of Alcohol and Other Drug Dependence. Liver Transplantation 13, 59-64.

Schiff, E. R. (1997). Hepatitis C and alcohol. *Hepatology* 26, 39S– 42S.

Schottenfeld, R. S., Pakes, J. R., and Kosten, T. R. (1998). Prognostic factors in buprenorphine- versus methadone-maintained patients. *Journal of Nervous and Mental Disease* 186, 35– 43.

Schut, J., File, K., and Wohlmuth, T. (1973). Alcohol use by narcotic addicts in methadone maintenance treatment. *Quarterly Journal of Studies on Alcohol* 34, 1356– 1359.

Selzer M.L. (1971). The Michigan Alcoholism Screening Test (MAST): the quest for a new diagnostic instrument. *American Journal Psychiatry* 127, 1653– 1658.

Senbanjo R, Wolff K, Marshall J. (2006) Excessive alcohol consumption is associated with reduced quality of life among methadone patients. *Addiction*; 102:257–63.

Serra A.V., Lima M.M. (1979). O uso do «Michigan Alcoholism Screening Test» como instrumento discriminador entre grupos de alcoólicos e de não-alcoólicos. *Coimbra Médica* 197, 39-5.

Simpson D., George J. and Grace A. (1997). Drug Abuse Treatment Retention and Process Effects on Follow-up Outcomes. *Drug and Alcohol Dependence*, 47, 227-235.

Sklar S. M; Annis H. M.; Turner N. E. (1997) Development and validation of the Drug-Taking Confidence Questionnaire : A measure of coping self-efficacy. *Addictive behaviors* 22, 655-670.

Soyka M, Zingg C, Koller G, Kuefner H. (2008) Retention rate and substance use in methadone and buprenorphine maintenance therapy and predictors of outcome: results. *Int J Neuropsychopharmacol.* 21, 1-13.

Srivastava, A., Kahan, M., Ross, S. (2008). The effect of methadone maintenance treatment on alcohol consumption: a systematic review. *J. Subst. Abuse Treat.* 34, 215–223.

Stacy AW, Widaman KF, Marlatt GA. (1990) Expectancy models of alcohol use. *Journal of Personality and Social Psychology* 58:918–928.

Staines, G. L., Magura, S., Foote, J. et al. (2001) Polysubstance use among alcoholics. *Journal of Addictive Diseases* 20, 53–69.

Strang, J., Griffiths, P., and Powis, B. (1999). Fountain, J., Williamson, S., and Gossop, M. (1999) Which drugs cause overdose among opiate misusers? Study of personal and witnessed overdoses. *Drug and Alcohol Review* 18, 253– 261.

Strang, J., Marsden, J., Cummins, M., Farrell, M., Finch, E., Gossop, M., Stewart D, Welch S. (2000). Randomized trial of supervised injectable versus oral methadone maintenance: Report of feasibility and 6-month outcome. *Addiction* 95, 1631– 1645.

Stein MD, Cioe P, Friedmann PD. (2005) Buprenorphine retention in primary care. *J Gen Intern Med.* 20(11), 1038-41.

Stenbacka, M., Beck, O., Leifman, A., Romelsjo, A., Helander, A. (2007). Problem drinking in relation to treatment outcome among opiate addicts in methadone maintenance treatment. *Drug Alcohol Rev.* 26, 55–63.

Stimmel, B., Vernace, S., and Tobias, H. (1972). Hepatic dysfunction in heroin addicts. The role of alcohol. *Journal of the American Medical Association* 222, 811 – 812.

Sullivan, J.L., Baenziger, J.C., Wagner, D.L. (1990) Platelet MAO in subtypes of alcoholism. *Biological Psychiatry* 27, 911-922.

Sumnall, H., Wagstaff, G., Cole, J. (2004). Self-reported psychopathology in polydrug users. *J. Psychopharmacol.* 18, 75–82.

Teplin, D., Raz, B., Daiter, J., Varenbut, M., Plater-Zyberk, C. (2007). Screening for alcohol use patterns among methadone maintenance patients. *Am. J. Drug Alcohol Abuse* 33, 179–183.

Turner, N. E., Annis, H. M., and Sklar, S. M. (1997). Measurement of Antecedents to Drug and Alcohol Use: Psychometric Properties of the Inventory of Drug-Taking Situations (IDTS). *Behav. Res. Ther.* 35, N. 5.

von Knorring, A. L., Bohman, M., von Knorring, L. and Oreland, L. (1985) Platelet MAO activity as a biological marker in subgroups of alcoholism. *Acta Psychiatrica Scandinavica* 72, 51–58.

von Knorring, A.L., Hallman, J., von Knorring, L., Oreland, L. (1998) Platelet monoamine oxidase activity in type 1 and type 2 alcoholism. *Alcoholism: Clinical and Experimental Research* 22, 598-604.

Waldrop A, Back S, Verduin M, Brady K. (2007).Triggers for cocaine and alcohol use in the presence and absence of posttraumatic. *Addictive behaviors* 32, 634-9.

Walter H; Ramskogler-Skala K; Dvorak A; Gutierrez-Lobos K; Hartl D; Hertling I; Munda P; Thau K; Lesch O; Witte P (2006) Glutamic acid in withdrawal and weaning in patients classified according to Cloninger's and Lesch's typologies. *Alcohol and Alcoholism* 41, 505-511.

West, S L, O'Neal, K K, Graham, C W. (2000) A meta-analysis comparing the effectiveness of buprenorphine and methadone. *J-Subst-Abuse*. 12(4), 405-14.

Westreich LM. (2005) Alcohol and mental illness: clinical focus. *Prim. Psychiatry* 12:41–6.

Williamson, A., Darke, S., Ross, J., Teesson, M., (2006). The effect of persistence of cocaine use on 12-month outcomes for the treatment of heroin dependence. Drug Alcohol Depend. 81, 293–300.

Windle, M. and Scheit, D. M. (2004) Alcoholic subtypes: are two sufficient? *Addiction* 99, 1508–1519.

Young, R. M., and Knight, R. G. (1989). The Drinking Expectancy Questionnaire: A revised measure of alcohol-related beliefs. *Journal of Psychopathology and Behavioral Assessment* 11, 99–112.

Zador S, Sunjic D. (2000) Deaths in methadone maintenance treatment in New South Wales, Australia, 1990–1995. *Addiction* 95:77–86.

In: Social Drinking: Uses, Abuses and Psychological Factors ISBN: 978-1-60876-219-4
Editors : K. T. Everly, E. M. Cosell, pp. 207-235 © 2010 Nova Science Publishers, Inc.

Chapter 5

DRINKING AMONG FEMALE VICTIMS OF INTIMATE PARTNER VIOLENCE: MECHANISMS AND INTERVENTION

Sonya B. Norman, Kendall C. Wilkins, Kimberly Baeressen, Steven R. Thorp, Regina Huelsenbeck, Erin Grimes, Carie Rodgers, and Carolyn Allard

Veterans Affairs San Diego Healthcare System
Veterans Affairs Center for Excellence for Stress and Mental Health
University of California, San Diego, CA, USA
San Diego State University/University of California San Diego, Joint Doctoral Program
San Diego, CA, USA

INTRODUCTION

As many as 1/3 of women in the general population (Kubany, Hill, and Owens, 2003; Tjaden, 2000) and 50% of women seen in primary care (Coker, Smith, Bethea, King, and McKeown, 2000) experience abuse by an intimate partner during adulthood. The consequences of having experienced intimate partner violence (IPV) are quite alarming. Female IPV victims represent one of the largest traumatized populations in the U.S. (Council on Scientific Affairs, 1992). More than 60% of women who present to domestic violence shelters meet criteria for posttraumatic stress disorder (PTSD; Saunders, 1994).

Alcohol use among female victims of IPV is common in the form of heavy, moderate or episodic drinking and appears to be both an outcome of and a risk factor for trauma (El-Bassel et al., 2003). Researchers have found that female victims of IPV use drinking to cope with a variety of symptoms associated with trauma and PTSD. Motives for drinking among females with PTSD include coping with anxiety, managing conflict with others, and dealing with sleep problems. Overall, research suggests that drinking is used as a method to cope with psychological distress related to PTSD rather than to create positive experiences. While drinking may serve to decrease the intensity of uncomfortable posttraumatic symptoms, this relief is only temporary. In the long-term, using substances has been associated with increased psychological distress, functional impairments, adverse health outcomes, and greater vulnerability to revictimization. It is important to understand the relationship between drinking, IPV, and IPV-related posttraumatic distress to help prevent and treat alcohol and other trauma related problems in women who have been abused.

In this chapter, we review the problems commonly associated with IPV, psychosocial treatments designed to help IPV victims, and research regarding the relationship between drinking and IPV. First, we review the prevalence of drinking and alcohol problems associated with IPV for women who are in the abusive relationship, transitioning out of such a relationship, and women who have terminated the abusive relationship. We then discuss the role of drinking in IPV and in trauma more generally. We review the literature on empirically supported psychosocial interventions for these three stages of IPV (i.e., current relationship, transitioning out, and terminated relationship) and organize our discussion around these three stages as well. Finally, we make recommendations for future research, specifically addressing the need for alcohol-related interventions for IPV victims.

For the purposes of this article, we address female victims of male violence. The review is focused in this way for a number of reasons: 85% of IPV victims are women (Greenfield et al., 1998), women suffer more severe physical injuries after IPV than men (Golding, 1999), and mental health sequelae for battered men have not been well researched (Golding, 1999). Little is known about mental health consequences of same-sex partner violence (Golding, 1999).

PREVALENCE OF SOCIAL DRINKING AND ALCOHOL PROBLEMS ASSOCIATED WITH IPV

In the Abusive Relationship

Prevalence of substance use and abuse is rarely assessed while a woman is actively in the abusive relationship. Rather this data is assembled from baseline interviews and self reports when women access services, having left (or in the process of leaving) the abusive relationship. In one study, 72% of women (n=191) entering assorted domestic violence shelters reported substance use in the three months immediately prior to entering the shelter (Poole, Greaves, Jategaonkar, McCullough, and Chabot, 2008). In a sample of 360 women entering various substance abuse treatment facilities, 47% reported they were currently experiencing intimate partner violence (Swan, Farber, and Campbell, 2000). Likewise, of 676 women seeking protective orders (PO) against an abusive male intimate partner for abuse within the last year, 66% met criteria for DSM-IV-TR alcohol abuse/dependence (Shannon, Logan, Cole, and Walker, 2008). The women within this alcohol abuse/dependence group were also significantly more likely to have experienced sexual assault (33.8%) by an intimate partner within the last year than the women who reported some or no alcohol use (20-22%).

During Transition from an IPV Relationship

When transitioning from an IPV relationship, women often access services such as domestic violence shelters or substance abuse treatment facilities. This point of contact and the period immediately leading up to it may be the woman's highest period of stress and substance use (Poole et al., 2008). In general, it is estimated that 67-80% of women in substance abuse treatment facilities are victims of IPV (Cohen et al., 2003) and conversely that 25% to 50% of women receiving victim services for IPV have substance abuse problems (Bennett and Lawson, 1994; Downs, 2001; Ogle and Baer, 2003).

After Terminating the IPV Relationship

Substance use is 1.5 to 5.5 times more prevalent in women with trauma histories than without (Council, 1996; Najavits, Weiss, and Shaw, 1997). Women who have been victims of IPV are more likely than non-victimized women to have problems with alcohol and illicit drug abuse (Briere and Jordan, 2004; Golding, 1999; El-Bassel et al., 2003). In an emergency room sample of 90 women, El-Bassel and colleagues (2003) found that women who had been abused were more likely than non-abused women to report a history of regular crack, cocaine, and heroin use.

Although the literature overall suggest that having experienced IPV in the past is associated with problem drinking, one study found evidence that substance use decreases significantly shortly after terminating the IPV relationship. Poole et al (2008) interviewed women (n=125) while they resided in one of 13 domestic violence (DV) shelters and three months after they left the shelter to track their substance use patterns. Women received DV counseling, including either a significant alcohol intervention or no/minimal alcohol intervention, depending on the shelter (no random assignment). Women reported significantly less substance use, specifically the frequency of alcohol and stimulant use, after leaving the shelter regardless of the type of intervention. Poole et al highlight that this result was consistent for both the minimal alcohol intervention group and the significant alcohol intervention group.

The Role of Alcohol in IPV

People who have experienced traumatic events and developed PTSD may seek short-term escape or avoidance of affective states that are unpleasant, and this may take the form of substance use problems (Follette, 1994). The self-medication hypothesis predicts that alcohol use can provide short-term relief from PTSD symptoms and that drinking is thus maintained by negative reinforcement (McFarlane, 1998). However, many individuals report an expectation that drinking alcohol will generate positive physical and emotional feelings, with less emphasis on alcohol's ability to ameliorate negative emotions (Brown, Goldman, Inn, and Anderson, 1980).

Cooper, Russell, Skinner, and Windle (1992) proposed three types of drinking motives based on expectations: (1) social motives, which involve drinking due to custom in a social context or for celebration; (2) enhancement motives, which involve seeking positive affect (e.g., excitement, getting high, having fun); and (3) coping motives ("self-medication"), which involve seeking to reduce negative or painful emotions (e.g., cheering up when feeling down, forgetting worries). Cooper et al found that enhancement motives and social motives were associated with drinking in social situations, and coping motives were associated with drinking alone. Enhancement motives were also associated with frequent, heavy drinking and use of marijuana, cocaine, and other stimulants, whereas coping motives were predictive of functional impairment and symptoms of tolerance and withdrawal and linked to greater use of barbiturates and tranquilizers. The researchers suggested that drinkers with enhancement motives may have more control over their drinking, perhaps due in part to more social feedback about their behavior.

Grayson and Nolen-Hoeksema (2005) suggest that an emotion regulation model of alcohol problems incorporates both the traditional focus on distress coping motives as well as the enhancement motives, and in testing this model found that indeed drinking with motives for both coping and enhancement partially mediated the association between childhood sexual abuse and drinking problems in women. Also consistent with a broad model of motivations for drinking, women with current PTSD reported greater expectancies that alcohol would reduce tension and had experienced more positive enhancement from alcohol compared to women without PTSD (Simpson, 2003). To underscore the importance of situational factors among women who were substance abusers, both PTSD symptoms and heavy alcohol use were higher in situations of physical discomfort, interpersonal conflict, and unpleasant emotions; PTSD symptoms were negatively correlated with heavy drinking when the women experienced pleasant emotions; and no link between PTSD symptoms and heavy alcohol use was apparent during pleasant social interactions or tempting-to-drink situations (Stewart, Conrod, Pihl, and Dongier, 2000). In a related vein, Marlatt and Gordon (1985) found that most cases of relapse among alcoholic individuals were triggered by negative events, though some were spurred by positive events such as celebrations or social gatherings.

Kaysen et al. (2007) examined drinking motives in a sample of women who had experienced IPV. The investigators limited their analyses to only the coping motives aspect of Cooper et al.'s (1992) model (which they stated was due to high correlations among scales measuring the three constructs and their theoretical interest in the coping scale), and found that coping motives mediated the association between drinking and trauma symptoms. Similarly, Ullman, Filipas, Townsend, and Starzynski (2006) found that women who had experienced sexual assault as adults were more likely to have drinking problems in addition to PTSD (as opposed to PTSD alone) if they believed that alcohol could help them cope and if they drank with the intention of reducing distress. Nishith, Resick, and Mueser (2001) found that coping motives for drinking (but not enhancement or social motives) among female rape victims were specifically associated with sleep disturbances (e.g., insomnia, nightmares, and physical discomfort) rather than with other symptoms of PTSD or depression.

Taken together, these findings suggest that a model of drinking problems among women who have experienced IPV (or other traumatic events) should incorporate motives of coping, enhancement, and social factors.

PHYSICAL, EMOTIONAL, AND FUNCTIONAL SEQUELAE ASSOCIATED WITH IPV

In addition to the role of drinking, it is also important to take into account all of the problems associated with IPV to fully consider how best to treat women who have experienced IPV. In this section, we review physical, emotional, and functional problems associated with IPV.

Physical Sequelae

Female victims of IPV perceive their physical health as poorer and report more somatic symptoms than non-traumatized women (Campbell, 2002). Women with present or past histories of IPV report higher rates of chronic illnesses including gastrointestinal and gynecological problems, respiratory disorders, migraines and other headaches, sexually transmitted diseases including HIV/AIDS, heart problems, hypertension, arthritis, and diabetes (Campbell, 2002; Campbell, Kub, Belknap, and Templin, 1997; Coker et al., 2000; Leserman, 2007; Salam, Alim, and Noguchi, 2006; Silverman, Decker, Saggurti, Balaigh, & Raj, 2008). IPV victims are more likely to suffer from chronic pain, including chronic pelvic pain, as well (Leserman, 2007; Meagher, 2004; Salam et al., 2006), and if pregnant during the abuse to experience miscarriages (Morland, Leskin, Block, Campbell, and Friedman, 2008).

The mechanisms by which IPV affects physical health are not fully understood. Some physical sequelae have an obvious direct link. Forty-two percent of women who reported a physical assault by a partner sustained an injury in a nationally representative large scale phone survey study (Tjaden and Thoennes, 2000). These injuries take many forms, including traumatic brain injury. Seventy-four percent of battered women in one study sustained one partner-induced brain injury from their partner, and 51% sustained multiple brain injuries (Valera and Berenbaum, 2003). Many abusers become most violent when they are at risk of losing control over their victim (Fleury, Bybee, and Davidson, 1998). Therefore, women can be especially at risk when trying to leave the abuser. In a study of IPV victims in transition shelters, 92% had received blows to the head in the course of battering incidents, 68% had been severely shaken by the partner, and 40% had lost consciousness (Jackson, Philip, Nuttall, and Diller, 2004). According to the national data collected by the Centers for Disease Control and Prevention (2003) about 1,300 women lose their lives as a result of IPV in the U.S. each year. Another national data collection agency reported that more than 3 women are murdered by intimate partners every day (Bureau of Justice Statistics Crime Data Brief, 2003).

In addition to physical health problems directly related to injury, researchers have posited that the long-term stress of IPV may contribute to the development or exacerbation of physical health problems (Coker et al., 2000; Norman et al., 2006; Sutherland, Bybee, and Sullivan, 2002). Initial research has revealed that PTSD symptoms mediate the association between IPV and proinflammatory cytokine levels (Woods et al., 2005). Researchers also have found a relationship between IPV and higher levels of evening cortisol and morning and evening dehydroepiandrosterone (DHEA), controlling for other potentially confounding factors including age, smoking, medications, lifetime history of victimization, and mental health status (Pico-Alfonso, Garcia-Linares, Celda-Navarro, Herbert, and Martinez, 2004). An association has also been shown to exist between trauma exposure and engaging in more negative health behaviors and fewer positive health behaviors (Lang et al., 2003). For example, IPV victims are more likely than women without abuse histories to engage in risky sexual behaviors (Rodgers, Norman, Thorp, Lebeck, and Lang, 2005).

Emotional Sequelae

The most prevalent mental health consequences of IPV are PTSD and depression (Marais, deVilliers, Moller, and Stein, 1999). Up to 90% of female victims of IPV have been found to meet criteria for PTSD at some time in their lives (Astin, Lawrence, and Foy, 1993; Eisenstat and Bancroft, 1999; Fedovskiy, Higgins, and Paranjape, 2008; Gallop and Everett, 2001; Gorde, Helfrich, and Finlayson, 2004; Humphreys, Lee, Neylan, and Marmar, 2001; Jones, Hughes, and Unterstaller, 2001; Saunders and Kindy, 1993; Saunders, 1994; Stein and Kennedy, 2001). This prevalence rate is especially alarming when compared to lifetime estimates of PTSD in the general population, which are as high as 8-12% (Golding, 1999; Kessler et al., 2005). Lifetime prevalence of clinically significant depression symptoms have been reported to be as high as 70% in IPV victims (Briere and Jordan, 2004; Campbell et al., 1997; Helfrich, Fujiura, and Rutkowski-Kimtta, 2008; Gerlock, 1999; Golding, 1999; Peterson, Gazmararian, and Andersen-Clark, 2001; Roberts, Lawerence, Williams, & Raphael, 1998; Stein and Kennedy, 2001; Zlotnick, Johnson, and Kohn, 2006), which stands in stark contrast to the 12% found in women in the general population (Kessler at el., 2005). Additionally, as many as 13% of IPV victims have comorbid PTSD and MDD (Stein and Kennedy, 2001).

Prevalence of anxiety disorders are as high as 54% in women with IPV histories (Helfrich et al., 2008; Gerlock, 1999; McCauley et al., 1995; Roberts et al., 1998) compared to 14% in women the general population (Kessler et al., 2005). Higher rates of insomnia, somatic symptomatology, hopelessness, dissociation, and suicidality, and lower self-esteem have been reported in women who have experienced IPV compared to non-abused women (Briere and Jordan, 2004; Golding, 1999; Hathaway et al., 2000; Herbert, Silver, and Ellard, 1991; Matud, 2005; Zlotnick et al., 2006). Female victims of IPV also have higher likelihood than women in the general population of having severe mental illness. In a study of women residing in a DV shelter 23% of residents reported having bipolar disorder compared to 0.7% of women in the general population; 14% had a personality disorder versus 0.6% of all U.S. women; and 3% had a diagnosis of schizophrenia and 8% paranoid or delusional disorder compared to 0.1% and 0.3%, respectively, in the general population of women (Helfrich et al., 2008).

Functional Sequelae

Another area of difficulty for IPV victims is daily functioning. IPV exposure is related to degree of impairment (Coker et al., 2000; Zlotnick et al., 2006). Thirty-five percent of women in a DV shelter identified themselves as disabled, compared to 4.6% American women in general (Helfrich et al., 2008). Women who experience IPV exhibit greater difficulty finding or keeping work, and decreased productivity, compared to U.S. women overall (Gilson, DePoy, and Cramer, 2001; Helfrich et al., 2008; Lloyd and Taluc, 1999; Riger, Raja, and Camacho, 2002; Wettersten et al., 2004; Wisner, Gilmer, Saltzman, and Zinc, 1999). Interpersonal problems are more commonly reported by IPV survivors and women in the general population (Helfrich et al., 2008). Compared to non-abused women, women who have experienced IPV are four times more likely to report housing instability, controlling for age, race and ethnicity, marital status and, notably, poverty (Pavao, Alvarez, Maumrind, Induni and Kimerling, 2007).

This functional impairment has been attributed to IPV correlates, including the common psychological sequelae mentioned earlier. Depression and anxiety disorders, in particular PTSD, are associated with functioning difficulties (Byrne and Riggs, 1996; Norman, Davidson, and Stein, 2007; Rapaport, Clary, Fayyad, and Endicott, 2005; Stein, Walker, Hazen, and Forde, 1997; Zatzick et al., 1997). Among IPV victims in one study, those with PTSD reported more problems with physical functioning, mental health, vitality, role limitations due to emotional health, and social functioning, after controlling for SES, age, depression symptoms, and extent of abuse (Laffaye, Kennedy, and Stein, 2003). In another study, PTSD was found to mediate the relationship between IPV severity and resource loss (Johnson, Zlotnick, and Perez, 2008).

Other common characteristics of IPV victims that appear to contribute to functioning difficulties include isolation, guilt and shame, and learned helplessness. Women in abusive relationships are frequently isolated, either as part of the pattern of abuse or out of shame and embarrassment of their situation. As a result, women who are able to leave abusive relationships often find themselves without social support (Howard, Riger, Campbell, and Wasco, 2003). But even when social support and other resources are available, abused women appear to have a diminished ability to access and utilize them effectively (Perez and Johnson, 2008).

Women in abusive relationships learn helplessness, which can interfere with their ability to leave the abusive relationships and to function effectively once out. Abusers often try to control even the minutia of their victim's actions and behavior, thus, after leaving the relationship women may find themselves struggling to problem solve or take care of daily responsibilities independently, including finding and keeping employment and parenting (Kubany et al., 2003). Compared to women in the general population, IPV survivors tend to be less assertive, be less likely to advocate for themselves, exhibit fewer help-seeking behaviors, and have decreased ability to effectively use available resources (Foa, Cascardi, Zoellner, and Feeny, 2000; Kubany et al., 2003; Kubany et al., 2004). Researchers also have found that guilt and shame are prevalent in IPV victims, which can place them at risk for other emotional problems and can be debilitating in and of itself (Kubany et al., 2004).

Finally, the rate of entering future abusive relationships is also quite high among female IPV victims. Up to 51% of IPV survivors reported having had more than one abusive partner (Kubany et al., 2004). Posttraumatic distress is associated with revictimization in other trauma populations (Orcutt, Erickson, and Wolfe, 2002). Recently, this association was reported in battered women as well, such that PTSD was more predictive of revictimization than women's previous experiences of violence, depression symptom severity, help-seeking behaviors, and social support (Perez and Johnson, 2008).

Financial Burden of IPV

IPV also poses a substantial societal and financial burden. The healthcare costs associated with IPV exceed $5.8 billion annually, nearly $4.1 billion of which is in direct medical and mental healthcare services (Centers for Disease Control and Prevention, 2003). Almost $1 billion is attributed to lost productivity, and close to another billion dollars is due to homicide-related lost earnings. These figures underestimate the problem of IPV because costs from some medical care (e.g., home health care, treatment for sexually transmitted diseases, and pregnancy terminations), social services, criminal justice proceedings, law enforcement, imprisonment, and services provided to children were not included.

Rivera and colleagues (2007) conducted a longitudinal cohort study to more accurately determine the healthcare utilization and medical care costs of IPV perpetrated against women. Notably, roughly half the women who participated in their telephone surveys reported IPV experiences (1546 out of 3333). Compared to no IPV history, IPV history was related to 20% higher healthcare utilization as late as 5 years after cessation of abuse and 19% higher adjusted annual total healthcare costs. These rates were used to estimate a healthcare cost of about $19.3 million per year per 100,000 women. This more inclusive conclusion about the burden of IPV may still be an underestimate. Coker and colleagues (2000) found that IPV victims more likely than non-abused women to be receiving disability compensation for physical (or emotional) problems.

Interventions

The previous sections have demonstrated the high prevalence of drinking among women who have experienced IPV, the functions that drinking have for these women, and the myriad of other problems experienced by these women. In this section, we review interventions that have been developed for IPV in order to evaluate whether currently existing interventions address alcohol related problems and the full gamut of physical, emotional, and functional problems experienced by these women.

In the Relationship

Social Drinking/Alcohol Interventions. At present there is a paucity of data evaluating the effectiveness of social drinking and alcohol interventions for women with the majority of alcohol treatment outcome research to date involving predominantly male samples (McCrady, Epstein, Cook, Jensen, & Hildebrant, 2009). This is also true of investigations of alcohol interventions related specifically to IPV with the overwhelming majority of studies examining alcohol use treatment in samples of male perpetrators. Research investigating treatments for female victims of IPV with alcohol use difficulties and/or disorders is scarce (Fals-Stewart and Kennedy, 2005). In fact, our review of the treatment literature yielded only four studies involving female victims of IPV currently in relationships, including a small descriptive study of an intensive outpatient treatment for alcohol use disorders (n = 10; Stuart et al., 2002) and three studies examining the same controversial intervention discussed in greater detail below,

Behavioral Couples Therapy (BCT; Fals-Stewart, Birchler, and Kelly, 2006; McCrady et al., 2009; Winters, Fals-Stewart, O'Farrell, Birchler, and Kelley, 2002). The general conclusion from these investigations is quite promising in that findings indicate treating alcohol use in either IPV perpetrators or victims seems to reduce IPV, particularly in the absence of relapse (Fals-Stewart and Kennedy, 2005). Given the lack of literature involving female victims of IPV, a more general review of social drinking and alcohol interventions and their empirical support is discussed with findings related specifically to women and IPV included whenever possible. Research is still needed to determine which, if any, of these services are most appropriate for IPV victims currently in an abusive relationship.

The use of Brief Interventions has been investigated in individuals with a variety of levels of alcohol consumption ranging from problematic to clinical levels of alcohol use. Two domains of brief interventions exist: 1) Opportunistic Brief Interventions (OBIs) found in community settings and used by non-specialized providers such as physicians to address problematic and/or excessive drinking and 2) Brief Treatments (BTs) used by mental health providers and often consisting of longer more intense treatment typically for more serious alcohol problems (Heather, 2004). OBI's may be particularly useful with IPV victims engaging in social drinking especially if access to treatment is limited. These services are very short (e.g. a portion of a visit to the doctor's office) and have been delivered in primary care (Flemming et al., 2002), via computers (Finfgeld-Connett, 2006), and in preliminary evaluations using pamphlets (Cunningham, Neighbors, Wild, and Humphreys, 2008). It should be noted that while research generally supports the effectiveness of brief interventions (for a review see Heather, 2004), Chang (2002) highlights that findings related specifically to women can be somewhat mixed. BTs include interventions such as Motivational Enhancement Therapy a brief treatment based on Motivational Interviewing techniques (Miller and Rollnick, 1991). Project MATCH, the largest alcohol treatment outcome study to date, investigated a 4-session MET approach and found it to be as effective as two more intensive treatments Cognitive Behavioral Therapy and Twelve-Step Facilitation (Project Match Research Group, 1997, 1998). Additionally, the brevity of this type of intervention may be particularly useful to IPV victims in relationships if they have limited access to services.

As noted above, Behavioral Couples Therapy (BCT), a couples-based treatment for alcohol and substance use disorders, is the one of two interventions found in our review that specifically examined female IPV victims with alcohol use disorders currently in an abusive relationship. BCT has been found to be effective in a variety of studies consisting mostly of male alcohol or substance users and their non-using female partners (Fals-Stewart, et al., 2006; McCrady, et al., 2009). Findings from the three existing studies of female IPV victims suggest that BCT reduces drinking, alcohol-related consequences, as well as partner violence (Fals-Stewart, et al., 2006; McCrady et al., 2009; Winters, et al., 2002). BCT encourages partner support towards abstinence and addresses relationship difficulties (Fals-Stewart, O'Farrell, and Birchler, 2004). Additionally, BCT includes coping skills and steps to increase safety during situations where partner violence is likely. Despite these findings the idea of conjoint therapy in IPV remains controversial with many feeling a couples approach to IPV treatment is possibly unethical and dangerous for the victim (Fals-Stewart and Kennedy, 2005). It is imperative that those considering implementing this technique review the literature and determine if their clients are appropriate candidates. Specifically, this approach is likely not appropriate for couples where the perpetrator engages in severe forms of abuse or in cases where the victim reports being fearful of death or significant injury at the hands of their partner, has been threatened with weapons in the past, is fearful of participating in the intervention, or wishes to leave the relationship (Fals-Stewart and Kennedy, 2005).

Cognitive Behavioral Treatments (CBT) for alcohol use disorders have consistently demonstrated effectiveness (Morgenstern and Longabaugh, 2000; Parks, Marlatt, and Anderson, 2004), however no studies were found looking at this approach in IPV victims. CBT includes techniques such as relapse prevention and a community reinforcement approach. CBT also encompasses behavioral interventions, including behavior contracting, aversive therapies, cue exposure, relaxation training, contingency management, and skills training as well as cognitive techniques such as examining appraisals, problem solving, and cognitive restructuring (for review see Parks, Anderson, and Marlatt, 2004). In addition to support for the overall treatment approach, some of the components listed above, such as relapse prevention, have been found to be effective in and of themselves (Parks, Anderson, and Marlatt, 2004).

Mutual aid and Twelve Step Facilitation approaches, such as Alcoholics Anonymous (AA), have also found support in the literature (Emrick, 2004; Project Match Research Group, 1997, 1998) and may be useful to female IPV victims in abusive relationships. As noted above, results from Project Match suggested that Twelve Step Facilitation, led by a trained clinician, was as effective as MET and CBT (Project Match Research Group, 1997, 1998). Additionally, research has supported the usefulness of community based AA meetings as well (Humphreys, Moos, & Cohen, 1997).

Physical sequelae. We found few studies designed to address the physical sequelae of IPV. Although safety interventions could be considered preventative measures by which to reduce the likelihood of further harm, we reviewed the literature discussing these interventions under functioning since these are generalizable behaviors that can help women function better in many contexts.

The body of literature most directly related to physical sequelae of IPV regards physician interventions to document abuse. Healthcare provider efforts to document abuse at primary care appointments are effective in reducing exposure to abuse (e.g. Morier-Genou, Bodenmann, Favrat, and Vannotti, 2006; Rhodes and Levinson, 2003; Rhodes et al., 2007). Coker and colleagues (2002) demonstrated that women benefited in several ways when physicians asked a single screening question. Physicians were more likely to document the abuse, which is helpful if women decide to get a restraining order, and were also able to make referrals to community agencies. Women were more likely to report taking action to improve their safety once they had disclosed to their physician. Similar results were found with a study done by McCloskey and colleagues (2006). This study investigated whether disclosure of IPV to health care providers increased the odds that women would leave the abusive relationship and whether leaving was associated with improvements in self-reported health status. Their results indicated that 1 year after disclosure 44% had exited the abusive relationship. Among those who were no longer with their partner, 55% received a domestic violence intervention (e.g. advocacy, shelter, restraining order), compared with 37% of those who remained with their partner. Talking to their health care provider about the abuse increased women's likelihood of using an intervention and those who received interventions were more likely to subsequently leave the relationship. Importantly, women no longer with the abuser reported better physical health based than women who stayed. Emergency room and prenatal clinics are other setting in which screenings can occur (Fanslow, Norton, and Robinson, 1999; Guo,

Wu, Qu, and Yan, 2004). Kendall and colleagues (2009) assessed the impact of emergency department (ED) IPV counseling and resource referrals on patient-perceived safety and safety planning. ED patients experiencing IPV were offered consultation with trained IPV advocacy counselors who completed safety assessments, provided resource referrals, and helped patients develop safety plans. Over 96% of patients perceived an increase in their safety after the intervention, and approximately 50% had completed a portion of their safety plan.

Unfortunately, screenings for domestic violence in medical settings rarely occur (e.g. Klap, Tang, Wells, Starks, and Rodriguez, 2007; Lindhorst, Meyers, and Casey, 2008; Rhodes and Levinson, 2003). Klap and colleagues (2007) examined whether 4,821 women were ever asked about domestic or family violence by any health care provider. Only 7% of women reported they were ever asked about domestic violence or family violence by a health care professional. Of women who were asked about abuse, nearly half (46%) were asked in a primary care setting, and 24% were asked in a specialty mental health setting. Lindhorst and colleagues (2008) found inadequacies with domestic violence screening in public welfare offices. Their study investigated domestic violence screening practices in welfare offices using 782 transcribed interviews between welfare workers and clients from 11 sites in four states. The analysis found that only 9.3% of case encounters involved screening for domestic violence. Screening rates differed by state, interview type, and length of worker employment. Qualitative analysis of the interviews showed that the majority of screening by workers consisted of informing clients of the domestic violence policy without asking about abuse. Only 1.2% of the interviews incorporated at procedures that increase the likelihood of disclosure among domestic violence survivors. Although medical residents receive significantly more hours of education about IPV than they did ten years ago, the likelihood of screening for domestic violence among residents has not improved (Miller, Coonrod, Brady, Moffitt, and Bay, 2004).

Barriers to screening for IPV in medical settings include provider perception that women may be offended if asked if they have been abused (Rhodes and Levinson, 2003; Varjavand, Cohen, Gracely, and Novack, 2004) and uncertainty about how to screen for and manage IPV (Varjavand et al., 2004). However, studies have found that despite previous notions, most patients are comfortable with healthcare staff inquiring about domestic violence (e.g. Boyle and Jones, 2006; Chen et al., 2007). In a study of 198 women presenting to an emergency room setting, 76% of the sample felt comfortable being asked about IPV and 60.5% felt that they should always or usually be asked about IPV in an emergency room setting (Sethi, Watts, Zwi, Watson, and McCarthy, 2004). However, healthcare providers may not understand the benefits of documenting IPV (Sethi et al., 2004). Bonds and colleagues (2006) noted that providers were more likely to administer interventions if the interventions were tailored to their environment. For example, each provider was allowed to select the screening instrument to be used in their clinic (from 5 previously tested instruments), the method of screening (verbal or written), the staff person responsible for screening (provider or nursing staff), the frequency of the screening, and the patient population to be screened.

Emotional Sequelae. We could not locate any studies that assessed or addressed PTSD in women currently experiencing IPV. However, it is possible that helping women to identify and label the abuse may bring some emotional relief. According to Walker (1987), women who are in violent relationships tend to minimize the extent of the abuse. Walker recommends that clinicians label the abuse and talk about it openly to help women commit to practicing safety behaviors.

Functional sequelae. Although interventions by the legal system are designed to address the victim's safety, psychosocial interventions can also improve safety behaviors and recognition of dangerous situations (for a review of legal interventions, see Mears, 2003). Psychosocial interventions to improve safety behaviors among victims of IPV have been effective in reducing the frequency of abuse that some women experience (McFarlane, 1998). Parker and colleagues (Parker, McFarlane, Soeken, Silva, and Reel, 1999) tested a three-session intervention to improve abused pregnant women's use of safety behaviors. They targeted this population because abused women are at risk for suicide attempts, substance abuse, and complications during pregnancy (Bacchus and Bewley, 2004; Parker et al., 1999). During the intervention, women met with a counselor to develop a safety plan. They were advised to secure copies of important documents and extra keys, establish a code with family and friends, hide extra clothes, and identify behaviors of the abuser that indicated increased danger. The intervention was effective in reducing incidents of abuse compared to a control group at 6-months and 12-months post-delivery. The authors found support for the efficacy of a similar intervention with pregnant women that focused on advocacy and community referrals in addition to safety issues (McFarlane, Parker, Soeken, Silva, Reed, 1998).

Another common intervention that focuses on decreasing IPV and improving victim's safety is couples therapy. Holtzworth-Munroe and colleagues (2003) note that, "over half of all couples seeking couples therapy have experienced husband physical aggression in the past year" (p. 208). While treatment involving both partners may be controversial, there is evidence that this type of intervention does not put women at increased risk for continued abuse (Stith, Rosen, & McCollum, 2003), and is as effective in reducing IPV as gender-specific therapies (Holtzworth-Munroe, Marshall, Meehan, & Reham, 2003; Stith et al., 2003). We were only able to locate one study specifically assessing the impact of PTSD diagnosis on treatment outcome in female victims of IPV (Schlee, Heyman, and O'Leary, 1998). Participants in this study were couples involved in a 14-week group treatment program focused on decreasing spouse abuse. Participants were randomly assigned to psychoeducational groups attended separately or conjointly with their spouses. Topics addressed in the conjoint group included anger control, violence cessation, and communication skills. The gender specific treatment groups also focused on violence cessation with the male only group also addressing power and control and the female only group addressing self-esteem and assertiveness. Across both treatment groups, the women reported a significant decrease in fear of their husbands, depressive symptomatology, and reports of their partners' physical and psychological abuse. There were no significant differences on any of these outcome measures between women with and without PTSD. However, the authors did not assess for changes in levels of PTSD in women pre- and post-treatment.

In Transition

Social Drinking/Alcohol Interventions. No studies were found specifically discussing social drinking or alcohol related interventions for IPV victims transitioning out of an abusive relationship. As noted in the previous Social Drinking/Alcohol Interventions section, research related to alcohol use treatment for women is limited and that pertaining to IPV victims is even scarcer. Given this it is difficult to make recommendations regarding appropriate services for women during this stage. If one uses empirical evidence of the general effectiveness of alcohol focused interventions as a guide then all of the interventions discussed previously, exclusive of BCT as it is a couples approach, could be possible interventions used during this stage of IPV. As noted above, future research is needed to continue to determine the effectiveness of these methods with women and with IPV victims in particular.

Physical Sequelae. We could not locate any studies for IPV victims in transition that focused specifically on the physical sequelae of IPV.

Emotional and Functional Sequelae. Most interventions designed to help women in transition focus on safety, improving social support and self-esteem, and helping women with assertive communication and problem solving. PTSD, depression, and substance abuse were generally not assessed or addressed in the intervention studies we reviewed. The transition out of an abusive relationship is an extremely stressful time for women. In fact, some women report greater stress during the process of leaving than they experienced while living in the abusive relationship (Anderson and Saunders, 2003). Experiencing high levels of stress during the transition appears to be a predictor for worsening mental health over time (Anderson and Saunders, 2003). Thus, this is an especially important time for psychosocial intervention.

Although a few studies have examined outcomes related to counseling or therapy that occurs within domestic violence shelters, these studies have generally used small, nonrandomized samples (Howard et al, 2003). Howard and colleagues (2003) looked at the effectiveness of individual counseling for 500 women residing in shelters or using counseling services for women in transition. Counselors were free to use whatever form of therapy they preferred. Questionnaires completed by participants following treatment indicated that most counseling included skills development, new perspectives on abuse, understanding of the effects of the abuse, psychoeducation regarding choices available to the women, developing a safety plan, and understanding domestic violence as a social problem. The authors compared counseling outcomes between women who had been both physically and sexually abused (n = 143) and women who had only experienced physical abuse (n = 357). Both groups improved in well-being and coping. Women who experienced both types of abuse had lower scores at baseline, but showed greater improvement through the study. Unfortunately, this was not a controlled study and the type of counseling was not specified.

Group counseling for women in transition has also received some attention (Tutty, Bidgood, and Rothery, 1993). Support groups for IPV appear to fall on a continuum from self-help groups to therapy groups, with a primary goal being for the group members to support and teach each other (Tutty, Bidgood, and Rothery, 1996). Other goals include reduction of social isolation, allowing women to see that their reactions to abuse are not unique, and being able to learn from women at further stages of leaving the abusive relationship.

Tutty and colleagues (1993) assessed the effect of a 10–12 session support group on 76 women who were transitioning out of an abusive relationship. Group participants showed positive changes on a number of measures including: Belonging Support, Locus of Control, Self-Esteem, Perceived Stress, Attitudes Towards Marriage and the Family, and marital functioning. Women still living with their abusive partners reported a reduction in physical and nonphysical abuse. Improvements in self-esteem, social support, locus of control, and perceived stress were maintained over twelve months (n = 32 women who completed follow-up assessments). Interestingly, older women benefited less from the groups, possibly because their exposure to the abuse had been longer (Tutty et al., 1996). The absence of a control group and lack of random assignment to treatment conditions limit the conclusions that can be drawn from this study.

Cox and Stoltenberg (1991) examined the effectiveness of a group intervention delivered to residents in a domestic violence shelter to provide personal and vocational counseling to women. The objective of the intervention was to help women deal effectively with personal adjustment, social interpersonal adjustment, and vocational problems. Women were assigned to either a control group or one of two identical experimental groups determined by the time of year in which they entered the shelter. The treatment was delivered in 5 modules including cognition, assertiveness and communication skills, problem solving, vocational counseling, and body-awareness. While the first experimental group improved significantly on measures of affect, assertiveness, and self-esteem, the second experimental group did not show similar improvement. Because the authors did not find changes on any vocational factors they speculated that the transition stage may be too early for women to focus on career issues. Unfortunately, the research design (e.g. lack of randomization, artifacts such as time of year) limits interpretation of the results of this study.

Several other studies have shown mixed results or no benefits for support groups to reduce emotional and functional sequelae of IPV (e.g., Holiman and Schilit, 1991; Ruben, 1991). However, these studies are limited by a small sample sizes, lack of random assignment, and usually a lack of control groups (Tutty et al., 1996).

We identified one intervention designed to address safety behaviors in women in transition. McFarlane and colleagues (2002) recruited women from a family violence unit of a large urban district attorney's office. They randomized 150 women to receive a six-week telephone intervention on safety behavior or standard care. The intervention covered topics similar to those used by Parker and colleagues (1999), reviewed above. Since these women were in transition, the authors stress the importance of discussing the risk of men becoming more violent when losing their victim. Results indicated significantly more women in the intervention condition were practicing safety behaviors at three- and twelve-month follow-up than women in standard care.

After the Relationship

Social Drinking/Alcohol Interventions. Integrated treatments addressing both trauma related symptoms that so often come with interpersonal violence as well as alcohol use may be particularly appropriate for women no longer in the relationship. While integrated treatment research is still in its infancy, there are some promising interventions that may be effective for female victims of IPV. Specifically, Seeking Safety, an integrated treatment for trauma or posttraumatic stress disorder and concomitant alcohol and or substance use, has been shown to be helpful to women in outpatient treatment, substance abuse treatment, and community mental health centers, as well as with female veterans, females in prison, and low income urban women (Cook, Walser, Kane, Ruzek, and Woody, 2006; Hien, Cohen, Litt, Miele, and Capstick, 2004; Holdcraft, and Comtois, 2002; Najavits, Weiss, Shaw, and Muenz,1998; Weller, 2005; Zlotnick, Najavits, and Rohsenow, 2003). Seeking Safety is a present-focused therapy that utilizes cognitive, behavioral, interpersonal, and case management techniques and aims to help clients attain safety from trauma/PTSD and alcohol/substance use. Establishing safety is often times one of the most important clinical needs of women struggling with difficulties related to both trauma and alcohol use. Through this integrated treatment this need is addressed by establishing safety with regard to abstinence, self-harming behaviors, and unsafe relationships. Seeking Safety can be delivered in a group or individual format and consists of 25 modules that can be conducted in any order, thus allowing for great clinician flexibility (Najavits, 2002). Seeking Safety is one of the most researched integrated treatments to date with several studies showing support for its usefulness; however, efficacy data on this intervention is still limited and a full randomized control trial has not yet been conducted. While future research investigating this intervention is still needed, given its preliminary support Seeking Safety may be useful for female victims of IPV struggling with difficulties related to alcohol use.

Several other studies have investigated integrated substance use/PTSD interventions as well. In general, these studies show that addressing PTSD symptoms in a trauma focused therapy typically leads to decreases in substance use and does not lead to increased use or relapse (Back, Waldrup, Brady, and Hien, 2006). Amaro and colleagues (2007) explored the effects of integrated trauma-informed services on the severity of substance abuse, mental health, and PTSD symptoms among women with histories of trauma. Women in the experimental condition had access to a clinical services intervention which included: trauma-informed assessments, treatment plans, service coordination, leadership skills building groups, and trauma-specific groups. The enhanced model also included the use of a common Co-Morbidity Screen and referral resource materials to assist providers in systematically screening for potential problem areas related to the client's substance abuse, mental health, and trauma as well as with appropriately referring clients to services, assessments, and/or education. Women in the comparison condition had access to services as usual which generally included primarily substance use treatment. Results indicated that at 6 and 12 month follow-ups, those in the trauma-informed intervention group, in contrast to the comparison group, had significantly better outcomes in drug abstinence rates in the past 30 days as well as in mental health and PTSD symptoms.

Additionally, Back and colleagues (2006) investigated the temporal course of improvement in PTSD and alcohol dependence symptoms among individuals with comorbid PTSD and alcohol dependence participating in a 12-week outpatient, double-blind, placebo-controlled medication trial of sertraline. Improvements in PTSD were associated with reductions in substance use; however, reduced substance use did not lead to improved PTSD symptoms. Improvement in hyperarousal symptoms, in particular, was related to substantially lower alcohol use. It should be noted that these interventions are not designed specifically for IPV victims.

Physical sequelae. We were not able to locate interventions studies to reduce physical sequelae of IPV for women who have left the abusive relationship.

Emotional and functional sequelae. Although many studies of interventions designed to reduce trauma sequelae have included IPV victims in their sample, we only located one intervention designed specifically for IPV victims (Kubany et al., 2003; Kubany et al., 2004). Interventions designed specifically for IPV victims may be crucial because of the factors that make IPV trauma unique. These include prolonged and repeated exposure to trauma (Kubany & Waston, 2002), exposure to multiple forms of abuse (physical, psychological, sexual), the perpetration of the trauma by a trusted loved one (Saunders, 1994,), the control and isolation experienced by women during the abusive relationship, and the experience of shame related to the abuse (Buchbinder and Eisikovits, 2003).

The intervention designed specifically for IPV victims is Cognitive Trauma Therapy for Battered Women with PTSD (CTT-BW; Kubany et al., 2003; Kubany et al., 2004). This therapy is based on the premise that guilt plays a role in maintaining chronic PTSD because guilt thoughts paired with the memory of the trauma maintain a highly distressed emotional response to the memory of the trauma. The 11-week treatment focuses heavily on assessing and correcting irrational guilt beliefs. Other psychological components of CTT-BW include psychoeducation regarding PTSD, stress management, and exposure to the trauma. To improve functioning, self-advocacy and empowerment strategies, problem solving skills, assertive communication, management of unwanted contact with the abuser, and ways to avoid revictimization are addressed.

Kubany and colleagues recently published the results of a clinical trial of CTT-BW (Kubany et al., 2004). The authors randomized 125 women who met criteria for PTSD to their treatment or a control group. Outcomes were measured pre, post, and at 3- and 6-month follow-up. Following study completion, 85% of women no longer met the numbing/avoidance criteria of PTSD and 69% achieved good end-state functioning. Results for depression were similarly promising. Therapy gains were maintained at both follow-up assessments. There were no differences between treatment delivered by professionals or paraprofessionals or male or female therapists. There were also no differences in effectiveness by ethnicity.

This intervention is impressive in that it targeted psychosocial problems and functional impairment, thus, touching upon many key issues that we have identified. A limitation is that women who were currently abusing alcohol or substances were excluded. This limitation compromises generalizability, since the prevalence of alcohol and substance abuse in IPV victims is high (e.g. El-Bassel et al., 2003; Frye, El-Bassel, Gilbert, Rajah, and Christie, 2001).

Other psychotherapies that have empirical support for the treatment of PTSD include prolonged exposure therapy (PE; e.g., Foa, Hembree, and Rothbaum, 2007) and cognitive processing therapy (CPT; e.g,. Resick and Schnicke, 1996). The Institute of Medicine (2007) recommends exposure based therapies such as these for the treatment of PTSD. Both have been tested in randomized clinical trials with female trauma victims with good results, although IPV specifically was not examined. Prolonged exposure therapy is modeled on the premise that people who develop PTSD after trauma are more likely to avoid memories and reminders of the trauma than those who recover naturally. In light of this, the therapy guides patients through en-vivo (from a ranked hierarchy of avoided situations put together by the patient and therapist) and imaginal exposures (recounting the memory in session and listening to recordings of the recounting between sessions) to counteract the avoidance. The premise of CPT is that those who develop PTSD have cognitive stuck points that keep them from recovering from trauma. The therapy uses cognitive restructuring techniques to help patients move past those stuck points.

RECOMMENDATIONS AND FUTURE DIRECTIONS

Social Drinking/Alcohol

Considering the high prevalence of problem drinking among women who have experienced IPV, the dearth of alcohol interventions is problematic. While more general interventions can be applied, these do not take into account the particular coping functions that alcohol use may serve for these women nor do they address the particular stressors these women face whether they are in the relationship, in transition out, or have terminated the relationship.

Interventions for women who have experienced IPV should use a "No blame model," meaning that women should never feel pressured to apologize to the abuser or be made to feel at fault for being victims of abuse. Davis, Combs-Lane, and Smith (2004) recommend addressing health risk behaviors in tandem with trauma interventions. Intervention would include psychoeducation regarding the pros and cons of behaviors such as drinking, correcting distorted cognitions regarding health risk behaviors, behavior change strategies, and addressing self-blame. The authors highlight that clinicians should be cautious to avoid delivering messages that victims may perceive as blaming them. For example, rather than asking victims if they were drinking when sexually assaulted, clinicians may ask if victims have any strategies they use to numb the pain, and use this method to introduce alternative coping strategies.

Resources should be available to women regardless of drinking status. For example, women in transition should not be refused from shelters because of drinking behavior. Because of the comorbidity between drinking and emotional problems such as PTSD and depression, dual diagnosis services should be available.

Physical Sequelae

Our review revealed that physical sequelae of IPV are least touched upon in psychosocial interventions. This may be driven by a belief that physical sequelae fall under the umbrella of physician interventions and should be addressed in the emergency room or the family practitioner's office. However, a look at some of the specific physical sequelae indicates that many are quite appropriate for psychosocial intervention.

One potential area of intervention is the mild traumatic brain injury (MBTI) associated with IPV. Jackson and colleagues (2004) make several recommendations for treating MTBI in IPV victims. First, those who work with IPV victims should become familiar with indicators of MTBI and post-concussion syndrome (PCS) and should recommend neurological evaluations when appropriate. Those who test positive for MTBI, should receive interventions that address their impairments. Recommended interventions are similar to other interventions recommended for IPV victims. These include safety issues, self-esteem, emotional support, isolation, daily functioning, and problem solving. In addition, Jackson and colleagues suggest education about head injury and strengthening cognitive capacities to process and interpret information. We recommend that future intervention research with IPV victims include pre- and post-evaluation of cognitive deficits and that the intervention include modules designed to alleviate difficulties associated with cognitive impairments.

IPV victims may also benefit from interventions to reduce chronic pain. Meagher (2004) points out that the neurocognitive pathways associated with PTSD are similar to those associated with chronic pain, a possible reason for why the two conditions co-occur with high frequency in IPV victims. Meagher recommends integrated cognitive behavioral treatments that address both chronic pain and PTSD. Such interventions would include education about both conditions, skill acquisition and rehearsal, as well as skill generalization and maintenance.

All of these interventions must be evaluated empirically before conclusions regarding their efficacy can be drawn. Finally, more research is needed to understand and overcome physician barriers to screening and documenting IPV. Future studies may also shed light on whether screening female victims of IPV for other negative sequelae such as PTSD, depression, and substance abuse, is efficacious and clinically useful.

Emotional Sequelae

Much of the research on interventions to reduce emotional sequelae of IPV assesses the effectiveness of supportive counseling. However, the results of these studies are inconclusive, in part based on the limitations of the study designs. Based on their review of the literature, Tutty, Bidgood, and Rothery (1993) published guidelines for groups for IPV victims in transition. These authors recommend that group content focus on the following points: 1) the future safety of the woman; 2) recognition of violence; 3) reduction of self-blame; 4) enhancing self-esteem; 5) increased understanding of why battering occurs, 6) expression of anger and mourning, and 7) developing a support network. While these recommendations appear theoretically sound, studies are needed to evaluate their efficacy.

Interestingly, most of the literature examining supportive counseling for IPV victims does not assess for the presence of PTSD, depression, or substance abuse. Some of the literature talks explicitly about the importance of not pathologizing IPV victims (e.g., Pagelow, 1992). However, more recent research seems to indicate that there are benefits to diagnosing IPV victims when appropriate. For example, Hughes and Jones (2000) noted that giving the diagnosis of PTSD to victims of IPV might improve treatment efficacy by reducing the victims' anxiety, self-blame, and sense of powerlessness. Jones and colleagues (2001) argue that not addressing PTSD and other diagnoses in treatment may be iatrogenic for IPV victims. Indeed, there is evidence that female victims of IPV with PTSD are significantly more impaired than female victims of IPV without PTSD (Laffaye et al., 2003). Ignoring these more severe symptoms in intervention efforts ignores significant impairment in the majority of female victims.

Based on the high prevalence rates of PTSD and depression among IPV victims, more research is needed on efficacious treatments to reduce the symptoms of these disorders. PE and CPT are PTSD treatments that have received the most empirical support. Although studies of these treatments have included women who experienced IPV, outcomes with IPV victims have not been examined specifically. Likely, these therapies would be effective with IPV as long as an index trauma can be identified (for PE) and women are willing to engage in a trauma processing therapy. As noted earlier, IPV-related trauma has several unique aspects to it, such that treatments should be tested specifically with this population before statements about their effectiveness with IPV can be made. Although many trauma therapies focus primarily on PTSD symptoms, studies have shown that as PTSD symptoms decrease, symptoms of depression tend to decrease as well (e.g. Kubany et al., 2004). Further research is needed to shed light on whether this relationship is true with IPV victims.

Functional Sequelae

Few studies to date have demonstrated that specific interventions are effective in improving the functioning of IPV victims. For example, Cox and Stoltenberg (1991) did not find their vocational intervention for women in transition to be effective. They speculated that the transition period is not a good time point at which to deal with vocational issues. Future studies are necessary to evaluate whether this statement is accurate and to identify the most appropriate time to introduce vocational interventions. Kubany and colleagues' (2004) intervention shows promise in helping women recover from PTSD, reduce revictimization and improve assertiveness and problem solving, but women with substantial drinking were excluded from this study.

Conclusions and Recommendations

We have identified a number of negative IPV sequelae that we propose should be the focus of intervention with IPV victims. In particular, given the high rates of drinking in relation to IPV, interventions that integrate addressing alcohol issues in tandem with other IPV-related issues are needed. The literature on motives for drinking related to IPV suggests that coping, enhancement, and social motives should be targets for intervention. Given the myriad of negative sequelae, it is doubtful that a single intervention could address such an abundance of issues. This is an empirical question that deserves further attention. In the meantime, there is some evidence that it may be possible to address multiple issues in a single intervention. For example, Seeking Safety (Najavits, Weiss, and Liese, 1996) and several other interventions target the emotional and functional sequelae of PTSD and alcohol use concurrently. One way to accomplish this is through a modular treatment format where treatment can be individualized by selecting the most pertinent modules for each patient. Another option is a stepped-care approach where issues are addressed one at a time, starting with the most pressing. Future studies must evaluate which approaches would be most effective.

This review is an integration of literature from the disciplines of psychiatry, public health, primary care, and sociology. Mears (2003) among others has recommended that a collaborative effort among many different fields that encounter IPV victims is necessary for best practices to be developed. This review reveals the dearth of empirically supported psychosocial interventions to help women recover from the debilitating aftereffects of IPV. Clearly, more empirically supported interventions are needed at every point at which clinicians may make contact with IPV victims. Quite encouraging is the fact is that many interventions that have been effective in reducing the effects of trauma exposure in other populations may be applicable to and effective with IPV victims as well. However, the unique aspects of IPV may need to be addressed in these interventions to facilitate efficacy with female victims of IPV. In particular, alcohol interventions are needed given the high rate of use and abuse among women and associated problems with those who have experienced IPV. Much more research is needed to understand how to best help women regain their physical and emotional health and functional independence after experiencing domestic violence.

REFERENCES

Amaro, H., Dai, J., Arevalo, S., Acevedo, A., Matsumoto, A., Nieves, R., & Prado, G. (2007). Effects of Integrated Trauma Treatment on Outcomes in a Racially/Ethnically Diverse Sample of Women in Urban Community-based Substance Abuse Treatment. [Journal]. *Journal of Urban Health: Bulletin of the New York Academy of Medicine, 84*(4), 508-522.

Anderson, D. K., & Saunders, D. G. (2003). Leaving an abusive partner: an empirical review of predictors, the process of leaving, and psychological well-being. *Trauma Violence & Abuse, 4*(2), 163-191.

Astin, M. C., Lawrence, K. J., & Foy, D. W. (1993). Posttraumatic stress disorder among battered women: Risk and resiliency factors. *Violence and Victims, 8*(1), 17-28.

Bacchus L, M. G., & Bewley S. (2004). Domestic violence: prevalence in pregnant women and associations with physical and psychological health. *European Journal of Obstretic and Gynecological Biology, 113*(1), 6-11.

Back, S. E., Brady, K. T., Sonne, S. C., & Verduin, M. L. (2006). Symptom Improvement in Co-Occurring PTSD and Alcohol Dependence. *Journal of Nervous and Mental Disease, 194*(9), 690-696.

Back, S.E., Waldrup, A.E., Brady, K.T., & Hien, D. (2006). Evidenced-Based Time-Limited Treatment of Co-occurring Substance-Use Disorders and Civilian-Related Posttraumatic Stress Disorder. *Brief Treatment and Crisis Intervention, 6*(4), 283-294.

Bennett, L. & Lawson, M. (1994). Barriers to cooperation between domestic violence and substance abuse programs. *Families In Society, 75* (5), 277-286.

Bonds, D., Ellis, S. D., Weeks, E., Palla, S. L., & Lichstein, P. (2006). A practice-centered intervention to increase screening for domestic violence in primary care practices. *BMC Family Practice, 7*(63), 1-8.

Boyle, A., & Jones, P. B. (2006). The acceptability of routine inquiry about domestic violence towards women: a survey in three healthcare settings. *British Journal of General Practice, 56*, 258-261.

Briere, J., & Jordan, C. E. (2004). Violence against women: Outcome complexity and implications for assessment and treatment. *Journal of Interpersonal Violence*. Special Issue: Toward a National Research Agenda on Violence Against Women--Part 1, *19*(11), 1252-1276.

Brown, S. A., Goldman, M. S., Inn, A., & Anderson, L. R. (1980). Expectations of reinforcement from alcohol: Their domain and relation to drinking patterns. *Journal of Consulting and Clinical Psychology, 48*, 419-426.

Buchbinder, E., & Eisikovits, Z. (2003). Battered women's entrapment in shame: a phenomenological study. *American Journal of Orthopsychiatry, 73*(4), 355-366.

Bureau of Justice Statistics Crime Data Brief, Intimate Partner Violence, 1993-2001, February 2003.

Byrne, C. A., & Riggs, D. S. (1996). The cycle of trauma: Relationship aggression in male Vietnam veterans with symptoms of posttraumatic stress disorder. *Violence and Victims, 11,* 213-225.

Campbell, J. C. (2002). Health consequence of intimate partner violence. *The Lancet, 359,* 1331-1336.

Campbell, J. C., Kub, J., Belknap, R. A., & Templin, T. N. (1997). Predictors of depression in battered women. *Violence Against Women, 3*(3), 271-293.

Centers for Disease Control and Prevention, N. C. f. I. P. a. C. (2003). *Costs of Intimate Partner Violence Against Women in the United States,* from http://www.cdc.gov/ncipc/pub-res/ipv_cost/ipv.htm

Chang, G. (2002). Brief interventions for problem drinking and women. *Journal of Substance Abuse Treatment, 23,* 1-7.

Chen, P.-H., Rovi, S., Washington, J., Jacobs, A., Vega, M., Pan, K.-Y., et al. (2007). Randomized comparison of 3 methods to screen for domestic violence in family practice. *Annals of Family Medicine, 5*(5), 430-435.

Cohen, J. B., Dickow, A., Horner, K., Zweben, J. E., Balabis, J., Vandersloot, D., & Reiber, C. (2003). Abuse and violence history of men and women in treatment for methamphetamine dependence. *American Journal on Addictions, 12* (5) , 377-385.

Coker, A. L., Bethea, L., Smith, P. H., Fadden, M. K., & Brandt, H. M. (2002). Missed opportunities: intimate partner violence in family practice settings. *Preventive Medicine., 34*(4), 445-454.

Coker, A. L., Smith, P. H., Bethea, L., King, M. R., & McKeown, R. E. (2000). Physical health consequences of physical and psychological intimate partner violence. *Archives of Family Medicine, 9*(5), 451-457.

Cook, J. M., Walser, R. D., Kane, V., Ruzek, J. I., & Woody, G. (2006). Dissemination and feasibility of a cognitive-behavioral treatment for substance use disorders and posttraumatic stress disorder in the Veterans Administration. *Journal of Psychoactive Drugs, 38,* 89-92.

Cooper, M. L., Russel, M., Skinner, J. B., & Windle, M. (1992). Development and validation of a three-dimensional measure of drinking motives. *Psychological Assessment, 4*, 123-132.

Council on Scientific Affairs, A. M. A. (1992). Violence against women. *Journal of the American Medical Association, 267*, 3184-3189.

Council, N. R. (1996). *Understanding violence against women.* Washington, DC: National Academy of Sciences.

Cox, J. W., & Stoltenberg, C. D. (1991). Evaluation of a treatment program for battered wives. *Journal of Family Violence, 6*(4), 395-413.

Cunnigham, J. A., Neighbors, C., Wild, C., & Humphreys, K. (2008). Ultra-brief intervention for problem drinkers: research protocol. *BMC Public Health, 8,* 1-12.

Davis, J., Combs-Lane, A. M., & Smith, D. W. (2004). *Victimization and health risk behaviors: Implication for prevention programs*. Washington DC: APA.

Downs, W. (2001). *Alcohol problems and violence against women: Report of summary findings.* United States Department of Justice, Document Number 188267, Grant No. 96-WT-NX-0005. Retrieved 5/1/09 from http://www.ncjrs.gov/pdffiles1/nij/grants/188267.pdf

El-Bassel, N., Gilbert, L., Witte, S., Wu, E., Gaeta, T., Schilling, R., et al. (2003). Intimate partner violence and substance abuse among minority women receiving care from an inner-city emergency department. *Womens Health Issues, 13*(1), 16-22.

Emrick, C. (2004). Alcoholics anonymous and other mutual aid groups. In N. Heather & T. Stockwell (Eds.) *The Essential Handbook of Treatment and Prevention of Alcohol Problems* (pp. 177-192). Hoboken, NJ: John Wiley & Sons.

Eisenstat, S. A., & Bancroft, L. (1999). Domestic violence. *New England Journal of Medicine, 341*(12), 886-892. Fals-Stewart, W. & Kennedy, C. (2005). Addressing intimate partner violence in substance-abuse treatment. *Journal of Substance Abuse Treatment, 29,* 5-17.

Fals-Stewart, W., Birchler, G. R., & Kelley, M. L. (2006). Learning sobriety together: A randomized clinical trial examining behavioral couples therapy with alcoholic female patients. *Journal of Consulting and Clinical Psychology, 74*, 579 –591.

Fals-Stewart, W., & Kennedy, C. (2005). Addressing intimate partner violence in substance-abuse treatment. *Journal of Substance Abuse Treatment, 29*, 5-17.

Fals-Stewart, W., O'Farrell, T. J., & Birchler, G. R. (2004). Behavioral couples therapy for substance abuse: Rationale, methods, and findings. *Science and Practice Perspectives, 2*, 30 – 41.

Fanslow, J. L., Norton, R. N., & Robinson, E. M. (1999). One year follow-up of an emergency department protocol for abused women. *Australian & New Zealand Journal of Public Health, 23*(4), 418-420.

Fedovskiy, K., Higgins, S., & Paranjape, A. (2008). Intimate partner violence: How does it impact major depressive disorder and post traumatic stress disorder among immigrant latinas? *Journal of Immigrant and Minority Health, 10*(1), 45-51.

Finfgeld-Connett, D. (2006). Web-based treatment for problem drinking. *Journal of Psychosocial Nursing, 44,* 20-27.

Fleming, M. F., Mundt, M. P., French, M. T., Manwell, L. B., Stauffacher, E. A., & Barry, K. L. (2002). Brief physician advice for problem drinkers: Long-term efficacy and benefit-cost analysis. *Alcoholism: Clinical and Experimental Review, 26,* 36-43.

Fleury R. E., S. C., Bybee D. I., & Davidson W. S. (1998). "Why don't they just call the cops?": Reasons for differential police contact among women with abusive partners. *Violence and Victims, 13*(4), 333-346.

Foa, E. B., Cascardi, M., Zoellner, L. A., & Feeny, N. C. (2000). Psychological and environmental factors associated with partner violence. *Trauma, Violence, & Abuse, 1*(1), 67-91.

Foa, E., Hembree, E., & Rothbaum, B. (2007). Prolonged Exposure Therapy for PTSD: Emotional Processing of Traumatic Experiences Therapist Guide (Treatments That Work). New York: Oxford University Press.

Follette, V. M. (1994). Survivors of child sexual abuse: Treatment using a contextual analysis. In S. C. Hayes, N. S. Jacobson, V. M. Follette, & M. J. Dougher (Eds.), *Acceptance and change: Content and context in psychotherapy* (pp. 255-258). Reno, NV: Context Press.

Frye, V., El-Bassel, N., Gilbert, L., Rajah, V., & Christie, N. (2001). Intimate partner sexual abuse among women on methadone. *Violence & Victims, 16*(5), 553-564.

Gallop, R., & Everett, B. (2001). Recognizing the signs and symptoms. In B. Everett&R. Gallop (Eds.), The link between childhood trauma and mental illness: Effective interventions for mental health professionals (pp. 57-79). Thousand Oaks, CA: Sage.

Gerlock, A. A. (1999). Health impact of domestic violence. *Issues in Mental Health Nursing, 20*(4), 373-385.

Gilson, S. F., DePoy, E., & Cramer, E. P. (2001). Linking the assessment of self-reported functional capacity with abuse experiences of women with disabilities. *Violence Against Women, 7*(4), 418-431.

Golding, J. M. (1999). Intimate partner violence as a risk factor for mental disorders: A meta analysis. *Journal of Family Violence, 14*(2), 99-132.

Gorde, M. W., Helfrich, C. A., & Finlayson, M. L. (2004). Trauma symptoms and life skill needs of domestic violence victims. *Journal of Interpersonal Violence, 19*(6), 691-708.

Grayson, C. E., & Nolen-Hoeksema, S. (2005). Motives to drink as mediators between childhood sexual assault and alcohol problems in adult women. *Journal of Traumatic Stress, 18*, 137-145.

Greenfield, L. A., Rand, M. R. Craven, D., Klaus, P. A., Perkins, C. A., Ringel C., et al. (1998). Violence by inmates: analysis of data on crimes by current or former spouses, boyfriends, and girlfriends. Washington, D. C.: US Department of Justice, Office of Justice Programs, Bureau of Justice Statistics.

Guo, S. F., Wu, J. L., Qu, C. Y., & Yan, R. Y. (2004). Domestic abuse on women in China before, during, and after pregnancy. *Chinese Medical Journal, 117*(3), 331-336.

Hathaway, J. E., Mucci, L. A., Silverman, J. G., Brooks, D. R., Mathews, R., & Pavlos, C. A. (2000). Health status and health care use of massachusetts women reporting partner abuse. *American Journal of Preventive Medicine, 19*(4), 302-307.

Heather, N. (2004) Brief interventions. In N. Heather & T. Stockwell (Eds.) *The Essential Handbook of Treatment and Prevention of Alcohol Problems* (pp. 117-138). Hoboken, NJ: John Wiley & Sons.

Helfrich, C. A., Fujiura, G. T., & Rutkowski-Kmitta, V. (2008). Mental health disorders and functioning of women in domestic violence shelters. *Journal of Interpersonal Violence, 23*(4), 437-453.

Herbert, T. B., Silver, R. C., & Ellard, J. H. (1991). Coping with an abusive relationship: I. How and why do women stay? *Journal of Marriage & the Family, 53*(2), 311-325.

Hien, D. A., Cohen, L. R., Litt, L. C., Miele, G. M., & Capstick, C. (2004). Promising empirically supported treatments for women with comorbid PTSD and substance use disorders. *American Journal of Psychiatry, 161,* 1426-1432.

Holdcraft, L. C. & Comtois, K. A. (2002). Description of and preliminary data from a women's dual diagnosis community mental health program. *Canadian Journal of Community Mental Health, 21*, 91-109.

Holiman, M. S. & Schilit, R.(1991). Aftercare for battered women: How to encourage the maintenance of change. *Psychotherapy: Theory, Research, Practice, Training, 28*(2), 345-353.

Holtzworth-Munroe A, M., Marshall, A. D., Meehan, J.C. & Rehman, U. (2003). *Physical Aggression.* In D.K. Snyder & M. A. Whisman (Eds.), *Treating Difficult Couples:*

Helping Clients with Coexisting Mental and Relationship Disorders (pp. 201-230). New York, NY: The Guilford Press.

Howard, A., Riger, S., Campbell, R., & Wasco, S. (2003). Counseling services for battered women: a comparison of outcomes for physical and sexual assault survivors. *Journal of Interpersonal Violence, 18*(7), 717-734.

Hughes, M. J., & Jones, L. (2000). Women, domestic violence, and posttraumatic stress disorder (PTSD). *Family Therapy, 27*(3), 125-139.

Humphreys, J., Lee, K., Neylan, T., & Marmar, C. (2001). Psychological and physical distress of sheltered battered women. *Health Care for Women International, 22*(4), 401-414.

Humphreys, K., Moos, R. H., & Cohen, C. (1997). Social and community resources and long-term recovery from treated and untreated alcoholism. *Journal of Studies on Alcohol, 58,* 231-238.

Institute of Medicine. (2007). *Treatment of posttraumatic stress disorder: An assessment of the evidence*. Washington, DC: National Academy of Sciences.

Jackson, H., Philip, E., Nuttall, R. L., & Diller, L. (2004). Battered women and traumatic brain injury. In K. A. Kendall-Tackett (Ed.), *Health consequences of abuse in the family: A clinical guide for evidence-based practice Application and practice in health psychology* (pp. 233-246). Washington, DC: American Psychological Association.

Johnson, D. M., Zlotnick, C., & Perez, S. (2008). The relative contribution of abuse severity and PTSD severity on the psychiatric and social morbidity of battered women in shelters. *Behavior Therapy, 39*(3), 232-241.

Jones, L., Hughes, M., & Unterstaller, U. (2001). Post-traumatic stress disorder (PTSD) in victims of domestic violence: A review of the research. *Trauma Violence & Abuse, 2*(2), 99-119.

Kaysen, D. L., Dillworth, T. M., Simpson, T. L., Waldrop, A. E., Larimer, M. E., & Resick, P. A. (2007). Domestic violence and alcohol use: Trauma related symptoms and motives for drinking. *Addictive Behaviors, 32*, 1272-1283.

Kendall, J., Pelucio, M. T., Casaletto, J., Thompson, K. P., Barnes, S., Pettit, E., et al. (2009). Impact of emergency department intimate partner violence intervention. *Journal of Interpersonal Violence, 24*(2), 280-306.

Kessler, R. C., Berglund, P., Demler, O., Jin, R., Merikangas, K. R., & Walters, E. E. (2005). Lifetime Prevalence and Age-of-Onset Distributions of *DSM- IV* Disorders in the National Comorbidity Survey Replication. *Archives General Psychiatry.* 62, 593-602.

Klap, R., Tang, L., Wells, K., Starks, S. L., & Rodriguez, M. (2007). Screening for Domestic Violence Among Adult Women in the United States. *Society of General Internal Medicine, 22*, 579-584.

Kubany, E. S. & Watson, E. B. (2002,). Cognitive trauma therapy for formerly battered women with PTSD: Conceptual bases and treatment outlines. *Cognitive & Behavioral Practice, 9*(2), 111-127.

Kubany, E. S., Hill, E. E., & Owens, J. A. (2003). Cognitive trauma therapy for battered women with PTSD: preliminary findings. *Journal of Traumatic Stress, 16*(1), 81-91.

Kubany, E. S., Hill, E. E., Owens, J. A., Iannce-Spencer, C., McCaig, M. A., Tremayne, K. J., et al. (2004). Cognitive trauma therapy for battered women with PTSD (CTT-BW). *Journal of Consulting & Clinical Psychology., 72*(1), 3-18.

Laffaye, C., Kennedy, C., & Stein, M. B. (2003). Post-traumatic stress disorder and health-related quality of life in female victims of intimate partner violence. *Violence & Victims, 18*(2), 227-238.

Lang, A. J., Rodgers, C. S., Laffaye, C., Satz, L. E., Dresselhaus, T. R., & Stein, M. B. (2003). Sexual trauma, PTSD, and health behavior. *Behavioral Medicine, 28*, 150-158.

Leserman, J. (2007). Association of sexual and physical abuse with functional gastrointestinal and pelvic pain. *Primary Psychiatry, 14*(4), 58-63.

Lindhorst, T., Meyers, M., & Casey, E. (2008). Screening for Domestic Violence in Public Welfare Offices: An Analysis of Case Manager and Client Interactions. *Violence Against Women, 14*(1), 5-28.

Lloyd, S., & Taluc, N. (1999). The Effects of Male Violence on Female Employment. *Violence Against Women, 5*, 370-392.

Marais, A., Villiers, P. J., Moller, A. T., & Stein, D. J. (1999). Domestic violence in patients visiting general practitioners--prevalence, phenomenology, and association with psychopathology, *South African Medical Journal, , 89(6),* 635-40.

Marlatt, G. A., & Gordon, J. R. (1985). *Relapse situations.* New York: Guilford Press.

Matud, M. P. (2005). The psychological impact of domestic violence on spanish women. *Journal of Applied Social Psychology, 35*(11), 2310-2322.

McCrady, B. S., Epstein, E. E., Cook, S., Jensen, N., & Hildebrandt, T. (2009). A randomized trail of individual and couple behavioral alcohol treatment for women. *Journal of Consulting and Clinical Psychology, 2,* 243-256.

McFarlane, J., Parker, B., Soeken, K., Silva, C., & Reed, S. (1998). Safety behaviors of abused women after an intervention during pregnancy. *Journal of Obstetric, Gynecologic and Neonatal Nursing, 27*(1), 244-250.

McCauley J, Kern, D. E., Kolodner, K., Dill, L., Schroeder, A. F., DeChant, H. K., et al., (1995). The 'battering syndrome': prevalence and clinical symptoms of domestic violence in primary care internal medicine practices. *Annals of Internal Medicine, 123,* 737–746.

McCloskey, L. A., Lichter, E., Williams, C., Gerber, M., Wittenberg, E., & Ganz, M. (2006). Assessing Intimate Partner Violence in Health Care Settings Leads to Women's Receipt of Interventions and Improved Health. *Public Health Reports, 121*, 435-444.

McFarlane, A. (1998). Epidemiological evidence about the relationship between PTSD and alcohol abuse: The nature of the association. *Addictive Behaviors, 23,* 813-826.

McFarlane, J., Malecha, A., Gist, J., Watson, K., Batten, E., Hall, I., et al. (2002). An Intervention to Increase Safety Behaviors of Abused Women: Results of a Randomized Clinical Trial. *Nursing Research, 51*(6), 347-354.

Meagher, M. (2004). *Lings between traumatic family vilence and chronic pain: Biopsychosocial pathways and treatment implications*. Washington DC: APA.

Mears, D. P. (2003). Research and interventions to reduce domestic violence revictimization. *Trauma Violence & Abuse, 4*(2), 127-147.

Miller, A. W., Coonrod, D. V., Brady, M. J., Moffitt, M. P., & Bay, R. C. (2004). Medical student training in domestic violence: a comparison of students entering residency training in 1995 and 2001. *Teaching & Learning in Medicine, 16*(1), 3-6.

Miller, W. R., & Rollnick, S. (1991). *Motivational Interviewing: Preparing People to Change Addictive Behavior.* New York: Guillford Press.

Morgenstern, J. & Longabaugh, R.. (2000). Cognitive-behavioral treatment for alcohol dependence: a review of the evidence for its hypothesized mechanisms of action. *Addiction, 95,* 1475-1490.

Morier-Genoud, C., Bodenmann, P., Favrat, B., & Vannotti, M. (2006). Violence in primary care: Prevalence and follow-up of victims. *BMC Family Practice, 7*(15).

Morland, L. A., Leskin, G. A., Block, C. R., Campbell, J. C., & Friedman, M. J. (2008). Intimate partner violence and miscarriage: Examination of the role of physical and psychological abuse and posttraumatic stress disorder. *Journal of Interpersonal Violence, 23*(5), 652-669.

Najavits, L.M. (2002). *Seeking Safety: A treatment manual for PTSD and substance abuse.* New York: Guilford.

Najavits, L. M. (2002). Clinicians' views on treating posttraumatic stress disorder and substance use disorder. *Journal of Substance Abuse Treatment, 22*(2), 79-85.

Najavits, L. M., Weiss, R. D., & Liese, B. S. (1996). Group cognitive-behavioral therapy for women with PTSD and substance use disorder. *Journal of Substance Abuse Treatment, 13*(1), 13-22.

Najavits, L. M., Weiss, R. D., Shaw, S. R., & Muenz, L. R. (1998). "Seeking safety": outcome of a new cognitive-behavioral psychotherapy for women with posttraumatic stress disorder and substance dependence. *Journal of Traumatic Stress, 11*(3), 437-456.

Najavits, L., Weiss R.D., & Shaw S.R. (1997). The link between substance abuse and posttraumatic stress disorder in women. A research review. *American Journal of Addictions, 6*(4), 273-283.

Nishith, P., Resick, P. A., & Mueser, K. T. (2001). Sleep difficulties and alcohol use motives in female rape victims with posttraumatic stress disorder. Journal of Traumatic Stress, 14, 469-479.

Norman, S.B. Davidson, J.T., & Stein, M.B. (2007). Profiling Posttraumatic Functional Impairment. *The Journal of Nervous and Mental Disease, 195(1),* 48-53.

Norman, S.B., Means-Christensen, A.J., Craske, M.G., Sherbourne, C.D., Roy-Byrne, P.P., & Stein, M.B. (2006). Associations between Psychological Trauma and Physical Illness in Primary Care. *Journal of Traumatic Stress,* 19(4), 461-470.

Ogle, R. L., & Baer, J. S. (2003). Addressing the service linkage problem: Increasing substance abuse treatment engagement using personalized feedback interventions in heavy-using female domestic violence shelter residents. *Journal of Interpersonal Violence, 18* (11), 1311-1324.

Orcutt, H. K., Erickson, D. J., & Wolfe, J. (2002). A prospective analysis of trauma exposure: The mediating role of PTSD symptomatology. *Journal of Traumatic Stress, 15*(3), 259-266.

Pagelow, M. D. (1992). Adult victims of domestic violence: Battered women. *Journal of Interpersonal Violence, 7*(1), 87-120.

Parker, B., McFarlane, J., Soeken, K., Silva, C., & Reel, S. (1999). Testing an intervention to prevent further abuse to pregnant women. *Research in Nursing & Health, 22*(1), 59-66.

Parks, G. A., Anderson, B. K., & Marlatt, G. A. (2004). Relapse prevention therapy. In N. Heather & T. Stockwell (Eds.) *The Essential Handbook of Treatment and Prevention of Alcohol Problems* (pp. 87-104). Hoboken, NJ: John Wiley & Sons.

Parks, G.A., Marlatt, G.A., & Anderson, B. K. (2004). Cognitive-behavioural alcohol treatment. In N. Heather & T. Stockwell (Eds.) *The Essential Handbook of Treatment and Prevention of Alcohol Problems* (pp. 69-86). Hoboken, NJ: John Wiley & Sons.

Pavao, J., Alvarez, J., Baumrind, N., Induni, M., & Kimerling, R. (2007). Intimate partner violence and housing instability. American Journal of Preventive Medicine, 32(2), 143-146.

Peterson, R., Gazmararian, J., & Anderson Clark, K. (2001). Partner violence: Implications for health and community settings. *Womens Health Issues, 11*, 116-125.

Perez, S., & Johnson, D. M. (2008). PTSD compromises battered women's future safety. *Journal of Interpersonal Violence, 23*(5), 635-651.

Pico-Alfonso, M. A., Garcia-Linares, M. I., Celda-Navarro, N., Herbert, J., & Martinez, M. (2004). Changes in cortisol and dehydroepiandrosterone in women victims of physical and psychological intimate partner violence. *Biological Psychiatry, 56*(4), 233-240.

Poole, N., Greaves, L., Jategaonkar, N., McCullough, L., & Chabot, C. (2008). Substance use by women using domestic violence shelters. *Substance Use and Misuse, 4,* 1129-1150.

Project MATCH Research Group. (1997). Matching alcoholism treatment to client heterogeneity: Project MATCH posttreatment drinking outcomes. *Journal of Studies on Alcohol, 58,* 7-29.

Project MATCH Research Group (1998). Matching alcoholism treatment to client heterogeneity: Project MATCH three-year drinking outcomes. *Alcoholism: Clinical and Experimental Research, 22,* 1300-1311.

Rapaport, M. H., Clary, C., Fayyad, R., & Endicott, J. (2005). Quality-of-life impairment in depressive and anxiety disorders. *American Journal of Psychiatry, 162*(6), 1171-1178.

Resick, P. A., & Schnicke, M. K. (1996). *Cognitive Processing Therapy for rape victims: A treatment manual.* Newbury Park, CA: Sage.

Rhodes, K. V., Frankel, R. M., Levinthal, N., Prenoveau, E., Bailey, J., & Levinson, W. (2007). "You're Not a Victim of Domestic Violence, Are You?" Provider–Patient Communication about Domestic Violence. *Annals of Internal Medicine, 147*(9), 620-627.

Rhodes, K. V., & Levinson, W. (2003). Interventions for intimate partner violence against women: Clinical applications. *Journal of the American Medical Association, 289*(5), 601-605

Riger, S., Raja, S., & Camacho, J. (2002). The radiating impact of intimate partner violence. *Journal of Interpersonal Violence, 17*(2), 184-205.

Rivara, F. P., Anderson, M. L., Fishman, P., Bonomi, A. E., Reid, R. J., Carrell, D., & Thompson, R. S. (2007). Healthcare Utilization and Costs for Women with a History of Intimate Partner Violence. *American Journal of Preventative Medicine, 32(2)*, 89-96

Roberts, G. L., Lawrence, J. M., Williams, G. M., & Raphael, B. (1998). The impact of domestic violence on women's mental health. *Australian and New Zealand Journal of Public Health, 22*(7), 796-801.

Rodgers, C. S., Norman, S. B., Thorp, S. R., Lebeck, M. M. & Lang, A. J. (2005). Trauma Exposure, Posttraumatic Stress Disorder and Health Behaviors: Impact on Special Populations. In Corales TA (Ed.), *Focus on Post-Traumatic Stress Disorder Research.* Hauppauge, NY: Nova Science Publishers, Inc, pp. 203-224.

Ruben, A. (1991). The effectiveness of outreach counseling and support groups for battered women: A preliminary investigation. *Research on Social Work and Practice, 1*(4), 332-357.

Salam, M. A., Alim, M. A., & Noguchi, T. (2006). Spousal abuse against women and its consequences on reproductive health: A study in the urban slums in Bangladesh. *Maternal & Child Health Journal, 10*(1), 83-94.

Saunders, D. (1994). Posttraumatic stress symptom profiles of battered women: a comparison of survivors in two settings. *Violence and Victims, 9*(1), 31-34.

Saunders, D.G. & Kindy, P. (1993). Predictors of physicians' responses to woman abuse: The role of gender, background, and brief training. *Journal of General Internal Medicine, 8,* 606-609.

Schlee, K. A., Heyman, R. E., & O'Leary, K. (1998). Group treatment for spouse abuse: Are women with PTSD appropriate participants? *Journal of Family Violence, 13*(1), 1-20.

Sethi, D., Watts, S., Zwi, A., Watson, J., & McCarthy, C. (2004). Experience of domestic violence by women attending an inner city accident and emergency department. *Emergency Medicine Journal, 21*(2), 180-184.

Shannon, L., Logan, T.K., Cole, J., & Walker, R. (2008). An examination of women's alcohol use and partner victimization experiences among women with protective orders. *Substance Use and Misuse, 43,*1110-1128

Silverman, J.G., Decker, M.R., Saggurti, N., Balaiah, D., & Raj, A. (2008). Intimate Partner Violence and HIV Infection Among Married Indian Women. *JAMA, 300(6),* 703-710.

Simpson, T. L. (2003). Childhood sexual abuse, PTSD, and the functional roles of alchol use among women drinkers. *Substance Use and Misuse, 38,* 249-270.

Stein, M., & Kennedy C. (2001). Major depressive and post-traumatic stress disorder comorbidity in female victims of intimate partner violence. *Journal of Affective Disorders, 66*(2-3), 133-138.

Stein M. B., Walker J. R., Hazen A. L., & Forde D.R. (1997). Full and partial posttraumatic stress disorder: Findings from a community survey. *American Journal of Psychiatry, 154,* 1114-1119.

Stewart, S. H., Conrod, P. J., Samoluk, S. B., Pihl, R. O., & Dongier, M. (2000). Posttraumatic stress disorder symptoms and situation-specific drinking in women substance abusers. *Alcoholism Treatment Quarterly, 18*, 31-47.

Stith, S., Rosen, K.H., & McCollum, E.E. (2003). Effectiveness of couples treatment for spouse abuse. *Journal of Marital and Family Therapy, 29*(3), 407-426.

Stuart, G. L., Ramsey, S. E., Moore, T. M., Kahler, C. W., Farrell, L. E., Recupero, P. R., et al. (2002). Marital violence victimization and perpetration among women substance abusers: A descriptive study. *Violence Against Women, 8*, 934 – 952.

Sutherland, C., Bybee, D.I., & Sullivan, C. M. (2002). Beyond bruises and broken bones: the joint effects of stress and injuries on battered women's health. *American Journal of Community Psychology, 60*(5), 606-636.

Swan, S., Farber, S., & Campbell, D. (2000). *Violence in the lives of women in substance abuse treatment: Service and policy implications*. National Online Resource Center on Violence Against Women. Retrieved 5/1/09 http://new.vawnet.org/category/documents.php?docid=1206

Tjaden, P., & Thoennes N. (2000). *Full Report of the Prevalence, Incidence, and Consequences of Intimate Partner Violence Against Women: Findings from the National Violence Against Women Survey.* Washington (DC): National Institute of Justice and the Centers for Disease Control and Prevention.

Tutty, L. M., Bidgood, B. A., & Rothery, M. A. (1993). Support groups for battered women: Research on their efficacy. *Journal of Family Violence, 8*(4), 325-343.

Tutty, L. M., Bidgood, B. A., & Rothery, M. A. (1996). Evaluating the effect of group process and client variables in support groups for battered women. *Research on Social Work Practice, 6*(3), 308-324.

Ullman, S. E., Fillipas, H. H., Townsend, S. M., & Starzynski, L. L. (2006). Correlates of comorbid PTSD and drinking problems among sexual assault survivors. *Addictive Behaviors, 31,* 128-132.

Valera, E. M., & Berenbaum, H. (2003). Brain injury in battered women. *Journal of Consulting and Clinical Psychology, 71*(4), 797-804.

Varjavand, N., Cohen, D. G., Gracely, E. J., & Novack, D. H. (2004). A survey of residents' attitudes and practices in screening for, managing, and documenting domestic violence. *Journal of the American Medical Womens Association., 59*(1), 48-53.

Walker, L. (1987). Treatment alternatives for battered women. *The Victimization of Women* (pp. 143-174). Beverly Hills, CA: Sage, 1978.

Weller, L.A. (2005). Group therapy to treat substance use and traumatic symptoms in female veterans. *Federal Practitioner,* 27-38.

Wettersten, K. B., Rudolph, S. E., Faul, K., Gallagher, K., Trangsrud, H. B., Adams, K., et al. (2004). Freedom through self-sufficiency: A qualitative examination of the impact of domestic violence on the working lives of women in shelter. *Journal of Counseling Psychology, 51*(4), 447-462.

Winters, J., Fals-Stewart, W., O'Farrell, T., Birchler, G., & Kelley, M. (2002). Behavioral couples therapy for female substance-abusing patients: Effects on substance use and relationship adjustment. *Journal of Consulting and Clinical Psychology, 70,* 344 –355.

Wisner, C. L., Gilmer, T. P., Saltzman, L. E., & Zinc, T. M. (1999). Intimate partner violence against women: Do victims cost health plans more? *Journal of Family Practice, 48*(6), 439-443.

Woods, A. B., Page, G. G., O'Campo, P., Pugh, L. C., Ford, D., & Campbell, J. C. (2005). The mediation effect of posttraumatic stress disorder symptoms on the relationship of intimate partner violence and IFN -Î³ levels. *American Journal of Community Psychology.* Special Issue: Theoretical and Methodological Innovations in Research on Intimate Partner Violence, 36(1-2), 159-175.

Zatzick D., Weiss D.S., Marmar C.R., Metzler T.J., Wells K., Golding J.M., Stewart A., & Schlenger W.E. (1997). Post-traumatic stress disorder and functioning and quality of life outcomes in female Vietnam veterans. *Military Medicine,* 162, 661-665.

Zlotnick, C., Johnson, D. M., & Kohn, R. (2006). Intimate partner violence and long-term psychosocial functioning in a national sample of American women. *Journal of Interpersonal Violence, 21*(2), 262-275.

Zlotnick, C., Najavits, L.M., & Rohsenow, D.J. (2003) A cognitive-behavioral treatment for incarcerated women with substance use disorder and posttraumatic stress disorder: Findings from a pilot study. *Journal of Substance Abuse Treatment, 25*, 99-105.

In: Social Drinking: Uses, Abuses and Psychological Factors ISBN: 978-1-60876-219-4
Editors : K. T. Everly, E. M. Cosell, pp. 237-259 © 2010 Nova Science Publishers, Inc.

Chapter 6

ACCESSORIES TO THE CRIME: "SECONDARY SERVERS" AND ALCOHOL SALES TO OBVIOUSLY INTOXICATED BARROOM PATRONS

***James C. Roberts*[1]**
The University of Scranton,
Department of Sociology/Criminal Justice Scranton, PA, USA

ABSTRACT

The primary goal of this study was to identify characteristics of licensed drinking establishments that predict alcohol sales to obviously intoxicated barroom patrons. Of particular interest was the relationship between "secondary servers" of alcohol and irresponsible alcohol service. Relying on a structured observation guide listing a large number of variables believed to be related to irresponsible alcohol service, trained observers spent a total of 444 hours collecting data in 25 licensed drinking establishments in Hoboken, New Jersey. Observations took place at two separate time periods, 7:30pm – 10:30pm and 11:00pm – 2:00am, on Thursday, Friday, and Saturday nights. Ordinary least squares (OLS) regression analyses revealed "number of secondary servers" as the strongest predictor of alcohol service to obviously intoxicated patrons in Hoboken barrooms. Another significant predictor of alcohol service to intoxicated patrons in this study was the presence of "aversive environmental stimuli" within licensed premises, such as excessive heat, smoke, and crowding. Several prevention strategies aimed at reducing irresponsible alcohol service in bars and associated problems with alcohol-related harm are proposed.

Keywords: *Alcohol, intoxication, licensed premises, bar staff, responsible beverage service*

1 James C. Roberts, Ph.D. The University of Scranton, Department of Sociology/Criminal Justice Scranton, PA 18510-4605, Direct dial: (570) 941-7435, Fax: (570) 941-6485, E-mail: robertsj7@scranton.edu.

INTRODUCTION

Despite the passage of laws in most countries that prohibit alcohol sales to obviously intoxicated individuals, barroom patrons are regularly served alcohol to the point of intoxication and beyond (McKnight, 1991; Nusbaumer and Reiling, 2003; Toomey, Wagenaar, Kilian, Fitch, Rothstein, and Fletcher, 1999; Toomey, Wagenaar, Erickson, Fletcher, Patrek, and Lenk, 2004). Furthermore, there is growing body of research that links continued alcohol service to obviously intoxicated patrons to alcohol-related harm occurring in and around licensed drinking establishments. Graham, La Rocque, Yetman, Ross, and Guistra (1980) conducted one of the first and most influential observational studies of barroom aggression. Teams of observers (male-female pairs) spent three months and a total of 633 hours conducting unobtrusive observations in 185 licensed premises in Vancouver, Canada. In addition to variables such as poor ventilation and shabby décor, these researchers identified irresponsible alcohol service and patron intoxication as important predictors of aggression in Vancouver barrooms. In describing the prototypical aggressive bar, Graham et al. (1980) state, "...extreme drunkenness is common and usually acceptable. The only reason for refusal of service seems to be that the person is unconscious – and some instances were seen in which a person was awakened to be served another drink" (p. 290).

It is important to note that research on alcohol-related harm occurring in and around licensed premises is grounded in the belief that social contexts have a direct effect on the behaviors of bar patrons. Furthermore, this research takes for granted that individuals bring to drinking episodes a variety of unique characteristics, including unique propensities for problem behavior, including acts of violence and aggressive alcohol consumption (Graham, 1980; Graham, Schmidt, and Gillis, 1996; Graham et al., 1998; Graham, West, and Wells, 2000). Homel, Tomsen, and Thommeny (1992) used insights from Graham et al.'s (1980) study of Vancouver barrooms as a starting point for their research in Sydney, Australia. They too relied on structured observations within barrooms to identify predictors of naturally occurring alcohol-related aggression. Teams of observers spent 300 hours conducting unobtrusive observations in 23 sites within 17 Sydney barrooms. Like Graham et al. (1980), Homel et al. (1992) identified high drunkenness, which is a byproduct of staff members' willingness to serve bar patrons to the point of intoxication and beyond, as one of the chief variables present during violent episodes. These researchers suggest that crowding, boredom, discounted drinks, high cover charges, and the absence of substantial amounts of food in most bars exacerbate problems with irresponsible alcohol service and high levels of intoxication. In their replication of the 1989 Sydney study, Home and Clark (1994) also identified irresponsible alcohol service and intoxication as key situational factors that increase the risk of violence in and around licensed drinking establishments.

Stockwell, Lang, and Rydon (1993) relied on a household survey of adults in Perth, Western Australia to explore drinkers' reports about the setting in which they drank and their experiences with alcohol-related harm, including involvement in violent arguments and fights, accidents, and drunk driving offenses. Findings from this study revealed that most experiences with alcohol-related harm occurred after the respondent had been drinking at licensed premises. Furthermore, these researchers identified bar staff continuing to serve "obviously intoxicated" patrons as the strongest predictor of whether drinkers themselves experienced some kind of harm. While discounted drinks and crowding were also found at places where intoxication was permitted, these variables did not significantly predict increased alcohol consumption or increased risk of harm to drinkers. However, as in Home et al.'s (1992) study of Sydney barrooms, both drink discounting and crowding demonstrated small but significant associations with continued alcohol service to intoxicated patrons, which, according to these researchers, may be of significance from a preventative point of view. Lang, Stockwell, Rydon, and Lockwood (1995), who analyzed the same survey results used by Stockwell et al. (1993), identified additional predictors of irresponsible alcohol service and high risk consumption, such as the presence of musical entertainment and dancing in bars.

Donnelly and Briscoe (2003) conducted a telephone-based survey of young adults in New South Wales, Australia in order to examine the extent of irresponsible alcohol service to patrons showing signs of intoxication in licensed drinking establishments. Individuals who indicated that they had shown at least one sign of intoxication during their last drinking occasion in a bar, such as loss of coordination or slurred speech, were asked how serving staff responded to their observable intoxication. Possible staff reactions included:

1) they refused to serve me any more alcoholic drinks;
2) they asked me to leave the premises;
3) they called the police;
4) they suggested I buy low- or non-alcoholic drinks;
5) they suggested that I buy some food;
6) they advised me on or organized transport home;
7) they suggested that I stop drinking; and
8) they continued to serve me alcoholic drinks" (Donnelly and Briscoe, 2003, p. 1289).

Findings from this study revealed that few individuals who said that they showed visible signs of intoxication during their last bar visit reported any attempt by serving staff to stop them from consuming alcohol. In fact, of those individuals who reported showing at least one sign of intoxication, less than 3% were refused alcohol and less than 4% were asked to leave the bar. Of those who reported three or more signs of intoxication, less than 4% were refused alcohol and only about 6% were asked to leave. The most common server response to visibly intoxicated patrons was continued alcohol service.

In addition to surveys with and observations of actual bar patrons, researchers have employed the use of "pseudo-intoxicated" bar patrons in an attempt to better understand the nature of irresponsible alcohol service in barrooms. McKnight (1991) was among the first to use covert actors trained in exhibiting signs of intoxication as a means of evaluating responsible beverage service (RBS) training programs. While the RBS program examined in this study led to significant overall changes in knowledge of, attitudes toward, and practices and policies pertaining to responsible alcohol service among bar staff, there was little increase in the refusal of alcohol service to observers feigning intoxication. Rydon, Stockwell, Lang, and Beel (1996) also employed pseudo-intoxicated patrons in a study of licensed premises in Western Australia. Over the course of 120 visits to 23 different establishments, pairs of pseudo-drunk actors placed more than 350 drink orders. Bar staff in this study refused alcohol service on only 10% of the visits and implemented partial interventions, such as offering food or low-alcohol or non-alcoholic drinks, in only 5% of these visits.

In yet another study employing the use of pseudo-intoxicated bar patrons, Lang, Stockwell, Rydon, and Beel (1998) examined the effectiveness of an RBS program implemented in a popular entertainment area in Western Australia. Like McKnight (1991), these researchers found the server training resulted in significant changes in knowledge about responsible beverage service practices and alcohol laws and regulations, but had little impact on actual server responses to obviously intoxicated patrons. Pseudo-drunks in this study were rarely refused alcohol service and their identification was rarely checked on most occasions. Toomey et al. (1999) report similar findings in their evaluation of Project ARM, a server training program implemented in Minnesota, USA. The majority of purchase attempts by pseudo-drunks in this study resulted in alcohol sales. Despite these rather disappointing evaluations of interventions aimed at reducing problem serving in bars, several studies employing the use of pseudo-intoxicated patrons have shown positive changes in responsible alcohol service following the implementation of RBS training (Geller, Russ, and Delphos, 1987; Gliksman, McKenzie, Single, Douglas, Brunet, and Moffatt, 1993; McKnight and Streff, 1994; Russ and Geller, 1987; Toomey, Wagenaar, Gehan, Kilian, Murray, and Perry, 2001; Wallin, Gripenberg, and Andreasson, 2002).

While there is a good deal of research that examines the extent of irresponsible alcohol service in bars, as well as that which links alcohol service to obviously intoxicated patrons to incidents of alcohol-related harm occurring in and around licensed premises, few studies have examined factors that "predict" alcohol sales to intoxicated bar patrons. This relatively new area of research was influenced by studies that have attempted to identify predictors of alcohol sales to underage patrons. For example, several studies suggest that younger servers are more likely to sell alcohol to underage patrons than are older servers (Forster, McGovern, Wagenaar, Wolfson, Perry, and Anstine, 1994; Forster, Murray, Wolfson, and Wagenaar, 1995). Other studies have found alcohol service to underage patrons to be more problematic in busier establishments (Forster et al., 1995) and in those without visible bar managers (Wolfson, Toomey, Forster, Wagenaar, McGovern, and Perry, 1996).

Andreasson, Lindewald, and Rehman (2000) offer one of the first studies to examine factors believed to predict alcohol sales to intoxicated bar patrons. These researchers employed pseudo-intoxicated patrons to illicit server responses to obvious alcohol impairment. The purpose of this study was to see whether intoxicated patrons would be served additional alcohol and whether variables such as age and gender of server, level of bar crowding, and general order within licensed premises affected server responses to alcohol impairment. Findings from this study revealed that pseudo-drunks were served alcohol at 95% of the licensed premises they visited. However, none of the independent variables examined in this study, such as lighting, music, and age and sex of servers, affected this outcome. Like Andreasson et al. (2000), Toomey et al. (2004) attempted to assess the likelihood of alcohol sales to obviously intoxicated patrons and whether server and/or establishment characteristics were related to the likelihood of illegal sales. These researchers also employed pseudo-intoxicated patrons to illicit server responses to obvious alcohol impairment. As in Andreasson et al.'s (2000) study, the likelihood of alcohol sales to obviously intoxicated bar patrons was very high. Findings from this study revealed age of alcohol servers to be an important predictor of alcohol service to intoxicated patrons, as servers who appeared to be less than 31 years of age were 2.7 times more likely to serve alcohol to pseudo-drunks than those who appeared to be age 31 or older.

Reiling and Nusbaumer (2006) relied on survey data collected from 911 alcoholic beverage servers in Indiana, USA to examine willingness to serve bar patrons beyond intoxication. These researchers examined the influence of various personal factors, location factors, management policies and practices, and external social control efforts on willingness to over-serve. Findings from this study revealed servers' personal drinking patterns as important predictors of alcohol service to obviously intoxicated patrons. Specifically, servers who reported drinking frequently, who reported frequently drinking to intoxication, and who reported drinking on-the-job were more likely to serve alcohol to obviously intoxicated bar patrons. Finding from this study also suggest that servers who are heavy drinkers might have distorted definitions of intoxication, which can further affect their ability to serve responsibly. According to Nusbaumer and Reiling (2002), "...previous research indicating the heavier one drinks, the more drinks they require for a definition of intoxication, draws into question their ability, as heavy drinkers, to accurately or appropriately evaluate intoxication" (p. 740). Finally, while some servers may be less capable of responsible alcohol service due to their personal drinking patterns, these researchers suggest that others may simply be choosing to over-serve because of economic incentives. As discussed by Reiling and Nusbaumer (2006), problems associated with the latter group are much more difficult to address and put added pressure on owner and managers to run an orderly bar.

Like Andreasson et al. (2000), Roberts (1998) focused on the characteristics of bars themselves rather than characteristics of serving staff in his attempt to identify predictors of alcohol service to obviously intoxicated bar patrons. This study entailed unobtrusive observations in several bars located in four different beach towns in Southern New Jersey, as well as semi-structured interviews with bar staff and managers working in these establishments. As in Homel et al.'s (1992) study of Sydney barrooms, drink specials and the absence of food in most bars were found to exacerbate problems with irresponsible alcohol service. Like Reiling and Nusbaumer (2006), Roberts (1998) identified serving staff drinking on-the-job as an important predictor of alcohol service to obviously intoxicated patrons. However, the strongest predictor of alcohol service to intoxicated patrons in this study was the presence of "secondary servers" of alcohol.

According to Roberts (1998), secondary servers distribute alcohol in areas within licensed premises away from "traditional bartenders" and bar stations and cater primarily to obviously intoxicated patrons who are either unable or unwilling to wait in long lines in order to purchase alcoholic beverages. "Shot-girls," one of the four types of secondary servers identified in this study, travel throughout barrooms carrying trays of pre-poured, attractively packaged "shots" of alcohol. One popular pre-poured shot in South Jersey barrooms was the "test tube" shot, which consisted of alcohol combined with different mixers and served in a plastic test tube. "Tub-girls" served two to three options of bottled beer from stationary, metal or plastic beer tubs strategically positioned throughout bars. "Cocktail waitresses" traveled throughout bars taking drink orders, placing them with traditional bartenders, and then running drinks back out to bar patrons. Finally, "service bar attendants" worked from behind compact, moveable bar stations that offered two to three choices of bottled beer and two to three choices of alcohol shots. Each of these secondary servers were found to reduce the effort it took for obviously intoxicated bar patrons to continue drinking, as in the case of shot-girls and waitresses, patrons did not have to move from where they were sitting, standing, or in some cases, leaning, to purchase alcoholic beverages.

It is important to note that the names given to secondary servers in Roberts' (1998) study were those used by staff members and management in South Jersey barrooms. In fact, many of the secondary servers interviewed in this study reported responding to employment advertisements posted by bars seeking shot-girls, tub-girls, etc. These were also the job titles they were instructed to apply for when completing work applications at various South Jersey barrooms. It should also be noted that only females were employed as secondary servers in South Jersey barrooms. Owners and managers interviewed in this study were very open about seeking out females, especially young, attractive females, for these positions, as they believed that they would appeal more to the most aggressive drinkers frequenting their establishments, that being young, college-aged males. Traditional bartenders interviewed by Roberts (1998) reported that the presence of secondary servers made it difficult to monitor patrons' alcohol consumption, which is a key component of RBS training programs. Interestingly, secondary servers interviewed in this study reported being exempt from RBS training, as owners and managers were said to view them not as fully functional servers of alcohol, but rather as "support staff" for traditional bartenders.

The primary goal of the present study was to identify characteristics of licensed drinking establishments that predict alcohol sales to obviously intoxicated barroom patrons. Of particular interest was the relationship between secondary servers of alcohol and irresponsible alcohol service. It was predicted that increased numbers of secondary servers working in barrooms and present during individual observation periods would lead to increased alcohol service to obviously intoxicated patrons. The present study also was also an attempt to investigate a number of other possible predictors of alcohol service to intoxicated patrons identified by past researchers.

METHODS

Sample of Bars

The present study focused on licensed drinking establishments that functioned primarily as entertainment venues for young, college-aged patrons in Hoboken, New Jersey. The total population of bars located in Hoboken's southeast quadrant was included in this study, with the exception of two venues that functioned primarily as restaurants. The southeast quadrant of Hoboken contains over half of the city's licensed drinking establishments, as well as a major hub for public transportation that attracts patrons both from within and outside the city. It should be noted that each of the bars included in this study (n = 25) were within reasonable walking distance from this transportation hub and were therefore capable of being visited by the same population of patrons. Bars ranged in capacity from about 100 to over 900 patrons. While the primary entertainment in most venues was prerecorded music, several bars also attracted patrons with televised sporting events, live bands, and disc jockeys. Bars included in this study catered primarily to young (e.g., 20s), white, professionals and college students from Hoboken and the surrounding areas. Male patrons outnumbered female patrons in most Hoboken barrooms.

Procedures

Observations took place at two separate time periods, 7:30pm – 10:30pm and 11:00pm – 2:00am, on Thursday, Friday, and Saturday nights. Each bar, with the exception of one venue that was only open on Fridays and Saturdays, was visited on six separate evenings, allowing for observations on each of the above-mentioned days and time periods. In total, the study entailed 148 individual observation periods lasting a total of 444 hours. Barrooms were assigned to nights and times of observation using a random start, the final result being a structured observation schedule. The present study employed one primary observer who participated in all 148 observation periods. In order to measure the reliability of observer responses in completing the data collection instrument, a second observer was employed who participated in approximately one third of the total number of observation periods. Once the observation schedule had been devised, indicating the days and times each bar was to be observed, the second observer was randomly assigned to 50 observation periods. The primary observer conducted observations alone during the remaining 98 observation periods.

During the months leading up to the study, the two observers studied the contents of a structured observation guide containing a large number of variables related to the physical and social setting of barrooms (e.g., smokiness, temperature, crowding, dancing, etc.), as well as numerous variables related to alcohol service and consumption (e.g., drink specials, drinking in rounds, servers of alcohol drinking on-the-job, etc). They also studied guidelines for identifying and recording the service of alcohol to obviously intoxicated bar patrons. Signs of intoxication included slurred speech, loss of coordination, stumbling, staggering, spilling drinks, crude or quarrelsome behavior, etc. While this list of intoxication signs is not exhaustive, it incorporates those identified by past researchers as being key behavioral indicators of persons who are "obviously intoxicated" (See Donnelly and Briscoe, 2003; Lang et al., 1995). Observers focused exclusively on those patrons who displayed multiple signs of intoxication and appeared severely intoxicated. It is important to note that the primary researcher in this study had seven years of experience as a bartender prior to the start of data collection and had been certified in several alcohol management programs that train serving staff to identify signs of intoxication and monitor patron drinking. In addition to counting the number of times obviously intoxicated patrons were served alcohol, observers also recorded other server responses to intoxicated patrons attempting to purchase alcoholic beverages, which included cutting the patron off and allowing them to stay in the bar, cutting the patron off and asking them to leave the bar, and refusing alcohol service but offering non-alcoholic beverages or food.

In the present study, each alcoholic beverage sold to an obviously intoxicated patron was considered an individual incident of serving intoxicated patrons. Therefore, a single encounter with an intoxicated patron may have resulted in multiple incidents of serving intoxicated patrons. In addition, there were occasions in which sober patrons purchased rounds of drinks for groups of intoxicated patrons. Each drink distributed to an obviously intoxicated patron, whether by a server or patron, was also considered an individual incident of serving intoxicated patrons. Therefore, each incident of serving intoxicated patrons does not necessarily represent a patron-server encounter. Observers in the present study moved from server to server and attempted to spend an equal amount of time observing the serving practices of each. During observation periods with two observers, the protocol was to stay together and observe the same server together. On nights with two observers, the average of their individual counts for the variable "number of incidents of serving intoxicated patrons" was recorded for analysis.

During observation periods, observers circulated throughout the premises, paying particular attention to situational variables contained in the observation guide. They did not consume any alcoholic beverages while conducting observations, but instead purchased beverages that closely resembled mixed drinks (e.g., sodas with lemons or limes, etc.). As in previous observational studies conducted in bars (Graham et al., 1980; Homel et al., 1992; Homel and Clark, 1994), only limited note taking was conducted while inside licensed premises and was done so in places that would not draw any unwanted attention, the most common location being bathroom stalls. Written recordings taken inside barrooms were limited to items in the observation guide that required observers to make counts of particular phenomena, including server responses to obviously intoxicated patrons.

Immediately following each observation period, observers independently rated items in the observation guide. For observation periods in which both observers were present, a third and final observation guide was prepared for analysis after differences in individual coding were resolved. The two observers maintained a high degree of inter-rater reliability throughout the study, with individual responses to items in the observation guide never varying to such a degree as to cause concern. For example, if individual coding of variables did vary, it rarely did so by more than a single response category (e.g., somewhat smoky vs. smoky).

Results

Server Responses to Obviously Intoxicated Patrons

An examination of observed server responses to obviously intoxicated bar patrons revealed that traditional bartenders were the only servers to "cut a patron off," or refrain from serving them alcohol. However, there was only one such incident observed over the course of the entire study. There were no incidents observed in which any server of alcohol offered obviously intoxicated patrons food or non-alcoholic beverages. Even more surprising was the extent of alcohol service to obviously intoxicated bar patrons. Traditional bartenders averaged 58.54 incidents of serving intoxicated patrons per observation period. Secondary servers of alcohol averaged 61.30 incidents of serving intoxicated patrons during those observation periods in which they were present (n = 56). There was a combined average of 81.74 incidents of serving intoxicated patrons per observation for "all servers" of alcohol over the course of the 148 observation periods. It is important to note that many Hoboken barrooms employed more than one type of secondary server of alcohol, including each of those identified by Roberts (1998) in his study of licensed drinking establishments in South Jersey (i.e., shot-girls, tub-girls, cocktail waitresses, and service bar attendants). However, the present study only examined the collective serving practices of this group of servers. As was the case in South Jersey barrooms, only females were hired as secondary servers in licensed drinking establishments throughout Hoboken.

While counts of alcohol service to intoxicated patrons in the present study were quite large, they are partly explained by the phenomenon of "drinking in rounds." Drinking in rounds involves a single patron purchasing three or more alcoholic beverages at one time. Furthermore, as already mentioned, each alcoholic beverage an obviously intoxicated patron was served was considered an individual incident of serving intoxicated patrons. In addition, there were occasions in which sober patrons purchased rounds of drinks for groups of intoxicated patrons. Each drink distributed to an obviously intoxicated patron, whether by a server or patron, was also considered an individual incident of serving intoxicated patrons.

Bivariate Analyses

Table 1 presents the relationship between the dependent variable, number of incidents of serving intoxicated patrons, and several variables related to the physical and social environment within barrooms. As indicated, the average number of times intoxicated patrons were served alcohol was significantly higher during observation periods in which barrooms were unattractive, smoky, hot, crowded, difficult to move around in, uncomfortable, and unclean. There was also more frequent alcohol service to intoxicated patrons during observation periods in which tables, ledges, and bar surfaces were rarely cleared or cleaned and left littered with discarded trash and empty bottles.

As indicated in Table 1, the average number of times intoxicated patrons were served alcohol was higher during observation periods taking place between 11:00 pm and 2:00 am, as well as during those taking place in bars other than "watering holes." Watering holes, which represented most of the establishments included in the present study, offered little in the way of entertainment, musical or otherwise. "Other" Hoboken barrooms, on the other hand, attracted patrons through some specialized, and usually well advertised, entertainment, such as live bands, disc jockeys, or televised sporting events. Dancing, a common feature of other bar types, also demonstrated a statistically significant relationship with number of incidents of serving intoxicated patrons ($p<.01$).

Table 2 presents the relationship between number of incidents of serving intoxicated patrons and several variables related to alcohol service and consumption. As indicated, the average number of times intoxicated patrons were served alcohol was higher during observations periods in which patrons were checked for identification at entry points into barrooms. Some of the more stringent door policies were observed at establishments that local law enforcement identified as being on probation for serving underage patrons. Alcohol service to intoxicated patrons was also significantly higher during observation periods in which there were cover charges, drink specials, and patrons frequently purchasing rounds of alcoholic beverages, as well as during those in which there was no food or snacks made available to bar patrons.

Table 2 also reveals statistically significant relationships between number of incidents of serving intoxicated patrons and the variables "bouncers and doormen drinking alcoholic beverages" ($p < .01$) and "servers of alcohol (any) drinking alcoholic beverages" ($p < .01$). As indicated, the average number of times obviously intoxicated patrons were served alcohol was 200.48 during observation periods in which bouncers were present ($N = 107$) and drinking alcohol, but only 60.74 during those in which they were present and not drinking alcohol. Similarly, the average number of times obviously intoxicated patrons were served alcohol was 155.09 during observation periods in which servers of alcohol (any) were drinking alcohol on-the-job, but only 35.79 during those in which they were not.

Table 1. "Number of incidents of serving intoxicated patrons" by variables related to the physical and social environment (N = 148 observation periods)

	N	# incidents of serving intoxicated patrons		F (df)
		Mean	sd	
Appearance of bar				$43.21_{(2)}$**
Attractive	66	29.71	37.70	
Somewhat unattractive	46	56.37	91.73	
Unattractive	36	209.53	157.17	
Smokiness in bar				$45.86_{(2)}$**
Mostly smoke free	91	34.86	65.53	
Somewhat smoky	34	96.24	99.54	
Smoky	23	245.78	164.08	
Temperature in bar				$48.97_{(2)}$**
Cool	70	26.16	34.57	
Somewhat warm	40	57.65	62.10	
Hot	38	209.47	167.61	
Crowding (maximum capacity) in bar				$64.76_{(2)}$**
Low[2]	95	29.88	46.16	
Medium	28	104.46	102.15	
High[3]	25	253.32	163.80	
Movement throughout bar				$47.11_{(2)}$**
Easy to move about	76	23.51	33.18	
Somewhat difficult to move about	35	75.71	85.79	
Difficult to move about	37	207.03	163.24	
Overall comfort of bar				$84.85_{(2)}$**
Comfortable	82	21.29	22.73	
Somewhat uncomfortable	31	66.42	68.36	
Uncomfortable	35	236.91	153.41	

[2] Low = approximately 1/3 bar's maximum capacity.
[3] High = at or exceeding bar's maximum capacity.

Clearing of tables and ledges		25.13	31.00	$42.27_{(2)}$**
Mostly kept clear	85	106.10	151.17	
Somewhat cluttered	29	202.47	137.73	
Cluttered	34			
Clearing of bar surfaces				$30.84_{(2)}$**
Mostly kept clear	89	30.81	42.98	
Somewhat cluttered	25	122.24	129.23	
Cluttered	34	185.26	168.07	
Overall cleanliness of bar				$49.85_{(2)}$**
Mostly clean	91	25.57	32.37	
Somewhat unclean	22	112.73	90.17	
Unclean	35	208.29	171.33	
Dancing				$89.81_{(1)}$**
No	100	30.42	40.38	
Yes	48	188.65	157.00	
Time				$35.35_{(1)}$**
T1 = 7:30pm – 10:30pm	74	28.74	67.05	
T2 = 11:00pm – 2:00am	74	134.73	137.89	
Bar type				$37.80_{(1)}$**
Watering hole	117	53.72	77.59	
Other (e.g., band bars, sports bars, dance clubs, etc.)	31	187.48	182.10	

* $p < .05$. ** $p < .01$.

Bivariate correlations revealed significant and positive relationships between number of incidents of serving intoxicated patrons and the variables "number of secondary servers of alcohol" ($p < .01$) and "number of traditional bartenders" ($p < .01$). These analyses also revealed significant and positive relationships between number of secondary servers and number of traditional bartenders ($p < .01$). Relationships between categorical independent variables were examined by running a series of cross-tabulations (chi-square tests). These analyses revealed statistically significant relationships between several variables described as aversive environmental stimuli, including: appearance of bar, smokiness in bar, temperature in bar, crowding (maximum capacity) in bar, movement throughout bar, overall comfort of bar, clearing of tables and ledges, clearing of bar surfaces, and overall cleanliness of bar. In order to address potential problems associated with multicollinearity in the multivariate analyses, a factor analysis was conducted to see if variables could be combined. This analysis resulted in the extraction of a single underlying factor, which explained 67.2% of the variability in the nine variables. This factor, labeled as "aversive environmental stimuli," was substituted into the multivariate analyses.

Table 2. "Number of incidents of serving intoxicated patrons" by variables related to alcohol service and consumption (N = 148 observation periods)

	N	# incidents of serving intoxicated patrons *Mean*	*sd*	*F (df)*
Cover Charge				$52.00_{(1)}$**
No	120	52.03	75.55	
Yes	28	209.07	181.83	
ID check				$57.74_{(1)}$**
No	108	42.85	62.36	
Yes	40	186.73	168.82	
Drink specials				$17.76_{(1)}$**
No	94	51.78	71.70	
Yes	54	133.89	163.83	
Food				$5.37_{(1)}$*
No	82	102.02	135.01	
Yes	66	56.53	94.42	
Drinking in rounds				$30.66_{(1)}$**
Infrequent	68	27.50	54.73	
Frequent	80	127.84	140.57	
Bouncers and doormen drinking alcoholic beverages (N = 107)				$27.30_{(1)}$**
No	80	60.74	88.23	
Yes	27	200.48	186.14	
Servers of alcohol (any) drinking alcoholic beverages				$44.59_{(1)}$**
No	91	35.79	62.69	
Yes	57	155.09	151.14	

* $p < .05$. ** $p < .01$.

In preparation of the multivariate analyses, it was also necessary to dummy code the variable "bouncers and doormen drinking alcoholic beverages." To account for observation periods in which bouncers and doormen were not present, this variable was dummy coded into: variable 1 = bouncers and doormen drinking (1 = yes, 0 = no) and variable 2 = bouncers and doormen not present (1 = not present, 0 = present). "Bouncers and doormen not drinking" was used as the reference category in the multivariate analyses.

Multivariate Analyses

Again, the primary hypothesis guiding this study was that increased numbers of secondary servers working in barrooms and present during individual observation periods would lead to increased incidents of serving intoxicated patrons. Testing this hypothesis involved regressing number of incidents of serving intoxicated patrons on number of secondary servers of alcohol while controlling for other variables demonstrating statistically significant relationships with number of incidents of serving intoxicated patrons in the bivariate analyses. Due to the significant and positive correlation between number of secondary servers and number of traditional bartenders, these variables could not be included in the same ordinary least squares (OLS) regression model. Instead, three OLS models were run, the first examining secondary servers independently from number of traditional bartenders, the second examining number of traditional bartenders independently from number of secondary servers of alcohol, and the third examining "total number of servers of alcohol" (i.e., number of secondary servers and number of traditional bartenders combined). By examining the Adjusted R-Square (R^2) for each model, it was possible to see which grouping of variables accounted for the greatest amount of variance in the dependent variable, number of incidents of serving intoxicated patrons.

Table 3 presents the results for the first OLS model examining the relative influence of "number of secondary servers of alcohol" on "number of incidents of serving intoxicated patrons." Collinearity diagnostics were run on all independent variables going into this model and variance inflation factors were examined in order to access the level of multicollinearity among these variables. All of the variables included in the first OLS model demonstrated VIFs of below 3.0, indicating that multicollinearity was not an issue. As indicated, three variables included in the first OLS model demonstrated significant unique effects on incidents of serving intoxicated patrons. These variables are aversive environmental stimuli ($p < .01$), dancing ($p < .05$), and number of secondary servers of alcohol ($p < .01$). Examining the slopes for these variables reveals that for every one-unit increase in the number of secondary servers of alcohol, the number of incidents of serving intoxicated patrons is predicted to increase by 30.216. This finding supports the primary hypothesis guiding this study that increased numbers of secondary servers working in barrooms leads to increased alcohol service to obviously intoxicated patrons.

Table 3 also reveals that for very one-unit increase in aversive environmental stimuli, the number of incidents of serving intoxicated patrons is predicted to increase by 47.444. In addition, when there is dancing, the number of incidents of serving intoxicated patrons is predicted to increase by 33.089. Examining the standardized beta coefficients for these variables reveals that number of secondary servers of alcohol is the strongest predictor of incidents of serving intoxicated patrons (Beta = .396), followed by aversive environmental stimuli (Beta = .394). The Adjusted R^2 reveals that the variables included in this OLS model explain approximately 72.9% of the variation in the dependent variable incidents of serving intoxicated patrons.

Again, due to the significant and positive correlation between number of secondary servers and number of traditional bartenders, these variables could not be included in the same OLS regression model. Table 4 presents the results for the second OLS model examining the relative influence of "number of traditional bartenders" on "number of incidents of serving intoxicated patrons."

Table 3. OLS regression model 1: Results for "number of secondary servers of alcohol" on "number of incidents of serving intoxicated patrons"

Variable	B	S.E.	Beta	T	P
(Constant)	-9.278	27.443		-.338	.736
Time	9.152	14.513	.038	.631	.529
Bar type	19.064	17.963	.065	1.061	.290
ID check	19.820	16.725	.073	1.185	.238
Aversive environmental stimuli	47.444	7.757	.394	6.116	.000
Dancing	33.089	16.433	.129	2.014	.046
Bouncers and doormen drinking alcoholic beverages	26.964	17.145	.087	1.573	.118
Bouncers and doormen not present	17.367	13.572	.065	1.280	.203
Cover charge	12.561	18.562	.041	.677	.500
Drink specials	-8.864	13.169	-.036	-.673	.502
Food	1.330	11.619	.006	.114	.909
Drinking in rounds	12.459	12.457	.052	1.000	.319
Servers of alcohol (any) drinking alcoholic beverages	17.272	13.891	.070	1.243	.216
Number of secondary servers of alcohol	30.216	4.497	.396	6.719	.000
R2 = .753 Adjusted R2 = .729					

Collinearity diagnostics were run on all independent variables going into this model and it was determined that multicollinearity was not an issue. As indicated, three variables included in the second OLS model demonstrated significant unique effects on incidents of serving intoxicated patrons. These variables are aversive environmental stimuli ($p < .01$), bouncers and doormen drinking alcoholic beverages ($p < .05$), and number of traditional bartenders ($p < .01$). Examining the slopes for these variables reveals that for every one-unit increase in the number of traditional bartenders, the number of incidents of serving intoxicated patrons is predicted to increase by 15.510.

Table 4 also reveals that for very one-unit increase in aversive environmental stimuli, the number of incidents of serving intoxicated patrons is predicted to increase by 53.027. Furthermore, when bouncers and doormen are present and drinking alcoholic beverages, the number of incidents of serving intoxicated patrons is predicted to increase by 45.325. Examining the standardized beta coefficients for these variables reveals that aversive environmental stimuli is the strongest predictor of incidents of serving intoxicated patrons (Beta = .440), followed by number of traditional bartenders (Beta = .185). The Adjusted R^2 reveals that the variables included in this OLS model explain approximately 65.6% of the variation in the dependent variable incidents of serving intoxicated patrons, less than that explained by the variables included in the first OLS model (72.9%).

Table 4. OLS Regression model 2: Results for "number of traditional bartenders" on "number of incidents of serving intoxicated patrons"

Variable	B	S.E.	Beta	T	P
(Constant)	1.674	33.659		.050	.960
Time	.853	16.354	.004	.052	.958
Bar type	-5.605	19.789	-.019	-.283	.777
ID check	37.352	18.551	.138	2.013	.046
Aversive environmental stimuli	53.027	8.700	.440	6.095	.000
Dancing	22.261	18.600	.087	1.197	.233
Bouncers and doormen drinking alcoholic beverages	45.325	19.004	.146	2.385	.018
Bouncers and doormen not present	25.871	15.348	.096	1.686	.094
Cover Charge	24.514	20.793	.080	1.179	.241
Drink specials	-6.765	15.416	-.027	-.439	.661
Food	5.460	13.097	.023	.417	.677
Drinking in rounds	13.523	14.148	.056	.956	.341
Servers of alcohol (any) drinking alcoholic beverages	8.395	15.559	.034	.540	.590
Number of traditional bartenders	15.510	5.791	.185	2.678	.008
$R^2 = .687$ Adjusted $R^2 = .656$					

Table 5 presents the results for the third and final OLS model examining the relative influence of "total number of servers of alcohol" on "number of incidents of serving intoxicated patrons." Once again, collinearity diagnostics were run on all independent variables going into this model and again it was determined that multicollinearity was not an issue. As indicated, two variables included in the third OLS model demonstrated significant unique effects on incidents of serving intoxicated patrons. These variables are aversive environmental stimuli ($p < .01$) and total number of servers of alcohol ($p < .01$). Examining the slopes for these variables reveals that for every one-unit increase in the total number of servers of alcohol, the number of incidents of serving intoxicated patrons is predicted to increase by 17.646. Furthermore, for very one-unit increase in aversive environmental stimuli, the number of incidents of serving intoxicated patrons is predicted to increase by 47.335.

Examining the standardized beta coefficients for the variables included in Table 5 reveals that total number of servers of alcohol is the strongest predictor of incidents of serving intoxicated patrons (Beta = .400), followed by aversive environmental stimuli (Beta = .393). The Adjusted R^2 reveals that the variables included in this OLS model explain approximately 71.2% of the variation in the dependent variable incidents of serving intoxicated patrons, which is still less than that explained by the variables included in the first OLS model (72.9%).

Table 5. OLS Regression model 3: Results for "total number of servers of alcohol" on "number of incidents of serving intoxicated patrons"

Variable	B	S.E.	Beta	T	P
(Constant)	-35.860	30.331		-1.182	.239
Time	10.699	15.052	.045	.711	.478
Bar type	17.401	18.621	.059	.934	.352
ID check	24.006	17.179	.089	1.397	.165
Aversive environmental stimuli	47.335	8.028	.393	5.897	.000
Dancing	24.675	16.929	.096	1.458	.147
Bouncers and doormen drinking alcoholic beverages	31.450	17.604	.101	1.787	.076
Bouncers and doormen not present	23.885	13.980	.089	1.708	.090
Cover Charge	14.543	19.128	.047	.760	.448
Drink specials	-17.485	13.976	-.070	-1.251	.213
Food	.352	12.012	.001	.029	.977
Drinking in rounds	8.780	12.923	.036	.679	.498
Servers of alcohol (any) drinking alcoholic beverages	15.320	14.304	.062	1.071	.286
Total number of servers of alcohol	17.646	3.002	.400	5.878	.000
R^2 = .738 Adjusted R^2 = .712					

CONCLUSION

A comparison of Adjusted R-Squares for the OLS models presented in the results section reveals that the grouping of variables contained in the first OLS model (See Table 3) accounted for the greatest amount of variation in the dependent variable, number of incidents of serving intoxicated patrons. Again, variables in this model, which includes number of secondary servers of alcohol, explain approximately 72.9% of the variation in the dependent variable incidents of serving intoxicated patrons. Furthermore, number of secondary servers of alcohol was the strongest predictor of incidents of serving intoxicated patrons in this model (Beta = .396), which supports the primary hypothesis guiding this study that increased numbers of secondary servers working in barrooms leads to increased alcohol service to obviously intoxicated patrons.

Before discussing secondary servers of alcohol and their impact on irresponsible alcohol service and associated problems of alcohol-related harm, it is important to mention the other variables that demonstrated significant unique effects on incidents of serving intoxicated patrons in the multivariate analyses. As mentioned, the factor "aversive environmental stimuli" was also a significant predictor of alcohol service to intoxicated patrons in each of the OLS models (See Tables 3-5). Furthermore, it was the second strongest predictor of alcohol service to intoxicated patrons in the first OLS model (Beta = .394), which again contained the variable number of secondary servers of alcohol. This finding is in keeping with past research that suggests that variables such as excessive heat, crowding, and smoke may lead patrons to drink more heavily and become more intoxicated in order to relieve their discomfort (Fox and Sobol, 2000; Graham, et al., 1980; Homel et al., 1992; Homel and Clark, 1994; Macintyre and Homel, 1997; Quigley, Leonard, and Collins, 2003; Roberts, 1998; Tomsen, 1997; Tomsen, Homel, and Thommeny, 1991).

While the presence of aversive environmental stimuli may be pervasive and problematic in high risk drinking settings, minor modifications of the barroom landscape may reduce their effect on alcohol service to intoxicated patrons, as well as associated problems of alcohol-related harm occurring in and around licensed drinking establishments. For example, problems associated with excessive heat may be avoided by installing air conditioning units or ceiling fans. Similarly, problems with excessive smoke may be addressed by installing "smoke eaters" or other air filtration systems. Homel, Carvolth, Hauritz, McIlwain, and Teague (2004) state that strategies aimed at improving the overall level of comfort within bars are critical to reducing problems with alcohol-related harm. A major component of Graham, Osgood, Zibrowski, Purcell, Gliksman, Leonard, et al.'s (2004) "Safer Bars" initiative in Toronto, Canada was helping owners and managers identify ways to reduce environmental irritants. These researchers suggest that environmental changes designed to reduce or prevent problem behaviors in bars should be easier to market to owners and managers than interventions that focus primarily on tightening controls on alcohol sales.

The variables number of traditional bartenders and total number of servers of alcohol also demonstrated significant unique effects on the dependent variable number of incidents of serving intoxicated patrons (See Tables 4 and 5). Increased numbers of serving staff likely results in increased alcohol sales in most barrooms, as patrons have greater access to alcoholic beverages. This may be especially true in large, packed to capacity bars in which inadequate numbers of serving staff could substantially hinder alcohol sales. It would make sense, therefore, that increased numbers of servers would lead to increased alcohol service to intoxicated bar patrons, as they, like their sober counterparts, would also have greater access to alcoholic beverages. One would also expect increased numbers of servers working in barrooms to make monitoring patrons' alcohol consumption more difficult, as patrons may wander from bar to bar ordering drinks from different serving staff. Related to this, having many servers spread throughout licensed drinking establishments might also make communication between servers more difficult. For example, it would be near impossible for bar staff working in large barrooms with multiple rooms and floors to warn each other about a patron's aggressive drinking or early signs of intoxication, which is important information for those wishing to serve responsibly. According to Roberts (1998), secondary servers of alcohol exacerbate problems with staff communication and patron monitoring, which contributes to increased alcohol service to obviously intoxicated patrons. In the words of a male bartender interviewed in this study:

> I remember this one night I had a guy coming up for a beer about once an hour. Well, after serving him about his fifth beer, a bar-back comes up to me and says, "hey man, be careful how much you serve that guy." Now I'm thinking to myself, there is no way this guy is drunk yet. As it turned out he had been buying shots off of one of our girls (tub-girls) out on the dance floor all night. This can make it tough on us up front who are trying to monitor each person's drinking (Roberts, 1998, p. 99).

In addition to making it more difficult for bar staff to server responsibly, secondary servers reduce the effort it takes to purchase alcoholic beverages. What separates secondary servers from traditional bartenders, however, is that they cater primarily to obviously intoxicated patrons who are either unable or unwilling to wait in long lines at traditional bar stations. According to Roberts (1998), secondary servers are employed for the sole purpose of increasing the flow of alcohol throughout licensed drinking establishments. While several owners and managers interviewed in Roberts' (1998) study of Jersey Shore barrooms reported hiring secondary servers to make things "more convenient" for bar patrons, others were very frank about their desire to sell more alcohol and make more money, regardless of the cost. Again, owners and managers in this study also reported only hiring females for these positions in hopes of increasing alcohol sales to young, college-aged males. Homel and Clark (1994) also identified a desire to maintain and increase profitability as the primary motivations for most of the observed barroom practices in their study of licensed premises in Sydney, Australia. Reiling and Nusbaumer (2006) suggest that the economic motives of bar owners and managers significantly influence the attitudes and practices of servers, as well as the service of alcohol to obviously intoxicated bar patrons, stating:

> Indeed, what the current analysis might be suggesting is that owners who see greater economic benefit that cost in continuing to serve may be more likely to retain servers whose definitions of intoxication are compatible with increased sales to patrons and the willingness to accommodate patrons' continued consumption, even if beyond intoxication (p. 663).

Because of the overriding concern for profit in most barrooms, it would be unlikely for owners and managers to willingly limit or reduce the number of servers they employ, including, and maybe especially, secondary servers of alcohol, as fewer servers would likely result in reduced alcohol sales. Again, Graham et al. (2004) state that interventions that focus primarily on tightening controls on alcohol sales are typically hard sells to bar owners and managers. RBS programs that train bar staff to serve alcohol responsibly may also be a hard sell, as promoting responsible alcohol service, like limiting the number of servers working in bars, would negatively affect alcohol sales. Research also suggest that servers themselves may not be very receptive to these programs, or responsible beverage service in general, as refusal of alcohol service to already intoxicated bar patrons may lead to loss of gratuities (McKnight, 1991), or some cases, physical altercations with individuals who are unhappy about being "cut off" (Felson et al., 1986). While several evaluations of these programs have shown positive changes in responsible alcohol service (Geller et al., 1987; Gliksman et al., 1993; McKnight and Streff, 1994; Russ and Geller, 1987; Toomey et al., 2001; Wallin et al., 2002), others have shown little increase in refusal of alcohol to intoxicated, or pseudo-intoxicated, bar patrons (McKnight, 1991; Lang et al., 1998; Rydon et al., 1996; Toomey et al., 1999).

Regardless of their potential for reducing irresponsible alcohol and associate problems with alcohol-related harm, RBS programs will not have the desired effect in establishments whose management and staff does not "truly" embrace responsible alcohol service. After all, some bars may participate in such programs just to "look" like they are doing something, possibly for insurance purposes or protection from potential lawsuits. Furthermore, Reiling and Nusbaumer (2006) suggest that one should not assume that all servers lack the ability to identity intoxication. As mentioned, some may simply be choosing to do so due too lack of incentives not to. Furthermore, these researchers suggest that focusing solely on the behaviors of servers puts the onus of responsibility on them rather than on unscrupulous bar owners and managers.

Finally, in considering RBS training as a solution to irresponsible alcohol service, findings from the present study suggest that even servers who are encouraged by barroom management to serve responsibly, and who have acquired such skills through participation in RBS training, may experience difficulty doing so in establishments that employ secondary servers of alcohol. Furthermore, as already mentioned, secondary servers interviewed in Roberts' (1998) study of Jersey Shore barrooms reported being exempt from RBS training, as owners and managers were said to view them not as fully functional servers of alcohol, but rather as "support staff" for traditional bartenders. In order for RBS programs to be effective, they must involve all servers of alcohol, not just traditional bartenders. After all, it makes little sense to expose only select members of a serving staff to RBS training in hopes of reducing irresponsible alcohol service, as bar patrons may simply seek out untrained servers who are less capable of serving responsibly. Furthermore, by not requiring that secondary servers participate in RBS training, owners and managers may inadvertently be sending a message to these staff members that they are somehow less accountable for their actions, which may contribute to their willingness to sell alcohol to intoxicated bar patrons. Again, this assumes that some servers sell alcohol to obviously intoxicated bar patrons not because of an inability to identify signs of intoxication, but rather because of lack of incentives not to. The inclusion of secondary servers in RBS training might also necessitate a complete overhaul of these programs, as they have been and continue to be designed with traditional bartenders in mind, not free-roaming secondary servers, such as shot-girls and cocktail waitresses.

Left to their own devises, it is unlikely that bar owners, managers, or staff members would do much to address irresponsible alcohol service and associated problems of alcohol-related harm occurring in and around these establishments. Knowing this, researchers have suggested the need for greater external regulation of barrooms by law enforcement agencies and alcohol beverage control (ABC) offices. According McKnight and Streff (1994), "...simple enforcement of existing laws and regulations prohibiting service of alcohol to already intoxicated patrons of bars and restaurants represents what appears to be a potentially cost-beneficial way of reducing accidental injury and death" (p. 87). Unfortunately, findings from the present study support claims that there is a gross lack of enforcement of existing liquor laws in many licensed drinking establishments (McKnight, 1991; Nusbaumer and Reiling, 2003; Toomey et al., 1999; Toomey et al., 2004).

In response to weak internal and external regulation of barrooms, a growing number of researchers have proposed and implemented community-based initiatives that seek to bring together all relevant "stakeholders," including bar owners, community members, and government regulators, in coordinated efforts to address problems in and around licensed premises. Stockwell (2001) stresses the importance of community support and involvement in interventions targeting barrooms, stating, "Even with a well-drafted liquor act with ample harm minimization provisions backed up by a well-organized system of regulation may be inadequate if the host community is hostile or otherwise unsupportive" (p. 264). Ross Homel and colleagues' "Surfers Paradise Safety Action Project" implemented in Australia (See Carvolth, Homel, Hauritz, Wortley, Clark, and McIlwain, 1996; Homel and Clark, 1994; Homel, Hauritz, Wortley, McIlwain, and Carvolth, 1997; Macintyre and Homel, 1997) and

Kathryn Graham and colleagues' "Safer Bars" program implemented in Canada (See Chandler Coutts, Graham, Braun, and Wells, 2000; Graham, 2000; Graham, Jelley, and Purcell, 2005) provide two examples of community-based initiatives that were successful in facilitating both internal and external regulation of bars and bringing about substantial reductions in irresponsible alcohol service and associated problems of alcohol-related harm. Again, for these initiatives to be successful, researchers such as Reiling and Nusbaumer (2006) suggest that they must seek to address owners' economic incentive to allow the overserving of bar patrons by increasing the economic cost of the consequences for doing so.

The present study was not without limitations or weaknesses. One specific limitation was the use of only one observer during 98 of the 148 observation periods. During observation periods with two observers, any discrepancies in individual coding were discussed and decisions on how to code items for the third and final observation guide were agreed upon. This type of cross validation was not possible during those observation periods with a single observer. However, as mentioned, observers in the present study maintained a high degree of inter-rater reliability throughout the present study. The consistency of observer responses to items contained in the observation guide was likely the result of the observer training and pilot-testing of the data collection instrument that preceded the study. When possible, however, future research should utilize multiple observers, not just to ensure that the individual coding of observation guides remains consistent, but also to better examine the many situational variables present in the barroom environment.

Due to the homogeneity of barrooms (i.e., mostly watering holes) and patrons (i.e., primarily young and white) in the present study, the findings cannot be generalized to all types of drinking establishments or all populations of bar patrons. Whether predictors of alcohol service to obviously intoxicated patrons identified in the present study hold up in barrooms catering primarily to non-white or older bar patrons is a question that future research should attempt to address. Future research might also examine whether situational variables found to be good predictors of alcohol service to obviously intoxicated patrons in the present study hold up in large samples of sports bars, dance clubs, or band bars. The present study provides only limited evidence that they do.

A final limitation of the present study is that it did not assess differences in serving practices among different types of secondary servers of alcohol. Instead, it examined the collective serving practices of four distinct types of secondary servers: shot-girls, tub-girls, cocktail waitresses, and service bar attendants. Future research is needed that examines whether certain types of secondary servers are better predictors of alcohol service to intoxicated barroom patrons than others. Furthermore, it might also be interesting to do a gender-based analysis of servers and serving responses to obviously intoxicated bar patrons. For example, it is unclear if female servers, whether they be traditional bartenders or secondary servers, are any more or less likely to serve alcohol to obviously intoxicated bar patrons than are male servers. Additionally, there is a need for continued studies of serving practices in barrooms throughout the United States, as most barroom research in general has been conducted in locations throughout Canada, Australia, and the UK. While research examining predictors of barroom aggression has been ongoing ever since Graham et al.'s (1980) groundbreaking study of licensed premises in Vancouver, Canada, the present study represents one of only a few studies to examine predictors of alcohol service to obviously intoxicated bar patrons. The identification of situational variables that predict alcohol service to intoxicated barroom patrons is critical to the developed of effective strategies for reducing irresponsible alcohol service in bars, as well as associated problems with alcohol-related harm occurring in and around licensed drinking establishments.

Acknowledgements

I gratefully acknowledge the Rutgers University School of Criminal Justice and the First Securities Service Corporation for providing funding for this study. The opinions expressed in this article are those of the author and do not necessarily reflect the views or policies of the funding sources. I am also forever grateful to Drs Ronald V. Clarke, Marcus Felson, Michael Maxfield, and Helene Raskin White for their insights, guidance, and feedback during this project. I would also like to acknowledge the second observer in this study, Kimberly Lutter, who served as my second pair of ears and eyes during the data collection. Finally, I would like to thank Phyllis Schultz for her kind and continuous support and assistance.

References

Andreasson, S., Lindewald, B., and Rehnman, C. (2000). Over-serving patrons in licensed premises in Stockholm. *Addiction, 95,* 359-363.

Carvolth, R., Homel, R., Hauritz, M., Wortley, R., Clark, J., and McIlwain, G. (1996). Swilling in Surfers: Responsible hospitality practice. *Community Quarterly: Community Development in Action, 38,* 22-28.

Chandler Coutts, M., Graham, K., Braun, K., and Wells, S. (2000). Results of a pilot program for training bar staff in preventing aggression. *Journal of Drug Education, 30,* 171-191.

Donnelly, N, and Briscoe, S. (2003). Signs of intoxication and server intervention among 18 – 39-year-olds drinking at licensed premises in New South Wales, Australia. *Addiction, 98,* 1287-1295.

Felson, R. B., Baccaglini, W., and Gmelch, G. (1986). Bar-room brawls: Aggression and violence in Irish and American bars. In A.Campbell and J. Gibbs (Eds.), *Violent transactions: The limits of personality* (pp. 153-166). Oxford, UK: Basil Blackwell.

Forster, J.L., McGovern, P.G., Wagenaar, A.C., Wolfson, M., Perry, C.L., and Anstine, P.S. (1994). The ability of young people to purchase alcohol without age identification in northeastern Minnesota, USA. *Addiction, 89,* 699-705.

Forster, J.L., Murray, D.M., Wolfson, M., and Wagenaar, A.C. (1995). Commercial availability of alcohol to young people: Results of alcohol purchase attempts. *Preventive Medicine, 24,* 342-347.

Fox, J.G., and Sobol, J.J. (2000). Drinking patterns, social interaction, and barroom behavior: A routine activities approach. *Deviant Behavior: An Interdisciplinary Journal, 21,* 429-450.

Geller, E.S., Russ, N.W., and Delphos, W.A. (1987). Does server intervention training make a difference? *Alcohol Health and Research World, 11,* 64-69.

Gliksman, L., McKenzie, D., Single, E., Douglas, R., Brunet, S., and Moffatt, K. (1993). The role of alcohol providers in prevention: An evaluation of a server intervention programme. *Addiction, 88,* 1195-1203.

Graham, K. (1980). Theories of intoxicated aggression. *Canadian Journal of Behavioral Science, 12,* 141-158.

Graham, K. (2000). Preventive interventions for on-premise drinking: A promising but underresearched area of prevention. *Contemporary Drug Problems, 27,* 593-668.

Graham, K., Jelley, J., and Purcell, J. (2005). Training bar staff in preventing and managing aggression in licensed premises. *Journal of Substance Use, 10,* 48-61.

Graham, K., La Rocque, L., Yetman, R., Ross, T.J., and Guistra, E. (1980). Aggression and barroom environments. *Journal of Studies on Alcohol, 41,* 277-292.

Graham, K., Leonard, K.E., Room, R., Wild, T.C., Pihl, R.O., Bois, C., and Single, E. (1998). Current directions in research on understanding and preventing intoxicated aggression. *Addiction, 93,* 659-676.

Graham, K., Osgood, D.W., Zibrowski, E., Purcell, J., Gliksman, L., Leonard, K., et al. (2004). The effect of the *Safer Bars* programme on physical aggression in bars: results of a randomized control trial. *Drug and Alcohol Review, 23,* 31-41.

Graham, K., Schmidt, G., Gillis, K. (1996). Circumstances when drinking leads to aggression: An overview if research findings. *Contemporary Drug Problems, 23,* 493-557.

Graham, K., West, P., and Wells, S. (2000). Evaluating theories of alcohol-related aggression using observations of young adult bars. *Addiction, 95,* 847-863.

Homel, R. Carvolth, R., Hauritz, M., McIlwain, G., and Teague, R. (2004). Making licensed venues safer for patrons: What environmental factors should be the focus of interventions? *Drug and Alcohol Review, 23,* 19-29.

Homel, R., Hauritz, M., Wortley, R., McIlwain, G., and Carvolth, R. (1997). Preventing alcohol-related crime through community action: The Surfers Paradise Safety Action Project. *Crime Prevention Studies, 7,* 35-90.

Homel, R., and Clark, J. (1994). The prediction and prevention of violence in pubs and clubs. *Crime Prevention Studies, 3,* 1-46.

Homel, R., Tomsen, S., and Thommeny, J. (1992). Public drinking and violence: Not just an alcohol problem. *The Journal of Drug Issues, 22,* 679-697.

Lang, E., Stockwell, T., Rydon, P., and Beel, A. (1998). Can training bar staff in responsible serving practices reduce alcohol-related harm? *Drug and Alcohol Review, 17,* 39-50.

Lang, E., Stockwell, T., Rydon, P., and Lockwood, A. (1995). Drinking settings and problems of intoxication. *Addiction Research, 3,* 141-149.

Macintyre, S., and Homel, R. (1997). Danger on the dance floor: A study of interior design, crowding and aggression in nightclubs. In R. Homel (Ed.), *Policing for prevention: Reducing crime, public intoxication and injury, Crime Prevention Studies* (Vol. 7, pp.91-113). Monsey, New York: Criminal Justice Press.

McKnight, A.J. (1991). Factors influencing the effectiveness of server-intervention education. *Journal of Studies on Alcohol, 52,* 389-397.

McKnight, A.J., and Streff, F.M. (1994). The effect of enforcement upon service of alcohol to intoxicated patrons of bars and restaurants. *Accident Analysis and Prevention, 26,* 79-88.

Nusbaumer, M.R., and Reiling, D.M. (2002). Environmental influences on alcohol consumption practices of alcoholic beverage servers. *The American Journal of Drug and Alcohol Abuse, 28,* 733-742.

Nusbaumer, M.R., and Reiling, D.M. (2003). Where problems and policy intersect: Servers, problem encounters and targeted policy. *Drugs: Education, prevention and policy, 10,* 21-29.

Quigley, B.M., Leonard, K.E., and Collins, R.L. (2003). Characteristics of violent bars and bar patrons. *Journal of Studies on Alcohol, 64,* 765-772.

Reiling, D.M., and Nusbaumer, M.R. (2006). When problem servers pour in problematic places: Alcoholic beverage servers' willingness to serve patrons beyond intoxication. *Substance Use and Misuse, 41,* 653-668.

Roberts, J.C. (1998). *Alcohol-related aggression in the barroom environment: A study of drinking establishments at the Jersey shore,* Unpublished master's thesis, Rutgers University School of Criminal Justice, Newark, New Jersey.

Russ, N.W., and Geller, E.S. (1987). Training bar personnel to prevent drunken driving: A field evaluation. *American Journal of Public Health, 77,* 952-954.

Rydon, P., Stockwell, T., Lang, E., and Beel, A. (1996). Pseudo-drunk-patron evaluation of bar-staff compliance with Western Australian liquor law. *Australian and New Zealand Journal of Public Health, 20,* 290-295.

Stockwell, T. (2001). Responsible alcohol service: Lessons from evaluations of server training and policing initiatives. *Drug and Alcohol Review, 20,* 257-265.

Stockwell, T., Lang, E., and Rydon, P. (1993). High risk drinking settings: The association of serving and promotional practices with harmful drinking. *Addiction, 88,* 1519-1526.

Tomsen, S. (1997). A top night: Social protest, masculinity and the culture of drinking violence. *British Journal of Criminology, 37,* 90-102.

Tomsen, S., Homel, R., and Thommeny, J. (1991). The causes of public violence: Situational "versus" other factors in drinking related assaults. In D. Chappell, P. Grabosky, and H. Strang (Eds.), *Australian violence: Contemporary perspectives* (pp. 177-194). Canberra: Australian Institute of Criminology.

Toomey, T.L., Wagenaar, A.C., Erickson, D.J., Fletcher, L.A., Patrek, W., and Lenk, K.M. (2004). Illegal alcohol sales to obviously intoxicated patrons at licensed establishments. *Alcoholism: Clinical and Experimental Research, 28,* 769-774.

Toomey, T.L., Wagenaar, A.C., Gehan, J.P., Kilian, G., Murray, D.M., and Perry, C.L. (2001). Project ARM: Alcohol risk management to prevent sales to underage and intoxicated patrons. *Health Education and Behavior, 28,* 186-199.

Toomey, T.L., Wagenaar, A.C., Kilian, G., Fitch, O., Rothstein, C., and Fletcher, L. (1999). Alcohol sales to pseudo-intoxicated bar patrons. *Public Health Reports, 114,* 337-342.

Wallin, E., Gripenberg, J., and Andreasson, S. (2002). Too drunk for a beer? A study of overserving in Stockholm. *Addiction, 97,* 901-907.

Wolfson, M., Toomey, T.L., Forster, J.L., Wagenaar, A.C., McGovern, P.G., and Perry, C.L. (1996). Characteristics, policies, and practices of alcohol outlets and sales to youth. *Journal of Studies on Alcohol, 57,* 670-674.

In: Social Drinking: Uses, Abuses and Psychological Factors ISBN: 978-1-60876-219-4
Editors : K. T. Everly, E. M. Cosell, pp. 261-278 © 2010 Nova Science Publishers, Inc.

Chapter 7

THE SOCIAL DRINKING AMONG WARSAW ADOLESCENTS

Katarzyna Okulicz-Kozaryn and Anna Borucka
Institute of Psychiatry and Neurology, Warsaw, Poland

ABSTRACT

Despite the fact that alcohol use is associated with high risk of adverse health and social effects great majority of teenagers drink alcoholic beverages. For this reason and because of data indicating good psychosocial functioning of adolescents who use but not abuse alcohol, alcohol drinking may be treated as an important factor in "the development to adulthood".

The aim of the study was to assess changes in the prevalence of social drinking (moderate drinking with peers) and other patterns of alcohol use ("risky", "solitary", "family" and "other" drinking) by adolescents in the past 20 years. Analysis were based on the data from the study aimed at monitoring trends in alcohol and other drug use by Warsaw 15-year-olds. The survey was repeated every four years, from 1988 to 2008, with comparable sampling approach and core questions. The sample size varied from above 3000 in 1988 to 1244 in 2008. In 2004 and 2008 some questions concerning adolescents lifestyle and mental health were added what allow to compare lifestyles of adolescent abstainers, social drinkers and other alcohol users.

Study results indicate that since the late 80's majority of Warsaw adolescents have been social drinkers (30%-40% of the population). Recently the prevalence of social drinking decreased (to 26%) while the increase of alcohol abstinence rates (from 11% in 2000 to 18% in 2008) and risky drinking among boys (from 14% in 1988 to 24% in 2008) was observed. Alcohol use alone is more prevalent among boys (4% to 7% across years) than girls (2% to 4%), while drinking with parents - among girls (16% - 22%) than boys (13% - 17%).

Regression analysis indicate that social drinkers lifestyle differs from other adolescents lifestyle in many aspects: they spend more time out of home, less time on their school homework, smoke more cigarettes and more often participate in parties were illicit drugs are used than abstainers and those, who drink alcohol with parents (family drinkers). Their cigarette use and partying is less intensive than in case of risky drinkers (those who abuse alcohol in peers company). Risky and solitary drinkers are at the higher risk of developing alcohol related problems. The finding that teenagers who drink alcohol in moderate quantities in company of parents (family drinkers) is associated with less risk of negative social and health consequences than drinking with peers, solitary or even being an abstainer, suggests the revision of zero-tolerance approach.

INTRODUCTION

In 2008 in Poland, in the national survey 72% of adults admitted that in the past 12 months they have been drinking alcohol (CBOS, 2008). In 2007, in ESPAD study, 79% of Polish 15-years old students gave positive answer to the same question (Sierosławski, 2007). So, we can say that drinking alcohol is, at least, as prevalent among teenagers as it is among adults. There is a risk of development of alcohol related problems for all users, too. But alcohol cause more harm to young, developing individuals than to matured ones. Alcohol use is the leading cause of death in accidents of people younger than 21 years of age (The Scope of the Problem, 2004/2005). Frequent alcohol use in adolescence increase the risk of alcohol dependence in young adulthood (Bonomo et. al., 2004). Early initiation of alcohol use (under 14 years of age) is associated with more intensive consumption in future (Hellandsjo Bu et. al., 2002), higher risk of accidents and risky sexual behaviors (Hingson, Winter, 2003; Hingson et al, 2003; Engels, Knibbe, 2000). The risk of depressive and psychosomatic disorders increase with the frequency of alcohol abuse by teenagers (Hoel et al., 2004). Studies conducted among Polish adolescents confirm that alcohol use is related to negative consequences: social and legal problems (Sierosławski, 2003; Ostaszewski, 2008), accidents and injuries (Mazur, Woynarowska, 1999) other risky behaviors (Bobrowski, 2008) and mental health problems (Bobrowski et al., 2005; Bobrowski, 2006).

For these reasons, alcohol policy usually makes a difference between adolescents and adults alcohol use assuming that it is reserved for adults and prohibited to youth. In Poland, like in many other countries, zero-tolerance policy are in force in regard to minors alcohol use (National Programme of Alcohol Problems Prevention and Solving for years 2006-2010). In the same time, national campaigns promoting responsible drinking are targeted exclusively to adults (PARPA, 2008). Epidemiological data provide support for this approach. While national statistics (CSO, 2007) indicate the increase of alcohol economic availability (e.g., in 1998 one could buy about 500 bottles of beer for an average month salary and in 2007 – more than 1000 bottles) and consumption in the whole population (pure alcohol per capita consumption increased from 7,02 liters in 1998 to 9,21 in 2007), among youth alcohol abstinence is more and more popular (Sierosławski, 2007; Okulicz-Kozaryn, Borucka, 2008). But still, 80% of Polish 15-years old students drink, 57% do it frequently (at least once in the past month) and 22% frequently get drunk (Sierosławski, 2007). So, the question about possibly useful harm reduction approach to teenagers alcohol use remain valid.

Since alcohol drinking by adults is legally and socially accepted phenomenon, while there are no such permissions for alcohol use by teenagers, the term "social drinking" is more often used with reference to adults than adolescents. But, even then, it does not have one, generally accepted definition and has been defined in different ways by researches across years. Normal social drinking, defined as non problem drinking was used in the mid 1960's. (Williams, 1966). Later, social drinking was defined by level of alcohol consumption combined with size and gender composition of drinking groups (Senchak et.all, 1998). In other study (Christiansen, 2002) the concept of social heavy drinker was defined as having a heavy-drinking episode but not drinking alone. Social drinking by teenagers or young adults was implied as drinking alcohol for social motives or because alcohol tastes good, but without getting drunk (Bogren, 2006). This group of drinkers was called "moderate" or "competent" drinkers – as those who know their limits and try to avoid risky situation related to drunkenness. The term of social drinking also refers to those, who have never drunk alone (Tucker et. all, 2006).

With reference to adolescents, the combination of social context with the amount of alcohol consumed seems to be the most adequate way of defining social drinking. That is because alcohol use plays a very important role in "the development to adulthood" (Stępień, 2004, p.79), because it permits to copy behavioral patterns of adults, is an easy (available) and attractive (forbidden) way of collecting new experiences, testing own abilities, affirming independence from authorities and gaining group appraisal (Stępień, 2001). Social context of alcohol use such as attending parties, discos, drinking with family members, parents, friends and in solitude can influence alcohol consumption (quantity and frequency) and provide some benefits as well as some negative consequences for individuals. The findings of several studies indicate that increasing acceptance and popularity among peers, having more friends and acquaintances are related to alcohol drinking by teenagers (Tucker et all, 2006, Bogren, 2006). Moreover, drinking is not only connected with increasing number of friends but also with improvement of quality of friendships (Hoel et all., 2004, Engels and Knibbe, 2000).

A lot of interesting information, that highlight the meaning of drinking alcohol in teenagers lifestyle come from qualitative researches (Jarvinen and Gundeelach, 2007, Demant and Jarvinen, 2006, Bogren, 2006). These studies findings indicate, that alcohol drinking by teenagers can fulfill the important function in "struggle for recognition" (Demant and Jarvinen, 2006, p.596). Hence the adolescents, who drink very little or not at all may have weak position and no respect and admiration among peers, who are more experienced in alcohol drinking. Teenagers, who often go to parties and discos and have been drunk are more popular and feel more accepted and mature, than those, who do not have such experiences. Abstainers or cautious drinker are not easily accepted by drinking peers and have problems in joining their group or participating in teenage parties (Jarvinen and Gundelach, 2007). Therefore, these authors raised an interesting issue: "To drink or not to drink is not only a question of alcohol consumption, but a vital importance for whom the teenagers are allowed to keep company with..." (Jarvinen and Gundelach, 2007, p. 65).

Now that we assumed that social drinking means drinking with peers and for building drinker's position within peers group a question about other patterns of adolescents alcohol use arise. What are the differences between teenage social drinkers and those who drink with parents or in solitude? Some answers come out from studies of Bourgault and Demers (1997) and Tucker et al. (2006). Bourgault and Demers (1997) defined solitary drinking as having an episode of drinking alone, which does not exclude drinking in company or even assumes customary social drinking. The findings of this study show that solitary drinking is not the single and sufficient factor explaining alcohol related problems. Tucker et al. (2006) found that adolescents who have had episode of drinking alone tended to be heavier alcohol users compared with adolescent social drinkers. Moreover, solitary users spend less time on homework, on hobbies and are less engaged in school than social drinkers. There is also some evidence (Pliner and Cappell, 1974), that when people drink in social settings they described their reaction for alcohol in terms of affect (more friendly, more euphoric, less bored) in contrary to people who drank alone, who report their feelings in terms of physical symptoms (less clear-thinking, more sleepy and dizzy).

Drinking with parents or in parental home is the next social context of alcohol drinking by adolescents. Studies' results suggest that drinking alcohol by teenagers in family environment is less risky (least likely to produce intoxication) than consuming alcohol in public places or in peers' houses (Forsyth and Barnad, 2000). Bellis et all (2007) found that being given alcohol by parents is the protective factor against getting drunk and that buying alcohol by parents prevents adolescents alcohol use in public places. Our previous study (Okulicz-Kozaryn, Borucka, 2008) indicate that drinking with peers is associated with higher consumption of alcohol, while alcohol use with parents is most typical amongst moderate drinkers.

The aim of the present study is to assess changes in the prevalence of social drinking and other patterns of alcohol use by adolescents in the past 20 years in Warsaw, as well as, to compare lifestyles of adolescent abstainers, social drinkers and other alcohol users. Having in mind all, above mentioned, explanations of social drinking we constructed our own definition of this term. By "social drinking" we mean alcohol use in peers company (social context) but in small amounts, not leading to drunkenness and rather not provoking risky behaviors (competent/moderate drinking). We agree with cited above qualitative studies' results, that even excessive alcohol use may help in gaining high position within peers group (Demant and Jarvinen, 2006), but we do not forget that alcohol abuse often leads to antisocial behaviors such as quarrels, fights and conflicts with friends (Sierosławski, 2003). So, we separate social drinkers from adolescents using high quantities of alcohol with peers. But this distinction triggers another problem. What does it mean "small" or "high" amounts of alcohol in regard to adolescents, who according to zero-tolerance approach, are not allowed to use any alcohol? The limits of "safe" drinking are usually formulated with reference to the whole population and they differ one from another. E.g. U.S. Dietary Guidelines for Americans (2005) define binge drinking as five drinks or more for men and four and more drinks for women. Australian Alcohol Guidelines (2001) recommend to use not more than six drinks in any one day for men and for women – up to four drinks in any one day. Polish adolescents asked, how many drinks they should have in order to get drunk most often indicated 3-4 and 5-6 standard drinks (Sierosławski, 2007). Therefore, for this study, we assume that moderate drinking means having up to two drinks for girls and no more than three drinks in a row for boys.

2. METHOD

3.1. Design

Analysis are based on the data from the study aimed at monitoring trends in alcohol and other drug use by Warsaw 15-year-olds. The survey was repeated every four years, from 1988 to 2008, with comparable sampling approach and core questions. In all editions data were collected at the beginning of the school year (Fall). Between 1988 and 2000 the participants of the survey were in the first grade of high school or vocational school and the majority of them was 15 years old. In 2004 and 2008 due to the structural changes in the educational system, the same age group was in the last (final) grade of 3-year middle school (gimnazja).

The survey is conducted in a part of Warsaw (in the 80' it was one district – Mokotow, now it is divided into several separate administrative units). In 1988 all first grade classes from all high and vocational schools in this district participated in the study. Since 1992 approximately 50% of classes were randomly chosen.

At all time points classroom surveys were conducted by trained research staff members, who had no connections with the schools. The anonymity of individual students, classes and schools was guaranteed.

3.2. Participants

The number of participants ranged from 1229 in 2008 to 3918 in 1988 (table 1). At all study time points, with only one exception in 2004, number of boys was smaller than girls (46%-49%). Every year the percentage of students absent from school on the day of the survey was similar and did not exceed 10%.

Significant changes across all study time points were observed in terms of delay from proceeding from one school grade to the next one. Until 2000 the percentage of students older than 15 years of age ranged from 11% in 1996 to 15% in 1988 and 2000, but in 2004 it decreased to 7% and in 2008 to 5%. Due to this disproportion adolescents who - at the time of the study were older than 15 years of age – were excluded from trend analysis (table 1).

Table 1. Sample size

Year	No. of participants	% of boys	% of 15 year old or younger students
1988	3918	47%	86%
1992	2000	46%	88%
1996	2484	47%	89%
2000	2471	49%	85%
2004	1461	52%	93%
2008	1229	49%	95%

3.3. Measurement

In the self-reported anonymous questionnaire respondents were asked three questions: when, in what quantity and with whom did they last use three kinds of alcoholic beverages (beer, wine, vodka) (Wolniewicz-Grzelak, 1995). With regard to the frequency questions (when?) the respondents were to choose one out of 9 answers (ranging from "I've never drunk" to "from 1 to 4 days ago"). Concerning the quantity questions (how much?) a 7-point answer was used. The answers scale ranged from "I've never drunk" to "more than 4 bottles" (for beer), "a bottle or more" (for wine), and "1/4 l. or more" (for vodka). In order to describe with whom adolescents had last been drinking, the respondents were to chose one of the given possibilities: "with parents", "with other adults", "only with teenagers", "alone", or they were allowed to mark more than one category if they were drinking with e.g. parents and other adults (coded as "mixed company").

By combining answers on quantity, frequency and company questions six categories of respondents were differentiated: (1) abstainers – those who have never drunk alcohol; (2) social drinkers – moderate drinkers (boys who, during their last drinking occasion, did not have more than 3 drinks and girls who did not drink more than 2 drinks) drinking with peers; (3) risky drinkers - alcohol abusers (boys who, during their last drinking occasion had 4 drinks or more and girls who drunk 3 drinks or more) drinking with peers; (4) family drinkers - moderate drinkers drinking with parents; (5) solitary drinkers – those, who during their last drinking occasion, drunk alone; (6) other drinkers – this category comprised those who were drinking with "other adults" or in a mixed company[1].

In 2004 and 2008 some questions concerning adolescents lifestyle and mental health were added. In this analysis included are measures of:

- Cigarette use ("no", "few times per month or year", "few times per week or everyday"), illicit drug and psychoactive medicines use without medical prescription in the past year ("no", "any use"), (Wolniewicz-Grzelak and Ostaszewski, 1983)
- Participation in youth parties on which illicit drugs were used (never in the past year, 1-2 times in the past year, several times), (Wolniewicz-Grzelak and Ostaszewski, 1983)
- Violence - indicated by participation in fights ("no" or at least once in the past year) and other forms of physical or psychological violence exertion (never or rarely versus "about once a week" or "more frequently") at school in the past year (Adlaf, Paglia, 2001)
- Victimization by any form of physical or psychological violence at school in the past year (never or rarely versus "about once a week" or "more frequently"), (Adlaf, Paglia, 2001)
- Delinquent behaviours – damaging things, thefts, hitting anybody, escaping from home, cheating in school (yes or now in the past year), (Zimmerman and Schemeelk-Cone, 2003)
- Everyday lifestyle – on average day, how much time an adolescent spent on: internet, doing school homework, his/her hobby, out of home (continuous variable measured on 5 point Likert's scale from none hours to 5 or more hours per day), (Bobrowski, Ostaszewski, Pisarska, 2007)
- Depressive symptoms – measured by shortened version of CES-D scale (Adlaf, Paglia, 2001), including 4 questions about feeling sad, lonely, low spirits and tearful in the past 7 days. Reporting all four symptoms "often" or "all the time" is treated as indicator of depressiveness.
- Current mental health problems – how many days in the past month an adolescent felt that his/her mental health was not as good as usually (14 days or more indicates poor health), (Department of Health and Human Services, 2000)

1 Adolescents abusing alcohol in company of parents were not included into any category, because they form a very small (less than 0,7% of studied population in all study time points) and probably, a very specific subset of teenagers – a high risk group.

Data Analysis

Besides descriptive statistics showing time changes in different drinking styles, binary logistic regression analysis, with stepwise forward conditional method, were used to compare abstainers, risky, family and solitary drinkers to social drinkers. Comparisons between social drinkers and "other drinkers" (adolescents drinking with "other adults" or in a mixed company) were not conducted because we have no data allowing understanding who exactly are this adults. All we know is that they are not adolescent's parents, what means that they could be other family relatives (uncles, parents' friends etc.) or older (matured) respondent's friends. This uncertainty would make meaningful interpretation of study results impossible.

As predictors of alcohol use style in regression analysis were used: gender, year of the survey (2004 and 2008 because in previous measures no comparable data was collected) and all variables listed above with three exceptions: victimization by violence, depressive symptoms and current mental health problems. These variables were excluded because preliminary bivariate analysis did not indicated their significant correlation with dependent variable.

3. Results

Prevalence of Different Patterns of Alcohol Use

Since the late 80's majority of Warsaw adolescents have been social drinkers – using alcohol in moderate amounts in company of their peers (graph 1). However, dynamic changes in the prevalence of social drinking occurred in the past 20 years. In the late 80's the percentage of social drinkers was 28%. Then it rapidly grow to 38% in 1992 and remind stable until 2000. In recent years it decreased to 26%.

The opposite changes have been observed for alcohol abstinence. In 1988 the prevalence of abstinence was equal with the prevalence of social drinking (28%). Than it has been decreasing when the prevalence of social drinking has been increasing and in recent years it grow from 11% in 2000 to 18% in 2008.

In the past decades two stable groups of adolescents can be identified. The first, consists of adolescents drinking alcohol alone, who represent about 4% of the population. The second, are teenagers drinking alcohol in moderate amounts in company of their parents (14% to 19% of studied population across 20 years).

Stable increase can be observed in the percentage of adolescents drinking alcohol in a mixed company (with parents and other adults or parents and peers or adults and peers), from 6% in 1988 to 13% in 2008. Similar changes are visible in the trend of alcohol abuse with peers. In the past 20 years the prevalence of drinking in high quantities in a company of peers grow from 15% in 1988 to 24% in 2008.

When we look at the trends of various types of alcohol use by girls (graph 2) and boys (graph 3) some differences are immediately visible. First, we can realize very dynamic decrease in the prevalence of social drinking among boys since the beginning of the 90's. Recently, social drinking is more prevalent among girls (30%) than boys (26%).

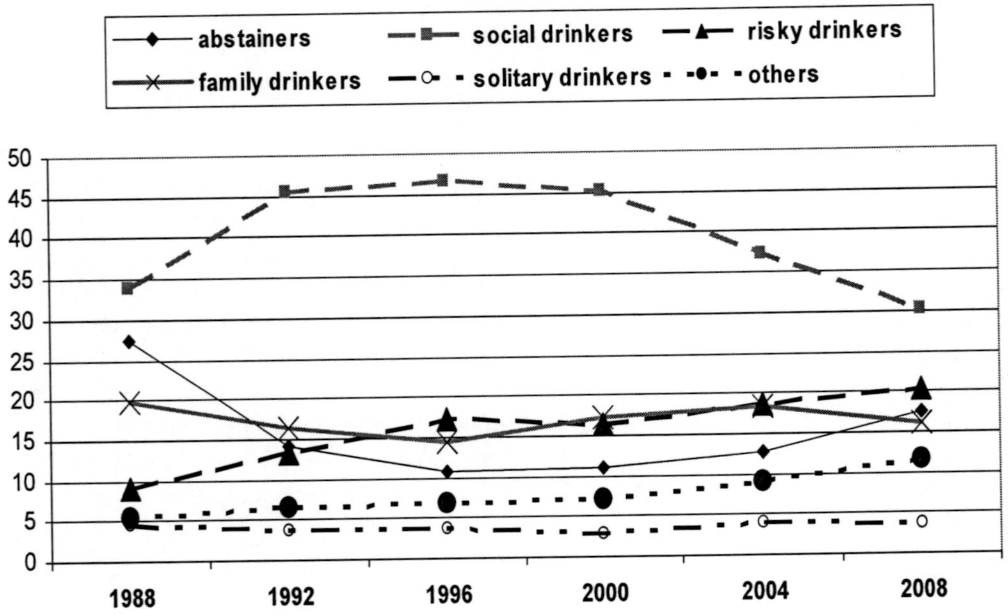

Grapg 1. Changes in patterns of 15 years old Warsaw adolescents alcohol use from 1988 to 2008.

Secondly, risky drinking (abusing alcohol with peers), traditionally has been more prevalent among boys than girls. In 1988 the gender gap was the highest – 6% and then it started to diminish and in 2004 this pattern of use was reported by more girls (24%) than boys (19%). Recently (2008), boys are "leading" again (risky drinking is reported by 21% of girls and 24% of boys).

From two trends stable in the whole population: alcohol use alone and drinking with parents, the first one is more prevalent among boys (4% to 7% across years) than girls (2% to 4%), while the second – among girls (16% - 22%) than boys (13% - 17%).

Social Drinkers and other Teenagers

Table 2 shows results of binary logistic regression analysis comparing various groups of teenagers to those, who are classified as social drinkers. As indicated by the pseudo R^2 Nagelkerke's coefficients the strongest differences exist between social drinkers and abstainers (the model explains 40% of differences between theses two groups). This model indicates that odds ratios of abstaining are significantly lower for adolescents smoking cigarettes, attending parties on which illicit drugs are used, cheating in school (0,3), spending more time out of home (0,7 per scale unit) and those who in the past year stroked anybody (0,6), than odds of social drinking. Odds of abstaining increase 1,2 times per scale unit with the time spent on school homework on average day. They are also 2,7 times higher for those who in the past year once a week or more often participated in physical or psychological violence at school compared to those who have no or rare such experiences. Moreover, regression results confirm that being an abstinent was more probable in 2008 than four years earlier.

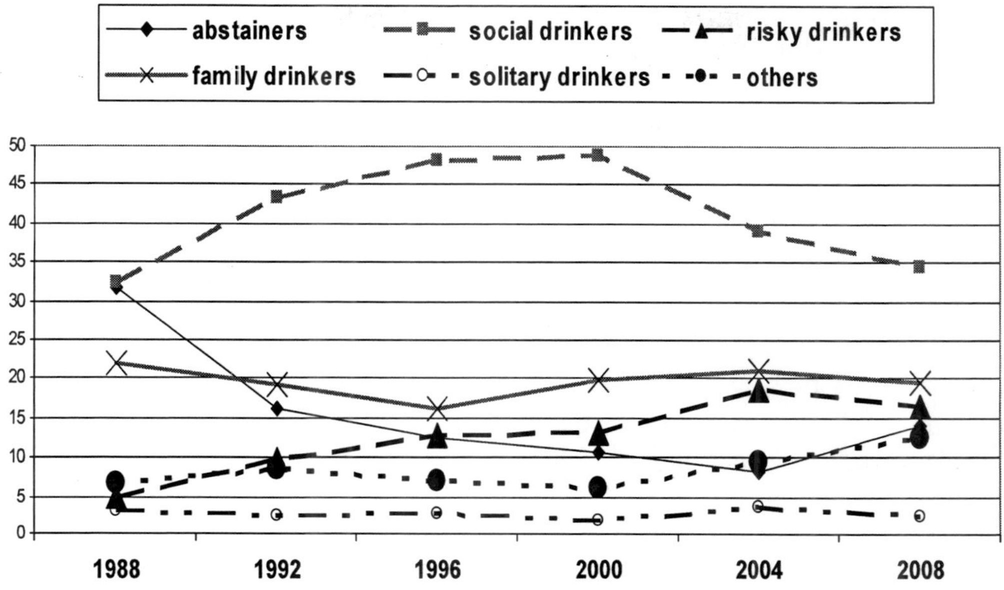

Graph 2. Changes in patterns of 15 years old Warsaw females alcohol use from 1988 to 2008.

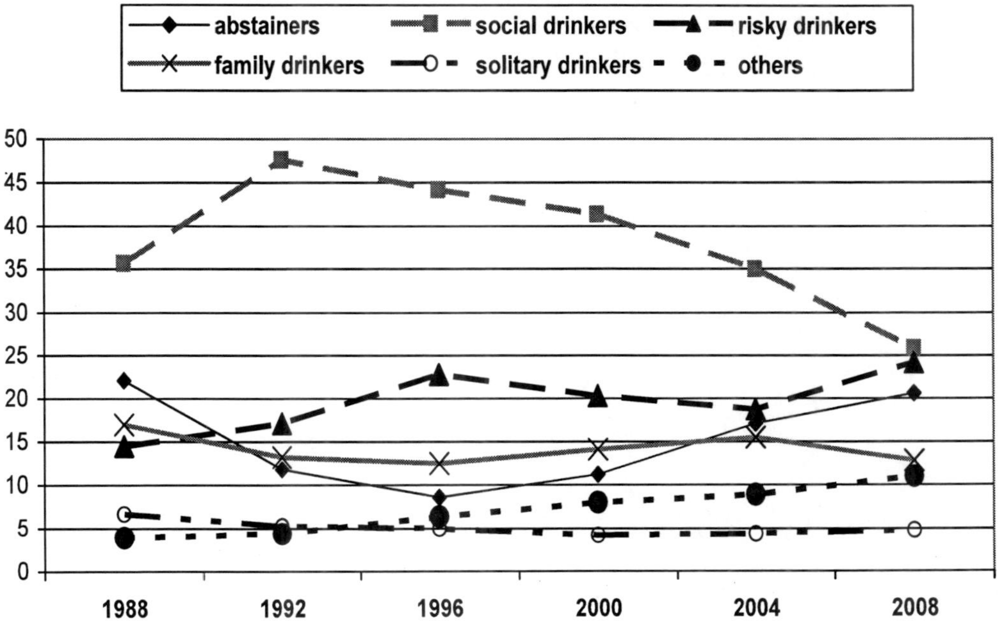

Graph 3. Changes in patterns of 15 years old Warsaw males alcohol use from 1988 to 2008.

The second in terms of explaining between groups variance is the equation for family drinkers compared to social drinkers (pseudo R^2 = 0,19). Similarly to abstainers – social drinkers model, significant predictors of moderate use of alcohol with parents are: fewer time spend out of home on average day (0,7 per scale unit), no participation in youth parties on which illicit drugs are available, no cigarette use and more time spend on school homework (1,3). Moreover, odds of family drinking increase with time usually spend by an adolescent on his/her hobby (1,2).

The model explaining differences between social drinkers and those who abuse alcohol in peers company (pseudo R^2 = 0,12) indicates that odds ratio of risky drinking for adolescents who smoke cigarettes few times per month or less frequently is 1,8, and for those who smoke more often 2,2 compared for those who do not smoke. Risk of alcohol abuse is significantly higher for those who several times per year participate in youth parties were illicit drugs are used (odds are 1,5 the odds for those who do not attend such parties). Moreover, odds of risky drinking with peers are higher for those who in the past year escaped from home (1,5), had fights at school (1,4), by purpose damaged some objects (1,4) and spent much time in internet (odds increase 1,1 per scale unit).

The less powerful (it explains just 6% of differences) is the model in which social drinkers are compared to solitary drinkers, but it suggests interesting differences between these groups of teenagers. First of all, solitary drinkers (similarly to abstainers) have higher odds (2,6) of participation in physical or psychological violence at school and they spent more time on school homework (1,3) than social drinkers. Secondly, the odds of solitary drinking are 2,3 the odds of social drinking for adolescents using psychoactive medicines without medical prescription.

Table 2. Binary logistic regressions comparing abstainers, risky drinkers, family drinkers and solitary drinkers to social drinkers (reference category in parenthesis)

		95,0% C.I.	
	Exp(B)	Lower	Upper
Abstainers	R^2=0,402 (N=1013)		
Year (2004)	1,912	1,396	2,621
Time spent on school homework	1,240	1,043	1,475
Time spent out of home	,670	,579	,777
Cheating in school (no)	,345	,233	,509
Striking anybody (no)	,619	,406	,945
Participation in violence (no or rare)	2,654	1,472	4,785
Parties with drugs (no)			
1-2 times in the past year	,391	,236	,648
Several times in the past year	,228	,107	,484
Cigarettes (no)			
Few times per month	,065	,023	,185
More often	,026	,003	,191
Risky drinkers	R^2=0,116 (N=1226)		
Time spent on internet	1,129	1,022	1,247
Fights at school (no)	1,406	1,073	1,843

		95,0% C.I.	
	Exp(B)	Lower	Upper
Escaping from home (no)	1,499	1,033	2,175
Damaging things (no)	1,374	1,039	1,818
Parties with drugs (no)			
1-2 times in the past year	1,174	,860	1,602
Several times in the past year	1,499	1,109	2,027
Cigarettes (no)			
Few times per month	1,846	1,340	2,543
More often	2,215	1,636	3,000
Family drinkers	R^2=0,187 (N=1055)		
Time spent on school homework	1,263	1,083	1,473
Time spent on hobby	1,207	1,060	1,375
Time spent out of home	,670	,586	,766
Parties with drugs (no)			
1-2 times in the past year	,582	,395	,856
Several times in the past year	,426	,263	,689
Cigarettes (no)			
Few times per month	,551	,353	,860
More often	,331	,175	,627
Solitary drinkers	R^2=0,064 (N=759)		
Time spent on school homework	1,298	1,006	1,674
Participation in violence (no or rare)	2,612	1,529	4,460
Psychoactive medicines use (no)	2,316	1,382	3,882

4. Discussion and Summary of Results

In our study five groups of Warsaw teenagers were distinguished: abstainers, social drinkers, risky drinkers, family drinkers, solitary drinkers and, not very well defined, group of "other" drinkers. Division of adolescents into these groups was based on the description of their last drinking occasion, what assumes, that this last occasion is representative for the typical pattern of alcohol use by individuals. Of course, it does not have to be always true. Moreover, we created our composite indicators of alcohol use by combining separate questions concerning use of various kinds of alcoholic beverages (beer, wine and vodka) in given time periods: "1-4 days ago", "5-7 days ago" etc., assuming that when a respondent indicated e.g. "1-4 days ago" for all three beverages means that he/she drunk beer and wine and vodka at the same occasion. It is another of this study limitations. But, in spite of these imprecise measures, our results are meaningful and consistent with other research findings.

Prevalence of Different Patterns of Alcohol Use

We defined teenage social drinker as a person, who drinks alcohol with friends, probably due to social motives (to be with friend, to have a good time) and who tries to avoid drunkenness and thus, probably does not experience negative consequences of alcohol drinking (lost of control, hangover, vomiting etc.). This pattern of alcohol use, in the 90's and in the beginning of 2000 was the most popular among Warsaw teenagers, characterizing nearly 40% of adolescents. However, its popularity is recently diminishing and in 2008 one in four adolescents was classified as social drinker. Good news is, that with the decrease in social drinking the prevalence of alcohol abstinence increase. Growing tendency of abstaining from alcohol is observed in national adolescents survey, too. ESPAD data indicate that from 2003 to 2007 the rate of 15 year old school students who declared that they never in the lifetime used alcohol increased from 7% to 10% (Sierosławski, 2007). But, in our study there is a bad news, too - the growing tendency, observed among boys, of drinking alcohol in more risky way – together with peers but in high amount (four drinks or more in a row). This negative trend, observed in Warsaw population, is not visible on the national scale. In ESPAD study (Sierosławski, 2007) the decrease in the prevalence of getting drunk in the lifetime was observed (for boys: from 68% in 2003 to 55% in 2007 and for girls: from 51% to 49%). In this context it is worth noting, that earlier studies suggest that, Warsaw boys are somehow trendsetters for other Polish youth. E.g. the decrease in the prevalence of alcohol abuse by boys was observed in Warsaw between 2000 and 2004 (Ostaszewski et al., 2005) while in Poland – not before 2007 (Sierosławski, 2007). Increase in boys alcohol abstinence is noted in Warsaw since 1996 (Ostaszewski et al., 2005) while in the national sample (Sierosławski, 2007) only recently (in 2007). So, probably in the near future, national data will show increase in alcohol abuse by adolescent boys, too.

It seems, that the most stable groups, in terms of the prevalence, are adolescents drinking with parents and adolescents drinking alone. The first of these drinking styles is more prevalent among girls. This may suggest that child-rearing practices in family are gender-based and parents use different approaches in introducing boys and girls to adults world, therein - alcohol drinking.

The result suggesting that solitary alcohol use is more prevalent among boys than girls is consistent with other studies (Tucker et al., 2006, Bourgault and Demers, 1997). However, these studies reported much higher prevalence of this phenomenon (17% in Tucker's et. al. and 27% in Bourgault and Demers study) than we stated in Warsaw (4%). This difference is probably due to various definitions of "solitary drinking". We assumed that those, who during their last drinking occasion drunk alone, usually drink in solitude, too. Tucker et. al. (2006) defined solitary drinking as any use of alcohol in solitude in the past year and Bourgault and Demers (1997) labeled as "solitary drinkers" those who had an episode of drinking alone in the past three months. Moreover, our respondents were younger than participants of other studies (in Tucker's et. al. study participated older adolescents and in Bourgault and Demers study – adults).

Among girls, we can observe increasing prevalence of alcohol use with "other adults" and in a mix company. It is difficult to interpret this result because, as mentioned above, we have no data allowing understanding who are these "other" adults. The same problem concerns answers indicating mix company of drinking – who exactly these companions have been? Anyway, without deciding this question we may suppose, that observed increase in this indicator shows growing acceptance of alcohol use by minors during various social and family gatherings.

Differences between Adolescents Presenting Different Patterns of Alcohol Use

In our study, social drinking is understood similarly to "competent drinking" (Bogren, 2006), as drinking for being in peer group without being drunk what is the sign of maturity. Regression analysis indicate that social drinkers lifestyle differs from other adolescents lifestyle in many aspects. First of all, they spend more time out of home, smoke more cigarettes and more often participate in parties were illicit drugs are used than abstainers and those, who drink alcohol with parents. But, their cigarette use and partying is less intensive than in case of risky drinkers (those who abuse alcohol in peers company). Social drinkers tend to spent less time on their school homework than abstainers, family and solitary drinkers, too. These findings are in line with studies showing that for social drinkers alcohol use plays positive role as an instrument facilitating realization of important developmental tasks such as: to maintain the close relationships with peers, to have opportunity to discuss with them some personal issues, to spend more time with friend and to become more independent from parents (Bogren, 2006). In such developmental context getting good marks at school is not so important (Engels and Knibbe, 2000).

Probably, for this group of teenagers, alcohol use is not the main risk factor. Their health risks are associated rather with cigarettes smoking (risk of respiratory system disease), participation in parties, where illegal drugs are available (risk of using such substances). These adolescents are also exposed to negative social consequences caused by more often cheating in school and aggressive reactions e.g. striking somebody (in comparison with abstainers).

"Family drinkers" – adolescents drinking alcohol with parents spend more time at home, are more engaged in school works and in their hobbies than social drinkers. The fact, they drink alcohol under parental supervision suggests their close relationship with parents. This study results indicate that family drinkers are generally well functioning youth, more focus on individual and educational development than social drinkers. Moreover, other studies proved that alcohol use with parents or under parental supervision is related to smaller amounts of alcohol consumed (Wells et al., 2005, Forsyth and Barnard, 2000; Okulicz-Kozaryn and Borucka, 2008) and not drinking in public places (Bellis et al. 2007). In general, early onset of alcohol use in well functioning family environment is much less likely to be associated with later development of alcohol related problems than early outside family initiation (Forsyth and Barnard, 2000; Bellis et al. 2007).

Family drinkers characteristic is similar to abstainers, however with one significant exception: abstainers have higher odds of participation in violence at school than social drinkers, while there are no differences in this measure between family and social drinkers. This result, needs closer look at the questions concerning violence included in our questionnaire. Two of them concern clearly physical violence: fights and striking (hitting) somebody by purpose. The other question, the one suggesting more favorable characteristic of family drinkers than abstainers, concerns not precisely defined, any forms of "psychological or physical violence". Therefore, it includes psychological violence, which might be a case for abstainers. Why abstainers exert more psychological violence than social drinkers? One answer, based on the other studies findings, indicate the association between being abstainer and week peer networks (Pedresen and Kolstad, 2000). They have weaker friendships, in terms of quantity and closeness, in comparison with moderately and heavily drinking peers

(Hoel et al., 2004). They may give vent to their feeling of loneliness and rejection by classmates in acts of psychological violence.

Not only abstainers, but adolescents drinking alcohol in solitude participate in psychological violence more often than social drinkers. This is consistent with Tucker's et al. (2006) founding that solitary drinkers were involved in more deviant behaviors (stealing, acting out at school), got lower grades and spent less time on homework compared with social users. In the same study, the association between solitary drinking and one's belief, that alcohol use is an effective strategy to cope with problems was established. In our study we did not ask adolescents about alcohol use related beliefs and personal problems, but we found that solitary drinkers more often use psychoactive medicines than other groups of adolescents. This finding may confirmed that those, who drink alcohol alone have some personal problems. Research on self-reported medicine use by adolescents show that youth took medicines to deal with psychological problem (Pisarska and Ostaszewski, 2009; Boyd et al., 2006) or to reduce negative effect of abusing alcohol or to intoxicate (Okulicz-Kozaryn et al., 2008).

In the context of Tucker's et al. (2006) findings, it is interesting, that Warsaw solitary drinkers, contrary to American school students spend much time on school homework than social drinkers. We suppose that it is another difference caused by the way "solitary drinking" was defined in both studies. For us, solitary drinking concern adolescents usually or, at least quite frequently, using alcohol alone, while for Tucker and colleagues – it was very intensive drinking style characterized by frequent use in company plus – use alone. So, it is obvious that Tuckers' "solitary drinkers" generally were more focused on partying and alcohol drinking and cared less about school, than adolescents given the same label in our study.

There are significant differences between those adolescents who moderately (socially) or more excessively (in more risky way) drink alcohol in peers company, too. Odds of risky drinking compared to social drinking are higher for those adolescents who in the past year escaped from home, damaged some objects, took part in fights at school, who several times attended parties where illicit drugs were used, and those who smoke more cigarettes. They probably drink alcohol in order to get drunk. There are some evidence that teenagers whose drink intensively regard themselves as more accepted and more popular among classmates than their peers, who do not drink alcohol at all or drink rarely (DemantandJarvinen, 2006). But on the other hand, other studies (consistent with our findings) indicate significant relationship between alcohol abuse and violent acts (Sierosławski, 2003; Wells et al., 2005). Moreover, some results suggest, that being frequently intoxicated increases the possibility not only of committing delinquent acts but of being victimized, too (Rossow, 1996).

To summarize this study results, we can say that social drinkers are more socially active than abstainers and family drinkers, which is indicated by less time they spend at home and their more frequent participation in youth parties on which illicit drugs are used (and probably in any other parties, too). They are also less involved in school activities (indicated by less time spend on homework) than abstainers, family and solitary drinkers, and less engaged in their hobbies than family drinkers. Social drinkers are more prone than abstainers and family drinkers to some problem behaviors, like cigarette use, cheating and fighting at school. Notwithstanding they are less engaged in psychological violence at school than peers who do not drink alcohol at all. On the other hand, their involvement in other socially disapproved behaviors e.g. illicit drug use and escaping from home and damaging objects is lower than in case of adolescents abusing alcohol in peers company (risky drinkers).

Interesting conclusions coming up from this study concern other groups of adolescents. First, it seems that abstainers and family drinkers characteristics are very similar when compared to social drinkers. They appear as groups most adjusted to adults expectations: they spend a lot of time at home, doing their homework or working on their hobby. They do not smoke cigarettes do not attend youth parties where drugs are available (and probably, other parties, neither) and do not fight. It suggests some benefits of being abstainer or being introduced to alcohol use by parents. The finding that teenagers who drink alcohol in moderate quantities in company of parents is associated with less risk of negative social and health consequences than drinking with peers, solitary or even being an abstainer, suggests the revision of zero-tolerance approach. Maybe, instead of regulating the issue be general laws, the possibility that parents, by themselves, decide about permitting their adolescent child to use alcohol should be considered?

Second, solitary drinkers seems to be a group which needs special interest and intervention because their alcohol use is related to other behaviors signalizing mental health problems: use of psychoactive medicines without medical prescription and participation in psychological violence.

Third, the result worth of further exploration is the positive relationship between participation in psychological violence and alcohol abstinence and solitary drinking. It may suggest, that these two groups of adolescents, contrary to social drinkers, do not feel really good in company of their peers. This interpretation is supported by findings that for adolescents alcohol use, especially in friends company is a factor promoting social integration (Demant and Jarvinen, 2006; Tucker et al., 2006; Bogren, 2006; Hoel et al., 2004; Engels and Knibbe, 2000).

References

Adlaf., E, Paglia A. (2001). The Mental Health and Well-Being of Ontario Students. Findings from the OSDUS. Toronto, Centre for Addiction and Mental Health.

Australian Alcohol Guidelines: *Health Risks and Benefits* (2001).. NHMRC, 6.

Bellis, M. A., Hughes, K., Morleo, M., Tocque, K., Hughes, S., Allen, T., et al. (2007). Predictors of risky alcohol consumption in schoolchildren and their implications for preventing alcohol-related harm. *Substance Abuse Treatment, Prevention, and Policy*, 2, 15.

Bobrowski, K. (2008). Fazy używania nielegalnych substancji psychoaktywnych a picie alkoholu wśród młodzieży i młodych dorosłych. *Alkoholizm i Narkomania,* Vol. 21, No. 4, 341-362.

Bobrowski, K., Ostaszewski K., Pisarska A. (2007). Rekomendacje narzędzi do oceny zagrożeń zdrowia psychicznego młodzieży do dalszego stosowania w badaniach mokotowskich oraz w innych badaniach ankietowych młodzieży szkolnej. Warszawa, Instytut Psychiatrii i Neurologii.

Bobrowski, K. (2006). Zdrowie psychiczne i zachowania ryzykowne 15-latków – badania mokotowskie. *Alkoholizm i Narkomania,* 19, 3, str. 225-242.

Bobrowski, K., Czabała, Cz., Brykczyńska, C. (2005). Zachowania ryzykowne jako wymiar oceny stanu zdrowia psychicznego młodzieży. *Postępy Psychiatrii i Neurologii,* 14(4), 285-292.

Bonomo, Y., A., Bowes, G., Coffey, C., Carlin, B.J., Patton, G., C. (2004). Teenage drinking and the onset of alcohol dependence: a cohort study over seven years. *Addiction,* 99, 1520-1528

Bogren, A. (2006). The competent drinker, the authentic person and strong person: lines of reasoning in Swedish young people's discussions about alcohol. *Journal of Youth Studies*, Vol. 9, No. 5, November, 515-538.

Bourgault, Ch., Demers, D. (1997). Solitary drinking: a risk factor for alcohol-related problems? *Addiction,* 92(3), 303-312.

Boyd, C., J., McCabe, S., E., Cranford, J., A., Young, A. (2006). Adolescents' motivation to abuse prescription medications. Pediatrics, Vol. 118, No. 6, December, 2472-2480.

Central Statistical Office (CSO). Ceny w gospodarce narodowej w 2007 roku. (2007), Warszawa, GUS.

Centrum Badania Opinii Społecznej (CBOS, 2008) Wzory konsumpcji alkoholu w Polsce http://www.parpa.pl/download/wyniki%20badania%20wzory%20konsumnpscji%202008_%202%20metody_poprMFdoc.pdf

Christiansen , M., Vik, P., W., Jarchow, A. (2002). College student heavy drinking in social context versus alone. *Addictive Behaviors* 27, 393-404.

Demant, J., Jarvinen, M. (2006). Constructing maturity through alcohol experience – Focus group interviews with teenagers. Addiction Research and Theory, December, 14(6), 589-602.

Department of Health and Human Services (2000) Measuring Healthy Days. Population Assessment of Heath-related Quality of Life. Centre for Disease Control and Prevention. National Center for Chronic Disease Prevention and Health Promotion. Division of Adult and Community Health. Atlanta, Georgia.

Dietary Guidelines for Americans 2005. U.S. Department of Health and Human Services, U.S. Department of Agriculture www.healthierus.gov/dietaryguidelines , p.44

Engels, R., Knibbe R., A. (2000). Young people's alchol consumption from a European perspective: risk and benefits. *European Journal of Clinical Nutrition*, 54, Suppl 1, S52-S55

Forsyth, A., Barnard, M. (2000). Preferred drinking locations of Scottish adolescents. *Health and Place* 6, 105-115.

Hellandsjo Bu, E., T., Watten, R., G., Foxcroft, D., R., Ingebrigtsen, J., E., Relling, G. (2002). Teenage alcohol and intoxication debut: the impact of family socialization factors, living area and participation in organized sports. *Alcohol and Alcoholism* Vol, 37, No, 1, 74-80.

Hingson, R., Heeren, T., Winter, M., R., Wechsler, H. (2003). Early age of first drunkenness as a factor in college students' unplanned and unprotected sex attributable to drink. *Pediatrics*, Vol. 111, No. 1, 34-40.

Hingson, R., Winter, M., (2003). Age of drinking onset and alcohol-related crash involvement Epidemiology and Consequences of Drinking and Driving, Vol. 27, No. 1, 75.

Hoel, S., Eriksen, B., Breidablik H., J., Meland, E. (2004). Adolescent alcohol use, psychological health, and social integration. *Scand. J. Public Health* 32, 361-367

Jarvinen, M., Gundelach, P. (2007). Teenage drinking, symbolic capital and distinction. *Journal of Youth Studies,* Vol. 10, No. 1, February, 55-71.

Mazur, J., Woynarowska, B. (1999). Zdrowie młodzieży szkolnej w Polsce. Wypadki i urazy. Katedra Biomedycznych Podstaw Rozwoju i Wychowania, Warszawa, Wydział Pedagogiczny Uniwersytetu Warszawskiego.

Narodowy Program Profilaktyki i Rozwiązywania Problemów Alkoholowych 2006-2010. (National Programme of Alcohol Problems Prevention and Solving for years 2006-2010). http://www.parpa.pl/index.php?option=com_contentandtask=viewandid=19andItemid=5

Okulicz-Kozaryn, K., Borucka, A. (2008). Warsaw adolescent alcohol use in period of social change in Poland: Cluster analyses of five consecutive surveys, 1988 to 2004. *Addictive Behaviors*. Vol. 33, 439-450.

Okulicz-Kozaryn, K., Borucka, A., Brykczyńska, C. Pisarska, A. (2008). Używanie poszczególnych rodzajów narkotyków przez młodzież: wzory i konsekwencje. *Alkoholizm i Narkomania*, Vol. 21, No.4, 391-412.

Ostaszewski, K. (2008). Problemy nastolatków związane z używaniem substancji psychoaktywnych. *Alkoholizm i Narkomania*, Vol. 21, No. 4, 363-390

Ostaszewski, K., Bobrowski, K., Borucka, A., Kocoń, K., Okulicz-Kozaryn, K., Pisarska, A. (2005). Raport techniczny z realizacji projektu badawczego PN. Monitorowanie trendów używania substancji psychoaktywnych oraz wskaźników innych wybranych aspektów zdrowia psychicznego u młodzieży szkolnej. Warszawa. Instytut Psychiatrii i Neurologii.

Państwowa Agencja Rozwiązywania Problemów Alkoholowych (PARPA) Wyhamuj w porę. (2008). http://www.wyhamujwpore.pl/

Pedersen, W., Kolstad, A. (2000). Adolescent alcohol abstainers: traditional patterns in new groups. Acta Sociologica, Vol. 43, 219-233.

Pisarska, A., Ostaszewski, K. (2009) Over-the-counter medicine use among 9th grade students from Warsaw. The article was submitted to Pharmacoepidemiol Drug Saf

Pliner, P., Cappell, H. (1974). Modification of affective consequences of alcohol: a comparison of social and solitary drinking. *Journal of Abnormal Psychology,* Vol. 83, No. 4, 418-425.

The Scope of the Problem (2004/2005). Alcohol Research and Health, Vol. 28, No. 3, 111-120.

Senchak, M., Leonard, K., E., Greene, B., W. (1998). Alcohol use among college students as a function of their typical social drinking context. *Psychology of Addictive Behaviors*, Vol. 12, No. 1, 62-70.

Sierosławski, J. (2007). Używanie alkoholu i narkotyków przez młodzież szkolną. Raport z ogólnopolskich badań ankietowych zrealizowanych w 2007 r. Warszawa, IPiN. http://parpa.pl/download/Raport%20ESPAD%202007%20Polska1.pdf (accessed 2 January 2009)

Sierosławski, J. (2003). Używanie alkoholu i narkotyków przez młodzież szkolną. Raport z ogólnopolskich badań ankietowych zrealizowanych w 2003 r. Eurpoejksi Program Badań Ankietowych w szkołach ESPAD. Warszawa, IPiN,

Stępień, E. (2004). Jakość życia młodych dorosłych a intensywność picia alkoholu w dorastaniu i we wczesnej dorosłości (badania katamnestyczne). *Alkoholizm i Narkomania,* 17 (1-2), 77-90.

Stępień, E. (2001). Doświadczenia i przekonania związane z alkoholem z okresu dorastania a intensywność picia alkoholu przez młodych dorosłych. Badania katamnestyczne. *Alkoholizm i Narkomania*, 14), 289-300.

Rossow, I. (1996). Alcohol-related violence: the impact of drinking pattern and drinking context. Addiction, 91(11), 1651-1661.

Tucker, J., S., Ellickson, P., L., Collins, R., L., Klein, D., J. (2006). Does solitary substance use increase adolescents' risk for poor psychosocial and behavioral outcomes? A 9-year longitudinal study comparing solitary and social users. *Psychology of Addictive Behavior*, Vol. 20, No, 4, 363-372.

Wells, S., Graham, K., Speechley, M., Koval, J.J. (2005). Drinking patterns, drinking contexts and alcohol-related aggression among late adolescent and young adult drinkers. *Addiction,* 100, 933-944.

Williams, A., F. (1966). Social drinking, anxiety, and depression. *Journal of Personality and Social Psychology,* Vol. 6, 689-693

Wolniewicz-Grzelak, B. (1995). Badanie picia napojów alkoholowych przez młodzież arkuszem "Piwo, wino, wódka". *Alkoholizm i Narkomania,* Nr 2/19, 117-127.

Wolniewicz-Grzelak, B., Ostaszewski, K.(1983). Badanie środowisk szkolnych w zakresie zagrożenia uzależnieniem od środków odurzających. *Biuletyn Instytutu Psychoneurologicznego,* Nr 4(52), s. 68-82.

Zimmerman, M.A. and Schmeelk-Cone, K.H. (2003). A longitudinal analysis of adolescent substance use and school motivation among African American youth. *Journal of Research on Adolescence*, 13(2), 185-210.

In: Social Drinking: Uses, Abuses and Psychological Factors ISBN: 978-1-60876-219-4
Editors : K. T. Everly, E. M. Cosell, pp. 279-290 © 2010 Nova Science Publishers, Inc.

Chapter 8

PROTECTIVE BEHAVIORAL STRATEGIES AS A MECHANISM FOR REDUCING HIGH-RISK DRINKING AMONG COLLEGE STUDENTS

Matthew P. Martens and James G. Murphy
University of Memphis, Memphis, TN, USA

ABSTRACT

Protective behavioral strategies (PBS) are cognitive-behavioral strategies that can be used to reduce high-risk drinking and related negative consequences. Such strategies may be useful to include in intervention efforts targeted at college students, who have been identified as a population at-risk for dangerous alcohol consumption. The purposes of this chapter are therefore to (a) review the research on college student alcohol use, (b) address existing research findings on the relationship between PBS and college student drinking, (c) discuss ways in which PBS have been incorporated into clinical interventions, and (d) provide recommendations for future research and clinical efforts in the area.

INTRODUCTION

Over the past decade researchers have documented that alcohol use among college students represents a public health problem for both the students themselves and those with whom they come into contact. A considerable number of efforts have been undertaken that were designed to curb excessive drinking among college students, with mixed results. For example, broad mass marketing educational campaigns have generally been shown to not be effective at reducing heavy drinking (e.g., Wechsler et al., 2003), whereas individualized motivational approaches have shown some success (Carey, Scott-Sheldon, Carey, and DeMartini, 2007; Larimer and Cronce, 2007). The use of specific behavioral strategies for reducing substance use or related harms has been addressed quite a bit in the general alcohol treatment literature, but less so in the domain of college drinking. Recently, though, researchers in the area of college drinking have explored the construct of protective behavioral strategies (PBS), which have been defined as "behaviors that individuals can engage in while drinking alcohol in order to limit negative alcohol-related consequences" (Martens et al., 2004, p. 390). PBS can include behaviors designed to slow the consumption of alcohol (e.g., avoiding "chugging" or keeping up with others' alcohol consumption; avoiding drinking games), behaviors designed specifically to avoid alcohol-related harms (e.g., using a designated driver, knowing where one's drink has been at all times), and self-control or planning-based strategies designed to curb alcohol consumption (e.g., choosing in advance how much to drink in a given night). Although studies on this construct are just emerging, initial findings suggest that incorporating PBS into clinical interventions may serve to reduce or limit high-risk drinking among college students.

This chapter is organized into three major sections. We first provide an overview of the public health problem associated with college student drinking. Next, we discuss studies that have examined the relationship between PBS and alcohol use, including clinical trials that examined the construct as a mediator of intervention effectiveness. Finally, we examine possible future directions for research and clinical activities in the area of PBS.

THE PROBLEM OF COLLEGE STUDENT DRINKING

Over the past two decades a number of epidemiological studies have been conducted that provide a fairly clear and consistent picture regarding the alcohol use habits of college students in the United States. The four most comprehensive sources of data come from the Monitoring the Future Study (Johnston , O'Malley, Bachman, and Schulenberg, 2008), the American College Health Association's national survey (American College Health Association, 2007), the Core Institute's national survey (Core Institute, 2005), and Wechsler and colleagues' College Alcohol Study (Wechsler et al., 2002). Each study included a national sample of college students, with sample sizes ranging from 1,250 (Johnston et al., 2008) to 91,379 (American College Health Association, 2007).

Results from these surveys indicated that between 80.9% and 84.5% of college students reported using alcohol in the previous year (Core Institute, 2005; Johnston et al., 2008). The typical student averaged 5.81 drinks per week, with men consuming more drinks per week than women (8.60 vs. 3.95; Core Institute, 2005). Although these weekly drinking totals are relatively moderate, college students often consume all or most of these drinks in one or two occasion. This pattern of consuming large quantities of alcohol over relatively brief time periods can result in dangerously high blood alcohol content (Fournier, Ehrhart, Glindemann, and Geller, 2004). Thus, researchers and clinicians in the area of college drinking prevention are often more concerned with reducing heavy drinking episodes than with reducing total weekly consumption. A heavy drinking episode is typically defined as 5+ drinks in one sitting for men and either 4+ or 5+ drinks in one sitting for women, with studies indicating that between 41.1% and 44.4% of college students reported engaging in at least one heavy drinking episode in the preceding two weeks (Johnston et al, 2008; Wechsler et al., 2002). Heavy episodic drinking has been associated with increased likelihood of experiencing multiple alcohol-related negative consequences, such as problems with schoolwork, engaging in unplanned sexual activity, driving while intoxicated, and getting into trouble with the authorities (Wechsler, Lee, Kuo, and Lee, 2000).

Another way to gauge the public health problem of college student drinking is to specifically examine the prevalence of alcohol-related problems in this group. Research has shown that such problems can be severe, as each year among college students there are approximately 1,700 deaths, 500,000 unintentional injuries, and 600,000 assaults that can be attributed to alcohol-related causes (Hingson, Hereren, Winter, and Wechsler, 2005). Data from a national epidemiological survey on alcohol use indicated that approximately 20% of college students met past-year diagnostic criteria for alcohol abuse or dependence, and that college students were more likely than their non-college peers to meet criteria for alcohol dependence (Dawson, Grant, Stinson, and Chou, 2004). These findings are consistent with other research indicating that 15.6% of college students reported using alcohol at least 10 times in the preceding 30 days (American College Health Association, 2007), and 19.4% of college student drinkers reported experiencing at least five or more different alcohol-related consequences (Wechsler et al., 2000).

A final way to assess the public health impact of college student drinking involves its impact on other students not using alcohol, as research has indicated that heavy drinking college students negatively impact those with whom they interact. For example, one national survey found that two-thirds of college students reported at least one adverse effect from another student's drinking, such as being assaulted, experiencing unwanted sexual advances, and study or sleep interruptions (Wechsler, Moeykens, Davenport, Castillo, and Hansen, 1995). Among students who live in dorms or fraternity/sorority houses but either abstain from alcohol or report non-binge drinking, 29.2% indicated that they had been insulted or humiliated, 15.2% had their property damaged, and 8.7% had been assaulted as a result of others' drinking. A majority of the students (60.0%) reported that they had their sleep or study interrupted as a result of others' drinking, and almost half (47.6%) reported having to care for an intoxicated student. Heavy drinking college students can negatively impact their academic institutions as well, in the form of property damage and time/energy needed to devote to problems caused by such individuals (Perkins, 2002). Therefore, even though the majority of college students either do not drink or generally do so in a responsible manner, those who do drink heavily are at-risk for negative health and social consequences to themselves, their peers, and those who work in their academic institution. Designing and implementing effective interventions for at-risk college drinkers is thus an important public health matter.

PBS and College Student Drinking

The idea of teaching individuals specific behavioral strategies that will help them reduce their alcohol use is not a new concept. Since the 1970s a number of studies have examined the effectiveness of "behavioral self-control training" on reducing alcohol consumption, with findings generally indicating that this treatment is effective among problem drinkers (Walters, 2000). One component of most self-control training treatments involves teaching specific behavioral strategies designed to reduce alcohol consumption and associated negative consequences. Although not referred to as "PBS," in this chapter we will use the term to refer to the behavioral strategies discussed in these studies. In general, these interventions addressed implementing specific PBS such as avoiding drinking straight spirits, taking smaller drinks, pacing one's drinking, and limiting total consumption (e.g., Alden, 1988; Foy, Nunn, and Rychtarik, 1984; Graber and Miller, 1988; Rychtarik, Foy, Scott, Lokey, and Prue, 1987; Sanchez-Craig, Annis, Bornet, and MacDonald, 1984).

Empirically supported interventions specific to college student drinkers have also incorporated the teaching of specific PBS. For example, the Brief Alcohol Screening and Intervention for College Students program (BASICS; Dimeff, Baer, Kivlahan, and Marlatt, 1999) incorporates behavioral strategies such as drink monitoring, slowing the pace of one's drinking, and alternating alcohol and non-alcoholic beverages. This intervention, or programs modeled after it, has been shown to reduce alcohol consumption and alcohol-related negative consequences among college student drinkers (e.g., Borsari and Carey, 2000; Larimer et al., 2001; Marlatt et al., 1998).

Although research has indicated that treatments that include the teaching of PBS are effective, it is generally not possible to determine from these studies if using the strategies themselves was associated with reduced alcohol use and/or alcohol-related problems. There are two somewhat related reasons for this state of affairs. First, researchers typically did not assess the degree to which participants used PBS to limit their alcohol use. Without such an assessment it was impossible to determine even the simple bivariate relationships between PBS use and alcohol use, much less if use of such strategies impacted treatment outcomes. Second, the aforementioned interventions that included instruction on PBS incorporated multiple additional components as well. For example, because most college drinkers do not view their drinking as a problem, interventions with college students generally include motivational enhancement components like reviewing personalized feedback on drinking levels relative to normative standards and engaging in decisional balance exercises regarding the pros and cons of drinking (e.g., Dimeff et al., 1999). Similarly, behavioral self-control treatments conducted with other populations also included components like blood alcohol discrimination training, thought stopping, and functional analysis exercises (e.g., Alden, 1988; Foy et al., 1984; Graber and Miller, 1988; Walters, 2000). We are aware of no studies that dismantled the effects of the components of these interventions, thereby leaving the effects specific to PBS unknown.

More recently, though, researchers have begun to develop and utilize measures that attempt to quantify the use of PBS, examine the specific relationships between PBS and alcohol use/alcohol-related problems, and address the role of PBS in treatment outcomes. The bulk of these studies have been conducted with the college student population, and are reviewed in more detail below.

Measuring PBS. Perhaps the first effort at formally measuring PBS was conducted by Werch and Gorman (1986), who developed the Self Control Questionnaire (SCQ) to assess behavioral self-control practices like drinking slowly, drinking in small sips, and setting drinking limits. This scale was infrequently used in the years after it was developed, but several groups of college drinking researchers have begun to use the measure in recent years (e.g., Barnett, Murphy, Colby, and Monti, 2007). One limitation of the SCQ, though, is that there exists fairly limited psychometric information regarding the measure. We could locate only one study whose primary purpose was to assess the reliability and validity of the measure (Werch and Gorman, 1986), and several contemporary tests of validity have not been examined with the SCQ (e.g., no confirmatory factor analytic studies have been conducted). Other measures of PBS, such as the 10-item measure on the National College Health Assessment (American College Health Association, 2007) and a 10-item measure used by

Benton and his colleagues (Benton et al., 2004) also have either questionable or largely unknown psychometric properties (see Martens et al., 2005).

There have been two measures that have been recently developed that have been subjected to more rigorous and comprehensive psychometric analyses. Martens and his colleagues (2005; 2007b) developed a 15-item measure of PBS that encompasses three subscales: Stopping/Limiting Drinking (e.g., "Alternate alcoholic and non-alcoholic drinks"), Manner of Drinking (e.g., "Avoid drinking games"), and Serious Harm Reduction (e.g., "Use a designated driver"). Results from an exploratory factor analysis provided initial support for this factor structure (Martens et al., 2005), which was subsequently replicated via confirmatory factor analysis in an independent sample (Martens et al., 2007b). Findings from these and other studies have also provided support for the convergent validity of the measure in the form of theoretically consistent relationships with alcohol-related variables (described in more detail below). Sugarman and Carey (2007) also developed a measure that assesses PBS, which they termed "drinking control strategies." The three subscales that emerged on this measure were labeled "Selective Avoidance" (e.g., choosing not to participate in drinking games), "Strategies While Drinking" (e.g., keeping track of the number of drinks consumed), and "Alternatives" (e.g., using other strategies to reduce stress). Their study involved rigorous and comprehensive item generation procedures (e.g., comprehensive literature review, a pilot study examining college students' drinking control strategies), exploratory factor analysis, and multiple tests of convergent validity. The exploratory factor analysis accounted for a considerable portion of the variability in the items (92.9%), and the convergent validity tests supported the measure's utility in predicting alcohol use and related problems (described in more detail below).

In sum, researchers and clinicians interested in assessing PBS use now have several self-report assessments that have at least promising empirical support as valid measures of the construct. Although additional studies addressing the psychometric properties of these measures are warranted, their existence has allowed researchers to begin to examine the relationship between PBS use and variables like alcohol use and alcohol-related problems.

The Relationship Between PBS and Alcohol Use/Problems. A number of studies have shown that among college students there is a direct relationship between PBS use and alcohol use. Several studies (e.g., Benton et al., 2004; Martens et al., 2007b; Sugarman and Carey, 2007) have examined the simple bivariate correlations between PBS use and alcohol consumption, with results generally suggesting that greater PBS use was associated with less alcohol consumption. Benton et al. (2004) reported correlations of -.44 and -.51 ($ps < .01$) in their two samples between use of PBS and number of drinks consumed when "partying," Martens et al. (2007b) reported correlations of -.15 to -.33 ($ps < .01$) between the PBS subscales on their measure and two indices of alcohol use (drinks per week and heavy episodic drinking), and Sugarman and Carey (2007) reported correlations of -.17 to -.19 ($ps < .05$) between two of the subscales on their measure and two indices of alcohol use (drinks per week and average blood alcohol content). They did, however, also report a finding that was contrary to other studies of PBS, in that one of the subscales on their measure (Strategies While Drinking) was actually positively correlated with measures of alcohol use. Although future research on the measure is needed, it is possible that this particularl subscale is not tapping into clear protective strategies. For example, one item assessed activities that might actually promote alcohol use (dancing, playing pool), while other items might be less relevant to college students (e.g., limiting drinking to certain nights of the week, which most college student drinkers already do). Finally, one study (Martens et al., 2005) conducted a more rigorous analysis of the relationship between PBS use and alcohol use by examining their relationship after controlling for the effects of relevant demographic variables (e.g., gender, body weight, age at first drink). They found that scores on their PBS measure accounted for an additional 10% to 18% of the variance ($p < .01$) on four measures of alcohol use (drinks per week, peak number of drinks on a single occasion, heavy episodic drinking, and drinking frequency). Thus, research generally suggests that higher self-reported PBS use is associated with less alcohol use among college students.

Although the aforementioned associations with drinking provide support for the clinical utility of PBS, the relationship between PBS use and alcohol-related problems or negative consequences may be a more meaningful indication of their centrality in alcohol abuse prevention. First, some PBS items explicitly measure drinking practices (e.g., deciding to drinks less or to set drinking limits), which might artificially inflate relations with drinking. Second, the primary goal of most intervention for college drinking, and especially the PBS component of these interventions, is to reduce harmful consequences associated with drinking. Many protective behaviors will result in a drinking reduction, but some (e.g., planning ahead to avoiding drinking and driving) could reduce harm without a concomitant change in drinking. The most rigorous research examining this question has been several studies that examined the relationship between PBS use and alcohol-related problems after controlling for the effects of alcohol consumption (Benton et al., 2004; Delva et al., 2004; Martens et al., 2004; Martens et al., 2007b). Such a design isolates the potentially unique contribution of PBS to harm reduction efforts. Two of these studies (Delva et al., 2004; Martens et al., 2004) examined the relationship between PBS use and likelihood of experiencing alcohol-related problems with the problems variable(s) coded categorically (i.e., yes/no). Delva et al. (2004) examined the relationship between PBS use and the likelihood of experiencing any negative alcohol-related consequence in the preceding year. After controlling for the effects of several demographic variables and frequency of heavy episodic drinking, they found that women in the lowest three quartiles of PBS use were 6.4, 6.6, and 3.2 times more likely ($p < .05$) to experience an alcohol-related problem than women in the highest quartile of PBS use. For men, though, there was no relationship between PBS use and likelihood of experiencing an alcohol-related problem. Martens et al. (2004) conducted their analyses separately for individual consequences, and found that greater PBS use was associated with less likelihood of experiencing the following alcohol-related problems in the previous 12-months: physically injuring someone else, being in a fight, doing something later regretted, having memory loss, and having unprotected sex. They compared the likelihood of experiencing each consequence between participants whose PBS value indicated that they "usually" used each strategy versus those who indicated that they "rarely" used each strategy, and found that the latter were 1.93 to 8.40 times more likely to report experiencing the individual negative consequence. The other two studies (Benton et al., 2004; Martens et al., 2007b) used a continuous measure of alcohol-related problems. Both studies found that after controlling for demographic factors (e.g., gender, body weight) and alcohol use, PBS use was associated with a statistically significant increase in variance accounted for on their measures of alcohol-related problems. Students who reported more frequent use of strategies reported fewer problems related to drinking even after taking into account consumption patterns. Together, this body of research provides strong support for the role of PBS in minimizing alcohol-related harm among students who choose to drink.

Predictors of PBS Use. Given the importance of PBS to minimizing alcohol-related harm, researchers have begun to investigate factors associated with students' use of PBS. One recent study found that in addition to the expected relationships with alcohol use itself, gender and having a problem drinker parent were associated with PBS use (women and those without a problem drinking parent reported greater PBS use) (Walters, Roudsari, Vader, and Harris, 2007). Thus, inadequate use of PBS may be one way in which family history confers risk for alcohol problems.

Associations between and Other Alcohol-Related Constructs Two studies have incorporated PBS use into more complex models of college student alcohol use, thereby addressing the manner in which PBS relate to other relevant constructs in understanding the phenomenon. In one study (Martens, Ferrier, and Cimini, 2007a) the researchers were interested in determining if PBS use might explain why certain types of drinking motives were associated with alcohol consumption and related harms (see Kuntsche, Knibbe, Gmel, and Engels, 2005). In this study the researchers found that PBS use mediated the relationship between positively reinforcing motives (e.g., drinking to have a good time or enhance pleasure) and alcohol use/problems, but that it did not mediate the relationship between negatively reinforcing motives and alcohol use/problems. This was primarily due to the fact that only positively reinforcing motives were associated with PBS use. These findings suggest that PBS-based interventions may be particularly effective for individuals who drink primarily to increase positive affect, rather than reduce negative affect. A second study (Martens et al., 2008) also examined PBS as a mediator variable, this time in terms of the relationship between depressive symptoms and alcohol-related problems. The authors hypothesized that depressed individuals would be less likely to engage in protective behaviors when drinking, and that the absence of PBS would account for the higher rates of drinking problems observed among depressed college drinkers. The researchers found that PBS use did in fact mediate this relationship, such that higher depressive symptoms were associated with less PBS use, which was associated with more alcohol-related problems. Although both studies were limited by the cross-sectional nature of the data, they do provide further support for the importance of PBS in alcohol problems, and also identify depressed mood and drinking for negatively reinforcing reasons as a risk factor for low levels of PBS

PBS and Intervention Outcomes. An important unanswered question from the aforementioned studies is whether or not PBS use actually causes reductions in alcohol use and/or alcohol-related problems. No study using an experimental design has focused on increasing or decreasing PBS use, making conclusions about causality impossible. This is a particularly important issue when considering how PBS can be incorporated into clinical interventions. However, several recent clinical trials have examined PBS use as a potential mediator of the effectiveness of brief motivational interventions (BMIs) among college student drinkers. These longitudinal studies provide a more thorough evaluation of the causal role of PBS in decreasing alcohol use and problems.

There have been three clinical trials that have examined whether or not PBS mediates the effectiveness of brief interventions among college student drinkers. In a trial that found that a BMI plus personalized feedback was more effective than a BMI without personalized feedback, a feedback-only condition, and an assessment-only condition, Walters and his colleagues (2009) did not find that use of PBS mediated the intervention main effects. The authors of this study noted, though, that their intervention did not specifically target PBS, which raises some questions regarding whether or not PBS should have been examined as a potential mediator. In contrast, findings from studies that did specifically target PBS have shown promising results. Larimer and colleagues (2007) examined the efficacy of an intervention that involved mailing participants personalized feedback about their drinking habits. This feedback included a summary of current drinking behavior, how that behavior compared to the typical student's behavior at his or her university (i.e., social norms information), information about alcohol-related expectancies, and instructions that encouraged the use of several PBS. Results at a one-year follow-up indicated that students in the personalized feedback condition reported less alcohol use than students in the assessment-only control condition, and that these intervention effects were mediated by PBS use. Students in the intervention condition reported greater PBS use at follow-up than students in the control condition, PBS use at follow-up was associated with alcohol use at follow-up, and the direct effects of the intervention condition on follow-up alcohol use were no longer statistically significant when controlling for follow-up PBS use. Surprisingly, the results also indicated that the intervention did not impact another theoretical mediator, namely social norms. Thus, in this trial PBS use served as a causal factor in explaining the efficacy of the intervention. Similar findings were reported by Barnett et al., (2007), in a trial examining the efficacy of a single-session in person BMI versus a computer-delivered intervention. The in-person BMI included, among other components, feedback on the specific PBS that participants' reported using to reduce alcohol-related harm and suggestions for additional PBS. Results indicated that the in-person BMI resulted in fewer drinks per drinking day than the computer delivered intervention at the 12-month follow-up, and that this effect was mediated by increases in PBS use at the 3-month follow-up. It should be noted, though, that PBS use mediated intervention effects for only one alcohol consumption variable, as the BMI was not more effective than the computer delivered intervention at reducing drinking days, heavy drinking days, or estimated BAC. Nonetheless, the findings from these latter two trials suggest that targeting PBS use in brief interventions with college students may result in reduced drinking among that population.

FUTURE DIRECTIONS

Teaching drinkers practical skills to make better decisions about when, where, and how much to drink, with whom to drink, how to plan for safer drinking evenings, when to stop drinking, and how to stop drinking is an intuitive means of reducing the net harm associated drinking. Such advice is now included in many cognitive behavioral alcohol treatments, brief motivational interventions, and public health level informational campaigns. Only recently have researchers begun to measure PBS and systematically examine their relation to drinking and treatment outcome. The development of psychometrically sound and multidimensional measures of PBS has set the stage for research that might more conclusively established the relevance of PBS to drinking outcomes, identify factors associated with engaging in protective behaviors, and develop intervention approaches for maximizing the potency of PBS within alcohol interventions. The following sections provide suggestions for each of these future research directions.

Specifying the Relations between Specific PBS and Drinking Outcomes. Existing PBS research has generally measured retrospective associations between PBS (either an entire measure or a subscale comprised of multiple behaviors) and global drinking outcomes (aggregated drinking amounts and alcohol problem totals over a month or some other timeframe). Although useful for establishing the general relevance of PBS and designing measures, these designs are incapable of isolating the specific behaviors that protect against specific alcohol related outcomes (e.g., drinking and driving, blacking out, vomiting). Prospective studies that more carefully measure the occurrence of specific PBS and drinking patterns/outcomes, such as ecological momentary assessments or other "real time" assessment strategies, can provide more specific information regarding the key protective behaviors that students engage in to avoid heavy drinking or to avoid negative consequences on those occasions when they do drink heavily. Such studies would be of particular use to clinicians because they may identify specific strategies that are most important to focus on in the context of clinical interventions.

Understanding Why Students Do or Do Not Engage in PBS. Although interventions have understandably attempted to encourage students to increase engagement in PBS, these efforts have not been guided by research on the naturalistic predictors of PBS use. There may be several levels of relevant predictors: individual difference variables such as impulsivity or subjective response to alcohol; state variables such as mood, craving, and intoxication from other drugs; cognitive variables such as risk perceptions and outcome expectancies; and situational factors such as the drinking location or the number and sex of peers, specific motives for drinking, and the presence of moderate drinking peer models. Research is needed to understand how these and other factors might interact to predict students' successful (or unsuccessful) use of PBS. This knowledge can then be used to guide the development of intervention approaches that can effectively increase PBS.

Developing Interventions to Increase PBS. Currently PBS are included in many intervention approaches for college drinkers, but no study has investigated approaches for specifically increasing engagement in PBS. For example, traditional cognitive-behavioral interventions for heavy drinking or alcohol dependence have favored in-vivo practice of moderate drinking or exposure to a moderate drinking model. Brief interventions typically target PBS by providing a generic list of PBS that may or may not be personalized in the context of a discussion with a clinician. To our knowledge only one study actually provided feedback on the student's reported PBS, along with a discussion of those and other potential PBS (Barnett et al., 2007). Developing effective strategies for increasing PBS could set the stage for dismantling studies that identify whether or not PBS in an active ingredient in efficacious drinking interventions. Future research might also explore innovative strategies for increasing PBS in groups of high risk students such as first year students, athletes, and students residing in fraternity or sorority houses. Social norms marketing, normative feedback, peer modeling, and education campaigns might create a culture that supports PBS.

CONCLUSION

Although encouraging college students who are drinking at unsafe levels to use strategies to limit such drinking is not a new phenomenon, it has only been recently that researchers have begun to explore how using PBS is related to less alcohol consumption and fewer alcohol-related problems among this group. Initial studies in this area have been promising, as research has demonstrated an inverse relationship between PBS use and both alcohol use and alcohol-related problems. Several promising findings have also emerged from clinical trials that suggest that incorporating PBS into interventions with college student drinkers may be an important aspect of successful outcomes. More research on this topic is needed, of course, but we believe that the combination of assessing for, providing feedback on, and engaging students in a discussion of PBS use can be an important component of effective treatment and prevention efforts within the population of college student drinkers.

References

Alden, L. E. (1988). Behavioral self-management controlled-drinking strategies in a context of secondary prevention. *Journal of Consulting and Clinical Psychology, 56,* 280-286.

American College Health Association (2007). American College Health Association National College Health Assessment Spring 2006 reference group data report (abridged). *Journal of American College Health, 55,* 195-206.

Barnett, N. P., Murphy, J. G., Colby, S. M., and Monti, P. M. (2007). Efficacy of counselor vs. computer-delivered intervention with mandated college students. *Addictive Behaviors, 32,* 2529-2548.

Benton, S. L., Schmidt, J. L., Newton, F. B., Shin, K., Benton, S. A., and Newton, D. W. (2004). College student protective strategies and drinking consequences. *Journal of Studies on Alcohol, 65,* 115-121.

Borsari, B., and Carey, K. B. (2000). Effects of a brief motivational intervention with college student drinkers. *Journal of Consulting and Clinical Psychology, 68,* 728-733.

Carey, K. B., Scott-Sheldon, L. A. J., Carey, M. P., and DeMartini, K. S. (2007). Individual-level interventions to reduce college student drinking: A meta-analytic review. *Addictive Behaviors, 32,* 2469-2494.

Core Institute (2005). *Results-2005.* Retrieved April 10, 2009, from Southern Illinois University-Carbondale, The Core Institute web site: http://www.siu.edu/~coreinst/.

Dawson, D. A., Grant, B. F., Stinson, F. S., and Chou, P. S. (2004). Another look at heavy episodic drinking and alcohol use disorders among college and noncollege youth. *Journal of Studies on Alcohol, 65,* 477-488.

Delva, J., Smith, M. P., Howell, R. L., Harrison, D. F., Wilke, D., and Jackson, D. L. (2004). A study of the relationship between protective behaviors and drinking consequences among undergraduate college students. *Journal of American College Health, 53,* 19-26.

Dimeff, L. A., Baer, J. S., Kivlahan, D. R., and Marlatt, G. A. (1999). *Brief alcohol screening and intervention for college students: A harm reduction approach.* New York: The Guilford Press.

Foy, D. W., Nunn, L. B., and Rychtgarik, R. G. (1984). Broad-spectrum behavioral treatment for chronic alcoholics: Effects of training controlled drinking skills. *Journal of Consulting and Clinical Psychology, 52,* 218-230.

Fournier, A. K., Ehrhart, I. J., Glindemann, K. E., and Geller, E. S. (2004). Intervening to decrease alcohol use at university parties: Differential reinforcement of intoxication level. *Behavior Modification, 28,* 167–181.

Graber, R. A., and Miller, W. R. (1988). Abstinence or controlled drinking goals for problem drinkers: A randomized clinical trial. *Psychology of Addictive Behaviors, 2,* 20-33.

Hingson, R., Heeren, T., Winter, M., and Wechsler, H. (2005). Magnitude of alcohol-related mortality and morbidity among U.S. college students ages 18-24: Changes from 1998-2001. *Annual Review of Public Health, 26,* 259-279.

Johnston, L. D., O'Malley, P. M., Bachman, J. G., and Schulenberg, J. E. (2008). *Monitoring the Future national survey results on drug use, 1975–2007: Volume II, College students and adults ages 19–45* (NIH Publication No. 08-6418B). Bethesda, MD: National Institute on Drug Abuse.

Kuntsche, E., Knibbe, R., Gmel, G., and Engels, R. (2005). Why do young people drink? A review of drinking motives. *Clinical Psychology Review, 25,* 841-861.

Larimer, M. E., and Cronce, J. M. (2007). Identification, prevention, and treatment revisited: Individual-focused college drinking prevention 1999-2006. *Addictive Behaviors, 32,* 2439-2468.

Larimer, M. E., Lee, C. M., Kilmer, J. R., Fabiano, P. M., Stark, C. B., Geisner, I. M., et al. (2007). Personalized mailed feedback for college drinking prevention: A randomized clinical trial. *Journal of Consulting and Clinical Psychology, 75,* 285-293.

Larmier, M. E., Turner, A. P., Anderson, B. K., Fader, J. S., Kilmer, J. R., Palmer, R. S., et al. (2001). Evaluating a brief alcohol intervention with fraternities. *Journal of Studies on Alcohol, 62,* 370-380.

Marlatt, G. A., Baer, J. S., Kivlahan, D. R., Dimeff, L. A., Larimer, M. E., Quigley, L. A., et al. (1998). Screening and brief intervention for high-risk college student drinkers: Results from a 2-year follow-up assessment. *Journal of Consulting and Clinical Psychology, 66,* 604-615.

Martens, M. P., Ferrier, A. G., and Cimini, M. D. (2007a). Do protective behavioral strategies mediate the relationship between drinking motives and alcohol use in college students? *Journal of Studies on Alcohol and Drugs, 68,* 106-114.

Martens, M. P., Ferrier, A. G., Sheehy, M. J., Corbett, K., Anderson, D. A., and Simmons, A. (2005). Development of the Protective Behavioral Strategies Survey. *Journal of Studies on Alcohol, 66,* 698-705.

Martens, M. P., Martin, J. L., Hatchett, E. S., Fowler, R. M., Fleming, K. M., Karakashian, M. A., et al. (2008). Protective behavioral strategies and the relationship between depressive symptoms and alcohol-related negative consequences among college students. *Journal of Counseling Psychology, 55,* 535-541.

Martens, M. P., Pedersen, E. R., LaBrie, J. W., Ferrier, A. G., and Cimini, M. D. (2007b). Measuring alcohol-related protective behavioral strategies among college students: Further examination of the Protective Behavioral Strategies Scale. *Psychology of Addictive Behaviors, 21,* 307-315.

Martens, M. P., Taylor, K. K., Damann, K. M., Page, J. C., Mowry, E. S., and Cimini, M. D. (2004). Protective factors when drinking alcohol and their relationship to negative alcohol-related consequences. *Psychology of Addictive Behaviors, 18,* 390-393.

Perkins, H. W. (2002). Social norms and the prevention of alcohol misuse in collegiate contexts. *Journal of Studies on Alcohol, 14,* 164-172.

Rychtarik, R. G., Foy, D. W., Scott, T., Lokey, L., and Prue, D. M. (1987). Five-six-year follow-up of broad-spectrum behavioral treatment for alcoholism: Effects of training controlled drinking skills. *Journal of Consulting and Clinical Psychology, 55,* 106-108.

Sanchez-Craig, M., Annis, H. M., Bornet, A. R., and MacDonald, K. R. (1984). Random assignment to abstinence and controlled drinking: Evaluation of a cognitive-behavioral program for problem drinkers. *Journal of Consulting and Clinical Psychology, 52,* 390-403.

Sugarman, D. E., and Carey, K. B. (2007). The relationship between drinking control strategies and college student alcohol use. *Psychology of Addictive Behaviors, 21,* 338-345.

Walters, G. D. (2000). Behavioral self-control training for problem drinkers: A meta-analysis of randomized control studies. *Behavior Therapy, 31,* 135-149.

Walters, S. T., Roudsari, B. S., Vader, A. M., and Harris, R. T. (2007). Correlates of protective behavior utilization among heavy-drinking college students. *Addictive Behaviors, 32,* 2633-2644.

Walters, S. T., Vader, A. M., Harris, T. R., Field, C. A., and Jouriles, E. N. (2009). Dismantling motivational interviewing and feedback for college drinkers: A randomized clinical trial. *Journal of Consulting and Clinical Psychology, 77,* 64-73.

Wechsler, H., Lee, J. E., Kuo, M., and Lee, H. (2000). College binge drinking in the 1990s: A continuing health problem. *Journal of American College Health, 48,* 199-210.

Wechsler, H., Lee, J .E., Kuo, M., Seibring, M., Nelson, T. F., and Lee, H. (2002). Trends in college binge drinking during a period of increased prevention efforts. *Journal of American College Health, 50,* 203-217.

Wechsler, H., Moeykens, B., Davenport, A., Castillo, S. and Hansen, J. (1995). The adverse impact of heavy episodic drinkers on other college students. *Journal of Studies on Alcohol, 56,* 628-634.

Wechsler, H., Nelson, T. F., Lee, J. E., Seibring, M., Lewis, C., and Keeling, R. P. (2003). Perception and reality: A national evaluation of social norms marketing interventions to reduce college students' heavy alcohol use. *Journal of Studies on Alcohol, 64,* 484-494.

Werch, C. E., and Gorman, D. R. (1986). Factor analysis of internal and external self-control practices for alcohol consumption. *Psychological Reports, 59,* 1207-1213.

In: Social Drinking: Uses, Abuses and Psychological Factors ISBN: 978-1-60876-219-4
Editors : K. T. Everly, E. M. Cosell, pp. 291-304 © 2010 Nova Science Publishers, Inc.

Chapter 9

ALCOHOL CUES, ALCOHOL EXPECTANCIES, AND AGGRESSION

Melissa Mayer and Kenneth Abrams[1]
Department of Psychology, Carleton College, Northfield, MN

The scientific community has long been aware of the relation between alcohol consumption and aggression through anecdotal and experimental evidence. Correlational studies have linked alcohol consumption to an increased likelihood of committing acts of aggression, including spousal abuse, sexual assault, and murder (see Bushman and Cooper, 1990). Further, a meta-analysis of thirty experimental studies on alcohol and aggression supported a causal relationship between alcohol consumption and aggressive behavior (Bushman and Cooper, 1990). By examining rates of crime in which alcohol was involved, Cook and Moore (1993) predicted that if alcohol consumption per capita decreased by 10%, there would be a 1% decrease in homicide, a 6% decrease in sexual assault, a 6% decrease in assault, and a 9% decrease in robberies nationwide. This potential for the reduction of violent crime offers a compelling argument for the continuation of research into the mechanisms through which alcohol increases the propensity to aggress.

Despite the growing body of evidence that alcohol consumption facilitates aggression, the effect appears to be more complicated than pure psychopharmacology. That alcohol influences aggressive behavior appears to be at least partially due to the anticipated effects of alcohol, as placebos can produce behavioral changes that reflect a person's expectations (Begue, et al., 2009). In particular, people who believe that they have consumed alcohol have been shown to engage in greater retaliation against an aggressive confederate (Begue, et al., 2009). Such findings support the notion that the mere belief that one has consumed alcohol contributes significantly to the behavioral effects of alcohol consumption.

Recent experimental efforts have looked beyond the placebo effect to examine the extent to which cues that prime alcohol expectancies, in the absence of alcohol consumption itself, can influence aggressive behavior. Of course, the propensity of alcohol consumption to

1 Correspondence concerning this chapter should be addressed to Kenneth Abrams, Department of Psychology, One North College St., Carleton College, Northfield, MN 55057, Phone: (507) 222-4380. Fax: (507) 222-7005. Email: kabrams@carleton.edu.

increase aggressive behavior is not consistent across the population, as the majority of people who consume alcohol do not aggress (Borders, Barnwell, and Earleywine, 2007). While some of this variance can be explained by physiological differences, there is also evidence that cognitive processes moderate the link between alcohol consumption and aggression (Bartholow and Heinz, 2006). Alcohol outcome expectancies (or simply "alcohol expectancies"), in particular, may partially account for individual differences in the alcohol consumption – aggression link (Goldman, 1999).

ALCOHOL EXPECTANCIES

Alcohol expectancies are beliefs about the outcomes of drinking on future behavior, emotions, physiology, and cognition. They exist in long-term memory, are formed through past personal or vicarious experiences that a person has had with alcohol (Goldman, 1999), and predict behavior following exposure to alcohol or alcohol-related cues (Friedman, McCarthy, Bartholow, and Hicks, 2007; Friedman, McCarthy, Forster, and Denzler, 2005). When a person encounters a context that they associate with alcohol, expectancies become available (or "activated") so as to guide the person's behavior (Goldman and Darkes, 2004).

Alcohol expectancies can be measured using questionnaires such as the Alcohol Expectancies Questionnaire (AEQ; Goldman and Brown, 2003). Such questionnaires contain lists of outcomes that could result from the consumption of alcohol, and participants are asked to indicate whether they agree or disagree that alcohol is associated with that particular outcome (Jones, Corbin, and Fromme, 2001). Using these questionnaires, past studies have found correlations between a range of specific alcohol expectancies and drinking behaviors. Prospective studies suggest that expectancies predict future drinking behavior, even among children who have never consumed alcohol (Goldman, Darkes, and Boca, 1999). The effect is bidirectional, as ongoing experiences with alcohol also alter expectancies (Leigh and Stacy, 2004).

Holding more generally negative expectancies is associated with abstention from alcohol, while holding more generally positive expectancies is associated with a higher frequency and quantity of alcohol consumption (Leigh and Stacy, 2004). The evidence so strongly supports the relationship between expectancies and drinking, that some researchers have recommended a cessation of simple correlational studies and instead called for further investigation into moderators of this relationship (Goldman, et al., 1999). Of particular importance to researchers now is an exploration of the contexts in which alcohol expectancies are activated. It is important to study the ease with which specific alcohol expectancies can be activated with particular environmental cues, as decision-making regarding alcohol consumption appears to be heavily influenced by the real-time accessibility of particular alcohol expectancies (Leigh and Stacy, 1998).

PRIMING EFFECTS ON ALCOHOL EXPECTANCIES

A growing body of research is finding support for the theory that alcohol expectancies can be primed to influence cognition and behavior. In one study participants were subliminally primed with alcohol-related or non-alcohol-related words and then asked to rate the attractiveness and intelligence of a young women featured in a series of photographs (Friedman, et al., 2005). Subliminal priming by alcohol cues interacted with alcohol expectancies such that, for those with high sexuality alcohol expectancies, alcohol cuing increased attractiveness ratings and sexual desire. No significant differences in ratings were found between those with high and low sexuality alcohol expectancies for the control trait of intelligence. This finding suggests that there is specificity of the effects of alcohol expectancies on behavioral outcomes. In other words, alcohol expectancies do not affect global changes in perception but rather shape perceptions specific to the activated expectancy.

Another study that primed alcohol expectancies with alcohol-related words showed that the mere presence of contextual alcohol cues can activate two disparate alcohol expectancies – tension reduction and aggression – and that this activation alters behavior (Friedman, et al., 2007). Of particular relevance to this chapter, following near-subliminal exposure to alcohol-related words, participants with stronger aggression alcohol expectancies displayed greater hostility to a stranger in an experimentally engineered dispute. For both Friedman studies, the specific alcohol expectancy manipulated significantly predicted behavior, whereas other expectancies (e.g. sociability and sexual arousal) did not. This specificity provides evidence that alcohol cues can promote varied behavioral outcomes, depending on which expectancies are activated by the task or situation in which participants are placed.

A recent study demonstrated that alcohol expectancies moderate the effect of alcohol consumption on aggressive behavior and hostility (Borders, et al., 2007). In particular, the authors found that those who expect alcohol to cause greater aggression display more aggressive behaviors as well as more hostile feelings after consuming alcohol. Additionally, typical alcohol consumption interacted with expectancies such that, for those individuals who held low or medium aggressive expectancies, high levels of typical alcohol consumption were associated with increased alcohol-related hostility. Individuals who held high aggression alcohol expectancies reported the highest alcohol-related hostility, regardless of typical alcohol consumption. These findings suggest that individuals with high aggression alcohol expectancies are more likely to exhibit alcohol-related aggression regardless of typical consumption.

Experimental studies support the notion that alcohol cues interact with alcohol expectancies to influence the evaluation of another person's hostility. In one study, experimenters primed participants with alcohol-related or non-alcohol-related advertisements and had participants rate the hostility of a character in a person perception task (Bartholow and Heinz, 2006). The person perception task, developed by Srull and Wyer (1979), presents participants with a fictional character engaged in a series of ambiguous behaviors and asks participants to rate the character on the relevant character trait (hostility in this case). Among participants with high and moderate aggression alcohol expectancies, those who had been primed with the alcohol advertisements rated the ambiguous actions of the character as more hostile than did participants primed with non-alcoholic ads. Participants with low alcohol expectancies for aggression rated the actions as less hostile, regardless of priming condition (Bartholow and Heinz, 2006). The study also found no main effects of alcohol use or aggression-related problems on hostility ratings, suggesting that the higher hostility ratings actually were the product of a specific interaction between cues and expectancies.

The justification for using hostile impression formation as a measure of an aggressive state comes from a model that suggests aggressive concepts are part of a semantic network that can be activated from long-term memory storage just as other concepts stored in long-term memory are activated (Anderson and Bushman, 2002). Once aggressive thoughts are activated, the accessibility of aggressive concepts is increased, and people are more likely to judge others' ambiguous behaviors as hostile. Further evidence for this characteristic of aggression comes from a study of the effects of video games on aggression (Bushman and Anderson, 2002). Undergraduates were randomly assigned to play violent or nonviolent video games for a brief period and then given ambiguous stories about situations that could potentially trigger an aggressive response. They were then asked to indicate how the main character of the story would respond to the situation. Compared to the control group, students who had played violent video games expected a significantly more aggressive response from the character. Apparently, the increased accessibility of aggressive thoughts shaped the perceptions of the participants.

Spreading Activation Model vs. Motives Theory

Two primary theories have been put forth to explain the processes through which alcohol cuing activates aggressive behavior in the absence of consumption (Friedman, et al., 2007). One theory attributes the effect to the spreading activation of concepts. In this "spreading activation model," first described by Collins and Loftus (1975), concepts are represented as "nodes" that are connected to other nodes through a network. When a concept is activated in long-term memory, the activation spreads to linked nodes and then continues to spread and activate related concepts. This model suggests that, for those with high aggression alcohol expectancies, alcohol cues first activate semantic representations of concepts related to alcohol, which in turn activate concepts associated with aggression. These activated concepts implicitly shape cognition in social situations, causing persons with high aggression alcohol expectancies to react more aggressively when presented with alcohol cues (Friedman, et al., 2007).

An alternate hypothesis for the interactive effects of alcohol cuing and alcohol expectancies on aggression is that alcohol cues *motivate* a person to aggress (Friedman, et al., 2007). Motives are action plans of behaviors, and these plans can be primed to influence behavior in much the same way as semantically represented concepts. Like other mental representations, motives are capable of being activated automatically by contextual cues (Bargh and Chartrand, 1999). Motivational states can be goals, needs, intentions, or concerns, and activation of these states leads linked concepts in long-term memory to become more accessible (Forster and Liberman, 2007).

Goals have been defined as "cognitive representations of desired endpoints that impacts evaluations, emotions and behaviors" (Fishbach and Ferguson, 2007). Goals, as well as motives, are stored in long-term memory. As items stored in long-term memory, these constructs vary in accessibility depending on their relevance to contextual and situational factors (Forster and Liberman, 2007). This characteristic means that motives vary in the extent to which they influence behavior at any given time.

There are features of the activation and maintenance of motives that enables their distinction from other semantic representations as the mechanism for the effects of alcohol cuing and alcohol expectancies on behavior (Friedman, et al., 2007). A key difference is that activated semantic representations rapidly decline in accessibility whereas activated motives remain accessible until "satisfied" (i.e. until the person engages in an action that would fulfill the motive). Of note, the "motives fulfillment hypothesis" and spreading activation model are not mutually exclusive but may each account for some of the interactive effects of alcohol cuing and alcohol expectancies.

Activation and Accessibility of Motives

Past research suggests that motives can be cued without conscious awareness. Further, even if people consciously perceive a stimulus, they may not be aware that it has activated associated memories and goal constructs (Fishbach and Ferguson, 2007). In one study consisting of five experiments, experimenters primed participants either consciously or unconsciously with behavioral goals and found that both can become activated without conscious choice. For example, in one experiment, participants were primed with words relating to cooperation (e.g. fair, friendly, and share) and then given a "resource management" game in which players could act cooperatively or selfishly. Those who had been primed with the cooperation goal demonstrated significantly greater cooperation (Bargh, Gollwizer, Lee-Chai, Barndollar, and Trötschel, 2001).

The study by Bargh et al. (2001) also supported the principle that activated motives maintain accessibility until goal fulfillment. The fourth experiment found that participants who were unconsciously primed with the goal to perform well, but were interrupted on a word-finding task, continued the task even after the signal to stop working. Participants who were not primed with the goal to perform well did not persist after the signal. This finding indicates that the participants ignored instructions in order to fulfill a previously formed goal. Of relevance, the activation of concepts related to the goal being pursued would help a person to achieve the goal more efficiently. It would be logical, too, that following goal fulfillment, those concepts related to the goal would become less accessible, allowing an individual to pursue other goals (Bargh, et al., 2001).

Recent studies in social cognition indicate that potential behavioral responses are represented in long-term memory and can be automatically activated without conscious awareness when a person encounters a context or situation appropriate to that goal (Bargh, Chen, and Burrows, 1996; Ferguson and Bargh, 2004). According to learning principles, if an individual responds consistently to a social stimulus, that response will eventually be activated automatically when the stimulus occurs (Bargh, et al., 1996). This automaticity translates into a consistent behavioral response to certain stimuli over time. In a series of three experiments, Bargh and colleagues (1996) demonstrated that participants primed with stereotyped-group traits displayed behavior consistent with the primed concept (such as rudeness, slowness, and hostility). Of particular relevance, in one of the experiments participants were primed by viewing images of members of a stereotyped group, African Americans. These participants showed more hostility towards the experimenter than a control group, as assessed by raters blind to condition.

These results suggest that hostile behavior can be primed by the mere exposure to contextual effects that a person associates with a hostile behavioral response. The authors argue that an additional requirement exists, though, for primes to automatically influence behavior: the primed behavior must be relevant to the experimental situation in which participants are placed (Bargh, et al., 1996). In other words, a cue may activate hostility if a person associates that cue with hostility, but the person must then encounter a situation that could trigger aggressive behavior in order for the activated concept to translate into behavior.

If a person holds strong aggression alcohol expectancies, exposing that person to alcohol cues should activate concepts related to aggression. As discussed, this activation has the potential to alter a person's interpretation of others' behaviors (Bargh and Chartrand, 1999). Further, if alcohol expectancies operate by activating motives, then aggression-related concepts should maintain their accessibility until the individual has the opportunity to aggress.

CATHARSIS AND AGGRESSION

Experiments supporting the motives theory suggest that motives to aggress are inhibited following the opportunity to aggress (Bargh and Chartrand, 1999). This idea, which can be traced back to Sigmund Freud, is consistent with the common belief in catharsis as a means of reducing anger. Freud believed that the repression of emotions could cause psychological symptoms and that the expression of emotions, including anger, was healthy. However, modern studies suggest that expressing aggression generally makes one even more aggressive (i.e., strengthens the motive to aggress). In a study by Bushman and colleagues (1999), one group of students was exposed to a pro-catharsis message, which claimed that direct aggressive action is a good way to relax and reduce anger and then asked to hit a punching bag. Participants in this group displayed a greater desire to subsequently hit a punching bag than members of the control group, who read an anti-catharsis message and did not have the opportunity to hit a punching bag. These results suggest that those who are given the opportunity to act out aggression subsequently demonstrate more aggressive behavior, even when given the message that acting out aggression will reduce aggression.

The Bushman study provides evidence that engaging in a direct expression of aggression (in this case, hitting a punching bag) will increase aggressive behavior in a subsequent opportunity to aggress. Hitting the punching bag increased physiological arousal, a factor that can heighten anger according to the excitation transfer theory (Anderson and Bushman, 2002). The excitation transfer theory suggests that physiological arousal produced by any source, such as exercise, can be misrecognized as anger and will subsequently increase the likelihood that a person will engage in aggressive behavior. It remains unclear, though, whether similar results would be found following aggressive behavior that does not directly promote physiological arousal (e.g., harsh written evaluations). If such results were found, it would suggest that the opportunity to aggress increases, rather than decreases, the accessibility of activated aggressive motives. In other words, if Bushman's findings generalize across contexts, there would be evidence that aggression is an exception to the motives fulfillment hypothesis. That is, drinking juice might *decrease* one's motive to drink something sweet (as one example), but acting aggressively would *increase* one's motive to act aggressively.

THE CARLETON STUDY

The recently-conducted and previously unpublished Carleton study examined the interaction of exposure to alcohol cues, aggression alcohol expectancies, and opportunity to evaluate a paper on hostile impression formation. Participants, half of whom were exposed to alcohol cues, were given a mildly offensive sample paper to read in order to provoke an aggressive response. Only half of those from each cuing condition were given the opportunity to evaluate the sample paper and leave comments. Finally, all participants completed a person perception task in which they were asked to evaluate the hostility of an ambiguously-characterized fictional character.

One strength of the study design is that it used a more externally-valid alcohol cuing methodology (alcohol containers and alcohol advertisements) relative to formerly-used computer priming methods. A previous study found that students who completed an experiment in a bar rather than a laboratory responded more quickly when asked to report alcohol expectancies (Wall, McKee, Hinson, and Goldstein, 2001). This finding suggests that environmental stimuli may facilitate the recall of alcohol expectancies.

In the Carleton study, we tested two competing hypotheses. The motives fulfillment hypothesis suggests that alcohol cues should activate a motive to aggress for those with high alcohol expectancies (Friedman, et al., 2007). Thus, participants who have the opportunity to evaluate the paper (and hence fulfill an aggression goal) should subsequently evaluate the fictional character as less hostile. Bushman's hypothesis, in contrast, suggests that those who have the opportunity to aggress should become more hostile (Bushman, et al., 1999). If those who have the opportunity to evaluate the paper rate the fictional character as more hostile, the results would support this hypothesis. It would follow that expressing aggression does not fulfill a motive but rather increases the activation of aggression motives.

As such, if the motives hypothesis is to be supported, participants with high aggression alcohol expectancies who are cued with alcohol containers and signs and who have *not* had the opportunity to evaluate the paper should show the highest hostility (Friedman, et al., 2007). However, if Bushman's hypothesis is to be supported, participants with high aggression alcohol expectancies who are exposed to alcohol cues and who *have* had the opportunity to evaluate the paper should display the most hostility (Bushman, et al., 1999). For participants who have low aggression alcohol expectancies and/or are exposed to non-alcoholic beverage cues, there were no predicted effects of paper evaluation condition.

METHODS

Participants

Sixty undergraduates at a Midwestern liberal arts college were recruited for this study from psychology courses and advertisements in campus publications. Participants were between the ages of eighteen and twenty three (M=20.3, SD=1.33). With respect to race, 82% of participants identified as Caucasian, 7% as Asian, 5% as multiracial, 3% as Hispanic, and 3% as other.

MATERIALS

Alcohol Expectancies Questionnaire

The questions used for analysis of aggression alcohol expectancies were drawn from the Alcohol Expectancies Regarding Sex, Aggression, and Sexual Vulnerability Questionnaire (AESAVQ; Abbey, McAuslan, Ross, and Zawacki, 1999). This questionnaire examines alcohol expectancies in four domains related to sexual assault: aggression, sexual affect, sexual drive, and vulnerability to sexual assault. The AESAVQ was chosen as the source for questions related to aggression alcohol expectancies because each of its subscales has high internal consistency and high test-retest reliability over a one-month period (Abbey, et al., 1999). Additional distraction questions were drawn from the tension reduction subscale of the Alcohol Expectancy Questionnaire (AEQ; Goldman and Brown, 2003) so that participants would be less likely to suspect that the true dependent measure related to hostility.

Person Perception Task

The present experiment utilized a methodology that is based on the "Donald" paragraph, developed by Srull and Wyer (1979) and used by Bartholow and Heinz (2006) to indirectly measure alcohol-cued aggression. In that paragraph, a character encounters a variety of scenarios and acts in ways that may be evaluated as hostile or defensible (for example, refusing to pay rent until his apartment is repainted). However, unlike in previous usages of the task, the modified version used for the present study featured a character that is acting ambiguously hostile towards the *reader*. Consistent with Bartholow and Heinz (2006), participants in the present study rated the character on six dimensions related to hostility (for example, unfriendly), and six unrelated dimensions (for example, boring) on a Likert scale ranging from 0 ("not at all") to 10 ("extremely"). Three positive and three (reverse scored) negative qualities were related to hostility, and scores on these were summed to calculate the primary outcome measure (range = 0 to 60, with higher numbers indicating greater impressions of hostility).

Procedure

To minimize demand characteristics, participants were recruited with the understanding that the study would be investigating links between "consumer brands, alcohol expectancies, and impression formation." Prior to experimental sessions, participants were randomly assigned to both cue condition (alcohol or non-alcohol) and paper evaluation condition (present or absent). After giving informed consent, participants completed the alcohol expectancies questionnaire and a simple measure of quantity and frequency of alcohol use.

Next, participants were given a brief (one page) paper to evaluate while seated directly in front of a shelf containing three beer bottles and a large beer promotional sign (alcohol cues condition) or three soda bottles and a large soda promotional sign (non-alcohol cues condition). The experimenter told participants that the paper would be the first of two impression formation tasks. The paper was intended to be mildly offensive to the majority of participants as it contained an argument against the utility of a liberal arts education. It also contained several obvious grammatical errors. After reviewing that paper, half the participants had the opportunity to rate the paper from A to F on the dimensions of spelling, grammar, style, and strength of argument, with room to leave comments (evaluation present condition).

Finally, all participants received the modified person perception task (described above).

RESULTS

Tests of Random Assignment

The means and standard deviations for demographic and alcohol consumption variables are presented in Table 1. We conducted 2 (beverage cue condition) x 2 (paper evaluation condition) ANOVAs to examine whether random assignment to groups successfully distributed participants with regard to age, number of drinking episodes per week, quantity of drinks consumed per drinking occasion, and number of drinks consumed per week. Indicating successful random assignment, there were no significant differences on these variables across groups.

A chi-square test was conducted to test for random assignment with regard to sex. There were no significant differences for sex between groups assigned to the alcohol cuing condition and the non-alcohol cuing condition [χ^2(.000, N=60)=1.000, p>.05] and between groups assigned to the paper evaluation condition and those assigned to the no paper evaluation condition. [χ^2 (3.068, N=60)=.143, p>.05].

Table 1. Descriptive Statistics by Conditions

	Alcohol Cues Condition				Non-alcohol Cues Condition			
	Paper Evaluation		No Paper Evaluation		Paper Evaluation		No Paper Evaluation	
	M	SD	M	SD	M	SD	M	SD
Age	20.13	1.73	20.40	1.12	20.20	1.26	20.33	1.29
Occasions/week	1.70	1.71	1.23	1.03	0.97	0.72	1.20	0.86
Drinks/occasion	2.80	2.66	3.13	2.39	2.03	1.27	2.23	1.47
Drinks/week	6.48	6.20	5.37	6.50	2.53	2.55	3.12	2.76

Paper Evaluation Task

An ANOVA was performed to test for the effects of alcohol expectancies (using a median split) and cue condition on paper evaluation ratings for each of the four scales: spelling, grammar, style, and strength of argument. There was a significant main effect of cue condition on evaluation of style [F(1,26)=1349.91, p<.05]. Participants exposed to alcohol cues graded style the most leniently. There were no other significant main effects or significant interactions for any of the scales.

Hostile Impression Formation

A three-way ANOVA examined the effects of cue condition, alcohol expectancies, and paper evaluation condition on hostile impression formation. This interaction was not significant. However, because of the limited sample size for detecting a significant 3-way interaction, we examined separately for those with low and high aggression alcohol expectancies (the quasi-independent variable) the effects of cue condition and paper evaluation condition (the two true independent variables) on hostile impression formation. For participants with high aggression alcohol expectancies, the interaction approached significance [$F(1,26)=3.50$, $p=.07$]. Consistent with study predictions, participants with high aggression alcohol expectancies who were exposed to alcohol cues and who did not have the opportunity to evaluate the paper displayed the most hostile evaluation of the character (Figure 1). For participants with low aggression alcohol expectancies, the two-way interaction for alcohol cues and paper evaluation condition was not significant.

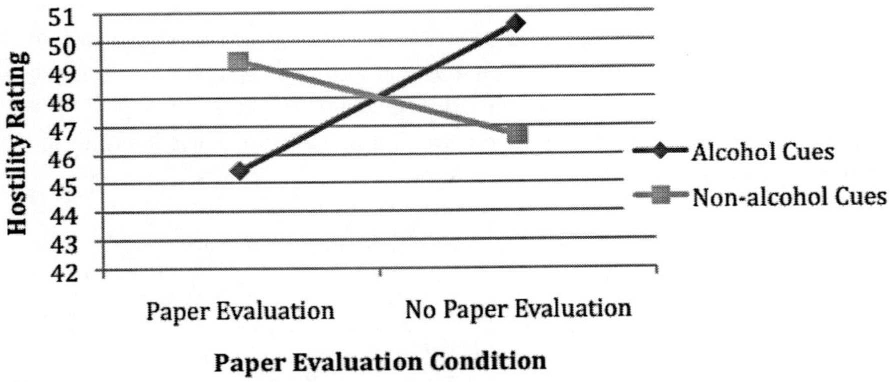

Figure 1. Hostile impression formation for participants with high aggressive AOEs.

IMPLICATIONS

We sought to examine, among those with high aggression alcohol expectancies who were exposed to alcohol cues, the effect of the opportunity to evaluate an offensive paper (and hence the opportunity to aggress) on subsequent hostile impression formation. For participants with high aggression alcohol expectancies, the two-way interaction between cuing condition and paper evaluation condition approached significance. Only for those exposed to alcohol cues, the opportunity to evaluate the paper resulted in reduced hostile impression formation on a subsequent task ($p=.07$). While this finding is consistent with the motives fulfillment hypothesis, the result should be interpreted cautiously because of failure to find significance at the traditional level. We found no support for Bushman's hypothesis –

that the opportunity to aggress should lesson subsequent hostile impression formation. (Bushman, et al., 1999).

Study Limitations

An open question and potential limitation is whether participants viewed the evaluation opportunity as an opportunity to aggress. The sample paper's message may not have been sufficiently offensive, or perhaps the participants did not see the opportunity to grade the paper as an act of aggression. Future studies may wish to make this task more clearly an opportunity to aggress, perhaps by informing participants that the author will actually read the assigned grades and comments.

Additionally, the cues themselves may not have been a sufficient prime for activating aggression alcohol expectancies. Ideally, this study would be replicated with the experimental group completing the experiment in a bar (Wall, et al., 2001). The context of a bar would be a more realistic context than a laboratory with alcohol cues for encountering alcohol-related aggression. At a minimum, future studies may wish to make alcohol cues more salient for all participants, possibly by converting the laboratory into a space that more closely resembles a bar.

The method used in this study to examine aggression was the evaluation of a fictional character's hostility. This methodology is based on the notion that, once aggressive thoughts are activated from long-term memory, other people's ambiguous behaviors are more likely to be interpreted as hostile (Bushman and Anderson, 2002). However, future studies could utilize a more direct measure of aggression. As one example, participants could be given the opportunity to put hot sauce into the drink of an aggressive confederate (Begue, et al., 2009). If direct aggression is used as the dependent measure instead of evaluation of another's hostility, then Bushman's hypothesis could be tested using the same methodology as the original study (Bushman, et al., 1999). If participants displayed reduced aggression following a direct expression of aggression, this would contradict Bushman's theory and suggest that alcohol expectancies influence aggressive behavior via the activation of aggression motives (Friedman, et al., 2007).

Concluding Remarks

The Carleton study evaluated one classical feature of motives – that their accessibility diminishes post-fulfillment (Bargh, et al., 1996). Since activated motives persist until goal attainment and appear to be relatively resistant to decay after time delay, future studies could assess the accessibility of aggression motives at various time points following the exposure to alcohol cues (Friedman, et al., 2007). A study of this nature would help to further isolate motives theory as a potential explanation for the effects of alcohol cues and alcohol expectancies on hostile impression formation.

Alcohol expectancy challenges, in which people's beliefs regarding the behavioral effects of alcohol are called into question, have shown initial promise as a means of reducing harmful behaviors that result from drinking, as well as the quantity and frequency of drinking itself (Lau-Barraco and Dunn, 2008; Wood, Capone, Laforge, Erickson, and Brand, 2007).

Expectancy challenges are designed to disconfirm expectancies of positive outcomes, such as sexual and social outcome expectancies. In fact, previous studies have shown that alcohol expectancies better predict aggressive behavior than actual alcohol consumption (Begue, et al., 2009). If heavy drinkers are made aware this finding, it may increase their motivation to challenge their aggression alcohol expectancies.

A fuller understanding of the mechanisms through which alcohol cues and expectancies influence behavior is important to help inform expectancy challenges and other efforts aimed at reducing problems associated with alcohol consumption. Specifically, if studies find that unfulfilled motives is how alcohol cues and alcohol expectancies promote aggression, interventions could be adjusted to incorporate motives. Future studies could then investigate whether, among persons with activated aggression motives, such motives could be safely altered or fulfilled so as to reduce the likelihood that a person would engage in antisocial aggressive behavior.

References

Abbey, A., McAuslan, P., Ross, L. T., and Zawacki, T. (1999). Alcohol expectancies regarding sex, aggression, and sexual vulnerability: Reliability and validity assessment. *Psychology of Addictive Bheaviors, 13*(3), 174-182.

Anderson, C. A., and Bushman, B. J. (2002). Human Aggression. *Annu. Rev. Psychol., 53*, 27-51.

Bargh, J. A., and Chartrand, T. L. (1999). The unbearable automaticity of being. *American Psychologist, 54*(7), 462-479.

Bargh, J. A., Chen, M., and Burrows, L. (1996). Automaticity of social behavior: Direct effects of trait construct and stereotype activation on action. *Journal of Personality and Social Psychology, 71*(2), 230-244.

Bargh, J. A., Gollwizer, P. M., Lee-Chai, A., Barndollar, K., and Trötschel, R. (2001). The automated will: nonconscious activation and pursuit of behavioral goals. *Journal of Personality and Social Psychology, 81*, 1014-1027.

Bartholow, B. D., and Heinz, A. (2006). Alcohol and aggression without conclusion. *Psychological Science, 17*(1), 30-37.

Begue, L., Subra, B., Arvers, P., Muller, D., Bricout, V., and Zorman, M. (2009). A message in a bottle: Extrapharmacological effects of alcohol on aggression. *Journal of Experimental Social Psychology, 45*, 137-142.

Borders, A., Barnwell, S. S., and Earleywine, M. (2007). Alcohol-aggression expectancies and dispositional rumination moderate the effect of alcohol consumption on alcohol-related aggression and hostility. *Aggressive Behavior, 33*, 327-338.

Bushman, B. J., and Anderson, C. A. (2002). Violent video games and hostile expectations: A test of the general aggression model. *Personality and Social Psychology Bulletin, 28*(12), 1679-1686.

Bushman, B. J., and Cooper, H. M. (1990). Effects of alcohol on human aggression: an integrative research review. *Psychological Bulletin, 107*(3), 341-354.

Bushman, B. J., Stack, A. D., and Baumeister, R. F. (1999). Catharsis, aggression, and persuasive influence: Self-fulfilling or self-defeating prophecies? *Journal of Personality and Social Psychology, 76*(3), 367-376.

Collins, A. M., and Loftus, E. F. (1975). A spreading-activation theory of semantic processing. *Psychological Review, 82*(6), 407-428.

Cook, P. J., and Moore, M. J. (1993). Violence reduction through restrictions on alcohol availability. *Alcohol Health and Research World, 17*(2).

Ferguson, M. J., and Bargh, J. A. (2004). How social perception can automatically influence behavior. *Trends in Cognitive Sciences, 8*(1), 33-39.

Fishbach, A., and Ferguson, M. (2007). The goal construct in social psychology. In E. T. Higgins (Ed.), *Social Psychology: Handbook of Basic Principles. 2nd edition* (2nd ed.). New York: Guilford Press.

Forster, J., and Liberman, N. (2007). Knowledge Activation. In A. W. Kruglanski and E. T. Higgins (Eds.), *Social Psychology: Handbook of Basic Principles* (2nd ed., pp. 201-231). New York.

Friedman, R. S., McCarthy, D. M., Bartholow, B. D., and Hicks, J. A. (2007). Interactive effects of alcohol outcome expectancies and alcohol cues on nonconsumptive behavior. *Experimental and Clinical Psychopharmacology, 15*(1), 102-114.

Friedman, R. S., McCarthy, D. M., Forster, J., and Denzler, M. (2005). Automatic effects of alcohol cues on sexual attraction. *Addiction, 100*, 672-681.

Goldman, M. S. (1999). Risk for substance abuse: memory as a common etiological pathway. *Psychological Science, 10*(3), 196-197.

Goldman, M. S., and Brown, S. A. (2003). Alcohol Expectancy Questionnaire (adult) AEQ. *Assessing alcohol problems: A guide for clinicians and researchers*.

Goldman, M. S., and Darkes, J. (2004). Alcohol expectancy mulitiaxial assessment: A memory network-based approach. *Psychological Assessment, 16*(1), 4-15.

Goldman, M. S., Darkes, J., and Boca, F. K. D. (1999). Expectancy mediation of biopsychosocial risk for alcohol use and alcoholism. In I. Kirsch (Ed.), *How Expectancies Shape Experiences* (pp. 233-262). Washington, D.C.: American Psychological Association.

Jones, B. T., Corbin, W., and Fromme, K. (2001). Conceptualizing addiction: a review of expectancy theory and alcohol consumption. *Addiction, 96*, 57-72.

Lau-Barraco, C., and Dunn, M. E. (2008). Evaluation of a single-session expectancy challenge intervention to reduce alcohol use among college students. *Psychology of Addictive Behaviors, 22*(2), 168-175.

Leigh, B. C., and Stacy, A. W. (1998). Individual differences in memory associations involving the positive and negative outcomes of alcohol use. *Psychology of Addictive Behaviors, 12*(1), 39-46.

Leigh, B. C., and Stacy, A. W. (2004). Alcohol expectancies and drinking in different age groups. *Addiction, 99*, 215-227.

Nolen-Hoeksema, S., and Hilt, L. (2006). Possible contributors to the gender differences in alcohol use and problems. *The Journal of General Psychology, 133*(4), 357-374.

Wall, A.-M., McKee, S. A., Hinson, R. E., and Goldstein, H. (2001). Examining alcohol outcome expectancies in laboratory and naturalistic bar settings: a within-subject experimental analysis. *Psychology of Addictive Behaviors, 15*(3), 219-226.

Wood, M. D., Capone, C., Laforge, R., Erickson, D. J., and Brand, N. H. (2007). Brief motivational intervention and alcohol expectancy challenge with heavy drinking college students: a randomized factorial study. *Addictive Behaviors, 32*, 2509-2528.

In: Social Drinking: Uses, Abuses and Psychological Factors ISBN: 978-1-60876-219-4
Editors : K. T. Everly, E. M. Cosell, pp. 305-310 © 2010 Nova Science Publishers, Inc.

Chapter 10

Examining Drinking Patterns: Future Implications for Research

Noriko Cable[1]
Department of Epidemiology and Public Health
University College London
1-19 Torrington Place, London, WC1E 6BT, United Kingdom

Drinking alcohol is a socially accepted behaviour; however, it becomes a social problem when it exceeds the accepted social boundary as identified as alcohol misuse. Alcohol misuse includes three patterns of alcohol use: hazardous alcohol use (drinking alcohol heavily that potentially cause physical or psychological harm)(Fuller, Jotangia, and Farrel, 2009; Singleton, Bumpstead, O'Brien et al., 2001), harmful alcohol use (an extreme form of hazardous drinking which likely damage physical or psychological health or both), and alcohol dependence. Implemented in 1995, adults were encouraged to drink within the recommended daily limit which was 3-4 units for men and 2-3 units for women (Prime Minister's Strategy Unit, 2004) to prevent incidence associated with alcohol misuse. There was a dose-response link between quantity of alcohol use and alcohol attributed diseases in men (Lau, Freyer-Adam, Coder et al., 2008) and between heavy alcohol use and traffic accidents (Valencia-Martin, Galan, and Rodriguez-Artalejo, 2008). Drinking alcohol "sensibly" by adhering with this recommended quantity of alcohol by English government (Department of Health, Home Office, Department of Education and Skills et al., 2007) appears to be an effective way to protect adults from physical harm induced by alcohol misuse.

Reflecting this public health campaign of "sensible alcohol use", recent alcohol related statistics in England showed that the proportions of adult men's hazardous alcohol use and alcohol dependence were slightly reduced from the past figures (Fuller et al., 2009; Singleton et al., 2001). However, the prevalence of harmful alcohol use in men was not changed, and adult women's patterns of alcohol misuse were not changed at all. Moreover, the prevalence of mild alcohol dependence in women increased by nearly 1% compared with the past figure

1 E-mail: n.cable@ucl.ac.uk.

(Fuller et al., 2009). According to the Health Survey for England 2007, around 30 to 40% of adults reported that they heard about the measurement for alcohol intake, "units", yet they did not know the recommended daily limit for alcohol intake for adults of either gender (The NHS Information Centre and Lifestyles Statistics, 2009). These indicate that public message of "sensible drinking" has not yet been reached to all of the population and therefore English public has not been responding well to reduce incidence and consequence of alcohol misuse. This figure shows that an urgent need for public education about recommended quantity of alcohol use.

While it is necessary to educate public for quantity of sensible alcohol use, the public health message of "sensible drinking" tended to emphasise quantity of alcohol use over frequency of alcohol use. However, low quantity of alcohol use was found to have increased risk of developing cirrhosis, cancer, and cardiac arrhythmia (Gutjahr, Gmel, and Rehm, 2001). It also did not alcohol dependent drinkers from mortality (Dawson, 2000). Long-term alcohol use, even it is only one drink a day, increased incidence of cancer among adult women (Allen, Beral, Casabonne et al., 2009). In addition, individuals who reported to have misused alcohol also reported to have drunk excessively in more than one occasion (The NHS Information Centre and Lifestyles Statistics, 2009). It is possible that a longitudinal effect of alcohol use on alcohol dependence appears not to follow the dose-response pattern because frequency and quantity related adolescent drinking patterns were risk for adult alcohol dependence for men, whereas adult women's alcohol dependency was associated with frequent adolescent alcohol use (Cable and Sacker, 2008). Although the trend is declining, in England about 13% of adult men and 7% of women reported to have consumed alcohol daily (The NHS Information Centre and Lifestyles Statistics, 2009) and 6% of the sampled adults showed symptoms of alcohol dependence (Fuller et al., 2009). Based on these findings, alcohol studies are required to include both quantity and quantity in their models of alcohol use to better understand the complex mechanisms of alcohol use and misuse.

Moreover, researchers need to examine the effects exerted by social factors on alcohol use and misuse, given the documented link between social positions and alcohol misuse (Bloomfield, Grittner, Kramer et al., 2006; Casswell, Pledger, and Hooper, 2003; Mäkelä and Paljärvi, 2007; Marmot, 1997; Petridou, Zavitsanos, Dessypris et al., 1997; Richter, Leppin, and Nic Gabhainn, 2006). Adding the relevant social context into behaviour oriented alcohol use and misuse would assist researchers to better understand the dimensions of quantity and frequency of alcohol use. In turn, it will assist to develop empirically supported effective alcohol related interventions. Alcohol related social factors can be at the level of individual, family, and society which are woven into individual life time alcohol use and misuse. Adopting the lifecourse approach is likely to capture complex socially patterned alcohol use and misuse which develop and change over time. This approach is also effectively to assess the effect of long term alcohol use and the trajectory of drinking patterns on physical and psychological health.

Positive alcohol expectancies, described as positive expectation to gain desired effects produced by drinking alcohol (Jones, Corbin, and Fromme, 2001), is thought to be an individual factor to promote alcohol use. Studies found multiple dimensions in positive alcohol expectancies with each dimension having an independent effect on quantity and frequency of alcohol use by gender (Mooney, Fromme, Kivlahan et al., 1987; Van Wersch and Walker, 2009). In young men and women, expectation to gain social assertion and physical and social pleasure from drinking alcohol was related to quantity of their alcohol use(Mooney et al., 1987). However, among young men, frequency of their alcohol use was related to expectation to gain physical and social pleasure from alcohol. On the other hand, young women's frequent alcohol use was driven by expectation to reduce tension. These findings indicate that researchers need gender specific model of alcohol use and misuse. Several models of alcohol expectancies (Gilles, Turk, and Fresco, 2006; Oei and Baldwin, 1994; Oei and Burrow, 2000) implies the inclusion of self-efficacy, as well as positive alcohol expectancies, explaining the link between risky alcohol use, self-efficacy and positive alcohol expectancies.

Findings of previous alcohol studies indicate a need for studying the roles of family and other socially related factors on the manner in which alcohol is used and misused. Individual alcohol expectancies are thought to be related to social learning process (Jones et al., 2001), and the same learning process can contribute to the development of self-efficacy likely to be determined by parents (Patock-Peckham, Cheong, Balhorn et al., 2001; Watkins, Howard-Barr, Moore et al., 2006). Since social patterns are often found in frequent (Casswell et al., 2003) and heavy and harmful alcohol use (Mäkelä et al., 2007), it is possible that family and individual level alcohol related factors are socially patterned, which in turn, may create socially patterned drinking behaviours.

Previous studies showed that the patterns of alcohol heavy alcohol use tended to have declined over time (Goddard, 2006; Karlamangla, Zhou, Reuben et al., 2006; Moore, Gould, Reuben et al., 2005). In a recent survey in England, hazardous drinking was more likely to be found among younger adults aged between 16 and 34 in men and 16 and 24 in women (Fuller et al., 2009). The trend of hazardous and harmful drinking was in declining in older age groups, especially among women. In women aged between 35 and 44, incidence of hazardous and harmful drinking dropped to less than 20% compared with younger age groups (Fuller et al., 2009). The incidence of alcohol dependence was low in the age group of 25 and 34; however, the incidence of alcohol misuse was higher than in the age group of 35 and 44 than the age group of 25 or older age groups. This was not found in men's age groups; the trend of alcohol misuse was peaked in the age group of 25 and 34 and systematically declined in all of the older age groups. A study showed that adolescent social disinhibition alcohol expectancies still predicted heavy alcohol use and misuse in midadulthood (Cable and Sacker, 2007); yet, it is possible that changes in alcohol misuse patterns can be ascribed to transitions in individual social roles such as taking up employment and engaging into partnership and parenthood, motivating people to change from risky or heavy alcohol use to sensible alcohol use (Kuntsche, Knibbe, and Gmel, 2009). Further studies are needed to explain the trajectory of drinking patterns across the lifecourse. Past studies which applied the lifecourse approach showed the accumulated effects of social disadvantages during childhood on adult health (Graham and Power, 2004; Hertzman, Power, Matthews et al., 2001). There is a suggested link between multiple incidence of early social disadvantages and certain drinking patterns (Caldwell, Rodgers, Clark et al., 2008). Using the lifecourse approach will allow researchers to examine the full spectrum of alcohol use and misuse, in relation to individual, family and society across time.

In summary, frequency of alcohol use has not been well reflected in the current alcohol related policies, which aim to reduce social problems associated with alcohol misuse. Alcohol use and misuse appear to have different individual, family and socially related factors by gender and age. Lifecourse approach is useful for researchers to better capture this complex picture of alcohol use and misuse across time which will provide evidence based alcohol related policies to manage incidence of alcohol misuse

REFERENCES

Allen, N. E., Beral, V., Casabonne, D. et al. (2009). Moderate alcohol intake and cancer incidence in women. *J.Natl.Canc.Inst., 101,* 296-305.

Bloomfield, K., Grittner, U., Kramer, S. et al. (2006). Social inequalities in alcohol consumption and alcohol-related problems in the study countries of the EU concerted action 'Gender, Culture and Alcohol Problems: a Multi-national Study'. *Alcohol Alcohol Suppl, 41,* i26-i36.

Cable, N. and Sacker, A. (2007). The role of adolescent social disinhibition expectancies in moderating the relationship between psychological distress and alcohol use and misuse. *Addict. Behav, 32,* 282-295.

Cable, N. and Sacker, A. (2008). Typologies of alcohol consumption in adolescence: predictors and adult outcomes. *Alcohol Alcohol, 43,* 81-90.

Caldwell, T. M., Rodgers, B., Clark, C. et al. (2008). Lifecourse socioeconomic predictors of midlife drinking patterns, problems and abstention: findings from the 1958 British Birth Cohort Study. *Drug Alcohol Depend., 95,* 269-278.

Casswell, S., Pledger, M., and Hooper, R. (2003). Socioeconomic status and drinking patterns in young adults. *Addiction, 98,* 601-610.

Dawson, D. A. (2000). Alcohol consumption, alcohol dependence, and all-cause mortality. *Alcohol Clin.Exp.Res., 24,* 72-81.

Department of Health, Home Office, Department of Education and Skills, and Department for Culture, M. a. S. (2007). Safe. Sensible. Social. The next steps in the National Alcohol Strategy. Department of Health [On-line]. Available: http://www.dh.gov.uk/

Fuller, E., Jotangia, D., and Farrel, M. (2009). Alcohol misuse and dependence. Adult psychiatric mobidity in England 2007 Results of a household survey [On-line]. Available: www.ic.nhs.uk

Gilles, D. M., Turk, C. L., and Fresco, D. M. (2006). Social anxiety, alcohol expectancies, and self-efficacy as predictors of heavy drinking in college students. *Addict.Behav., 31,* 388-398.

Goddard, E. (2006). *Smoking and drinking among adults, 2006* Newport: Office for National Statistics.

Graham, H. and Power, C. (2004). Childhood disadvantage and health inequalities: a framework for policy based on lifecourse research. *Child Care Health Dev., 30,* 671-678.

Gutjahr, E., Gmel, G., and Rehm, J. (2001). Relation between average alcohol consumption and disease: An overview. *Eur.Addict.Res., 7,* 117-127.

Hertzman, C., Power, C., Matthews, S. et al. (2001). Using an interactive framework of society and lifecourse to explain self-rated health in early adulthood. *Soc.Sci.Med., 53,* 1575-1585.

Jones, B. T., Corbin, W., and Fromme, K. (2001). A review of expectancy theory and alcohol consumption. *Addiction, 96,* 57-72.

Karlamangla, A., Zhou, K., Reuben, D. et al. (2006). Longitudinal trajectories of heavy drinking in adults in the United States of America. *Addiction, 101,* 91-99.

Kuntsche, S., Knibbe, R. A., and Gmel, G. (2009). Social roles and alcohol consumption: a study of 10 industrialised countries. *Soc.Sci.Med., 68,* 1263-1270.

Lau, K., Freyer-Adam, J., Coder, B. et al. (2008). Dose-response relation between volume of drinking and alcohol-related disease in male general hospital inpatients. *Alcohol Alcohohol, 43,* 34-38.

Mäkelä, P. and Paljärvi, T. (2007). Do consequences of a given pattern of drinking vary by socioeconomic status? A mortality and hospitalisation follow-up for alcohol-related causes of the Finnish Drinking Habits Survey. *J Epidemiol Community Health, 62,* 728-733.

Marmot, M. (1997). Inequality, deprivation and alcohol use. *Addiction, 1997,* S13-S20.

Mooney, D. K., Fromme, K., Kivlahan, D. R. et al. (1987). Correlates of alcohol consumption: sex, age, and expectancies relate differentially to quantity and frequency. *Addict.Behav., 12,* 235-240.

Moore, A. A., Gould, R., Reuben, D. B. et al. (2005). Longitudinal patterns and predictors of alcohol consumption in the United States. *Am.J.Public Health, 95,* 458-465.

Oei, T. P. and Baldwin, A. R. (1994). Expectancy theory: a two-process model of alcohol use and abuse. *J Stud.Alcohol, 55,* 525-534.

Oei, T. P. and Burrow, T. (2000). Alcohol expectancy and drinking refusal self-efficacy: a test of specificity theory. *Addict.Behav., 25,* 499-507.

Patock-Peckham, J. A., Cheong, J., Balhorn, M. E. et al. (2001). A social learning perspective: a model of parenting styles, self-regulation, perceived drinking control, and alcohol use and problems. *Alcohol Clin.Exp.Res., 25,* 1284-1292.

Petridou, E., Zavitsanos, X., Dessypris, N. et al. (1997). Adolescents in high-risk trajectory: clustering of risky behavior and the origins of socioeconomic health differentials. *Prev.Med., 26,* 215-219.

Prime Minister's Strategy Unit (2004). Alcohol harm reduction strategy for England. Cabinet Office [On-line]. Available: http://www.cabinetoffice.gov.uk/strategy/work_areas/alcohol_misuse/index.asp

Richter, M., Leppin, A., and Nic Gabhainn, S. (2006). The relationship between parental socio-economic status and episodes of drunkenness among adolescents: findings from a cross-national survey. *BMC.Public Health, 6,* 289.

Singleton, N., Bumpstead, R., O'Brien, M., Lee, A., and Meltzer, H. (2001). Psychiatric mobidity among adult living in private households, 2000. Office for National Statistics [On-line]. Available: http://www.data-archive.ac.uk/

The NHS Information Centre and Lifestyles Statistics. (2009). Statistics on Alcohol: England, 2009. The NHS Information Centre [On-line]. Available: http://www.ic.nhs.uk/statistics-and-data-collections/health-and-lifestyles/alcohol

Valencia-Martin, J. L., Galan, I., and Rodriguez-Artalejo, F. (2008). The joint association of average volume of alcohol and binge drinking with hazardous driving behaviour and traffic crashes. *Addiction, 103,* 749-757.

Van Wersch, A., and Walker, W. (2009). Binge-drinking in Britain as a social and cultural phenomenon: the development of a grounded theoretical model. *J Health Psychol., 14,* 124-134.

Watkins, J. A. Howard-Barr, E. M., Moore, M. J. et al. (2006). The mediating role of adolescent self-efficacy in the relationship between parental practices and adolescent alcohol use. *J Adolesc Health, 38,* 448-450.

In: Social Drinking: Uses, Abuses and Psychological Factors ISBN: 978-1-60876-219-4
Editors : K. T. Everly, E. M. Cosell, pp. 311-314 © 2010 Nova Science Publishers, Inc.

Chapter 11

ABSTINENCE VS. CONTROLLED DRINKING: TRENDS AND FUTURE DIRECTIONS

Kenneth Abrams[1] and Melissa Mayer
Department of Psychology, Carleton College, Northfield, MN, USA

"An alcoholic is always one drink away from a drunk" is one of many catch-phrases of the popular organization Alcoholics Anonymous (AA; Vannicelli, 2002). AA upholds a popular view of alcoholism – that it is a disease and abstinence is the only effective goal for preventing relapse. In other words, a sip of alcohol is assumed to lead to irresistible cravings for more.

However, many individuals with alcohol use disorders (AUDs) are not interested in abstinence or are unable to commit to it (Gastfriend, Garbutt, Pettinati, and Forman, 2007). In fact fewer than 20 percent of individuals with AUDs choose to follow an abstinence-based treatment program (Vannicelli, 2002). Controlled drinking (or "moderation"), by contrast, aims to reduce a person's alcohol consumption and minimize the potential harm associated with drinking (Heather, 2006).

This topic – abstinence vs. controlled drinking – remains among the most contentious in the field of substance abuse treatment. Current clinical standards for treatment of AUDs in the US typically recommend complete abstinence, especially for those with alcohol dependence (Gastfriend et al., 2007). Controlled drinking, though, is employed widely in the UK and other European countries as a treatment goal (Heather, 2006).

EMPIRICAL STUDIES

Unfortunately, results from studies comparing controlled drinking and abstinence as outcome goals are rather mixed. For example, in one study, 420 individuals with AUDs who

---

1 Correspondence concerning this commentary should be addressed to Kenneth Abrams, Department of Psychology, One North College St., Carleton College, Northfield, MN 55057, Phone: (507) 222-4380. Fax: (507) 222-7005. Email: kabrams@carleton.edu.

sought different treatments were followed across time. At the one-year follow-up, 16% of participants reported controlled, non-problem drinking. After 16 years, 48% of these individuals continued to report problem-free drinking. Among the 48% of participants who reported abstinence at one year, 77% maintained abstinence after 16 years. These results suggest that controlled drinking is a less stable outcome than is abstinence (Ilgen, Wilbourne, Moos, and Moos, 2008). On the other hand, a few studies have found evidence that controlled drinking may be an achievable goal for a subset of problem drinkers (e.g., Walitzer and Connors, 2007).

INDIVIDUAL DIFFERENCES

Several studies have identified individual differences that moderate the relationship between treatment goal (abstinence vs. controlled drinking) and treatment success. For example, Miller and Hester (1980) concluded that controlled drinking is best suited for those who are younger (under 40) and socially stable (married and employed), have only a brief history of AUDs (fewer than 10 years), and have not suffered severe withdrawal symptoms. Other researchers have found that a lower severity of drinking impairment, fewer alcohol dependent symptoms, the absence of familial alcoholism, and being female were each associated with greater success at controlled drinking (Miller, Leckman, Delaney, and Tinkcom,1992; Rosenberg, 1993; Humphreys, Moos, and Finney, 1995; Ilgen et al., 2008).

Complementing these findings, members of Moderation Management (MM; a self-help group aimed at controlled drinking), relative to members of AA, have at the initiation of membership a lower frequency of drinking and fewer alcohol dependence symptoms. Additionally, MM members are more likely to be female, younger than 35, and currently employed (Humphreys, 2003).

A key question is whether programs like MM discourage severely-dependent persons from seeking or continuing in abstinence-only programs (arguably undesirable) and/or encourage less-dependent persons to seek treatment at all (clearly desirable). Somewhat inconsistent with the former possibility, many MM members have never participated in a professional alcoholism-treatment program (77% have not), have negative feelings about AA, and indicate they would attend only programs that offer moderate drinking as a possible goal (Humphreys and Klaw, 2001). Humphreys (2003) succinctly articulated the dilemma: "Should something be denied to those who may benefit from it so that it cannot be obtained by others who may be harmed?"

On the other hand, a meta-analysis of randomized, controlled drinking studies found that the severity of one's drinking problem does not predict the success of controlled-drinking treatment (Walters, 2000). Further, because controlled drinking programs have historically been reserved for non-dependent problem drinkers, controlled drinking interventions for alcohol-dependent individuals have received minimal attention in research circles (Dawe, Heather, Rees, Mattick, and Sitharthan, 2002).

Behavioral self-control training (BSCT) represents the most recent attempt to tailor treatment to a client's goals. BSCT provides strategies for goal setting, for self-monitoring, for identifying high-risk situations, and (if desired) for engaging in moderate social drinking. In line with the meta-analysis results (Walters, 2000), a recent study of BSCT found that this model of treatment can be effective for people with or without alcohol dependence (Koerkel, 2006). That is, even participants who had very high levels of alcohol consumption or demonstrated alcohol dependence consistently showed a significant decrease in alcohol consumption following BSCT (Koerkel, 2006).

A Call for Research

The cloudy picture that emerges from past studies could become clearer with additional studies that employ specific methods of participant recruitment, of assignment to treatment condition, and of outcome measurement, as outlined below.

1) Additional research is needed to examine individual characteristics that predict success in abstinence- or moderation-based treatment. Such research should employ participants with various self-selected goals (abstinence vs. moderation) and severity of alcohol dependence (mild, moderate, or severe).
2) Studies are needed that randomly assign participants to treatment goal selector (self vs. researcher), treatment goal for researcher-selected treatment conditions (abstinence vs. moderation), and booster sessions status (present vs. absent). Regarding treatment goal selector, there exists preliminary evidence that those who abuse alcohol will expend greater effort for self-set (vs. clinician- or researcher-set) goals (Hodgins, Leigh, Milne, and Gerrish, 1997). Booster sessions (i.e., periodic refresher sessions) have been found to assist heavy-drinking women maintain moderation-based treatment gains (Walitzer et al., 2007), and future studies might examine the value of booster sessions following the potentially-promising BSCT protocol (Koerkel, 2006).
3) Outcome variables (both research and clinical) should include continuous measures of alcohol use/harm (e.g., percent of weeks meeting goal, percent of days of heavy drinking) rather than simply the oft-used "percent of days abstinent." One recent study found that, when permitted to choose one's treatment goal, those who chose moderation were equally successful in achieving the goal during a six-month treatment period as those who chose abstinence (Al-Otaiba, Worden, McCrady, and Epstein, 2008). As such, abstinence as a primary outcome measure may underestimate true success rates.
4) Finally, future studies should examine factors that lead to mid-treatment adjustments in treatment goal (abstinence vs. moderation). Candidate factors include failure with initial goal, negative attitudes toward initial goal, and negative perceived social norms regarding initial goal (Al-Otaiba, et al., 2008).

Well-designed studies that incorporate one or more of these suggestions and gather longer-term outcome data (e.g., two years post-treatment) would help clarify some of the contradictory findings and unresolved issues in the literature.

REFERENCES

Al-Otaiba, Z., Worden, B. L., McCrady, B. S., and Epstein E. E. (2008). Accounting for self-selected drinking goals in the assessment of treatment outcome. *Psychology of Addictive Behaviors, 22* (3), 439-443.

Dawe, S., Heather, N., Rees, V. W., Mattick, R., and Sitharthan, T. (2002). Efficacy of moderation-oriented cue exposure for problem drinkers: A randomized controlled trial. *Journal of Consulting and Clinical Psychology, 70*(4), 1045-1050.

Gastfriend, D. R., Garbutt, J. C., Pettinati, H. M., and Forman, R. F. (2007). Reduction in heavy drinking as a treatment outcome in alcohol dependence. *Journal of Substance Abuse Treatment*, 71-80.

Heather, N. (2006). Controlled drinking, harm reduction and their roles in the response to alcohol-related problems. *Addiction Research and Theory, 14*(1), 7-18.

Hodgins, D.C., Leigh, G., Milne, R., and Gerrish, R. (1997). Drinking goal selection in behavioral self-management treatment of chronic alcoholics. *Addictive Behaviors, 22*(2), 247-255.

Humphreys, K., Moos, R. H., and Finney, J. W. (1995). Two pathways out of drinking problems without professional treatment. *Addictive Behaviors, 20,* 427-441.

Humphreys, K., and Klaw, E. (2001). Can targeting non-dependent problem drinkers and providing Internet-based services expand access to assistance for alcohol problems? A study of the Moderation Management self-help/mutual aid organization. *Journal of Studies on Alcohol, 62,* 528-532.

Humphreys, K. (2003). A research-based analysis of the Moderation Management controversy. *Psychiatric Services, 54*(5), 621-622.

Ilgen, M. A., Wilbourne, P. L., Moos, B. S., and Moos, R. H. (2008). Problem-free drinking over 16 years among individuals with alcohol use disorders. *Drug and Alcohol Dependence*, 116-122.

Miller, W. R., Leckman, A. L., Delaney, H. D., and Tinkcom, M. (1992). Long term follow-up on behavioral self-control training. *Journals of Studies on Alcohol, 53,* 249-261.

Miller, W. R., and Hester, R. K. (1980). Treating the problem drinker: Modern approaches. In W.R. Miller (Ed.), *The addictive behaviors* (pp. 11-141). Oxford, England: Pergamon Press.

Koerkel, J. (2006). Behavioural self-management with problem drinkers: One-year follow-up of a controlled drinking group treatment approach. *Addiction Research and Theory, 14*(1), 35-49.

Rosenberg, H. (1993). Prediction of controlled drinking by alcoholics and problem drinkers. *Psychological Bulletin* 113:129-139.

Vannicelli, M. (2002). A dualistic model for group treatment of alcohol problems: Abstinence-based treatment for alcoholics, moderation training for problem driners. *International Journal of Group Psychotherapy, 52*(2), 189-213.

Walitzer, K., and Connors, G. J. (2007). Thirty-month follow-up of drinking moderation training for women: a randomized clinical trial. *Journal of Consulting and Clinical Psychology, 75* (3), 501-507.

Walters, G. D. (2000). Behavioral self-control training for problem drinkers: A meta analysis of randomized control studies. *Behavior Therapy, 31*(1), 135-149.

In: Social Drinking: Uses, Abuses and Psychological Factors ISBN: 978-1-60876-219-4
Editors : K. T. Everly, E. M. Cosell, pp. 315-317 © 2010 Nova Science Publishers, Inc.

Chapter 12

BINGE AND SOCIAL DRINKING

Napoleon Waszkiewicz*[1] *and Agata Szulc
Department of Psychiatry, Medical University of Białystok,
16-070 Choroszcz, Poland

A large segment of the population drinks moderately [1]. It is called social or "safe" drinking [2]. Social drinkers usually drink not more than 2-3 units of alcohol per day. The Royal College of Physicians, Psychiatrists, and General Practitioners advise a safe weekly limit of alcohol intake of 21 units (168 g) for men and 14 units (112 g) for women. Although binge drinkers can remain within safe weekly limits of alcohol consumption, bingeing-induced harm is reliably observed. Binge drinking is characterized by the consumption of alcohol leading to intoxication (drinking to get drunk), often measured as having more than 5/4 (men/women) number of drinks on one occasion or bringing blood alcohol concentration (BAC) above 0.08 gram percent in about 2 hrs. Other binge measures include drinking over half the "sensible" number of units per week (1–14 units per week for women and 1–21 for men), or double the recommended daily guidelines in one session [3]. Binge drinking occurs in a third of the drinking occasions and increases the risk for numerous acute adverse health and social events including alcohol poisoning, acute myocardial infarction, injuries, accidents, suicide, interpersonal violence, etc [4]. However, for most bingeing people, none of the abovementioned health and social harms result and drinkers think they remain within the recommended "safe" weekly limits of alcohol consumption or think their drinking is social or slightly risky at the worst [5]. The Royal College of Physicians points out that "one third of the population is drinking at potentially hazardous levels" [6]. Nothing unusual in that since an increasing number of working young adults use alcohol as a recreational drug, tending to concentrate their drinking at weekends [7]. The type of drinks preferred in single drinking episodes are beer and spirits. Moderate drinking has been proven to be beneficial and this pattern seems to be less than risky [1]. In terms of total alcohol consumption most of binge drinkers can be classified as moderate drinkers or social drinkers [8]. However, binge

1 Corresponding author: Napoleon Waszkiewicz, Department of Psychiatry, Medical University of Białystok, 16-070 Choroszcz, Poland; Phone number/fax: +48 85 7193977, e-mail: napoleonwas@yahoo.com; napwas@wp.pl.

drinking is characterized by occasional high alcohol intake, being much more intensive during the single episode than social drinking [1,3]. Thus binge drinking is referred to as hazardous or even a harmful pattern of drinking [5]. Moreover, few studies compare “bingeing” to episodic heavy drinking or even to a heavy drinking [5,9]. As there is a wide variation in individual susceptibility to alcohol-induced harm, the “safe” limits for alcohol intake seem to be controversial. Although, the term binge drinking is usually considered a subset of at-risk (hazardous) drinking, the term of hazardous drinking is often used loosely to cover also the forms of drinking that cause harm- even if minimal [10]. Thus, other alternative terms of binge drinking/risky single occasion drinking appeared e.g. heavy episodic drinking, heavy sessional drinking or simply heavy drinking [9]. Routine laboratory tests are not sensitive enough to detect harmful effects of single occasion drinking, since pronounced changes are only measurable after very high and prolonged ethanol consumption. However an acute high alcohol intake has been shown to increase moderately serum level of aspartate aminotransferase in healthy subjects or elevated other biomarkers as salivary, serum and urinary β-hexosaminidase, hemoglobin-associated acetaldehyde or salivary immunoglobulin A [2,3,11,12]. Thus, it may be concluded that the binge drinking session can induce harmful effects, even if acute adverse health and social events are not apparent and drinkers remain within the recommended “safe social” weekly limits of alcohol consumption. Changes in laboratory tests, after bingeing, can help us in fully understanding the implications of the binge drinking session within a broader context, e.g. in context of more effective opportunities for intervention. Evidence exists for the effectiveness of “brief intervention” in reduction in binge drinking episodes per month [1]. In general populations questionnaires and physical examination are superior for alcohol-related problems screening [2]. The value of biomarkers in screening appears insufficient to justify their cost but little is known about biofeedback properties of such a markers. Providing the results of elevated laboratory test together with the specific information about binge drinking to the patient may enhance the impact on the patient’s drinking behaviour with possible risk or harm reduction [4]. Saliva-based testing in particular shows much promise, since material can be obtained in a simple non-invasive way.

Generally, in the literature, less attention has been paid to bingeing-induced toxicity, even though binge drinking is more common than chronic alcoholism [13]. The majority of alcohol-related problems are found among binge drinkers, not among alcoholics. Thus prevention strategies applies better to binge drinking cultures, where occasional heavy drinking is a common part of the drinking pattern. It is referred to as the “prevention paradox”. Frequent binge drinking may precede the sequence of events leading to alcoholism [14]. In particular young people who have symptoms of conduct disorder, anxiety, or depression, have an increased risk of alcohol dependence [15]. Thus, it is important to detect binge drinking as early as possible to prevent these events. Current prevention strategies that include increased alcohol excise taxes, minimum legal drinking age, restrictions on hours of sale, banning advertising, as well as reduced alcohol outlet density, seem not to be effective enough to stop accelerated binge drinking phenomenon. Thus a shift in public education seems to be required from safe weekly limits of alcohol consumption to safe limits per one occasion, to effectively minimize the level of harm caused by alcohol bingeing. Since the binge drinking levels are better and more rapidly accepted as a part of primary health care physician’s daily work than weekly drinking levels [16], new guidelines for alcohol consumption framed also in terms of the number of drinks consumed on a particular occasion may be satisfactory appreciated.

In conclusion, binge drinking is not a subset of a social drinking. Although binge drinkers can remain within the recommended social weekly levels of alcohol consumption, they drink more than social drinkers on particular occasion and what is the most important- they become intoxicated. Thus, the binge drinking is risky and may result in harm.

REFERENCES

[1] Saitz R. Unhealthy alcohol use. *N. Engl. J. Med.* 2005;352:596-607.

[2] Sharpe PC. Biochemical detection and monitoring of alcohol abuse and abstinence. *Ann. Clin. Biochem.* 2001;38:652–664.

[3] Waszkiewicz N, Szajda SD, Jankowska A, Kępka A, Dobryniewski J, Szulc A, Zwierz K. The effect of the binge drinking session on the activity of salivary, serum and urinary β-hexosaminidase: preliminary data. *Alcohol Alcohol* 2008;43:446-450.

[4] Waszkiewicz N and Szulc A. Can we better prevent binge drinking? *J. Epidemiol. Community Health* 2009;63:589.

[5] Murgraff V, Parrott A, Bennett P. Risky single-occasion drinking amongst young people--definition, correlates, policy, and intervention: a broad overview of research findings. *Alcohol Alcohol* 1999;34:3-14.

[6] The Lancet. Time for coordinated action on alcohol. *Lancet* 2004;363:1001.

[7] Kuntsche E, Rehm J, Gmel G. Characteristics of binge drinkers in Europe. *Soc. Sci. Med.* 2004;59:113-127.

[8] Jackson R, Beaglehole R. Alcohol consumption guidelines: relative safety vs absolute risks and benefits. *Lancet* 1995;346:716.

[9] Herring R, Berridge V, Thom B. Binge drinking: an exploration of a confused concept. *J. Epidemiol. Community Health* 2008;62:476-479.

[10] Mokdad AH, Brewer RD, Naimi T, Warner L. Binge drinking is a problem that cannot be ignored. *Prev. Med.* 2007;44:303-304.

[11] Waszkiewicz N, Szajda SD, Jankowska A, Zwierz P, Czernikiewicz A, Szulc A, Zwierz K. The effect of acute ethanol intoxication on salivary proteins of innate and adaptive immunity. *Alcohol Clin. Exp. Res.* 2008;32:652-656.

[12] Sillanaukee P, Seppa K, Koivula T, Israel Y, Niemela O. Acetaldehyde-modified hemoglobin as a marker of alcohol consumption: comparison of two new methods. *J. Lab. Clin. Med.* 1992;120:42-47.

[13] Rossow I, Romelsjo A. The extent of the 'prevention paradox' in alcohol problems as a function of population drinking patterns. *Addiction* 2006;101:84-90.

[14] Savola O, Niemela O, Hillbom M. Blood alcohol is the best indicator of hazardous alcohol drinking in young adults and working-age patients with trauma. *Alcohol Alcohol* 2004;39:340-345.

[15] Anonymous. Calling time on young people's alcohol consumption. Lancet 2008;371:871.

[16] Aalto M, Seppa K. Primary health care physicians' definitions on when to advise a patient about weekly and binge drinking. *Addict Behav.* 2007;32:1321-1330.

INDEX

A

B

C

D

E

F

G

H

I

J

K

L

M

N

O

P

S

V

W

Y

Z